ALTERNATIVE
LEARNING
ENVIRONMENTS

COMMUNITY DEVELOPMENT SERIES

Series Editor: Richard P. Dober, AIP

Volumes Published and in Preparation

Community
Development Series

ALTERNATIVE
LEARNING
ENVIRONMENTS

Edited by
Gary Coates

Dowden, Hutchinson
& Ross, Inc.
Stroudsburg, Pennsylvania

To my parents

Library of Congress Cataloging in Publication Data

Coates, Gary, 1947-   comp.
   Alternative learning environments.

   (Community development series, v. 7)
   Bibliography: p.
   1. School environment--Addresses, essays, lectures.
2. School facilities--Addresses, essays, lectures.
I. Title.
LC203.C55   690.7   74-1268
ISBN 0-87933-037-6

Manufactured in the United States of America.

Exclusive distributor outside the United States and
Canada:
John Wiley & Sons, Inc.

SERIES EDITOR'S PREFACE

Chirping, churlish, chastising, or cheerful, the pronouncements come tumbling from chancelleries and critics, insiders and outsiders: The time has come for applying new ways to educate children. Given the weight of publication in recent years, the importance this challenge has for our time and place in history must surely be self-evident by now.

What Gary Coates has done in this book is not a critical reiteration, but a drawing together of current thought so that planners, architects, and others involved in designing the environment for education can have reference points for solving particular problems, at hand and on the horizon.

Although pointed at those searching for alternatives, the book has a larger audience in concept and application. I refer to but one of his fundamental premises: " . . . the art of planning and design itself must become part of the curriculum."

One may interpret this in several ways. Coates is committed as much to a process of thought that allows redefinition as he is to the products of his process. But I think that the following interpretation, among many possible, is unassailable and gives a special dimension to his book.

How to recognize, interpret, and deal with continuity and change must be learned and must be taught. First, the oscillations of technology and urbanization will increase in tempo, duration, and effect. Second, the time interval between the acknowledgement of causative factors and finding a personal or group response will be, in many instances, shorter than our institutions have been able to handle. Adaptation of existing institutional responses to societal problems and probably the creation of new institutions is a likely prospect. Thus the conceptual and pragmatic understanding of *alternatives* at the earliest possible moment in cognitive development would seem to be a matter of fundamental importance. Affecting one's environment is one way this can be done.

These and similar issues are presented more

fully in the pages that follow by Coates and his collaborators. Here, then, is a useful book, one we are particularly pleased to publish, because it touches immediately the lives of those who will inherit the communities we now design.

Richard P. Dober, AIP

PREFACE

From its inception this book has been aimed at filling a vacuum in the existing literature. Most books on learning environments prepared for use by architects are little more than visual case studies of school buildings (usually award-winning). At best, such efforts constitute a statement of professional esthetic and functional standards which, it is supposed, practicing designers would do well to emulate if not directly copy. Seldom is there any critical analysis of the aims or processes of education which these buildings are meant to house. The assumption seems to be that everyone knows what goes on (and should go on) in schools and that the problem is merely one of designing the best-looking school for the least amount of money.

However, as evidenced by the flood of writing on education in the past fifteen years, educators, social policy planners, parents, and students are beginning to challenge the assumptions underlying the American system of compulsory education. This is the well-known "crisis" in education, and the controversy surrounding such issues as equality of educational opportunity and outcome, community control of the schools, decentralization of large school bureaucracies, and even "deschooling" have become a permanent part of the American scene. During the last decade alone millions of dollars were poured into such "innovations" as team teaching and programmed instruction, the "new" math, and a host of compensatory education programs such as Head Start. And now we are witnessing a period of experimentation with "free" schools, alternative schools within the public schools, and a wide variety of nonschool learning networks.

Yet where does the literature in environmental design reflect these concerns? In part, this book represents an attempt to fill this gap. During the past year and a half in which the manuscript has

viii   *Preface*

been in preparation, I have come to realize that, indeed, many people in the world of design share these concerns and have been actively involved in experiments in educational as well as environmental change. In fact, many have been so caught up in the world of action that they have not yet had the time to publish material concerning their efforts. One of the most rewarding aspects of the usually thankless task of editing such a book has been the opportunity I have had to get to know many of the contributors and to share the excitement of their ongoing efforts. I am especially indebted to authors Doreen Nelson, Robert Lloyd, Michael Southworth, Charles Rusch, George Peterson, Richard Chase, Mayer Spivack, Asher Derman, Jim Zien, and Anne-Marie Pollowy for their critical comments and helpful suggestions throughout the preparation of this volume.

I may never have "discovered" these contributors if it were not for the many helpful leads suggested by a grapevine of interested persons. Special thanks in this regard go to Roger Hart, Florence Shelton Ladd, and David Stea.

Without the intellectual stimulation provided by my own students, many ideas about the selection and organization of materials would have never been fully developed. In particular I am grateful to Karen Kobrosky for her assistance in searches of existing literature and her tireless travels for discussions with potential contributors. Much of what the book has become can be traced to her efforts. Also, Ellen Bussard and Lindsey Alley, former graduate students and research assistants, have been most helpful.

Frank Becker, Harriet Becker, Larry Friedberg, and Edward Ostrander have also contributed many useful comments concerning the manuscript. I am grateful to Richard P. Dober and Charles Hutchinson for their patience concerning missed deadlines, their thorough analyses of work in progress, and their generous assistance in all phases of manuscript preparation.

I would like to express my special appreciation to David Alpaugh for his initial help in formulating the concept of the book, for his many hours of footwork checking out projects on the West Coast, and for his ongoing help as critic, advisor, and friend. Had we been less separated geographically we would have been co-editors.

As always I am indebted to Joan and Henry Sanoff, my teachers and most helpful critics, whose thinking is so intertwined with my own that it is impossible to properly acknowledge the full extent of their contribution. Without their help this book would not have been possible.

Finally, I owe Julie, my wife and best friend, another kind of debt. It is because of her work as a tutor and community organizer for Black, Indian, and Appalachian communities in North Carolina that I first became aware of the need for and the value of alternatives in education. Many of the ideas represented in this volume are a continuing elaboration of what she and countless others began nearly a decade ago. In a very real sense this is our book.

Ithaca, N.Y.   Gary Coates
March 1974

Contents

List of Contributors

George Barbour, *Sandhills Mental Health Center, Pinehurst, North Carolina*

Anthony Barton, *Ontario Institute for Studies in Education, Toronto*

John Benyon, *Head of the School Buildings Section, Department of Education Planning and Financing at UNESCO*

Robert L. Bishop, *Northwestern University*

Peter Brown, *Brown & Goldfarb, Philadelphia*

Gian Carlo de Carlo, *Milan, Italy*

Topper Carew, *New Thing Art and Architecture Center, Washington, D.C.*

Richard Allen Chase, *The Johns Hopkins University School of Medicine*

Clare Cooper Marcus, *University of California at Berkeley*

Asher Derman, *University of Texas at Austin*

Michael J. Ellis, *University of Illinois at Urbana-Champaign*

Leonard B. Finkelstein, *The Parkway Program, Philadelphia*

Thomas Gallagher, *Brown & Goldfarb, Philadelphia*

Lawrence Goldfarb, *Brown & Goldfarb, Philadelphia*

Robert Goodman, *Author, Lecturer and Architect, Plainfield, Vermont*

C. Richard Hatch, *C. Richard Hatch Associates, Inc., New York*

George von Hilsheimer, *Green Valley School, Orangeville, Florida*

Sybil Kritchevsky, *Pacific Oaks College, Pasadena, California*

Robert Lloyd, *Phillips Academy, Andover, Massachusetts*

Stanley Madeja, *CEMREL, Inc., St. Ann, Missouri*

Richard M. Michaels, *Northwestern University*

Robin Moore, *University of California at Berkeley*

Doreen Nelson, *City Building Educational Program, Saugus, California*

Simon Nicholson, *The Open University, Milton Keynes, England*

George L. Peterson, *Northwestern University*

Luther W. Pfluger, *Mansfield State College, Mansfield, Pennsylvania*

Anne-Marie Pollowy, *Université de Montréal*

Elizabeth Prescott, *Pacific Oaks College*

Everett Reimer, *Centro Intercultural de Documentacion, Cuernavaca*

Charles W. Rusch, *University of California at Los Angeles*

Henry Sanoff, *North Carolina State University*

Michael Southworth, *Michael and Susan Southworth, Planners and Designers, Boston*

Susan Southworth, *Michael and Susan Southworth, Planners and Designers, Boston*

Mayer Spivack, *Harvard Medical School*

Lisa W. Strick, *The Parkway Program, Philadelphia*

Mark Terry, *Teacher and Co-chairman, Science Department, Oakwood School, North Hollywood, California*

Lee Walling, *Pacific Oaks College, Pasadena California*

Jim Zien, *The Children's Museum, Boston*

Jessie M. Zola, *University of Wisconsin at Milwaukee*

Introduction

We are living in an age of rapid and widespread social, economic, and political change. In the United States, the overall pattern and specific nature of these changes are fundamentally altering the character of American society. For the first time in the history of any society, there are more people employed in services than in goods-producing industries, with growth in the public sector—health, education, research, and government—accounting for the major share of this change. This transformation to a service economy has led naturally to a shift to white-collar occupations. Since 1956, white-collar workers have outnumbered blue-collar workers, and this trend is expected to continue. Significantly, the growth rate of jobs in the professional and technical areas has been twice that of average. It is expected that by 1975 professional and technical employment will become the second-largest occupational category in the American occupational structure, second only to semiskilled workers.[1]

According to Daniel Bell, these and related changes in the economy and the occupational structure suggest that the United States is now becoming a "postindustrial society." Whereas industrial society is focused on the coordination of people, resources, and machines for the most efficient production of goods, the emerging postindustrial society is

organized around knowledge, for the purpose of social control and the directing of innovation and change . . . and this in turn gives rise to new social relationships and new structures which have to be managed politically.

What has become decisive for the organization of decisions and the direction of change is the centrality of theoretical knowledge–the primacy of theory over empiricism and the codification of knowledge into abstract systems of symbols that, as in any axiomatic system, can be used to illuminate many different and varied areas of experience.

Every modern society now lives by innovation and tries to anticipate the future in order to plan ahead. This commitment to social control introduces the need for planning and forecasting into society . . . .[2]

While the shift to a postindustrial society does not *cause* every change that is occurring today, it does generate certain conflicts that must be resolved by both individuals and institutions. In this volume, the concern is primarily with how these conflicts are affecting the roles and problem-solving methods of professional educators, designers, and planners and their relationships to their various clients—students, parents, community residents, paying clients, user clients, and the general public.

In this context, the most important consequence of the postindustrial revolution is that issues related to education are now major public issues. By increasing the centrality of theoretical knowledge and the scientific and technical professions that are based on it, education becomes the primary means of access to positions of social, economic, and political importance. As a result it is no longer possible for educators to maintain the ivory tower myth that their decisions are apolitical and objective, even if it is claimed that they are based on scientific knowledge and "expert" opinion. The ongoing struggle for school control is the main arena in which the conflict between professional jurisdiction and public accountability comes into sharp focus.

Similarly, in a society in which more and more people are affected adversely by planning and design decisions, the major question becomes who are the *planners* and who are the planned *for*. Because of the revolutions in communications and the increased scale and complexity of environmental and social problems, this issue becomes even more problematic. It is no longer clear whether planning and design problems are purely technical and should be solved privately by experts, or whether they are primarily questions of values and priorities and should be settled publicly by means of democratic participation. The advocacy design movement, which first emerged in the last decade, illustrates the growing schism between those who accept the notion that professionals are experts who plan *for* people, and those who believe that it is necessary to plan *with* people. Advocate planners and designers are also attempting to expand the definition of client to include not only the paying client but also all those who are significantly affected by environmental design decisions. Since these user clients are seldom also paying clients, this movement represents a fundamental challenge to the traditional model of professional roles and obligations.

By accelerating the trend toward the bureaucratization of work, the postindustrial society also amplifies the already existing tension between institutional demands and individual freedom. This has become especially apparent in the rapidly growing white-collar sector. In the world of education, two recent trends can be traced directly to this conflict: (1) the movement toward "informal" or "open" education represents a reformist thrust toward a teaching–learning style that both accepts and enhances individual differences in interests and abilities and attempts to define the teacher as a facilitator of learning rather than as an authoritarian source of knowledge, and (2) the more radical demand for the disestablishment of schools, which are seen as "dominating" institutions, and, in their place, the establishment of learning "networks," which are characterized as "democratic" institutions. These are some of the recent changes which are calling into question the existing attitudes, values, and institutional forms in the areas of education and environmental design. This book should be of interest to anyone who is dissatisfied with existing approaches and is in search of alternatives. Articles have been included because of their relevance to the following issues:

1. *Participatory decision making versus expert decision making*. Articles have been selected that advocate the idea of user participation, both in educational and design decision making.
2. *Individual freedom versus institutional control*. Although this is clearly not an either/or question, the selection of material leans in the direction

of institutions and practices that maximize opportunities for individual self-enhancement and community self-determination.

3. *Traditional design methods versus systematic design methods*. Because of the increased scale and complexity of problems, it has become necessary for designers and planners to become more systematic when making design decisions. Although this tends to increase reliance on technical expertise, it also offers an opportunity for more effective community participation. Selections dealing with environmental evaluation illustrate how the "new" design methods can make public the traditionally private process of design decision making.

Since awareness of the issues and a desire to change are in themselves insufficient to lead to effective action, there has been a deliberate effort to select case studies of attempts to operationalize global concepts in the concrete circumstances of everyday life. Where large gaps have been found in existing literature, papers describing work in progress have been solicited. Consequently, nearly one third of the articles are being published for the first time. Hopefully, this collection of readings will encourage dialogue among people of diverse backgrounds and interests and stimulate further communication among them.

The volume is organized into three major parts, which parallel the steps that occur in any rational problem-solving activity. First there must be an *awareness* of issues and problems, followed by a decision to do something about them, which leads to some kind of *action*, and is followed by an *evaluation* of that action and its effects in terms of original intentions and an ongoing reevaluation of the issues and problems. Although it is clear that all three processes are present in all the articles, selections in each part are unified by a shared concern and emphasis on the issues central to that particular stage of this general process model.

The articles in Part One reflect the changes that

are occurring in basic attitudes about the aims of education, the process of teaching and learning, and the ways in which children grow and develop. Although clearly identified with the trend toward open education, the focus here is on environmental education. The authors, who include social and behavioral scientists, professional educators, architects, and city planners, seem unified in the belief that in a complex technical society in which nearly every decision has some effect on everybody, it is the responsibility of every citizen, not just the design professional, to have access to the information and skills necessary to generate the alternatives, as well as to choose from among them. Thus, it is argued that the art of planning and designing itself must become the curriculum.

Included in Part One are both detailed case studies and curriculum descriptions. The selections cover a wide range of age groups from preschool to high school in both public and private institutions. The underlying approach is to teach children problem-solving skills by first heightening their awareness of the effect that their environment (both natural and man-made) has on them, and the effect that they have and could have on their environment. Because such changes are limited to issues of pedagogy, what is to be learned and how, any of these programs can be adapted to and implemented within the framework of existing schools.

Whereas the articles in Part One do not specifically address the issues of school control and accountability or the more basic question of whether or not schools in their present form should continue to exist, these issues of institutional form are a major concern in Part Two. Closely related to the idea of community participation in educational decision making is the notion of user participation in design decision making. This, too, is treated in some detail in the second part.

The alternatives in education range from community-centered schools and mobile schools to nonschool learning webs, deschooled networks of resources which distribute the learning activity throughout the entire fabric of the city and throughout the lifetime of the learner. In all these experiments conventional boundaries between learning and nonlearning environments become more ambiguous, barriers between the environments of adults and children become more permeable, and distinctions between play and work, education and design, and living and learning become almost nonexistent. Processes and relationships become the new building blocks and the design activity becomes a search for adaptable, manipulable systems (comprised of both "hardware," the physical components, and "software," the rules governing relationships among people and between people and material resources) that are responsive to the evolving needs of the users of the system.

Finally, the papers in Part Three reflect the movement in the design professions toward the use of systematic design and planning methods, which are based on a commitment to ongoing evaluation research. Without high quality, relevant information about the actual performance of complex environmental and social systems finding its way back into the "awareness" and "action" phases of the design activity, designers and planners will continue to be unable to account for either their successes or failures. Rather than forgetting about a project once it is "completed," the scientists and practitioners represented here argue that the design, evaluation, and redesign cycle must continue throughout the life of a given setting.

These papers, which include both case studies and position papers, range in scope from market-type research into children's preferences for proposed environments to observational studies of children's use of existing environments. While demonstrating the importance of such research efforts for the design and management of play/learning environments, it is clear that there are still many unsolved problems in conceptualizing and carrying out effective research; our ability to be aware of problems and to act on them remains far ahead of our ability to either anticipate future consequences or to evaluate present circumstances in terms of desired outcomes.

NOTES AND REFERENCES

1. Daniel Bell, *The Coming of Post-industrial Society: A Venture in Social Forecasting*, New York: Basic Books, Inc., Publishers, 1973, p. 17. For anyone trying to understand what is going on today and what problems can be expected in the future, this is must reading.
2. *Ibid.*, p. 20.

PART ONE
ENVIRONMENTAL AWARENESS: EDUCATING FOR DESIGN

In recent years social critics such as Paul Goodman, Edgar Friedenberg, and Jules Henry and teachers such as Jon Kozol, Herb Kohl, and James Herndon have made it clear that traditional authoritarian educational practices have often had a devastating effect on the minds and spirits of our children.[1] In the suburbs as well as the ghettos this system of public education has been found to lead to suppression in the name of discipline, irrelevance in the form of fixed and mandatory curricula, passivity instead of independence, conformity instead of creativity, and a limited and grudging ability to learn by rote rather than a desire and ability to learn how to learn throughout life. The image that emerged by the end of the last decade was that of an institutional environment in which all the participants seemed to be unwillingly locked into roles that not only inhibited learning but also limited their freedom and ability to change the situation. It had become clear that any alternative to existing conditions would have to involve fundamental changes in the aims, content, and process of education.

Fortunately, we now seem to be in the midst of a period of change in our basic attitudes about the process of education and the ways in which children grow and develop. It seems that the once "radical" critique of the public schools has now become the common wisdom. Charles Silberman has described this as a "change in atmosphere— toward more humaneness and understanding" and a "change in learning style . . . ." away from the teacher as the source of all knowledge to the teacher as facilitator of learning, away from the traditional whole-class orientation to more concern with individualized learning."[2]

Following the lead of the primary schools of England, this movement has been variously described by the terms "informal education," "open education," "the open classroom." As many advocates of this approach have pointed out, these terms do not denote a fixed model of education or a neat set of learning or teaching techniques. Rather, it is a shared set of attitudes and values about the goals and processes of teaching and learning, the function and importance of childhood and adolescence, and the role of schools in a technological society. By contrast to the traditional model of education, this approach asserts that the goal of education is to instill in children the desire and capacity to continue to learn throughout life rather than to produce completely "educated" people. Rather than viewing children as passive recipients of predetermined packages of knowledge, children are viewed as active learners with unique and individual needs and abilities who learn because they need and want to know and understand. Rather than teaching basic facts and bodies of knowledge, it is necessary for the teacher to create situations that reflect individual differences and encourage exploration and invention. Rather than teaching basic skills to be used later as tools for learning, it is first necessary to create a reason for their acquisition. Rather than viewing childhood and school as a period of preparation for life, childhood and the time spent in school is in itself viewed as an important stage in life. Rather than standardizing teaching methods and content, and homogenizing and segregating children according to differences in age, ability, or race, the "curriculum" grows out of respect for individual and cultural differences. Rather than a competition with peers for extrinsic rewards, learning is viewed as a cooperative effort motivated by the intrinsic rewards of increased competence. The measure of success for the educational enterprise is not to be found in how much a child knows but in what kind of person he becomes.

These new attitudes are fast becoming transformed into changed practices, especially in preschool and elementary school programs. Although the movement does not specifically address the crucial issues of decentralized control of local schools, or the broader questions of whether or not schools should continue to exist, it is clear that open education represents an important new trend toward making existing schools more meaningful, humane, and supportive places to be. At the very least, any alternative in education should attempt to achieve this.

The articles in Part One clearly reflect the values, processes, and goals of open education, and therefore share the underlying assumptions about the nature of children and the ways in which they grow and develop. However, since the authors in Part One include architects and planners as well as psychologists and educators, there is an additional perspective which makes the specific content and focus somewhat different. In addition to sharing process goals with other advocates of open education, these authors are concerned with environmental design education as a means for providing a concrete referent for learning abstract concepts, and, most importantly, for integrating the knowledge from different disciplines and linking such knowledge to collective problem-solving action.

This should not be surprising since designers and planners are intimately concerned with making decisions that transform the man-made and natural environment. What is surprising, as well as particularly important, is that professional designers should now be concerned with teaching nonprofessionals (and children, at that) the mysteries of their trade. This phenomenon, too, can be traced to broader social forces which came to light during the last decade.

Because of the massive, unsolved environmental problems, such as traffic congestion, inadequate and indecent housing, and outdated and inappropriate educational facilities, planners and designers have become more concerned with process than ever before. This concern for finding better methods and techniques for making design decisions and the need for interprofessional and interdisciplinary collaboration to deal with the increased scale and complexity of design problems has led quite naturally to a reassessment of the role of the designer in society.

During the second half of the 1960s many designers came to realize that they tended to serve the needs of the establishment because they provided services for a fee. Those who could not pay, such as the urban poor, could not expect the help of the planning and design professions and the response to this recognition of the politics of planning led many young designers to offer their services on the basis of need rather than ability to pay. This new "advocacy" role heightened the importance of understanding and identifying the lifestyles and perceptions of user clients, with whom the designers often shared few values. This served to intensify the application of social science research to identify and solve design problems and opened up the design decision-making process to user participation by a greatly enlarged public.

One of the many reasons for the generally recognized failures of the advocacy design movement was that the designer was forced into a role of being an advocate *for* people, to plan *for* rather than *with* people. All of a sudden designers began to feel the need to educate people to act as their own advocates in solving their own environmental problems.

So, as a result of the trends toward open education and user participation in design and planning, we find that there is now a new breed of designer–educators and educator–designers who are deeply committed to teaching children how to identify, learn about, and solve environmental problems.

What, then, are the shared goals of environmental design education as exemplified by the teachers and designers writing in Part One?

1. To learn from life as well as about life. The concrete problems of the child's everyday environment provide an immediate and relevant focus for learning by doing.
2. To provide learning opportunities that allow the child to see the world as whole and interrelated rather than fragmented into disciplines.
3. To develop an awareness of how the natural and man-made environment affects and is affected by human values, activities, and decisions. This is basic to the idea of "environmental" design.
4. To foster an action orientation to collective environmental problems and to provide the skills necessary for their solution now, and later as aware, concerned, and competent adults. This is the political meaning of educating for design.

All the programs described in Part One are intended to be implemented within existing schools, without calling for either a radical change in organization or control of the institution. They are pragmatic attempts to create alternative learning environments by redesigning the ways in which existing people, places, and things are perceived and used in the process of learning and designing.

Although the design and education professions have come to accept the importance of considering the relationship between the man-made environment and human behavior, the article by Mark Terry reminds us of the importance of also considering the effect of the designed environment on the natural processes of our life-supporting ecosystem. He suggests that environmental education should begin by examining the impact that the schools themselves have on the environment. Unless our educational institutions become actively involved in finding and implementing solutions to school-caused environmental problems, it is unlikely that anything but hypocrisy will be taught. Focusing on the classroom as an environmental unit, Terry proceeds to show how students and teachers can sensitize themselves to their everyday environment. These sensory-awareness exercises then become the basis for common concern and collective action through a process of analysis, evaluation, and experimentation. Both students and teachers collaborate in becoming expert in sensing the environment and effecting changes in their own immediate surroundings.

Another approach to introducing environmental planning education into existing schools is illustrated by Space Place, which was created by an interdisciplinary team of designers and educators to provide an opportunity for children to directly manipulate their own environments. Designed as an "instructional tool" that can be introduced into any classroom setting, the Space Place constitutes a complete multimedia learning environment.

The planning curricula described by C. Richard Hatch, an architect and planner, and Doreen Nelson, an elementary school teacher, are addressed to the growing need to create a more humane environment out of the chaos of our cities, a task that cannot be accomplished without the effective participation of a knowledgeable citizenry. Unfortunately, the techniques and skills necessary for community development are not taught in the schools. These two papers exemplify the commitment of the authors in Part One to prepare our children for active involvement as adults in planning and designing the urban environment.

It is out of this perspective that these two authors conceived of their curricula for educating children to become their own advocates in their own communities. The Hatch curriculum has, since this article was written, been published as a multimedia educational program[3] and has been received enthusiastically by more than 2,000 New York City public school students, ranging from ten to seventeen years of age. Since this program emphasizes actual involvement in urban planning in the student's own community, there is little danger that it will become a sterile intellectual exercise. Rather, success in mastery of skills is measured in the world of action.

The City Building Educational Program described by Doreen Nelson has been experimentally applied to a socioeconomic cross section of fifth- and sixth-grade children in the Los Angeles public schools. Standard school curricula such as math, geography, and social studies are studied through the use of a city "model," and the participants (students, teachers, and professionals) all interact in solving problems emanating from the task of re-creating their community physically and socially. This program shows the exciting possibilities of integrating the arts and sciences into a unified approach to environmental planning education.

These two planning curricula go a long way toward establishing the relevance of the school in the community and in helping children to develop the interpersonal skills and sensitivities necessary for collective problem-solving action.

Robert Lloyd, a teacher in an art program at a private high school, describes the many problems of implementing an architectural program within the constraints of an existing high school curriculum. The intention is to engage the student in a meaningful progression of problem-solving studio experiences, beginning with abstract exercises in visual expression and culminating in real world design and construction projects. Of particular interest to those who may be concerned with implementing similar courses is the attention paid to the complex teacher–student relationship in each phase of the course of study.

As the article by Pfluger and Zola points out, even 3- and 4-year-olds can be involved and competent environmental planners. In this brief case study, the authors report on the results of an experiment in child-centered education, in which children in a preschool program were allowed to equip and arrange their room as they pleased. Perhaps the teachers, parents, and child-development experts were the true learners in this experiment.

Taken as a group, the papers in Part One provide a representative sample of the wide range of planning and environmental education programs which are currently being tried with all age groups all over the country. Yet it should be clear that we have not yet begun to tap the enormous potential of this approach to education. Hopefully, other teachers, parents, designers, and social scientists will be motivated to experiment with similarly innovative responses to the need for every individual to be a lifelong learner and an aware and competent planner of our collective future. Such an education is necessary if our children are to be capable of adapting to change in a complex world.

NOTES AND REFERENCES

1. For criticisms of public education within a broader social perspective, see Paul Goodman, *Compulsory Mis-education and the Community of Scholars,* New York: Random House, Inc.—Vintage Books, 1962; Edgar Z. Friedenburg, *Coming of Age in America,* New York: Random House—Vintage Books, 1965, and *The Vanishing Adolescent,* New York: Dell Publishing Co., 1972; Jules Henry, *Culture Against Man,* New York: Random House, Inc., 1963. For a more graphic picture based on a teacher's point of view, see Jonathan Kozol, *Death at an Early Age,* Boston: Houghton Mifflin Company, 1967; Herbert Kohl, *36 Children,* New York: The New American Library, Inc.—NAL Books, 1967; James Herndon, *How to Survive in Your Native Land,* New York: Bantam Books, Inc., 1972. For an excellent anthology covering the writings of all of the above, see Ronald and Beatrice Gross (eds.), *Radical School Reform,* New York: Clarion Books, 1969.
2. Charles Silberman (ed.), *The Open Classroom Reader*, New York: Random House, Inc.—Vintage Books, 1973, p. xvi. This is the best single reference on open education and is a book well worth having.
3. *Urban Action: Planning for Change*, Lexington, Mass.: Ginn and Company, 1971.

The Need For Environmental Education*

Mark Terry

The justifications given for interest in environmental education have traditionally been two. In American public education, we educate to produce an enlightened electorate. For our representative democracy to function, our citizenry must be aware of and must understand their environment. The management of natural resources requires environmental understanding and participation on the part of the voting public. A certain amount of conservation education has long been recognized as necessary to meet this demand for an informed electorate.

The second major argument for environmental education has usually been the aesthetic. Appreciation of nature is somehow recognized as the rightful pursuit of the American citizen. Our

mandate to secure the good life has included this enjoyment of the continent's natural wonders. The call for environmental education in the past has often been based on this need for the capacity to delight in nature.

With these main justifications, environmental education in one form or another has been subject to the same calls for development as the other subject areas. Education conferences have repeatedly suggested the need for environment textbooks, environment curriculum guides, and required environment units for teachers and students. Major developments following these suggestions have been slow in coming until recently.

The environmental revolution that has grown in the public mind through the final years of the 1960s has ended the dormancy of efforts in environmental education. The pressures of population growth and environmental deterioration have grown fast enough to cause great concern for our present and future environmental health. The pressing of great amounts of environmental litigation has been accompanied by the entrance of environmental quality as a major political issue. Educators have renewed their calls for development of environmental education and have found an unusually attentive audience. Funds for environmental curricular development have begun flowing from federal, state, and private sources. Initial texts produced in the heat of this concern are already on the market and many more are in development stages. Special committees of state legislatures are seriously considering requirements of specified units of environmental study for students and for beginning teachers. A statement by the American Association of School Administrators, from their 1966 volume *Imperatives in Education*, typifies the concern with which the sudden upsurge in environmental education efforts is growing:

As the prince in the ancient legend took the broken sword that the cringing knight had jealously broken in two and discarded and turned the tide of the battle, so must administrators and teachers—even when the circumstances are difficult— meet the challenge of instilling in the minds and hearts of a generation of young people the understanding and commitment necessary to use the natural resources of this country successfully.

The Association's statement also typifies the problems that the environmental education movement is creating for itself. New curriculum development, student and teacher course requirements, assigning someone responsibility for environmental education, these are the actions most often and most eagerly proposed. The implication of such actions, proposals, and statements is that environmental education is a new and long-awaited development that must take its place in the traditional order of subject "coverage"; that someone can teach it as a subject; and that such education can cure our environmental ills. These implications indicate a misunderstanding of the nature of environmental education. This is

written with the hope of making clear this misunderstanding and of suggesting a different approach to environmental education.

In brief, my thesis is that all education is environmental education. The pleas for development of environmental education as a new subject have misrepresented the problem, which is to change the environmental education that is provided in the study of any subject and in any classroom according to our best understanding of environmental realities. We must realize that all educational situations contribute to environmental education. Environment is no single subject and is certainly not the property of a given teacher or classroom. Attempts to delegate responsibility for environmental education to such a teacher compound misunderstanding of the environment, which is dealt with in *every* teacher's classroom.

Though environmental education in schools can reasonably be expected to help our efforts to improve our environmental relationships, it should not be burdened with the unrealistic responsibility of stopping pollution or solving the deterioration of the environment. Aiming toward such goals tends to breed insensitivity to practical issues and to foster the growth of an already overwhelming rhetoric. A goal far more practical for schools and far more conducive to environmental education is to do all that is possible to improve the school's environmental relationships.

At all levels, institutions of learning contribute to overuse and overgrowth. Our first responsibility as educators is to tend to our own nests, to eliminate overuse and overgrowth in our own classrooms, buildings, and districts.

This must sound like either heresy or insanity to teachers whose schools seem always to lack the materials and resources they want. As with the world's food and minerals, we are not sharing equally in the schools. There are obviously districts and schools within districts that are truly in need of help. But for the majority of schools, I believe the problem is one of wise use rather than insufficient supply. Teachers must learn to conserve and reuse materials they now treat as expendable, no matter how they may complain about shortages.

How can we possibly educate for solutions to environmental exploitation while we ourselves remain so important a part of the problem? I fear that all the discussions about environment, all the projects, all the readings, cannot compete with the sight of this Everest of wastepaper that was somehow a part of our learning for the year. Was it really necessary?

Cutting back on our own exploitation, finding better ways to use and to reuse the resources we have, redistributing resources to share with other schools, these are all measures necessary to reduce the man-caused environmental imbalance. These measures are also necessary, however, to give meaning to any attempts we may make to offer our students an environmental education. Only if educators are demonstrably involved in finding and carrying out solutions will they have a reasonable chance of achieving the following objectives of environmental education:

1. *The ability to perceive and to conceive of nonlinear causal relationships:* We must leave Aristotle behind. We cannot afford to continue teaching the myth of simple cause and effect. We and our students must develop the awareness of causal webs operating in all areas of our environment. We must develop the vocabulary necessary to describe such causal webs. We must develop predictive abilities through gaming and experimenting with real and model webs.

2. *The habit of speaking of the deepest implications of our world views:* We must not let the ideas of sphericity, gravity, indestructibility of matter, mutability of compounds and energy, and similar ideas pass for inconsequential platitudes. Our habit of speaking of the Earth as round must become the habit of speaking of the Earth as finite. To achieve this we must develop models, games, investigations that allow sphericity, for example, to speak for itself.

3. *The ability to sense and describe the role of any activity in shaping the environment:* Developing a combination of awareness and concern, we must see how all activities and all studies are environmental. A great help in achieving this must be the development of both formal and informal interdisciplinary offerings. The mere observation that a group of seemingly unrelated teachers can communicate and jointly understand the environmental connection between their subjects can be an education in itself.

4. *The ability to plan and carry out personal solutions to environmental problems:* We and our students must be able to consider our own behavior and to act to make that behavior ecologically sound. Crucial to the development of this ability is an understanding of the relationships between individual needs and institutional drains on the environment. There could be no better laboratory for demonstrating and investigating these relationships than the school. Equally crucial to the development of "competence" in students is the example of competence set (or not set) by the teacher.

5. *The ability to locate and use ecological knowledge:* The school must provide access to the best ecological information it can. Its environmental courses should be built around the application of ecological research to local situations. The environmental curriculum packages that are being developed should become cores of practical information for use in the school, not simply additional articles to occupy bookshelves and lockers.

THE CLASSROOM AS ENVIRONMENT

As a subdivision of the world environment the classroom is as deserving as any other of receiving separate consideration. In light of the amount of time that students and teachers occupy their classrooms, these environmental boxes most certainly deserve close attention. To evaluate and explore classrooms we must keep in mind that they are both simple physical environments and purposeful, goal-oriented constructions. They may thus be evaluated both according to their basic physical nature and according to their success in attaining their specified goals.

Make an Environmental Inventory

Become acquainted with the shape and content of your classroom. There is no limit to the depth in which you can explore any environment, and these suggestions are only a beginning.

Begin with basic matter. Perhaps with the help of a custodian, determine all the materials out of which your classroom is constructed. What woods, metals, or plastics make up the walls, desks, floor? Glass, blackboards, linoleum, what are they? Any material can be considered in its molecular or elemental forms, and from these you can estimate the actual amounts and percentages of various kinds of matter that *are* your classroom. Gases, liquids, suspended dust? What are your clothes and books and papers and pencils and inks made of? Perhaps useful would be two categories, one of transient the other of permanent materials.

On another level, consider why the different forms of matter are used for the various structures in which you find them. Could they be interchanged and still make a useful classroom? Are some significantly stronger or more durable than others? What happens to those that seem to disintegrate with time? How old, in fact, are the materials surrounding you? How old are the elements composing these materials?

Move on to energy. What various forms of energy can be found? What seem to be the sources of chemical, radiant, electrical, or other forms of energy within the room? What is the energy accomplishing? What forms of matter seem particularly involved with the energy?

With a basis in matter content and energy, other levels of the classroom begin to open. What colors are to be found in the room? Examine all the materials and all the energy forms for color. Compare sensitivities and impressions about the colors. What are the light sources? How do they affect the colors?

Smell is a way of identifying matter (which you may have used to make the initial inventory). What are the smells in the room? Why do they change from day to day? With what materials and energy processes are they associated? Enlist the help of a dog. Compare our sensitivities to light and to smell; compare the vocabularies with which we describe these sensations.

What are the various surfaces of the classroom's materials? Does the same material always present the same texture? With what surfaces are we used to coming into contact? What surfaces do we avoid? Assess the variety present in the room with regard to color, smell, surface texture.

Are there sounds in the room? How does the room affect the sounds? Which sounds does the room generate?

Is there a variety of temperatures within the room? What materials and energies seem to be associated with particular temperatures? Are temperature changes or gradients abrupt or gradual? Does temperature seem to affect color, texture, smell, or vice versa?

Are there any things to be tasted in the classroom? Taste, more than the other senses, is restricted to use with specific intent to determine edibility. Is there any variety of tastes in the room? How easy is it to be fooled into eating an inedible material?

The environmental inventory so far is at least as much an inventory and exercise of sense abilities. This is anything but coincidental, and the opportunity should not be lost to explore where individual and environment become separate, if indeed they do.

Consider the overall shape and structure of the classroom. What parts of it are fixed, what parts movable? Just how permanent is any of it likely to be, given a long enough period of time? Are there any processes similar to erosion or deposition occurring within the room and changing its form? How does the distribution of materials affect the usable area? How do different distributions affect the "feeling" of the room?

Compared to basic sensory information, how much verbal information is being displayed or presented in the room? What forms does communication of verbal information take? Of all the material in the room, how much is used to present verbal information? Of all the energy used in the room, how much is used to present verbal information? In communication of verbal information, what are the roles played by the various senses?

Determine what attitudes affect the appearance of the classroom environment. Is there an emotional environment? How is it independent of the information environment or the physical environment? Determine what factors in the appearance of the environment affect the emotional environment.

Evaluate the Classroom Environment

Through analysis and evaluation, the inventory can become more than an awareness exercise: it can become the basis for a common concern.

Try to determine with your students what the objectives of your classroom are. "Learning" does not describe them sufficiently. The concepts should be at least as concrete as "facilitation of communication," "access to information," "experimentation with objects and processes." The discussion of just why any of you are in the classroom is always interesting and may help release a good deal of honest but pent-up opinion about the way things in general are going. To avoid such a discussion is to hide from the true environment of a classroom.

In deciding on, or at least in compiling some objectives for the classroom environment, question the items in your inventory as to their contribu tion toward or detraction from achieving you

goals. Is access to information, for instance, better promoted by more or by less nonverbal sensory stimulation? Does the shape of the classroom contribute to full communication of all members, or does it channel communication one way? Does the classroom suffer from particular environmental problems? Does it enjoy any particular environmental benefits?

Experiment with the Classroom Environment

Your inventory and evaluation are bound to raise questions about better ways of proceeding. Awareness and concern, as was mentioned earlier, are of little value in the absence of competent action. The object of the evaluation, therefore, should be to plan alternative classroom styles, and these should then be tried.

Experimentation need not mean a wholesale disruption of traditional methods and arrangements. In fact true experimentation should begin modestly with the alteration of one variable, keeping other conditions constant. Pursuing and evaluating experiments on the classroom environment can become the most significant learning experience in which we engage.

Alter the configuration of the room. It is finally becoming widely recognized that the traditional row and column seating arrangement is seldom the best for facilitation of communication. Try a circle or an arc, not necessarily with you at the center. See what can be done without desks.

The easiest kinds of experiments are deprivation experiments. To determine if a material is needed or not, or if it contributes to or inhibits communication, do without it for a week. Of how much advantage *is* a blackboard, a textbook, an overhead projector, notepaper? Likewise, try to do without a given sense for some length of time. Conduct a class with all of you blind, mute, or deaf. Do without electric power. Try to discover just what your dependencies are and in what ways your classroom might be improved by the withdrawal or addition of energy or materials.

Experiment with using each of the senses sometime during each day, or with providing greater variety of stimuli for a given sense. See how much of the communication and information that passes in the class is presentable in other than printed form.

These experiments should be undertaken to improve the classroom environment's contribution to the learning processes and whatever other goals are suggested in the evaluation. Seemingly distant from the problems of environmental education, I believe they lay essential foundations for further environmental investigations. Moving beyond our consideration of the classroom as a learning environment, we may now look for expanded relationships of the classroom to the outside environment.

THE CLASSROOM AS NATURE

Besides being purposefully constructed to achieve educational objectives, a classroom is also a natural object. It is easiest to see it and speak of it as artificial, but it is in truth natural, made of the matter and energy of the Earth, constructed by one of Earth's living organisms, and somehow subject to all the natural processes of the world. When the classroom seems not to be subject to natural processes, that is the fault of our limited insight rather than a reflection of reality. Leaving educational considerations behind, then, the classroom is a useful object of study to discover how it is natural, what is happening to it, how it participates in the rest of nature, and to experiment with it as a representative part of nature.

Make an Inventory of the Classroom's Natural Relationships

The inventory of the classroom as an isolated environment could not have avoided problems of

artificiality: ultimately it makes no sense to cut any one part of the environment off from any other. The atmosphere, energy, materials, position, and all other aspects of the classroom are connected to the larger environment. The connecting relationships all involve some process or collection of processes that can become the objects of this new inventory.

How is the content of the classroom atmosphere dependent upon the local environment? In urban areas it would be easy to demonstrate a direct connection as the smog content varies both in and out of the classroom. Amplifying the question to cover dependence on the regional environment, it could be demonstrated that prevailing winds bring in airs of various humidities, pressures, and temperatures, from which the classroom receives regular samples.

How does the classroom provide habitats for various organisms, inside or out? How are these organisms changing the classroom? Are mosses or lichens gradually disengaging bricks and mortar? Are carpenter ants digesting a wall? Will the young tree that has started growing impossibly close to the wall die before its roots crack the foundations? Are any particular plants or animals flourishing on the sides shielded from the wind or sun?

Perhaps the key question that ought to guide the entire classroom-as-nature survey is: How is the classroom changing? On a daily basis, its changes are due to daily cycles of light, temperature, activity. Seasonally it takes part in weather cycles and animal and plant life cycles. Over many years it changes according to the actions of geologic cycles, eroding, settling, perhaps being shaken by an earthquake.

Evaluate the Classroom's Participation in Nature

Having inventoried the classroom as a natural object, constructed from and participating in the natural world, it becomes possible to compare its performance in nature with other areas. The connections to nature disclosed during the inventory will most often be parts of processes and cycles. These same processes and cycles involve areas outside the classroom. For evaluation, standards of efficiency or speed might be used. In itself the choosing of standards for evaluation will raise important questions, many no doubt answerless: What should be the function of a natural area? Is one collection of organisms more valuable than another? On the time scale of Earth's existence, are any standards of comparison meaningful? Are there any clues in nature that suggest real standards do exist? Do men's actions already suggest man has decided on standards?

A final evaluation could be based on number and kind of learning opportunities. For what sorts of education is the classroom particularly suited? For what sorts of education is the area outside particularly suited? How many different learning devices are to be found in the classroom; how many outside? In which environment are the tests more relevant to the subject matter?

Experiment with the Classroom as a Model of Nature

Whether or not the preceding evaluation shows the classroom to be a good natural environment, the classroom can be effectively used as a model in which environmental principles may be examined. Though few classrooms can qualify as spheres, all classrooms qualify as Earth models by sharing Earth's finiteness. In some schools the effects of overcrowded classes directly parallels the lack of resources available to a species in an overcrowded environment.

Within a classroom it is perhaps easiest to observe finiteness by initiating an inanimate population explosion. Chairs, for instance, borrowed from the custodian's assembly supply could be used as follows: Day 1, place one chair at back of classroom; Day 2, add one chair; Day 3, add two; Day 4, add four; and continue to double the chair population regularly, as the human population doubles regularly. The effects of such growth will go from hardly noticeable through curious to disruptive in a few days. If possible do not stop short of the disruptive stage. That unlimited growth leads to disruption is the lesson to be learned.

To demonstrate the ultimate indestructibility of matter, allow the janitorial service a month's vacation from your room. When the tide of trash becomes noticeable, perhaps students can agree on a plan to render as much waste reusable as possible. Stemming the tide of waste would be a first and very difficult goal; reversing it would be an imaginative exercise.

Experiment with Earth's energy ration by issuing each student a daily energy voucher. With this, he is limited to a specified number of statements and movements for the day. Situate a pool of fossil-fuel vouchers within reach of one corner of the class, but out of the possible range of the other students. Some form of pollution should be generated with each use of an increment of the limited fossil-fuel pool.

The classroom is well suited to the exploration of causal webs and feedback. As a student gets up, moves across the room, and sharpens a pencil, his seemingly simple actions start waves of complicated effects. The spatial distribution in the room is altered; the sound environment is significantly affected. Visual or sound communication may be impaired for other students. The action may stimulate other students to check their own pencils and may start a series of movements across the room to the sharpener which makes it necessary, eventually, to empty the accumulated residue. The student is also that much closer to having to obtain a new pencil.

The feedback to the student for his action might come in any number of forms. In some classrooms he will receive a rebuke of some sort from the teacher. He may discover his pencil is now too short to be of use to him. Upon returning to his seat, if his action has stimulated others to follow suit, he may find his own verbal and visual environments impaired. In any event, he can be sure that he will not have done "merely one thing."

Communication itself can be explored as essentially nothing other than highly structured feedback. The teacher, teaching aids, and other students have come to the classroom in order to subject themselves to the causal web and to trade the feedback that is learning. In some classrooms it might be interesting to deprive either students or teacher of making a response, preventing the feedback connection for a certain length of time. The learning accomplished might then be evaluated.

The interface between organism and environment is being explored in any of the activities suggested above (and in any activities undertaken for whatever purpose at whatever time!). Additionally, it would be informative to alter the shape, size, or stimuli of the classroom in order then to analyze the effects these alterations have on students and teachers. Would any specific alterations of the environment make it uninhabitable for any of the individuals in the classroom or for all humans? Older classrooms offer rich opportunities for examining the effects of organisms on their environment in the worn floors and desks. It might be interesting to compare photographs, movies, or tapes of the classroom as it exists without human beings and as it exists with human beings. Returning to the notion of feedback, the class could also consider whether any normal activities of the dominant organisms themselves would affect the classroom environment so severely as to make it uncomfortable or uninhabitable for themselves.

Finally, once the classroom's connections to nature have been explored, and once it has been used as a model of nature for games and experiments, one could reconsider man. Man constructed the classroom out of nature, man receives the energy or matter of many natural cycles through his use of the classroom, and man mediates the return of energy and materials to nature from the classroom. In light of these connections, of what use is it to consider the classroom as separate from nature? And if the classroom is seen to be fully a part of nature, of what use is it to consider man apart from nature?

THE CLASSROOM AS INSTITUTION

The classroom is a collection of individuals meeting together for the accomplishment of common purposes. Resources are ordered for the classroom to meet the collective demands of the group. Individual needs are summed, and the classroom mediates the fulfilling of these needs from the outside environment. This conforms to the essential nature of any of the institutions of civilization. It conforms so well, in fact, that it is useful to consider the classroom as a consuming institution and to examine the effects of its use of environmental resources.

A major obstacle to adequate understanding and to effective action regarding environmental problems is the comfortable shield of institutional consumption. We all hide behind this shield, which protects us from seeing the direct connection between our own acts and their environmental effects. Paying a water bill is distantly removed from observing the lowering of the water table, yet the act of paying has assumed the connotations of being the source of our water. In the classroom, needs and suppliers can easily be identified because of the limited number of individuals participating and the nearness to the school's ordering procedures. And because of the concreteness of some of the resources used, it is easy to experiment with efficiency of use and volume of demand. The classroom is ideal for the exploration of individual–institution–environment relationships and for the development of competence in proposing and carrying out alternative systems of usage.

Inventory the Individual Needs That the Classroom Meets

It would be useful first to set up two categories of needs: (1) survival needs, and (2) additional needs. The activity of deciding which needs fall into which category may prove to be the most informative lesson of all. It is likely to become apparent that the classroom does not provide for a great many basic survival needs. Some of these may be provided by the larger institution of the school, but some may still remain unsupplied.

There are two totals that should be derived from the inventory. Each would probably be best expressed in the form of a rate per day, though different time scales could be used. The first total: the class rate of use of each material and of each form of energy. This is the total institutional demand that the class makes for each resource. The second total: each student should arrive at a complete list of his individual daily consumption of each resource. This is his total environmental requirement per day. The figures might be more or less manageable if computed for a month's or year's duration.

Having calculated the above totals, it might be enlightening to make subtotals of energy used for survival, and energy used other than for survival, and similarly for materials. Totaling up the inventory on class consumption is but the first step in exploring the individual–institution–environment connections.

Trace the Class's Materials and Energy to Their Sources

You may already have begun something like this in locating the classroom's connections to nature. Now it is imperative to concentrate on the class as a group of individuals making collective demands on the environment. Following the principles of causal webs, an effort should be made to locate all the effects of the various processes involved in obtaining the class's resources. If any attempt to compute costs is made, do not pass over side effects that are usually not included in official economic calculations. Side benefits or side injuries are no less caused by the relevant activities simply because they may not have been intended or expected.

Direct observation of the processes and visits to the pertinent locations should provide an active focus for the investigation. If facilities for field trips are available, then they are obviously in order. It might be less complicated, yet even more valuable, to send individual students to observe with notes or camera the various processes of supplying a classroom. Indeed, it would be difficult in the extreme to find time for a full class to explore all the ramifications of the provision of a single resource, but individual students following up individual leads could assemble a nearly complete picture.

The attempt to follow up each of the resources used in a single classroom would undoubtedly turn that class, whatever its original subject, into "Introduction to the Following Up of Resources." It would simply be impossible to do an adequate job, in a reasonable amount of time, with more than a very few kinds of materials and energy. Discuss and select one or two resources, initially, that are of interest and that seem to promise tangible results.

For example, electric power is an obvious possibility, and might be pursued in something like the following manner. Electricity makes its appearance in the room at more or less convenient wall outlets. Without tearing apart the classroom it should be demonstrable that electricity is transported by wire, generally by copper wire, and that the wire in turn must be wrapped in some sort of insulating material. Stop. Already there is the discovery that this form of energy is inextricably related to use of certain materials, notably copper and plastics or rubber. This might be called "Branch 1," for it leads to investigation of the mining of copper and the world's supplies of copper, both topics of great environmental interest. Also implicated is the entire synthetic plastics process, which has import both in its use of hydrocarbons derived from petrochemicals and in the problem of disposal of the durable synthetics.

Depending on how far-reaching the original classroom-as-environment inventory was, it might already be necessary to make a revision and add the estimated amount of wire and insulation needed to carry the room's electric power. With the help of custodians it should be possible to locate the connecting terminals that pass electricity in from the outside. The manufacture of the terminals and the materials involved could become Branch 2.

Power lines, of course, involve more materials, and estimates of just how much of which material might be obtainable from the local power company. If they are above ground, however, they may have greater interest from their effects on the environment through which they are strung. Branch 3 could follow both the visual and physical impact of the poles and wires, considering elements of aesthetics and safety. Again with help from the power company, information on the efficiency, the relative power leakage, might be obtainable. If the local company is at all concerned about the power lines, an extension of Branch 3 could involve interviews with citizens and an exploration of the problems of changing from poles to underground wiring. (And, of course, most poles were once trees—from where?)

The local power substation may take up a significant amount of land. Branch 4 could explore its impact on property values, the reasons for building on a particular site, and perhaps the succession of a living community on its protected soil.

Before reaching a generating plant, the class may encounter a long stretch of high-tension wires. Whether these lines with their great supports travel through wilderness or tilled fields, the effects of their placement will be of interest: Branch 5.

When you have finally reached the source of the electricity, your problem will be deciding just what is a branch and what is a main trunk. This should not be a cause of alarm, rather one of celebration: it indicates that you and your students are seeing the environment as a web.

Do not lose sight of your original classification of needs into survival and nonsurvival categories. As much of a game as the investigation of resources can and should probably be, it is also an investigation of the involvement of a group of individuals in use of the environment. Questions of whether that use, as it becomes fully investigated, is wise or not are particularly germane.

Experiment with the Classroom's Impact on the Environment

In every classroom some decisions can be made and some actions can be taken that will help restore environmental balance. The excuses for avoiding the decisions and not taking the actions range from ignorance through negligence, tradition, despair, perhaps to vested interest. In all cases, the effect of avoiding decision and actions is an education in incompetence, and often in hypocrisy.

Once the figures have been gathered from the class's investigation into their rate of consumption, discussions should follow on the magnitude of the class's environmental impact. With the collected data on at least some of the resources, proposals for altering or lessening the class's environmental influence should be made. Evaluating the proposals will be that much easier and more meaningful because of your quantitative equivalents established between class use and environmental effects. Notify the suppliers, transporters, and middlemen of the actions you are taking and your reasons for acting. Solicit their advice and opinions.

The most important outcome of your classroom efforts to recycle and conserve resources may not be the minuscule lowering of our gross national pollution or consumption that will ensue. You cannot do merely one thing, however, and you cannot proceed with such activities in a school and not expect to be noticed. The most important outcome of your efforts may well be the school's efforts, or even the community's efforts to follow in your small but definite tracks.

For your students, the most important outcome will be the beginning of an education in competence. They will have discovered some ways of behaving, individually, which when multiplied through a group have an appreciable effect on the real environment. They will also have begun to discover where they, as individuals, begin, what they need, and what they can do without. This is, unfortunately, a revolutionary education in a society in which we are continually told that we need everything and anything in ever greater amounts.

Space Place[1]

Stanley Madeja

INTRODUCTION

A ten-year-old girl described her reaction to her experiences in the Space Place as follows: "I really thought the Space Place was exciting because we could work projectors and because we could use our imagination. When we cleaned up everybody worked together to get the job done. I think I learned if you put your mind together you can create wonderful things. I think to make these things, you have to cooperate. When you have big blocks to build with and a low roof over your head, you can really imagine all kinds of things. The Space Place was where you could learn as well as to have a good time." — Stephanie Sommers, Grade 5.

This is a typical feeling children have as they enjoy the Space Place environment. A child who is allowed to manipulate his environment and make choices which please him apparently becomes a happier and more satisfied child.

The physical world surrounding children is usually determined by adults; the house is divided into spaces by an architect or builder, rooms are divided into spaces with furniture selected by parents, and the schoolroom offers little or no choice in its arrangement. The outside world is spatially determined by a host of forces. There is rarely an opportunity for children to make their own decisions about the environment they live in, learn in, and play in.

The Space Place was created to provide children with these experiences that are usually denied them. Developed not as a toy but as an instructional tool, the components of the Space Place are manipulative in nature and children can arrange them in various configurations. The components consist of a false ceiling of stretch panels which become a series of large or small spaces by using weighted blocks to pull down sections of the ceiling panels. The ceiling component is flexible, creating an undulating surface

under which styrofoam blocks can be stacked and arranged to create spaces within a space.

Opaque and translucent panels can be hung tentlike to create walls and serve as projection surfaces.

The use of 35-mm slides and 8-mm film loops creates various types of visual phenomena within the environment.

A tape recorder or sound system provides options for various sounds to complement the visual environment.

Multicolored modules are used as seating arrangements or additional building components to further develop an environment as simple or as complex as the children desire. Manipulation of these components by the children is the basis of the activities. The Space Place provides an opportunity for a free experimental kind of activity or a highly structured design problem.

EDUCATIONAL GOALS

The Space Place was designed as a manipulative environment that could be introduced into the classroom setting. The environment that the Space Place creates is not static. It is one in which the student has alternative choices or decisions to make about how the various components can be arranged. The following outlines the educational outcomes which the designers feel are applicable to the Space Place.

1. The student will be able to make aesthetic and functional decisions about the arrangement of space within the context of the school. The decision-making process will be reinforced in the process of manipulating the structural components of the environment, such as styrofoam blocks, ceiling panels, and the visual and aural dimensions or components.
2. The student will be able to define and solve problems which deal with the division of space and the aesthetic use of space.

3. The student will become aware of the effect of the environment on the individual, a group within the context of the environment, or a community. The Space Place is a setting which is immediate in the school and gives the student an opportunity to experience first hand the individual and/or group process of making aesthetic decisions about the environment.

STRUCTURAL COMPONENTS

White styrofoam blocks are of three sizes, 6 by 12 by 12, 6 by 12 by 24, and 6 by 12 by 36 inches, and are extremely durable. The material most widely used by the children are the blocks. The similarity between these blocks and ordinary wooden building blocks and bricks makes this material the one children readily relate to and feel most confident in using.

Ceiling membrane panels are of three sizes, 24 by 24, 24 by 48, and 48 by 48 inches, and are in a variety of colors, opaque white, opaque black, and translucent. In addition to using the panels to make up the ceiling membrane, extra panels can be used in a variety of creative ways, such as for walls, as an alternative to blocks, or simply to hang to create a form or sculptural effect. The translucent panels function as a dual projection screen or wall, with the visual image reversed on the back side of the panel.

Elastic connectors are of two lengths, 6 and 12 inches, made of shock cord with an S hook attached at each end to hold the ceiling panels in place, and allow the flexibility for the ceiling membrane. They can also be used to hang extra panels *without* altering connectors in the ceiling membrane. The 12-inch elastic connectors are used to attach panels to the steel cable.

Weighted blocks are provided so students can lower the ceiling as desired.

35-mm slides and 8-mm film loops provide additional colors, shapes, patterns, visual textures, images, and movement to the environment. Three slide projectors and one film-loop projector create almost as much student interest as the styrofoam blocks and are considered exotic machines.

Tape recorder or record player can be used to provide options for various sounds to complement the visual environment. It is suggested that students create their own Space Place music in addition to the tapes or records.

SEQUENCE OF ACTIVITIES

The initial experience with the Space Place is to provide acquaintance with the structural components of the environment. The manipulation of these structural components is fairly simple and can be accomplished by students at almost any age level. The teacher's role in the Space Place then becomes one of setting or creating problem-solving situations that the students can be involved in. It is not necessary to follow any set procedure; however, a sequence of experiences for student movement through the Space Place experience is suggested. Individual teachers may, and are encouraged to, adapt the following sequence when it seems applicable.

1. The first session acquaints the students with the various components of the Space Place, and show them how these can be manipulated. The points to emphasize in this initial contact are:
   (a) The ceiling can be lowered or raised in various ways.
   (b) The blocks can be used as support for the ceiling, but also as separating members or modules of the existing space.
   (c) The extra panels can be hung vertically to be used as space dividers and projection surfaces.
   (d) Additional dimensions can be added to the environment through projected images both static and moving, through the use of 8-mm or 16-mm films or loops. Sound

tapes or records can be used to complement the spatial relationships that have been established.

2. The second activity is built around either a further expansion in problem solving, using and manipulating the elements, or in a motivational context for the students. Motivational problems which can be used to manipulate the structural elements are illustrated by the following example:

Problem-Solving Approach

1. Construct a space that has the following requirements:
   (a) It should contain enough room for three people.
   (b) It should be divided into three activity areas: one quiet area, one activity work area, and one conversation area.
   (c) The spaces should reflect the function related to one another and should be aesthetically pleasing. Also discuss how the spaces they construct can be made visually and aurally more attractive. What should be added or deleted to accomplish this?
2. Using only the ceiling and the hanging panels, create a geometric space which is not a square. Use the visuals in such a way that you create an open feeling within each space you have defined. Topics can be selected from the visuals to create a city feeling, an outdoor feeling, a closed-in feeling, etc., within the space.
   Variation: Using the ceiling and the blocks create a geometric space which is not a square. Once the children understand their constuction problem divide the class into small groups of two to four children per group and begin construction.
3. The third phase would be to further delineate problems which are culminating in nature. For

instance, a problem which is built upon a social situation, an imaginary situation, or a functional situation could be used. An example of the imaginary situation is given below.

We are ants — build an ant colony!

Discussion questions:

If you were an ant, what would you look like?

How would you move?

Do ants talk?

How would you communicate to each other?

What is an ant colony?

What is an ant colony used for?

How do ants build or construct their colony?

How many rooms make up an ant colony?

Are all the rooms the same size and shape?

How do the ants go from one room to another?

Once you have the children involved in making decisions and imagining the forms and shapes that they need to build, discuss the various types of structural components they are to build with. Add further motivational cues if needed. From this point on allow the children to create their colony, but remind them that this is a group activity which will involve cooperation and planning as a unit. They are now ready to begin building.

4. The last activity should be a summation of what the students have worked through. There should be emphasis on the fact that our environment affects us as individuals and as groups of people living in it. The students should be aware that the decisions that are made about the environment very much affects them and how they live. The relevance of the aesthetic component of the environment should be stressed as it provides an approach to the quality of total life experience. Correlated areas of study, such as the role of the urban designer or the architect in shaping the environment, could be related to instructional activities on the city or on city planning.

NOTE

1. The Space Place was created by a team of designers: Theo. Van Groll, School of Architecture, University of Virginia; Atilla Bilgutay, School of Architecture, Washington University; and Stanley Madeja, CEMREL, Inc. The design project was supported by a grant to the University City School District of Missouri from the JDR 3rd fund.

    The Space Place has been in a number of school and museum settings, among them, the Oklahoma Arts Center, the St. Louis Art Museum, and the Philbrook Art Center, Tulsa, Oklahoma. It is now part of a traveling exhibit entitled *"The Five Sense Store,"* designed by the Aesthetic Education Program of CEMREL, Inc. The exhibit is being circulated by the Smithsonian Exhibition Service and opened at the National Collection of Fine Arts in Washington, D.C., April 1973. The exhibit will tour the United States and Canada over the next two years.

Planning for Change: Neighborhood Design and Urban Politics in the Public Schools*

C. Richard Hatch

All lovely architecture was designed for cities in cloudless air . . . cities built that men might live happily in them. . . . But our cities [are] cities in which the streets are not the avenues for the passing and procession of a happy people, but the drains for the discharge of a tormented mob, in which the only object in reaching any spot is to be transferred to another; in which existence becomes mere transition, and every creature is only one atom in a drift of human dust and current of interchanging particles, circulating here by tunnels underground, and there by tubes in the air, for a city, or cities, such as this no architecture is possible—nay, no desire of it is possible to their inhabitants.

John Ruskin, Lecture to the Royal
Institute of British Architects, 1865

This is an age, even more than his own, that Ruskin prophetically described in 1865. One hundred years later in the United States nearly 70 percent of our population lives in or near

*From *Teaching Urban Action: Planning for Change* and *Community Planning Handbook, Urban Action: Planning for Change,* created by C. Richard Hatch Associates, Inc., © Copyright, 1970, by Ginn and Company. Used by permission.

such cities. Four million urban families occupy "dwellings of such disrepair as to violate decent housing standards," according to the President's recent housing message. One quarter of our urban population lives in poverty; the rest lives in fear. Our neighborhoods are marked by a paucity of open space, staggering unemployment rate, inadequate schools, squalor, increasing crime and a pervasive sense of individual powerlessness.

In 1831, Alexis de Tocqueville found American townships in New England "so constituted as to excite the warmest of human affections." We must return the cities to their people and eliminate poverty and white racism. In so doing, we may create a desire for architecture where none now exists.

During the past few years the government has created a vast array of benefit programs designed to ameliorate the present critical situation. With the exception of the most sophisticated, city residents now look upon these programs with either open skepticism or fear. Communities, ignored in the initial planning, have learned to build effective organizations to resist outside-directed efforts. It is becoming apparent that planning, urban renewal, and social service activities cannot be carried out at the scale necessary to rebuild our cities without the effective participation of a knowledgeable citizenry. Without the active support of those who most desperately need assistance, the level of public renewal and welfare efforts will remain unequal to the task—and the task is nothing less than the creation of a humane environment from the chaos of our cities.

The scale and intensity of the violent outbursts in many cities during the summers of 1967 and 1968 leave no doubt that the minority poor have lost faith in the willingness of white America to deal purposefully with the issues of race and poverty. The very institutions that have sustained the poor have come under sharp attack along with the slumlord and the exploitative merchant. The urban school, the traditional vehicle for socialization and advancement, is now accused of fostering "genocide" and has become the focus of the ghetto community's anger born of frustration and discrimination.

Planning and programming for community development require social and technical skills that are not now taught in our schools. Yet such knowledge is increasingly important to adult performance in an urban world. A school curriculum that deals directly with the development issues central to our urban neighborhoods can go a long way toward reestablishing the relevance of the school in the community. The practice of these skills is also important to the child, for it requires the careful analysis of social indicators and the understanding of rights and responsibilities and the process of government; it also requires the child to evaluate alternative future states and to determine how they may be achieved.

DEVELOPING THE PLANNING CURRICULUM

In the summer of 1965, during my tenure as Executive Director of the Architects' Renewal Committee in Harlem (ARCH), a group of graduate students were hired to prepare reports of the history and condition of the Harlem area and its inhabitants. ARCH had been created some months earlier to provide free professional services to organizations of the poor in Harlem that were attempting to deal with the complexities and dangers of urban renewal and federal housing programs. Community education was a major thrust of our work, and the summer's program produced widely circulated manuals on tenant action, welfare action, housing program procedures, and similar matters of urgent concern in the ghetto.

In the course of their work the students unearthed a good deal of graphic material, which, it occurred to me, would make a fascinating social studies unit in the public schools. With the half-hearted support of the Board of Education, I developed and taught a brief course on the past and future of Harlem in two seventh-grade classrooms. The classroom discussion ranged from the first Negro real estate agent's success to Malcolm X's vision, to the design of African cities, to strategies to deal with slumlords. After Christmas vacation, when the experiment ended, sixty of the sixty-two students signed a petition to continue. When the principal insisted that the children return to their study of New York State history instead, they started appearing in our office on Lenox Avenue to watch us at the drawing board or to listen as we discussed our planning work. The excitement the program had generated convinced me that the idea was worth pursuing.

During the spring of 1966, with the strong support of the Center for Urban Education, New York's Title IV Regional Laboratory, and its director, sociologist Robert Dentler, a refined program was developed and arrangements made with the Board of Education for installation in nine ghetto schools. Curriculum planning began with the assumption that the satisfaction of the middle-class professional derives in large part from his ability to comprehend and manipulate his environment, to demand a response from our semimono-lithic contemporary institutions, and to determine the course of his own life, and that the apathy of the poor reflects a *real* inability to understand and cope with a social and political framework of power that consciously excludes them and deni-grates their cultural patterns. No mobility, no learning, and no long-term gratification are possible to the child who sees his entire immediate society powerless to affect the decline of his community, and the style and scale of our political institutions make direct participation increasingly difficult.

Clearly, very specific social and technical skills are required in order to play an effective role in the present decision-making processes. With these things in mind, we set out to develop a curriculum in the social sciences that, by making children expert in their own environment, knowledgeable of the neighborhood power structure, and familiar with the men and processes of government, would strengthen their self-images and prepare them for active political roles as adults. To do this, a curriculum must be realistic—it must deal directly with the conflict in our society and must support the child in his first engagements with it. It must involve him in evaluating the role of the groups and agencies competing for power in his milieu and direct his attention to *critical* struggles from which he can derive a functional understanding of political power.

The staff assigned to the project developed detailed information on the history of Harlem, Bedford-Stuyvesant, and Mott Haven, and made contact with the numerous local citizen groups with which the children and teachers would be working on projects in their neighborhoods. A student handbook was also produced. Called *Planning for Change,* it contained survey forms for the investi-gation of neighborhood housing and services, information on public agency responsibilities, and case studies of successful community action projects.

In my mind the course was intended to achieve five objectives:

1. An awareness that the environment is the creation of man, and is the result of decisions that can be located, understood, and changed by individual and group action.
2. To enable the student to see himself as an actor, rather than a passive recipient, in educa-tion and life, and a participant in community process.
3. To open new areas of choice by making stu-dents aware of both practical and utopian alternatives.
4. To make school relevant to life in the commu-nity, thus increasing the child's willingness to learn essential verbal and computational skills.
5. To increase the teachers' knowledge of and sensitivity to the special problems and strengths of minority group children.

Action was and is the key. Teachers were encouraged to let children take the lead in determining what should be studied within the neighborhood and what should be done about it. Teachers were encouraged to adopt the posture of good community organizers: not to do things that students could do, but to help the students do things for themselves. Recorded comments from participating teachers are revealing:

Well, I think it has vastly improved the student-teacher relation-ship in my classroom, for two reasons: the students are pleased to see my participation, they know much more than I do; they also like my vulnerability. I can't be a steady, impene-

trable institution in the class when we set goals together and cooperate.

At the beginning of the year I said to the kids that we may eventually become involved in solving some problems that they had identified—air pollution, the war in Vietnam, general poverty in the country. When I said, "what about here—what about something in the school that should be changed" they said, "you can't change the school; how can we do anything about the school?" It was so close that it loomed so large, that they were willing to take on the whole world. They've reviewed this thought and they have now reached the realistic point: "Maybe we can begin to attack here . . ." In effect, we can start; we can follow it for years; we can become aware and involved now—but we're going to start with something close, not in the clouds.

Another teacher who has my class happened to mention that she was having trouble getting her apartment painted; she was having problems with her landlord. This was immediately seized upon by my class and they came up with very concrete proposals. They brought in the book You and Your Landlord *and told her that she could demand certain things. They really gave her the steps to follow.*

There are all sorts of names for our community—a community within a community within a community. The students named all the possibilities, except one. They didn't say, "This is part of Harlem." To me this was very obviously and clearly left out; so the next question was, "Would you say you lived in Harlem?" which was followed by, "Is Harlem a place?" "Is Harlem an idea?" "What is Harlem like?" A lot of the kids' own prejudices, feelings, and ideas toward Harlem really started coming out in my class. With that one question posed in a variety of different ways, we discussed it for two or three weeks.

After going out on several surveys, comparing neighborhoods and housing, one of the students said to me, "You know, a man looked at me and said, 'you're too young to be doing this.'" And the student said, "but we're doing it and we're learning something." The realization that I'm here and I don't have to hide from it, and in it, and to it—make it better for myself and others.

Students' comments are even *more* interesting:

Right now, we divided the class into three committees (housing, consumer problems, and welfare). I'm on the housing committee. We're interviewing people from rent-controlled buildings. There are lots of different violations in the old houses. We're going to hand out the [*Rent and Rehabilitation Administration*] *form, A1, to help them lower their rents.*

If you don't have a group you can't do nothing in the community, because people aren't interested. Well, I think that the people are interested, but you know, they just say "let the other fellow do it." And everybody keeps on saying, "let the other fellow do it." And nothing gets done. They're waiting for one person to make the first move. And I think that if a person just gets up enough courage—one person or a couple of people in the neighborhood—they keep on talking about it and go around to the other people. Then they could get a group to get something done.

Well, I think the city or the state, they should plant some trees and try at least to fix it up. Clean up the place and try to clean up the bums that hang around there [*a park*]. *If people wouldn't pressure, the city or state wouldn't do nothing. Well, they should form groups and sign petitions and say, "what type of park is this?" It's supposed to be a beautiful city, like on postcards—all fancied up.*

Although the children in the program were only twelve and thirteen years old, they were able to accomplish a great deal. Brooklyn students organized their parents and neighbors into permanent block associations and wrote and distributed their own Spanish–English handbook called *Tenant Power.* Two enterprising students in Upper Harlem became and remain full-fledged members of the official local planning board. Other Harlem students undertook a consumer-education program involving extensive price surveys and newsletters. Still others, working with volunteer landscape architects, architects, and planners, produced proposals for neighborhood housing and recreation facilities. At least one—a small park—appears about to be realized.

Early in 1970, based on these extensive field tests, *Urban Action: Planning for Change* became widely available as a multimedia course for use in grade seven and above.[1] The specific content of this course is the structure, function, and growth of the urban or suburban (community) neighborhood. Information for study and analysis will come from field trips; mapping; interviews with parents, political figures, community service workers, businessmen, doctors, real estate brokers, and others; and visits from architects, planners, and neighborhood leaders. These data will be supplemented and interpreted with the aid of the materials in the *Planning for Change* kit.

The Six Units

Unit 1 — Cities: Purposes, Problems, and Planning. Why do people come together in the cities? Brief comparative studies of cities in history. How planning can help solve social and political problems. How city plans are made. A case study of one urban community in action. An investigation into local government and how its resources and responsibilities relate to community problems. (This introductory unit is a prerequisite to all the others.)

Unit 2 — Who Lives and Works in the City? Why? Why parents and neighbors have come to the community. What opportunities and satisfactions they find there. Their experience is compared with that of other immigrants to the city. Students identify important economic functions of the city and the neighborhood. They inquire into the distribution of economic activities and of income in the city. They investigate the growth of the city as an economic and social institution and inquire into the changing role of local government.

Unit 3 — The Art and Culture of the Neighborhood. Artists, as well as social scientists, have sought to express the meaning of the city and urban life. Students examine painters' changing views of the city and experiment with words and images to capture the flavor of their own community and its people. They investigate the culture of their neighborhood—its music, food, customs, and languages—and discover those unique aspects of the neighborhood that help create a sense of the community.

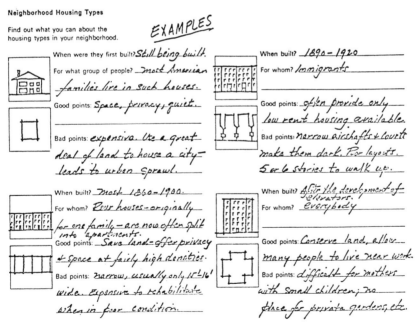

Figure 1

The Land Use Map.

A land use map shows how every piece of land in the community is being used. It gives a good picture of what goes on in an area. You make a land use map by adding colors to a base map, using a different color for each different use of land.   Here is a review of the land use categories and color code.

Planning Land Use Code

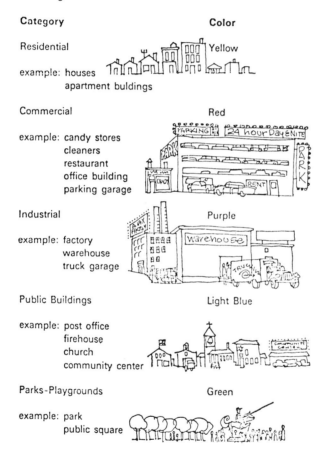

Category	Color
Residential	Yellow
example: houses apartment buldings	
Commercial	Red
example: candy stores cleaners restaurant office building parking garage	
Industrial	Purple
example: factory warehouse truck garage	
Public Buildings	Light Blue
example: post office firehouse church community center	
Parks-Playgrounds	Green
example: park public square	

Vacant lots and vacant buildings are not colored in at all. Mark them with an X. An apartment house with a store on the ground floor is colored yellow with a strip of red on the street side to show the store.

Figure 2

The Building Condition Map.

A building condition map shows the physical condition of every building in the community. It points up clearly what areas of the neighborhood need the most attention. The planner usually gets his information about condition by studying carefully the outside of the buildings. Like the land use map, a building condition map is made by adding colors to a base map. A different color is used for each condition.

Planning Condition Code

Category	Color
Good—building in need of no repairs or only minor ones	Yellow
example: needs painting slight damage to front steps a few, small cracks in walls	
Fair—building is basically sound but needs some major repairs	Orange
example: rotten window frames broken stair treads chipping plaster	
Poor—building in such bad condition that it is dangerous	Brown
example: large, open holes in floor, walls, or roof major damage from fire	

Mapping Your Own Neighborhood

You are ready to begin making a base map of your neighborhood. You will have to take careful measurements of every block and every building on every block. Then you will have to draw them to the scale your class has decided on, like 1 inch = 100 feet. Be sure to note the type of each building so that you draw the proper shape.

This is a very big job. It will go faster and easier if teams of students work on small areas of the neighborhood and put them together later into one large map. You will need at least 3 copies of the map. One for building condition, one for land use, and one for your future plan. The maps will last longer and look better if they are pasted onto stiff pieces of cardboard.

Once the base maps are complete, you will want to gather land use and building condition information. This will mean going to every block and marking on the map the condition and the use of every building.

Unit 4 — What Makes Up a City Neighborhood? Students learn to use planning maps and charts to gather and interpret data about the physical and social nature of their area (see Figures 1 and 2). They inquire into the uses of land and the condition of structures. They investigate the adequacy of the commercial, social, recreation, and transportation services of the community. They investigate the internal distribution of power and of "interest groups" and compare community needs with existing plans for change.

Unit 5 — Designs for Ideal Communities. Are there alternatives to the way we live today? Can planning influence social values? Students examine utopian architectural and political solutions to contemporary urban problems and evaluate the applicability and desirability of each in their own neighborhood. They inquire into the nature of good urban design and apply the principles to projects in their study area.

Unit 6 — Making a Plan for Change. How is a plan designed and presented to the public? What are the politics of plan acceptance and implementation? Students review their neighborhood data and set preliminary goals for future change. They analyze the positions of relevant political forces of major urban issues, and they develop an understanding of the conflict over scarce resources that marks city planning. In a simulated political context, they make final decisions on goals and projects for inclusion in their plan. They present their plan to the community and to outside agencies and seek to organize a neighborhood coalition in support of it. Through this, they learn how individuals and groups use the formal and informal mechanisms of politics to change a city. At least 6 weeks must be given to this unit. If a plan is not completed and presented, the learning value of the earlier units will be seriously undermined.

NOTE

1. Building on the experience of the eighth grade program, we have just completed a more extensive curriculum designed for the fourth and fifth grades throughout the city. The ages of the children using the new material dictate a more restricted action orientation. We have greatly expanded the time given to the study of utopian solutions to our urban problems, drawing heavily on Le Corbusier, Frank Lloyd Wright, and the Goodmans' *Communitas*. Greater attention is also given to ethnic, racial, and neighborhood history. But the idea of action remains.

   Since the above article was written, the elementary school program in planning for New York City has been tested in some forty public school classrooms. It has been well received and, following revisions and improvements made during the summer, is to be used in over one hundred schools (including the decentralized schools) during the present school year. We believe that we have proved the validity of "Planning for Change" in the public schools.

The City Building Educational Program: A Decision-Making Approach to Education

Doreen Nelson
with the assistance of
Teri Fox, Ty Miller, Dan Benjamin, Greg Spiess, Alexis Smith

The City Building Educational Program, or CBEP, developed in response to a concern for urban living and the changes that individuals and groups face as they move toward an unknown future. In the past, children were able to follow the paths of their parents, but the rate of change in our society has become so accelerated that, in addition to imitating the example set by adults, the child of today must be ready to make choices that will help him to take an active part in predicting and directing his future. The primary goal of the program is to make this possible—to broaden the vision of the learner out into the world in which he lives, to help him discover resources there, and to prepare him to make choices that will benefit him, his teachers, his family, and ultimately the total community.

The program grew out of both social and educational considerations. An Environmental Goals Committee, established in Los Angeles in 1967 to formulate environmental objectives for the metro-politan Los Angeles region, conducted interviews with citizens on how the city could or would look. It was apparent from the interviews that few people could envision the possibilities for any alternative environment. They know only the noise and confusion of traffic congestion, inadequate public transportation, overcrowded facilities, and cluttered open spaces. They had experienced no other surroundings and could not conceive of effecting changes. From a social standpoint, it was hoped that our program would provide the participating children with an opportunity to experience the alternatives that their parents could not imagine. These alternatives would be both concrete, in terms of decision making and effecting changes within groups, and fantasy-oriented (e.g., actually building scale cities and structures).

The educational concerns of the program were perhaps more specific and came about in response to the limitations of traditional teaching methods. In elementary education, the teaching process is a centralized system with information and problem contexts generated by a single source, the teacher, and information can be exchanged only along one line of communication. If this link between the student and teacher is weak—if the teacher is unable to "reach" a particular student—the process stops for that individual.

The CBEP maintains this organization to some extent, but the program involves a gradual decentralization over the course of the school year as multiple lines of communication are created. Each person within the classroom is seen as a potential teacher as well as a student, and it is each person's responsibility to take advantage of the information available. Real problems that interest students are dealt with, community resources are made available, and tools can be mastered within a context that is relevant to all the students.

The initial activities were chosen to provide situations in which organization by the students at various levels would be necessary to generate a solution. Greater organization is demanded by each successive problem until eventually the students can initate their own activities, analyze their own problems, and carry out group decision making by themselves.

Another aspect of current elementary teaching to which we chose to address our project is the rigidly structured and detached method by which children are taught their relationship as individuals to society. Early education generally begins with a study of the home and moves gradually toward a study of the community, then the society, and finally the world. The child is supposed to assimilate his role with relation to these complex organizations by studying their structure and extrapolating the connection between himself and the individuals of which they are composed. We feel that this connection can be made more successfully by giving the children an opportunity to experience these relationships for themselves on many levels.

Through activities that constantly force the child to examine the relationship of himself to the small group, to the large group, to the community, and to the society, activities that call for decision making and necessarily generate conflict, the child develops a concrete understanding of how individuals form organizations and how organizations work. This understanding is more than academic, for it becomes part of the child's working knowledge and can be applied to everyday situations.

The idea of conflict necessitating action, touched on briefly, is integral to the CBEP. Formal education often fails to prepare students for real life because it generally presents them with problems that have only one "correct" answer. This may, in a certain sense, make problem solving easier or less frustrating, but it does not encourage children to deal with complicated issues for which many solutions may be partially correct (see Figure 1). In our model we set up problems with built-in obstacles or complications, which do not allow for any easy solutions. The final solutions are amalgams of many people's "correct" answers. In this way, we try to create a more accurate approximation of real life and accustom students to applying information to many facets of the same problem.

The CBEP began after the results of the Los Angeles Goals Program had led many of us to conclude that education was the only way to raise community consciousness toward city goals. In

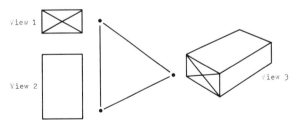

Figure 1
Three views of reality, each unique and correct.

1969 the children and their teachers in grades 3–6 in a Venice (Los Angeles) elementary school decided to give up the past (the district-scheduled study of the westward movement) to explore the present and future. In September the children began to study and redesign the Venice community. It wasn't a new idea; we know that giving children cameras and letting them photograph their world helps them learn to read. As one child explored her life she said, "I don't want to take a picture of my house; it's so ugly." At that time she couldn't envision it differently. After the children had evaluated their neighborhood, they started a basic study of physical change. They began by taking common objects like forks and pencils and coat hangers and making simple transformations. In one exercise they picked everyday objects, studied them, and fabricated the objects to their scale as costumes, learning about structure and space as the object changed in size. We thought that if the children experienced a transformation of their own bodies, they would begin to see similar possibilities for other things like the "ugly house."

As the objectives of the program crystallized and we began to acquire a perspective on what worked, the "transformation" concept gained importance. This can be applied to objects made larger or smaller by a change of scale or to natural changes, such as the growth of a caterpillar from a cocoon to a butterfly.

The children always had to consider their relationship to the subjects or objects they studied: "What are the consequences of living in your house? being in a classroom? How would you change it? What would you do instead?" The first transformations were done with paper and pencil, some as drawings (fantasy collages of houses made after walking trips to see real houses), some as stories or just lists ("A snail increased in scale could cover an indoor swimming pool"; "The school playground, open twenty-four hours, could

become a community center"). But these were only ideas and needed to be substantiated by research.

After seeing photographs and books on famous architects, the students formed groups and studied the work of each architect. Using mainly visual analysis, they described the common features of the buildings. They examined each architect by describing their personal reactions to his style, and were able to discover who had influenced whom as well as how the architect's work had changed over his lifetime.

One girl chose Gaudi, and after several weeks of study, came to me and said, "You know Gaudi's stuff looks like that guy Sam Whatchamacallit who did the Watts Towers." She had never seen Watts Towers other than in photos, and her ability to make this connection proved that she was beginning to analyze the world of ideas and where they came from. She went on to say that the buildings also looked like some of those old churches in Europe, and showed photographs of the cathedrals in Milan and Chartres.

One interesting thing we noticed was that many children were suspicious of being able to do art for schoolwork. Most felt that if they didn't do pages of math or spelling, it couldn't be real schoolwork. At first we kept to the type of problems they were used to, incorporating the visual aspect of their environment as the main resource by asking them to measure their room, draw a piece of furniture to scale, draw their room to scale, their house or their block to scale, count trees, count cars on the freeway at 5:00 with the number of people in each car, average them, etc. Finally I was able to say, use twenty-five words to tell about anything; make up your own homework!

During the first half of the year the students examined Venice, and discovered what existed there and what the consequences were. Then they went on to do what proved to be a giant simulation of the community planning and government process. Boundaries were formed around the community, and by decreasing the scale the students brought a large section of the Venice landscape into their classroom. Each child became a property owner through what might be called a "land grab," and the job of redesigning Venice began. It was at this point that the need for professional planners to work with the children became apparent. In response to a call for help, two University of Southern California graduate architecture students came to visit the class. They subsequently became involved with the project, and spent several mornings helping to bring about a fantasy city of the future.

The experiment of bringing in outside professionals was a success. The graduate students were able to give the students more specialized information about the planning process and about structures. But more importantly, the introduction of outside adults helped to decentralize teaching and set up a complex network of communication lines. The presence of "architects" also gave the project a special quality, as it reinforced the idea that what the children were doing was important.

Acceptance of and support for the program in its experimental stage were readily received from the children, their parents, and the Venice community as a whole. The children were very proud of their work, and the number of people who came to see their fantasy city of Venice gave increased weight to their ideas. One of the few elements of disappointment came when the child mayor and his city council were given an audience with the real Los Angeles City Planning Commission to describe their plan for Venice of the future. After the Commission had heard the plan, the Director hit his gavel on the table and said facetiously that he recommended that the Commission accept the children's plan. The mayor of the class shrugged his shoulders and said, "They think we're just little kids and that our ideas can't work, but they haven't done such a great job!"

During the fall of the second year, I was invited to the University of Michigan to present the project before an urban gaming seminar. Over the course of the two-week conference, I participated in many games of widely different designs, and I came away amazed at the similarities between our giant Venice puzzle and the computer-generated simulation games such as *Metro, CLUG, APEX,* etc. We were using all the same components without the hardware, and having a success with children that was rare among groups of adults. Seeing the project in this light prompted me, together with architect Frank Gehry, who had already conducted some workshops, called "Fantastic Cities," for underprivileged children, to devise a short-term game simulation based on some of the ideas I had been working with in the Venice classroom. The game, called "Purium," was conducted at the Smithsonian Institution in Washington for one summer. It was offered for both children and adults, and the adult courses eventually came to form the basis for our teacher training sessions. I must say here that I was extremely reticent at first about presenting these children's games to adults, and was especially intimidated by the idea of professionals, such as architects, playing city building games with styrofoam and cardboard. But their comments and the correspondence that I have maintained with them indicate that they feel the game actually contained the essence of the planning experience.

The first in a series of teacher training courses was held at the Smithsonian Institution during the summer of 1972. This experimental workshop was, to the best of our knowledge, the first funded attempt at placing both adults and children from a variety of socioeconomic and ethnic backgrounds together in a learning setting in which participants could experience role changes, that is, act the part of the concerned citizen, student, teacher, planner, and/or decision maker.

Our specific goal was to develop a core of

teachers who would be able, at the end of the summer's workshop, to return to their school districts and design and implement similar programs within their own setting. It was hoped that through the summer workshop we would be able to identify more people qualified to conduct the program in schools throughout the country, to continue experimentation, and to consult with project personnel on the further development of materials and systems for perpetuating this process of visual and experimental education.

Although the CBEP began as an attempt to raise the environmental awareness of children, it has since evolved into an innovative method of teaching upper-grade elementary students the subjects required by state law through the use of gaming. The gaming, or "simulation," deals with the city process and is used to examine current issues. The curriculum establishes a vocabulary related to the organization of things and how this organization is perceived. Emphasis is placed on the meaning of structure, function, transformation, and other changes and attributes discovered within these arrangements. The vocabulary then is applied to the organization of both physical and social systems through exercises which cover the teaching of urban government, mapping, scale relationships, and the use of diversity in materials. Actual building experiments allow the children to design a future fantasy city. This final stage, the building of a city model out of styrofoam, demonstrates the children's ability to apply the information gained from participation in the CBEP workshop.

The current goal of the program is to help the youngsters become critical thinkers, able to apply their information in new settings, and to actively participate in the formation of future life styles. Granted, this is not the traditional sort of problem solving. New lessons are improvised from existing situations, and the teaching is spontaneous. The learner must find the necessary tools to solve problems as they occur, rather than learning the tools by rote and applying them when it seems appropriate. With direction by teachers and professionals, the learner, by reexamining his basic assumptions, develops the ability to determine the appropriate problems on which to focus. Within the context of the model, he must ultimately ask, "Do we want cities at all, and, if so, in what form?" This is the issue that must be raised and dealt with by human beings who live, work, and communicate in an urban environment.

PROGRAM ACTIVITIES: (WHAT THE KIDS DO AND WHY)

The CBEP in an experimental form has been conducted on a year-long basis in various locations; this was made possible through joint funding from the National Endowment for the Arts and the U.S. Office of Education. Each classroom was made up of a typical group of public school children, most of whom were average students. Throughout the study, the activities and techniques used by the CBEP staff were aimed at examining and experimenting with individual and collective efforts to raise problems, bring about their solution, and regenerate new problems and solutions.

Included here are some of the major events in each classroom, as well as a description of the children's activities in the study of city building and the identification of the systems, structures, and specific activities of which the city is composed. These events should be considered in light of the basic objectives that we used to establish a course of study. These objectives were to

1. Bring the child to a greater understanding of his environment and world.
2. Introduce him to the use of group dynamics as an approach to solving problems too complex for the individual.

3. Meet the educational objectives of existing state-wide curriculums.

Pretest and Orientation

Initiation to the concept of structure occurred through a series of exercises and experiments beginning with the Purium City Simulation Game. For this game, the children were told they were "future people" (meaning technology could accomplish anything they wanted to build), and presented with a ready-made landscape of mountains and valleys, with a river flowing through the valley. The major problem for the participants was to fulfill the needs of a city whose population was doubling every year (one hour of playing time equaled one year of real time). The massive population explosion had resulted from the discovery of Purium, a miracle material that made everything biodegradable. An introduction was presented to the participants in the form of a discussion about cities, and the children listed on a chart what they felt they didn't want and what they thought their city needed. The players had to plan housing, transportation, services, mining, and refining under a strict time pressure, which was applied by the adults acting as "the federal government." In a half-hour a land-use map of their city plan was made, and a mayor and city council were elected along with officials in charge of housing, transportation, utilities, air control, land control, and water control.

The intention of the game is to have the children decide what they feel is bad about a big city and help them understand that time and communication problems in a city pressure individuals and groups into making mistakes. When it was time for the children to build, the land-use map was ignored, and with a miner's cabin and a sailboat as scale references, the participants completed building Purium City to house 1,200,000 people. The federal government would step in when necessary to see that housing and transportation facilities were developing fast enough to accommodate the influx of people.

"You know the Purium City we just did? It's just like any other city. It's got squares and stuff, it's boring really, if you know what I mean. It's fun to make, but it's boring when you look at it."

"Today we made our first city. And it didn't turn out too good. It was supposed to be a city of the future but it looked like cities nowadays. And we had a list of things we wanted or didn't want in our city, but that got messed up a little."

Another such exercise was the redesign of the classroom space. For this activity the students

were given building materials, such as large cardboard tubes and refrigerator boxes, and asked to create a new, life-size interior of their classroom. After the exercise the room was called a "disaster" by the students who evaluated their ability as individuals and as a group to create work spaces, desk spaces, and storage spaces that could function and remain stable as structures: "Things don't stand up!," "No one was talking to anyone else," etc. In one classroom a boy built a room for himself with two doors to connect him with the rest of the class. Another boy built a telephone system; when the rest of the class didn't use it the way he wanted, he tore it down. The class had a meeting and decided that he had to build it again for everyone to use. The finished furnishings were also useful for evaluating the ability of the learner to organize space visually, as well as to simply make things stand up, and several small exercises followed the simulation to reinforce and elaborate on the concept of structure.

The pretests served as a general introduction to the program's ideas for the children, and were a means of evaluating the child's understanding of his city and of learning something of his perceptions of his environment. Many pretest forms have been used. The students have been asked to

1. Draw their neighborhood to identify landmarks, signs, etc.
2. Take twelve photos (black and white) of what they think is "good" in their environment, describing the reasons for their selection. The process was repeated with "bad" environment photos.
3. Study, identify, and draw the shape and location of the seven continents.
4. Establish techniques evaluating their own success or failure. (These change with each activity.)

Scale Transformation

The teaching of scale transformation was primarily accomplished by having the students select objects that they would become (for Halloween) and fabricate those objects at their own scale (as costumes). For example, one child decided to become a motion picture camera. By studying the object he discovered that several rectangular box shapes of different sizes join together to make the camera. By applying the proper ratio to increase each shape, the total camera could be produced much larger. After much experimentation with building rectangular

boxes, the student was forced to abandon his original idea in order to meet the building project deadline. Instead of a camera, he became a Kodak film box, which required only one rectangular shape to enclose his volume. Two girls joined together to become dice. First building one, then the other, they had to increase the size of the cube and dots to fit their body proportions. When the first die was completed, that child thought that she was finished and stopped working on the second. The other child was ready to give up on having an object to wear, so a group meeting was held, and the second die was successfully completed. (The importance of the children's discussion and resolution of their own problems, without the intervention of adult authority, cannot be overstressed. We addressed this entire program to the examination of decision making and the conflict or struggle it involves and to each person's potential as a teacher of others.)

Field Trips

Trips to the Watts Towers, the Bradbury Building, the Gamble House, the Los Angeles Arboretum, the Southwest Indian Museum, and the California Institute of the Arts gave the children a perspective on individual and collective efforts in the city building experience.

"I think a lot of buildings should feel soft. Some-

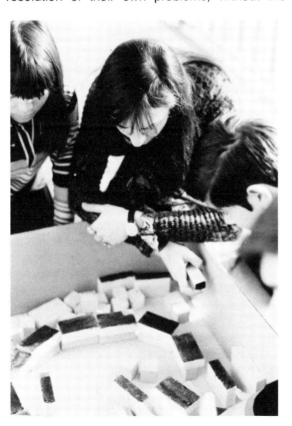
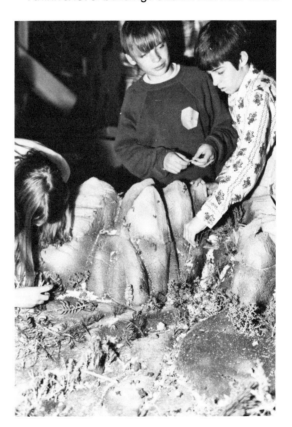

thing like the person who built the Watts Towers, he did that same sort of thing, but in a different way. Like he did make soft buildings, soft looking, but they weren't soft at all, they were very hard buildings. Well he makes it kind of rounded. I like the way he builds because they're not like sharp looking."

In one class a field trip provided an opportunity for the children to use their own initiative to overcome an obstacle. The trip was planned early in the school year by the students and professionals and was to include four stops over an entire day. The trip was actually cut short by the bus driver, whose schedule did not permit her to complete the last two stops. The children were angry and disappointed, but they were able to examine the cause of the failure—no one had understood all the details of the bussing regulations—and see it as a communication breakdown within the system. The children successfully rescheduled the trip themselves. They met several times with the head of bussing and studied the rules and organization of the system. They learned how busses are used and scheduled in school districts and compared the costs of private bussing as an alternative. The students had written letters of protest immediately after the original trip, but were asked not to send them until they had done their research. In the end, they decided not to send the letters after all.

Classroom Planning

The students designed two-dimensional scale plans showing arrangements of furniture for activities in a classroom. The fantasy classrooms were designed to be interesting, functional, and responsive to the students' particular learning needs. Some of the better plans were chosen to be tested in 1-inch scale models. Formal presentations and criticism of each individual or group plan were held. The children attempted to put some plans into action by changing their classroom furniture as much as possible. They found that there

is a difference in volume as scale increases; several students complained that what worked in the scale models did not work in the real classroom.

Natural Structures

The idea of the imagination game illustrated was to have the children learn more about structures, societies, natural materials, and survival. Before the game everyone was asked to bring in natural things, such as leaves, wood, or feathers. Each child who brought in natural objects became a member of the group, which took a time-machine trip back to 1 million B.C. With the aid of a scale model, the children used the natural objects for building materials to make shelters to protect them from the rain and wild animals on the island where the time machine had taken them.

Each day, as more students brought natural objects to class, they became members of the "tribe." In this way a society began developing to organize the food gatherers, fire tenders, and other workers. Campfire rituals, including songs, chants, and dances, also developed. Through this gaming simulation a sense of responsibility for and identification with a group was established. The beginning of community participation and concern was evident.

One outgrowth of this activity was the study of tribal societies. Three classrooms joined together to become a tribe, forming clans, councils, and governing rules. A composite tribe based on their research information was simulated, the children accenting the rule that in order to make a decision a 100 percent vote of the tribe was needed. Since planning for classroom activities was handled by the clan leaders and tribal chief, many meetings took several hours to get a consensus. It had been decided that the tribe simulation would last one month. At the final tribe meeting, reports of new systems of government were presented, and the acceptance of a democracy instead of a dictatorship was held up by six children who insisted that simulating a dictatorship would be fun. The children sat it out and made each student defend his reasons until the total tribe agreed on a democracy.

Claes Oldenburg's Film and Exhibit

After seeing Claes Oldenburg's film and his sculpture "London Knees," the children were reintroduced to object transformation and scale change. "Ice Bag," the name of both the film and the sculpture, was shown to the children at the Pasadena Art Museum. The students took their object costumes to the exhibit.

Maps

All the classes used opaque projectors to help draw maps of their communities on the larger map of the city with its council districts. This exercise was a continuation of having the children think about their city in a two-dimensional perspective. Streets were located on the maps. This was a lesson in scale, direction, and map legends.

Discussion of Communities

The students were instructed to identify functionally styled buildings and those which were overly decorated and nonfunctional.

Questions were formulated by planning consultants to help each class decide which areas of the city they would study and redesign. During this time the students studied the Los Angeles city and county governments. Following the real example, the children elected their own city council members, mayors, and planning commissioners or Board of Supervisors, after speeches were given by the student candidates. Surveys, designed by the children, were prepared for the communities each class was to study. These were taken, and the community supported the students in gathering data.

Boundaries were formed around the communities the classes were to study. The students used professional surveying equipment to measure the street boundary angles so that their communities could be scaled down and reproduced in their correct shape. Architects helped the classes measure the angles of their community with a transit and protractor as they walked the designated boundaries. On their playgrounds the classes reproduced their communities' boundaries at twice the scale to be used in the classrooms: 1 inch to 25 feet or 1 inch to 20 feet.

Choosing Properties

In each class the children experimented with different ways of choosing pieces of property. Ownership helped demonstrate the economics of private property and the logic behind urban planning, or the lack of it.

Walking Trip Around Community

The architecture students and advisers accompanied each class on a walking trip through their own communities. These walks gave the children a chance to take pictures and study their communities' boundaries, landmarks, good points, and bad points. They examined their communities as a planner might study the existing area before redevelopment. "If we had tall buildings out there on the beach, then the short buildings couldn't see the beach, or the water, or nothing."

Los Angeles City Hall Field Trip

The classes visited the Los Angeles City Hall for a city council meeting and then met with Councilman Edelman, Councilwoman Russell, and Councilman Braude. The children asked questions about population, transportation, and air pollution.

Sand City

Another simulation exercise of city building was done on the beach at Venice. The children's ideas for building were tested in the sand. The children reproduced the shapes of their own communities, using protractors, a transit, yardsticks, and string.

Plans for Private Property

With the background from their community surveys, elections, and study of the real city, the classes began to plan their properties with regard to individual, group, and community needs. This kind of in-depth planning required identifying the wants and needs of the property owner, the neighborhood and the community at large.

Individual properties were drawn on paper shaped the same as the child's plot of property. The pieces of paper fit together like a huge puzzle to form a map of the area under study. The properties were irregular, and this helped the children to think of city planning other than on a grid plan.

Development of Plans

Each classroom developed their community's fantasy city into a plan, some with no private ownership of land, others with total private ownership. Three classrooms working together completed a community-owned city with private interests dominating over public interests. The architectural consultants showed the class how a "bubble diagram" helps experts relate uses of certain areas to uses of other areas. This idea provided a bridge from the concept of private ownership and land development to that of overall urban design. The bubble-diagram method led the students to develop a map with housing (low cost, elderly, and suburban), industry, government services, parks, shopping centers, schools, and amusement areas that related to each other in terms of distance, noise, height of buildings, and landscape.

Transportation systems, such as rapid transit, pathways, bikeways, and moving classrooms, were planned with the minimum of roads and cars necessary for cases of emergency. Color coding was introduced so that the map could explain itself.

Transferring Private Properties to a Large Map

All the children began by designing their individual properties, which were then transferred to a large map the size of the fantasy model. The large map was then mounted on styrofoam blocks and color coded. Children experienced many perceptual difficulties in placing their pieces in the correct location, as well as when reversing the total plan by drawing it in a mirror image.

Planning Commissions and Governments

To simulate city government and ensure a well-planned community without housing problems, a planning commission was established. At regular meetings, discussions of the feasibility of plans took place. Rules, regulations, and procedures for having plans adopted were designed and communicated to the "citizens" to help them in building on their properties. Often citizens' interest groups formed in response to unacceptable decisions made by the planning commission.

Working with the total government organization, some classes simulated city government with a mayor and city council; others simulated county government by electing supervisors, a chief administrator, and a regional planning commission. In all cases, once the form of government was established, it remained until the final model was completed.

One supervisor who was also an individual property owner with land on a hillside zoned as public open space, decided to level the hillside and make individual swimming pools. The group he represented and the planning commissioners whom he had helped to select forbade him to complete his plan. The citizens' groups representing people with interest in open space brought about a zoning law aimed at preventing the destruction of nature. In the final city evaluation, buildings were kept or rejected by the commissioners based on this law. In other instances, aesthetic principles dominated so that one class actually gave power to the city planning commission to move buildings in arrangements that "blended together" and "looked good."

Los Angeles City Council Members and Planning Commission as Resources

Students had a chance to really use the resources of Los Angeles' elected officials when questions of city procedure came up in the class city council meetings. Such problems as how to replace a suspended city councilman and how a planning commission is selected and operated were answered by Councilman Edelman's office and the Los Angeles Planning Commission's office.

Helium City

Some classes created a floating city from balloons filled with helium. "Packing" the space above the city map was done to demonstrate three-dimensional filling of an unframed space. Strings were attached to the balloons and anchored with pins to the styrofoam-mounted map. Buildings were shaped with balloons as closely to the student's designs as possible. Some, such as the butterfly school, were very recognizable in balloon shape. The day's purpose was to define a given shape in an alternative form. This applied to the shapes of the buildings, as well as to the shape of the fantasy city.

Consultation with Architects

Throughout the school year architects and planning students were in-class resource people.

Both teachers and children used their professional advice in projects that were new and difficult. The professionals, who would begin making a structure or a drawing, helped stimulate the children to begin physical activities such as construction, drawing, or painting. The architects were especially useful to the students when the two-dimensional map was changed to a three-dimensional model. Group and individual problems were discussed and solved through reasoning between novices and professionals.

Building a Finished Model

The final stage of the CBEP began with the construction of three-dimensional buildings. After plans had been passed by the appropriate commissioners, styrofoam was carved into the shapes each child wanted. Then the buildings were painted and embellished as the buildings' designers wanted. The buildings were placed on the model in relation to each other as they had been on the map, with changes occurring when necessary. Transportation systems were then pinned onto the base or painted; in some cases, fabric landscape was wrapped around the styrofoam base connecting the buildings to each other.

Evolution of Ideas for Individual Buildings

One example of the transition of an idea to a reality was an apartment house shaped like a big yellow bird. On the school's two-dimensional map, the proposed housing complex overlooked a park with a lake. As the three-dimensional city model was being built, the designer asked for some "professional" assistance from one of the architects. He did the rough sawing of the styrofoam. There was also some consultation on decorating the structure, and the student drew elevation sketches of the styrofoam bird building to get a better idea of what people would see if they lived in her building. The huge yellow beak became a community restaurant, and the finished

building supported itself and gave the city a monumental structure that was a useful landmark.

Another child's idea for a "butterfly school" was voted by the class as the plan to be used in the educational area of the city. The original concept of a school with mobile classrooms was accomplished by creating a special transportation system to move the classrooms. Several attempts were made to create a building that did justice to the idea behind the school. The final butterfly school was stylized, well-proportioned, and maintained the designer's original concept. The green park area where the school was situated was a large community cultural center with museums, a theater, a symphony hall, and a library.

The "community flower" building was a group effort to fulfill the need for housing for the elderly and a convenient shopping center, with housing in the petals and the shopping area in the center of the flower. A transportation system was also provided for the apartment complex.

The "Herman the hermit" building was designed by two children who joined their properties to-

gether and built a "megastructure." The structure included apartments, a shopping center, and a restaurant. The scale was not proportional to the rest of the city, but the huge building was a monument everyone in the city could see.

The following questionnaire indicates the kinds of considerations the children used in evaluating their building and land uses.

HOUSING
(single and multi-dwellings)

Questions by Terri Meadows and Norma Proctor, Lisa Mandelsohn and Socorro Moldonado, ages 10, 11

1. Do you have a place for people to live without paying a lot for rent? _____

2. Will your property have a high cost, a medium cost, or a low cost? _____

3. How many apartments do you have? _____

4. How many single houses do you have? _____

5. What is the average of how many people can live in one of your multi-dwellings (apartments)?
_____

6. Do you have enough room in your structure to move around in it? _____

7. Will each person have a nice view of something that is pretty to look at? Either an open space or a view of the city? _____

8. Will each person have some place that they can go in or near your structure where they can have privacy at least once a day? _____

9. Will there be some sort of recreation in or around the building? _____

10. Will your living units or structures be close to all the transportation for moving about inside and outside the Venice area? _____

11. Will they be close to all the services that a person needs in order to live comfortably? _____

12. Will the sun go on every side of every building?
_____

13. Will the apartments allow people to have pets?
_____

14. Will all your buildings look alike? _____

15. Will there be schools near your housing?
_____

16. Will there be churches near your housing?
_____

17. Will there be community centers near your houses? _____

18. Will there be any empty lots available for people to buy and build? _____

19. Will there be strict building laws for people who build in the future? _____

20. Will the apartments have security? _____

21. Will the dwellings be checked for bugs and fumigated? _____

22. Will sunlight and fresh air be let into the apartments? _____

23. How will a person go about getting an apartment?
_____

24. How will a person go about getting a house?
_____

25. What laws will there be to avoid overcrowding?
_____

More Buildings

The "telephone-off-the-hook" building was a monument to the telephone company and to the poor people who could not afford to have telephones. (Monuments were significant because they represented objects that might not exist in the real future cities.)

The "convertible stadium" was finally made functional after many attempts to construct a building that would support itself and also many people.

The "H2O building" was the city's water and power center, and its function was easily recognized by its shape.

The "tooth building" housed dental-care facilities.

The "information building" provided a readable map of the community for one of the fantasy cities.

Parks were common in some of the cities. Several parks included rivers, lakes with bridges, hills, trees, and a waterfall.

The forbidding "hypodermic needle" building, a community clinic, showed its function graphically.

A building to store bikes that could be bought or rented was in the shape of a bike—the wheels serve as the storage area; the handlebars are a receiving station to which the customer calls in his order; the information is programmed, and the bike is available at the wheel when the customer arrives.

Major Decision in the Planning Process

The year 2000 or beyond was selected to allow development of technology to accomplish imaginative proposals. The project stimulated a great many creative concepts for providing community services. For example, as a consequence of the decision to have no automotive transportation, an alternative means of transportation was a vehicle that flew on a cushion of air and had the shape of a top. All "tops" were of the same size, and the passenger vehicles were designed to carry a maximum of twenty people. Tops landed and departed at designated stations strategically located within the area and placed within an approximate three-minute walk from any given

point. To accommodate automobiles for use outside the area, nine of the top stations bordering the area were situated on top of car collectors, two-story circular buildings used for parking.

Another example of the class's imaginative ideas was future planning for utilities. Solar energy, transformed and stored by converters atop each structure, provided the primary source of energy. Telephone lines and poles were eliminated through the use of technologically advanced portable telephones. To cope with the serious problem of pollution and water purification, special prefilters for water and sewage were installed in each structure. In each instance an attempt was made to address both esthetic and physical needs.

NEW ROLES AND A NEW CURRICULUM

Opportunities to participate on many levels gave the children a new depth of experience in addition to the regularly prescribed subject areas of elementary education. The students became *change agents* in the classroom while working on the educational city model. Critical thinking and physical building were as much a part of the classroom activities as was consultation with resource people and planning with peers.

The development of an idea from beginning to end provided a new experience for the children. Their own ideas became realities in the CBEP. In many ways, they became their own teachers. As the children first experienced in the Purium simulation, an idea might seem worthwhile, but as it is developed and built, the finished result (in this instance, a city) might not be as well accomplished as originally hoped. This occurs when the physical restrictions (materials, craftsmanship, and time pressure) become part of the original idea. In some cases the children redesigned a property or building until it was a success visually and functionally. The butterfly school and the sports stadium are examples of this trial, error, and eventual success. In other cases the students became discouraged with a failure, as demonstrated by the fact that they would either give up or they would ask another student or resource person to help them redesign the building. Making ideas a reality was an important experience in the CBEP.

The girls in all the classes had new opportunities in leadership roles, as decision makers, change agents, and as responsible citizens. There were girl mayors, city councilwomen, tribal chiefs, and property owners. At one point a girl had chosen property surrounded by property held by boys, but they refused to listen to the girl's ideas and ignored or laughed at her. She complained to the teacher, and was moved to another piece of property, but agreed to take her property back and stand up to the boys when the situation was brought out into the open. As a result, she became a recognized member of the group whom the boys listened to and worked with. Several girls were especially talented in designing buildings, for example, the butterfly school building.

Probably the most important new role was that of students as future decision makers for their communities. Not only were the children dealing with contemporary urban problems, but they were also learning the differences between individuals and communities, between what a community wants and what it really needs, and between feasible ideas and fantasies.

Huge gaps between ideas and their feasibility were discovered and became a positive aspect, rather than a negative experience, for the students. A sports arena was started by one boy; after successive failures, but with a growing number of student helpers and consultants, the stadium was completed.

The kind of curriculum described here is still one that teaches children math (via scale mapping and building geometric shapes), physical science (climate study, earth cycles), botany, zoology, geography, economics, sociology, psychology, history, and government (by writing their own documented history of their own constructions and serving as officials). Because the children are dealing with their own present and future lifestyles, and not some historical "event" with little or no relation to them, the skills of reading, writing, and speaking evolve naturally.

It has been observed that CBEP doesn't cover all subject areas, nor does it deal with all learning problems. The program has experimented with ways of presenting the planning process, and has mainly been conducted with upper-grade elementary students. Through the years of its evolution, the program itself has remained dedicated to change. As each year is evaluated, the original purpose is restructured, opening up new directions.

EVALUATION AND FUTURE DIRECTIONS (KINDS OF SUCCESSES)

Children's Cities

Classes differ in their approaches to building cities. Although the teachers and resource people in each class helped define approaches to city building within each class, the children were the most important decision makers about what kinds of cities were designed and built. The two main approaches were those of the individual, thinking of and accomplishing his own ideas, as opposed to the group, executing ideas thought up by a few individuals. These attitudes related directly to how well individuals worked with each other and in groups.

In some instances children had great difficulty in working together. Each child wanted individual attention and was unwilling to pool his ideas and work with even one or two of his peers. Because certain children were more vocal than physical, they spent more time arguing than trying to make different ideas work together. City council meetings accomplished little, and individual property owners often regarded their wants and needs as more important than those of the community. This problem diminished later in the school year because of the constant pressure of the program to learn to work and think together (although students were not encouraged to think alike).

Other children found working in groups easiest and apparently cared for the community's desires more than their individual wants. Part of this might have been due to an urge to do less thinking and avoid decision making. Most of the class leaned on a few brighter and more vocal students, and they were busiest when their city became "socialized" and individuals were no longer responsible for their own properties. Even buildings were often invented by one individual and built by a group. The city itself reflected this group thought in an overall sameness of size, scale, and color. There was more of a collective pride and understanding of the city among some students, and they appeared to have an understanding of how their city "worked."

Both the individual and collective approaches presented problems. When each child was responsible for his or her own property, the children were so busy filling the space that careless planning and craftsmanship produced an overcrowded and out-of-scale city. Strong group orientation produced a city that had far fewer buildings. Each was well crafted, but the effect of the city was cold and impersonal. Although the housing was undiversified and stoic, the transportation system was highly effective in the group effort; but there were few parks and only one specific recreation area to connect with the rest of the city. On the other hand, the individually oriented city had many parks, amusement areas, and people-oriented buildings, but it lacked a reliable transportation system and other needed services.

Through the processes of city council meetings, simulation activities, and model building, it was hoped that children would become thinkers and workers as well as individuals and members of groups. Group discussions, such as the city council meetings and simulations, encouraged intelligent verbal expression. Model building helped form working groups, which utilized the best abilities of each individual. Toward the end of the school year the project's adult resources began applying heavier time restrictions, forcing the children to complete the city. Because of this pressure, the children often became more cohesive and "went on strike," saying that the city was their city, not the teacher's or other adult's. This show of independence was an important step, making it clear that the children identified strongly with their cities. It was a goal of the project to develop independence, leadership, and determination.

Use of Resources

National Endowment funding made a variety of resources available to each classroom. These resources went beyond the usual materials available to public elementary school classes. It was hoped that they would enrich the educational environment by providing the children with more outside information and experience, which would stimulate them into thinking in greater depth about their school subjects. This goal was accomplished with the help of field trips, professional people, magazines, newspapers, and building materials.

Probably the most important and most innovative aspect of this program was the intense help received from professional architects, planners, photographers, video artists, and other resource participants. Besides paid consultants, volunteer university students within related fields provided many insights not usually presented to an average class. The college-age students conveyed a relaxed, informal attitude in the way they dealt with both the subject areas and the children. They were available for consultation and help with physically difficult projects. These older students helped the teachers by explaining in some detail why certain techniques and methods should be applied to the project and how these ideas could be accomplished. The university students also added aesthetic and vocabulary input for the teachers who had no architectural or planning experience.

Other resources for ideas and techniques were available in the magazines, newspapers, and library books sent to each classroom by subscription or requisition. The *Los Angeles Times, Artforum, Art in America,* and Los Angeles City Library books were chosen for their pertinence to the CBEP. By flipping through the magazines and books, the children could get some idea of what people had already thought of, built, or dreamed about. There were also explanations and technical information on how to build things like air buses, buildings, and super garbage systems. The *Los Angeles Times* helped keep the classes up to date on governmental decisions in Los Angeles that might affect their communities in the future.

Field trips allowed the children to see things firsthand which they would not have been able to see in their classrooms. These trips also gave them the opportunity to participate in activities, such as building a sand city and a huge kite. With firsthand knowledge of places and ideas, the children returned to their classes armed with new information and new perspectives on their projects.

In the classrooms the materials ranged from Super-8 movie cameras, video tape equipment, and Kodak Instamatics, to art supplies and building materials for the city model. Because of this range of materials, many different kinds of activities could take place inside the classroom. City council meetings were taped on the video tape equipment and replayed to the children to give them pointers on how to make their meetings more effective. Steps in building the city were filmed by children who had been given special technical instruction. Helping to document and record activities gave the children more perspective on the planning process. Classroom materials such as poster paints, paper, and masking tape

were used a great deal. These and other art materials allowed for experimentation, while styrofoam and wood helped to make structures that could support their own weight. A professional transit was used for surveying and determining angles of the communities of which the classes built their scale models. Fabrics and decorative materials were also incorporated in the project to give the fantasy cities color and variety. The use of fabric was an attempt to have the children make their city aesthetic and pleasing to the eye, rather than to abandon aesthetic decision making to professionals, as is the case in a real city.

As the program expanded, greater emphasis was placed on the use of natural materials and standard classroom instructional supplies. Utilizing professional and community support as a major resource, the concept explored by the natural structures simulation was incorporated into some of the later cities, reducing further the use of "special supplies."

The use of standard state texts for teaching mathematics, reading, and the social sciences has proved invaluable, because the books provide a wealth of historical information that children can examine, criticize, and expand upon. The state math texts, for example, include an in-depth explanation of the major concepts touched upon by the project.

Follow-Through

An important part of the program was the need for follow-through of ideas and activities that were begun and that related to the city building process. Vocabulary, surveys, trips, lectures, and films contributed to the development of each concept. Teachers, project directors, and students also helped develop the momentum and direction of the program.

Although not all the ideas and activities that were begun were finished, every class did have a city model to present at the end of the school year.

Some aspects of the program were not successfully completed. In particular, none of the teachers kept the detailed logs in which they were asked to record events to help evaluate the program. The teachers and children in several instances were willing to give up when parts of the program became difficult, and no complete diaries were kept to explain their feelings about the project. The post-tests in some cases were failures, with one teacher admitting dictating answers to the children to speed along the end of a very demanding school year.

Unfortunately, as the program expanded, few new teaching techniques were recorded for future use by the teachers. The teachers were either not interested in or unable to use, in depth, the written materials made available to them. The daily newspapers were used only occasionally, and the specially selected library books were seldom used in class plans. It is understandable that the cameras and video tape equipment might be too technical for the teachers' use and could have been more effective with the help of an outside person.

The program suffered because of the undefined roles of the teachers. Without confining the teachers' roles, it would have been helpful to have provided goals and directions along with the available subject areas and other requirements. The need for developing new teaching methods and accountability is an important factor that should have been stressed along with greater depth of instruction in subject areas. The project did provide experimental study courses for each main area of study orientation and a year-long plan of activities. The teachers did not participate in redefining this material as was intended.

The Smithsonian Institution summer workshop was planned to orient teachers to the first experimental course of study, to have them play and design simulations, and to broaden their knowledge of planning and architecture. In a morning session teachers played the part of the children, participating in simulated lessons; afternoon sessions were conducted to define the purpose of each activity, and evening sessions were conducted by architects and planners in hopes of familiarizing teachers with the planning vocabulary.

Some teachers, in returning to their classrooms, were able to put their experience into action in a total year-long program; others used only parts of what they learned. In one case, a trained teacher returned to her home school in Sulphur Springs Union School District and directed a team-teaching approach to the CBEP with five other untrained teachers, but she elected not to use the program's resources. She delved heavily into government processes and the history of cities, offering the children an alternative to their usual education. Unfortunately, her omission of the architect–planner and the programs methodology put her project at a disadvantage. Rather than addressing themselves to the concepts and conflicts inherent in redesigning a community, the children were arbitrarily given the traditional tract home development as a basis from which alternative city arrangements could emanate. Thus the children failed to experience and participate in the initial stage, which contains the steps critical to a successful decision-making process.

In another case, the teacher conducted her own year-long class, and trained her team partner, who had not attended the summer workshop. Their classroom of sixty children was an excellent example of the application of the program's ideas. There was a minimum of guidance from architect–planners; instead the focus was on the regular use of the study guide and other project resources.

ORGANIZATIONAL DIFFICULTIES

Several problems became apparent during the course of the program. School schedules, classroom locations and space, teachers' understanding of the program, and the amount of time the teachers were willing to devote to the program were some of the major areas of conflict within the CBEP.

Playground recesses can be ignored if the children are intensely involved with a subject or activity, but rotating classes for math and sciences cannot be ignored. The rotating of subjects mitigated against the program, because this project requires periods of indeterminate length for thought and concentration by the children. The active school day is already short for those participants interested and enthusiastic about their projects, and for some the daily change of math classes and the selection of many students for chorus helped to dampen enthusiasm for the CBEP. The effectiveness of visiting professionals was inhibited by numerous interruptions.

Insufficient classroom space was a problem in some locations, because the use of materials required work space separate from the tables and other teaching areas of the classroom. One class did most of their building on the stairs and balcony outside their room.

The requirements of accountability also posed a problem because, as with any new educational program, the CBEP has not yet developed ways of measuring children's intellectual growth, and data have not yet been developed to show computable advancement. Although it is possible to know when a child understands math, it is difficult to chart what he knows about problem solving as it relates to city planning and decision making. Written and oral language can be fully used in this program. Math, social studies, and the sciences are endemic in the CBEP because scale, structures, and social involvement are major parts of the building process. Because this city is a "teaching model," the teachers are the catalysts responsible for relating "the City" to all academic subjects required in the public school. Some lessons were hard to present in lesson-plan form. Decision making, for example, was taught by trial-and-error reasoning and the use of the scientific method. Sequential flow charts also emphasized that the child select the tool appropriate to his needs when preparing to solve a problem.

As the school year progressed, it became increasingly difficult for the teachers to make connections between the city building process and their own lesson plans. As the time limits became more apparent, less time was spent explaining the concepts behind decisions and more time was spent on building the physical model. The professionals felt this lack of adequate continuity on the part of the teachers, and this created tension between them.

Some of these problems were overcome as a result of the teacher-training workshop, yet certain weaknesses were still apparent. Many of the summer-trained teachers returned to their home schools to find no administrative understanding or support for their ideas. Another difficulty was the teachers' inability to relate the program to specific statewide mandated subject study skills.

RECOMMENDATIONS

Because an important aspect of the CBEP is its experimental nature, which requires flexibility and cooperation among all participants, several changes are necessary for its continuation. Many apparent difficulties within the past years were related to the teachers' participation in the program. It is felt that criteria for selecting these teachers should take into consideration their willingness to work under time pressure, willingness to work with outside resource personnel, and attitudes about completing activities. Rather than leaving the selection of the teachers to school administrators, it might be helpful to develop screening techniques. The project's teacher selection process could be combined with an intensive session that would allow interested teachers to experience the teaching model in much the same way as a child might. Those teachers who reacted well to the project would be encouraged to continue the CBEP within their classrooms. Weekend planning retreats among the adults chosen to participate could allow the "sounding" of ideas and help establish basic communication and cooperation. This activity could also help establish a community feeling among the teachers, resource people, and administrators of the program.

Another way to eliminate areas of misunderstanding among participants would be to institute a written agreement. The agreement would state exactly those things required of each teacher, such as logs, lesson plans, and the completion of program activities. It would also be clear what the teachers should expect of the project resources and the professional people. The teachers' roles would be defined before the program got underway, making it possible for everyone to agree on fulfilling certain obligations. It might also be helpful to establish regular weekly or biweekly meetings for the professional resource people and the teachers, at which time ideas and problems could be freely discussed. Disagreements and misunderstandings could be talked about. In this way, encouragement and support could be shared among the participants to provide an atmosphere of exchange and understanding. Participating teachers could also be freed from the pressure to make every phase of the project "successful" if they were allowed the opportunity of regular exchange with the other participants. (Problems sometimes occurred when the teachers felt they might be reprimanded if their class did not live up to predetermined standards.) The meetings could also create new leadership roles among the adult participants. Chairing of the meetings could be rotated, allowing each adult to emphasize areas of need and interest. In this way, teachers could participate more fully in the

direction of the program. Such an arena might also help eliminate any competition between the teachers and professionals for the control of the children's time for responsiveness.

As I have mentioned, over the past years the program has shifted from a strictly environmental emphasis to one of general education. We feel this trend is valid and should continue. Courses offered by accredited schools of education (including teacher training workshops with children, similar to the Smithsonian design) should be held with selected teachers and their school administrators. This would give teachers and administrators the necessary experience and background information to design their own curriculum based on our preliminary research. It would also provide us with an evaluation of the program from the viewpoint of both the teachers and administrators—often two differing positions—and would hopefully generate a dialogue between the two. The use of the film "Kid City" made in the Los Angeles City Schools and video tapes made at the Sulphur Springs Union School District could provide further access to the program's activities and content. Through a year-long training program in which the teachers experience the program firsthand with children and then put it into practice with supervision, it is hoped that highly qualified teachers would be trained to carry out the program's objectives. In this "teacher force" it is essential that leadership roles emerge so that the use of the project's resources is transmitted by the most successful teachers, and that they in turn begin to train others.

A positive aspect of the program that has never been fully developed is that of supporting the teachers in expressing their own creativity in the area of lesson plans. Each individual has a responsibility to contribute his own ideas and efforts, just as the children are encouraged to create and build new kinds of cities, so the teachers should be encouraged to demonstrate new teaching methods and develop their own lessons relating math, reading, and science to the many facets of the project.

The school administration could be helpful in encouraging the teachers to be flexible and experimental. This attitude might be expressed in something as simple as providing a custodial service that is not rigid and demanding on the teacher. The CBEP is messy, and constant attention to neatness is often a hindrance to creativity in styrofoam and paint. The school principals should also be aware of any special pressure imposed on the program teachers by other teachers in the school. The principal might choose to provide other teachers with alternative benefits to relieve any tensions or envy resulting from benefits received by the program teachers. Morale could be improved by inviting other teachers into the program's "workshop–classroom" to see for themselves the amount of work required from the program teachers for the resources they are given. This exchange would also provide the visiting teachers with new information and would allow the program teacher to explain and describe the activities and goals of the CBEP.

The "workshop–classroom" idea requires the teacher to provide a workable environment for the children, an atmosphere that allows them to receive and make the best use of individual and group attention. Some teachers have a tendency to give their students a total democracy, which allows the children to express their ideas freely, without direction. In the extreme, this policy leads to confusion about the children's roles in the classroom. Other teachers try to establish order and discipline, sometimes at the expense of the children's individuality. We feel that the teacher involved in this program needs to establish an environment, within the classroom and out of it, that promotes both effective learning and teaching and individual expression by providing direction and leadership without rigid discipline. It is easier to create this type of learning situation when uninterrupted blocks of time are available so that

activities which are begun stand a fair chance of being completed within the school day, week, or year. When math and language are taught to the same group of students each day, there is a greater opportunity for the teacher to relate lessons successfully to the teaching model.

One of the greatest single needs is for the program participants to be committed to the idea of completing an experiment or activity. If the experiment proves to be unsatisfactory, the participants should be expected to provide new, alternative experiments. If the wear and tear caused by interruptions and conflicting schedules can be minimized, teachers and other participants will be less likely to become discouraged and abandon experimentation.

The program's materials and resources were provided to make possible as many different kinds of experiences as could be worked into a public school framework. Cameras, film, and field trips were freely available; but the teachers often avoided using the equipment and trips, perhaps because of a lack of technical know-how. These extra activities appeared to put additional strain on the teachers, because special effort was required to relate the activities effectively to conventional subject areas. The addition of a "media" resource person appeared to be an answer to this problem. This person was able to assume the responsibility for providing technical assistance, while relating photography, music, art, and various other outside experiences to traditional academic subjects.

Both public documentation, such as television and news media reports, and private documentation, such as the film made on the Los Angeles City Schools and the video tapes showing each major segment of the program, are valuable experiences for the children. Documentation helps the students define their city, show leadership qualities, develop better speech and language, and relate to their fantasy city as a real and important activity. The news media can provide the children with an opportunity to explain their ideas and with encouragement to complete those ideas. The city model presents a tangible example of the children's thoughts, creativity, and craftsmanship. Private or in-house documentation of the program should become so commonplace to the children and teachers that the video tape machine, cameras, and other equipment are not distractions. The video equipment and film should be seen as teaching tools. The children can use film making as an educational experience, and as another way of expressing their ideas and knowledge about their real and fantasy cities.

To promote the experimental idea of the CBEP, it seems necessary to tailor each year's process to the special needs and abilities of each group of children who are participants. In this way the program ensures change and adaptation that relates directly to the children, minimizing the adult urge to adapt the children to the program.

Through university, school district, and community involvement, the CBEP could be placed into a state-supported framework encouraging these studies. Such involvement could be strengthened by special meetings at which the documentation of the program (books, photos, video tapes, and films is presented. Parents might be even more supportive of the program were they to experience firsthand some of the simulation activities offered to their children. They might have reactions similar to those of the adults in the Smithsonian program.

Major formal evaluation and measurement of the CBEP has been intentionally withheld as field testing of the program continues to allow for further experimentation. Changes in learners' behavior have been noted through their ability to withhold "snap judgments" on information they have collected and through their ability to select resources to solve a given problem. Experience reports written by children describing their activities could become a means for evaluating their ability to take a body of information, plan it, organize it, and put it in a reasonable form. Children

could be tested on their understanding of what a structure is prior to beginning the study of structures, and then tested at the completion of that phase of the program. These tests on specific concepts could offer the program more information than the general tests given at the beginning and end of the program.

Finally, it was proposed that further experimentation be done using the completed physical model as a format for discussion with professionals from a variety of disciplines. In one class a physicist–mathematician did relate concepts of trash disposal and sewage to the fantasy design. An economist worked with children on land values, banking systems, and trade. From this experience, it seems that the introduction of outside disciplines presents almost unlimited possibilities, and eventually we would like to see an Urban Education Center, where further experiments in learning and in visual education could be conducted with an interdisciplinary mix of professionals as well as both children and adults. Such a center might not only train teachers but a variety of interested persons from various disciplines. The aim might be to produce a core of environmentalists or persons sensitive to and aware of their environment and able to communicate to others a new perspective on effecting change and improving the quality of our world.

In any public school the children's progress and welfare are the primary concerns. This is why it is necessary to encourage new ideas in education. To provide better educational methods requires experimentation and time. Accountability, designed to define good approaches, must be measured in more than quantitative methods, for this kind of experimentation is largely a qualitative educational device. The administrative, public, and professional support of their CBEP can help allow new and exciting approaches to public education as it relates to our urban environment. With this support, accountability for innovative programs will lead to a greater acceptance of new educational ideas.

Architecture: A Course of Study for High School Students

Robert Lloyd

Architectural design as a subject of study for a high school student serves as an immediate way to draw his attention to the relationships between a person and his environment.

In teaching architecture I am concerned that a young person should choose to regard his physical environment as important and as distinct from his social environment, his intellectual environment, his cultural environment, his interpersonal environment, or his eventual occupational environment. Although the ramifications of the word "physical" are many and ancient, here I mean those parts of a person's environment that immediately stimulate his senses. I want him to make sensory connection with what is around him and to keep that connection alive. Understanding that the strength of this connection is perceptual as well as sensory—that we tend to see what we choose to look for—I assume that its development is intentional and hence educable. Schooling strongly influences the perceptual choices a person makes, and a small deflec-

tion at an early age makes a great difference (for better or worse) later in life.

How can a young person's interest in his environment be encouraged, and how can his perceptual radar be best directed? The most basic answer to these questions is obvious: he develops his interest and skills by becoming actively engaged with his environment. Clearly, almost any activity provides opportunity for such engagement, and if one looks at a typical school curriculum, one finds that many engaging activities are provided, from football to computer work. Most of these are not, however, specifically environmental in their goals, nor specifically designed to enhance perception. I wish to describe a two-part program that several of us have developed at Andover, a program that does have these specific goals. The first part is a perceptual course, called Visual Studies, which, in addition to being a diploma requirement for most students, is a prerequisite for the second part, an elective architecture course. I shall describe the

Visual Studies course only briefly, confining my-self to a single, exemplary exercise picked for its relevance to the architecture course, which is my major interest here.

Each student in Visual Studies has two teachers. One teacher gives him exposure to basic photography, concentrating on the development of selective seeing, and in addition, via movies, slide-tapes, and discussion, suggests some of the broader range of the visual arts in history and in a variety of media. The other teacher introduces the student to a combination of two- and three-dimensional design exercises, including drawing, collage, paper bending, sheet metal, wire, and other media not particularly difficult to deal with. By sequencing exercises, each of which is highly structured, demanding, and open to many different solutions, the studio teacher attempts to involve the student in structured perception, in problem solving, and in the rewards of doing the job well. But let me give an example.

The problem I shall describe follows in sequence another problem in which each student has been asked to draw a series of objects held in his hand beneath the table: felt but not seen. Without thinking about it much, most of the students have drawn the unseen object with conventional line technique, recording an outline and any sharp edges within it (Figure 1). Imagine the complexity of the perception required to translate a set of tactile sensations into an assumed, fictitious, single point of view and a fairly well-proportioned drawing of the object! After complimenting the class on its unconscious skill, I observe that in using this technique a student is obeying a convention in which a line can do two things: (1) delineate an enclosed area as singular and distinct from what lies outside it; and (2) function as an interior edge in such a way as to create our sense of the volume of the object (Figure 2). Suppose that we look for some entirely different conventions, some new ways in which lines on a page can suggest to us a thing and its volume?

Given an object on the table before you (I say), imagine a series of parallel, vertical, equidistant planes, ¼ to ½ inch apart, in plain view perpendicular to your line of sight as you face the object. From your actual point of view, draw the inter-

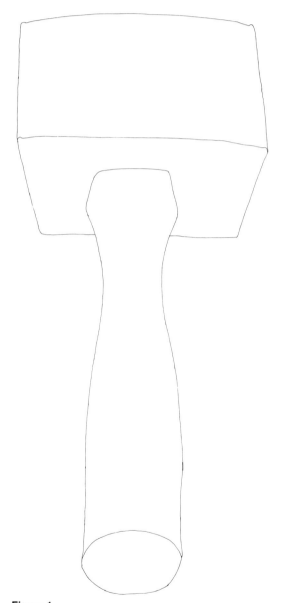

Figure 1

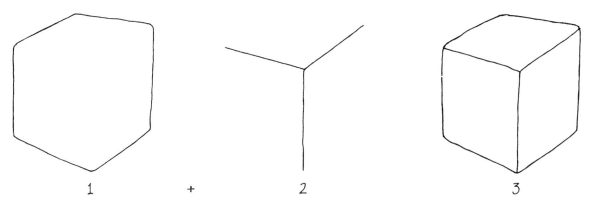

1   +   2   3

Figure 2

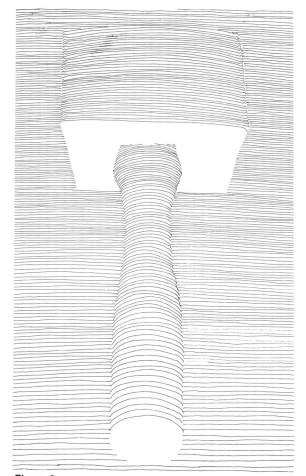

Figure 3

section of each plane with the table top and the surface of the object, omitting those lines which, if actually drawn on the table and the object, would be obscured by the opacity of the object.

In addition to the fact that the resulting drawings are often quite elegant (Figure 3), if the instructions are carefully followed, a number of new kinds of articulation appear. These can be categorized roughly into two groups: edge definition and surface definition (Figure 4). Without burrowing into any extended theoretical discussion of the mechanisms of perception, let me point out that, in fact, all these examples have one thing in common: in every case, the perceived articulation is composed of lines but is not itself a line. In every case the system of lines induces us to perceive an edge or a shaped surface where, in fact, there is no specific stimulus —on the paper *between* the lines. It is apparent, then, that this perception does not occur on the paper but *within the perceiver*. These articulations cannot be perceived at all without this degree of engagement.

Anticipating for a moment the architecture course, let me point out that this perceptual engagement—the capture of one's eye and attention—is occurring at the same time as the student is drawing lines on his pad of paper. That is, at the same time that he must attend to the physical characteristics of the line (is it straight?

Edge Definition:

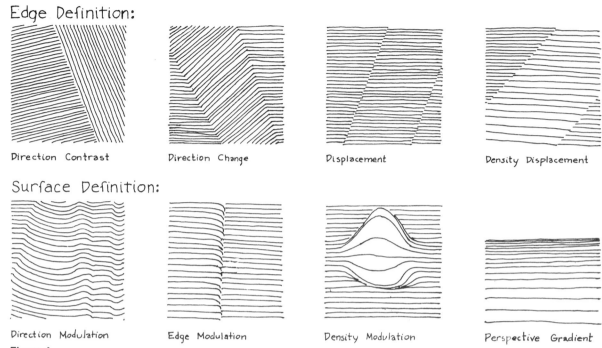

Direction Contrast   Direction Change   Displacement   Density Displacement

Surface Definition:

Direction Modulation   Edge Modulation   Density Modulation   Perspective Gradient

Figure 4

is it of an even darkness? is it in the right place? is it equidistant from the line next to it? at what point should it disappear behind a section of opacity in the object? etc.), he must be aware of what is happening to his total perception of the drawing, which includes the almost magical element of the blank spaces between the lines coming into a new, strong order and life. This new order and life are both imaginary and undeniably seen. That is, out of one's rather measly efforts with a pencil have come—from nowhere, apparently—powerful communicative results: a new thing is seen, the major components of which are not the lines one has drawn at all, but result from the way one has drawn them. The appreciation that one can depend on this result (and many similar results) coming to meet him "from nowhere" is, I would say, the basic faith of the designer: that by his skill he can draw upon and greatly amplify the *perceived* bounty of an already bountiful environment.

In combining concrete effort with communicative imagination, the student in Architecture develops his capacities for design in the same directions established in Visual Studies. Problems are assigned to which a concrete solution is required. By the time a student has made his "answer" to the problem a real solution, all sorts of additional meanings have attached themselves to the problem, and his imagination has been given a disciplined workout. By definition, problem solving is an active engagement, and if the problem given is environmental, the engagement is going to strengthen a student's environmental perceptions—and prejudices. What kind of environmental problem, then, best introduces a student to the broad area of environmental design? What kind of design problem best introduces a student to the concerns of an architect? What kind of course dynamic establishes a direction of rewarding exploration and continuous development for an imaginative student? I shall try to share some of my experience in answering these questions.

In the context of our school there is an additional fact that may make my experience unique. Because our school year is divided into three ten-week trimesters, each with a new registration, each trimester's enrollment includes some new students and some old. The needs of both must be satisfied. For this reason I have had to design three different introductions to architecture, each of which will satisfy a new student, and which, when put in sequence, will still progress somewhere for the continuing enrollee.

The first course is a basic design-and-scale-model-building course of a traditional kind. The second is a problem-solving course involving the techniques of wood and metal working. In the third, the class has a real client for whom they must design and construct a piece of environment.

INTRODUCTION TO ARCHITECTURE I

The first ten-week trimester requires each student to design and build a scale model of four different human environments. The eighty hours of class meeting are divided among four projects as follows:

Project 1 (ten hours)

Two hours In small groups the students are asked to walk around the campus, trading off leadership. Each leader is to become like the counter on a Ouija board and to let each outdoor space lead him through itself and on to the next. The group should discuss what have been the influences on the choice of path.

Six hours I assign the first project, to design and make a scale model (¼ inch = 1 foot) of a small environment (the site is 25 by 50 feet) that defines an entrance, a central event, and an exit. The design may allow a person to walk only hori-

zontally. The project employs only horizontal ground surface and only vertical walls (of any shape or ground plan). My teaching function is to answer questions without suggesting specific solutions.

Two hours A class criticism of the completed project in which I concentrate on four things: (1) clarity of the scale relationship and connection between the imagined scale person (1½ inches tall = 6 feet) and the spaces; (2) clarity of the distinction between the three parts of the project, and the successful organization of each within itself (does the entrance invite, is the central experience interesting and satisfying, does the exit lead the person out with some defined "farewell" experience?); (3) the successful organization of the whole structure as a sequence of events experienced by the imagined scale person and as a formal structure appreciated from our bird's-eye view; (4) craftsmanship.

Project 2 (fourteen hours)

Twelve hours I assign the second project, which is the same as the first with the following additional considerations: (1) the site is larger (48 by 92 feet); (2) instead of a single central event, the pathway between entrance and exit may contain a number of contrasting events; (3) as a result, a wall may begin to function with regard to a designed space on each side of it; (4) although more complex, the design still must be controlled; (5) better quality of design and craftsmanship can be expected.

Two hours A class critique. The main difference between this critique and the first is that the students participate more as the source of judgment, offering on the one hand points of disagreement and reactions to confused design, and, on the other, encouragement on aspects that they like.

Project 3 (twenty-two hours)

Twenty hours The third project specifies a structure with the same function as the first two— an environment to enter, walk through, and leave. This time we take another jump in complexity by adding the possibility of the inhabitant's moving in other-than-horizontal directions and by allowing the designer to employ other-than-vertical planes in defining the collection of volumes. The additional problems of design are considerable, doubling the amount of time allowed. By this time it is clear that this kind of assignment can be thought of in a number of different ways: it could be described as the opposite of a maze—as an environment designed to please and direct rather than to frustrate and confuse; or it could be described as a building with two functions, walking through and looking at; or it could be described as an organic composition of man-holding volumes.

Two hours   Class critique. By this time I feel that I can give more summary criticism and be understood. As time has passed, the students have become willing to be more self-critical along the way and to discuss portions of their own projects with which they are not pleased.

Project 4 (twenty-six hours)

Twenty-four hours   The fourth project I assign in response to a growing restiveness with white cardboard, gray Homasote, and the abstractness of the assignments. O.K., I say, here is the program for a real building.[1] Design it, make a model of it, and use any materials you consider appropriate. I suggest that it may be possible to design the shape of five walls and a roof or two that will more simply communicate the idea of a design—and result in a better grade—than a laborious, complicated presentation of a less-thought-through idea. I suggest this idea, which is to some students almost heretical in its dis-

regard for normal school values, because the major transition from simple (walk–look) function to complex (multifaceted) function is a very difficult one to make, particularly in the face of the sudden (unmentioned) possibility of imitation. Each student is almost inevitably going to retreat to buildings he has known as models for his thought. It is difficult to keep his thoughts connected with the previous course work; yet, with urging, the connections he can make between the preceding abstractions and the design of an "actual" building can be exciting.

Two or three hours   Critique of this final project is focused on the definition of a *parti,* the idea of the design. By pointing out that two or more different designs have arrived at the same diagramatic, functional arrangement, and that another design would be diagramed differently, I have arrived at a point where many architectural design courses begin—with a diagramatic language for design. In contrast to those courses, this ten-week course has provided a set of materials that are readily visualized. During the hours spent fiddling with white cardboard, trying to wrap it around air in such a way that the air becomes a collection of human-scale spaces, a student develops a mental "substance" for his imagination to work with. He can begin to dream of his project whenever and wherever he turns his mind to it, and the vocabulary of his dreaming —most basically the opaque surface as it combines with transparent volume—is immediately applicable to any environment in which he finds himself. The language can be useful both in analyzing our natural environment and in evaluating the ideas of an environmental designer.

INTRODUCTION TO ARCHITECTURE II

The contrasts between Architecture II and Architecture I are several. First, the entire ten-week (eighty-hour) period of time is devoted to solving a single design problem. Second, instead of working alone, each student is teamed with another. Third, instead of designing a human environment, the task is to design and build a "life-support" system for some inanimate object—usually a rolling, bouncing ball. Fourth, the finished product is the actual environment specified rather than a scale model of a fictitious environment. Finally, the construction of the project involves the student in full use of the metal and woodworking shop. Instead of sitting around cutting and gluing cardboard in abstract model patterns, he is using the table saw, welding steel, designing and building electric circuits, gluing Plexiglas, and directing air jets.

Over the years I have described the problem in various degrees of elaboration,[2] but this year I decided that simplicity was more effective:

November 28, 1972
Job: to provide an environment for a number of different kinds of balls (e.g., BB's, Ping-Pong, super, squash, soccer, tennis, beach, base, foot, you name it). The basic requirement is to keep x number of a given kind of ball in perpetual motion. The class will be divided into groups of two. Each group will design and build at least one contraption to keep a specific kind of ball in motion. Toward the end of the term we will organize all the contraptions into one great super-contraption which will then be installed in the Gallery for the Winter Term Art Show—but only if it all works perfectly.

There are several different aspects of the problem which must be considered, each of which will require your attention and my evaluation:
1. *Organizing a motion-giving and motion-controlling environment for the selected inhabitant.*
2. *Selecting and harnessing an appropriate power source.*
3. *Designing and manufacturing an error-free contraption.*
4. *Developing teamwork and constructive communication.*
5. *Learning the skills and the overall discipline in the use of the shop.*
6. *Coping with frustrations and failures of complex mechanisms.*
7. *Adapting to a schedule of deadlines.*
8. *Having a good time. You will enjoy yourself!*

Schedule of deadlines:
December 12, 4:15 Preliminary plans (model or drawings)
January 12, 4:15 Plans finalized
February 22, Contraptions complete
March 1, all installation in the Gallery complete

As the schedule suggests, the time flow of this problem-solving venture breaks down into three distinct periods, each of which involves the expansion of a student's initial sense of how long each step should involve. Most students seem to think that, given a problem, the best procedure is to think of a solution and to demonstrate that solution as fast as possible. They have been taught that the quick answer is rewarded and that every problem has a single solution—or at least a best solution. An introductory design course must contradict those assumptions as strongly as possible. My approach is to try to establish a discipline of design that subverts the quick-answer, single-solution assumptions without substituting disorder or discouragement. I ask for five ideas for solutions. The most interesting and important occupation is to develop a notion of what a design "idea" is. Can you imagine a student's shock when, after he and his partner have spent four earnest hours designing five elaborate ways of lifting a ball up and letting it roll and bounce down again, they show them to me and I tell them that all five are simply the same idea? That they have four more to go? One of them will start to argue with me, and I will be stubborn and see that they are simply taking the ball up and letting it drop down again; finally, in exasperation one of them will say, "Well, what *is* another idea?," and I will say, "How about floating the ball around on currents of water? Or how about moving the environment instead of the ball?" And the student usually sees immediately what I mean by "a totally different idea." Initial frustration turns into a stimulus to reach further.

The first period of time ends when we post all the diagrams on the wall and take turns having each one explained by a student who has not previously seen it. This method accomplishes three objectives: first, together we undergo the processes of understanding a visual, diagramatic language; second, failures in that language are immediately exposed; and third, a large variety of approaches to the problem can be seen and compared at once.

The second time period begins with a conference in which each team and I discuss which one of their several ideas they are going to proceed with. The temptation has always been present to submit one good and five bad ideas, but they feel content with the thought that they may spend the rest of the term making any one of their plans. If a team is already committed to one of the plans, there is no real decision to be made, whereas if the decision requires that some good, hard thinking be discarded, the decision makers have a real stake in making the *best* decision.

Once we have negotiated a decision and selected the idea to develop, my next task as a teacher is immediately to frustrate any notion a team may have that in possessing an idea they also possess a design. This I do by saying, very simply, that what we have accepted is *only* the idea. Having insisted on a totally nonverbal description, I now insist on an only-verbal description as a next filter. Let me give an example. Two students have selected a preliminary idea having to do with floating Ping-Pong balls through two different densities of water. At this point I suggest that they establish their idea only as floating balls in moving water and forget any drawings they have made. We discuss some of the obvious difficulties of working with their scheme as planned. In a couple of class periods they have decided to concentrate simply on moving the water, and have designed a structure that by means of a pump will keep three Plexiglas cubes enclosing Ping-Pong balls filling with water and then emptying as they rotate about a central axis. From a fairly sloppy diagram they have progressed to a fairly elegant design. I am confident that sloughing off their bad drawing allowed them to move ahead.

By my description so far you could suspect my method to be crudely dialectical. (1. Talk about the problem with each other. 2. Forget your talk and draw an abstract, nonverbal description. 3. Forget your drawing and verbalize your solution. 4. Turn that verbalization into a concrete, visible design.) Indeed it is, but my intent is not only to exercise the student in some kind of mental gymnasium. I am also anticipating all kinds of mechanical and technical difficulties that many of the projects will have—difficulties that in the rush of the term's end may be insurmountable. In suggesting at the beginning of the second phase that the student feel committed only to the verbal idea, my intent is that he have an assurance of what he is going to do in general, yet at the same time be free to use his common sense as he begins to think concretely about the actual, physical design. My intent is to maintain maximal freedom, so that his prior commitments, necessary to his self-confidence, will not prove simply frustrating or discouraging.

During the third and final stage of this project my role as delayer and pseudo-obstructionist is taken over by the problems of manufacturing

Figure 5

the designed environments. Just getting the things made neatly and operational is enough of a challenge so that my own role can become more supportive (rather than entirely adverse). The value of cooperation and mutual aid becomes organically apparent. If one member of the team doesn't come to class, his teammate has many problems—should he push ahead and make important decisions on his own? Is he doing right by their plan? Can he remember all they had discussed? Why should he keep on working by himself, anyway? Normally, when both are there, the problem becomes that of both people working efficiently on separate tasks, rather than their doing every operation together. Throughout this final period of time the sense of pressure as the deadline approaches gradually increases until (almost inevitably) half the work remains to be done in the final two weeks. Here is the final test of cooperation, and it is almost necessary that the emergency occur before the lesson is really learned.

Figure 6

I should not exaggerate the quality of the final results. Some of the projects are not particularly good. Some don't quite work. Some of the students don't have a great deal of fun: a few cut corners and end up with a bad feeling. But most of them have learned much about design and manufacture that they will not rapidly forget. Much of what they have experienced is identical with the architectural designer's experience. All the critical values are identical, as well as the forms of self-discipline. The process has been a long, engaging encounter with a structured environment—the shop—in order finally to assist at the birth of an additional structured environment.

INTRODUCTION TO ARCHITECTURE III

The goal of the third ten-week course is to design and construct a real project for a real client. We have tried this here at Andover twice, each under somewhat different conditions, and I am about to engage in a third attempt. Two years ago my colleague, John McMurray, taught the architecture course, which at that time was a year-long minor meeting three and a half hours per week. During the fall the students designed some playground equipment, persuaded our public school officials to buy some of it, and spent the winter and spring constructing and installing the pieces on the site of a local public school (Figure 5). Last year, having been convinced that such a project was feasible, I assigned my class the job of designing and building a practice-climbing tower for our school's Search and Rescue program, an outdoor training group similar to the Outward Bound program. The task was to simulate as many rock-climbing situations as possible (Figure 6). At the present moment I am organizing a project to design and build a playground for a local nursery school.

I do not yet feel that I could present any of these projects as a model for teaching. Each has been significantly different, and each has had significant problems. All the projects were organized into an initial design phase, an indoor construction phase, and an outdoor installation phase. Given this organization as a parti and with no pretense of having a blueprint in hand, let me describe some of the problems that have arisen with the hope that foreknowledge can help to avoid some of them. I shall suggest, too, some of the limitations that I have accepted to begin with and that seem to be unavoidable.

Problems of the Beginning

1. Choice of Client   The first considerations have to do with finding a client with the right kind of project. It is hard to say which should be the first thing to think about, client or project, but I suspect that the client is the place to start. It is clear that you need a client who will be willing and able to spend time with the class as needed. Probably such a client will be in the field of education, will be able to see the importance of the class's learning as paramount, and thus will be relatively relaxed about matters that are ordinarily more important. This fact explains why all the projects we have done have been for schools. I suspect that a situation in which the client placed low priority on my educational goals would be a disaster.

In addition, the client should be somewhat sophisticated in his appreciation of environmental design—somebody who has enthusiasm to spare for good design, and who will be able to tell a student when he likes the student's work. The client will be functioning as a teacher in this situation. To look at this from a longer range, probably most of the students in this class will not become architects, but many of them *will* at some time function as architectural clients, and it is well to give them a good example of how a client should behave. Designers aside, people generally get the kind of environmental design they want.

2. Choice of Project   It is no accident that the projects we have undertaken have all been to build environments for students—the first year for elementary school children, last year for adolescent mountain climbers, this year for preschoolers. My guess is that it is essential for the young designer to feel that he has some real, nonartificial authority in his relationship to his clientele (the users of this environment, as opposed to the client).

A more mechanical and "pedagogical" consideration in choosing a project is how the work, in all its stages, can easily be divided among students in the class. One factor is the size of the class. Another is the tone of cooperation that may have developed in the preceding part of the course. Another is the kind of project you undertake: can it be subdivided into relatively autonomous units? Do you want your students to work singly or in groups—or a bit of both? Is the project such that in its different stages you can tackle it in a number of different ways? In other words, to what degree does a particular project leave you, the design teacher, with as many teaching options as possible? I mention this, too, with respect to the problem of coordinating, or even synthesizing, a number of students' designs. I will return to this problem later (Group Design).

A final consideration is the question of finances. Here is where the "real client" idea becomes real. It is important that the client spend money to define the stakes. It is important that the students take on the job of becoming responsible for their expenses. Indeed, they should be estimating the costs of their designs all the way along. In this area it is tempting for the teacher, if he is knowledgeable to do most of the figuring:

it is much more efficient, and it may be that class time seems too valuable to spend in this way. However, it is really important for each student to begin to develop the sense of contact with the nonschool world by pricing out his designs.

Problems of the Middle

1. Relationship of Client to Class   A client newly confronting a class of budding designers may have some difficulties—and vice versa. Some difficulties are simple and human: mutual shyness and uncertainty, lack of coherent mutual perception, lack of an established form of interaction and communication, contradictory or unknown agenda, and so forth. This last touches on what becomes more specifically a design problem—or rather a central question about the differentiated perceptions and roles of client and designer. It is, after all, because they have different roles that they can be useful to each other. The client can surprise the designer by being pleased with his work; the designer can surprise the client by getting done more than the client dreamed of. The question, in this context, is whether the mutual surprise is pleasant or not.

If the teacher is functioning within an art program, he should recognize that this relationship (of client to designer) distinguishes the designer from the artist, the teacher of design from the teacher of art, the student of design from the student of art. I do not mean that there is no art within design or design in art, but simply that the designer without a client is not an architect. He may be a valuable contributor to civilization in exposing his thoughts about design, but he is not responsible in the same way that an architect is. The measure of an architect is the degree to which he can "instruct" his client without displeasing, and please his client without prostituting his perceptions of the client's needs. Need-

less to say, to create this sense in students, and for them to make it happen, is hard work of a subtle sort.

2. Group Design   Group design is impossible. When the crunch comes, various crucial decisions are not made *en masse* but by individuals. A total design can well contain a number of decisions made by different individuals, and such a design need not be a "camel" (a horse designed by a committee). It is important to realize from the outset that a successful group project is comprised not of a group decision—there is no such animal—but of a number of individual decisions.

The teacher is not the least person who needs help, but his problem is peculiar to his situation, although it is analogous to the students'. Just as the student–designer must learn to instruct *and* please the client, so must the teacher learn to instruct *and* please his students. The particular bone of contention in this case is the design itself: to what extent is it to be the students', to what extent will it be modified by the teacher's criticism, to what extent will its central cohesion be provided by the teacher? It would be simple if one could say that all self-generated ideas are (by definition, perhaps) pleasing to a student. But that is not the case, and often the teacher must intervene to keep the student on the right track.

It would be simple if one could teach entirely on the principle of deferred gratification: so long as the project ends up looking good, it doesn't matter what happens along the way; the student will be satisfied to be associated with the project even if his own contribution has been negligible. But such is clearly not true. Once the student becomes disengaged, he surely becomes bored, and once he becomes bored, he will surely stay that way, independent of the project's completion, until he gets tired of boredom. Under these circumstances, the fact that the project goes well may just be depressing.

The resolution to this problem—of mutually satisfying and constructive teacher–student participation—is as I said: there must be created an idea for the design that is mutually understood and appreciated. This idea is ideally expressed as having been generated by all the participating designers, whether the entire class or a sub-group, including the teacher. Once the design begins to take shape, its continuing life and growth can also be experienced as participatory. Under these circumstances, both students and teacher can be both creative and critical.

3. Constructions Problems   The largest problem in construction that I have run into is that most teenagers don't know how to drive a nail. When I stop to think about it, I can understand. They simply haven't done any nail driving, and nail driving (contrary to what you might suppose) is very difficult. It involves sophisticated skills, much more sophisticated, say, than soldering circuits in an amplifier or inserting a program into a computer. To watch somebody hammer who really knows how is to watch something extraordinary, which is just the problem.

John McMurray and I have both found that, when a project enters construction, the operation changes entirely. Not only does the class get into hand work, it also gets into a new kind of head work, a kind of thinking that is entirely foreign to most students. Even students who have learned some of the intricacies of working with tools and machines on small projects in the shop are really thrown off when it comes to man-handling sheets of plywood, climbing ladders, hitting their thumbs with a hammer, fitting a two-way scribe, locating a stud within a wall, and learning to pace their efforts in order to keep going for a couple of hours or more.

The leadership in the group changes, and the value system shifts ground. Some of the students don't make it over the hump. Some lapse into inaction, which looks like laziness but may be simple bewilderment. Others suddenly reveal obscure prejudices against common labor. Others somehow manage to be absent more than usual. The challenge at this point is clear: how to bring the class over into the new state.

Partly the answer is to give each student some nitty-gritty instruction in basic carpentry. Partly the answer is to remind those who have taken previous sections of the course how much they have enjoyed the end results, and that they will again. Mainly the answer (again!) is to get under way. As soon as something large begins to take shape, most students become involved, often to the point of obsession. As an antidote to boredom, or whatever you call lack of enthusiasm, there is nothing like accomplishment.

There are more overt pleasures, too. Acting in a large team that can get a lot done quickly is fun. Being outdoors in the spring, even in the rain, is enjoyable. As the project begins to take shape, it may attract volunteers from outside the class, and the resultant sociability is a great dividend.

End Problems

1. Completion   The greatest problem at the end is to complete the project. Unlike most construction projects, the circumstances here are hampering in two ways: first, the student labor force has many other daily commitments and usually can work only during the class periods; second, at the end of the school year all students disappear into thin air. The second fact puts pressure on the first, and as the term end approaches it becomes apparent that class time will not be sufficient.

I suppose one could insist that if I planned the

course properly this problem could be avoided, but to do so would be to forget Parkinson's law: work expands to fill the time available. In this case the law must be modified. The student perceives the job to be done in conceptual terms (first this must be done, then that, then the next thing) and has little or no knowledge of how long even simple matters take to accomplish, particularly when he has no experience in working efficiently. The modified law for students says: work expands to take *more* than the time available. No project can be perfectly programmed. There are too many unpredictable variables to insist that the project fall together neatly on schedule—particularly when working within the fragmented schedule of a school week. Teacher and class alike had better plan from the outset to expend some extracurricular time toward the end of the term, Saturdays, Sundays, whatever it will take. Mention it ahead of time and there will be less difficulty when the time comes. There still may be a student or two who cannot or will not give the extra time. This can be difficult to live with—I have found it so—and a teacher has to struggle to be fair in such cases. It is important to accept the fact that every student has other obligations.

The existence of this conflict was dramatized for me last spring by the contrast in behavior between two students. The first had been in the course all year and had played it very low key. He hardly ever spoke, worked very slowly, showed no signs of interest, and when the end of the year came and most of the class was spending extra time on the practice-climbing tower, he never came extra. Here he was surrounded by some pretty excited students, building a rather large structure, and he didn't flicker an eyelid, played the course requirements by the book, and after the last day of class simply disappeared. Contrast him to another boy who was not even enrolled in the course, a member of the Search and Rescue group, who spent a great deal of time on the project, was an enthusiastic contributor to the group's morale, and probably was the most responsible toward the project in his behavior. He spent much time that he could have spent to good effect on his other studies.

Two contrasting students, two contrasting personalities, two contrasting resolutions of the conflict between the demands of this kind of project and the demands of the institution. The contrasts point to a larger issue that a teacher in a similar situation should not ignore and should be prepared to deal with. The issue lies between autonomous obligations of the architecture project—obligations to the client, to the investment in materials, to the "project-in-itself"—and the institutional structure, which has certain expectations of both students and teacher.

At the present time it is tempting to see these conflicts as analogous to conflicts between radical and conservative: the designer–builder is by definition engaged in changing things, and it is simple for him to perceive the institution, when it interferes with completing the project, as somehow standing for no change. Certainly there is a tradition of revolutionary thinking and feeling on the part of the artist or (less often) designer, making him prone to antiestablishmentarian rhetoric. The mainstream of architectural development in the twentieth century has insisted on the analysis of design in terms of what people really need, understood in total, organic, and developmental terms, rather than on using design as a form of tradition or imitation. Even the beginning designer has a liberal frame of mind toward his clientele. The contemporary designer assumes that he starts with the client's needs, and that these needs are centered in the client's free will.

Equally, the designer accepts the need for his work to fit responsibly into the existing environment, with minimal damage, disruption, and waste. The common sense of this obligation is also one that has developed primarily within this century, although the roots of this idea go back at least to Rousseau. It was Rousseau, after all, who postulated that it is intuitively self-evident that every individual is undeniably free. And it was Rousseau, too, who postulated that it is undeniably self-evident that the free individual must choose to honor the freedom of others by freely accepting his obligations to them. Rousseau's elegant and paradoxical synthesis of the needs of the individual with the needs of a social structure is an excellent model for the synthesis by design of the architectural client's need with his responsibilities both to his neighbors and to the total system of resources and energy to which we all belong. In building a playground it makes no sense at all to create an environment that children, in the freshness of their special freedom, will not choose to use. Nor does it make sense to build something that offends neighbors, is drastically wasteful, or creates a nuisance. The solution may be something startling in its imagination and generosity, but it must be well knit into the needs, uses, and tastes of the community.

Taking this general model of design as a starting point, the idea of a successful synthesis between the individual's freedom and the responsible structuring of his relationships with his environs has become for me the operational basis for understanding the relationship between my students and our institution. At times when my demands on a student in some way put stress on his obligations to the institution, I accept my own responsibility—I realize I may be rebuked—but at the same time I expect that nine out of ten students will clearly benefit from the experience of stress. Unless you have students who freely accept extrainstitutional responsibilities, your project will probably not get done. Paradoxically, it seems that those students who most freely do this are those who most enjoy being part of our institution.

2. Evaluation   Another point of stress between a project of this sort and the school is the institutional necessity to grade a student on his contribution. I do not at all mean to raise the clichéd question of whether one can grade work in "nonacademic" areas such art or even creative writing. I have no great difficulty in assessing the comparative value of student work, nor in explaining my assessment to a student. It is wrong to imply that art cannot be evaluated. Not only can it be, it must be.

When a situation is clearly "artificial," as it is when one is teaching in a classroom, the process of evaluation is a necessary part of the student's experience, because it is his most significant feedback. However, in a situation such as the one I am describing it is questionable whether it makes sense to bring forward this kind of evaluation. The reasons I raise the question are three: first, there have been many other kinds of feedback, large and significant, from the exasperations of normal construction to a range of comments from passersby; second, my role in the process has been much more participatory and less overtly authoritarian, and hence any act of evaluation on the project would be confused with an evaluation of myself; and third, out in the "real world"—the situation we are specifically trying to more than simulate—evaluation of such work is never clear, consistent, or even finally known. Willy-nilly there is no voice that ever speaks with an ultimate authority. So my instincts have been to play down any expressions of a superordinate judgment on the project as a whole, and to concentrate my attention on making sure that each person knows that I see what he has done and am grateful for his efforts.

Grades, then, I base on whatever I can clearly distinguish as belonging to the individual student: level of effort both on his own and in participation, particular contributions he has made to the design, his sense of craftsmanship. The total result of the total effort must make its own way and for each student is somehow separated from his individual efforts.

CONCLUSIONS

What has the progression been for those students who have been with the course all year? What common ingredients do the three trimesters possess that allow me to be confident that in each course the short-term student has touched the bases of an "introduction to architecture"?

The year-long progression can be described in a number of ways: first, as a progression from ideal design through an encounter with physical, mechanical problems to a large, real combination of the two; second, as a gradual increase in complexity; third, as a progression from individual to more cooperative effort; fourth, as a gradual widening of the student's field of view; fifth, as a gradual movement toward a student's sense of independent responsibility within a more open and realistic context; and sixth (correspondingly), an increasing sense of equality with the teacher and a decreasing sense of subordination to his authority.

The second question—that of the common ground between the courses—is more difficult to answer. Partly the difficulty comes from my assumption that I can trust my training, my intuitions, and my limitations to make my underlying pedagogical intentions consistent over a period of time. Partly the difficulty stems from the complexity of the connections involved: they are both metaphorical and more than metaphorical. Partly the difficulty comes from my belief that the most important things are taught primarily by example: they elude description, are often unconscious, and if one tries directly to mention them, he often ends up *un*teaching them because they seem too theoretical or too personal; from the contour lines of my behavior each student must yet construct

his perception of my intentions as a teacher. Partly one must recognize that such a question is very large. It asks, in effect, how sets of clearly different experiences (in this case three sets) can teach "the same thing"? This is comparable to asking whether there are permanent principles of design that are equally applicable to all situations. Or whether there are perceptions of design that can be equally held by people of diverse experience, even diverse cultures. Without any sure knowledge that I can answer this question, let me conclude this article by summarizing the principles of design that I suspect I teach in any situation, over any period of time, whether with a constant consciousness or not:

1. A student is a student in order to change himself for the better.
2. A sequence of events, set in order, is necessary to get something done. A project has a beginning, a middle, and an end, each of which is a different kind of experience, making different demands.
3. One should not be satisfied with the first cut at a problem. One's beginning assumptions are always open to question, even much later on when it is painful to raise a question.
4. In the visual universe, the basic differentiation is between the seen and the not seen. There is something new to be seen at all times: it will constantly appear from out of the not seen. One must keep one's eyes open and be prepared to respond before the newly seen disappears into the old.
5. A stimulus (the seen) is always attached to something else not yet seen. That something else (the not seen), the source of all our anticipation, thereby connects all discrete stimuli. In design, one is attempting strongly to communicate to others that sense of connection between things seen via the not seen.

The well-designed environment allows the new inhabitant to feel anticipated, welcomed, and at home—to feel like an old friend, surprised in his humanity.

6. A design idea is always attached to a concrete objective that must be accomplished. The goal of environmental design is not gratification of the designer, but a sense of belonging bestowed on the inhabitant.

7. Between teacher and student this basic differentiation is also centrally important to their relationship, and therefore to the changes that take place between them, and therefore to the education accomplished. What happens between them when they are present to each other (see each other) contrasts to what happens between them when they are absent to each other (do not see each other). How do those two states affect each other in both parties?

8. Economy is perhaps the central value, the means by which a good idea becomes a good design. Evaluation refers to economy of materials, of energy, of effort, of disappointment, of involvement with others, and the lack of waste, of superfluous information, of unclear communication.

9. In speaking of environmental design one is speaking of the relationships between discrete, autonomous pieces of being, some animate and some inanimate. The principle of economy applies to the transactions between the parts of a granular universe.

10. The goal of the designer is to create a sense of generosity; his economies are practiced in order to convey a sense of bounty rather than stinginess; his motive is to give rather than to be ambitious, to control others, or to impose order.

NOTES AND REFERENCES

1. A small church, a parking garage, a small theater are programs I have given out. It is important to keep it simple!
2. See *The Andover Bulletin,* Feb. 1968, p. 1.

A Room Planned by Children*

Luther W. Pfluger

Jessie M. Zola

"We talk about child-centered rooms, but they are always arranged by adults." "Everyone starts with the idea of a child-centered room, but no one actually does anything about the room itself."

These two statements became a challenge to us at the nursery school at Campus Elementary School, The University of Wisconsin–Milwaukee. If the room was to be child-centered, then why not involve children in planning the arrangement?

THE SETTING

The seventeen children in this project were typical of previous morning nursery groups at Campus School. Since this was a two-year pro-

gram, the nine four-year-olds were in the room for the second year; the eight three-year-olds were new. The teaching staff consisted of a full-time teacher, a graduate assistant, and two student teachers; interested adults from the University and the community visited frequently.

The large, cheerful nursery room is located in a wing of the school that houses all programs for young children, and is easily accessible to the outdoor play area. Interest areas were arranged in the usual manner, with tables for art and manipulative activities close to the cupboards, shelves for blocks away from the traffic patterns, and trucks nearby. The housekeeping area was near the quiet corner, which had book shelves and a rug on which the children could sit and rest. A work bench, a science table, and a water table were in another part of the room. A large area of floor space was reserved for block building, trucks, and rhythms.

Every effort was made to create an atmosphere in which children were free to experiment and manipulate, one rich in learning experiences. In order that children had opportunities to make mistakes and experiment, their activities were unstructured. The teachers accepted diversity and encouraged ingenuity on the part of the children.

PLANNING THE PROJECT

As members of the staff discussed the idea of a child-centered room planned by the children, two areas of concern developed. First, questions were raised regarding the behavior of the children. What type of environment would the children create if given the opportunity? What equipment would they choose to put into their room? How would they arrange the equipment? What would be the reactions of the individual children? A second set of questions concerned the teachers in the room. How well would they function when the physical environment was arranged by the children? Would the program (as seen by the teachers) be as rich in learning experiences with this arrangement? What attitudes would they express?

In order to give the children maximum freedom to make decisions about the arrangement of their room, as many obstacles as possible were eliminated. It was feasible for the children to take all the movable furniture and equipment from the room into the adjoining workroom and the hall, if they desired, because the room had two other exits to the outside of the building. Since the doors on the cupboards were a deterrent to children in securing their supplies easily, they were removed. The door to a large walk-in storage closet was removed and most of the items from the closet were discarded as they had little relevance for the present program. Since three- and four-year-old children do not generally feel the need for privacy in the bathroom, it was decided that those doors could also be removed.

Because the children's reactions to this project were of great concern to the staff, several methods were used to keep records of their reactions. A tape recorder capable of picking up voices anywhere in the room was used to record individual children's actual comments. This equipment was new to the children, so everyone who was interested was given a chance to become familiar with it before the project began. The two student teachers served as recorders throughout the project, writing down as many comments and reactions of the children and teachers as possible.

IMPLEMENTATION

The teacher initiated the project one Tuesday by asking the children, "Where would you put the furniture and toys in this room if you had a chance to change them?" There were many ideas and suggestions. Children were quite excited as they talked about their ideas or walked around to illustrate their plans. They were told that the next day they could carry everything into the hall until the room and the shelves were empty. Teachers and children would work together to accomplish this task. The children were also assured that they could bring the things back into the room as they wanted to use them, with a teacher to help if necessary. When they were through playing, they could place the equipment anywhere they wanted to in the room. Everyone was so enthusiastic that they wanted to begin at once; however, the morning was almost over and mothers would soon be calling for their children. Wednesday morning another short planning session was needed. The children decided the blocks, tables, and chairs would be the first things removed. They worked together, asking for assistance from an adult whenever it was needed. One teacher was stationed in the hall to ensure that an area remained open for traffic and to help arrange the various items. The children appeared excited and happy as they worked to empty the room.

After about fifteen minutes, when the children seemed tired, the teacher suggested they gather on the rug. Though the children were enthused about all the open space they were creating, they did have some real concerns. Erik asked, "Where can we have our juice and crackers?" David wondered, "How will my sister get through (the hall and workroom) when she calls for me?" Andy stated, "We have more room to play." Mary observed, "Now we can sweep the dirty floor." The teacher suggested that the children leave the remainder of the things in the room for that day, and they could finish the task tomorrow. Since some of the things were in the room and some were out in the hall, Becky observed, "We can have a mixed-up day."

While the children were still sitting on the rug, Erik wondered how the heavy piano could be moved. David suggested that it would be easy to roll it on the big wheels, and Margaret added, "All you have to do is just push it." Under the supervision of the teacher, two children found they could begin to move the piano, and with additional assistance, it gained momentum. They encountered difficulty moving the piano through the door, but the children were able to solve this problem through a discussion with each other, and soon the piano was in the hallway. Jenny's concluding remark for the morning was: "Do you know what my Mom will say? My Mom is going to say when she looks into the room tomorrow, 'Hey, the stuff is moved out!'"

On Thursday morning the children worked and played in both their room and the hall. Some things were moved back into the room for a short period; however, by the end of that day, all equipment had been removed from the room. Three large trucks and a wooden slatted box, large enough to accommodate two children, had recently been purchased. By including these with the other items outside the room, the children could now select from new as well as from familiar pieces of equipment.

Friday morning a few children went directly into the large empty room, while others went quickly to the hallway and selected equipment to take into the room. Several of the children ran back and forth in the room; others found the open space an excellent area in which to race their cars and trucks. The quieter children selected manipulative materials from the shelves and played close by, preferring not to become too involved in the activities of the more exuberant children, while other children chose to play in the hallway. Children discovered that the large walk-in closet could now be used as a "special place." They looked forward to the opportunity to play there alone or in cooperation with others.

The children had complete freedom to choose whatever equipment they wanted. The trucks, blocks, and housekeeping furniture were the first things brought back into the room. At juice time, when Cheryl's mother brought in treats for her birthday, the children decided they did not need tables and chairs; so everyone, including the children from another room who had been invited, sat on the floor and enjoyed the cupcakes and juice.

After the first two days, almost all the activities centered in the large room. Occasionally a child would go into the hall or workroom for something he wanted; by Thanksgiving recess, most of the equipment and materials were returned to the room. However, the large tables, intended for manipulative and creative activities, remained in the hall. Everything that was brought back was placed against a wall; nothing protruded into the room. It was interesting to see the children get their supplies for creative projects from the shelves and spread them out on the floor, since they were no longer limited to projects that "fit on a table." A table placed under the window was rarely used; if the children chose to carry out some activity on it, they used only a small space.

One day, when they were making popcorn and the other table was in use, they agreed to bring in a second table, but insisted that it be removed as soon as they finished with the project.

Because the children did not want tables in the room, juice and crackers were served to children and adults sitting on the floor or in whatever location seemed appropriate to them. Some youngsters sat alone; others visited with friends. At this stage of the program the children became interested in shapes. One day Becky said, "I have a crazy idea. Every day we will change the way we sit. We will make a square, a circle, a design." So it was not unusual to find a group of children seated on the floor enjoying their juice and at the same time forming a geometric shape or some "fun shape" such as a lollipop.

Even though a number of children played on the piano in the hall from time to time, they did not request that it be brought back into the room until Wednesday of the second week. Then they decided that it should be placed in front of the fireplace, which was not usable at that time. When they brought the rug back, they returned it to the corner of the room where it had been originally.

The use of the water table by a hyperactive child provided interesting observations. After being involved in strenuous play with other children, the boy frequently chose to use the water table as a means of relaxation. He would bring it into the room with the assistance of an adult or another child, fill it by himself, and use it in various ways.

The housekeeping corner continued to be a major center for dramatic play. While the basic unit remained very small and occupied only a small space near one wall, the children brought equipment and materials out of the corner and combined them with the blocks or other equipment to form a spaceship, a hospital unit, or anything they chose to make. On some days the children returned the equipment to the small area within the housekeeping corner; at other times the structures they made remained for play the next day.

EVALUATION

Throughout the project it was evident to the teachers and other adults that the children enjoyed the roominess and openness of their environment. The children appeared to be more relaxed than they had been. They knew that when they developed a particular interest they could pursue it within the limits of the space and equipment available to them. The decisions they made reflected their desire to maintain the open space.

Observers who viewed the program noted activities quite similar to those prior to the inception of the project. The children organized the equipment in such a way that meaningful learning activities could continue. The significant difference was that the youngsters were constructively occupied in a setting which they had established and for which they could take responsibility. They now felt free to structure their own environment and were not forced to adjust their activities to conform to a prearranged structure developed by adults.

Parents became interested in the project and many stopped in each day to see how the room was changing. They commented that the children talked at home about the changes that were taking place "in their room."

The children were deeply involved with materials and equipment. They were constructively occupied in their room. Because adults did not insist that the room be arranged in a specific way and that items be returned to a specific place in the room, fewer conflicts developed between children. The rule established early in the project that "wherever the children want the equipment to be, that is where it goes" continued to be honored. Throughout the school year, when a child asked, "Where does this truck go?" the response was, "Where do *you* think it should go?" Although much interaction took place during a variety of activities, children were usually able to solve the conflicts by themselves with little or no help from the teachers.

The adults too felt more relaxed and were ready to accept the decisions made by the children. The entire project appeared to foster positive attitudes on the part of all individuals involved. This attitude of acceptance continued throughout the school year. Even though the adults felt that they had always listened to what the children were saying, they found that now they were listening even more carefully than before. An even greater attempt was made to utilize the children's ideas. For example, a proposed unit on sound was replaced by activities involving the use of maps and globes because this idea came from the children.

We know that three- and four-year-olds work individually or in small groups according to their own interests and abilities. The major purpose of the project was to give children the opportunity to create their own environment. By allowing the children to satisfy their need to have space and equipment organized in ways that were comfortable and functional for them, we found that their room truly became "a child-centered room."

PART TWO
ENVIRONMENTAL
ACTION: DESIGNING
FOR EDUCATION

As a nation we are just beginning to recognize the inherently political nature of the public educational system. To assume, as many professional educators have done in the past, that schools are solely concerned with instruction is to greatly misunderstand the socialization function of schools. Students learn not only required facts, concepts, and skills but also the implicit rule system which tells them which behavior patterns and attitudes are rewarded and which are punished. Many critics[1] have referred to the school's rules, routines, and administrative procedures as the "hidden curriculum," which shapes individual behavior into conformity with the expectations of the institution. Often the messages students (and teachers) receive from this hidden curriculum contradict the messages coming from the pedagogical goals and classroom procedures of the formal curriculum. The effect has often been to undermine attempts at educational reform which are conceived only in terms of change in teaching techniques.

Neither is this hidden curriculum, the institutional environment of schools, based on a series of apolitical administrative decisions. Rather, compulsory attendance, standardized curriculum and teaching methods, state certification of teachers, and the financing of school buildings and programs are all outcomes of political decisions. This is so because what goes on in the public schools is of such vital importance to every citizen in our advanced technological society. As Charles Silberman has observed, it has become more and more obvious that

education is becoming the gateway to the middle and upper reaches of society, which means that schools and colleges thereby become the gatekeepers of the society. And this transforms the nature of educational institutions. They are inevitably politicized, for whoever controls the gateways to affluence and social position exercises political power, whether he likes it or not, and whether he is conscious of the fact or not.[2]

These realizations have led many young teachers, parents, and students to conclude that meaningful change in the total quality of the learning experience is impossible within the constraints of the existing organization of the formal educational system. Consequently, within the last ten years we have seen the flowering of a variety of alternative educational institutions, both within and outside of the public schools, and a growing movement for community control and decentralization of large bureaucratic educational systems.

Despite considerable differences in the specific nature of the educational alternatives proposed in Part Two, all the authors seem unified in their critique of the hidden curriculum of existing schools and in their desire to develop more supportive environments within which children can learn and grow.

Similarly, many professional designers have come to recognize that the design activity is inherently political. Just as the educational system is set up to serve the needs of the existing society, the design professions survive on fees paid by the institutions and people with money, influence, and power. This is, of course, true of every society. However, when the social and economic inequities of the existing organization of power become generally recognized, as happened during the last decade, it becomes increasingly difficult for responsible professionals to continue with "business as usual."

The response of some designers has been similar to the response of some educators—to increasingly open up the decision-making process to participation by people whose lives are most directly affected by those decisions. Not only is there a growing pressure for the design process to become more publicly accountable, but there is also a growing number of young designers who are determined to change society rather than to simply manage it. In the process, they are defining new roles based on advocacy of the interests and values of nonpaying user clients.

This seems to be at the heart of the issues in Part Two: To what extent should the community of users of professional services and institutions participate in and have control over the decision-making process? This question is central to the ideal of professional responsibility and public accountability in an open society. The message of Part Two, and, indeed, of this entire volume, seems clear: People and communities are increasingly unwilling to be planned for, even if the product, whether it is a school or an urban renewal plan, is viewed as basically desirable. It is real participation in the process of deciding what is needed and how to get it that is important. This principle reflects the broader movement for self-determination which found its most recent impetus in the civil rights movement of the last two decades and continues to spread to other minority groups, such as Chicanos, Puerto Ricans, women, and the disaffected young people of the middle class.

It is clear that how we resolve these issues will have a profound effect on our traditional models of apolitical professions and institutions. The authors in Part Two provide a glimpse of the kinds of change that can be expected: in the process by which learning environments are designed, in the roles of professional designers and educators, and in the kinds of alternative learning environments that become possible as a result of these changes.

Part Two is divided into three parts. The alternative schools in the first section are concerned with the organization and control of schools—aspects of the hidden curriculum. In one way or another, all the authors attempt to overcome the existing limitations of large class size, bureaucratic regimentation, age segregation, and institutional control of activities. These articles reflect a growing movement aimed at discovering new institutional forms which are responsive to the needs of all the participants—parents, staff, and children.

The outdoor play–learning environments in the second section are examples of the search for nonschool neighborhood scale learning options. Although these alternatives share much of the philosophy and practices of the open education movement, it is important to note that the learning which takes place is not required, evaluated, or certified. It is initiated by the children and the rewards are intrinsic to the activities. Learning is not an institutionally mediated service and children are not a captive audience of knowledge consumers.

The articles in the last section of Part Two address the need to replace existing schools with "opportunity networks" that make educational resources more accessible to those who desire them. Just as in the case of the neighborhood play–learning environments, the number and diversity of learning possibilities are directly proportional to the educative quality of the total man-made and natural environment.

NOTES AND REFERENCES

1. This idea has been analyzed from many perspectives. Benson R. Snyder, in *The Hidden Curriculum,* Cambridge, Mass.: The MIT Press, 1971, explores the "two curricula" of college students. Melvin Silberman (ed.), *The Experience of Schooling,* New York: Holt, Rinehart and Winston, Inc., 1971, is a general source. Of course, Ivan Illich, in *Deschooling Society,* New York: Harper & Row, Publishers, 1971 and Everett Reimer, in *School Is Dead: Alternatives in Education,* Garden City, N.Y.: Doubleday and Co., Inc., 1971, both base their indictments of schooling on the manipulative effect of the hidden curriculum.
2. As quoted by Ray C. Rist (ed.), *Restructuring American Education: Innovations and Alternatives,* New Brunswick, N.J.: Transaction Books, 1972, p. 9.

As the blurred and often confused outline of what has come to be called the "free school movement" has finally begun to come into clearer focus, it seems that there are two distinct ideological perspectives on the meaning of the concept of freedom. Although the two different kinds of alternative schools that result share a common opposition to the organization, teaching methods, and outcomes of the public schools, one trend is decidedly political in its ideology, while the other is more concerned with individual growth and development free from any form of coercive institutional control.[1]

The basis for these two distinct and often divisive trends can be traced to disillusionment with the public education system's performance in fulfilling the traditional expectations Americans have had for their schools. Public compulsory education has been justified by the twin beliefs that schooling provides the aware and competent citizenry that is so necessary to the functioning of democratic institutions and that the schools provide every child, regardless of ethnic or cultural background, an equal chance at social and economic success based on merit and performance alone. Underlying both trends in the movement for alternative education is a growing recognition that the schools have largely failed to fulfill either of these expectations.[2]

For many on the bottom of the socioeconomic ladder, it is clear that the schools do not provide a means of upward mobility but reinforce and reproduce existing patterns of class stratification based on racial and cultural distinctions. As several prominent educators and social critics have pointed out, the public education system functions to "Americanize" students by sorting out, filtering and accrediting students based on middle-class values. The response by many minority groups has been a demand for full community participation in educational policy making and decentralization of control of local schools.

The politically oriented alternatives find their origins in the "freedom" schools that sprang up in the early 1960s in the rural South and the ghettos of the urban North. In these schools minority groups sought to regain control over the brutalizing processes of the public educational system. For these blacks, Chicanos, Indians, and others, freedom means having control over education—who says what goes. These schools emphasize the role of the school in the broader struggle for political, social, and economic equality.

As a consequence, many of these minority-group community schools still evidence a high degree of authoritarian organization and formal structure, including teacher-directed courses and intensive drilling in basic skills. Until ghetto children possess the technical know-how to regain power over their lives in a social and economic sense, there is little value attached to attempts to reform the process of education.

For the middle class, who already tend to have well-equipped physical facilities and school boards responsive to parental pressures, the thrust for reform is a reaction against the passivity, conformity, and vicious competition induced by the organization and values of existing schools. By contrast, this trend in the alternative school movement can trace its origins to the theory of freedom which is best exemplified in the Summerhill[3] tradition. This movement asserts that children are naturally curious and motivated to learn for the intrinsic rewards of increased joy and understanding. Any forms of coercion, regimentation, or authoritarian approaches to learning and socialization are viewed as destructive to healthy growth and development of full human potential. There is less emphasis on who controls the institution and more concern for nurturing the natural curiosity of the child in an environment rich in learning resources and supported by concerned adults who guide to understanding rather than compel to learn.

In spite of these differences in ideology, it is clear that the issue of freedom is central to the overall movement for alternative education. Schools as they now exist are seen as an abridgement of freedom for all participants—parents, administrators, teachers, and children. It is the form of the institution itself that locks people into roles that inhibit dialogue and pit one group against the other. If meaningful alternatives are to be found, it will be necessary to provide opportunities for all participants to share responsibility for making major decisions, ranging from those which are related to institutional form and administrative procedure to those concerned with curriculum content and teaching–learning style.

The papers in this section of Part Two represent efforts to find such alternatives. In many cases, the schism between the trend toward political reform and the trend toward pedagogical reform can be seen clearly. However, the beginnings of a reconciliation are also visible. There is a pervasive desire to overcome the existing institutional limitations of large classes; segregation by age, race, and place; and the exclusion of community people from the design, administrative, and pedagogic decision-making processes.

In the first selection, John Beynon, who heads the School Building Section at UNESCO, analyzes some emerging trends in education which are likely to have far-reaching implications for the design of educational facilities in the future. This overview of educational change and architectural consequence serves to introduce the reader to the issues discussed in more detail in the rest of Part Two.

Most proposals for alternatives to existing schools are aimed at breaking down the barriers that isolate living from learning, that separate black children from white, rich from poor, the young from the old, and the world of action from the world of reflection. In order to counteract the segregating tendencies of schools, Gian Carlo de Carlo advocates the disintegration of the school building as a specific place for a specific group, intended for a specific function. As an alternative, a nonplace school is suggested that would be a double network, composed of specialized and concentrated "nucleus" and an "orbit" that could be broken up and dispersed throughout the city to meet changing demands. It is clear that such a "school" can only be designed with the intervention of the user at every stage. Echoing a theme that recurs throughout this volume, de Carlo sees the architect as necessary to help restore the capacity of the nonexpert public to make an effective and imaginative input. Thus, both the process and product in this model leave the greatest possible latitude for user-initiated change in the future.

Reacting to the age-segregating nature of large bureaucratic educational institutions, George von Hilsheimer calls for a return to the small community school. Rather than dispersing the school into the fabric of the city to bring the child into direct meaningful contact with adults and the world of work, he proposes that the adults and children be integrated under one roof. Citing research findings that self-directed learning is more effective than an authoritarian approach and that curriculum and pedagogy are less important than community and values, von Hilsheimer describes his own experiences in a cooperatively run and owned 24-hour-a-day community of adults and children living and learning together.

The New Thing Art and Architecture Center is very similar in concept to a community-centered school, except that it is not a school. It is a community-based organization in Washington, D.C., dedicated to the development of the black community through art and education. In the best tradition of a mixed-age community of learners, anyone who has an ability to relate to the kids and a commitment to the community can participate as a teacher–learner. Topper Carew, who is an architect, criticizes traditional architectural education for failing to provide exposure to cross-cultural traditions and values, and an awareness

of the political reality of the design and planning process. The New Thing center illustrates how architecture and education can be used as tools to strengthen cultural identity and prepare community children for meaningful participation in the "outside world."

Anthony Barton's Hard–Soft school outlines a similar two-way link with the larger community: first, through community service projects, children would be brought out into the "real world," and second, both uncertified teachers and professionals such as artists, craftsmen, scientists, and media specialists would be paid to do some of their work in the school environment. In addition to desegregating age and interest groups, Barton's paradigm calls for a rich variety of physical milieus that would encourage the child to actively explore his relationship to his surroundings.

Architect and educator Charles Rusch sees the existing institutional and architectural form of the public schools as a barrier between the child and the people, places, and processes of the urban environment. His alternative to existing public schools is a mobile school that integrates both the political and pedagogical approaches to reform: (1) by reallocating school funds, and involving parents, teachers, and kids in all phases of administrative and curriculum planning; (2) by building the curriculum around the discovery and use of vast resources of the urban–rural environment in Los Angeles; and (3) by focusing on the development of the mental, physical, and "spiritual" needs of the child. He describes his plans to start a cooperative "Toy Store for Learning Things" as a home base for certain learning activities and as a means for providing financial support for the school's growing program. This unique alternative, Rusch feels, could eventually be adopted by the public education system.

The remaining three papers are primarily concerned with ways in which architects can facilitate user participation in the planning and development of alternative schools. These authors reflect the growing awareness within the environmental design professions that designing and planning are inherently political activities. In these case studies it is clear that the process as well as the product of designing can be an effective means for making the process of education open to participation by administrators, teachers, parents, and children.

To Robert Goodman, an architect and planner well known for his indictment of the design professions, this advocacy role means helping "disenfranchised" users create their own learning environment. Effective participation in these terms necessarily involves a transfer of power, in this case from adults (parents and educators) to children (high school students). Goodman attempts to raise environmental issues through a design process involving users. The designer thus becomes a "kind of environmental idea man" advocating alternative social institutions for people without power.

Rather than adopting such a confrontation approach, architect Henry Sanoff and psychologist George Barbour have chosen to act as neutral planning facilitators in the creation of a parent–teacher–child coalition aimed at developing an educational as well as an architectural program. A variety of group facilitation techniques are described, including "wish" poems to establish learning objectives, role playing to allow children to understand the design and development process, and a decision-making "game" aimed at relating learning goals to an architectural program. Just as in the Goodman paper, Sanoff asserts that a major benefit of this approach to design is the feeling of understanding and group unity that results from the very struggle of planning together. This case study is a clear example of a growing awareness among designers that the design activity must include the design of the process of design and the activities to be accommodated (the program), as well as the traditional job of designing the physical environment.

A third approach to advocacy design is illustrated by Goldfarb, Brown, and Gallagher, acting as staff architects of a community-owned architectural and development office in a low-income area of Philadelphia. Unlike the previous two authors, their experience extends to the entire design and development process for seven schools. All these schools are to some extent community controlled and based on a wide variety of nontraditional models of the learning process, including: the "open classroom" approach; an experiment in racial, social, and economic integration; totally black enrollment, aimed at reinforcing a sense of pride and cultural identity; a scattered site middle school, aimed at facilitating more individualized instruction; and a variety of schemes for decentralization within the public school system, ranging from complete community control to a program of shared responsibility and control between the local community and the central administration. This extraordinary set of case studies contains many general and specific lessons for any group planning an alternative school within or outside the public school system. Once again it is clear that it is impossible to consider questions of design process or product without also considering the related issues of school control, administration, and the aims and processes of education.

NOTES AND REFERENCES

1. For an excellent general reference, see Ronald and Beatrice Gross (eds.), *Radical School Reform,* New York: Clarion Books, 1969. Jonathan Kozol has written the best single review of the free school movement from an inside point of view. In it he cites the growing split between the "genuine" politically oriented freedom schools and the new "wheat germers" as a major threat to the movement. See Jonathan Kozol, *Free Schools,* Boston Houghton Mifflin Company, 1972. The *Harvard Educational Review* published a special issue on alternative education Vol. 42, No. 3, Aug. 1972. Among the many fine articles, the one by Alan Graubard, "The Free School Movement," is of particular importance. It is an attempt to analyze the data on the nature and extent of the movement. The distinction made in this volume between politi-

cal and pedagogical trends is based largely on Dr. Grau-bard's excellent analysis.

2. See, for example, Colin Greer, *The Great School Legend: A Revisionist Interpretation of American Public Education,* New York: Basic Books, Inc., Publishers, 1972. While most discussions of school reform refer to a failure to realize traditional expectations of public education, the clear and succinct treatment in an anthology by Ray C. Rist greatly influenced the development of my thinking. See Ray C. Rist (ed.), *Restructuring American Education: Innovations and Alternatives,* New Brunswick, N.J.: Transaction Books, 1972.

3. Founded in Britain in 1921, Summerhill is one of the most famous experimental schools in the world, and the theories of freedom espoused by its founder and headmaster, A. S. Neil, remain central to any discussion of alternative education. Although the literature related to Summerhill is vast, Neil's book, *Summerhill: A Radical Approach to Child Rearing,* New York: 1960, is basic reading.

Accommodating the Education Revolution*

John Beynon

Leading educational thinkers are increasingly using a revolutionary vocabulary when discussing education of the future; the new watchwords are change, innovation, reform, and regeneration. Students want changes in the traditional teaching systems; educators complain that innovations are difficult or impossible to disseminate; reforms are often sabotaged by the inflexibility of systems which have become rigid; and regeneration, even after serious upheaval, is often a patchy reassembly of the old elements rather than a serious renewal of the system. In developed countries the problems are many, and in developing countries they are magnified by the difficulties of coping with systems imported from old colonial or economic powers and superimposed on the Third World cultures.

*Reprinted by permission of UNESCO from *Prospects: Quarterly Review of Education,* Vol. 2, Spring 1972; © UNESCO 1972.

The implication is clear: we are entering a period in which the vast public education systems assembled with great sacrifice over the last 200 years are being severely challenged as inappropriate for today's society.

The problems—real and supposed—are many. Means have dominated ends. Respect for authority and apparent order has become more important than the transfer of knowledge.

Arbitrary goals, such as that of producing more graduates, have sometimes oriented entire educational systems toward university preparatory programs when, in fact, only a small minority of the population ever attend university, much less obtain degrees.

EDUCATION FOR WHAT?

In the light of the fact that in many countries educated people cannot find work, it is little wonder that educational planners when asked to organize continued expansion of educational output reply "education for what?" There are few people in society more frustrated than the educated unemployed and few governments wish the right to education to become a right to unemployment. Thus the planners' question is a poignant one, especially since studies reveal that even vocational education does not necessarily improve employment opportunities. Students ask the same questions—they quite rightly demand that they should get both intellectual and economic return for their investment of time and effort in school and postsecondary education.

But the revolutionary vocabulary does not assure us of real changes in the educational system, nor is it yet clear which specific innovations will find broad acceptance.

Not surprisingly, we can expect that the Third World, with its limited accumulated investment in educational facilities, will provide international leadership in these changes. Before considering some of the most important tendencies for change and their implications for educational architecture, it is important to note some of the major factors affecting school building, particularly in developing countries. An understanding of some of the constraints might help in highlighting major problems and in facing realistically the possibilities and potentialities for change:

1. Initial cost: having to spend money on such "noneducational" items as buildings creates budgetary constraints which restrict the buildings' role to that of providing shelter without amenity; raw space without regard for the processes going on within.
2. Shortage of professionals often means that individual buildings cannot be given proper professional attention and means costly use or misuse of standard plans. While standardization sometimes yields savings in an industrialized economy, the converse is often true in a developing country. In the case of schools,

regional or national standardization of school buildings often means losing the advantage of particular local conditions which could effect considerable construction savings.
3. Official class size. Buildings are planned with "standard" areas per class and per child which are based on very carefully worked out studies of the exact minimum areas required by students and teachers. Often overlooked are the facts that the actual size of classes rarely matches the "official" size; the number of students available for each grade is practically never the same and often changes drastically over the course of a year; the minister can change the official class size with the stroke of a pen; changing the size of even one classroom may be more difficult to accomplish.
4. Once the required area per class is decided, the factors of sun and wind often determine the final shape and orientation of the building overriding the advice of the educator.
5. Too often designs are generated by ideas borrowed from foreign architectural publications rather than by a penetrating analysis of actual conditions. The not uncommon result is inappropriate and uncomfortable buildings.

It is important, keeping in mind the above points, for those who plan educational buildings to recognize and analyze important tendencies in the educational system which are likely to have the strongest influence on architecture. Four of these are discussed below.

RELATING EDUCATION TO DAILY LIFE

Educators are searching a number of avenues to enable them to change educational methods by building educational programs around the realities of individual communities.

In rural areas "development" education will train people specifically for increasing crop production, development of handicrafts or improvement of health facilities. Thus one can foresee the traditional, narrowly conceived primary school replaced by a local community center with a broad role: providing a variety of services, education among them, to all members of the community.

The architectural form of such centers will be as radical a change from existing primary schools, as will be the content. The building itself must be conceived as an example for community development. Rather than being constructed of imported foreign materials it should be made of local materials, with experimental modifications which could gain acceptance and improve local building techniques. The center could in itself be a full-scale learning aid, involving local people in its planning and construction.

Such a center would be an educational marketplace. At least part of its functions will have to take place in the center of town where people normally congregate; location thus becomes an even more important factor. At the same time education would include the operation of experimental farm plots and possibly a small local craft industry. These activities may take place in branches located at the edge of the community.

The educational needs of people in urban areas can be interpreted in the same community-development light. Here transportation, pollution, and urban sociology may become some of the key issues on which educational programs might be based. Just as farming and crafts cannot be properly taught as academic classroom subjects, urban problems can best be learned firsthand through direct contact and involvement; short periods of working in transportation centers, local industry, local shops, or social-service activities may become part of the new curriculum.

Again it is easy to see that educational architecture will have to be something different from the monolithic, centralized facilities that typify educational buildings in today's cities. Facilities will include a proliferation of small, special-interest centers integrated into the functional parts of the

community such as those mentioned above. Thus educational space in urban areas will be found almost anywhere—old stores, warehouses, industries, office buildings, rooftops, basements—anywhere that will permit education to become an essential factor in the economic and social life of a community.

LIFELONG EDUCATION

If education is no longer to be a privilege afforded to the young and everyone is to have a right to continue his education whenever he pleases, a vast expansion in facilities will be necessary. How can governments of developing countries, struggling with the high cost of providing education to only a small part of the school-age population, afford to expand their educational systems? The answer lies in the utilization for educational purposes of spaces that normally are used for other things or are not used at all.

Let us assume that existing school spaces can be converted into the kinds of community centers mentioned above—most existing schools, primary and secondary, are used no more than 30 hours per week and for no more than 30 weeks per year, i.e., 900 hours per year. A man's waking hours are 16 hours a day, 7 days a week, 52 weeks per year—a total of 5,824 hours per year. Is it not reasonable to suggest, therefore, that the use of existing schools could be quadrupled or even increased fivefold? A wide range of activities can take place in such an educational center, since it would be intended for uses varying from formal classes to individual artisan project work and community functions. It should serve all age levels from preprimary to adult—and it would be used every day of the week and as long as possible during each day.

To serve such a wide range of functions, this center must be an integral part of the community, virtually indistinguishable from the surrounding structures; it must be easily accessible both as to place and time; it must be located to serve community functions such as dances, sport, or films; and it must take into consideration the needs of workers, farmers, and housewives as well as those of the children.

DEINSTITUTIONALIZING

The significant characteristic of these neighborhood or village educational centers and the specialized branches will be the deinstitutionalizing of education.

Communities must therefore insist on an architecture that will be radically more humane than that which institutionally minded administrators are all too eager to accept from architects who are anxious to create viable, monumental, photogenic buildings. A new design vocabulary must be adopted by designers in order to provide a suitable environment for the new education. Educational spaces will be evaluated for their reflection of social needs—for their warmth, for the extent to which they invite the entire community to enter, for the extent to which these facilities demonstrate the challenge to participate in learning.

Another feature of the new educational environment will be that, just as the curriculum and program have to become so flexible that they can be changed from one year, one week, or one day to the next in order to reflect changes in community life, buildings will have a much more temporary quality than today's concrete and steel educational fortresses designed to defend the existing educational system.

The evolving demographic composition of communities changes school needs. High-income districts which once had few school-age children become low-income districts, densely inhabited with large families, while low-income districts developed for young families become ghettos for the aged. School attendance boundaries exist only for a relatively short period of time. New forms and new locations will have to be found for educational

space, adaptable to these changes. Movable space is one answer to this problem. Another is mutable space which might be used for commercial, social, or educational purposes depending on the needs of any given generation.

INDIVIDUALIZATION

Any school administrator knows that many of the changes discussed above are not possible within the existing educational systems because of the variety of educational aims of people of different ages and different interests. The variety of subject interest and levels of competence of those using the centers will necessitate the development of an educational system based around teaching individuals instead of groups. The idea that thirty or forty students are sufficiently alike to be subjected to identical educational programs is increasingly in dispute. The architectural consequence is that community-centered educational nuclei cannot be designed as an assemblage of classrooms. Rather, one must think in terms of creating spaces that educate; and of carving these spaces out of large envelopes the inside of which can be altered, changed, and revised to serve education. Large, interior, open spaces, with small groups working on a variety of subjects in different corners, will replace rigid classrooms with children neatly lined up in rows. Resource material centers where students can come and teach themselves with books, films, slides, and individualized electronic equipment will grow at the expense of spaces traditionally provided for large groups. The guidance center will be where close teacher–student contact can take place. The library will be the source of information for the pursuit of individual interests and will provide a place to study from these sources.

Spinning out from this hub will be the specialized branches and group orientation areas.

While some of the educational changes may seem difficult to achieve and far in the future for many countries, these are not such radical departures from present systems that architects and administrators cannot now begin to accept the need for such changes. Nothing should prevent architects from designing schools that welcome children and adults alike. Nor is it impossible to design facilities which have the kind of flexibility and convertibility indicated above. To build educational centers of local materials in tune with local environments is probably both less expensive and easier to achieve than the pseudo-sophisticated schools so frequently encountered.

Architects have an educational responsibility that is a heavy one. Static outmoded educational buildings of today are a major impediment to educational change. Imaginative forward-looking facilities could help to stimulate educational change and become a positive force in turning the educator's new vocabulary into reality.

Why/How To Build School Buildings*

Gian Carlo de Carlo

In a period of crisis of values like the one which we are going through at present, we cannot deal with problems of "how to" without first posing the problems of "why." If we were to begin discussing immediately the best way to build school buildings for contemporary society without first clarifying the reasons for which contemporary society needs school buildings, we would run the risk of taking for granted definitions and judgments which may not make sense any more; and our speculations would turn out to be sand castles.

We will begin, therefore, with four elementary questions, well aware that often the most elementary questions—which no one has posed for a long time because they seem so obvious—can help us to discover the hidden thread in the evolution of a new reality.

*Reprinted from *Harvard Educational Review,* Vol. 39, No. 4, 1969. Copyright © 1969 by President and Fellows of Harvard College.

W1. The first question: "Is it really necessary for contemporary society that educational activity be organized in a stable and codified institution?"

W2. The second question: "Must educational activity take place in buildings designed especially for that purpose?"

W3. The third question: "Is there a direct and reciprocal relationship between educational activity and the quality of the buildings in which it goes on?"

W4. The fourth question: "Must the planning and construction of buildings for educational activity be entrusted to specialists?"

The fourth question leads into problems of "how," but at the same time it is connected to the first question, on "why." In fact, it could be formulated more exactly in this way: "Must the planning and construction of a school building be entrusted to specialists trained by means of an institutional education which has specialized them in such a way that they consider fundamental the requirements of the institution?"

The four questions are therefore four points of a circular relationship which can be interrupted or continued at any point. We will examine them one at a time, looking for the most reasonable crossover points into the problems of "how."

A1. Education is the result of experience. The wider and more complex the experience, the deeper and more intense the education. The field of experience widens in direct relation to the frequency of contacts, and its complexity grows with the increase in their variety.

Ideally, to ensure a really profound and intense education, no kind of experience should be denied: all possible contacts of whatever nature should be not only permitted but encouraged.

But institutions are organizational structures constituted for the attainment of preestablished goals: they can permit and encourage only those experiences which serve the attainment of their goals.

Institutions limit both contacts and education. They institutionalize education so that it will be useful to the institutions, first for their consolidation, then for their defense.

During periods of expansion, societies had no need to organize educational activity. The problem arose only when the societies began to generate institutions, that is, when they passed from the stage of self-definition to the stage of accumulation and preservation. At this point education ceased to be coterminous with the entire field of experience of the society and became limited to the field of experiences permitted by the institutions.

For example, the Greeks had no forms for real organization of educational activity up until the late Macedonian period; the Romans, up until the consolidation of the Empire; the Renaissance, up until the Reformation and the Counter Reformation. For that matter, all the revolutionary periods of human history coincide with a suspension of institutionalized educational activity: education takes place where the opportunity for experience is most intense, that is, in the exercise of revolutionary activity.

During the French Revolution the real centers of public education were the clubs, the streets (and the stage of the guillotine); during the Russian Revolution, the soviets, the factories, the ateliers (and the people's courts); in the course of the Chinese Revolution, which is still going on, the army of liberation, the communes, the assemblies of the Red Guards (and the Tatzebo); in the Cuban Revolution, the guerrilla war, the work brigades, the committees of defense (and the combat battalions), etc.

But while these forms of direct and total education were expanding, the authoritarian and restrictive structures of institutional education were taking shape by a process of internal contradiction. In France, for example, the Constituent Assembly and the Convention had already begun to lay the foundations of an educational system functional to the necessities of the state apparatus, which the Napoleonic Empire and all modern states took as a model—independently of their different political and ideological orientations.

The definition of education as the "means of directing opinions," stated by Napoleon, sums up precisely what institutional education had been not only before him (conditioned to accept the power of religion or absolutism), but after him as well (conditioned to accept the power of capital or the state bureaucracy).

In fact, since then the two problems—of teaching and of opinion control—have never been separated; every necessity in the former has opened up necessities in the latter and vice versa. The expansion of culture, increasing objectively the critical potentialities of the social body, has necessitated an increasingly articulated opinion control which, in order to be efficient, has had to restrict the sphere in which culture is formed and, therefore, organize a rigid and unified structure of teaching. The development of industry and technology has pushed this development to extremes, generating the necessity of mass education in order to face up to the demands of production and consumption at the same time that it has generated the necessity of conditioning the educated masses, by means of a controlled educational system, to prevent their becoming aware of their exclusion from the processes of decision making and the manipulation of power.

For quite some time specialization seemed to be the most expedient means of solving the contradiction between these two opposing necessities. Its economic motivation, even though limited and banal, was sufficient to justify its alienating effects: the specialist was supposed to possess only that knowledge which was necessary and sufficient to fulfill efficiently a role in a process which, for lack of a wider vision, would escape his capacities of judgment.

Today, however, the expedient which has functioned almost perfectly for so long has begun to show its fallacy. The student revolt which is flaring up all over the world at every level of education, and which has begun to infiltrate the professions as well, reveals a radical refusal of the condition of exclusion caused by an aprioristic, codified limitation of the field of cultural action. Perhaps specialization is indispensable, but the opinion is growing increasingly strong that it is acceptable only when the specialist has first achieved a broader understanding so that he is capable of maintaining the capacity to criticize—to accept, reject, or somehow choose, with a political consciousness of his action—the role which the individual assumes in the social context. The equation "specialization = participation" is replacing the equation "specialization = estrange-

ment," implying the revolutionary overthrow of the whole existing institutional system and, in particular, the revolutionary overthrow of educational institutions.

With the student revolt, education has returned to the city and to the streets and has, thus, found a field of rich and diversified experience which is much more formative than that offered by the old school system. Perhaps we are headed toward an era in which education and total experience will again coincide, in which school as an established and codified institution no longer has any reason for existence.

A2. Education has always been conceived as a segregated activity. Plato taught while walking back and forth in the grove of Academe, and Aristotle in the enclosure of Apollo Lyceum, but these were cases, as we have said, of education which was not yet organized. When education began to become an institution, buildings were immediately made for the purpose of containing it and, at the same time, isolating it from contacts with the surrounding environment. In the High Middle Ages monasteries were built, in the Late Middle Ages the first campuses, in the Renaissance period the Academies, between the Reformation and the Counter Reformation the theological schools, under absolutism the first great university complexes, in the period dominated by capitalism and state bureaucracy a wide variety of scholastic complexes of different types corresponding to different kinds and levels of education.

Since the end of the nineteenth century, as the principle of specialization has consolidated itself, the subjects of specialization have multiplied and, with them, the types of scholastic building. Each branch of learning has had its type of building, specifically designed for its use and more or less differentiated from an organizational and structural point of view.

But in spite of the precise differences of definition and the vague differences of configuration, all these types have one feature in common: the strictest adherence to the principle of segregation. The school is a physical structure designed exclusively for education, for teachers and students, just as a prison is a physical structure designed exclusively for imprisonment, for jailors and for prisoners; its function is to house a specific activity, but also to isolate it from other activities.

The reason for this function is the preservation of the institutional and class integrity of educational activity.

Isolation in a single spot acts as a filter for experiences which are not permitted by the institution and as a barrier to the classes which do not control the institutions. We know that, with time, this model has undergone a series of deformations. The expansion of mass education has caused a wrench which has continued to alter the bars of the cage without changing, however, its nature as a cage. In certain cases the spaces between the bars have actually widened —for example, in the case of elementary and professional education—when the necessity for a greater diffusion of centers of learning has made it necessary to mix them in with the fabric of the city. But the cage has continued to be a cage: the school building has continued to be a very distinct and autonomous physical structure, a point which sticks out, breaking the continuity of the fabric in which it finds itself.

The representation of this concept of education becomes clear in the conception of the buildings, where we always find closed organizational structures and monumental architectural forms. No matter how different their appearances, the organizational structures of a school building can always be brought back to outlines based on the principle of authority: hierarchy of spaces, absence of osmosis between the different parts, interruption and control of internal and external communications, etc. The formal configurations, on the other hand, correspond to the authoritarian formulation of the organizational structures for whose

anonymity they try to compensate by loading themselves down with symbols and monumental characteristics.

To the inevitable observation that these authoritarian and monumental characteristics are more typical of nineteenth-century schools than of present ones, we can reply that a series of classrooms served by a corridor is substantially equivalent to a series of classrooms served by a common space and that the monumentalness of the columns and decorations in cement is substantially equivalent to that of the steel framework and curtain wall. In architecture, in fact, organizational structures can be defined as authoritarian when the articulation of the spaces does not stimulate the community to exchange communications at any moment and at a level of complete equality. The formal configurations are considered monumental when they adapt themselves to the esthetic codes of the institutions and are not receptive to the users' free expression.

In fact, very little has been done in the contemporary epoch to modify the authoritarian and monumental characteristics which school buildings have always had. Schools in cities or anywhere in the territory can be distinguished immediately; they stand there, isolated and emphatic, even when they are inserted into the most closely woven urban fabric. All the tricks which have been conjured up to humanize their formal expression have concentrated on defining in terms of an elementary and schematic language, as always happens when the real idea of "people" (plurality of individuals which gives rise to a variable field of interrelations) is confused with the abstract idea of "mass" (amorphous aggregation of human units, made amorphous by the simple fact of being lumped together). In any case all the devices used to reduce the appearance of their isolation have turned out to be useless, because the problem was attacked from the outside instead of from the inside, wherein lay the real source of the difficulty. Considering the school as a point of convergence for an area of influence or even as a possible neighborhood center, establishing the greatest possible access to it in terms of time or conditions of protection for its access routes would not change in any way its physical "apartness" with respect to the urban or territorial context.

School buildings built especially to house educational activity can house, therefore, only that part of this activity which is in the interest of the institutions which construct the school buildings. The rest of education—the richest and most active part—goes on elsewhere and has no need of buildings; or perhaps it has not yet found the appropriate spaces in which it could take place as a whole, becoming part of a sphere of total experiences.

A3. Socrates taught in the gymnasiums of Athens, and many centuries later Pestalozzi began his activity as an educator in a farm building at Neuhof near Zurich. Besides these two exemplary cases, there are many others in the history of education which show that a school can be excellent even though it is housed in an inappropriate, or even ugly, building. On the contrary, there are many cases of buildings considered excellent which house schools of very poor quality. We can be certain, then, that there is no direct and reciprocal relationship between architectural quality and the quality of the educational system. Architecture, because of its superstructural nature, can modify the environment directly; but it cannot dictate the activities that go on in the environment.

We know, however, that architecture, by acting on the environment, can exert influences on activities, orient or deviate their ways of coming about in the network of the complicated interplay of feedback through which form establishes a dynamic relationship with society.

However, if it is true that today educational activity remains indifferent to the influences exerted by architecture, if its being good or bad is in-

dependent of the influences of the physical environment in which it goes on, and if this is the case even in the presence of school buildings considered excellent in quality, then it is the very definition of quality which must be brought into discussion. That is, we must ask ourselves if, in judging a school building excellent or poor, we are not referring to a conventional outworn esthetic code, by now lacking in universal significance.

In fact, the esthetic code taken as a model for the measurement of a building—scholastic or otherwise—is the result of a long manipulation of renaissance standards made to reconcile them with the ideology of order.

But what is order in a formal configuration, if not the expulsion of every expression which is inconsistent with the requirements of representation of the institutions? And what is this expulsion, if not a repressive act with regard to collective participation, an act which corresponds perfectly with the repression which the same institutions carry out in the political and social sphere? The correspondence is particularly evident in the school buildings where the principle of formal order which governs the architectural composition mirrors the principle of disciplinary order which is given as the definition of the purpose of educational activity. Contemporary school buildings—both those considered poor in quality and those considered excellent—do not escape this law of symmetry which mirrors the disciplinary order in the formal order. Underneath an architectural language which is different, the same compositional structures can be seen which organized the medieval cloister schools or the barracks schools of the late nineteenth century: distinct separation between interior and exterior, plans based on simple addition, rhythmic cadences of the facade elements, monocentric views, monotony of materials, technical austerity, decorative repetitivity, etc. And this compositional structure mirrors the authoritarian procedure of educating an elite to exert cultural control over the whole society in the name of a particular social class to which the elite itself belongs. Authoritarianism and esthetics of order are correlated products of the rule of the class in power.

Today this rule continues to survive in different forms, but the contradictions generated by its own mechanisms continue to tear it apart. In fact, education is tending to become a universal requirement; and the effects of the contradictions in this process are being felt not only in the most advanced educational circles, but even more clearly in the tensions that agitate the very cultural elites and, above all, the students.

Even though authoritarianism is still the mainstay of educational activity, it is clear by now that teaching cannot go on being authoritarian for very long. Likewise, it can be said that, even though the ideology of order is still the mainstay of the esthetic code which governs scholastic architecture, it is clear by now that the architectural values of the future will be organized on the basis of a radical reevaluation of disorder.

The very sound of the word "disorder" generally provokes uncontrollable nervousness. Therefore, it must be explained that disorder does not mean accumulations of systematic malfunctioning but, on the contrary, the expression of a higher type of functionality, capable of taking in and manifesting the complex interplay of all the variables involved in a spatial event. Order comes from a selection which isolates the variables considered significant and organizes them in a system which is as simple as possible, i.e., so as to offer a stable solution. We know that there is an increasing tendency toward the organization of physical space according to this reductive principle, and we know that it is the origin of all the methods based on addition which are universally applied to the construction of the environment, for example, the method based on the search for a typological order according to which it is possible to separate and attribute spatial prototypes—or a series of prototypes—to them. The combination by addition

of these gives rise to an environmental whole: the street, the neighborhood, the city. We also know that a city, a neighborhood, or a street, even a building, is interesting to us exactly for all that which manages to escape from the controls of these rules, for the expressions which are "not permitted" but which insinuate themselves through cracks in the order and reveal themselves with all the wealth of stimuli which is the property of contradictions.

The breakthrough of the unallowed expressions gives rise to an imperfect configuration of disorder. The perfect configuration would be achieved if these expressions were included in a complex system organized from the beginning to include them. But that would imply a condition based on collective participation—on the creative collaboration of the entire collectivity—much different from the discriminatory and segregational participation which we find in reality. In that case, the organization of the physical environment would come about by means of a process and not by means of authoritative acts; the solutions would not be stable but in continual formation; the esthetic code would not be exclusive and secret but comprehensive and open.

We are still very far away from this condition; but, on the other hand, we are faced with the objective necessity of reaching it. The salvation of the world—in all fields, from politics to esthetics—lies in "disorder," as an alternative to restrictive and abusively overwhelming order which can no longer be tolerated.

To return to school buildings and to the problem of their qualitative turning point, we can conclude that the only possible way for them to exert a positive influence on educational activity is to revolutionize the procedure according to which they are planned and constructed. The school should not be an island but part of the physical context, or more precisely, the physical context as a whole, conceived as a function of the requirements of education. It should not be a closed apparatus but a structure spread out in the network of social activities, capable of articulating itself to their continual variations. It should not be an object represented according to the rules of an aprioristic esthetic code, but an unstable configuration continually re-created by the direct participation of the collectivity that uses it, introducing into it the disorder of its unforeseeable expressions.

A4. Collective participation in the formation of the environment implies radical changes in the role of the architect.

If it is agreed that all expressions should be permitted, even if they give rise to situations of disorder; if it is established that these situations of disorder are legitimate, even though they are in contrast with the official esthetic code based on the ideology of order; if to this disorder is attributed an inner logic which has not yet been revealed, only because it is complex and, therefore, beyond the elementary schemes which we are used to manipulating; if it is accepted that the impulses which bring about the definition of an environmental configuration should link themselves together freely in a process which generates solutions in continual renewal; if all this is considered consistent with the most progressive tendencies of society and, therefore, desirable; then the function of the architect must change in the same way that the functions of all the specialists operating in the different professional fields must change.

The architect's profession—as all the other professions—is defined and circumscribed by the proxy with which the institutions invest him to carry on a particular specialized activity for them, with the implicit commitment to accept their objectives in exchange for a relative freedom of choice with regard to the technical aspects of the problems with which he deals. The exercise of criticism is permitted as long as it remains inside the system and does not corrode the foundations on which the system is based.

In a situation of collective participation, the proxy does not come from the institutions but from the entire collectivity; or, more exactly, it is not a question of a proxy, but of an agreement which is continually renewed by means of a continual confrontation. The exercise of criticism not only is permitted but becomes necessary, and cannot be limited to the technical aspects of problems but must be extended to the whole range of problems, which runs from the motivations to the consequences of every decision along a line of permanent control which continually brings into discussion the general objectives as well.

The dimensions of the field of action are also made problematic. The architect, like most professional people, confronts the problem which he is asked to solve without worrying too much about the repercussions which the solutions produce in the general context in which they are inserted. He ignores the entire network of interrelations; or he reduces it radically in order to simplify his problem or in order to raise, as much as possible, the level of his own personal interpretation.

In a situation of collective participation, the consideration of the network of interrelations which are established between every new project and the context to which it is destined becomes fundamental. To design a school building in this situation means to design a piece of the city, to enter into the city with a project which will be homogeneous, to change the city to make it homogeneous with the project which is being designed, to act upon the whole field of urban forces and put it all into movement, foreseeing the consequences of this movement.

And finally the methodology of action is in question. The architect—more than any other professional—plans circumscribed and finished objects. His specific task is a function which he receives extracted from its context; he plans a structure suitable to its realization, within the limits of isolation from context, and shapes this structure into a physical form which represents the full context, giving it expression in physical space. But the procedure suffers at every stage from the abstractness accepted at the beginning when the activity was taken out of its context, cutting its ties with reality. The initial authoritarian decision reflects its burden of authoritarianism on the succeeding stages, which become in their turn authoritarian. The structures act as exclusive organizational systems; and the physical forms shape themselves as finished, inflexible representations, presumed to be that much nearer to esthetic perfection the less space they leave for the accidental character of time and use.

The institutional objective pursued—and worse, rarely reached because of a recurring technical imperfection—is the least possible entropy, which means the minimum quantity of connotations necessary to designate the event, the contrary of what happens in every spatial situation endowed with universal meanings and, therefore, rich in signs accumulated and stratified, in time, through a continual involvement with society.

In a situation of collective participation, the organizational systems are necessarily included and inclusive as parts of a more general system which makes the whole of the activities indivisible. On the other hand, the forms must necessarily be open, which means defined only in the essential elements which generate and regulate their evolutionary process.

To design a school building for a situation of collective participation does not mean to lay down a succession of spaces connected by a single line of communication, but rather to organize a place for opportunities for experience and to represent it in the physical space by means of a system of forms already oriented to the reception of the multiple and variable lines of expression of those who have the experiences.

Can a specialist design a school building according to this conception? Generally he doesn't know how and he is not capable of doing it, for two basic reasons. First of all, because his professional horizon does not extend beyond the circle of institutional requests advanced by the institutions, the inclusion of collective participation would push him toward a sphere of criticism which is denied him by definition. In the second place, his specialization has made him clever at designing in terms of autonomous and self-sufficient organizational systems and of formal configurations which are concluded and stable. He has been prepared for this and he identifies his own function in it.

Only those few architects who have liberated themselves from their specialistic and professional preclusions can contribute to a design which is appropriate for the requirements of a new educational activity. But many would be needed, a number proportionate to the dimensions of the problem.

According to our plan, proceeding along the line of the "whys," we have penetrated deep into the problem of "how." Now we must conclude the analysis and focus on its consequences in terms of action without, however, having gone beyond the enunciation of a few general points of orientation. In fact, every prescriptive norm would turn out to be useless and contradictory with regard to the mobility of the panorama which has emerged. From this point of view, we will now take up some of the principal questions, in the same order in which they have been treated so far.

H1. The institutional school furnishes a limited education because it makes possible only those experiences which are permitted by the institutions, while it excludes those which the institutions do not permit. The experiences which are not permitted, however, are often those that teach the most, if for no other reason than that they contain the seeds of refusal which make them critically more active.

Che Guevara maintained that the whole society should be an immense school, and he was right, if we understand his statement as he meant it, to refer to a society which should not be organized on the existing institutional basis nor on other bases which produce the same authoritarian and discriminating situations as the existing institutions.

The experiences which are not permitted by the institutions can be obtained only in the city and in the territory where they coexist with the experiences which are permitted, insinuating themselves into the established pattern and making it burst open with the contradiction of concrete reality.

The city and the territory, until society changes, are the immense school which we have at our disposition. We must work therefore with energy and imagination to make the school identify itself with the city and the territory, to make the enormous growth of the demand for education, typical of our time, spread into the city and territory.

The design of schools which are purified of their institutional limitations should begin with the noninstitutional design of the physical environment.

H2. The least suitable place in which to carry out educational activity is the school building, because by incapsulating teaching and learning in a unitary, isolated, and closed off space, it tends to cut off contacts with the complex content of society. On the other hand, it seems that the necessity of mass education makes the rapid proliferation of educational structures necessary. Therefore, we must reconcile the two opposing requirements which deny or confirm the utility of schools, which advise their elimination or multiplication.

The solution can only be the disintegration of the school building as a specific place, intended exclusively for a specific function.

It is a question of identifying its essential "nucleus," which must be maintained intact and multiplied, and its nonessential "orbit"—nonessential except in relation to the unacceptable desire for autonomy and exclusion—which can be broken up and dispersed. Educational activity consists in the search, potentially identical for students and teachers, for knowledge and types of behavior which help each individual to find an appropriate role in society. The search for knowledge implies a technical apparatus (the "nucleus") which can be specialized; the search for types of behavior implies the formation of places (the "orbit") where a continual and generalized confrontation can take place. To obtain the generalization and continuity of the confrontation, the physical structures of the school "orbit" must be spread out in the city and in the territory, mixed together, superimposed and integrated with other physical structures intended for other activities, and, therefore, generators of other experiences. To specialize the technical apparatus, on the other hand, the physical structures of the school's "nucleus" must be concentrated and unified, maintaining, at the same time, the possibility of aggregating themselves with the structures of the "orbit" and, through these, with the city and territory, from time to time as the necessity arises.

In this prospective we can imagine the school as a double network—laid out in the environmental context—of places in which multiple activities go on, including education, and places in which the more specific instruments of educational activity necessary for the finding, elaboration, and transmission of knowledge are concentrated. The intersection of the two networks should not necessarily coincide or even stand still; on the contrary, they should be as distinct and mobile as possible, so as to place themselves always in the best conditions—the first where social experiences are most intense and the second when specialized cultural services are required. It is not unthinkable (and moreover, for other reasons and with other aims, it has already been almost outlined)[1] that a scholastic structure could consist of capsules which include libraries, laboratories, studies, teaching machines, learning models, etc., and which can move about in the urbanized areas to reach the places where groups of students and teachers live and carry on their research, using structures intended for other activities as well.

In this way the principle of the school building as a spatial unity—generator of exclusive organizational types and monumental compositions—would become a thing of the past, and education would become an omnipresent pattern, capable of penetrating everywhere and of being continually penetrated by the happenings of society.

In comparison with this image, it becomes clear how much vanity and mystification was contained in the nineteenth-century program of using the school as a reassuring and celebrative materialization of Progress, or in the more recent proposals, only apparently more modest, to attribute to the school a polarizing energy that would make it a center around which the physical environment could reorganize itself spontaneously. The non-place school, disaggregated and dispersed, seems to be a more believable opportunity for renewal, if only because it proposes the distraction of its own organizational preconceptions as an example of the more general upheaval which involves the whole urbanized territory and, through it, the entire society.

The noninstitutional design of the physical environment is, therefore, not only a premise but also a consequence of the design of schools purged of institutional limitations.

H3. The situation of omnipresence of the school in the territory is probaby very far away, but it can be taken as an ideal which has the possibility of becoming real, if unhoped-for opportunities should arise among the vacuums opened up by institutional inefficiencies. It happens to architecture, in the wanderings of its superstructural existence, suddenly to run into these vacuums; it depends on the intensity of its universal commitment whether or not it will be ready to fill them up with subversive architectural material capable of causing feedback on the most protected structures.

We may, therefore, consider the ideal as though it were real and, in order to avoid the risk of abstraction, consider at the same time the real as though it were tending very slowly toward the ideal.

The introduction of educational activities into physical structures intended for other activities, as well as the inclusion of other activities in the physical structures intended for education, cannot come about without a profound reconstruction of the entire environmental pattern. This implies an intense activity of design—but at what level, with what procedures, and by whom?

All levels, from the territorial to that of the smallest associational unit, must be taken into consideration, because the urgency and the dimensions of the consequences remain constant from the highest to the lowest level. We know not only that the present organization of the territory and the city is not conceived for their contribution to education, but also that it is obtusely calculated for just the opposite effect: to unify experiences, to flatten every emergence to uniform levels, to hide conflicts by separating everything that can conflict. The emotional stimuli which can be obtained from the city and the territory (more from the city than from the territory because of the relative accumulation of contradictions) are all received in spite of the organization. At the higher level, therefore, it is a question of liberating the suffocated potential energy and making it explode in a myriad of opportunities for experience. Design can lead to this result, if it overthrows the organizational and formal preconceptions which it goes on passively accepting, if it restates in critical terms the scope and aims of its action.

The assumption of the idea of a school disaggregated and dispersed in the territory, immersed in the more general context of the environmental structures, imposes a verification of the legitimacy of all the physical structures which have been used so far to represent human activities in physical space. It makes it necessary to ask if it is still reasonable to divide up the physical context according to exclusive types, corresponding to isolated activities—street, residence, places for production and leisure—or if it would not be better to reunify it in a way which corresponds to how activities really go on, through the definition of new comprehensive structures (inside which education, because it is ubiquitous, disappears).

The same critical procedure is still valid on the lower level, in the observation of the smallest associational unit, the actual building for the school. But while at the higher level the revolution consists of proposing an objective of integration to restore unity to the environmental context, here it consists of proposing one of disintegration to aim at the destruction of the school's autonomy as a force which is antagonistic to the recomposition of the environmental unity.

In the traditional type of organization, considered exhaustive with regard to the teaching sector to which it is attributed, the design must first of all separate the parts which compose it and extract them from their conventional unity. Classrooms, laboratories, cafeterias, theaters, gymnasiums, sports and amusement facilities—there is no reason why they cannot be shared, at least for limited periods of time, with other activities which, although not defined as educational, educate, nonetheless, if not institutionally, beyond the school. Each part can, therefore, remain inside the scholastic structure but open to the use of the whole collectivity, or can be relocated in other structures remaining accessible to the school, or, finally, can be put together with other parts similar to itself to create a new organism used by different structures which can offer fertile opportunities for contacts and exchange.

Thus, operation at the higher or lower level can converge toward a single aim; and every vacuum which unexpectedly appears at either extreme can be filled up immediately. The double pretense of expecting from the renewal of the school the reconstruction of the environment and of expecting from the reconstruction of the environment the renewal of the school is merely a fiction to explain a lack of imagination or a desire for conservation.

H4. The formation of a new totally educational physical environment and the achievement of new scholastic structures projected into the context of social activity are inconceivable as products of an imperative type of design, which, as we have seen, tends to exclude from its field of operation all complex variables in order to organize simple systems which correspond to the limitations of an authoritarian vision concerned, above all, with order. Its choices are categorical and its procedures summary. Its products are monofunctional structures and formal configurations conditioned by the premises of uncontamination prescribed by the esthetic code of the institutions.

But the refusal to produce objects finished and defined in every aspect, whatever their scale, and the proposal to organize structures articulated so as to make possible any integration of different activities in open and variable configurations create the necessity for more sophisticated procedures and demand the inclusion of the totality of the variables in question. In this case, design becomes a process, a development of the successive events whose movement must be oriented, whose direction must be corrected, whose time must be regulated without ever limiting the free expression of the desires of the participants, when they are legitimate and organic with the development itself. No prefigured model can be given as the final goal to reach, especially no morphological type of model. The form, in fact, because of its intrinsic property of generating feedbacks, constitutes an indispensable regulating ingredient. It cannot remain outside the development as its preestablished conclusion, but it must be within it as an evaluation reproposed at every stage.

These differences of method and operation,

which distinguish imperative design from procedural design, involve an even more distinctive difference of content: in the former the relationship between objectives and decisions is concluded within a limited and preconstituted field of consensus, while in the latter it goes on in the unlimited and indeterminable field of collective participation. In the process-design the intervention of those who, directly or indirectly, will use the finished product must count in every stage, not only in order to furnish a complete picture of the real needs and to guarantee that the decisions be examined exhaustively, but also to introduce at the formal and structural level the powerful contribution of the collective creativity.

It cannot be excluded, or rather it should be assumed as an ultimate goal which could become real, that in the future the process of planning the physical environment can be entirely governed by the collectivity, that the carrying out of its different stages, from the elaboration of the decisions to the creation of the formal configurations, can come about through a sequence of choices, verifications, and inventions capable of regulating themselves within a continual polyphonic confrontation. At that point the ambiguous and insidious function of the specialists (of the architect) will be deprived of all authority. But that point is a long way off, and how long it will take to reach it depends not only on the rapidity of the libertarian transformation of society, but also on how quickly the exercise of freedom will be able to destroy the barriers of alienation which the exercise of power has erected.[2]

In the present situation, the architect is still necessary, and more intensely necessary as he contributes to the speeding up of the restoration of creative capacity to the collectivity.

The planning of schools, whether it comes about by means of transforming the entire physical environment to make it comprehensively educational or through the design of school buildings, must take this prospect into consideration. It is no longer a question of designing sacred enclosures as eloquent on the outside and rigid on the inside as is necessary to impose a will for order. It is rather a question of initiating a process which generates multiple active experiences and, therefore, intense education.

The design is the process itself, its reiterated transcription into spatial terms; therefore, it goes on without ever concluding itself along the path drawn by its formulator (the architect) and continually readjusted by those who appropriate it (the students, the teachers, the people who use it for other things as well).

H5. The job of the architect who designs a school is to outline the organizational structure which should realize educational activities in space, whatever the complexity and the degree of contamination with other activities which they may take on with time. The organizational structure will contain within itself the seeds of the formal configuration to which it will give rise or the basic ingredients of which it will be composed, or completely defined fragments around which its future development will evolve according to the circumstances, the intentions, and the reactivity of the situation in which one is working. The most important thing is that structure and form leave the greatest possible space for future evolution, because the real and most important designer of the school should be the collectivity which uses it.

The work of the architect should be limited to the definition of the supporting framework—which is not neutral but full of tensions—on which should be able to develop the most disparate organizational modes and the formal configurations which stimulate the richest disorder. At this point we can ask, in conclusion, if there exist, in the concrete or in the imaginary production, episodes oriented in this direction.

The schools which we see in the cities and in the territory throughout the world all resemble each other and equally resemble the schools of the past. They are torpid mirrors of a worn-out educational system. Not even among the schools selected by specialized books and periodicals as exemplary cases to be called to the public's attention is it possible to find something new, except for clever little formal or distributive devices. Nor do really new suggestions emerge from the studies carried out by the research institutes which are exploring the problem in different countries; the courtyard, linear, nuclear, or cluster outlines represent more or less suggestive acrobatics which do not go beyond the enclosure of traditional limits.

Actually, some few episodes are to be found only where collective participation, in exceptional and unforeseen circumstances, has manifested itself. Newspaper photographs illustrating the events of the student revolt all over the world have shown us a new architecture of the school which neither architects nor educators had ever imagined.[3] Internal spaces radically transformed by the introduction of new uses, objects and signs of extemporaneous invention superimposed on the immobile insignia of the authorities, colorful and irreverent lacerations of the gray austere expressions of order, facades disintegrated by signs and banners communicating with the world outside, parks and gardens rescued from their decorative existences and filled with activities and communications, overflow into the surrounding environment, invasion of the streets, overturning of automobiles, ballets with the police, continual and impassioned contact with the people, and so on and so forth.

NOTES AND REFERENCES

1. A few years ago in an architectural school in the United States some students studied a unique project for the scholastic organization of a city. The basic idea was to organize the special teaching equipment on mobile units which could move about the city, going from school to school as the need for it arose. The organization, in this case as well, was distinguished in two parts: the system of stationary school buildings in the various zones of the city and the fleet of special mobile facilities which could be combined with the buildings in many different ways.

   It should be noted that this use of special equipment permits its full utilization and, therefore, makes possible a high level of technological development and specialization without wasting money.

2. Centuries of being left out of the process of transforming the physical environment have firmly convinced people that there is no possibility for collective expression to intervene directly in this process. By now there seem to be no alternatives to the models elaborated by the ruling class and the functional, organizational, and esthetic principles on which they are based seem to be the only possible ones. This numbness of the consciousness and the senses gives rise to alienation; and for this reason, even the rare cases in which direct action is possible, people go on choosing expressive typologies and languages exactly like the ones which are imposed.

3. For some concrete references we can see how the students of the architecture department of Yale or MIT have transformed their working spaces when they have been able to appropriate them (the *Architectural Forum,* July–Aug. 1967 and *Architectural Design,* Aug. 1968); but even more significant is what can be found in leafing through the French, German, and Italian illustrated magazines which report on the student revolt in the universities and secondary schools.

Children, Schools, and Utopias*

George von Hilsheimer

The structure of the public education system is now badly out of date and new forms will have to be found, more relevant to contemporary society. The structure we are stuck with at the present time was designed for the mass education of an illiterate, poor, and educationally well-motivated population who lived in close-knit communities where children could get their ethics, their social values, and their personality choices from the community around them. Then, centralized schools had a real professional function. Today, on the other hand, they are serving a literate, affluent population conditioned to entertainment and advertising in a community-less society. The time has come, therefore, to reexamine the root assumptions of "comprehensive, centralized, public education."

*From *This Book Is About Schools,* edited by Satu Repo. Copyright © 1970 by Random House, Inc. Reprinted by permission of Pantheon Books, a Division of Random House, Inc.

The key problem with the mass schools today is that they exacerbate the poverty of real persons in a child's life. While on paper the central school presents a rich display of human (as well as technical) resources, the child, in fact, experiences it as culturally poverty stricken. He is never treated as an individual and he has no continuing relationships with the adults there who are the only transmitters of culture.

In many ways the child was better off in the one-room schoolhouse. There the teacher had, in most cases, a continuity of years in which to get to know her children and more importantly, to be known herself. She also had the enormous resource of the social authority of older children to share with the little ones. And she had the tremendous advantage of being forced to leave the children to their own devices for most of the school day, thus enabling them to move on at their own pace. Even if a child came from an isolated farm in which he was the only child, he found, in this structure of schooling, a vital and real experience.

Our children today live in a startlingly different world, a world where there is no longer an adult community. For the first time in the history of man children do not associate with adults except in peripheral, stylized, symbolic, and ritual ways which do not teach anything other than the ritual style.

Let's take a look at what has happened in the past twenty years: old urban neighborhoods are being broken up. The magnificent complex of small towns is progressively turned into a series of bedroom communities with limited economic determination for themselves. The neighborhood store and the specialty shop are rapidly disappearing. Jobs are progressively removed, not only in time and space, but also psychologically from the world of the child; jobs are becoming increasingly difficult to explain. Not only are more people crowded into more anonymous dwellings with an increasingly higher background of meaningless noise, but these people have less and less to do with each other on a consistent and personal basis. For the first time in history the majority of Americans are living this way.

Today a child's only adult contacts tend to be with his mother—oppressed and harried as she is in the small-child-raising phase—and a series of vestal maidens in school who must forever remain symbolic and ritual in their importance to him. For a child knows that his teacher is with him only a year or less. In addition, she has thirty other kids to serve and usually has no social contact with the family. Most likely he is attending a consolidated school, far removed from his home —both geographically and socially. It can in fact be argued that the school in America is an alienating experience for children of all social classes, including the middle class, which professionally dominates it.

It was different when we grew up. Adults of only thirty years and even younger can remember urban neighborhoods—small enclaves remain in the New York Lower East Side and elsewhere—in which the corner candy-store man was an adviser, counselor, friend . . or enemy. The druggist, the grocer, the butcher, the greengrocer, the janitor, the neighbors, all played a vital role in the life of the child. They have disappeared or are rapidly disappearing. Most children never see their fathers working. If there *is* an exception, the father's work is usually incomprehensible. Servicemen, salesmen, and other adults who come into the child's home are only briefly a part of his life and their work is too complicated to follow. Furthermore, the "respected" character type is one that rejects children's natural interest. Adults have become symbolic, alien, ritual figures in a barren field. Their values are mediated to the child in a distorted, mechanistic way through the school system. To grow up emotionally healthy a child needs a rich culture of adults from whom to select psychological reactions, patterns, and values. He no longer has this choice. As a result we have the apathetic, robot-like, nihilistic adolescent of our time.

Let's take a look at this adolescent our community-less society has created. I have often thought that if every teacher was forced at the beginning of the year to watch a filmstrip of teenagers watching the Beatles or the Ladybugs and had time to reflect upon the expressions on the faces of these entertainers, they would be so profoundly terrorized that they might go out and do something.

I recently watched the Ladybugs, who are apparently one of the most popular female singing groups. They sang a song called "The Leader of the Pack." It is very popular. I'm sure it's at least in your subliminal consciousness. It's about a leader of a gang who dies in an automobile crash.

The song is full of sound effects and somebody shouts, "Look out." As they shout, their faces don't move. The emotional tone and quality of the voice does not change. At the end of the song, I became a little hopeful because when they were getting applause they did smile, just a little. This is now the cultural ideal of our adolescents. That's why I really recognize myself as a reactionary rather than a radical in eduation. This is not the control of the Victorians that we are all so much against. This is not the cold Canadian reserve. This is not active, intellectualized control over emotions that enables you to move forward. *It is catatonia!* I haven't seen faces like that other than in the back wards of hospitals for schizophrenics. This is the most precise description I can give of the socially idealized goal of adolescents. The more I have worked with them all over the face of America, the more terrified I am because their goal is to keep cool. To keep cool is not the old Eton idea of keeping your head while the world around you is falling to pieces, but it is *not to be there.* It is not to possess your body at all, not to perceive at all that the world is falling to ruin, not to be hurt, not to have anger to channelize and focus at the howling savages, not to have any anger at all. It is not even to notice that the howling savages are there but to be detached from reality which is intolerable because there are no exits. This is a profoundly different generation. I think I am the first old man starting to scream at teen-agers. "You will not rebel. You are too damn well-behaved."

What then should a community's relationship to its children be? Ideally, a "school" in a separated sense is not necessary at all, especially our big centralized ones. "School" as presently understood in America was developed for the lower classes. Its infliction on the upper classes is an historic irony that proves some justice is possible in the world. The generation of our founding fathers educated its leadership class at home: tu-

toring was not simply the job of professionals, but of the whole family. Boys went off to college at twelve or thirteen, and while social discipline was severe, it was surprisingly self-inflicted. Intellectual discipline was almost entirely self-administered at this class level by the time the boy was in his teens.

My proposal, then, is reactionary rather than novel. In a "school" which is really a living community of adults—with a very high ratio of adults to children, ideally outnumbering them—classes would be unthinkable. Children would learn to read and write in relationship to their mothers, fathers, nurses, peers. They would learn most of their science as they moved freely about in the community. They would specialize and discipline their intellectual abilities in their teens in tutorial relations. Their dependence on adult teachers in the ordinary sense would be negligible by the time they were fourteen or fifteen.

Is my proposal hopelessly Utopian? I think not. That teenagers can be intellectually and industrially self-starting and -directing should be no more surprising than the fact that some adults are that way, even though our society is aggressively organized to destroy such abilities. A few colleges—Reed, Antioch, Dartmouth, Bard—and most of the monster land-grant colleges demonstrate that American teenagers even today can be remarkably self-directing. Actually universities like Michigan, Illinois, Ohio State, *et monstrous al.* probably prove the point better than the officially liberal schools. It is simply impossible to police, to inflict a constant social control, in such large colleges. Students either make it or they don't. Of course, the majority don't, but their "successful" fellows prove that self-direction can work.

But let's get back to the public schools as they are today. They have contributed to the creation of the cool generation both by their emotionally and socially impoverished atmosphere and by their program of instruction which places a minimum amount of initiative on the child. The system is based on the assumption that individuals cannot make effective decisions and that those who are older and wiser and more powerful shall make the decisions for those who are weaker, younger, more ignorant. Besides inducing apathy, this approach also inhibits learning. It is a widely held myth that academic excellence, at least, is a result of rigid, authoritarian teacher-and-curriculum-centered education. This simply isn't so. Any research comparing authoritarian versus self-directive teaching methods indicates that the latter is more effective, even using such conventional measuring sticks as grades, college achievement, and success on jobs. Here is a sample of such experiments.

The most impressive comparative study along these lines was done in the 1930s. Several foundations, notably the Carnegie Foundation, put up over $4 million for a study which is known as the "Eight Year Study."[1] The "Eight Year Study" took in thirty schools, ranging from luxurious private schools to slum public schools. There was a special twenty-point outline for the kind of changes in curriculum and teaching methods that these schools agreed to make. Essentially the changes were in the direction of giving more authority and responsibility to the children and making curricula more flexible. In the most extreme school the teachers refused to teach altogether. They just stayed around as guardians and facilitators for the children, answering their questions, helping them to find books in the library, etc., but refused to tell what to study and would not give lectures. The 1,500 children in these thirty schools were tracked down through their four years of high school and through the subsequent four years of college—thus the name "Eight Year Study." Next, a survey was made of how they did when they got into the real grim world of dog eat dog, individualism and competition.

The final step was to compare these 1,500 children with 1,500 children from schools using conventional teaching methods. Each student was matched and paired for age, sex, social background, aptitude test scores, vocational and avocational interests, etc. The results were astounding: on every parameter, on every variable—their grades in high school and college, their academic honors, their leadership capacity, their job attitude while they were in school, and their success in maintaining themselves after they were out of school—the children from the experimental schools were superior to those in teacher-and-curriculum-centered schools. The children in the most experimental of the schools, including the one mentioned where the teachers refused to teach, had the highest scores of all.

The "Eight Year Study" is a powerful indictment of traditional, authoritarian methods of teaching children. But there are also many smaller experiments that can be repeated by anybody at a very small cost, which are equally persuasive.

1. There are the Lewin experiments in group leadership. Groups of ten- and eleven-year-old boys were given the opportunity to be released from class for a workshop club period. They, of course, readily responded. A great deal of care was given to the experimental situation. Rooms were prepared so that recordings and photographic records could be made. The leaders of the groups were given careful training in three types of leadership: laissez faire, authoritarian, democratic. The groups led by the laissez faire leader were, of course, not "led" at all in the ordinary sense. They came into a room where an adult was present. He cursorily greeted them, mumbled something about, "Do what you want to; there's stuff over there," and failed further to respond.

The authoritarian leadership was done up very well. The leader stood tall and erect, was dressed in severe and formal clothing. He was domineering, firm, and fair. "This is a handicraft group; your name is the Green Dragons; we will make wallets; you will bring the leather, you the knives, you the thread, etc. . . ." The children were quickly organized, and as quickly put to work, which was closely and continuously supervised.

The democratic leader greeted the group informally; he discussed with them the function of the club; he asked them to choose a name; he suggested various possibilities for handicraft and had them choose. After the choice was made, he discussed the implications of the work, where the materials were, what tasks had to be performed. At every point his task was to focus the group on its goal, to bring out of the group its information and skills, and to force the group to make decisions for itself.

There were a number of groups in each leadership category. Each group followed one form of leadership for a time, and then the leaders changed, changing their own leadership style at the same time. Comparisons were made of many things: production of goods, involvement of individuals in the groups, group morale, etc.

The democratic and the authoritarian groups were both high producers of handicraft articles. The laissez faire groups, as expected, produced little but mayhem and noise. The significance of the difference in leadership, however, became apparent when the leaders left the group.

When the authoritarian leader would leave the group for any length of time the production of goods in his group would decline to less than that of the laissez faire groups, while their noise and mayhem level exceeded them. In the democratic groups production actually went up when the leader was absent.

When leadership was changed, either simply to another leader or to another leader with a different leadership style, the democratic groups made the easiest transition. They resisted, however, change to authoritarian leadership, not primarily by noise and mayhem, but by retaining their own organic leadership developed under the democratic regime. They simply anticipated and made irrelevant the authoritarian leader. In all important regards, the democratically led groups were not only better satisfied, more fully involved, but also more efficient than the authoritarian groups, particularly in times of stress, change, or absence of accustomed leadership.

2. There was another experiment done with retention of objective data. Similar groups of students were given groups of leaves in order to learn the classifications, groupings, names, and morphology of the leaves. One set of students was given the leaves in a prepared fashion, carefully packaged in plastic, labeled well, with the most modern techniques of lettering and presentation. The other set of students was simply given a box of leaves and told to see if they could find out the natural relationships of the leaves. Since the classifications are not arbitrary, but based on the evolutionary relationship, the children could, after a time, get the leaves properly organized. They were then told the names, the groupings, and shown the morphology and the developmental relationships of the leaves. Quite naturally the first group—taught by what I call the "entertainment" concept of education—learned the names and so got on much more quickly than the second. However, the groups were taught until both tested with no significant difference. When tested after six months, the first group had forgotten almost all of what they had "learned." The second group retained a significant amount of the data. When retested at the end of the year the first group had no statistically significant recall of the material, while the second retained a useful grasp of the principles and a solid portion of the data.

3. A good friend of mine, an art resource teacher in Richmond, Virginia, reported an excellent experiment with third graders. The children entered the room and found two pieces of construction paper on their desks. The teacher held up a folded fan—the sort we have all made. She asked, "Do you know what this is?" "Yes." "Can you make one?" "Sure." "Well, go ahead." All of the children very quickly folded their papers into little fans. The teacher then had them put the fans on their desks and listen as she slowly read the instructions on how properly to fold a fan. Then she told them to make fans. Not one child could make a fan. She went around the room and tried to get them to go back to their old fan and make one like it. They could not. The verbal instructions had gotten in the way. This is an easily repeatable experiment, but one I do not recommend because it is damaging to the children. The evidence is already overwhelming that verbal, curriculum-centered instruction is destructive of an individual's ability.

Finally, I would like to describe one of my own projects in democratic education, Green Valley School in Orangeville, Florida. Green Valley is a community of teachers and students. It is owned by its teachers. There are no administrators that do not teach. There are no teachers who do not also sweep, saw, hammer, and cook. Teachers join Green Valley only as partners. A lack of "employee mentality" makes a difference both in the atmosphere of the school and how children learn. Green Valley teachers don't go home at 3:00 P.M. or 5:00 P.M. The whole place is sort of a larger-than-life family and school therefore becomes a twenty-four-hour process. Students and teachers live together and eat together and struggle together with the problems of both learning and living.

Our school is often referred to as an "experimental school," but Green Valley is not truly an experiment. It is a school that demonstrates a well-conceived, adequately proved and essentially conservative philosophy of education which has been neglected and ignored by the main stream in education. It exists in a tradition that includes the Ford Republic, Summerhill, The Gorky Colony, The Ferrer Modern School, Finchden Manor, Prestolee (a Lancashire County School), and many others. These schools are based on the "Commonwealth idea," which makes the following postulates: (1) the adults' legitimate rule-making authority is limited to health, safety, and the requirement of public law; (2) adults and children have an equal voice and vote in the establishment of all other rules; (3) a sort of basic "Bill of Rights" limits the kind of rules the school community can make—no bills of attainder or *ex post facto* laws, etc.; (4) children are not compelled to attend classes; (5) the staff's primary goal is a healthy psychological and social climate, and only incidentally intellectual education.

The "Commonwealth concept" assumes that cooperative, loving, social, and constructive behavior is a natural and healthy potential of children. It does not say that children are *intrinsically* good. Children are not intrinsically anything other than the potentials permitted by their societies. There are societies in which no children, other than those with organic pathologies, are antisocial, but our society is obviously not one of them. Unfortunately, there have been a few societies which, like ours, seem to expect all children, particularly adolescents, to be antisocial.

At Green Valley no self-conscious attempt is made to encourage manners, although an adult or a child has a perfect right to ask someone to take offensive behavior out of his room or out of public rooms. No attempt to persuade intellectual interest is made; a teacher may demand discipline as a requisite of a class, but the student does not have to attend. Since we pay a great deal more attention to pedagogy at Green Valley than at some schools, I cannot say that intellectual interest is not encouraged. The encouragement, however, is by competence, relevance, and interest. It is not by moral suasion. The only regular complaint about classes at Green Valley is that there are not enough of them—despite the fact that for teenagers classes go on in the evening as well as during regular school hours.

One of the objectives of the school is to force the responsibility of freedom on the children. This is why we require the student to stay at the school for at least a year—with reasonable exceptions. Children will otherwise seek the escape valve of their often queerly permissive authoritarian home to avoid the responsibilities of freedom. We insist that children not go home for weekends. They will stay up late into the night for a week and then run home where Mama will make them sleep. When they are *required* to face their own need, they begin to discipline themselves. Although it may offend common sense, the disciplinarian family is often the most indulgent. A rigid psychological consistency, if not necessity, appears in those families which most often inflict irrelevant disciplines such as appearance, cleanliness, noise, deportment on their children. These families collapse most easily when a serious conflict such as wanting to leave school, getting married, or buying a car arrives. It is ironic that as a headmaster of a free school I far more often have to counsel parents in how to say "no" than otherwise.

I want to emphasize that the Green Valley philosophy is not a "permissive" philosophy. Nor do I think that it legitimately belongs to the progressive tradition. Progressive education is preoccupied with curriculum and pedagogy. We at Green Valley are preoccupied with community and values.

A teacher at Green Valley must not see herself as a manipulator in community and personal relationships. Technique is valid and necessary in the classroom, but it is out of place in honest friendship. We have increasingly found that our opinions can be safely shared with students. Misbehavior can be openly reported and discussed. A teacher, as well as a student, must be willing to admit her mistakes and accept the consequences of them.

This is the most important difference between Green Valley School and the progressive movement. Progressives, on the whole, cannot stand idly by and watch a child dally in a puddle of water. It must be turned into a "learning experience," which is to say that the teacher must interpose her abstract structures between the child and the reality he is experiencing and learning. The model for education, progressive or traditional, has always been a wrestling match—the student trying to put something over on the superior teacher who must find ways to win him. If he does not learn through drill, then he must through work or through play, but learn he must. Unfortunately, the verb "to learn" has come to mean a quite artificial and abstract kind of talking about the world rather than experiencing it.

For the education of adolescents who have been brought up in Green Valley, there is little the teacher does that is not an ordinary part of interaction of an intellectual community. That is, someone writes, someone produces, someone directs and someone plays a drama. The events themselves are comparative and evaluative. There is discourse, argument, and ego protection. The disciplined, cultured, knowledgeable individuals in the community exercise the authority of their discipline, culture, and knowledge. They cannot fake it in this kind of living community. Individuals read and read and read. They talk. They debate. An authority delivers himself of a new idea buttressed by such evidence as he can marshal. The community reacts. Essentially, once a child has learned to read and to compose and to put some distance between criticism of his effort and his personality needs, there is little a teacher can do except to enjoy the growth and cultivation of another unique and precious individual.

There is somewhat more structure in our elementary education. The elementary classroom always has at least two teachers, often as many as ten. The number of students is always under thirty. The room is large and has an easily accessible half-second-story for reading and solitary quiet study, or sloth. The main room is organized with messy corners, book corners, and display corners, and it leads into a small shed with a shop and very messy things. The two core teachers establish themselves as active and emotional "poles" in the room.

Without directing the children to either teacher, each teacher moves into his own activity as the day begins. One is active, outgoing, paying loud attention to painting, clay modeling, building, and rambling outside. The other is quieter and more passive—the reader, the writer and composer of songs, and other scholastic activities. It is important that these divisions are not made in a merely mechanistic fashion and that either teacher may perform any task in the schoolroom. Every effort is made to associate books, schooling, reading with relaxed purposiveness.

The children move freely between the teachers or take up their own activity. Reading, writing on paper or on the board, drawing, painting, making things, or simply crooning to the floor go on all the time. Some children seldom, if ever, cross from one teacher pole to the other; most oscillate without self-consciousness or concern. All elementary and kindergarten ages are present.

Reading periods are about the same time each morning. They are sometimes skipped entirely as the teacher senses the tone of the children—or they tell her, "None of that stuff today." Sometimes reading classes consume all day. The smallest children are asked what words they would like. They are printed on a card and given to them, or they are written on the board and the teacher builds a sentence suggested by others, sometimes grammatically and developmentally, sometimes working the sentence out from the middle or ungrammatically. This kind of linguistic analysis goes on from the earliest classes.

Writing is developed in much the same way. Children write what interests them, and they read the writing with others. Tape recordings or transcripts of their own little stories or nonsense or refusals are made, typed or mimeographed, and reading proceeds apace. There is no "Up, up, up, John," at Green Valley. Illustrations of words made by the children, collages of words and illustrations, "dada" stories made up by pasting word cards and other techniques well known to all good teachers are part of our regular armament.

Rather than bringing bits and pieces of the world into the classroom, we make every effort to take children out into the world. Children are are not interested in seedlings in eggshells when they have eggs in eggshells and seedlings in the ground. Nature corners are redundant when an important part of the day is given to rambles with teacher to point, question, prod, and leave alone. The city, no less than the countryside, is a vital classroom and this does not mean guided museum tours. Quite young children can see the dramatic change of neighborhood lines, the abrupt economic change at a state line, the significant flow of foot traffic, the flow of vehicular traffic seen from the street and a high building, the difference in taste of commercial bread and home-baked bread or salad dressings. They can ask and answer penetrating questions about reasons for such phenomena.

And above all, we try never to forget that for adolescents and elementary school children alike the role of the teacher is to point, prod, to prick, to question, and always, to draw back from and to look and learn from what the children are seeing and asking. A cultured teacher, living in a community of cultured persons, cannot avoid communicating that culture to children when she is actively involved with the children. The only textbooks she needs are the ones which she uses herself.

REFERENCE

1. Commission on the Relation of School and College, *Adventure in American Education,* New York: Harper & Row, Publishers, 1942.

The Hard–Soft School*

Anthony Barton

It appears that there was an information explosion in the realm of finance before the stock market crash of 1929. Now it seems that there is an information explosion in education.

Pieces of paper are exchanging hands, but the exchange bears less and less resemblance to the real-life education of children, most of which now takes place outside the schools. Paper studies, paper seminars, paper diplomas, and paper tapes carry records of student attendance, age, and grade: information on which to base provincial grants, not information of help to students trying to learn . . . all this is an overexpansion of credit. The learning which is going on in our schools does not seem to justify the mountain of paper in departments of education and research institutes. If our self-interest does not permit us to put a match to the mountain, let us at least change the schools to permit learning which is more relevant to the present day. Let us have new schools which provide the kind of learning which it is very difficult to obtain in everyday life: the valuable kind. Instead of rationing facts, let children learn ways to understand and to work with film, television, and sound: the pen, pencil, and paper of the electric age.

If we can raise the true value of education to something approaching its paper value, we can stave off for another decade the Education Crash, the day when we tear up the journals of applied psychology, attendence sheets, and all the paraphernalia of the Myth.

So we need a new kind of school.
Should it be hard or soft?

HARD

A barred gate in a brick wall opens into an asphalt playground. A notice on the wall reads BICYCLE RIDING, HANDBALL PLAYING, HARDBALL PLAYING, PROHIBITED BY THE TORONTO BOARD OF EDUCATION. Fifth-grade children are standing in groups, one or two are skipping. An electric bell rings and a teacher marshals the children into a line. They walk up three steps and enter the concrete school building.

Inside, they are marched down a wide, clean corridor, their footsteps echoing. Private lockers line the corridor, all identical, every one secured by a combination padlock. The children are led into a classroom and seated in alphabetical order at desk chairs with built-in book racks. After calling the roll, the teacher talks to them about Canadian History for forty minutes, using an epidiascope to project onto a canvas screen some illustrations from the textbook prescribed for the course.

The teacher talks to them about logarithms for the next forty minutes, pausing from time to time to ask questions, to maintain order, and to dictate examination notes which the children write down on the left-hand pages of preruled hardback notebooks with 1-inch margins.

There is a twenty-minute break during which each child consumes half a pint of milk, followed by a practical science lesson in a laboratory with waxed benches, identical stools, identical gas taps, and identical sets of apparatus. During this lesson, all the children perform the same preconceived dummy experiment and write a third-person account under the headings Object, Method, and Conclusion. This is followed by an art lesson in which each pupil is seated 12 feet from a daffodil and told to draw it. Lunch, prepared by a catering staff, is eaten in a self-service canteen, served in stainless steel trays with compartments for meat, vegetables, and dessert.

After the meal there is a compulsory rest period, and then organized team games. The day ends with forty minutes of mathematics drill in a classroom equipped with thirty computer terminals dispensing the same programmed instruction to all.

SOFT

A tangle of mud, trees, grass, and children's constructions leads gradually into a covered, heated area. As the ground changes from mud to linoleum, a wooden grid appears low overhead. From this lattice of unfinished pine, many things are hanging: electronic sculptures, measuring instruments, polyethylene curtains, stage flats, mirrors, and microphones. The grid carries power and communications outlets and is festooned with mobile lamps and television screens. It is so low that an adult has to stoop, thus it is within easy reach of most of the children, some of whom are climbing about on top of it. In one corner, they are setting up the lighting for a protest play about the slavery of newspaper delivery in their locality. In another corner, a Spasm Band is rehearsing. In the middle of the open area, a group of five talkative children have hung mobile walls in a rough circle to make a projection room. They are discussing some slides which they made on a visit to a potash mine in Saskatchewan. Over on the far side of the area, there are three great bins, the first is full of paperback books, the second is full of scraps of film and tape, the third is a sea of magazines, journals, and newspapers. A boy is rummaging in the film bin, and two girls are making a pile of magazines. Several children are lying and sitting by themselves, reading and thinking. The noise is indescribable.

Posters abound. Typewriters, paper, and pieces of circuitry litter the floor. Safety has been built into the equipment and the environment: fire and electricity dangers are small. In the heart of the confusion, a teacher is busy painting a mural of dinosaurs; the children treat him as an equal and seek his advice on various matters from time to time. Close by, there is a computer terminal, a refrigerator, and a large gas cooker, all in constant use. People pause in their work to make themselves coffee or to cook a meal for themselves or their friends. Occasionally someone leaves a group to wander outside and roll in the mud, or to gaze up at the sky and dream.

EDUCATIONAL ADVANTAGES

THE HARD LIFE
prepares children for the illogicalities and hardships of our present-day regimented existence—war, business, taboos.

points out the drawbacks of organized efficiency—forced to read set books.

shows how boredom can arise from enforced activity and lead to inactivity—dozing in class.

saflsfies a child's need for simplified, structured surroundings—you know where you are.

permits nervous teachers to avoid personal relations with children—retreat to the staff room.

THE SOFT LIFE
prepares children for life as active individuals—try it my way.

points out the drawbacks of organized inefficiency—can't find my book.

shows how boredom may arise from freedom, also, and lead to activity—mustn't waste opportunities.

satisfies a child's need for diversity in exploratory play—this is just a model.

permits teachers to get to know children well, on equal terms—no talking down.

THE HARD–SOFT LIFE
enjoys the advantages of the hard and the soft—contrast.

shows how environment affects people and their work—graph-paper airplanes.

allows children to learn how to get the best of both hard and soft worlds—computergraphic painting.

demonstrates the need to work in an intermediate zone—drama in a frame.

permits teachers to teach the way they like best—chalkdust for me.

The school needs:

HARD AND SOFT
in equal measure. Both hard and soft have their advantages, both should be a part of everyone's experience.

A COMPUTER
tapping upon request a vast store of sound, vision, and audiovision. The computer will help to push the information level inside the school above the information level in the television-soaked surroundings.

FLEXIBILITY
Free access to materials and equipment with which the children can manipulate the modern media.

COURAGEOUS ARCHITECTS
with the imagination to include purposeless structures and interesting but unlabelled areas in their school designs. Children can learn a great deal by completion: an educational structure should be incomplete.

UNTRAINED TEACHERS
as well as trained professionals. Artists, scientists, craftsmen, and technologists should be paid to carry out part of their work in the school environment where they can interact with the children. Ideas will flow both ways.

LINKS WITH THE WORLD
Children should work, but *not* in a classroom to no immediate purpose. Their school should help the community. They themselves should carry out practical projects such as the relief of the elderly or the laying of school sewer pipes. Children need to visit law courts and power stations with an aim in view: to discover the laws relating to the care of the elderly, or the ways to imbed piping in concrete. They are easily bored by conducted tours in which they are mere observers, tiny tourists.

COURAGEOUS SCHOOL BOARD MEMBERS
These community leaders must be as willing to experiment with buildings as with gadgets and expensive computers to do payrolls.

Proposal: The school should be designed and built with a physically hard area leading to a flexible intermediate zone, which in turn fades into a physically soft area.

Alternatively, the school might consist of hard, soft, and intermediate modules in a pattern. The idea is to embody in the design a *complete* spectrum of environments, to help a child learn better how his surroundings affect him and what he does.

An *intermediate zone* seems to be an inescapable part of a hard–soft system. In this zone, hard structures, such as television receivers, screens, and thumb tacks, have to be moved at will. This requires a rigid framework of power and support and we suggest a hard overhead grid made of soft wood.

Where possible, the grid may be extended up and down the walls, to give greater flexibility to the area as a whole.

There should be power and communication outlets at every intersection of the grid.

Where Is the Computer in the Hard–Soft School? It Has Tentacles. It would be a mistake to draw clear boundaries between hard, intermediate, and soft. The computer itself might have to be situated in the hard zone, but its terminals could be placed in both the hard and the intermediate zones. A terminal or two might even find its way into the soft zone; that would be a milestone in education: a computer terminal in the mud.

The terminals in the HARD zone are used for organizational work, record keeping, accounting, budgeting, scheduling. (There may be two computers in the computer room, one for this kind of thing and one for educational purposes.) The terminals in the SOFT zone are used for free interaction with the machine, indescribable.

The terminals in the INTERMEDIATE zone are situated in a computer-controlled environment. Each terminal sits in a room of its own and the computer controls the lighting, sound, smell, and tactile surfaces of this room.

Bricks are not enough. What would happen if a hard–soft school were built and placed in the hands of teachers who did not understand it? They would turn the flexible grid into a gymnasium, screw electric bells onto the trees, remove the junk, level the mud, and put up signs saying KEEP OFF THE GRASS. It's a hard life.

So we need new teachers for new schools, people who can change their teaching to match their surroundings, and do it all day. Are there flexible, committed teachers who can splice videotape, discuss the subconscious, and climb trees? Yes, there are good teachers.

People are not enough. Good teachers exist, but they have few schools worthy of them. Those that stay in teaching tend to take on slowly the shape of the hard-walled mold.

Build hard–soft. Give them the school's real teaching needs. Half-measures will not do. There is at present a trend toward semiflexibility which is deceptive in that it is an architectural answer but not an educational one. There is little to be said for a mobile wall if it can be moved only by a teacher. Moving walls is education: children learn when they manipulate their environment themselves, because they want to do so.

HARD–SOFT EDUCATION: A READING LIST

Hard

Circular 14, Ontario Department of Education, Toronto. Classic document of educational bureaucracy.
The Republic, Plato. The idea of control as a basis of education.
Teaching Disadvantaged Children in the Preschool, Bereiter. The idea of control carried to extremes.
Walden Two, Skinner. A novel by a behavioral scientist suggesting indirect control.

Soft

Summerhill, Neill. Account of a free school forty years old, by its headmaster.
This Magazine Is About Schools journal. Accounts of Toronto's own free school, Everdale.
Rochdale College Calendar, Toronto. Free education at the university level.
Walden, Thoreau. Life in the woods as philosophical ideal.

Intermediate

Island, Aldous Huxley. Balanced education through experience in a realistic utopia.
Understanding Media, Marshall McLuhan. Hard formal education balanced by soft TV education in the home.
Misunderstanding Media, Gordon Martin, National Film Board of Canada. A paper pointing out how the hard school misuses the media.

Emile, J. J. Rousseau. The idea of allowing the child to develop freely in a hard frame.

Lord of the Flies. Golding. Novel about hard-reared children thrown into a soft environment.

Overview

SEF Report E1. The Metropolitan Toronto School Board, Study of Educational Facilities. Quotes from Dewey, many references for further reading.

Interview with Topper Carew*

The average architectural student does not come out of school being an architect—I mean a complete architect—because his architectural education is limited to one-third of the world, to thinking that represents only one third of the world, and certainly he has a responsibility to himself and to environments generally to explore what is happening in the rest of the world—what is happening that is of architectural significance in Africa, and what is happening of architectural

*This selection is excerpted from a transcription of two interviews with Topper Carew, Director of The New Thing, a community organization in Washington, D.C., dedicated to the development of the black community through art and education. The interviews took place in Cambridge and at The New Thing and were conducted by Arthur Blackman, Ken Freidus, David Robinson, and Florence Shelton Ladd, H.G.S.E. lecturer. Reprinted from *Harvard Educational Review,* Vol. 39, No. 4, 1969. Copyright © 1969 by President and Fellows of Harvard College.

significance in Asia, and it seems to me if he began to explore those things he would be a much better architect.

My own architectural education was such that I was led to believe that the only thing that happened of architectural significance in the world with some minor exceptions, like Egypt which we touched on very briefly, like the Orient which we also touched on very briefly—but beyond those things the only thing that really happened in the world happened to have its origins in Greece and Rome.

What I'm trying to say is that the education of most architects has been inadequate, so when it comes time for them to develop an educational environment for a group of people who have essentially different origins, it's a very difficult and almost impossible task.

The education at present is inadequate, because it's just studied as an art form and nothing else. You know, art is nice and sweet and all that other kind of stuff, but there are just too many people out there who just can't afford that art, but who are continually being asked to live in environments which have been designed by those artists, who, as far as I'm concerned, are in most cases insensitive to the needs of those people that must live in those environments. So, I mean, one place where you can begin to break that cycle is to bring students to meet with people, say, come and study for a week with Willy Vasquez, who is an organizer of Puerto Ricans in East Harlem, or talk to two guys in Watts who've been running what's called the Urban Workshop. This would be an attempt to politicize students, to encourage them to think differently about their work, and their involvement in the profession . . . and about the profession.

One of the problems for architects particularly is that they get almost no political education in architectural school. Or nothing that would encourage them to do any kind of community work. Most architectural schools are kind of ivory towerish. So it becomes a very difficult process for the average architect to get to the point where he can even talk to people about what they want.

Certainly most architects come out of school being fairly naive politically. There is no separation between art and politics, given that architecture is an art.

You talk to the average architect and the thing he wants to do for a school in a black community is design the same groovy school he designed for Montgomery County, which is the richest county in the United States. And he thinks he's solved the problem. What he's forgotten is that this little kid on 18th Street is going through a different thing than your white kid in Montgomery County. This means that the school's got to be pro-

grammed differently, and the school's got to be designed to reflect that program, and reflect what that cat's got going through his head.

Any time that you have a group of people that are subjected to a set of standards, whether they be cultural, aesthetic, artistic, or architectural or whatever, and that group of people does not share the same origin as those standards, you have racism. So I contend that most architecture that has its practice in the black community or any minority community happens to be racist because it does not respect the origins of those particular people. I contend that Afro-Americans have a life style which relates specifically to who they are as a people—on the basis of that we could probably define a set of cultural, aesthetic, artistic standards which relate specifically to them as a people. That they have an origin in Africa, have a life in Afro-America, have assimilated a given amount of Western culture, but are not Westernized. And that sort of defines what is the modern Afro-American.

The thing I'm interested in, in architecture, is how—architecture doesn't become object-oriented, it becomes more of a process whereby you start to humanize the individual. Most architects somehow think the solution to school problems—the design of educational facilities is, you just take that same basic form which is sort of a large rectangle in an urban area and we have to worry about things like security, etc. You know, vandalism and all that sort of stuff. And just do something to the inside of that space. But I think there's a lot more that we have to address ourselves to. You have to address yourself to the whole liberation struggle, what is being viewed as the black power movement, which is making certain demands of architects, of anyone who has anything to say about an environment, or the environment of a black community.

I'm concerned about who the sole power rests with. Most advocate planners end up being middle men between the establishment and a given community, rather than recognizing that the sole problem is the given community. And the community for whom they are working runs the risk of being sold out. I could document almost every case in Washington where someone has come in as an advocate planner, and show you in two out of three cases where people have been sold out.

If he doesn't recognize that his sole responsibility is that community, then the community is in trouble. This is the same argument, the thing about biting the hand that feeds you. When they initiated to give most of the local control of community action programs to communities, they found out that most of those communities were turning around complaining to the federal government and the federal government got very up tight because they thought they were funding this. Why fund an organization—they could not understand—complaining about how we operate. An advocate implies that you're a middle man rather than working directly for that community.

I'm interested in how communities can control architects to work for them, rather than how some character can just come in—some of these characters are really bad—guys who come in as advocate planners, sort of like a missionary who went to Africa, maybe fifty years ago. And these characters really have torn loyalties. The reason their loyalties are torn is because of the architectural profession as set up in this country. It can be disastrous.

The problem that really bothers me if you examine for example the code of ethics of the American Institute of Architects. They continually hassle me because I continually do work for nothing. Now the reason they hassle me for doing work for nothing, they say it's unethical because you're undercutting everybody. If you do it for nothing they can't get their 4 percent fee. They hassled me for working on Morgan School for nothing. They say that's unethical. But I have serious questions about their ethics. Why do they allow Skidmore, Owings and Merrill, which is one of the largest firms in the country, to work in South Africa and do work in the black community at the same time. They're doing the tallest concrete building in South Africa. The program stipulates that there'll be separate bathrooms. Every time you do one you've got to do three—for blacks, colored, and white. There are no cafeteria facilities for blacks and colored and the AIA doesn't say a damn thing—and the ethics of it, knowing South Africa is hell to a lot of people, and they come around looking for me because I work for people who can't afford services.

I sort of make a separation between myself and the profession in that I'm not interested in playing by a lot of rules they've established. The separation is that I'm thoroughly committed to working for the black community, even at the sacrifice of bread, etc. The initial state was just to get the hell out of downtown and come uptown and plant myself there, and start from that point.

What I did was, I decided there was a community which would probably best benefit from my services, if they decided they wanted that kind of services. I lived there . . . I live on the street. My physical facilities for working are located there, which I think is also important. People didn't really understand what an architect was, you know, most people would call me an archi-tect, and the first thing they'd say to you, after they find out what you do, is are you going to design me a house.

Most people in poorer communities really don't have a notion of what that's about. So what that means is that you've got to take some time to try to explain that. And there are several ways you can do that. Setting yourself up in a situation where people can actually watch you work, or do that and teach at the same time. What I do is to teach first, and then allow people to come in, just sort of an open operation, come in and watch you work. Of course, interest increases as you become more involved in any kind of issue that is related directly to that community. But the thing is, you somehow have to establish yourself as being part of that community, just as a liquor store, more so than a liquor store. I mean, everybody recognizes that liquor stores exist and knows the people who work in there. But the difference between you and the liquor store is that the liquor store people pack up and go home at night and you stay. So, you know, what you're doing is sort of molding an image, and just by being there, you expand the respect of a lot of kids, because they now have something else they can identify with. And what that does, it sort of provides them with another opportunity for themselves in terms of vocational possibilities, professional possibilities. I'm sure that most of those kids that are now working had very little idea of what an architect was. In fact, at our place, if you mentioned the word architect, they immediately identified with me. A lot of them think I'm the only architect that ever existed in the world.

We've been employing all kinds of different things, from rock and roll bands and films, to get people out to really make decisions about their environment. That's one of the parts of our operation, because there are a lot of different things that we can do. When I go to Columbia tomorrow, I'm going to speak . . . I'm going with fifteen drummers, fifteen voices, and a jazz quintet, to get an idea across about the whole African aesthetic, so what we do, I can go with this group, the Atlanta Blues Band, or a jazz quintet, or a dance crew, and try to present a very concrete example of what I'm talking about.

The same thing applies when you're trying to get a community aroused about any issue that affects their environment. One thing we did was very successful. Once, when we were involved in the Morgan School site, the thing we did was to make an eight-minute film. The problem was that the majority of people could not translate from the second and third dimension in their heads. So we went out and shot a film the day before, and that film included every piece of property that was at stake, the whole site, you know, vision. Then we showed the film and everybody knew exactly what we were talking about. And then we boosted that with slides, we kept going back to the plans, the drawings, and every time we talked about a piece of property, we'd show a slide. And when those people went downtown and they had their rhetorical thing to get through, and they sat there and talked about land and all that stuff, and the people downtown didn't know what had happened, because here was this lady sitting there in her old raggedy coat, talking about property just like an architect. One of the most difficult processes is bringing people to a point where they can make those kinds of decisions, and it's not just a thing where you sit there and go through a long discussion about thus and thus, and break it down rationally and all that kind of stuff, it just doesn't work. So we go into theatrical stuff, productions, to get ideas across.

Like in one particular situation we've proved to be much better comprehensive planners than some of those downtown planners, which is why, in this one particular instance, they won out over the planners. The planners were saying public housing, public housing. We were saying no more public housing in this area, and we documented a case which proved that the schools were overcrowded, and if you added more housing the schools would be that much more overcrowded. We documented another case which showed that they could not use medical facilities in that part of town—they had to go all the way across the city to get medical facilities. So they were saying, why should you add more housing when we need medical facilities, why should you add more housing when we need more schools, why should you add more housing when we need more commercial facilities, and documented a beautiful case.

I think the profession has to be changed. I make no bones about that, because I view it as being racist at the present; it has to be either changed or destroyed. I make no bones about that either.

I have this view of the system—that capitalism is a system which has put objects before people, has put material values before human values, and on the basis of that it's dehumanizing individuals in our society. I believe very strongly in change. I make no bones about that. I make no bones about being against the war, about being for black power. On the basis of that my work has more meaning.

I'm interested in developing some kind of architecture that I think is a reflection of the life-style of Afro-Americans. That's particularly important for black people who decide that they want to stay in a black community rather than leave it, and this isn't an argument for separatism—it's just for people who decide they want to stay in a black community and want to get a good education there.

What you do, you start setting up your own schools that are in spaces to which people can relate. They don't feel intimidated by those spaces. Now you're not going to have as many of them. I mean, instead of spending a lot of gray matter on developing those factories that they run those kids through, they should start spending money maybe on schools that have no more than 150 kids.

So there's a problem, there's a very real problem that we face in Washington. You can't get rid of those oppressive schools, because they're going to continue to build them like that for a long time. So what we've got to do is maybe set up a parallel structure. You see, in my architecture I don't separate politics from architecture or economics from architecture, I mean everything just comes together. That's the African thing too. Everything is interwoven.

That's why I think that right now existing spaces might be very suitable. I would say, let's stop new building and turn existing elementary schools into warehouses and look to existing facilities of lesser scale in those communities and let them serve as the educational plant—renovate, rehabilitate them, so they're more suitable.

First we'd have to find a vacancy. You look for a spot that's vacant . . . a storefront, an old row house, and that's your place. Then you send your teacher around the block to organize, that teacher does all that homework. They spend the three months prior to that September just organizing their school. And they don't have the summer off any more, because they want a summer program, which is sort of a nice break, I suppose, for the kids. Because, there's more fun involved.

How do you make those spaces more conducive for learning? It may be that you just put a fresh coat of paint on it, polish the floors, add a little life to the walls. The most important thing is creating a feeling of belonging, ownership, some attachment to that space for the people who have to use it. That's the kind of thing I'm interested in getting into right now, doing some research and writing on it, trying to develop that idea. I'm going to take this area, develop a model. If we talked about turning this area into that kind of model school district, and using the Morgan and the Adams Schools as the two warehouses, and then a whole system generating around that on the block, and using what I know about each block to determine whether or not and where that should go . . .

And staffing would be like . . . you take one or two teachers from the existing elementary school and put him or her on the block, and also require that they live there, and then you take graduate students in education, high school students, neighborhood youth corps, you use whatever you can to beef up the staff. But the important thing is that people from that block should be involved in working in that school. Some very interesting things could happen. Because that little model begins to function as a community organization on that block, and a teacher becomes a lot of other things than just a teacher, just someone who has to transfer those academic skills—he becomes sort of a personality on the block. He or she has got to work, got to do a good job, because the people on the block will run them right out. And it becomes more than just setting up a little PTA. You really set up a little community organization with parents' support, parents baking cookies, etc., all the things you need to help support that thing. You don't need truant officers, because the teacher can just run up the block to see where Johnny is today. It certainly utilizes energies of other people, other than just the teacher, who now has to comply to some standard that has to have some kind of certificate to teach. It certainly cuts that out for all the people who are sort of assistant teachers . . . you just look for good people, people who can relate, people who have good politics. . . .

One of the contentions on which I would base this new kind of school is that you provide them with extra incentives by having some elderly types there.

They do that in Scandinavia, old folk, grandparents who really dig kids, who are retired, who don't have anything to do, so why not take them off the block and put them in there and let them just love the kid in this block school, all week. If the kid's not getting it at home, it really is a good thing for that kid just to have that elderly person around. So you add all kinds of things in there, so you can give the kid the personal attention he needs, those extra incentives that he may not be getting at home. You bribe him with those things, so that when he's ten years old, his learning ability is just as—you've boosted him whereas the middle class kid is already getting the boost, and at the age of ten they're both capable of learning at the same pace. So that school becomes something else, because that grandfather is going to be there well beyond 3 o'clock. He's going to be there as long as he can be there, and probably be there early the next morning. There will be kids who'll have emotional problems necessitating even further attention, but my guess is that that kid will probably fall in love with the place—he feels security, he's getting attention. He's getting all those extra incentives he might not get out in the street and might not get at home.

Because of the size and the impersonality of the school systems it's impossible for people to make a commitment to it and to build something. Which might be a very important factor in the block school, because the teacher will have, like, her own school and will be able to make a commitment to building it, which is a different thing than going into a public school and having an institutional classroom and trying to make a commitment to something. We have a top salary of seven thousand bucks a year, but people stay because they feel they own a piece of it, and everybody's got something invested in it.

If we call this a school, we're in violation of the law, it means you've got to get fire doors, you've got to enclose your stairwells. They tried to close us down, but we convinced them it was to their advantage to keep all these kids in here, not to put them in the street, because they'd raise absolute hell. So they sort of let us slide by, turn their head when they walk by. So that's a real design problem. Because if we started calling all those things block schools and try to put them on the block, you even institutionalize those small buildings . . . by having to enclose your stairways, putting in fire doors, and that begins to really change the character of that building, and it's more like a tenement than a house.

Just having our stairwell open is important—it makes the building feel a lot freer. Once we enclose that stairway, something else happens.

One thing we don't have to worry about, if we find we're doing something wrong, we can just stop, and change directions or something. You don't have to go through a lot of hassle about doing that. One of the theories by which we operate is that we need maximum flexibility and we just ask people to trust our judgment. Flexibility to continue to develop models, and programs for working with kids. I'm not sure you can do that in the existing framework of public education. I know you can't, so that's one given. There may be a design problem in that they may not be able to capture this kind of space, the same feeling that exists within this space. Another thing is that probably, the requirements, the stipulations for who was or wasn't a teacher might be so stringent that you might not be able to get the kind of people you need.

The little boys have a cat named Eric, who's their idol, teaches them percussion, but it's more than just teaching percussion, it's a whole relationship. . . . When he comes in, he just has a whole line of kids walking behind him. It's partly because they can go see him at the jazz workshop, and because he talks to them. They can touch him and they know he's good. . . . But that whole worldly thing is important, how do you stretch kids out. One way is by having someone like Eric, who is very willing to place himself at their disposal. They know he's good, because they go to the jazz workshop, and they see the people clap for him, and they figure, that's a nice cat to identify with.

What's more, people like Eric like to share this with kids. And that's one of the bad things about schools—they lock out these people like Eric and whole lots of people who are moving in a much broader world and like to share this with other people, and schools say no, you can only do it if you have a certain kind of certificate.

Eric's twenty-one. He's played with Pharoah Sanders, he's recorded about three albums, Miles Davis wants him to play, but the public schools aren't going to take him.

We've got good teachers because none of them are teachers. Everyone teaches because they feel it's important, no one's teaching because they don't have anything else to do. The people who come to work for us, the only stipulation is that they have good politics and good sensitivities, and in almost all cases we've been right. We haven't lost one person since we've started, full-time.

The staff is interesting, and I'm not sure we could put another staff together like this, so the only thing to do is to encourage it to grow. No one here is trained as a teacher. There are two kinds of people. Most of the administrative people are old movement people, which means they've had some real experience in working with people. Now the artists, with good sensitivity, most of them have never been involved in working with people before. So you've got the administrators honest, talking about you've got to work with people, and you've got the artists injecting their enthusiasm and all that other stuff into the administrators, so they keep flipping back and forth. The administrators getting very artsy, the artists getting concerned about people. We've got five people on the administrative staff, four of them worked in the Movement, including myself, and only one didn't and he's my half brother so he was close enough to experience it.

Let me tell you how we work. We make very little distinction between a guy like Rhythm who is forty-seven and a kid like Perry who's eight. If we have a party, everybody's there. It's very important to develop a sort of communal feeling around education. We sort of have a little community here. You know how you get hung up on having a babysitter so you can go to a party. You don't need a babysitter, just bring the kid, the kid can either go to sleep or play until he gets tired, he can play with the other kids, so you've got that level occurring, and the kids running through the party, it's fun. Everybody digs the kids anyway. Then you have the teenagers, fourteen or fifteen, who every now and then take a little shot of rum and you have to sort of keep them away from the rum bottle. Then you have the people in our age bracket, and then the older people. But that, for us, becomes a real reinforcement, because sometimes the kids hang onto Rhythm, sometimes onto me, sometimes onto other kids. But because you have everybody, many different age levels involved, that's sort of a built-in reinforcement for us. Sometimes Rhythm provides a father image for me, or we make him feel good, because today's his birthday, and he wouldn't have a cake anywhere else. And he's sort of part of the community we're trying to generate. Rhythm comes in some afternoons and will just pick up a kid and kiss him. It does just as much to that kid as it does to him.

The way we teach reading—we recognize that in Africa storytelling is an old tradition which plays a strong part in every community. Now given that, we get involved in the whole idea of storytelling— you take the story as it's been told, you write it out in, you know, like 2½ inch-high letters, and you even display the stories as pieces of art. And they're all around this room and the kids look at them and they sort of get hung up on the notion, "Gee, I wrote that." But that sort of teaches reading backwards—on the basis of something that they do, something that's creative, and you teach them to read on that basis. But certainly if you begin to teach reading like that in the black community, given the history of the African community has been oral, it just happens that the Western tradition is one in which you must read. Given those three things, how to develop a more meaningful process whereby kids can learn to read. Now if that's true, it means that classrooms have to take on a different shape, a different form. They can't be just a very structured kind of thing. It becomes the kind of thing where the teacher becomes the head storyteller, and any assistants become sort of assistant storytellers, and you develop a whole learning experience on the basis of the story she tells, and then the stories that you tell back to her. But if you had some different kind of classroom, a different kind of scale, it may mean that you have to employ the kind of system we employ where you take an old house and you get a combination of people, one who's sort of chief storyteller, and that means that you have an ability to relate to the kids. And then you have some people who will help you — maybe college students or certainly people who really respond to that, or some of the older people in that community, who tell some of the best stories, and that's another kind of educational environment.

One problem certainly is that the average kid who, say, goes to an elementary school and grows up in this community, like in the *Cool World,* you see the *Cool World*? The fourteen-year-old prostitute who wants to see the ocean?

That's what I'm talking about. Seeing the ocean is a resource.

But there are cats on that corner there who never go downtown to shop, or never go to New York. So we also recognize as part of the experience taking the kids to New York. That's why I've booked our dance group when I can. So they can all thirty-six of them jump on a bus and go somewhere, just to stretch out and perform before a big audience, so they can feel what they've been doing on the street hasn't just been on the street, but it goes a lot farther than that . . . just to inject those little things all the time. You can only take kids to the zoo for so long.

The main resources are the people. It's our function, because of what we do, because I go on the airplane once a week, because I may go to Africa in a month. That's a resource. If I come back, and they say, "Gee, man, here's the cat that's been to Africa. Never knew a cat that's been to Africa before."

It's a different thing if an elementary school teacher takes a summer trip to Africa and then brings the slides in September and shows them to the kids. It's a different sort of thing if the kids are there, sort of helping you pack, you live in the same community they do, everybody knows you're going to Africa, people see you off, they're there when you get back, and you sort of unpack with everybody. That's a different kind of experience. When I go to Yale, someone from here usually takes me to the airport, someone picks me up, and I call back the next day to see how everything's going, call every day, and call a couple of people in the evening. So it's like I'm never really gone, and the Yale thing and my trip is just a part of this thing.

We see it as important. I said to Yale, I won't come unless you let me bring people from my organization here, if I decide I want to bring them, take people there and check them into a hotel, take them to my class, meet my students. My students have been here, I've encouraged that on the other hand. You come down here to see what we're doing. My students walk in here and people know them, people from here walk in there, and my students know them.

Maybe that's it. You bring part of the outside world to the village, and you take the village outside. Maybe those are the two things that make the kid worldly, expand his vision, even in the block school. Like the film, the day before yesterday, substantiated—the outside world is represented by a TV film, something done on national television, to them that's the outside world and we brought it right down here to show it to them—substantiated. So maybe it's a combination of those two things—bringing the capital to the village, taking the village to the capital.

MOBOC: A Mobile Learning Environment

Charles W. Rusch*

On the first day of school we had lunch in one of the Los Angeles city parks. After lunch I gathered eveyone, and I said, "Let's do some tree identification," and they all moaned. So I said, "Aw, come on, you live with these plants, you could at least know their names. What's the name of these trees we're sitting under?"

They all looked up, and in unison said "Sycamores." So I said, "What kind of sycamore?" and no one knew. I got out my Trees of North America book, and said, "Let's find out." There were only three kinds of sycamore in the book, only one on the West Coast, and it was called the California Sycamore. I thought it was all over, but I persisted, "We'd better make sure by checking these trees against the description in the book." So I started reading the text, "Leaves, 6 to 8 inches." I fished a cloth measuring tape out of a box, handed it to Jeff, and said, "Go check out those leaves." He found that the leaves were indeed 6 to 8 inches.

*I would like to thank David Alpaugh for his assistance in developing the manuscript for this article.

I went back to the book and read, " 'Height of mature trees, 30 to 50 feet.' How are we going to check that?" A big discussion followed, and we finally decided that I should stand up against one of the trees; they would back off as far as they could and estimate how many "Rusches" high the tree was. A little simple multiplication followed and we had an approximate tree height. Everyone was pretty involved by now, so I asked them "How else could you do it?" Eric was in the seventh grade and knew a little geometry, so he taught us how to measure the height by triangulation.

I was delighted just to have everyone's attention, so I went back to the book and kept reading. Near the bottom of the paragraph came the clincher, "Diameter: 1 to 3 feet." So I handed over the measuring tape and said, "Get me the diameter of that tree over there." They went over to the tree, and it wasn't until they were right on top of it that they realized that the only way to measure the diameter of a tree directly is to cut it down. But I insisted that we had to know the diameter of the tree, so two of them stretched out the tape next to the tree, and by eyeballing along one "edge" and then the other, they came up with 18 inches.

I said, "Is that an accurate answer or just approximate?" They agreed it was only a guess, so I said, "How else could you do it?"

Right off, Daniel said, "Well you could measure all the way around it, lay that circle out in the dirt, and then measure across it." I was really impressed, and said, "Go to it." Meanwhile, I turned to rest of the group, and said, "How else could you do it?"

Eric, who turned out to be a visualizer and was perhaps visualizing the tree as having two sides, said, "Well, you could measure all the way around it, and divide by two." Since I believe you learn at least as much from mistakes as from successes, I said, "Okay, try it." Meanwhile, Daniel was measuring across the circle on the ground, and by picking the right points on a somewhat lopsided circle came up with the same answer, "18 inches." So I gave the tape to Eric, he measured around the tree, got 60 inches, divided by 2, and got 30 for the diameter. He was naturally a little disappointed, so I said, "Well, I like your idea, maybe you just have the wrong number. Is there a better number to divide with than two?"

Right off, Michael said, "Well you could divide by 3," and then thinking ahead added, "and subtract 2."

I said, "Great! Now you have a formula; check it out on that tree over there," pointing to one only about 6 inches in diameter. They went over, measured the circumference, divided by 3, subtracted 2, and checked it against a circle on the ground. The result was disappointing, so I told them to try some more trees. They checked about three more trees and came back. "How did it work?"

"Well," Mark said, "Dividing by 3 works pretty well, but subtracting isn't so good."

"How good is dividing by 3?" I asked, and Michael replied, "It's not quite big enough."

"How big should it be?"

"About 3½," said Daniel.

"No!" said Michael, "It's more like 3⅛."

At that point, these five kids, ranging in age from 9 to 12 were within 2 one hundredths of discovering π and I was having trouble containing myself. I suppose I could have extended the lesson by having them convert ⅛ to decimals, but I was too excited.

"Look," I said, "I want to tell you a secret. There's a magic number which is so special it has its own name. It's called π. And the magic is that once you know how big it is, you can take any circle, no matter how big or how small, and go from circumference to diameter, or diameter to circumference. Now here is how it works . . ."

After my explanation, we went around the park, estimating the circumferences of trees by guessing their diameter, or figuring the diameter by measuring the circumference and dividing by π. Later when I had taught them how to use a slide rule, I pointed out π to them and gave them a whole series of "tree" problems. Later still, I reviewed the whole thing with telephone poles and lighting standards, just to make sure that the concept of π didn't disappear into the obscurity of abstract mathematics. I know that I didn't really understand π until I got to college, despite an excellent math program in high school. But for those five kids at least, π is something real; it "lives" in trees and telephone poles. Some teachers will say they can do the same thing in a classroom, that you don't have to go to a park to learn about π. Maybe so, but for me the critical moment was when I realized that you can't measure the diameter of a tree directly without cutting it down, and that when the children were confronted with that fact, they were on their way to discovering π.

BACKGROUND

Today's classroom, as it has derived from the schoolhouse of American tradition, is a window on a world dramatically changed from the rural America of its inception. As a device in rural society, the classroom served a vital need to extend the vision and understanding of a child from the several acres of his farm or village to the world of recorded knowledge and experience beyond. This made sense, and continues to make sense, under conditions that financially or practically prohibit the child's movement from his personal world to the origins of that knowledge and experience. It makes less sense if the view is distorted by third-hand reportage, as the grounds for belief become insubstantial and understanding becomes inconsistent and confused. It makes least sense, however, if the information is passed on wrongly *and* the constraints on the child's movement no longer exist. The classroom window in an *urban* world becomes an artificial barrier between knowledge and experience, between the world as the child is told about it and the one he sees every day.

The aim of the experiment reported here is to bring the child to the world, rather than vice versa, so that his view is firsthand and his knowledge and ability to deal with the world are integral with the experience of his life. The Mobile Open Classroom (MOBOC) was conceived as an alternative to existing forms of schooling, and has addressed itself to the deficiencies of those systems. It has been carried on outside the traditional school classroom because of that system's growing inability to adequately and meaningfully represent the world to its students. Most public schools are divorced from life, separating the child from his environment and hence from direct-experience learning. The child's ability to proceed through life and handle the many levels of problems confronted each day is hampered by his lack of preparation. This disadvantage is compounded by the refusal of most schools to develop problem-solving skills in anything more than an academic manner, if at all.

Public schools also pay insufficient attention to affective and social development. Socialization is seen as the incorporation of the child into society, which is done poorly; socializing with peers is stifled by rules that are built in the name of a "better learning environment," and is limited in essence to the hours not reserved for "teaching." Furthermore, public schools are often understaffed, forcing teachers to treat children as if they were all the same, and to concentrate on uniformity of behavior instead of creativity and individuality.

Private schools, on the other hand, tend to be of two kinds, traditional or "free." Traditional private schools tend to be "more of the same" vis-à-

vis public schools. The more expensive ones have a lower student–teacher ratio and thus are more individualistic in their training; but they are often still mentalistic, in that they still concentrate on teaching the three R's through secondary learning sources, but they work harder and longer at it. The free schools have a different collection of problems. Most free schools concentrate first on training the emotional or affective side of the child. They are determined to release the child from the external controls of the public school classroom, but they often do little to help the child replace that external control with an internal one; nor do the ones I have visited replace the classroom with a sufficiently varied learning environment to keep the child stimulated and growing. The environment often seems chaotic, noisy, and distracting to attempts toward concentration on serious individual learning. Group interaction is usually quite high, but, again, there is often little teaching of cooperative skills, and the children seem to be mercilessly and endlessly putting each other down. As a result, the free schools, in my opinion, tend to be weak in skill development (even the social skills) and prepare the child inadequately for life and a role in society.

This indictment of public and private schools, of course, does not apply to all schools, some of which are excellent in a wide variety of areas. However, there is no school that I know of that is educating what I would call the whole child.

THE IDEAL SCHOOL

If society is to educate the whole child, a new school model is needed. "Educating the whole child" means the development of the body, mind, and spirit of the child in a social context which imparts to the child the skills, knowledge, attitudes, and awareness that he will need later as an imaginative, creative, and competent member of society. The school system at present trains *the body* in certain narrowly defined areas connected with strength and sports. It does little to give the child a sound understanding of his body in terms of nutrition, health, flexibility, endurance, and body–mind relationships. As for the *mind,* the schools of the country spend most of their time training the mind, but they only train one portion of it, largely ignoring the creative, artistic, and poetic aspects of mental life. Finally, the *spiritual* side of life is completely avoided by the schools, partly because of an absurd misunderstanding of the need to separate church and state. Man has a profound need to transcend himself, yet even most churches have lost sight of their early objective of bringing such transcendent experience to every church member. Students from junior high school to college are expressing this need to transcend themselves by taking drugs, meditating, and exploring the esoteric religious cults. Even sexual exploration can be seen as an effort to transcend the self. Spiritual transcendence in its most positive form is dependent upon the mental and physical well-being of the individual, and a strong case can be made for the integration of spiritual education with mental and physical education.

Having the proper social context for such a complete education is extremely important. As long as man lives his life through societies, his children will be subject to the experience of socialization. As long as man creates cultures, the culturalization of his children will be necessary. Many persons involved in the free-school movement object to the emphasis of the public schools on socialization processes, but the only objection can be to the form such socialization takes, not to the fact itself. Every institution in society acts to socialize its members, be it public school, free school, or bank. What is needed in a new school model is a process that explains society and social process as fully as is possible to its children. But such an explanation, to be complete, should be largely direct, and only partly experienced through secondary sources, such as books and teachers. The child must be brought into contact with his environment, with the people of that environment, how they act, and what they do. He must experience the objects that people make, how they are made, and how they work. In addition, he should be brought into direct contact with the natural environment and the sensitive ecological systems that exist between nature and man. Much of this experience must be firsthand and direct if we are to counter the tremendous loss of meaning and insensitivity that has engulfed society.

The new school, then, if it is to educate the whole child, must concern itself with all levels of mind, body, and spirit. It should concentrate on direct-experience learning, bringing the child to a deep understanding of his social and physical environment. It should stimulate his curiosity through individualized instruction and independent study. Finally, it should be skill oriented, fostering the development both of social–interpersonal skills and problem-solving skills.

To accomplish these objectives, the school first needs to establish a one-to-one trusting relationship between the child and the teacher. There must be no fear in this relationship. Fear comes from punishment or dominance; punishment comes from having rules. Thus the ideal school should have few rules, only those necessary to mediate the interaction of the children as part of the social group. The teacher–student relationship must be built on trust, love, and mutual respect. Given that initial contact, the teacher should first bring out the strengths of the student to reveal his competencies to himself and to the others. These strengths should be developed before weaknesses are addressed. From competence flows confidence. As self-confidence expands, self-image improves. With an improvement in self-image comes improvement in relations with others. Emotional stability follows from love, trust, self-confidence, and successful relations with others. At this point the child has a solid base on which to build and is ready to work on weaknesses, incompetence, emotional blockages, and so forth. Throughout this process, the teacher must work to transfer the locus of control from external reward to internal satisfaction. The emotionally stable child has little need for praise, much less gold stars or grades. He must learn to be his own judge of the activities and performance levels that he finds satisfying. He must be allowed to love learning for its own sake. Children know this as preschoolers. It is our schools that teach them differently.

THE MOBILE SCHOOL IDEA

The Mobile Open Classroom (MOBOC) was entirely mobile for the first year. This emphasis on mobility was not simply for the sake of being different; it has a strong logic behind it. Mobility is the most characteristic feature of MOBOC, but there are three additional conceptual features that follow from the mobile school idea:

1. A radically different allocation of school funds.
2. A maximal use of urban resources.
3. A total restructuring of the curriculum around direct-experience learning.

Each feature depends upon mobility as the liberating concept. First, by making the school primarily mobile, school funds can be redistributed to the students' and teachers' advantage. By not building or renting a building, by not having to pay janitors, gardeners, and maintenance men to maintain the building, and by reducing administrative costs to a minimum (no principals, vice principals, secretaries, superintendents, etc.), it becomes possible to put almost the entire school budget into teaching or direct pupil costs. To oversimplify, by eliminating the building and the salaries of all those persons who do not directly

work with the children, the student–teacher ratio can be reduced from something like 35 to 1 to 10 to 1. In this one stroke, many of the most pressing public school problems can be eliminated at no extra cost to the school or school district.

Second, mobility allows us to use our public and private urban resources more wisely. In most cities, public libraries have restricted hours in the mornings. Children's rooms sit virtually empty all day because the children are in school. Many children's rooms have very large collections of fiction, nonfiction, and reference books for children. They almost all have a special librarian trained in helping children to find information or satisfying reading material. The only ingredient missing for a first-class learning event are the children themselves. MOBOC took advantage of this lacuna by bringing the children to the libraries during the day.

It is not just the libraries that have underused learning facilities. The children's areas of city parks stand unused until school lets out. Factories, professional offices, boy's clubs, beaches, yacht harbors, stores, and so forth, are never visited by children during the day, although they often provide excellent learning opportunities, including guided tours, demonstration models, and underused equipment. Why? Because the children are all in school. Once one becomes aware of the richness of the city's learning opportunities, the concept of the self-contained classroom becomes an absurd, unconscionable misuse of valuable resources.

Third, mobility allows the teacher to restructure the curriculum around direct-experience learning, which brings relevance and meaning to its subject matter. It is cruel to force children to sit in chairs for five hours a day. Children want and need to be moving constantly, to be talking to each other, and to be exploring their environments. To try to cut out, digest, and condense some piece of the world, and bring it to children shut up in a room just does not make sense. They need to see, touch, taste, hear, and smell life firsthand. No one can convince me (not even the most efficient behavior-mod type) that he knows what a child is learning at any given moment. I do not allow myself the luxury of that pretense. I therefore cannot justify restricting a child's learning to narrowly predetermined concepts. Let the child explore, explore with him, tell him everything you can about what you are learning at any given moment, and help him structure his learning into understandable wholes; but do not arbitrarily restrict it.

By taking the child out of the classroom, you open up the whole world to him as a learning laboratory. Ivan Illich, in his book *Deschooling Society,* makes the point that the city is full of teachers. Indeed, everyone can be considered a teacher of something. The children in MOBOC have talked to orchid growers, fishermen, architects, lawyers, writers, artists, assemblymen, telephone operators, disc jockeys, stock clerks, filmmakers, farmers, engineers (and on and on) about their work. Each of these people has enthusiastically related to the children what they do, whether they enjoy it, what their life is like, and so forth. Each encounter takes usually ten to thirty minutes and leaves a lasting impression on the child, because the contact was face to face and backed by love and interest. There can be no comparison with reading about those jobs in a book or even seeing them in a movie. In many cases the children were allowed to participate in the actual work experience.

The preceding features of the MOBOC experience describe some of the benefits of mobility; but there is much more to MOBOC than mobility. The most important additional premise is that teachers as well as children have a right to learn and grow. Probably the most important feature of MOBOC that promotes teacher growth is that they have to teach only eight children instead of thirty-five. You cannot teach thirty-five children; you can only control them. When I tell prospective teachers of MOBOC that they will have only eight children, they realize immediately that they can begin to

teach again. Actually, what happens is more like learning than teaching. The teachers soon discover, when they take their children out into the city, that they don't know everything about the city, and they must learn together with the children. The people in the city become the teachers, and the teachers of MOBOC become learners along with the children. MOBOC is as close to a learning community as any group with which I have been associated. Another feature which promotes teacher growth is that each teacher is almost entirely responsible for the administration of his own program. This comes about through the effort to reduce administrative overhead to a minimum. At the beginning of the year the teachers are uncomfortable with this type of responsibility; they are used to considerable administrative support. But as the year moves on they begin to discover the freedom that comes from running one's own program, and they grow through that freedom. By the end of the year, each teacher has seemingly become a new person, renewed and excited by his own effectiveness at administering and teaching his own program. Public schools, on the other hand, operate on just the opposite premise. First the school gives the teacher a narrowly defined task. Then, because the teacher doesn't respond well to this narrowly defined task, the school administration finds it has to supervise the teachers to make sure that they maintain the desired level of quality. The administrators then become watchdogs or supervisors of the teachers, who have not been given much responsibility to start with. The administrative burden of supervising people who are put in a no-trust, no-responsibility situation is enormous. The administrative burden of supervising teachers who have been given full responsibility for their program, a great deal of trust, and much support and encouragement is almost nil.

The third major feature of MOBOC that operates toward the promotion of teacher growth is the effect the program has on the children themselves. Teachers fully responsible for designing their program and administrating it can take full credit for the effectiveness of that program. With only eight or ten children to teach, each child can be given a great deal of individualized instruction. Unconfined to the classroom, the child expands at an enormous rate, his curiosity is stimulated, and he is continually excited about the variety of places and people that he meets as his classroom explores the city. Sometimes it almost seems as if he awakens out a deep sleep. Children who couldn't read begin to read; children who blocked over math begin to see the relevance of learning math. Children who are bored and not excited by anything become highly stimulated and excited by everything. At times it seems the entire personality has changed both at school and at home. The parents of the children of MOBOC are our most supporting group. When the teachers begin to see these changes in the children, they know that they are the only adult responsible on a day-to-day basis for the daily learning activities and behavior of the children. They become transformed themselves as they see the effectiveness of their efforts unfold. One of the basic problems of the public school system is not only that it does not recognize children as people, but that it does not recognize teachers as people.

Finally, in this list of conceptual features of the mobile school idea, I should mention the MOBOC school rules. It is my contention that an elaborate rule system can only result in the breaking of rules. At that point the administration or teacher is confronted with the problem of what to do to the child who has broken rules. The result is punishment or ostracization of some sort, and the child's reaction can only be one of resentment or fear. So in MOBOC we have as few rules as possible. There *are* some rules that are necessary, because MOBOC is an institution and as such forms a part of the larger socialization process in which individual behavior has to be attuned to that of the social group. But MOBOC finds that it can operate fairly successfully on three rules:

1. The first rule is that school is for learning. Although this rule may seem somewhat obvious and almost not necessary to state, we have found that it is very useful in clarifying for the children what goes on in school and what does not go on in school. It tells them what they can bring to school and what they should not bring to school, because school is for learning. MOBOC children can bring cards to school as long as they are learning from card games; but once the card games become routine, the cards are no longer appropriate school items. Water guns, on the other hand, cannot be brought to school unless the point of bringing them is to study the physical principles of their operation and not the results of their use upon each other. A corollary of this rule is that learning should be fun, which means that reading should be fun, mathematics should be fun, exploring the city should be fun, and time spent in the van should be fun. But all those activities should take place around real learning events. What we strive for in MOBOC is zero wasted time. This does not mean that we are pushing the children hard, but merely that, because school is for learning, we concentrate at every moment on maximizing what the child is learning at that moment.

2. Rule 2 states that no one gets hurt at MOBOC. By this we mean that no one gets hurt either physically or psychologically; that is, MOBOC is a nonviolent school. Once again it may seem like such a rule need not be stated. Yet I know some schools where the children are allowed to "work out" their problems on one another. I believe that violence breeds violence, and it is far better to have the children work out their differences verbally in an open discussion than physically in a brawl or cruelly through verbal abuse. When we tell the children about this rule at the beginning of the year, we are careful to state that we realize this rule is impossible to fulfill all the time, but that what we would like them to be doing is to be working on

it at all times. Children are going to hurt each other, both physically and psychologically. In fact, quite often children cannot even recognize when they are hurting each other, particularly psychologically; so we find that children have to be helped and reminded of this rule continuously throughout the year. There is no particular punishment for violating the rule, only another reminder, and perhaps the ordeal of sitting through a long discussion trying to work out personal differences.

3. Rule 3 states that when we are somewhere else we play by their rules. We find this rule necessary to cover the wide range of situations in which we find ourselves throughout the week. It means that when we go some place which requires that we be well dressed, we dress well, or if we go some place where we have to behave quietly, we behave quietly. This minimizes the number of conflicts we have and usually guarantees a return invitation. However, as soon as we are back in the bus, our own rules apply. There the students can dress the way they want, can talk to each other the way they want, and can use the words they want to use to express themselves—as long as what they are doing is done in the context of learning and is not hurting themselves or each other.

There is much more to MOBOC than this brief summary of conceptual features. However, I believe that it contains the essence of the mobile school idea.

THE IDEA IN PRACTICE

MOBOC has always been, even in its initial conception, a demonstration school for the public school system. We found, however, that the climate was not conducive in the Los Angeles School District to start this school within the system itself. On the other hand, the laws governing private schools in Southern California are fairly flexible, and we found that it would be quite easy to start MOBOC as a private school. We thereby avoided the constraints imposed by operating within the public school system. Of course, private schools have their own problems, most of which are concerned with the financing of the school program. We decided that it seemed much more feasible to tackle those financial problems than to tackle the constraints of the public school system.

The year before I started MOBOC a group of us had set up a nonprofit corporation called *Open Space,* which was devoted to working on school alternatives within the public schools. MOBOC was established as a division of Open Space and thereby became part of a nonprofit corporation in good legal standing. My initial plan was to start with a small five- or seven-row school bus and fourteen kids, with Gail Bass, one of my graduate students at the School of Architecture and Urban Planning, and myself as teachers. I was to go on half-sabbatical from the University of California at Los Angeles (UCLA) in order to begin the school. After hours and hours of meetings held over the summer with enthusiastic groups of parents, when school finally opened in the fall, we had enrolled only five children, two of which were mine. This was my first eye-opening disappointment, and it has continued to be the most severe problem that we face as an innovative school. Almost all parents, no matter of what political persuasion, become quite conservative when the subject is their children's education. Because of the low enrollment, we could not afford to have two teachers, and so I had to ask Gail to step aside and let me do it. By December I had seven children, and in February one child dropped out and one new one joined. For the rest of the year, the school consisted of seven children, one bus, and myself as teacher, bus driver, principal, secretary, financial manager, and janitor.

We started in my Volkswagen camper bus, but by October it was clear that we needed more space, particularly if I was going to attract more children to the school. We set about finding and buying a lager vehicle. Of course, I involved the children in this operation. We went from used-car lot to used-car lot, and I taught them everything I could about what to look out for in buying a used vehicle. We finally settled on a Ford SuperVan. I wanted to get the children involved in building their own classroom environment, so I bought a straight cargo van with no windows and almost no seats. We then proceeded to a complete architectural procedure on the van. We did measured drawings before it was even out of the used-car lot. Design drawings followed a complete architectural analysis of our needs and space requirements.

Then the fun began. First we built a small working model. Then for the next three weeks we worked on converting the van itself. Picture, if you will, one child leaning against the van with a scale and a set of working drawings reading off the exact measurements as to where the windows should be located to another child standing on a concrete block with a ruler and a crayon. Then picture the same child drilling a hole in the side of the van, which we had just purchased for several thousand dollars, and cutting out the window with a saber saw. In a similar way we built the storage floor and seating arrangement, which had a small table in it that could be raised and lowered. The storage floor had storage boxes for each child's equipment and all the items that the school would have to carry around on its daily excursions through the city. During this period, I taught the children about electricity when I wired the van, about the use of hand tools in building the storage floor, and about heat transfer when we insulated the van walls.

The curricular structure Gail and I had decided upon the summer before was simply to divide the region into four ecological areas—the beaches, the mountains, the deserts, and the city itself—and then set about to learn as much as we could about each of those areas. I did not know exactly how to start; but I found a little book called *What to Do with Your Kids in L.A.,* and I asked the children to pick out those places they most wanted to visit and then I screened the list for educational value. And we simply began. Three mornings a week we spent in the public libraries doing our reading, writing, and arithmetic for the week. Public libraries proved to be an excellent resource and locale for such activity, and as the children became more and more excited about school, they were able to accomplish in those six or seven hours what had taken a week in the previous year in public school. The rest of the week we explored the city.

It wasn't very long before I discovered that the places we were visiting were related to each other in a systemic way, and before we knew it we were working on an urban-systems curriculum. We studied the legal systems by visiting a variety of different courtrooms, the city council chambers, the police department, and law offices. We studied the food distribution system by growing our own garden in someone's backyard, by visiting a dairy outside of town, by visiting a tuna packaging plant in San Pedro, and by getting up at 4:00 A.M. and going downtown to the produce market to find out how the food gets from the farm to the market. In a similar way we studied the distribution of electricity in the city, the distribution of water, the distribution of magazines and newspapers, and we spent a considerable amount of time studying the communication systems of the city, that is, radio, television, telephones, and mail. I helped the children cognitively structure these diverse systems by asking them the question, "Tell me all the things that come into your home." Through discussion we decided that, besides ants and dust we should include gas, water, food, electricity, mail, newspapers, magazines, radio, TV, phone calls, and people. I then asked, "Where do all those things come from?" And from their scattered and partial answers I built a curriculum with considerable interest and relevance to their lives.

We found the public and private facilities to be explored in the city almost endless. Wherever we went one week we found three or four more places to go the next week. We stopped at twenty-six different parks in the course of the year, using them primarily for sports and lunches and stopping always at the one closest to where we happened to be. We visited twelve public libraries through the course of the year, finally settling on three favorites, which had fantastic collections in the children's room, friendly personnel, and modern carpeted buildings.

I had no idea how long the school would last that first year, and so I found it extremely important to maintain a normal rate of development in the traditional skill areas—that is reading, writing, and arithmetic. As it turned out we did much more reading and writing than the children had been doing in public school, and I maintained their normal rate of progress in mathematics by having them work in the state workbook series in math. For reading, I merely went around each week and asked the child what he had read that week. If it was a book that he had finished, I wrote it down on the list. Two thirds of the way through the year the children were trading lists, recommending books to one another, and even arguing over who was going to get the next book in the series. The best way to encourage reading in children is to communicate a love of books and reading to them, and then simply have them do a lot of it. Occasionally, I would have them read to make sure they were reading well and comprehending what they were reading. In this way one child read almost fifty books, most of them read over thirty books during the year, and one child, who was having great difficulty reading when he entered the school, read ten to twelve books. I approached writing in a very similar way. The children had to write something every week. We decided it did not make any difference what it was as long as they were learning how to express their ideas in complete, correct sentences and paragraphs. Each child wrote about a page and a half to two pages each week on a wide variety of subjects, ranging from tide-pool life to quite imaginative stories and high-quality poetry. In addition, we did quite a bit of math and physics by using objects we found in the environment. We were weaker that first year on history, social science, art, and music, although we did study each to a certain extent. History we studied by visiting historical sites and seeing a lot of movies, which we checked out of the public library. Social science we studied by visiting the institutions of the city and studying their purpose and function. The world of art was explored by visits to at least a dozen art exhibits, by seeing artists at work, and through the usual arts and crafts activities of children. Although music was approached mainly through appreciation, it included exposure to music of different cultures and demonstration of a variety of instruments.

Probably the most important learning events of the year, at least the most rewarding to me, were the ones we just happened upon on the way to or back from someplace else. Some of these are revealed in the anecdotes at the beginning and end of this article. I began to call these events "found learning." When we went to the dairy, we discovered the scales on which they weigh the trucks, and proceeded to do a whole unit on weight measurement. Walking down the street, we discovered that the reflections in curved glass are quite different from those in flat glass, and a discussion followed that revealed the physics of light. And we discovered that the entrance of a parking lot had, hidden in its asphalt, a whole lesson on electronic circuitry. A playground swing and a children's merry-go-round revealed the physical laws of momentum and inertia. The list seems endless; the world is there waiting to be explained to eager young minds.

The natural environment similarly fell away to our inquiring determination. In the fall we visited beaches because the tides were right; that is, the low tides occurred during school hours. We spent many hours learning the names and habits of all the little animals that live in tide pools. We were supported in this effort by the Marine Museum in San Pedro and untold books from several public libraries. In the winter the climate is perfect for exploring the desert, so we chose it for our first overnight camping trip. We spent three days in the desert in Anza Borrego Desert State Park studying desert life, survival, the logistics of camping, camping skills, and astronomy at night. In the spring the mountains are ripe for exploring, and we spent another three days in the mountains behind Santa Barbara, discovering how plants live in relationship to one another, in relationship to the climate, in relationship to the side of the hill they are growing on or the altitude at which they are found. We learned how different kinds of birds have adapted themselves to finding different kinds of insects and how to classify the birds according to these categories. Finally, we wound up the whole year with a four-day rubber raft trip down the Colorado River, starting with a tour of Hoover Dam, which helped fill out our understanding of where electricity comes from. The trip itself was an exciting culmination of the year's activity and allowed us to explore many different natural environments along the thirteen-mile trip. At this time the children were pretty accomplished campers and took care of themselves with very little effort on my part.

Although I did not fully understand it at the beginning of the year, the MOBOC experience turned out to be an excellent learning situation for the development of social skills. In public school, if a child has a falling out with a group with which he's involved, often he simply finds another group and reestablishes his relationship with that one. In MOBOC the child is confined to a situation where he has to interact successfully with eight or ten children. There is very little opportunity to switch groups. If the child is to stay in the school and be happy there, he is confronted with the fact that he must work out his differences with the other children. There is no easy escape. He must face his problems and work them out with the group. For the first month and a half it took a considerable effort on my part to get the group working together harmoniously. But once they came together, it was a joy to behold. They began to appreciate one another's strengths and ignore one another's weaknesses. They became quite supportive and extremely interested in interacting with one another. This was indicated in an increasing number of group projects that developed over the course of the year, and a decreasing number of arguments, backbiting, or cruel remarks.

The first year, however, did have certain serious shortcomings that I felt had to be addressed before we could begin the second year. The first was that the social group was considerably too small. Seven, eight, or ten children are a perfect learning group size. The teacher can get to know each child on an individual basis and can work very effectively with every child, correcting his weaknesses and developing his strengths. On the other hand, each child has a sense that he can develop a personal relationship with the teacher that has great depth and meaning. But children need many other children their own age to draw from for friendships. In short, our friendship pool was too small. I decided that next year I would expand the size of the school to something between twenty and thirty children, thereby giving each child a wider group of children to draw upon to establish friendships.

The second shortcoming of the first year was that the age range was too wide. We had children from the fourth grade through the seventh. With only seven children, that does not allow for many children in any particular age group. To be teaching many different levels of math, spelling, and English puts additional strain on the teacher, and the limited number of interactions with children their own age puts particular strain on the children. I knew that it would be better the second year if we had more children in each age group. Perhaps the age range could be just as wide, but with more children they could fill out each age group more completely.

The third shortcoming was that we did miss having some sort of permanent facilities. Being totally mobile, there were some things that we could not do the first year. It was difficult, for example, to work on arts and crafts, even though we did some of that in our homes. We needed a place where we could lay out our work, where we could let it dry, where we could hang it up and store our materials. We also had no place the first year to conduct indoor sports. Parks were perfectly adequate for outdoor activities, but on rainy days and for those sports that require an indoor space, we had no facilities. We also needed some sort of room to conduct group discussion, such as the group teaching of math skills. When several children are working on the same aspect of their mathematical sequence and each has to be taught individually because of the circumstances, time is not used efficiently. Some libraries did have group study rooms, but these were rather rare, and the parks were too distracting. In addition, we needed some sort of administrative headquarters where we could keep our records, where we had a telephone in case of emergencies or to answer inquiries into enrollment or for other operational problems. It seemed that in the second year we were going to have to back off from our total-mobility concept somewhat and arrange to have some sort of room, however limited in size and usage.

The fourth shortcoming was that, in fact, I needed some sort of administrative support. Although it was beneficial to me as a teacher to take total responsibility for the program and the development of the children, I found it somewhat of an overload to do all the scheduling and paper work, as well

as all the financial records for the school; I hoped that by the second year, we could have a half-time administrative assistant to help out in these matters.

THE SECOND-YEAR EXPERIMENT

The second year was set up to correct the first year's shortcomings. The enrollment problem that we had in the first year was greatly diminished. We were still unable to obtain the maximum number of children that we wanted, but at least we were at the point where parents were finding us rather than vice versa. Most of the year we operated with twenty-four children, four teachers (three full time, two half time), three buses, and a small room. I had to return to UCLA to teach full time, but managed to spend one long day each week with the school doing administrative business and teaching the children for a few hours. The latter part of the year I was able to get a half-time assistant to help with the administrative matters. Most of the shortcomings of the first year's program were ostensibly overcome in the operation of the second year.

In my opinion, the second-year curriculum was at least as successful as the first year's. Most of the teachers chose not to run the curriculum on an urban-systems basis as I had. Instead they presented the children with long lists of learning categories and let the children pick which categories held the most interest for them. The year started with an extensive exploration of mapping for the whole school. The children were given a long lecture by a geographer on the history of maps, on the different kinds of maps, and on the meaning of different scales of maps. They then went to a local park and laid out a grid on the ground and created their own map of that part of the park. This map-making experience was then followed up by a visit to the UCLA Map Library, one of the best in the country, and finally was translated to the city maps themselves, which the children would be using throughout the year to follow their travels as they moved around the city.

By this time, the list of places visited in the city was becoming quite long. A card catalog was kept as to the most beneficial trips, the kinds of reception they had, the kinds of reactions the children had to the trips, and the educational value of each trip. The impact of the year began to unfold.

In addition the teachers were learning over the course of the year how to work better and better together. I had selected the teachers on the basis of complementary skills. As the year unfolded they began to learn ways of trading skills and trading children so that their full range of skills could be applied to the individual needs of each child. By the end of the year they were grouping the children on Monday, Wednesday, and Friday by academic skill levels, and these were the primary groups for each teacher; but on Tuesday and Thursday they grouped according to interests, and the children chose which teacher and which interest area they were going to participate in that day. In this way, both the children and the teachers were mixed in their interaction with one another.

Meanwhile, over the course of the year, the children were beginning to change. In the second year we undertook an academic testing program to check the children along all the normal skill dimensions before the year began and after it was over. We found the testing had several beneficial results. In the first place it told us at the beginning of the year where each child stood academically in terms of mathematics, reading level, and so forth. At the end of the year it told us how the child had achieved on all those levels. These were standard tests, the same ones used in the public school system. In this way we were able to get a comparison between the progress of our children and the progress of public school children. Although we were spending only six to seven hours per week on academic subjects, at the end of the year we found that our children

overall, improved one and a half to two grade levels in each area. Sometimes this improvement took place even though no emphasis had been put on a subject throughout the entire year. For example, one boy who had never had particular problems with spelling was given no spelling instruction over the course of the year, yet his test score in spelling improved over 200 percent. These results seemed to confirm my belief that, if you concentrate on the whole child, get his natural curiosity about the world up, and get him interested in learning at all levels, his interest and curiosity will generalize to all skill areas. This is not to say that we do not have the responsibility to teach in the traditional subject areas, but it is an indication that we can legitimately concentrate on the child's weaknesses only after we have established in his mind and ours what his strengths are.

I might add that we have a wide range of achievement levels represented in the school. One child in the third grade could not read when he entered the school; three others, even older, could barely read or write. One child, although quite bright, is hyperkinetic, had been on medication for four years, but was taken off upon entering MOBOC. Another child, who was almost deaf, moved after only one-half year, but still showed considerable improvement in both personal and social development. Many of the children were considered "problem children" in public school, but have caused us very little difficulty. Finally, four or five of the twenty-four children have been "tested gifted" by the public schools.

The major problem in the second year again seemed to be the financial one. We never reached full enrollment. With three buses full enrollment would be thirty children, and we never had more than twenty-four. Since we were on such a close margin, we operated most of the year at some financial loss. However, even at full enrollment, we are not competitive on a financial level with public schools. We cannot afford to pay our teachers a salary comparable with the city school system salary. And we cannot spend the minimal amount of money that we need for administration. At full enrollment we can pay our teachers $7,000 for nine months. The public school beginning pay is something like $8,000. In addition, we had very little money for equipment or supplies to spend throughout the year. My teachers were more than happy to continue to work throughout the year at a reduced salary, but I felt uncomfortable with it, because I knew they were making sacrifices to work in my school, which I did not feel they should have to make under ideal circumstances. Finally, we have been financially unable so far to give scholarships to the children. This means that most of the children are middle-class children, although the socioeconomic range still varies considerably from those who can easily afford the $125 per month tuition to those that have to make extreme sacrifices to keep their children in school. By the end of the year we were looking very hard for ways to ease the financial problem.

We became aware that most of our trips were more observation than participation. As the kids got more and more sophisticated in their observation, as they learned more and more about the city, there was a stronger need to participate more. We needed to find places where the children could use the materials, could work with the people, could join in their activities. This need for greater involvement and less observation has become a continuing criteria in our search for meaningful things to do in the city.

We are presently searching for the basic unit for the mobile-school idea. At first the unit seemed to be seven kids, one teacher, and a bus. When that social group proved to be too small, it seemed best to have thirty kids, three teachers, three buses, and a room. Now, because of certain financial problems, it would seem that the basic unit might be fifty kids, five teachers, five buses, an administrator, and a store. Once it is financially on its feet, the store would be expected to underwrite the teachers' salaries, to provide some money for scholarships, to provide the additional materials for the store, to give the children an experience in learning economics and business through running the store and to give them practical experience through building some of the things to be sold in the store.

For example, the store might be called the "Toy Store for Learning Things," and would operate in the following way: in the front of the store would be the store itself; this would be essentially a toy store, but with a very special collection; each item would be there for learning. The store would include all kinds of puzzles, games of strategy, construction kits (both large and small), and it would include a small collection of books devoted to learning games or the construction of objects. In the back of the store would be our demonstration classroom. The store would only be a small part of the child's day; the rest of the day would be spent doing city learning.

Once the basic unit size model has been successfully established, we think that the way to expand upon it is to duplicate the unit in its entirety in another location in the city. Each unit would be autonomous, but would cooperate with others in the exchange of people and information. The units will then be kept administratively simple and unencumbered by people who do not have contact with children but draw heavily upon the school resources for their salaries. The basic features of the mobile school idea must be preserved. A radical reallocation of school funds, a new use of the resources of the city, and a restructuring of the curriculum around direct-experience learning, but now based on a storefront school.

CONCLUSIONS

To summarize briefly, almost all people connected with MOBOC during these first few years have seen it as a fantastic learning experience for the children. The teachers, in addition, have seen it as a positive growth experience of their own. In fact, the third year can be characterized by the teachers taking increased initiative, not only for running their own buses, but also almost total responsibility for daily operation and administration of the whole school. Parents have witnessed, by and large, remarkable changes in their children over the two years. Of the thirty or so children who have been with MOBOC at least part-time during the two years, there have only been two that we feel that we have been unable to reach. We have come to believe that the concept of mobility as applied to elementary school and junior high is an idea of sufficient power to transform the public school system should it be recognized and implemented. Through this system teachers are brought back into an effective teaching role where they can grow as creative people. Children are brought into contact with their environment and the objects and people in that environment. They find out how things work and what people do. Their curiosity is stimulated, and their interest in learning increases at a tremendous rate.

Some critics have told me that what I am doing is unique and not generalizable. And although I would be willing to admit that once one tries to handle large numbers of students in this way additional problems will be encountered, I so far do not find any of those problems insurmountable. Certainly you wouldn't want to teach all children this way. But I would guess that something like 75 percent of the school population could learn effectively from mobile experience. But if 75 percent is too large a figure for you, try 10 percent. In Los Angeles alone that would be something like 50,000 children in this age range learning through mobile education. 50,000 children at 10 children per bus is 5,000 buses, which seems like a huge number. But you must realize that the city of Los Angeles is vast, and its resources are almost limitless. Five thousand buses would be absorbed quite easily with no appreciable disruption of the

city's normal processes. As far as the administrative overhead for such large numbers, perhaps computerized scheduling would be required so that all 5,000 buses would not arrive at the city council chambers or some other place at the same time; but as long as each unit of five buses is autonomous, there would be little administrative buildup. For those 50,000 children there might be something like 1 million people in Los Angeles capable of teaching something significant about their lives. If handled carefully it would be many years before the same "teacher" were asked a second time to give twenty or thirty minutes of his time to such a group of children. But most of the people we came in contact with were eager to do it again next year or even within a few months.

However, when you start thinking about mobile education in large numbers, some of the city's public resources might become overloaded. Let us look at the library system, for example. There are only about two hundred public libraries in Los Angeles. But most of the branch libraries in the city are closed in the mornings. This is a public resource that is going unused for half the day. The vacant building sits there; the books sit there unused because there are not enough children or people coming in in the mornings to use them. Why not open them up and let the children in to maximize the utilization of these public resources? Furthermore, private resources are sometimes carefully guarded or protected. What we need is a change in attitude toward public education. We need to get the average citizen excited about the fact that he has something to contribute, something to tell to the society's children. We want him to change his attitude toward teaching and learning, to see himself as a potential teacher, and to see that he has a responsibility toward children to pass on what he knows to the next generation. Once the city becomes transformed in this way so that the people of the city see teaching children as part of their normal activities, we think that any problems with growth or expansion or numbers connected with the idea of mobile learning will fall by the side.

There are, however, some warnings that have to be passed on, some caveats about the difficulty of running a mobile operation. First, it is a tremendous challenge to teach in this kind of situation. It does take a very special kind of teacher. In MOBOC the teacher is given almost sole responsibility for the development of his or her curriculum. He is expected to work along with the children in developing that curriculum. But it demands of him great flexibility and imagination. No two days in this school are alike. Every day brings its own new adventure. The teacher has to be able to respond flexibly to changes in schedule, and has to have backup activities ready in case cancellations occur in the day's activities. I have the impression that some public school teachers have the whole year laid out in the fall and that each day unfolds according to that schedule. But in MOBOC the best you can do is lay out the next week. And then, after the fact, you and the children reconstruct what happened into meaningful, understandable, whole learning units.

Another warning to those who might want to try the idea of mobile education somewhere else in the country is to reemphasize how difficult it is to get parents to see that this is an exciting, meaningful experience for their children, at least equivalent to any other form of education they might give them. Children see this immediately. I show them my slides and tell them what the school is like, and they are immediately attracted to it. I could have hundreds of children in the school today if it were left up to the children. But most parents are quite conservative when it comes to their children's education, and perhaps rightfully so. Yet I think our two-year trial tends to support our claims that this type of education is as good as we dreamed it would be.

A third warning would be that so far this is a very limited trial. We have tried it only with a certain class of children, and with a very small group of children at that. It is perhaps dangerous to generalize beyond that group to the implications of using such a system on different socioeconomic groups. I cannot help believing, however, that for the lower socioeconomic groups, the disadvantaged children, this type of education would be a great boon indeed. I only wish that we had the funds to support an experimental effort with ghetto children. But perhaps the idea does not generalize for all situations. Perhaps it is best in some climates. Los Angeles has a very mild climate, and perhaps the idea would work less well in Denver or Wisconsin. Perhaps it is appropriate for some children and not others; for example, it might work well only with self-starters or children who have somehow maintained their sense of curiosity and excitement for learning. Perhaps it is best in some public school districts and not in others. Certainly, the idea fits urban learning better than it does rural learning. I know it makes more sense financially in overcrowded districts or in districts with schools damaged by earthquakes, floods, or storms, in schools that find themselves short of classrooms, in school districts experiencing a baby boom passing through their schools, or in other schools with populations that might shrink in the future. Instead of running double sessions during the day, why not put four-fifths of those overcrowded children in buses, move them around the city, have them learn from people in the city, have them structure their learning through the environment, and then come back to the limited number of classrooms as a home base to do arts and crafts, group math exercises, and other such classroom-oriented activities? Certainly, all new schools should incorporate some degree of mobility in their earliest planning sessions.

The final additional warning is that school districts which might be excited about this idea, but which are not presently overcrowded, will find that mobile education is an additional financial burden. We are operating successfully because we did not build a schoolhouse, and we do not pay vice principals, janitors, secretaries, bus drivers, and gardeners. But schools which already have all these financial burdens will find that starting a mobile learning experience is going to be a financial burden above and beyond their normal operating expenses. For those school districts, by and large, the idea is probably impossible.

Finally, I should like to say something about alternatives to a totally mobile school concept. Certainly, there are many other combinations of part mobile, part stable schools. We seem to be coming to a ratio of something like one-third of our time spent in a stable classroom and two-thirds of our time out on the road in a mobile condition. Next year, we are going to try one-fifth of our time in the classroom and four-fifths of our time in the environment. We do not know exactly what the proper ratio is yet. But we have found out that total mobility is somewhat difficult to achieve and total stability is something that we are no longer interested in. So what we are sure of is that the mobile idea is an idea that should integrate well with any school that wants to cut down on capital expenditures. Perhaps it should be stated that mobility does not primarily save school funds. Instead, it uses that money in a different way; it uses it for teaching children. There will probably be tax-payer groups that will jump at the idea and say, "Hey, if we had four mobile classrooms for every one traditional classroom, we could cut our school expenses by four-fifths." But that is not true. You cannot take a bus of thirty-five children out into the city and have any kind of meaningful experience. The learning group has to be eight to ten children and no greater. That is, eight to ten children for each teacher, and if you try to do it with more than ten children, the learning experience itself is going to deteriorate into something chaotic. The issue, then, is the reallocation of resources, not a radical saving of

resources. We are trying to put the money back into teaching and to take it out of capital expenditures and administrative overhead.

In conclusion I would like to make a few hypothetical remarks about the mobile school idea in regard to the larger concept of deschooling as espoused by Ivan Illich and others. I believe that the mobile school is a step toward deschooling. Certainly it reduces the number of children per teacher, even though that teacher is still a paid professional responsible for the learning efforts of a small group of children. In addition, the mobile school brings a lot of people who did not know they were teachers into active participation in the teaching role. And this is certainly another step toward deschooling. Perhaps if the mobile school idea spreads throughout the nation, we shall eventually get to the point where everyone in society considers himself a teacher, with a shared sense of responsibility toward raising and educating society's children. When that realization really hits us as a nation, perhaps we shall truly have a deschooled society.

We arrived at the Bradbury building about 8 in the morning and no one was there except the elevator operator. The Bradbury building was built in 1893 and had recently been restored to a magnificent structure. The elevator itself is something to behold, rising up through a large central space. It is entirely wrought iron and totally exposed to public view. The children had a need to let off a little steam at this point. I didn't see any harm in letting them run up and down the stairs, ride the elevator, and in general enjoy themselves in this unique architectural space.

They were just settling down somewhat when, standing on the fourth floor looking down, I overheard one of them say to another, "You know what's so neat about that elevator? You don't have to lift the weight of the elevator itself; you just have to lift the weight of the people." Then he went on, "See that counterweight over there? It must weigh exactly the same as the elevator itself. The cable goes up and over those pullies and down to the elevator so that when the elevator comes down, the counterweight goes up, and when the counterweight comes down, the elevator goes up. The two just exactly balance each other, and all the motor has to do is get the thing going and lift the weight of the people."

When I overheard this, I was just dumbfounded. Here was a sixth grader looking at a complicated mechanical piece of the environment, and totally understanding its operation. Having been architecturally trained in design, I was profoundly affected. It occurred to me that we are no longer designing the artifacts of our environment for learning. Actually the student was wrong about that elevator; that is not what is unique to it. What he said about the counterweight system is true of almost all elevators except perhaps hydraulic ones. What is unique about that elevator is that it is totally exposed to view. Most elevators are hidden inside shafts covered by walls and metallic coverings. We hide the mechanical contrivances of our society these days when we should be exposing them to view. We could be designing them for learning as they did in the 1890s, but instead we design for some esthetic principle which is rendered more important than the learning which could be achieved through exposure.

Having been sensitized to that type of design by that child, I then began to look for other objects that had a similar design ethic. I discovered that almost everything designed over fifty years ago was designed for learning. Our two old typewriters which were donated to the school held the same design ethic. Everything was exposed–keys, ribbon, mechanical linkages. The child could press one of the keys and see the entire linkage which caused the key to strike the paper. What a great loss that we no longer design for learning.

Liberated Zone: An Evolving Learning Space*

Robert Goodman

I was driving down from Boston to New York City with Dick Magidoff, a friend who teaches at a suburban high school near Boston. He was obviously excited as he told me about an idea he'd been exploring with a group of his students. How he or anyone else could get excited about anything that was happening in high school took getting used to. I could only think back to my own high school days as something I had to suffer through. But as he went on and got caught up in his enthusiasm, some things troubling me about my own work began to take on a new perspective.

Many of Dick's students were reacting to high school as I had, only he thought they might be able to create an alternative. The idea was to make a place where students could come together on their own for discussions, to drink cof-

*Reprinted from *Harvard Educational Review,* Vol. 39, No. 4, 1969. Copyright © 1969 by President and Fellows of Harvard College.

fee, or do other things that might interest them, a place where they might invite someone to speak to them in a more personal context for learning than school. This could be a place where students discuss what they want their education to be and how to get it. "A coffee house, you might call it—or a youth center—but that's a bad word for it." It sure was, I thought; a "youth center" sounded like the product of some bureaucrat trying to keep kids off the streets. But this place was going to be different. It seems some people in town "gave" the kids a "youth center" several years ago, complete with an adult to supervise things. The kids stayed away in droves.

The new youth center could be a place that was built and run by the students themselves. They had already had some experience in running programs outside the usual school context. Some time ago the school sent students and teachers to a conference to discuss the local "drug problem," putting students together with psychologists and teachers. The result did not solve the drug problem, but it did give the students an opportunity to experience a new group situation outside the framework of the classroom where they were able to have more control over what was being discussed. They continued other discussion groups, this time by themselves with only a few teachers, including Magidoff. They met at an elegant colonial house that was lent them on Sunday afternoons by one of the townspeople. Would I be interested in helping to design a more permanent place where this could happen? "Well, Dick, maybe—let me think about it. I'll let you know—it could be interesting."

ADVOCACY PLANNING AND HIGH SCHOOL STUDENTS

High school students and suburbia, these things were very far from my head. For the past three years I had been an "advocate planner." That's the term to describe planners and architects who work directly for the poor, trying to help them plan and design their own neighborhoods. All of this had taken place in central city areas and the clients were always adults.

The role of advocate planner for the poor was to help right the balance of planning powers. But many advocates find themselves delivering the goods to their clients—a program to build low-income housing for example. But they often find their clients are unable to make an intimate connection between the goods and their own needs because of the highly complex and bureaucratic nature of the goods. They put their clients in a position of going through years of planning studies, getting private foundation and government grants, dealing with private developers before any serious environmental changes can be made. A few "leaders" become "educated," and master the bureaucratic jargon of planning. But the mass

of people are still unable to create a direct response to their needs. People can't just say we've had it, we're going to rebuild our community, our apartment, what have you, and simply do it. Advocacy, when unrelated to more basic system changes as the redistribution of wealth and power, becomes simply another crutch that allows and, in the end, promotes business as usual.

The architect concerned with promoting social and environmental change is further limited working in low-income neighborhoods. Faced with the possibility of new environmental conditions, the goals of the poor are limited by their conditioned behavior as a result of their economic position in a capitalist consumer economy. Their goals for new environments have been shaped by television, the magazines, and the newspapers. It's not unlikely that you find many poor families striving for the fifth of an acre lot and the single family house. With so much forced "community living" with people who have a whole range of social pathology (as the sociologists call it), it is little wonder they have been sold on the suburban ideal of freedom through isolation.

What did working in the suburbs have to do with this? People in the suburbs have "arrived." They are presumably recipients of the material benefits our society has to offer to those who perform well. The single family house and the "good" schools controlled by the community—just the kind of control black people in the city center are fighting for. What need did the suburbs have for advocate planners?

Advocate planning is founded on the idea of providing adequate representation for all interest groups in decisions which affect their lives. Here was a group of disenfranchised people, white middle-class fifteen- to seventeen-year-olds, attempting to find a way to gain more control over their own lives—attempting to make a positive alternative to the institutionalized "learning place" not of their own making. In effect the building of a youth center would be the creation of a learning environment by the actual people who used that environment. For me this was the critical element in making it a relevant advocacy project.

The difficulty of creating socially relevant environmental form in the center city considered against the more hopeful possibility of doing this in the suburban situation also intrigued me. If the most potent model that the "have nots" use to make choices is the environment of the "haves," and it turns out that the "haves" environment is not working, then it could be that building more relevant alternatives for the "haves" could present the "have nots" with a more significant range of choice. If the school environment and program of the "haves" are as regressive in their own way as those of the "have nots," it makes little sense for black community leaders, for example, to promote ghetto schools (even though controlled by the community) which are based on the suburban model.

Generating new possibilities for learning places in the suburban situation would expose the problems of the existing schools. These possibilities would present models for students, parents, and teachers to evaluate against their existing situation. Getting people to look at the content of institutions—in addition to who controls them—would elaborate the present argument of community control versus city control. Youth centers, or whatever they're called, as places created by people who are exploring new patterns of becoming educated could be part of the broader cultural revolution by many young people who reject the values of a society which promotes an economic system that accepts the inevitability of "haves" and "have nots."

As these general goals began to jell, I began to share Magidoff's enthusiasm for the center. After discussing it with my architecture students at the Massachusetts Institute of Technology, I suggested that not only I get involved but that we make the center our class project, in which the class, the high school students, and I would work to design the building.

BEGINNING STEPS

I felt like the idea of what this place was going to be, what purpose it was going to serve, should evolve from the ideas of the high school students themselves, as they got closer to these ideas through discussion and design. The important thing was not to be limited to preconceived activities and architectural form based on the existing "teaching" spaces. Instead of the usual program—with so many square feet of this or that kind of space, I thought we should deal with the special nature of this environment. "What do you want this place to be?" I asked at one of our first sessions.

"Something very different than the school we have."

". . . If I had to use one word to describe it, it would have to be something improbable."

". . . a liberated zone."

". . . a coffee house that's always open."

But beyond these general descriptions, it was difficult to go much further. If my MIT students or I asked what do you want to do at this liberated zone, we usually got a description of a place identified with a specific activity.

"a place where groups can meet for discussions"

"yes, and a place for meditation"

"and a place for karate"

"we want a room to hear stereo music"

"we'll also have jam sessions"

"an auto shop"

"pottery and art studios"

"a padded room"

"a place to dance"

At first it seemed this approach might lead us to a dead end, where we would find ourselves with the usual laundry list program. But in the end the description of a program and the designs that followed acted as an important "opener." Having something specific to react to would be a way for all of us to learn about the kind of learning experience and environment the high school students were looking for.

Looking over their program I asked the students why they didn't get the school to give them space for these activities. After all it was an especially well-equipped place.

"Because it wouldn't work out. There'd be special times when they could be used—and they give us someone to supervise it."

"We need our own place where we can go any time we want."

We began to design by using the student's program as a point of departure for developing a number of alternatives. The designs seemed to move in the direction of satisfying all the requests by including a space for everything the students asked for. But somehow it wasn't right. Everything was there, but the youth center as a specially designed place wasn't. One of my students discussing his design noted "this doesn't look much better than the school they now have—it's only smaller." The designs were characterized by the same bundle of isolated activity areas strung together by a circulation system that typify most suburban schools.

We all discussed this; maybe the unique feature of the youth center should be its ability to bring people together in more communal ways than now exist. After all, many of the students could have privacy at home for listening to music, practicing meditation, and study. Instead of just providing a compendium of facilities, we could create an environment that induced people to be together. Eating seemed the one common activity that ostensibly brings people together to fulfill individual desires, but often allows people the "opening" for communal activities. Some restaurants and most coffee houses are places where

this happens. The kitchen during a party at home is often the most used space for discussions. Somehow it's easier for people to get together over passing each other food than simply introducing themselves. Perhaps coming into the kitchen for food means you don't have to make a commitment to talk to someone too long since your primary purpose was obviously to satisfy your hunger. This being done you can always leave in the middle of a conversation since you weren't there to talk in the first place. The kitchen–coffee shop in the center could be a serve-yourself operation quite open in form to the areas adjacent to it. This "heart" might also be one of the first contact points for people entering the building, allowing them to be near "what's happening" without having to wander through the building. While there was agreement on emphasizing the communal activity, there was still a strong sense for some private spaces where people could get away; one of the MIT students designed a tower of space cubicles, some of which were entered by climbing a ladder. Having to climb into the space could further exaggerate a feeling of isolation when someone moved away from the group activities.

The design of the center was both a threat and a promise to the students. The fact that something might actually get built promised the opportunity of something real and tangible. This motivation made those students involved want to think about how they would use it, giving the architects and themselves more concrete material to work with. The threat was that having no real experience with either designing or promoting the kind of learning place they were talking about, they were uncertain about what the design should be. Would people use it? Would they actually get it done? There was the threat of raising your hopes and then failing; failing not only yourself but also failing in the eyes of your fellow students whose hopes you have helped raise.

KNOW YOURSELF THROUGH DESIGN

There are already benefits from our design process aside from the possibility of constructing the building. By raising certain physical alternatives for this center, the students had to consider and develop ideas about how they saw themselves relating to each other and to the outside world. In one of the sessions for example, I asked what impression they would like the youth center to have on someone driving past it on the way home from work.

We should make it colonial on the outside and do what we want inside. That way people driving by will not get upset by it.

What do you mean colonial on the outside—we'll make it the way we want all over. Let's not worry about what other people think.

They also considered the problem of how the adults in the community would react to it. As some saw it, they had the power to close the place. The students saw the building as a display of their ideas, like a badge worn on their sleeve.

I don't think my parents will like it. Right now I'm home after school, and my parents like that. If the center gets built, I'll go there after school, be home for supper, and go there again at night. They're not going to like that.

How can they solve that problem—the fact is you are isolating them.

I don't know—maybe have another baby.

Is this place just for kids? What about adults? Can they come?

Adults can come, but on our terms. They can't come in like they usually do, judging us as adults, giving us a lot of bullshit about how they're going to close the place down if they don't like it. They can come in and argue, but they have to do it on the basis of equals. We can argue but they can't pull rank on us.

This has got to be a place where people can feel free. If they want to come on that basis, why not?

THE GROWNUPS

The reaction of parents is obviously crucial to the future of the center. No doubt there will be a range of opinions. The building of a place run by the people who use it, making decisions about how they want to educate themselves, can easily become a threat to those who view the school as a place where their children can be prepared to fit into the world as it exists. Those who have accustomed themselves to a situation in which they have little freedom to make choices about their own environment and the way they live may either react negatively, or they may accept the center more on the basis that they want to give their children something better than they themselves have been through.

There can also be another positive side to this. Rather than an alienated force, the center can serve as a model that adults might choose to emulate. Suburban parents suffer from many of the same problems as their children—the physical and often personal isolation of people from each other, the inability to develop communal activities beyond the ritualized town meeting and PTA meeting. The suburbs also lack places where controversial plays can be performed and controversial material discussed without being stopped by conservative school boards. There is no reason why the sensitivity groups, meditation yoga, body awareness exercises, and communitarian attitudes that engage many young people in the suburbs should become their exclusive preserve.

Not long ago people in the suburbs with "liberal" leanings could try to tackle the problems outside their areas. The civil rights movement, the problems of the ghettos, the so-called urban crisis could be seen as a kind of burden for the white man who had made it to the green lawns, shopping centers, and one-story campus schools of the suburbs. But with the growing cultural self-awareness, political sophistication and go-it-alone attitude of the intown Black neighborhoods, the suburbanite has been left holding his own bag. He has been forced to turn inward to his community, his children, and finally to himself.

This situation makes for an opportunity to begin exploring new attitudes for suburban living. It is an opportunity for white suburbanites to become less ideological and morally concerned about the lives of the poor unfortunates living somewhere else, and more involved in their own personal attitudes. They could become less concerned about the rhetoric of individual freedom for others and begin to examine whether or not their lives are really as free as they might think. They could begin to examine the roles the existing schools play in shaping the lives of children—going beyond the debate of whether to add a new wing to the school. They could look at the values that are promoted by the school system itself; for what kind of world are the schools preparing the children? They could go beyond the questions of racial integration of the present schools to examining the kind of attitudes in their own lives which produce the racism that in turn becomes a problem in the context of a larger society.

POOR POWER AND STUDENT POWER

One of the discoveries of such an inward analysis would be the realization that the school is neither an environment nor an institution created by people who use it. No amount of extracurricular activities nor "permissive" attitudes can correct this. The school is created by parents to train young people for a pattern of life that they think their children should be trained for. In this sense, it is a reflection of the larger world around it in that existing structures tend to maintain themselves by imposing their values on groups they can control. In doing so, these institutions become increasingly remote from the people who are being controlled. The student, as the poor resident living in the center city, finds himself in the position of reacting to programs of the administration rather than being able to initiate his own programs. For the student the issue might involve reacting to curriculum or grading policies; for the low-income intown resident it may take the form of reacting to the threat of urban renewal proposed by the city, rather than initiating their own housing programs. Because of this conditioning, people controlled often see their ideas initially in the context of how the controllers see them.

This thing (the youth center) might be a good idea, but if they (the faculty and administration) don't want us to do it, what can we do?

Even in the case of a "liberal" administration, many students recognize where they stand!

We wanted to wear blue jeans to school, we organized the students to fight for this . . . what happened when we presented our demands was they had a meeting . . . then they told us we could wear anything we wanted, grow our hair long or have a beard.

But the thing is those are the things they thought we should want . . . maybe they are but the thing is that we always have to wait till they see it that way . . . we can't do it just because we want it.

To solve this problem is not simply to ask the school for more student control over and participation in programs which are overseen by administrators politically responsible to parents rather than students. "Participation" and "recommendations" by students will not help unless the basic goals of the institution can be changed. Can an administrator running the school make the decision that the concept of "schools" is obsolete and therefore they should be abolished?

The crucial question of "participation" in the low-income neighborhood or in the school is whether such participation involves any power over one's own existence or simply going through the forms of predetermined ritual. A government official in charge of secondary schools, in discussing the problems he was having with students, said that he was "interested in what the young people had to say." He wanted to meet with them regularly so they could make "recommendations." Urban renewal administration frequently speaks the rhetoric of "citizen participation" and "planning with people." But who makes the final decisions after the public hearings? Chancellor Kurt George Kiesenger of Germany described what is perhaps the classic "liberal" attitude of those in power to those who are disenfranchised:

We must not meet these young people in an attitude of self-assurance and self-esteem. The young must feel they are listened to. Our task is to know that responsibility is still in our hands, and at the same time to be open to the arguments of the young people.[1] (my emphasis)

Former Vice President Hubert H. Humphrey set the matter straight on this side of the ocean:

I think this younger generation has got something to say to us, and I'm not sure that what they say all the time is necessarily the final word. I always believed in the right of a person to speak. I don't think he always has to be taken seriously, but he ought to have a right to say what he wants to say.[2]

That is, those in power decide who should be taken seriously or not, but let everybody talk as much as they like.

THE ARCHITECT AND NEW LIFE STYLES

At present, the youth center is still only a gleam in the students' eyes. There is land to be acquired and money to be raised. Talk is now of foundation support, help from some parents, and a benefit rock concert. As an idea, however, it has continued to grow and become more defined as a possible social phenomenon in no small part by raising environmental issues through a design process involving the users. For the designer to operate this way, as a kind of environmental idea man for promoting new social institutions for the

disenfranchised, he faces the possiblity of "failure," in the conventional sense of getting something built, more often than in the operation of a traditional architectural office. The usual client, who comes to the architect with a reasonably well-defined program of what he wants together with an easily financed project, is a much safer bet for getting something built and getting pictures in the architectural magazines.

Such is the paradox of the architect in this country. His theory is embellished with the social relevance of his work, designing bright new cities with housing and justice for all, but the real application of all this is that he performs as the agent of the real estate entrepreneur, the school administrator, parents, factory owners, and others who manipulate the environments of other people to serve their own ends. If the architect's work is to have social relevance in the sense of producing nonrepressive environments, then he must attempt to raise the possibilities of a new architecture for the disenfranchised user. Since the pattern of human interaction sets the requirements for architectural form, establishing new contexts for interaction, such as a liberated zone, helps move in this direction. The resultant architecture should reflect the way people get together in either personal one-to-one relationships or in more complex social organization. In the case of complex social interactions, an architectural complexity results not from formal, preconceived attitudes about "jazz," "richness," or "variety," but by allowing as many actions to take place as the users require. Such environments become the result of users as individuals or groups trading architectural interests with each other, negotiating these interests in ad hoc situations.

NOTES AND REFERENCES

1. "Chancellor Kiesenger Talks About Youth," *Look Magazine,* Nov. 12, 1966, p. 44.
2. *Boston Sunday Globe,* March 16, 1969, p. 18A.

An Alternative Strategy for Planning an Alternative School

Henry Sanoff

George Barbour

INTRODUCTION

In the past decade, there has been a growing body of literature on the concepts of alternative schools, free schools, open schools, and non-graded schools. Unfortunately, there has been little documentation of the process by which these educational options have been accepted and implemented in individual schools. This paper focuses on a strategy for developing an alternative school and on techniques which can facilitate the planning process.

The process began when the board members of the Wallace O'Neal Day School, a newly formed private school in Pinehurst, North Carolina, developed a long-range building plan which included a new facility for a proposed kindergarten-through-ninth-grade program. In the course of interviewing architects for the design of the new school, the building committee encountered one architect who suggested a participatory planning approach involving members of the school community as well as architects and consultants. In sharp contrast to other presentations based on the architect's experience in planning educational facilities, the building committee was invited to become involved with students, teachers, architects, and consultants in the creation of an educational program as well as a building. Their acceptance of this pluralistic approach is a measure of the commitment of the Wallace O'Neal community to their school.

The major objective of this proposal was the creation of a parent–child coalition to develop an alternative educational program and to plan and implement physical spaces to complement that program. The process for reaching this objective is frequently referred to as a *charrette*, from the French term which in architecture implies a period of brief but intensive planning.

In its present adaptation, a charrette is an activity that brings community members and experts together, for a limited time period, to study specific community problems. The essential ingredients are

1. A problem to be solved.
2. Community members willing to participate.
3. Experts in both substantive and process issues.
4. A commitment to implement the plans and recommendations of the charrette.

The concept of community participation is fundamental to a charrette, and sets it apart from problem-solving methods which involve experts but exclude people. A school planning charrette involves the consumers: the teachers, parents, and children who will have to use and "live with" the results. The most valuable by-product, one which in many ways gives life to the results, is the sense of commitment and cohesiveness which grows from the struggle of planning together.

THE SCHOOL

The Moore County Public School System, which includes the Pinehurst–Southern Pines area, is in many ways one of the most progressive in North Carolina. Several of the schools in the area provide open classrooms, nongraded classes, team teaching, and other innovations that are still relatively rare in public education.

Even so, the Wallace O'Neal School was created as an alternative to this public system, and the motives for this shift were fundamental to the emerging educational program. There was an expressed desire for "quality" education of a kind to be achieved through energetic, well-paid teachers and relatively small classes. (To some, the notion of "quality" was inextricable from the prestige of a private school.) Equally significant was a determination to develop a school that would be responsive to both the needs of the children and the wishes of the parents. There was a feeling that the public schools were too large, too bureau-

cratic, too inert to be affected by any individual, whether teacher, child, or parent. The desire to participate and to have an effect is an important motive in the creation of any alternative school, and the charrette process is an especially appropriate planning mode in such a situation.

These ideas were the beginnings of an educational program, but there has been little articulation of their relevance to the day-to-day workings of a school; in fact, there were, within the school community, some latent but very strongly felt disagreements about the best way to implement the program. The parents had discussed their objectives in general terms; the structure and techniques of the school were left to the headmaster, who was selected because he shared these objectives.

The school's orientation had been relatively traditional in its distinction between "academics," which are emphasized, and "nonacademics," which occur during semistructured "activity periods." The major academic areas were English, math, science, social studies, and art, which were taught in age-graded classes involving lecture, discussion, and individual or small group assignments. The school day was divided into uniform time periods with movement from subject to subject according to an established schedule. On a continuum between child-centered and teacher-centered approaches, the Wallace O'Neal program was best described as teacher-centered, with emphasis on the teaching of subject matter rather than on student learning. There were points at which this structure did not fully match the philosophical orientation of some parents and board members, but potential disagreements were muffled by apprehension about an alternative structure.

THE CHARRETTE TEAM

The planning team for the charrette consisted of William Laslett, the project architect, and members of his staff; Henry Sanoff, architectural consultant and charrette planner; and George Barbour, psychologist at the local mental health center. Also involved on a less regular basis were architects from the Department of Public Instruction, representatives from the Learning Institute of North Carolina (LINC); and Joan Sanoff, the child development specialist who conducted the children's sessions. This team was responsible for planning the charrette period of three evenings and three full days bridging a weekend.

A series of team meetings was held during the months prior to the charrette itself. These sessions proved essential to the effectiveness of the team by clarifying the roles of the participants, both within the team and in relation to the Wallace O'Neal community. This latter point was particularly important because it raised the issue of potential philosophical conflict between the team and its clients.

The probable traditionalism of the Wallace O'Neal community was recognized (and somewhat exaggerated) in the early team meetings, and we were aware that at least some of the client group were apprehensive that we might have a hidden agenda of propagandizing for a "radical" school program. Since many of the team members were, in fact, interested in developing a nontraditional program and building, the problem was genuine and carried the risk of a disintegration of the working relationship.

Within the team the issue was dealt with in terms of relative emphasis. Was the team composed of "experts" whose responsibility was to advocate their own opinions of the best educational direction for the school, or was it to be a group of "consultants" whose obligation was to help the Wallace O'Neal community articulate and implement its own ideas? Although the question could not be resolved completely (for this particular group or as a general consideration), one decisive factor was that the original charrette presentation had emphasized the "consultant" role and had been accepted on that basis. For this reason, it was generally agreed that the team

would serve a facilitative role and that our biases, though present, should not be allowed to interfere with the growth of consensus within the client group.

The charrette began with a morning-long children's session conducted by Joan Sanoff. In the following week, charrette sessions were scheduled for Tuesday, Wednesday, and Thursday evenings as well as the following Saturday and Sunday afternoon. Invitations were extended to the entire Wallace O'Neal adult community: parents, board members, building committee members, and faculty. The desirability of representativeness and continuity of participation was emphasized; but, although this ideal was approached in the early sessions, the group was soon reduced to the faculty and those building committee and board members who would carry the greatest responsibility for implementing the decisions emerging from the charrette.

THE CHILDREN'S SESSION

The charrette team felt that it was important to have the children of the school understand the events that would be taking place and to give them an opportunity to generate ideas of their own about the kind of school they would like to have. Because their direct participation in the charrette was not considered feasible, Joan Sanoff agreed to conduct a session at the school in which the children could, through various exercises, be made a part of the planning process. Although the children's group was limited to fourteen children, the involvement, enjoyment, and productivity of these children suggest that their wider participation can and should be considered an integral part of any school planning process.

The "Wish Poem"

The session opened with the construction of a collaborative poem, a group of statements composed of responses to the phrase, "I wish my school . . . ." This approach was developed to minimize the effort children expend in finding rhymes, an effort which usually stops the free flow of their feelings and associations. The formal repetition of the same words is designed to encourage freedom and imagination. The results show a number of clear educational and architectural objectives: spatial and temporal freedom, variety, spontaneity, and a sensuous appreciation of objects and settings.

I Wish My School

I wish my school to be the neatest place in the world.
I wish my school to be very unusual.
I wish my school to be out-of-the-ordinary.
I wish my school to be a nice place to go instead
  of a torture chamber.
I wish my school to have many different things
  going on.
I wish my school would be pleasant to come to
  and still be learning all the things
  we need to know.
I wish my school to be
  as free as it could be
    unless we broke a rule
    and destroyed the privilege.
I wish my school to be a place you
  can go
  anytime of the day.
I wish my school could be
  as fun
  as it is hard.
I wish my school to have freedom of choice.
I wish my school to be as long as I want it.
I wish my school to be without classes
  and mostly recess.
I wish my school to be beautiful
  with lots of trees
  and not big brick buildings.
I wish my school to have bright colors.
I wish my school to be seen and be noticed
  when someone is driving
  on the road.
I wish my school to be nicely planted
  with bushes and flowers.
I wish my school to have many things
  you can play on,
  inside and outside.
I wish my school to be a racetrack,
  a baseball diamond,
  a horse stable.
I wish my school to be with teachers
  who don't boss you around.

I wish my school to have breaks
  after every class.
I wish my school to have a
  little store
  where you can buy cokes,
    candies,
    sandwiches.
I wish my school room to have
  an upstairs
  and to have stairs that
  go around and around.
I wish my school to have lots of room to run.

The Rating Scale

The second exercise asked the children to rate, on a bipolar adjective scale, their present school environment and their conception of an ideal environment. The resulting comparison shows that, in general, the children liked many features of their present facility, but wished for a school that was more "unusual" and "imaginative," more "spacious" and "colorful," and had more "free space" than presently available. Since the school was located in three semipermanent modular units, these expressed desires for variety and space are not particularly critical of the way in which the school was using the limited space available.

School Drawings

The third exercise asked the children to draw pictures of four archetypical schools: an African school, a Japanese school, a "typical" American school, and their "dream" school. While the sketching ability of the children varied, their perception and portrayal of the archetypical cues of each model were very astute. It is particularly interesting to note the contrast between the "typical" American school, usually portrayed as a monotonous, factory-like brick box, and their "dream" schools. These ideal representations are remarkable in their innovativeness and frequent complexity; many were multilevel, and an elevated "tree house" structure was a common theme.

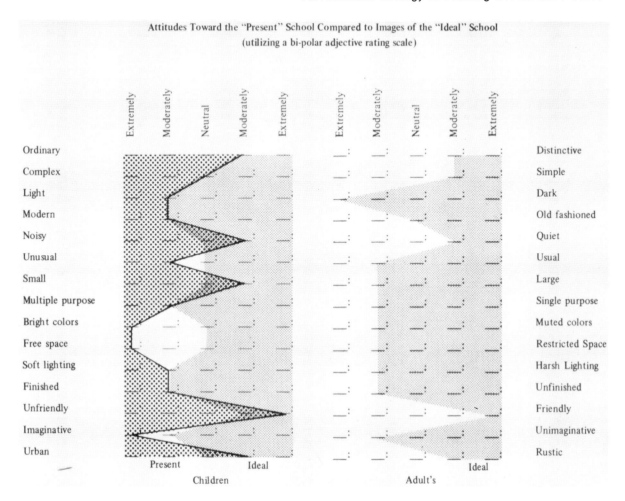

Attitudes Toward the "Present" School Compared to Images of the "Ideal" School
(utilizing a bi-polar adjective rating scale)

Here, as in the Wish Poem, the desire for variety and spontaneity, and for the sensuousness of sunlight and texture and color were apparent. The children wanted an environment they could enjoy, where they could be attracted to variation in color, texture, and spatial configuration.

Role Play

The fourth exercise was an introduction to the process of planning a school through a role-play simulation of the charrette itself. Children assumed various roles, each prescribed by the group leader to represent clearly defined and in some cases antagonistic viewpoints about the kind of school they would create. Some children had difficulty in taking part, but others were quickly transformed into sophisticated and uncompromising advocates for their point of view.

Instructions The purpose of this game is to decide what you want your school to be. By as-

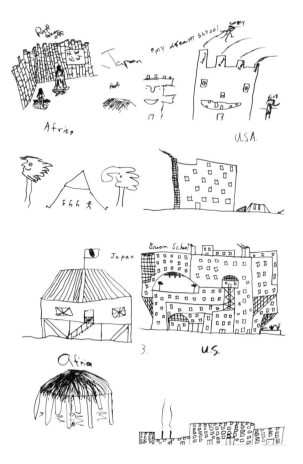

suming these different decision-making roles, you will be taking various positions which may be in conflict with each other, and presenting different viewpoints.

The Architect: You are designing a school for this community. In order to successfully achieve this end, you must find out from the building committee, parents, teachers, and headmaster what the educational objectives are. Each of the participants contributing ideas may create conflict. Your role is to direct the group to reach some agreement about goals and objectives.

Building Committee Member-Minister: You, the minister, are concerned with religious education.

You desire that more time be committed to the teaching of the *Bible* as an important part of the educational objectives.

Building Committee Member-Doctor: You, the doctor, feel that academic achievement is of utmost importance. There should be an emphasis on learning facts and information and do away with all this freedom nonsense of the child pursuing his own interests. Learn and get good grades so the child can get into a good college.

Building Committee Member-Builder: You, as the builder, are concerned with cost of construction. To you, a good school means sound brick construction at a low cost. You will support most ideas about education as long as they do not interfere with a sound building.

Parent 1: You are sending your child to this school so he can be with children of his own social level. The public schools expose your child to children you would not want him to become involved with—"children not of his own kind."

Parent 2: You feel that this school can offer your child better academic opportunities. You are interested in your child learning the three R's and getting good grades so that he can succeed in life.

Parent 3: You feel that the public schools don't understand your child. He does not get along with the teachers. They pick on him for things he does not do and accuse him wrongly. You feel that in this school, with small classes and better teachers, he will be better understood and do well.

Teacher 1: You believe in a strict schedule. All children do all activities together. They are assigned tasks and must fulfill their assignments. One afternoon a week is set aside for "free time."

Teacher 2: You believe that, with appropriate materials and guidance in their use, children can proceed at their own rate and interest. They are free to question the teacher and ask for help when needed. Children can move about freely with the teacher's permission.

Headmaster: You, the headmaster, feel that

education is self-directed. Each child pursues his own interests at his own rate of development. Each child receives individual instruction as required.

These role-play activities provided at least some of the Wallace O'Neal students with an opportunity to understand and to feel a part of the school-planning process. More generally, the results establish the principle that, as members of a school community, students can grasp the nature of the process (including the practical "adult" concerns) and can make effective contributions to the design of programs and facilities. Client groups will differ, of course, in the legitimacy or importance they ascribe to the ideas of the students, but it seems clear that those who are willing to listen can learn from their children.

THE CHARRETTE SESSIONS

The overall goal of the charrette was to help the Wallace O'Neal community compile information about itself, information that could then be used to create and evaluate an architectural design. Over the course of the charrette, the team used a number of techniques and strategies, each designed to generate, summarize, contrast, and translate into spatial terms the information and ideas of the client group.

The first evening session opened with introductions and general statements about the goals of the charrette. Joan Sanoff, as coordinator, then introduced the procedures of the Children's Session by having the group produce a Wish Poem of their own, a combined statement of their aspirations for their school.

I Wish Our School

I wish our school to begin with the piney woods.
I wish our school to be one built for the activities of those involved in it.
I wish the structure to be as exciting for those who use it as it is for those who view it.

I wish our school to be free.
I wish our school to be a fun place to learn for children and teachers alike.
I wish our school could be spacious, full of good books and free for each child to express himself and grow in body and mind.
I wish the school would be a place to look forward to, a place to do lots of different things.
I wish our school would develop into a model after which the public school would follow because they are far from perfect —far from good or adequate.
I wish our school could work with the less fortunate children in Moore County, who must go to public schools.
I wish our school a happy future, one in which new ideas can be tried out—and discarded if need be—a school of happy children learning to learn.
I wish my school to be a place where I want to go and no one has to tell me to.
I wish my school to have teachers who will talk to me and help me find out what I want to do.
I wish my school to have people to talk to about who I am and who will talk to me about who they are.
I wish that we had a school where children are turned on, not off to education.
I wish the children to be able to experience far more than textbook learning; more than just academics.
I wish our school could make books, blackboards, pencils, and papers to be more than mere tangible things.
I wish our school could respond to the emotional needs of our children.
I wish our school could foster social awareness and display by its existence, alternatives to narrow-mindedness, inequality and social injustice.
I wish our school could give a sense of awareness, to teach sight, sound, taste, touch, and smell.
I wish our school could cultivate a sense of responsibility for community, nature, and all mankind.
I wish our school could stimulate, prod, and provide, inspire questions, and provide avenues to find answers.
I wish our school could excite and stir the imaginations of parent, child, and teacher alike.
I wish our school were fun and free
  Where children love to learn and see.

The children's poem and their drawings of archetypical schools were presented and discussed, and the role-play session was described. It was clear that the meaning of this material varied within the group; some participants, particularly the faculty, seemed to feel that it was an important contribution in its own right, while others used the discussion as a basis for raising concerns about the nature and goals of the charrette.

Some parents were distressed by the stereotyped roles given the children for the role-play session; they were concerned that these exaggerations reflected the consultants' perceptions of the Wallace O'Neal group. This discussion (which might have been avoided with a clearer description of the role-play rationale) was useful in allowing an airing of this issue and seemed to establish a greater trust in the consultants as facilitators rather than potentially critical "outsiders."

Another issue had to do with the format of the charrette itself. The planning team had decided that a sound building program could be derived only from a clear and consensual educational program, and for this reason the bulk of the charrette time was scheduled for discussion of education issues. This choice was questioned from a number of viewpoints: some felt that the educational program was already clear and that they should begin planning the building, others felt that they had nothing to contribute to a discussion of educational objectives, still others seemed to feel that the consultants were avoiding their responsibilities by expecting the school community to produce its own plans and ideas. Again, this discussion was based on vital issues and helped to clarify both the goals of the charrette and the roles that the consultants felt that they could legitimately play in reaching those goals.

Not everyone accepted the results of these discussions; some dropped out and others remained skeptical, but most accepted the opportunity to become a part of the process.

With these issues partially resolved, the second and third evenings were used to formulate a consensual educational program. The primary technique for this purpose was the use of The Game, a simulation of the school design process developed by Henry Sanoff and the Community Development Group, for the Learning Institute of North Carolina (LINC). The game consists of four decision-making steps, with each part contingent on the product of the preceding steps. At each step, the individual participant is required to select from a limited universe of choices, and to define and discuss their own selections in the process of agreeing on a group product.

GAME

The four steps of the Game are

1. Objectives: The group is presented with a list of thirty-nine educational objectives, covering a wide range of philosophies. Each participant selects the four which are important to him; through discussion the group then reduces these to four which represent their generally agreed goals.
2. Techniques: Given their four chosen objectives, the group is presented with a list of educational techniques, again reflecting a wide range of possible instructional philosophies. Individually, and then as a group, they are required to select four techniques which seem most appropriate to each of their original objectives.
3. Interactions: The group is presented with a series of cards, each representing in an abstract drawing a type of interaction of relationship among the elements of a school (teachers, students, boundaries, equipment, etc.). Through individual and then group decisions, the group selects an interaction mode most representative of each of their chosen techniques.
4. Settings: This represents the final step in a simulated movement from abstract goals through concrete techniques to a physical setting. The participants are given cards showing sketches of learning places (classrooms, offices, lounges, etc.). They are required to select two settings to match each objective and the techniques and interactions connoted by that objective.

In order to work through the Game, the participants were divided into groups of four to six members, with one of the consultants assigned to each group. The consultants did not participate in decision making (and were not invited to); they were available to explain the rules, to help define terms, and to facilitate the process of explanation, argument, and agreement within the group.

It was found that the groups varied in their ability to use the process productively and that different groups faltered on different steps of the Game. In general, the objectives step was helpful in providing each individual with a framework for articulating his own ideas. However, it seemed less useful in the creation of a group agreement because of the compromise necessary in reducing the individual objectives to a single set. It was clear, though, that the exercise provided each group member with a greater understanding of the interests and goals of his fellow participants, and some working bonds were established in this phase.

Some participants felt unable to deal with the Techniques step because of the seeming infringement on "professional" grounds. Others rather mechanically assigned techniques to the objectives without considerable thought. For most groups and participants, though, this step was the beginning of discussion about the relevance, desirability, and implications of unconventional techniques such as nongradedness and student decision making.

Though designed as a bridge from the conceptual to the graphic modes, the Interaction series was, in general, too complex and abstract for many of the participants. In most cases, the process was one of simply locating the interaction card which described the technique they had selected; and little additional information about the nature of that technique was generated.

The groups varied widely in the ability to use the Settings discussion. Most of the groups were able to advance meaningful educational choices by considering the wide range of spatial alternatives in which their objectives and techniques might be implemented.

Over all, it was clear that each member of each group had been given an opportunity, at some stage of the Game, to define and defend his own ideas and to reach out for agreement and shared understanding within his group.

The five groups participating in the gaming sessions selected a total of ten different goals, two of which were common to four of the groups. These goals were "developing a sense of responsibility" and "developing motivation for learning . . . ." The goals and associated techniques for each of the groups are described in the accompanying table.

The game props provided an opportunity for the participants to involve themselves in the group problem-solving process as well as to begin to consciously define educational objectives. This was the preliminary to the weekend sessions, which were devoted to the actual goal setting for the new Wallace O'Neal School.

Resolution of Gaming Session

The weekend session began with board members, teachers, and parents assembling to reevaluate the findings of the previous game sessions, and to reword, clarify, and amend the material into a new set of goals that the entire group could support. A few new participants joined the planning group and were readily accepted and acquainted with the previous processes and decisions.

The collaborative Wish Poem was reviewed, and from it the following educational objectives were distilled:

1. Fostering social awareness.
2. Working with less fortunate children.
3. Experiential learning.
4. Responding to emotional needs.
5. Challenging students.
6. Being one's self.
7. Learning for children and teachers.

8. A sense of awareness.
9. Freedom of self-expression.
10. Community responsibility.
11. Happy children learning to learn.
12. Teacher responsiveness to parents.

With these statements and the Game Objectives in mind, the group was asked to meet without the consultants and to produce a set of goals, written in their own words, that would stand as the objectives of their school. They returned after a long and often boisterous discussion with a list of thirteen statements that they felt satisfied with.

Example of Goals and Techniques Selected by One Group from the Gaming Process

Goal	Developing a sense of responsibility
Techniques	Independent study
	Nongraded classes
	Field trips
	Competition
Goal	Developing motivation for learning
Techniques	Lecture–demonstration
	One-to-one student–teacher
	Accessibility of resources
	Student planning
Goal	Developing communication skills
Techniques	One-to-one student–teacher
	Peer counseling
	Accessibility to resources
	Self-presentation
Goal	Developing self-actualization
Techniques	Nongraded classes
	Independent study
	Student planning
	One-to-one student–teacher
Goal	Developing resourcefulness
Techniques	Accessibility of resources
	Lecture–demonstration
	Competition
	Student planning

Two techniques were then used to establish the school's priorities within this list. In the first, the thirteen goal statements were randomly divided into four groups. The participants then chose, by voting, the most important goal statements in each group.

The second procedure used a paired-comparison technique to establish a rank ordering for the entire list of statements. The participants were asked to compare each goal statement with every other one and to select, from each pair, the one that was most important. Although this required seventy-eight separate decisions (12 objectives by thirteen comparisons, divided by two), the procedure was carried out easily and the results were tabulated immediately.

The same three goal statements were selected as most important in both procedures; the fifth most important according to the paired comparisons had been among the first in the voting process. This provided a believable level of agreement between the two procedures.

The final thirteen goal statements, ranked according to the paired-comparison process, are listed in order below:

1. Developing a sense of responsibility.
2. Providing an atmosphere of trust.
3. Developing motivation for learning.
4. Developing a realistic self-image.
5. Encouraging student's sense of community, identity, and social awareness.
6. Developing and encouraging resourcefulness.
7. Stimulating curiosity and imagination with an initiative toward creativity.
8. Developing communication skills.
9. Developing persistence toward a goal.
10. Developing a tolerance of differences.
11. Developing a sense of achievement.
12. Involving parents in the education experience.
13. Developing motor skills.

This product, their own goals clearly ranked according to their own priorities, provided a great sense of satisfaction for the school community. They were especially pleased that their overall objectives emphasized personal growth rather than a concentration on academic achievement.

From this consensual base, a model was proposed for translating the community's objectives into instructional procedures and subsequently into educational settings. The first goal statement, "Developing a Sense of Responsibility," was used as an illustration by soliciting responses for instructional methods to implement this goal, using the alternatives already familiar from the techniques session of the Game. Some of the methods suggested were: Independent study, experimentation, Small group activity, Problem solving, Role playing, Lecture–demonstration, and Group discussion. A notation system was produced for classifying these instructional methods according to the student/teacher relationship: TD, teacher-directed; CD, child-directed; TR, teacher as resource; C, collaborative learning.

Each proposed method was then coded according to student–teacher relationship and evaluated against the thirteen goal statements in order to determine the methods and relationships best suited to the program objectives. This analytic process enabled the group to more fully understand the means by which their goals could be realized. It also held in abeyance emotionally loaded discussions of "open" or "nongraded" classrooms until some general understanding of children's learning processes was shared by all participants. This helped prevent the "fixing" of concepts too early in the planning stages by allowing solutions to evolve through goal-oriented discussion rather than arguments based on prejudgment. In this way, the architect (who participated in all the sessions) was given a more complete view of the intention and direction of the school program, and as a result

was in a position to generate alternatives appropriate to this community's needs rather than having to follow currently fashionable prototype.

This session heightened the confrontation between the faculty and the parents as, during the process of associating learning methods with objectives, it became clear that the student–teacher relationship should be a function of the goals intended, irrespective of the popularity or convenience of any "teaching" model. The teachers were made aware of the fact that, while they had a body of knowledge to convey through the academic curriculum, the school's objectives were to determine the way in which students were to be exposed to "content" areas.

All preceding discussions had centered on the development of a consensual educational base from which a building program could generate. The following session attempted to synthesize previous discussions through the pictorial representation of the newly formulated goal statements and methods. While the charrette participants suggested learning methods and activities, a team of architects responded with spontaneous sketches depicting the physical realization of the proposed ideas.

This session had a twofold impact on the community group. First, it permitted the participants to view the architects' interpretations of verbal statements into physical form; second, the participants became more sensitive to the processes designers utilize in shaping space. While it was evident that the emerging forms were merely illustrative suggestions, the group's awareness of the linkages between learning techniques and appropriate spaces was substantially sharpened.

Although this marked the end of the planned activities, the charrette was extended at the request of the participants in order to provide more specific design directives to the architect. The intention was to describe all of the activities that the children would engage in (the activities that the facility would be designed to serve) and to select the learning methods most appropriate to the objectives of the school.

The primary activities of the school day were initially defined as follows:

math	art
science	construction
social studies	sports
English	independent study
drama	language arts
music	

It was clear, however, that there are secondary activities which are necessary to support the fulfillment of the primary activities: food preparation, storage, toilets, circulation, etc. It was agreed that the architect had sufficient technical knowledge to resolve the requirements of the secondary activities and that discussion should focus on the primary activities.

In order to facilitate a productive discussion, data sheets were prepared whereby each activity could be treated independently. This allowed an assessment of appropriate learning methods,

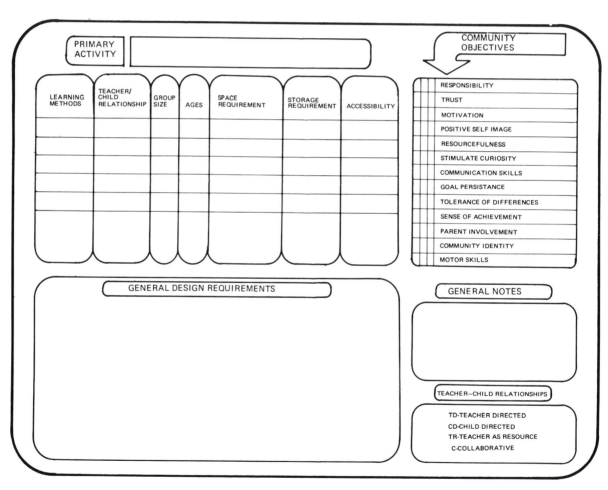

student–teacher relationships, and the spatial and material requirements. The data sheet became a permanent record of the requirements of the facility as the development of each of the primary activities suggested its relative importance in terms of the allocation of spaces. This provided the architect with a reasonable starting point for the development of a building design as he assumed the role of translating objectives, methods, and activities into an accommodating organization.

The charrette had reached this point through a series of structured techniques which had enabled the participants to define, with increasing confidence and independence, their educational objectives and the type of environment they would need to implement those objectives.

Innovation in the Philadelphia School System*

**Lawrence Goldfarb,
Peter Brown, and
Thomas Gallagher**

Innovation in the Philadelphia schools in recent years has been indistinguishable from Dr. Mark Shedd, who was hired away from Englewood, New Jersey, in 1967 to become superintendent of the Philadelphia system. His appointment coincided with the election of a new progressive school board, from which he has had constant support. Shedd's supporters refer to his record as a revolution designed to make the Philadelphia school system relevant to the needs of its students. Others, less comfortable with change, think his programs reflect a trend toward permissiveness and overindulgence. As a result, he has accomplished only a portion of the changes which he has sought. Under his direction a comprehensive study was undertaken to identify alternatives for decentralizing the system. Among his first recommendations to the school board were the establishment

*Excerpts from "Seven Schools," YGS Building Foundation, Inc., 1972.

of a talent pool of teachers from which principals could select a staff, decentralization of the budget, and discretionary funds to be used by principals and teachers for experimental projects.

Funds were allocated to enable schools to be open during evenings and weekends for recreation and adult education, and experimental programs emphasizing new approaches to learning were initiated throughout the city. One of these, the Advancement School, was attracted to Philadelphia from North Carolina. Ths school is geared to so-called underachievers who are exposed, usually for one school year, to a curriculum designed by a multidisciplinary staff to "turn them on."

Courses range from the "Consumer Game," a math course taught by simulating the marketplace; to "Boxing–Reading," a reading course that relates everything to boxing and includes visits by professional boxers and simulated in-school fights for which the students prepare the ringside commentary; to a gymnastics class in which young boys perform intricate ballet maneuvers to jazz rhythms.

The Advancement School is a curriculum development center; as such, it is open for observation with the objective of stimulating changes in the rest of the system with its innovations.

Another more or less renowned experiment has been the Parkway Program, often called the "School Without Walls." The Parkway Program, a high school for 500 students who are selected from applicants from all parts of the city, has no facilities of its own. All classes are held in existing city institutions: churches, museums, etc. Many of the courses are taught by professionals—stockbrokers, bankers, doctors, curators, etc.

A third experiment is the Learning Centers Project, which, like the Advancement School, was established to function as an agent for change within the system. In nine schools and one laboratory (set up for observation), the project conducts "open classrooms" based on the model of the British Infant Schools, an educational approach which places more emphasis on the students and less on the teacher. In this system, the teacher becomes a resource rather than an authoritarian figure always in control. Open classroom teaching is usually carried on in spaces larger—or at least more varied—than typical classrooms. Many of the teaching materials are self-correcting, and students are often allowed to choose their own. The Learning Centers Project also offers consulting services and workshops for teachers from other schools.

In spite of these and other innovations, the educational experience for the majority of students in the Philadelphia system has changed little in the last five years. One reason for this is the difficulty of moving an entrenched bureaucracy; another, more basic, is the acute financial crisis facing the school district.

This crisis has steadily worsened over the past few years, as necessary budget increases to meet rising salaries and overall inflation have averaged 11 to 17 percent. Thus an increase in the operating budget by this amount has been required just to maintain present staff and programs; however, the increase in revenue to offset these rising costs has only averaged 3 to 5 percent. Numerous attempts to legislate new taxes have met with delays and obstacles, and a sales tax on alcohol sold over the bar was recently vetoed by an unsympathetic mayor.

The budget crisis is only the most malignant of a number of ailments the Philadelphia school system shares with other major cities. Segregated, dilapidated, and overcrowded facilities, a high dropout and truancy rate, and a ponderous and ineffectual bureaucracy are typical items on a long, familiar list.

Shedd's revolution has probably done as much to accent these deficiencies as to eradicate them. Such seems to be the painful irony of reform.

A CONTEXT FOR THE SEVEN SCHOOLS

The Mantua community, in which five of the seven schools are located and from which all draw students, is a community of 17,000 people located one mile west of Philadelphia's City Hall, a half mile north of the University of Pennsylvania, and several feet up from the Schuylkill River and the tracks of the Penn Central Railroad's 30th Street Station. It is a ghetto, 95 percent black. The unemployment rate is estimated by a local planning office at 16 percent, and the majority of working-men have skills that qualify them only for manual jobs. Half of Mantua's 3,000 residential buildings are dilapidated and 17 percent are vacant and vandalized. There is a high rate of drug addiction and an accompanying high crime rate. Youngsters who drop out of school are the rule rather than the exception, and many are members of one of the half-dozen well-organized gangs.

Although the conditions in Mantua are in many respects less severe than those in the vast im-

Figure 1
Haverford Avenue—the "heart" of Mantua.

poverished area of North Philadelphia, it is unquestionably the most depressed section of West Philadelphia.

The seven schools are all, to one degree or another, community controlled and based on untraditional educational models. All but two of them originated with community groups, and there isn't one that isn't indebted to the Shedd administration for its existence.

Other than these similarities, and a more or less common location, the schools differ greatly. They range from a day-care center for infants to a high school. One of them is defunct, one is still in the planning stage.

As an introduction to the seven schools, a brief description of each is given below. The order in which the schools are described corresponds to the ages of children who attend, beginning with the youngest.

1. *The Young Great Society Infant Day-Care*

Center: A Day-Care Center for Welfare Mothers: The Young Great Society Infant Day-Care Center is a community-owned-and-run day-care center for twenty-two children aged six months to three years. It operates in one half of a remodeled duplex and is the first day-care facility in the state designed solely for infants. It opened in September 1970 as a service to welfare mothers and as an educational experience for young children. The center is funded ($77,000 in 1972) almost entirely from state Department of Public Welfare.

2. *The Mantua–Powelton Children's School: A Cooperative Nursery School Utilizing the Concept of the Open Classroom:* The Mantua-Powelton Children's School is a racially integrated school for thirty-six children. It opened in October 1970 in a rehabilitated dwelling on Spring Garden Street, the border between Mantua and Powelton Village. The school is an outgrowth of a parent cooperative nursery

which utilized the principles of the "open class-room," a concept borrowed from the British Infant Schools. The physical facility was developed privately by the Powelton–Mantua Educational Fund, a trust formed by the parents for the purpose of building the school. The Philadelphia School District leases the facility from the fund for $7,500 a year.

3. *The Walnut Center: A Public Demonstration School Emphasizing Racial and Social Balance:* The Walnut Center is a "demonstration" public school operated by the Philadelphia School District; the center enrolls 200 pre-kindergarten to first grade students. It is designed primarily as an experiment in racial, social, and economic integration. In addition to its regular program, the center operates a day-care service for another seventy-five children. The center is funded ($200,000 this year) entirely from the federal Department of Health, Education, and Welfare with special monies made available for poverty areas under Title I of the Elementary and Secondary Education Act of 1965.

4. *The Mantua–Powelton Mini-School: An Experiment in Total Community Control of a Public School:* The Mantua–Powelton Mini-School was a public middle school for 150 fifth through eighth graders. It operated from September 1968 to June 1970 in an abandoned factory in Powelton Village and was designed as an experiment in total community control. One of objectives was to attempt to utilize the techniques of the "affective curriculum" (which concentrates on the emotional as well as intellectual growth of the student) and to serve as a prototype for the house plan of the proposed McDevitt Middle School. It was financed the first year by a grant from the Rockefeller Foundation, the second out of the Philadelphia School District's operating budget.

5. *The Benjamin Banneker Urban Center: A Private Black Secondary School:* The Benjamin Banneker Urban Center is a privately owned and operated secondary school currently housed in facilities rented from the University City Science Center (located between the University of Pennsylvania and Mantua). It opened in February 1971 with a class made up of seventy-five seventh graders recruited from neighboring junior high schools. Banneker eventually plans to enroll over 500 seventh-through twelfth-grade students, including former dropouts. The school stresses the importance of individual as well as group counseling, and encourages tactile learning through independent projects utilizing the most advanced educational technology. The school presently operates on funds from the school district, issued in the form of a contract for services ($850 per student per year), and contributions from private donors.

6. *The McDevitt Middle School: A Public Middle School to Be Constructed on Four Scattered Sites:* The McDevitt Middle School is planned to be built on four scattered sites in the Mantua, Belmont, and Powelton Village communities. When complete, it will serve 1,600 fifth through eighth graders. The plan is an outgrowth of a confrontation in which the community successfully opposed a school district plan to build a typical middle school in a single building on a site adjacent to the Penn Central Railroad tracks. Practically all the decisions regarding sites and the distribution of facilities on these sites have been made by community groups utilizing the technical assistance of professional staff of the Philadelphia School District and of the Young Great Society Building Foundation.

7. *The West Philadelphia Community Free School: An Experiment in High School Decentralization Within the System:* The West Philadelphia Community Free School is a decentralized annex of West Philadelphia High School. All policy decisions are made by a thirteen-member Com-

munity Board, with the help of a full-time director who oversees the operation of three independent houses located in widely scattered areas of West Philadelphia. The school opened in February 1970 and operates with a non-graded curriculum (no grades or divisions of students by year); it seeks to make the learning experience more relevant by utilizing community businesses, institutions, and professionals as learning resources. Funds for the school come primarily from the school district's operating budget, and the amount is determined on a per-student basis and deducted from West Philadephia High's budget. Thus the Free School represents no increase in the city's overall operating budget.

It would be misleading to attribute this intensive development in innovative schools solely to the Shedd administration. For this aspect of Shedd's "revolution" echoes a growing political movement to return "power to the people." And it is people of all colors and abilities that have, through protest and sheer insistence, made these schools. They have made them not only because they desired alternatives to the public school system, but also out of a hunger for political control of the institutions which affect their daily lives, whether it be the schools, the police, or government. Thus the seven schools represent significant landmarks in a wider struggle.

West Philadelphia provides an apt context for this kind of dynamic. The area, especially the eastern portion where all seven schools are located, is dominated by the University of Pennsylvania, Drexel University, and an intense concentration of hospitals.

Of these, Penn has been heavily involved in the creation of two of the schools and indirectly involved in three others. Penn privately financed the construction of the new half-million-dollar facility for the Walnut Center and has donated $60,000 to

the Free School, as well as the services of an educational consultant and others from the university administration. The Benjamin Banneker Urban Center has benefited from the assistance of the director and staff of Penn's Management Science Center, who have been active in promoting the project with foundations and other funding sources.

Unfortunately, both institutional involvements (with the Walnut Center and with the Free School) were made only after and in response to direct confrontations with strong-willed community groups. Its involvement is thus interpreted by many as a defensive reaction, not as a carrying out of a coherent policy toward education in West Philadelphia.

Penn agreed to finance the construction of the Walnut Center only after strong community opposition to the planned demolition of the school's original facility in order to construct a parking garage for university use. Later the same year they became involved in the Free School when they were confronted with a demand that the university relinquish the building which houses its business school in order to relieve overcrowding at West Philadelphia High.

If the university is one promontory in the landscape of West Philadelphia politics, the Young Great Society is its counterpart in the community.

The Young Great Society (YGS) is a community self-help organization concerned primarily with the social and physical rebuilding of Mantua. It has programs in drug addiction, housing development, medicine, recreation, employment, job training, and education. Formed as the outgrowth of a corner gang, YGS's first major grant was $36,000 from the school district to pay salaries for several young community men to serve as "nonteaching assistants" (NTAs) in area schools. The NTAs' duties were essentially to work with disruptive pupils, especially young gang members.

Since then YGS has organized Little League teams in elementary schools, has placed occasional staff members in schools to teach special subjects (a secretary teaches typing; a planner, a design course), and regularly advises and counsels teachers and principals.

YGS owns the Infant Day Care Center and is almost solely responsible for the creation of Banneker. The organization had considerable influence in the creation of the Children's School, and it is unlikely that without the reputation of YGS the school board would have endorsed the Mantua–Powelton Mini-School.

We should not leave the impression that YGS is the only, or even the most crucial, community factor in the development of the schools discussed in this report. For it is, in the last analysis, individuals who have made these schools. And the schools represent human, not organizational or institutional, concerns. Toward YGS, the school board, Penn, and the "system," people hold differing and often opposing attitudes. What hardly varies at all, however, is their enthusiasm and commitment to the process of improving the quality of education for their children.

DESIGN AND DEVELOPMENT

In this section we change roles, from reporters to architects advocating an approach to the design of schools in the inner city. Since our experience has included the development, buying land, negotiating construction loans and mortgages, etc., as well as the design of these schools, we have attempted to generalize on this aspect of our experience in order to offer advice to others. The text is divided into two parts: the first is a discussion of design issues, the second, of the development process. The design ideas which are illustrated were developed during the course of this study. All seven participating schools were offered, in return for their assistance in preparing the case studies, planning and architectural services by the staff of the YGS Building Foundation.

In doing this we hoped to accomplish several objectives. First, we wanted to make the design component of this report as relevant as possible to the issues and concerns of real people and real programs. We wanted to avoid a theoretical design study which focused on architectural matters of interest only to other architects. Second, we were anxious to utilize the resources of this study to maximum advantage. Utilizing the seven groups as clients enabled us to provide design studies which would be useful in fund raising and in gaining community support for expansion of the schools.

For this report the authors have chosen not to present the design as seven separate proposals, but rather to use them as a basis for discussing general issues affecting the design of all schools.

The second part is a summary of the development issues raised by our experience with the seven schools and is intended to point out the alternative approaches open to a group that wants to sponsor its own program. This concludes with a series of recommendations as to what should be done first and what to avoid doing.

The issues which we have attempted to clarify with planning and design studies are

1. The staging of construction.
2. Flexibility of space use.
3. The choice between new construction and the rehabilitation of existing structures.
4. The quality of the interior environment.
5. The quality of the exterior environment.

Each of these issues is treated separately, and each concludes with specific recommendations. While the particulars of these discussions will not in all cases be transferable to other situations in other cities, many of the general ideas will.

At a minimum it is hoped that these ideas can provide information which groups can use as a basis for communication with their architects. Thus we conclude each part of this section with recommendations under the heading "Tell Your Architect."

DESIGN ISSUES

The Staging of Construction

There are a number of reasons why it is recommended that designs for community-sponsored school facilities be prepared with a view toward staging the project (i.e., constructing a facility, or facilities, in a series of predetermined phases). Staging is especially crucial in the event that only a portion of the required funds can be obtained. Often a preliminary design for a project is necessary even to find out how much money is required to get the program into operation. There are some basic first questions. For instance, how large a building will zoning regulations allow on a particular site and how many students will the building hold? What are the possibilities for future expansion onto adjacent sites? Or, if the first site is more than adequate, what is the minimum construction which makes sense in a first stage?

The design for the YGS Infant Day Care Center relates specifically to these issues. The facility, which is currently in operation for twenty-two children, occupies a previously vacant half of a semidetached house. At the time of its purchase the adjacent house, also vacant, was put under agreement of sale in order to guarantee the pos-

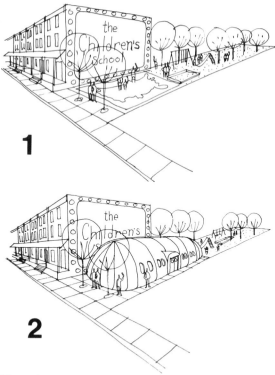

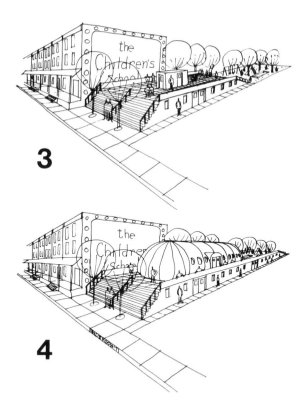

Figure 2
The Childrens' School—expansion is designed to take place in four phases.

sibility of future expansion. Beyond this, the plan is for the school to expand further into a new structure around the corner.

One rationale for clustering day care units on a single block rather than scattering them throughout the community is that state requirements for professional staff and kitchen facilities make a plan which centralizes these services more economical.

Another approach to the issue of staging is illustrated in the design for the expansion of the Mantua–Powelton Children's School. The first phase of this expansion calls for a playground on the vacant lot adjacent to the present building. This is to be constructed in the near future. Subsequent phases could proceed as follows: a proposed inflatable structure (more about inflatables later) could be constructed on a portion of the playground, and later disassembled and moved to the roof of a low one-story industrial-type building.

This proposal provides the option of constructing the relatively inexpensive inflatable and the one-story building either simultaneously (if the funds are available) or at different times (if the funds are not).

The lesson here is that a design concept should build in options which make it possible to respond to unpredictable circumstances.

The other side of the phasing question is illustrated by the proposed McDevitt scattered-site middle school. In this case the staff of the Philadelphia School District is recommending that the various units of the school be constructed in four phases, the development of each scattered site representing one phase.

The community Advisory Board is arguing that staging a 1,600-student middle school makes little sense, since all of the "core" facilities for physical education, art and dramatics, industrial arts, and the instructional materials center would have to be built first for a middle-school program to function at all. And when this minimal first phase of construction (as the community puts it) is added to the general academic space required for only half the proposed enrollment, it equals 75 percent of the total proposed construction. On the basis of this, the community has argued that it would be false economy not to build the school in a single phase.

Tell your architect to prepare his design with a clear idea of the possibility of staging the construction process in two or more phases, and to illustrate the minimum feasible first phase. Alternatively, if he recommends against phasing, his argument should clearly explain the false economy of a phased building program.

Flexibility of Use

Innovative educational programs, especially those that encourage the free movement of students or stress (as do Banneker and the Free School) the importance of students and teachers

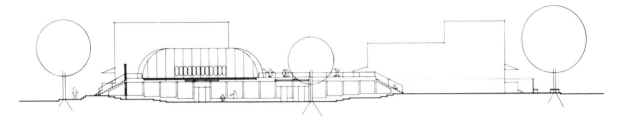

Figure 3
Cross section through the proposed expansion of the Children's School.

CHILDREN'S SCHOOL 3

meeting in variously sized groups for various forms of instruction, require facilities whose spatial arrangement can be altered at minimum cost and with minimum effort.

Ideally all school buildings should be constructed with enough flexibility so that their arrangements of space can be constantly altered to suit evolving methods of teaching.

A great amount of flexibility can be achieved by utilizing loft-type industrial construction of the kind traditionally used by industry. Such a building, with the advantage of large interior open spaces, is proposed for the Benjamin Banneker Urban Center. In this case, the decision was made primarily on the basis of economics and has resulted in a building with immense possibilities for the spontaneous rearrangement of space.

The plan of a typical Banneker floor illustrates one possible arrangement. The fixed elements consist only of the stairs, toilets, service elevator, and the grid of columns that support the building. All the remaining interior walls are removable. These can be made easily from a variety of lightweight panel materials held in place with wood or steel frames. The frames can be fitted with blackboards, attached together with bolts, easily carried, stacked in a storage closet, and erected by students themselves.

It is one of the rationales for the partitions, as well as for designing flexible space to begin with, that the experience of arranging their own environment can become part of the students' educational program. Banneker's director, Charles Askew, hopes this is one way his students can move toward greater self-awareness.

At the Steuart Hill Elementary School in Baltimore—a recently built school designed as a series of large open rooms which are subdivided by simple panels—students and teachers decide together on the best arrangement, and the process itself becomes a geometry lesson.

Another rationale for flexibility has to do with economics. The high cost of construction results in a large investment in interior partitions, doors, and ceilings; when the interior spaces are left unfinished and subdivided by the users themselves, either the overall cost is lowered or additional money is made available to be spent elsewhere in the building.

Another aspect of the economic considerations of phasing is related to the reluctance of lenders to provide mortgages for community projects. One problem, even with those institutions that are sympathetic to a group's objectives, is that most programs are funded with one- or two-year grants. Mortgages, on the other hand, usually have a ten- to twenty-year life. So if the group is not funded beyond its first grant, then the bank is left with the building. The community group's position is helped somewhat if the building is designed for easy conversion to another use. The term "programing for failure" may sound overly pessimistic, but it's real; and those groups that have thought out "what happens if . . ." will be in a stronger position than those who have not.

Tell your architect to plan for flexible space use within the building and consider how students might participate in making their environment within this flexibility.

To consider what other uses might be accommodated in the building should the school program terminate before the mortgage is retired.

Rehabilitation Versus New Construction

There are too many good arguments to be made on each side of this question for there to be a single answer which is applicable to all situations. On the side of rehabilitating existing structures, the following arguments are most often put forth:

It's cheaper. This should be so, but it's not always true. It depends on the type of construction and the present condition of the building. The Mantua–Powelton Mini-School, occupying an abandoned cookie factory, cost practically nothing to put into operation, but the program suffered as a result of the minimal investment in fixing up the building. On the other hand, the decision to construct a new building for the Banneker Center, instead of converting the old apartment house now on the site, was based primarily on cost. Unfortunately, until a full set of architectural drawings and specifications was prepared and put out for contractors' bids, this cost was not known.

A related economic consideration in the choice of new or rehabilitated construction concerns the number of students that can be accommodated. In the case of Banneker, the rehabilitated building would have had space for about 250, and the cost would have been $27.00 per square foot; by constructing a slightly larger building which would cost $22.50 per square foot, over 500 students could be accommodated. Since many school programs are funded on a per-student basis, this factor can drastically change the financial feasibility of a project.

Rebuild structures will fit better into a neighborhood environment. In many cases this is ture. Old warehouses and vacant factory buildings can sometimes be renewed, and with minor modifica-

tions the architectural result can be superior — in terms of the amount and quality of space — to anything possible within the rigid budget limitations under which most new schools are built.

As an example, the intimate quality of the interior spaces in the Children's School could never have been built into a new building without a much higher construction budget. The small building built for the Walnut Center is the inevitable result or a low budget and the stringent code limitations imposed on school construction by the state.

Other arguments, equally persuasive, are put forth by those who think new construction is the more logical approach.

There are too many hidden costs in rehabilitation. You never know what it's going to cost until you're underway and then it's often too late. This, too, depends on the circumstances. The cost of renovating a large building with many partitions is more difficult to estimate accurately than if the structure were a "shell" with only the basic structure remaining. This is especially true if the interior partitions are structural, that is, if they support the floors above. In many cases it is not

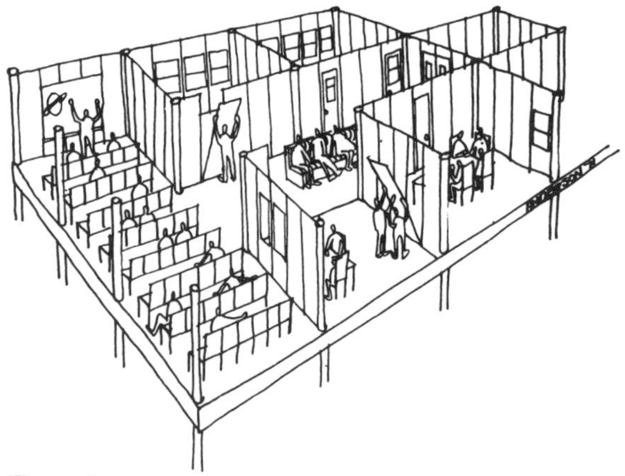

Figure 4
In a loft-type building such as Banneker, lightweight panels can be easily rearranged to create a variety of teaching spaces.

Figure 5
The proposed loft building to house the Banneker Center. The learning process on the inside becomes the architectural expression on the outside.

possible for an architect or a contractor to accurately predict the final cost of rehabilitation, because old buildings inevitably contain hidden problems not immediately apparent. These translate later into unplanned-for expenses. As a result, experienced contractors overestimate and less experienced firms, anxious for work, underestimate. It was partly as a result of hidden costs that the YGS Infant Day Care Center, originally estimated at $35,000, ultimately cost $55,000.

It's easier to get funding for a new structure, since it will have more of an impact on the surrounding area. This may not always be true, but in the case of the Banneker project it seems to be. Funding for the project is being sought through HUD under the Multi-Purpose Neighborhood Facilities Program. HUD does in fact favor a new

structure for Banneker in preference to rebuilding the apartment building now on the site.

In addition to the rational arguments for new construction in this particular case, our experience has been that there is a strong emotional preference for new facilities. It is not surprising that newness has a strong emotional attraction for people who have traditionally been dealt society's leftovers.

So there is no formula for resolving this issue; the arguments for rehabilitation or for new construction can go either way. It's important to consider the particular circumstances before making a decision to proceed with one or the other approach.

Tell your architect to evaluate carefully the particular circumstances of your project and to recommend whether rehabilitation of an existing

Figure 6
Portable desk units can be used to subdivide "great rooms"; designing the arrangement of these can become a lesson in geometry.

building or the construction of a new one is the more logical choice.

The Interior Environment

The central theme of this section is that a school does not have to be designed as a series of class-rooms lining a central corridor, each with standardized rows of desks and a teacher up front. As an environment for sparking the imagination of children, most schools which are built today fail miserably.

The Steuart Hill Elementary School in Baltimore, Maryland, provides a good example of how a more open classroom arrangement encourages growth and self-confidence. Instead of a single blackboard in front of the room, which "belongs" to the teacher, each student has his or her own blackboard which is part of a flexible unit that can either be placed separately or arranged with other units for group instruction.

Ronald Beckman, director of the Research and Design Institute of Providence, Rhode Island, and a design consultant of the Steuart Hill School, points out the enormous psychological difference between the situation in which a child goes to the teacher's blackboard in front of the entire class—knowing that making a mistake will bring laughter and humiliation—and the more supportive and confidence-building situation in which the teacher comes to the student's blackboard. Beckman believes these portable desk units are also ideal for subdividing what he calls "great rooms": large open spaces for many students, undivided by permanent partitions.

The great room represents the ultimate disintegration of the traditional corridors and classrooms plan. In a project for the expansion of an existing high school, Beckman's organization proposed a single great room, measuring 210 by 150 feet; the only fixed elements were to be the columns supporting the structure above.

On a much smaller scale the renovation of the present facility for the Mantua–Powelton Children's School utilizes the same principle. Since the only walls necessary for structural support in a row house are those on either side of the building, the second floor is a continuous open area from the front to the rear of the building.

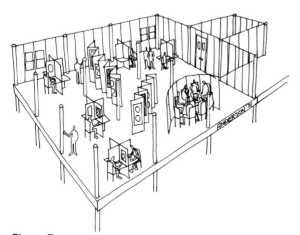

Figure 7
The only fixed elements in the Banneker Center will be the stairway core and columns holding the structure above.

Figure 8
The proposed inflatable for the Children's School will create a single large room.

Another variation of the great room concept is the proposed addition to the Children's School. The proposal calls for the use of an inflatable structure. Inflatables are constructed with a giant sheet of transparent plastic, held up against a web of cables by an airblower. This type of structure has been used as field houses for schools and universities and by industry for a variety of storage purposes.

Inflatables are cheap. A finished support covering the Children's School site would cost—complete with a foundation, bathrooms, carpeting, and lighting—$9 a square foot, less than half the cost of a new building. Inflatables can be erected in hours. The life of an air-supported skin, the plastic itself, is seven years and after that time it is easily replaceable at $2 a square foot.

The Mantua–Powelton Children's School's inflatable would accommodate forty-five children. There would be no walls. Portable partitions could be set up to divide the space. In addition to being economical, the inflatable has a great deal of esthetic appeal: it is translucent; it glows at night; during the day it lets in light; it is weather controlled like any other interior space, but plants can be grown in it in December—the list goes on.

While the structure is cheap in comparison with more conventional construction, there are, nevertheless a few problems. One is the inflatable's vulnerability to vandalism. Although rips in the plastic covering can be easily repaired with small plastic patches, it seems almost too tempting a target for youthful horseplay to be placed directly on the ground without some protection. A fence is one obvious solution; placing the structure on the roof of another building is another.

A second problem with the inflatable is getting it financed. It would probably be difficult to place a conventional mortgage on such an unconventional structure.

Another way to deinstitutionalize the interior space of school buildings, as well as to save money, is to avoid covering up the structure with hung ceilings and the walls with finished surfaces. In the proposed building for Banneker, wiring, which would otherwise be injected into walls, will be hung like a great web from the ceiling, making outlets available almost anywhere in the school. The educational motive is to encourage students to learn how their building works. This is impossible if its vital functionings are hidden away. This is also the reason why the bare concrete exterior walls won't be finished but left raw, why exposed beams and joints will be painted different bright colors which will be keyed to explain how the building is supported, and why there won't be any acoustical tile ceilings in Banneker.

Another aspect of Banneker's design represents an attempt to overcome the typical school building approach, which produces a fortress-like separation of interior and exterior environments. On the ground floor, stretching along Haverford Avenue, there will be a large glass-enclosed interior street with vending machines, tables, and display areas. Askew hopes this will encourage others in the neighborhood to use the facilities of the school and to identify with its purposes.

Likewise, in one early sketch for the core building of the McDevitt scattered site middle school (also to be located on Haverford Avenue, two blocks to the west of Banneker), a large open court is shown opening onto the street. The proposal calls for this court, measuring 100 by 120 feet, to be roofed, lit at night, and heated with radiant lamps. The court will be a place to sit, play basketball, or hang displays. Its primary intent would be to provide an improved physical environment for an extension of the spontaneous street life that already exists, thereby intimately connecting the school to the street and the people of the neighborhood.

Tell your architect to provide a rich variety of interior spaces for many kinds of learning situations.

To design interiors in such a way that, in some sense, they echo or open out into the street.

To design your school so that children can un-

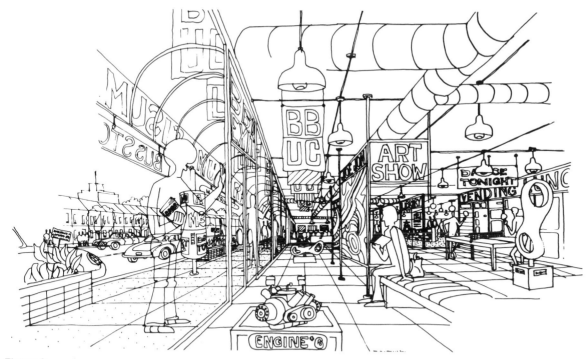

Figure 9
An all-year outdoor space is proposed for the Core build-
ing of the McDevitt Middle School.

Figure 10
The linear ground-floor lobby of the Banneker Center will
extend the adjacent street into the building.

derstand it: how people as well heat, electricity, and water flow through it, and how it is held up.

The Exterior Environment

The two examples which conclude the previous section provide an introduction to this discussion of the ways in which neighborhood school facilities can have a more positive influence on the surrounding physical environment. The central theme in this discussion revolves around the street and the way in which schools and streets can interact. In the previous examples, Banneker and McDevitt achieve this interaction by echoing the street and by providing an interior–exterior environment for street life. A third example of the same general approach is illustrated by a proposal which was developed by the staff and students of the mini-school several years ago. Their proposal was to close a small residential street and roof it with a glass dome. The houses on each side were to be used as classroom and laboratory space, and the covered street as a commons where students could meet and work on special projects, and where the public could view the work of the school.

In the examples discussed below, the interaction between buildings and streets takes another form, through the use of banners and graphics. In some cases these are purely decorative—broadcasting the message that education can be fun and advertising the fact that the physical environment is improving; in other cases, particular information is being transmitted.

The design for the facade of the expansion of the YGS Infant Day Care Center attempts to create a dialogue between the street and the school. A low concrete wall running between the pavement and the porch will be punctured with holes for children to look through. Correspondingly, large colorful lettering, spelling DAY CARE CENTER and stretching along the exterior of the porch below the railing, will be punctured here and there with little windows, so the children inside can peek out to the children on the pavement peeking in. In front of the wall will be little variously shaped hunks of concrete designed for climbing.

The play lot behind the center is designed with rugged materials, mostly telephone poles; it's intended for older neighborhood children as well

Figure 11
The Infant Day-Care Center will have punctured wall between street and building—creating a dialogue between the street and school.

Figure 12
The playlot behind the Day Care Center is intended for other neighborhood children as well as for the younger children of the center itself.

as for the younger children of the center itself. Mrs. Stokes, the director, likes this idea, since it allows all neighborhood kids to become involved, if only peripherally, in the Infant Day Care Center's activities.

The mural on the side of the Children's School (designed by Steven Isenour) is called a supergraphic; it not only boldly identifies the school but, in a sense, multiplies the effect of a rather minor rehab job with bright colors that can be seen from three blocks away. "It is clear that the city gives the neighborhood less than the needed maintenance," says Ronald Beckman, a consultant to this report. "These rebuilt efforts should stand as islands in the mess, until enough of them join together to leave the clutter as an exception." Successes, Beckman is saying, especially when they are scarce, should be capitalized and underlined.

"The result," he says, "is a feeling that things are being done."

Banneker's facade will be a constantly changing display. Student art will be displayed on removable plywood panels, as will announcements of community news, maps, pictures of neighborhood heroes, quotes from students' poetry. The second and third stories of the facade will also be decorated with flags, banners, balloons, and a mural depicting the life of Benjamin Banneker, an eighteenth-century black mathematician who many believe was the principal planner of Washington, D.C.

If there is a common theme running through all the projects illustrated in this section, it is that of trying to come to terms with rising construction costs and inadequate construction budgets. They all represent an attempt to find a basis for archi-

Figure 13
The broad steps leading to the Children's School inflatable will serve as a stepped plaza for adult sitting and children's play.

Figure 14
A community playlot to be built by neighborhood youths out of telephone poles.

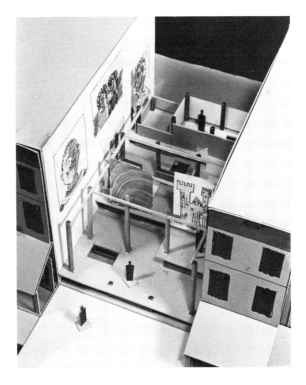

tectural expression in reality, and to create schools which support, rather than oppress, chil-den. "If you can give them confidence and turn them on to learning," says Charles Askew, "the rest is easy."

Thus there is a preference for simple factory-type buildings, which become architecture with the addition of inexpensive two-dimensional ele-ments such as painted graphics, panels of student art, banners designed by the students themselves, giant photographs of the school's football team, and exhibitions of the work going on inside the school.

If there is a philosophy beneath all this, perhaps it's one of seeking a new kind of monumentality; not the kind that architects are generally accused of—"He's trying to build a monument to himself" —but a more human kind of monumentality in which the people who live and work in and around the buildings, not the architects, become the heroes.

Tell your architect to design the exterior of your school to tell the story of what's going on inside.

To use the facade to advertise community im-provement and the message that a new kind of education is happening.

To extend the life of the street into the school and eliminate the usual fortress-like separation between interior and exterior.

THE DEVELOPMENT PROCESS

The physical development of school buildings is time-consuming and expensive. Public school systems spend a good portion of their annual bud-gets paying interest and principal costs on physical plant and paying the staff that administers the con-struction and management program.

Too often, groups involved in educational proj-ects attempt to alter this development process or to develop their own facilities without a full appreciation of the complexities or costs involved. Groups can easily lose sight of the fact that ad-vocating educational changes is very different from organizing, funding, building, and administering a school. Once a group has decided that it does want to operate its own program, it assumes re-sponsibility for providing a suitable building for it, and the implications of that responsibility should be thoroughly understood from the start.

The seven schools represent alternatives to the traditional design and ownership of public school facilities. The process by which some of the seven came into being differs greatly from the usual situa-tion, in which the Board of Education controls all phases of physical development. Some of the al-ternatives chosen by the seven schools have proved to be successful innovations, chosen to fulfill program objectives; others were less suc-cessful. Most of the problems encountered by these schools were the result of inexperience with the complexities of the development process, ad-ministrative short-sightedness, or the circum-stances surrounding the creation of the school.

As an example of this latter type, the mini-school was supposed to have had two renovated houses to accommodate its students. It settled for an aban-doned factory with unacceptable noise characteris-tics and an ugly, undifferentiated interior space. Poor planning was primarily responsible for the physical environment which contributed, in its own way, to the school's failure. The staff of the mini-school failed to decide what, at a minimum, the building had to provide for the students. They also failed to allow enough time or money to have the building ready by the time the students arrived.

The mini-school was unusual because, for better or worse, the school district left it completely to its own devices. The mini-school never had to satisfy, in advance, the stringent physical require-ments for school buildings. Once the school was open, however, visits by the municipal building inspectors became a common feature of administrative life; the mini-school never managed to satisfy the code requirements.

Of the seven schools, the YGS Infant Day Care

Center and the Mantua–Powelton Children's School are good examples of schools for which small scale and modest design have been a definite advantage. The facilities meet the minimum health and safety standards of the city, and the minimum space standards of the state and the Board of Education. Meeting these requirements and organizing the development program remained entirely the responsibility of the community groups which initiated the programs.

Of the two, the YGS Infant Day Care Center had the greater obstacles to overcome. In addition to resistance from the state Department of Public Welfare to the concept of group care for infants, YGS had to overcome its own inexperience with the development process, which requires the coordination of architects, contractors, banks, private funding agencies, and government authorities.

Well before the state had agreed to fund the operating budget, YGS decided to undertake renovation of the facility. The group had raised some $13,000 from alumnae of the University of Pennsylvania and had hired a small builder to renovate the structure, using local gang members as part of the labor force. Shortly thereafter the builder went bankrupt, leaving the job one third complete. YGS took over the builder's payroll and promoted the lead carpenter on the job to foreman. Another $20,000 brought the building to partial completion.

At about this time the YGS Building Foundation was organized to coordinate development projects in which YGS had an interest. It started with assets of $15,000 in cash and a $75,000 line of credit with a local bank. The foundation's first project was to complete the Infant Day Care Center, which by this time had been under construction for nearly one year. The foundation hired a better qualified contractor and spent $15,000 to complete the building. It was dedicated in May 1970 and finally occupied by the Infant Day Care Center in September 1970.

In order to replenish its exhausted cash, the foundation negotiated a fifteen-year mortgage with a mutual savings bank. The mortgage was not approved until all construction was complete and the state had finally signed the operating contract.

Inevitably, the poorly organized construction program has troubled the operation of the center. The plumber incorrectly connected the toilets to the hot water supply, with predictably unfortunate results. Torrential rains in the summer of 1970 caused the roof to leak excessively; the center had to be closed for several weeks for repairs. Minor physical problems constantly tax the patience of staff and the resources of the budget.

To complete the troubled story, the state payments have consistently been late, causing delinquencies in the mortgage payments, which in their turn have made it more difficult to finance the expansion program.

In many direct ways the Mantua–Powelton Children's School benefited from the mistakes that plagued the Infant Day Care Center. The Powelton–Mantua Educational Fund hired the YGS Building Foundation to act as project manager. The foundation negotiated a realistic construction price with a reasonably able contractor, and itself guaranteed sufficient funds to permit quick completion of construction. The foundation also negotiated the permanent mortgage with the same savings bank that had financed the Infant Day Care Center.

The educational fund ran into difficulties negotiating its financial arrangements with the Board of Education and requested that the YGS Building Foundation proceed with construction, even though a permanent loan was not assured. As with the Infant Day Care Center, the organizers reasoned that a completed building was a more compelling argument than a roll of architectural drawings.

The Fund had $10,000 of its own funds, Mrs. Britton Chance provided $11,000, and the YGS Building Foundation guaranteed $18,000 in short-term loans. Construction began in July 1970, and was substantially completed in October 1970.

The Board of Education agreed to lease the building from the educational fund for five years at an annual rent of $7,500 to finance the lease. The board used funds available in its ordinary budget category of "leased space." Legally, the educational fund is a landlord, the school board is a tenant, and the Children's School is an annex to the nearby Powel Elementary School. This arrangement is a good example of how an unusual project can get funding through already existing procedures of the school board.

Both the Infant Day Care Center and the Children's School demonstrate that groups who undertake their own development programs should expect to invest a great deal of time and to risk what, for a small group, can be a sizable amount of money. In addition, groups who undertake physical development risk their overall credibility in an enterprise where even experienced builders have difficulty surviving.

Despite these pitfalls, private development of the school building has some definite advantages. It places site selection and design in the hands of those planning the innovative program. Private development can produce buildings on a more "human" scale. This is a real virtue in buildings meant to serve young children. Completing the Infant Day Care Center and the Children's School gave people involved a real sense of having improved the opportunities for their children to learn. In cases where institutional resistance to change is high, a completed facility may be a compelling argument for a group to advance.

The Banneker Urban Center has taken the spirit of private development much further than either the Infant Day Care Center or the Children's School. The planned facility, which is intended to be financed with federal grant funds, is to be a multipurpose center whose ultimate cost, including land, could exceed $1,000,000.

In order to quality for federal Multi-Purpose Neighborhood Facilities funding, a group must demonstrate that its facility will serve a variety of community needs. In addition to space for the Banneker School, the plan is for the Banneker Center to house a branch library, medical service, and facilities for adult education. If approved, the Neighborhood Facilities grant will reduce Banneker's capital debt by two thirds. Groups considering such an ambitious facility should contact their local HUD office for information on project criteria. The development period could easily consume three years.

The development of facilities for the McDevitt Middle School and Walnut Center remained primarily the responsibility of the Philadelphia School District. In the case of the Walnut Center, the University of Pennsylvania and the school district made the arrangements for financing the building and hired the architect; the community organizations in the area had little to do with the planning process. But the decision to build a new Walnut Center was the result of pressure and threats by outspoken parents of children enrolled in the school. Compared to other public school facilities the Walnut Center is quite small.

The ultimate financial arrangement for the Walnut Center is quite similar to the arrangement made with the Powelton–Mantua Educational Fund for the Children's School. The facility for the Walnut Center is owned by a private group, in this case the University of Pennsylvania, which leases space to the Board of Education. The board operates the program and pays rent.

In contrast to this, the West Philadelphia Community Free School buildings were purchased and renovated by the school district, but were picked by the Free School staff with the assistance of the staff of the university's Office of Community Affairs.

The McDevitt Middle School represents by far the largest capital expense of any of the seven schools. It will cost in excess of $6,000,000. Strong community pressure stopped the planning of this school which was originally to be built as a typical middle school housing 1,600 students in a single building. By sheer insistence, community groups involved have gained a voice in the development process.

Unlike Banneker or the Infant Day Care Center or, indeed, any of the other six schools, McDevitt had an identity before any neighborhood groups became involved with it. For a good while McDevitt had been part of the school district's long-term capital program. Community pressure forced them to abandon the original one-site concept in favor of the scattered approach discussed earlier. The community groups which became involved in the planning insisted that issues such as gang territories and neighborhood boundaries should be given weight in selecting sites, and that the sites themselves should be scattered over a wider area.

Although delayed by the current moratorium on the building of new schools in Philadelphia, planning for McDevitt has advanced to the point at which sites are now being acquired.

While it is difficult to generalize about the issues of physical development which are illuminated by the experiences of these seven schools, we nevertheless feel that the following represents sound advice for any group planning to become involved in the development process.

1. Before making any commitments for land or buildings, define your educational objectives; then seek professional advice from an architect (experienced in low-budget projects) on the most economical kind of space within which to achieve these objectives.
2. Decide if your objectives can be met by influencing and modifying existing programs rather than beginning a new one.
3. Find out if your local school district is legally able to lease space. If so, this may be the most expedient way to obtain operating money.
4. Find out about the availability of mortgage financing. Savings banks are possible candidates for long-term mortgage funding if some stable source of income can be identified. School district leases are ideal for this purpose.

AFTERTHOUGHTS

In the midst of an overcrowded and increasingly obsolete educational system, these seven schools seem small and insignificant. The incredible effort required to bring them into existence, the continuing problems of keeping them going, and the sheer luck which separates some of them from the dozens of projects which never made it make it clear that even under the most favorable circumstances only a limited number of innovative projects can survive. Ultimately, reform of public education will have to come from within the system itself, because ultimately that is where the responsibility for public education rests and where the financial resources to make it work are to be found.

Our experience has made us very aware of the complexities involved in changing any single element of the system of public education, so it is not our intent to conclude with simplistic proposals for major reform, but only to summarize some personal observations about our experience and suggest the usefulness of this story for others.

Our major conclusions concern decentralized school facilities and decentralized control. On the question of school buildings, we are convinced that decentralized schools in smaller structures for fewer students can begin to establish the physical and psychological conditions for an improved educational environment in the inner city. In such a situation a different form of personal relationship becomes possible: between teachers and administrators, between teachers and students, and among students. If Askew is right and self-confidence is a prerequisite for learning, then we are convinced that the physical environment of the school is directly related to a child's ability to achieve this confidence. A school designed to allow this confidence to be expressed by manipulating and changing the building itself becomes a natural extension of the process of learning.

A second conclusion concerns community control and decision making and is probably the most complex of all the repeating themes running through this report. We have come to see it as a false slogan, overused, oversimplified, and overgeneralized, usually having little to do with education or children.

Our feelings are similar to those of Dr. Shedd, who came to Philadelphia full of bold concepts for turning the schools over to the communities. In those days we shared his optimism, but several years later it seems clear that the most successful experiments have been those based on a concept of shared control and responsibility, rather than exclusive control by a community group.

The success of community control is largely dependent upon a rare breed of administrators and educators, working within and outside the community, gifted people with unique vision, understanding, technical expertise, and patience.

The three forms which the concept of community control takes in the seven schools range from an explicit contractual relationship (Banneker, Infant Day Care Center) to a somewhat more ambiguous relationship (Children's School, Free School, McDevitt, Walnut Center) to the one example of total community control, the mini-school. It's probably not fair to draw conclusions from the fact that of the seven, only the mini-school is now out of business—unfair because in all cases these schools depend on outside resources for survival, and ultimately this means some form of shared control.

In our experience the least successful groups are those which have insisted on rigid definitions of powers. In contrast, those that have been able to respond to circumstances in a more flexible way have done much better. Leaving the situation a little ambiguous at the beginning often works to everyone's advantage, since it's impossible to anticipate the problems of running a school before you start.

Regarding innovative educational programs for the inner city, our experience has not led us to definite conclusions; only that there is an obvious conflict between the ideas of young white graduates of schools of education, anxious to reject the middle-class values of their parents, and the objectives of black community leaders, who want schools that prepare their children for the so-called mainstream of American life.

Finally, it's our conclusion that the most overlooked aspect of the problem of making a school work is that of administration. It's a rare individual that combines the necessary talents to make a school work in the midst of all the confusion and pressures surrounding the creation of a new kind of institution.

If all these observations add up to a conclusion, it is that experimental projects like the ones described in this report ought to be possible within the system of public education and not forced to exist as outside experiments. Any major reform of the system should accommodate and encourage the decentralized approach which these schools represent. Unless this occurs, schools like these will continue to exist as a handful of isolated experiments about which reports like this are written but which, in the end, have an effect on the lives of very few.

OUTDOOR PLAY–
LEARNING ENVIRONMENTS

Although the alternative schools proposed in the previous section overcome many of the institutional limitations of existing schools, most of them still exhibit what has been called the "invariant structure of the school." According to Ivan Illich, this hidden structure

constitutes a course of instruction that stays forever beyond the control of the teacher or of his school board . . . The hidden curriculum is always the same regardless of school or place. It requires all children of a certain age to assemble in groups of about 30, under the authority of a certified teacher, for some 500 to 1000 or more hours each year. It doesn't matter whether the curriculum is designed to teach the principles of fascism, liberalism, Catholicism or socialism . . . It makes no difference whether the teacher is authoritarian or permissive, whether he imposes his own creed or teaches the students to think for themselves. What is important is that students learn that education is valuable when it is acquired in the school through a graded process of consumption; that the degree of success the individual will enjoy in society depends on the amount of learning he consumes; and that learning about the world is more valuable than learning from the world.

It must be clearly understood that the hidden curriculum translates learning from an activity into a commodity—for which the school monopolizes the market. In all countries knowledge is regarded as the first necessity for survival, but also as a form of currency more liquid than rubles or dollars. We have become accustomed, through Karl Marx's writings, to speak about the alienation of the worker from his work in a class society. We must now recognize the estrangement of man from his learning when it becomes the product of a service profession and he becomes the consumer.[1]

While alternative schools can move us in the direction of a "deschooled society," they cannot, by definition, get us there. Translating the attitudes of open education into classroom practices that allow the child to become an active participant in his own learning rather than a passive recipient of required facts is also a step toward the Illich–Reimer ideal society. Similarly, the movement toward decentralization and community control of educational institutions begins to restore power to people so that they can begin to shape their own lives. These changes, so well illustrated in both Parts One and Two of this volume, are necessary precursors to the radical changes implied by the notion of a deschooled society. Yet they still fail to escape the invariant structure of schools as institutions which are the "gateways" to the benefits of our technological society.

Of course the changes called for by Illich and Reimer are likely to remain unfulfilled without still more fundamental changes in our entire social system. For such a cultural revolution to occur it would be necessary to undermine the technocratic ethos: the prevailing belief that all the ingredients of human happiness can be identified, produced, and delivered by benevolent institutions informed and guided by professional experts. Thus, for the foreseeable future the question still remains: What are we to do now? How can knowledge and learning increasingly become the result of individual initiative rather than the product of an "institutional enterprise or as the fulfillment of institutional objectives"?

This is the question that is addressed by the remaining papers in Part Two. In this section, which focuses on neighborhood scale alternatives for nonschool learning environments, there is an attempt to provide learning options which are not institutionally mediated. In these four papers it is assumed that (1) children learn whenever and wherever they enjoy what they are doing, (2) they are naturally curious and will attempt to give meaning to whatever situation they encounter, and (3) meaningful learning takes place in settings that allow the child to actively manipulate the environment in his own way, in his own time, and for his own ends. The critical difference between these alternatives and those discussed in Part One and the first section of Part Two is that such learning is not undertaken for any institutional purposes nor is it certified as the product of any institutional process.

For those who have come to accept the messages of the hidden curriculum of schooling, i.e.,

that the only education that is valuable is acquired in school and that learning about the world (formal education) is more valuable than learning from the world (incidental learning or just living), it is difficult to accept that play is indeed a form of learning. Yet the importance of play in children's intellectual, emotional, and physical growth is now becoming generally accepted.

Although the definition of play is greatly disputed, there is a growing body of evidence that such activities as exploration of the local environment, interaction with other children in both formal and informal situations, and the testing of physical and mental skills against physical obstacles—activities often identified as play—are essential for the healthy development of every human being.[2]

It is also clear that the child makes little distinction between these activities and those activities which adults consider work, and that the child will play whenever and wherever he is free to do so—not just in special adult-designated and supervised areas called playgrounds.

Unfortunately, this need to be able to move about freely and play in the total environment, especially within close proximity of home, has been increasingly frustrated by the process of urbanization and suburbanization brought by the industrial revolution. The child's world is increasingly reduced both in the size and diversity of settings. In the heavily populated urban centers automobile traffic and the decreasing availability of open space conspire to limit the child's free exploration of his neighborhood environment. Combined with overcrowding in the home and related social problems such as working mothers, fatherless households, and intolerance by neighbors of the presence of children and the noise they create, it is clear that the urban child's freedom is severely restricted. The child in the suburb, who is dependent on adults and the automobile for access to playgrounds, stores, movie theaters, and other meaningful settings, is not very much better off.

Even more than in the case of schools, the possibilities for learning provided by the designed environment are critical to out-of-school and out-of-house play–learning options. Merely improving the environment of the school will make little difference to the total growth and development of the child if the home-based environment to which he returns does not reinforce and enrich the opportunities for self-directed learning.

An adventure playground, as described by Clare Cooper, is both a place and a neighborhood-based program of play activities which allow children to build, tear down, and rebuild their own play environment with a minimum of adult supervision to ensure safety. Reviewing the history of this playground concept in Scandinavia and England, Cooper notes that adventure playgrounds have so far failed to gain widespread acceptance in the United States. However, the evidence in favor of such an alternative play–learning environment suggests that we may begin to see increased acceptance in the years to come, especially in high-density urban neighborhoods.

In this light, the article by Mayer Spivack provides some perspective on the kinds of problems that can be anticipated, not from the children but from adults—both parents and neighbors. Quite unintentionally, it seems, Spivack became a play leader while he was engaged in constructing a playground in a white working-class neighborhood in Boston. By joint agreement with the children the process of planning and constructing this facility became the product, leading Spivack to observe that "when a child makes something, or attempts to change his environment, he becomes invested in the object and in his work on it." Unfortunately, the adults in the neighborhood were not similarly involved in this process of creating and did not share the children's attachment to the effort. The result of this conflict in environmental values raises many issues about the nature of play and childhood, the environmental needs of inner-city children, and the conflict between adult and child perceptions of what is good and desirable. It points out the need for continuity and cooperation between the major socializing agents in the child's life—the school, the peer group, the family, and the neighborhood community. Any comprehensive attempt to provide real learning options must synthesize these often-competing viewpoints.

According to Simon Nicholson, "Children learn most readily and easily in a laboratory-type environment where they can experiment, enjoy, and find out things for themselves." Although this idea is increasingly accepted by advocates of open education in the schools, it is clear that our culture and traditional education lead us to believe otherwise. Nicholson reviews recent developments in such fields as art, education, architecture, and planning. He states that trends in these diverse areas can be viewed as different facets of a growing movement toward the kind of world in which everyone, both adults and children, can interact creatively with the total environment. To speed up this process, Nicholson closes with a proposal based on his principle of "loose parts," which would begin by addressing the learning needs of children wherever they are to be found.

One of these suggestions is to make more imaginative use of the often sterile asphalt area known as the public school playground. Not only are these places used by children while they are in school, but they are at least available for intensive use by neighborhood children in the evenings and on the weekends. They are, at present, greatly underutilized community open spaces. Robin Moore describes a project in which one such schoolyard was converted into a resource-rich play–learning environment. Unlike the case study by Mayer Spivack, all the participants—parents, teachers, and children—as well as students and designers from a nearby university, were involved as both planners and users of the yard. Although this particular effort grew out of an environmental education orientation in the school and is directly related to the school-based program, Moore views the yard as "a vehicle for the development of an environmental education process within the total school–community." From the point of view of an "action–research–designer–manager," Moore shares his thoughts about "the possibilities of environmental learning with and without the help of adults." He quite correctly believes that learning and play can and should happen all the time and everywhere that children are—"in the streets, shopping centers, factories, parks of our cities." To realize this aim it is clear that the total physical environment must be redesigned to restore free and safe access to the diverse resources of the urban environment. However, the Washington Environmental Yard seems to be a good beginning.

NOTES AND REFERENCES

1. Ivan Illich, "The Alternative to Schooling," in *Restructuring American Education: Innovations and Alternatives*, Ray C. Rist (ed.), New Brunswick, N.J.: Transaction Books, 1972, p. 259 (first published in *Saturday Review*, June 19, 1971). See also Alan Gartner, Colin Greer, and Frank Riessman (eds.), *After Deschooling, What?*, New York: Harper & Row, Publishers, 1973.
2. See, for example, the articles from Piaget, Froebel, and Isaacs in *The Open Classroom Reader*, Charles Silberman (ed.), New York: Random House, Inc.—Vintage Books, 1973. Two very good books on the nature and meaning of play are R. E. Herron and Brian Sutton-Smith (eds.), *Child's Play*, New York: John Wiley & Sons, Inc., 1971 and Susanna Millar, *The Psychology of Play*, Baltimore, Md.: Penguin Books, Inc., 1968.

Adventure Playgrounds*

Clare C. Cooper

Most people, talking of their happiest childhood experiences, will describe places that were wild, overgrown, mysterious, hidden from adult eyes; trees where they built houses, undergrowth where they created smugglers' passages, dumps where they could find scraps of wood and empty boxes. Rarely if ever will their treasured memories revolve around schoolyards or parks or other formal places provided for play.

Even systematic research attempts to get people to recall what they remember of the landscapes of their youth have come up with the same results; play was happiest and long-remembered in an unstructured, wild environment where fantasy, imagination and spontaneity were given free rein.[1] In an urban environment where every space is rapidly being planned, zoned, paved over, tidied up, designed, and ordered, it is imperative that children be reunited with that lost landscape of spontaneity.

*Reprinted from *Landscape Architecture,* Oct. 1970.

An adventure playground is a recreational space where children are permitted and encouraged to build their own play environment under adult supervision. The ground surface is left in its natural state. Building materials such as wood, cardboard boxes, pipes, planks, bricks, and rope are provided for the children to work with. The atmosphere is one in which children are encouraged to "do their thing" with minimum interference from adults, but with adequate supervision to ensure safety. There is no expanse of asphalt, no fixed equipment, no organized program. But there are endless opportunities to engage in creative play and adventure— to build houses, plant gardens, dig tunnels, hang rope swings from the trees.

DEVELOPMENT OF THE ADVENTURE-PLAYGROUND CONCEPT

Although children have been engaging in such activities for generations in the yards of their homes, in the countryside, or in vacant lots in the city, it is only in the last two decades that particular supervised locales for this activity have begun to be provided in the city. And it is probably only in the last few decades with increasing urbanization that the *need* for such playgrounds has become particularly crucial.

In the early 1930s a Danish landscape architect, C. T. Sorenson, who had designed many conventional playgrounds, noticed that children seemed to enjoy playing with the construction materials on the playground sites after workmen had left. In fact, they seemed to gain more pleasure from this than from playing on the completed playground. This gave him the idea for a different kind of play area, and in 1931 he suggested laying out a site where children could create their own playground using surplus building materials.

As in the case of most innovative ideas, there was a delay of some years before the first such playground came into existence. That the first experiment took place in a country not only at war, but also occupied by enemy troops, is perhaps some indication of the strength of the idea and the persistence of its first proponents.

In 1943 the Workers Cooperative Housing Association in the Copenhagen suburb of Emdrup laid out the first adventure playground. It was on a grassy site, 7,000 square yards in size, and surrounded by a 6-foot earthen bank. Despite early difficulties, the playground survived and prospered and is still visited by an average 200 children daily.

The success of Emdrup prompted the opening of a similar playground in Stockholm known as "Freetown," and the first experiment in the United States. *McCall's* magazine, impressed with the Scandinavian playgrounds, decided in 1950 to sponsor a demonstration adventure playground in the United States, and selected Minneapolis—with progressive park and school systems—as the setting. The suggestion was received enthusiastically. The Board of Education lent a 1⅓-acre vacant lot beside Edith Cavell grade school; the PTA unanimously approved the experiment; the neighbors

formed a Citizen's Committee to help plan and manage the playground; members of a local teamsters union contributed time to erect a fence around the site; the City's Welfare Department lent a trailer for a toolroom and office; and a committee of educators, social workers, psychiatrists, and city administrators was formed to undertake a long-range evaluation of the experiment.

All the ingredients for a successful adventure playground were present, and indeed "The Yard," as it became known, was an enormous success. Any child between eight and sixteen could come to the playground and stake out a lot measuring 10 by 16 feet, on which to build a house, dig a tunnel, or do anything else within reasonable safety limits. To boys, the shacks were generally forts; to girls they were homes, and after construction, the business of decoration, furnishing, and "visiting" began.

Because they're doing it for themselves, they figure out problems of design and construction which would probably floor them if presented in school as arithmetic. They're making most of mankind's great discoveries all over again . . . "That's a right-angle triangle," one of the boys told Jim, pointing to his gable roof. "I invented it."

After a windstorm one day, the children hurried back to the playground to see how their shacks were standing up . . . "A neighbor of ours lost half the shingles off his garage," said Ronny Randlo, aged eleven. "Look at my fort—not a board missing."[2]

The Yard was an undoubted success, but was only a one year experiment; despite considerable publicity, it seems not to have been copied elsewhere in the United States.

Meanwhile in Europe, the adventure playground idea was being taken up with enthusiasm in London where numerous bombed sites offered ideal rough locations for such playgrounds. The first recorded playground was in Camberwell, London, in 1948; other playgrounds followed in Liverpool, Bristol, Grimsby, London, and in some of the new towns. By 1962, the concept had become so well known and the demand for information so insistent that a

London Adventure Playgrounds Association was set up to provide new playgrounds with information on sites, fencing, materials, leaders' salaries, insurance, etc.

At the present time, the Greater London Council is providing sites for adventure playgrounds in all its new public housing projects, and a school system in the North of England is providing a small such playground in each of its new grade schools.

Unfortunately, the United States, in its acceptance and adoption of this innovation, is where Denmark was in the 1940s and England in the early 1950s. After the successful Minneapolis playground of 1950, there seems to have been little progress. A British graduate student at the Massachusetts Institute of Technology established a successful playground with an adventure component in a housing project in Lower Roxbury, Massachusetts, in 1966. It was a great success and survived until very recently when the site was needed for an urban renewal project.[3]

A successful adventure playground was run for several weeks on a Berkeley, California, school-yard in 1967, but this was only a short-term experiment. An adventure playground established by People Pledged for Community Progress on a 100 by 60-foot vacant lot in Richmond, California, operated for just over a year in 1969–1970. This latter example indicates that city authorities and neighbors *can* be persuaded to approve innovative ideas, and insurance companies *will* provide the necessary accident insurance.[4] The need now is for more publicity and understanding of the idea, more practical information about past experience.

THE OBJECTIVE OF AN ADVENTURE PLAYGROUND

One can look at the objectives of the adventure playground from two viewpoints. In the more limited, negative sense, one could argue that children —being naturally inquisitive and adventurous—

will inevitably seek out places where they can dig, build, destroy, light fires, and dam streams, and our best way of controlling such activity in an urban area is to provide places where it can take place under reasonably safe conditions. In a more positive sense, one could argue that the city child, deprived of the opportunities afforded the country child to play in woods, trees, fields, and farmyards, is being deprived in a much deeper, psychological sense of the ability to learn through experimenting in these kinds of activities, and it is imperative that we provide an urban equivalent of rural play.

The urban child is cut off from all natural life, from growth of plant and tree, from water, stream, or river, from sand on the seashore. Not surprisingly when he does get into the country he thinks of birds as targets for catapults and trees as things to be hacked down for firewood. If he finds crabs in a rock pool it will not be long before he is stoning them to death. The urban child is psychologically disoriented, cut off from man's natural roots, seldom called upon to battle with the elements or to learn to cooperate with nature. This is a deep sickness which no playground movement can as yet hope to cure. But it can make a beginning . . .[5]

There is evidence to suggest that the greater the *variety* of experience of a child in his formative years, the more rapid the development of his cognitive skills. Our present arrangements for supplying areas for play provide little variety and rarely—if ever—provide the child with the experience of manipulating and experimenting with the physical environment.

It has been suggested that play is compounded of four major elements: physical development, fantasy, imitation, and adventure.[6] The blacktopped play yard with fixed equipment adequately fulfills the need for play as physical coordination, as do sports programs run by the schools and recreation departments. Fantasy may be indulged in anywhere—in the suburban backyard, in front of the TV, in the schoolroom, in the automobile.

But opportunities to imitate the behavior of adults such as building "dens" and "houses," or for adventure in the form of climbing, building, tunnelling and fire lighting, are practically nonexistent for the urban child.[7] It is for this reason that the opportunities to play on an adventure playground are felt to be of particular, maybe even crucial, importance to the child growing up in the city.

We think nothing of busing hundreds of children to a museum to see a piece of moon rock, but shudder at the thought of providing them with a vacant lot and some wood to build themselves "dens." Who is to say which is more important?

MERITS OF AN ADVENTURE PLAYGROUND

Variety of Activities

One of the chief merits of an adventure playground is the great variety of activities—and consequently of age and interest groups—it can absorb. Perhaps the following list of activity observations, made on a London adventure playground by the author on a warm, Saturday afternoon in September 1967, can illustrate better than any subjective description the extent of that variety—not only the variety of things being done, but also of ages and group sizes.[8]

The fact that all these activities can go on amicably within a very small site (about 150 by 120 feet) suggests that we reconsider our penchant for age-segregated play areas. These observations also illustrate a point noted in a recent study of outdoor play, notably, that a considerable proportion of children's playing time is spent in watching others.[9]

Girl (5) rolling tire, alone.
Three boys (10) bouncing on roof of "house" to break it, two others watching.
Boy (6), alone, filling can with water from puddle and emptying over log.
Three boys (14) playing catch with ball, up and down steps.
Two boys (16) playing Ping-Pong; three others watching.
Three boys (8) climbing rope-climbing net together.
Three boys (18) sitting and talking.

Two girls (17) sitting and talking and watching three boys.
Two boys (7) standing on ladder and watching bonfire.
Eight boys and girls (7 to 9) playing softball; two girls (7) watching.
Girl (7) alone, swinging on rope.
Two boys (11) taking turns swinging on rope.
Six boys (15 to 17) taking turns on pulley ride which runs across playground; two boys (5) watching.
Two boys (18) playing cards on roof of playground building; six others watching.
Three boys (8) sitting on roof of building watching activity.
Girl (6) on rope swing being pushed by boy (9).
Boy (11) balancing on wooden beam.
Four boys and girls (7 to 8) climbing onto roof of "house" and jumping off.
Five boys (16 to 18) sitting on steps and talking.
Girl (6) dragging old chair up slope.
Boy (16) swinging on rope; boy (6) watching him from roof of "house."
Two boys (7) collecting water in cans from tap on building and pouring down concrete slope.
Girl (5) swinging alone in rubber tire.
Boy (8) talking to two male leaders by bonfire.
Two girls (14) sitting on steps, smoking and talking.
Four girls and boys (6 to 8) sliding down slide from roof of building to playground.
Two boys (12) banging brick on roof of "house," then sawing off plank; two boys (9) watching.
Male leader listening at door of shed where steel-drumband is practicing.
Boy (9) pushing barrel up concrete slope, lets roll down, leaves it, and climbs wooden "tower."
Four boys (10) playing on pulley ride, waiting turns.
Two boys (8) swinging together on end of rope.
Boy (7) brushing dust from ground into fire.
Girl (6) digging alone in sand.
Boy (17) climbing to top of rope net and down other side, watched by two other boys, same age.
Four boys (14 to 16) standing at door of shed listening to band.

Two girls (12 to 14) standing talking to female play
leader.

Boy (16) picks old toy dog on wheels off rubbish
pile, pushes along on wheels, picks up, flings
into fire.

Boys (5) standing tugging at hand of male leader.

Boy (5) digging alone in sand.

Three boys (6) playing on slide.

Two boys (16) taking turns swinging on rope.

Two girls (13) stand leaning on rope net, talking
to male leader.

Two leaders stand watching boy (7) sweeping dirt
into fire.

Boy (7) swinging alone on rope.

Two girls (7 to 9) pulling trolley on track up slope
and then riding down on it.

Boy (7) sitting on log watching softball game.

Boy (9) with shovel, flipping water from puddle into
sand box.

The advantage of this variety of activities within
a small space is that a child can circulate around
the playground finding many different things to do
that interest him; hence the tendency for children
to stay much longer on this kind of playground
than on a playground with fixed equipment. Variety
has a further advantage; with so many things to
do, there is generally something at which any one
child can excel. With our societal emphasis on
competitive sports, it is important to provide a locale where children who do not excel at or enjoy
these activities can find a place. For this reason
such playgrounds have particularly appealed to
children who are loners, or who don't enjoy the
"team spirit" of organized sport.

Not all activity on adventure playgrounds, however, is lone activity. Indeed, the very nature of
building often requires cooperation, and children
who started as "loners" end up as "cooperators."
An account of activities at The Yard in Minneapolis
documents this process:

*When The Yard first opened it was every child for himself.
The initial stockpile of secondhand lumber disappeared like*

*ice on a hot stove. Children helped themselves to all they
could carry . . . Some hoarded tools and supplies in secret
caches. Everybody wanted to build the biggest shack in the
shortest time . . . Highjacking raids were staged on half-
finished shacks. Grumbling and bickering broke out . . . But
on the second day of the great depression most of the youngsters banded together spontaneously for a salvage drive.
Tools and nails came out of hiding . . . Rugged individualists
who had insisted on building alone invited others to join in –
and bring their supplies along . . . New ideas popped up for
joint projects. By the time a fresh supply of lumber arrived, a
community had been born.*[10]

Perhaps one of the most important psychological merits of this form of permissive recreation
is that it provides a complete contrast with that
other institution which structures most of a child's
waking hours—the school.

Most urban children's school experience is that
it is organized, structured, and must of necessity
be largely nonpermissive. But children—like most
healthy human beings—require varied and
opposite experiences to become truly rounded
personalities. Thus the freewheeling, anything
goes atmosphere of an adventure playground
may have significant mental health merits for the
users of our increasingly crowded classrooms,
as the following quotation describing a British
adventure playground suggests.

*The appeal that the playground had for them was the differ-
ence that it presented from the school. As one boy said:
"It's the place I can come and do my mischief." What we
believe he needed, if he was to grow responsibly, was the
experience of being destructive and yet not losing the confidence of a stable adult–the experience which most children
get in a reasonably affectionate home, and which these children lacked. Some might get it at school, but this is chancy
business in classes of over forty, where the nuisance is easier
to suppress than to treat . . . The playground was in fact
complementary to the school. It was an "escape valve" where
many of the children came to let off steam after school. Though
many of the most difficult children on the playground were
also difficult in school, there were others who were well-
behaved, apparently model children in school, yet up to every
kind of mischief while on the playground.*[11]

As well as contrasting with the school environment, the adventure playground provides a locale

where children can engage in that essential element of play largely denied them in the city—the manipulation of the physical environment; for in moving and arranging objects in space, a child unconsciously communicates feelings about himself—a fact which of course forms the basis of most contemporary play therapy. It may be that when a child builds, rearranges, or knocks down a structure in play—whether of toy blocks in his bedroom, or empty crates on a vacant lot—he is symbolically testing his powers to change himself. If we deny children the chance to do this, it may well be that we are depriving them of an essential learning experience on the road toward self-actualization.

Numbers of Children Accommodated

Another merit of the adventure playground is that it tends to attract and absorb the interest of more children per unit of site area than a regular fitted playground. As urban land becomes more valuable, this may be a crucial element in its favor.

Counts have been made at a number of British adventure playgrounds and there is no reason to believe that attendance figures would be much different in American neighborhoods of similar densities.

A ¾-acre adventure playground in a row-house neighborhood of a British town opened in 1955 had a total user group of more than 400 children aged one to sixteen: the chief age group was eight to fourteen. The peak-hour attendance figures in the summer averaged eighty, and the winter figure was approximately forty.[12]

In a working-class moderate-to-high density area of South London, a 1¼-acre playground (Lolland Adventure Playground) attracted up to 250 children at a time on peak summer days.[13]

In a middle-income, single-family and row-house neighborhood in Stevenage New Town, summer vacation counts indicate an average attendance of ninety-five. The maximum and minimum counts of children present at any one time were 305 and 26, respectively. The playground is ⅓ acre.

Those under seven came on foot from as far as ½ mile away, and those in the eight-to-twelve age group (the chief users) often cycled ½ mile or farther to the playground.[14]

Many children bypassed a regular fitted playground that was actually closer to their homes in favor of the more interesting activities on the adventure playground.

These figures, limited though they be, do give some indication of the intensity of use of an adventure playground. They suggest that we should be less concerned about the *amount* of open space we provide for children's play than with what we put *into* that space.

If our job is to provide for people's needs, isn't the presence of 300 children on a ⅓-acre site a greater indication of success than 5 acres of flat grassy lawn with not a soul in sight?

Reduction in Vandalism

Vandalism might be defined as an adult and/or institutional view of deliberate damage, generally though not exclusively inflicted by minors on the property of others. In New York City, the cost of school vandalism alone in 1969 amounted to $6.5 million. The U.S. Office of Education in Washington sets the annual cost of destruction in public schools throughout the country at more than $100 million.[15] In 1967, $100,000 was spent on repairing damage caused by vandals in buses and subways in New York City, $650,000 on damage in public parks and repairs to vandalized phones.[16]

Research into the motivations for vandalism is relatively sparse, but one study suggests that schools with severe vandalism problems tended to be those where the students felt frustrated and alienated, where relationships between students, teachers, and administrators were poor, and where parents had little involvement in the schools' activities. Teachers attributed boredom, disinterest in school, and peer group pressure as the chief motivations for vandalism; the students themselves rated their prime motivation as boredom.[17]

It has always been hoped by the proponents of adventure playgrounds that a space where children could build—and destroy—in relative freedom from adult interference would lure off the streets some of those children who formerly turned to vandalism as an outlet for their creative—destructive urges. Although few systematic studies have been carried out on the social effects of adventure playgrounds, some evidence suggests that reduction of vandalism may be an additional "payoff" of this form of permissive recreation.

With regard to a playground in Grimsby, England, the Chief of the Fire Department stated that

. . . the area in which the playground is situated is considered a dangerous one, as the children lit fires on the streets and caused accidents . . . Since the playground has been open the Fire Department's chart for that area has been a blank.[18]

A similar report has come more recently (1968) from experience with a playground in a middle-income neighborhood in Stevenage New Town.

. . . the Police and Welfare Departments have expressed their approval of the playground. The police have indicated that the amount of vandalism in the area has been reduced since the playground opened, and the Headmaster of Bandley Primary School which is next to the playground has said that only one window has been broken after school hours and during school holidays since the opening of the Adventure Playground, whereas, prior to the opening of the playground, broken windows were a regular occurrence at this school. There would seem to be some justification for concluding from these facts that the playground is attracting those children who might otherwise cause vandalism.[19]

The only documented U.S. example reported the police as saying that since the opening of an adventure playground in a Minneapolis suburb

. . . we haven't had a call out that way. It used to be a headache, with kids breaking street lamps and picking up stuff from houses under construction to build their shacks along the railroad tracks.[20]

Although the evidence is limited as yet, it would seem reasonable to assume that at least some antisocial activities are forestalled by the attraction of these unconventional playgrounds. As the frustrations of growing up in the city become more acute, it is imperative that we think more seriously about the provision of places, such as adventure playgrounds, where the need to be energetically destructive as well as thoughtfully constructive can be acted out without hindrance.

Community Involvement

The initial adoption of most innovations comes about when one or a number of convinced persons persuade others of the worth of that innovation, and try it out on a small-scale, experimental basis.

It is particularly true of many social innovations that those "one or a number of convinced persons" are private citizens, and that only after some experience with the innovation on a private, volunteer-based arrangement does the City or national bureaucracy begin to take notice. This has certainly been true so far with the adoption of the adventure playground. In every documented case, it has been a group of volunteers—usually parents of the children who will benefit—which has initially banded together to promote the idea to their neighbors, obtain a site, raise funds to pay a leader, and persuade the requisite city authorities of the playground's worth.

For example, in the Stevenage New Town neighborhood of Bandley Hill, it was a group of mothers who persuaded the City to provide them with a site and building, stimulated interest in the innovation, raised funds, and hired a permanent play leader. The playground, now in its third year, is a great success; up to 200 children use it daily in the summer and some 500 local households contribute twenty-five cents a week to a lottery which gives prizes and pays the salary of the play leader.[21]

In some cases, it has been a neighborhood crisis which has precipitated the setting up of the playground. In the low-income West Indian and Irish neighborhood of Notting Hill Gate in London, a minor race riot in the late 1950s initially brought strife and tension to the residents, and subsequently was an impetus for their drawing together in an attempt to improve community relations.

That this was a playground on which neighbors chose to work together is perhaps not altogether surprising. This was a high-density neighborhood with many families sharing dwellings, many small children, poor access to parks or playgrounds, and many dangerous streets. There was thus a need; but a playground project also supplied something else in terms of community organization. It was a fairly simple, visible, tangible facility which all with children could benefit from and about which people from very different backgrounds and political affiliations could agree.

The adventure playground also has three real advantages for voluntary groups. (1) The capital costs are low (see section on needs of an adventure playground); there is little need for site improvement, no equipment to be installed. A group approaching the city for financial assistance has therefore a good selling point; this is probably one of the least expensive (per-site-area) recreation improvements that one could propose. (2) It is an ideal temporary use of vacant land, and if the city authorities are somewhat dubious about its value, they may offer a temporary use permit, and at the end of the period the playground can be removed with little capital loss. (3) The need for supervision on such a playground means that it creates jobs; with numerous federal programs for employing unemployed persons in subprofessional positions, the problem of finding financing for the playleaders need not be an overwhelming burden to either the voluntary group itself, or to the city.[22]

Because this kind of playground is—for the United States at least—a relatively new idea, it may take some persuasive selling in the neighborhood and in the city. This too may be an advantage to the voluntary group in that persuasive selling requires communication, and without communication, there can be no community.

Not only is an adventure-playground project a good one to form an initial rallying point for a neighborhood; the playground itself, because of the probable need for voluntary as well as paid supervisors, and because of the necessity of fund raising to keep it going, may well become a focus of neighborhood involvement long after its successful opening.

In a number of successful British examples, a project which started out as strictly a playground has become far more than just that. In Notting Hill Gate, London, the project was initially a temporary playground on a small vacant lot with a movable building; it was run and paid for by neighborhood volunteers. But as its success became obvious, the local parks department was persuaded to provide a larger, permanent site, money for a permanent playground building, and salaries of the leaders. Children who had played on the earlier playground were now older teenagers; facilities for them were provided within the building (TV, record player, table tennis, etc.), club meetings were held in the evenings, and a group of young Jamaicans among them built their own steel-band practice hut on the playground site. The playground which had originally been intended for eight to fourteen year olds began to be extended to other groups; a separate section was made for the under-fives and the Save the Children Fund provided paid child-care workers to organize a daily drop-in play group for the children of working mothers. The mothers in the neighborhood began to look on the playground as a community center and used the building one evening a week for a Young Wives Club. On other nights they and the teenagers organized a club for the many lonely, elderly people in the neighborhood. Similarly, the role of the leader has been extended; he no longer has to scout the neighborhood for waste materials, or wonder where his next paycheck is coming from, but has become a significant neighborhood figure, part social worker, part probation officer, part therapist, part policeman—and a father figure to innumerable children.

An adventure playground can thus be the nucleus of real community involvement in its planning and initiation, in its running, and in its expansion and adaptation to new demands. For this reason, it is perhaps best that it be run by a volunteer group, and not by a city department. As the playground proves itself, it may be beneficial that the salary of the leader be paid by the city; but it would be advantageous to the neighborhood it serves if the administration of the playground remains in the hands of local parents.

Recreation in Low-Income High-Density Neighborhoods

Although equally suitable as a play environment in any part of the city, the adventure playground has particular merit as a play area in low-income, moderate- to high-density neighborhoods. As stated above, it does not require a large site—even an area formerly occupied by only one or two houses could be large enough; it is an ideal temporary use—say, of some lots awaiting redevelopment; and it creates jobs. There must be at least one fulltime supervisor on the playground at all times, and depending on its size and popularity, the number may rise to five or six. Training need not be elaborate, and the work time (fulltime in the summer, after school during the school year) makes it particularly suitable for high school or college-age students.

These are some pragmatic advantages of the adventure playground in a low-income neighborhood. But it also has social and psychological merits. Where families live at such a density that few have access to private yards, the opportunity

to build, dig, plant seeds, light fires, and take care of pets on an adventure playground offers poorer children some of the learning experiences which middle-class children may enjoy in their own yards, or on family outings to the country. In addition, many low-income black families are female-headed; a trip to the playground can offer the children of such families the needed contact with father surrogates in the form of playground leaders, most of whom tend to be men. In a conversation in the summer of 1969 between the author and a leader of a London adventure playground drawing largely on children from housing projects, the young male leader remarked sheepishly, "I hate to think how many children call me Daddy."

In one British case, where the playground served mostly large, low-income families, a study of some of the regular users revealed:

> . . . *although relationships with the mother appear generally to be good, among over half the children, those with the father were poor, or the father was absent from the family. This reflection certainly adds weight to our general assumption that it was a substitute father that the children sought most of all—albeit unconsciously—from the playground.*[23]

This feature—the presence of adults, particularly men, who can be observed working at playground maintenance, assisting in building projects, and so on—has special merit for all urban children, not just those in low-income neighborhoods. Increasingly in urban residential areas, not only do children never see their own fathers at work, but rarely do they have the opportunity of seeing *any* men working. The fascination for children of men fixing the phone lines or digging a hole in a suburban street is a simple example of the need that children have to observe adults at work.

Low-income and particularly ghetto residents, however, may react negatively to the idea of an adventure playground for a number of reasons.[24] The playground often looks chaotic and untidy, and to some ghetto residents this is too much a reflection of the environment they see all around them. They prefer their children's playgrounds to be instead neat, ordered, tidy, and safe. This is not a universal of ghetto residents; among the few adventure playgrounds that have been established in this country, one was in Lower Roxbury, Massachusetts, and another in West Richmond, California, both in low-income black neighborhoods.

A reaction of one ghetto community group in West Oakland, California, was that the rich, white children in Piedmont (a wealthy community nearby) were the ones who were deprived since poor children are likely to find vacant lots and empty buildings in which to have "adventurous play" even if an official adventure playground is not provided, whereas rich children are stuck with an ordered environment of manicured lawns and trimmed privet hedges. This reaction bears thinking about.

SOME OBJECTIONS TO ADVENTURE PLAYGROUNDS

The chief objections which people are apt to raise to adventure playgrounds are that they are untidy, noisy, and unsafe.

That they are untidy can hardly be denied. Untidy is in the eyes of adults; tidiness is a learned value which most children do not share. Part of the philosophy of such a playground is that it *should* be untidy, flexible, changeable, freewheeling. Describing the early objectives of these playgrounds, an experienced leader has written:

. . . it was to be the workshop of the child. It was to be a place in which he would have the tools and materials to hand; where he could build, destroy and build again; where he could invent and try out, but, perhaps above all, it was to be a place which, without conscience, could be left untidy—like the workshop of the adult world.[25]

Untidiness need not go to excess; most adventure playgrounds have a clean-up time once a week when wood and other materials no longer usable are collected and burned—the resultant bonfire forming another treat often denied the urban child.

The fear of noisiness is rarely borne out in reality. Children absorbed in playing house, or building, or digging tunnels create far less noise than does, for example, a Little League game plus vocal supporters. The kind of solid fence created to screen the playground's untidyness will also generally provide adequate noise-screening.

Another objection is that the playground is potentially dangerous. It is partly this "potential danger" that attracts children; in perceiving the possible hazards, they, like all self-preservative species, are extra cautious in their behavior. True, the site is often rough, structures built by children may be hazardous, tools could be used in a dangerous way—but all available evidence indicates that the children are so absorbed in what they are doing, and so cautious in attempting anything beyond their present capacities, that the accident rate is in fact lower than that on conventional playgrounds with fixed equipment.

. . . in all the ten years' experience [with adventure playgrounds] in the United Kingdom there has been nothing more serious than cuts and bruises, and no parent has ever made a claim. Children are prone to danger whatever they are doing; many fatal accidents occur when they play in the streets amid the traffic, and very serious accidents occur when, because of boredom, they play monkey tricks on the fixed equipment on orthodox playgrounds.[26]

The truth seems to be that, when not offered challenges, children will seemingly use "safe" equipment in a potentially dangerous way to make their own challenges.

Similarly in the Minneapolis playground:

. . . the safety record astonished everybody. After a year of operation, injuries consist of some banged thumbs, small cuts and bruises for the entire involvement of over 200 children. No child has ever used a tool to hit another person.[27]

On a Liverpool adventure playground incorporating a hard-surface section with regular equipment, it was reported:

Statistically the slide appeared to be the highest risk while the permanent ironwork equipment generally produced more accidents than the junk and scrap materials in the Adventure Playground proper.[28]

The London Adventure Playgrounds Association—an organization set up in 1962 to publicize and advise on the concept—advises new playgrounds to take out the following forms of insurance: public liability (third party risk); employers' liability; burglary, house-breaking, and fire insurance. Recent experience in opening such a playground in Richmond, California, has indicated that U.S. insurance companies *are* willing to insure such playgrounds.

The American legal profession has instilled into public officials and citizens such a fear of being sued that this is the first objection brought up when discussing the concept. But if we can withdraw from our official roles as "Parks Director" or "school principal" and look at the community-wide costs and benefits of this form of recreation, we can perhaps get this "suing complex" into perspective, and ask ourselves some pertinent questions. Which is better for the community—a playground where children can experience challenge and excitement under reasonable supervision, or the courting of these necessary ingredients of life in busy streets and empty buildings? Which costs the community more—an occasional law suit for injury on a playground or loss of life and limb on neighborhood streets? Which financial "burden" would the community rather bear— the salary of a playleader on an adventure playground or the costs of repairing damage to institutional buildings by juvenile vandals who have nothing more interesting to do? Unless we learn to provide for children's natural appetites for excitement, adventure, and danger, we will face the antisocial results of the thwarting of these appetites.

We accept, and even applaud, the expansion of such exhilarating, challenging and danger-courting adult sports as skydiving, sailing, surfing, skiing, and drag racing, and yet are surprised and hurt when our children desert the costly designed playgrounds provided for their leisure, and seek enjoyment on waste land, abandoned quarries, parking lots, and half-built freeways.

We should learn from this behavior, instead of merely trying to thwart it. Children, like all human beings, tell the truth with their actions. Those of us in the business of improving the physical environment should learn to interpret what they are telling us; we must learn to observe and really "see," to listen and really "hear."

Another form of danger which adults fear on such a playground is that of children fighting and injuring each other. Ironically, their justification for such fears often stem from observations of children playing on asphalt play yards where pushing, shoving, teasing, and fighting are frequently engaged in out of boredom. Children at a Berkeley, California, grade school, asked what they did in recess periods and why, replied that they mostly "pushed the other kids around" because there was nothing else to do.[29] Their play yard comprises a vast expanse of asphalt, and one small set of balancing bars.

In the most detailed study ever undertaken of children's games in a contemporary urban society, the authors remarked:

We have noticed that when children are herded together in the playground . . . their play is markedly more aggressive than when they are in the street or in the wild places . . . Often, when we have asked children what games they played in the playground we have been told "we just go around aggravating people."[30]

In a flat featureless, hardtop playground in which there are no physical objects that can become the focus of play—to climb on, hide behind, run around, crawl through, and so on—it may be that children unconsciously turn their fellows into "physical objects" and interact with them accordingly. Suffice it to say that on an adventure playground, with its multiplicity of objects, surfaces, tools, and therefore, of potential activities, fighting and bullying rarely, if ever, occur. There is too much else to do.

THE NEEDS OF AN ADVENTURE PLAYGROUND[31]

Although the children will eventually build their own play environment, certain basic features must be provided by the local voluntary committee or city department responsible for setting up the playground. These include the following:

The Site

It is essential that much of the site be left unimproved so that the children who come to use it find a completely unstructured space free from implicit messages to "do this here—do that there."

But this does not mean that there is no designing to be done. The site must be chosen and demarked, the fencing selected, a playground building designed and located on the site, spaces for different kinds of adventure play delimited and enclosed. Especially if the site is small, this latter endeavour must be approached with great subtlety and care. In a particularly successful case—that of Notting Hill Gate playground in London—a very small site is carefully divided into six areas of play: a large dirt-surfaced adventure play section, a smaller hard-surfaced play area, an area for gardening and children's pets, a section for the under-fives, an area for indoor play inside the playground building, and a hanging-out place for teenagers on the roof of the building. Low picket fencing, a concrete berm, and the building itself form the boundaries between these areas.[32] Thus there is plenty of work for the designer even though most of the playground "equipment" is designed and built by the children.

The site should preferably be somewhere between ¼ and 1½ acres in size. Anything smaller than ¼ acre can soon be too overcrowded; anything larger than 1½ acres can be difficult to supervise and often lacks the intensity of use which children seem to enjoy. The shape of the site is of little importance, though perhaps a square or rectangular site would be easier to supervise than an irregular shape. The site should not be completely flat, since the change in level offers opportunities for digging, etc. If the site contains a number of mature trees—for climbing, tree houses, aerial ropeways, etc., the trees suffer no damage and add shade and beauty to the site. The site surface should ideally be part hard-surfaced, for use of wheeled toys, playing balls, etc., and partially dirt-surfaced for digging, making gardens, hammering in corner posts of "houses," and so on.

The site should ideally be located in the center of the area it is intended to serve and should be easily and safely accessible to children on foot, not on a busy road so that children congregating outside before opening time would be in danger. There should be access—separate from children's pedestrian access—for trucks delivering lumber and other materials. The site should not be located so that the noise or unsightliness will disturb neighboring homes, but it should not be tucked away so that children have difficulty finding it or potential nighttime vandals have the opportunity to work undisturbed.

Fencing

The site should ideally be fenced with some form of high, solid fencing material so that the children inside gain a sense of privacy and enclosure, and so that passing adults are "spared' the untidy, sometimes chaotic, appearance which such playgrounds inevitably take on. A small section of chain-link or other fencing that can be seen through might be inset near the entrance so that curious newcomers can peep in before they commit themselves to entering, and so that police can check on the site after closing hours.

The most successful vandal-proof fencing has been found to be 8 feet of concrete planks topped with 4 feet of chain link. Wooden board fencing looks better but lasts a shorter time. Perhaps the ideal arrangement is either a high earthen bank topped with a fence and planting (as at the original Emdrup playground) or a concrete plank fence screened with planting on the outside. On the inside, the concrete fencing can be used for bouncing balls against, chalking, painting, or building a lean-to structure, as well as providing the privacy that children need.

Playground Building

Some form of building, however primitive, is essential in which children can play in bad weather, and where the supervisor can have a small office and the children access to toilets. The building need not be elaborate; if the site is temporary, the demountable accommodations used on building sites may be a good solution.

Where the playground is intended as a permanent facility, the building should be a permanent structure and should ideally contain the following: large indoor playroom for games, meetings, dances, table tennis, pool, etc.; activities room with work tops for painting, clay modeling, and crafts; toilets and storage space for childre outdoor clothes; small kitchen and office for play leaders with a view over the entire pl ground; and storage for tools used on the pl ground. The building should be sited near entrance so that it can be used at night with children having to reach it via unlighted stretches of the playground.

Materials and Tools

The two most crucial elements leading to the success (or otherwise) of the playground are the personality of the leader, and a continuous supply of tools and materials. Tools for the children to work with—including hammers, mallets, nails, saws, buckets, shovels, wheelbarrows, trowels, etc.—are supplied by the city department or voluntary committee running the playground and if an imaginative method for ensuring their safe return is devised, there need be little loss through "attrition." One London playground uses the method of requiring the child to give up something of his own to the leader—pocket knife, shirt, book, etc.—which he gets back when he safely returns the borrowed tool. It is essential that the playground leader make good arrangements with local building material firms, or construction companies, or local factories for a steady supply of their "waste" materials which the children can use in building (packing cases, pieces of lumber, sand, brick, rope, cardboard boxes). Other kinds of materials for children playing inside would be old clothes for dressing up, and supplies for painting, modeling, woodworking, and art work.

The Leader

The site, fencing, building, and materials thus form the raw materials of the playground, but to come to life it must have two more ingredients— a sympathetic and talented leader, and a steady "supply" of children. These two are inextricably bound up, for it has been found in years of experience in England and Scandinavia that the success of the playground—and by success we mean numbers of children using it with obvious enthusiasm and relish—depends very largely on the personality of the leader.

In some of the most successful cases, the playground has become inextricably associated in the minds of the children with its leader, as in the following case of a playground in Bristol, England:

Children do not see the playground through adult eyes. For them its meaning comes from the dens they build, the games they play, the friends they meet, and above all else from the warmth and understanding of the leader. The Upfield Playground became known in the neighborhood as "Donald's," and it was of "Donald" or "Shorty," as some of the children nicknamed him, that they spoke first whenever the playground was mentioned.[33]

A quote from Donald's logbook of playground activities illustrates in a very human, personal way how the leader may become slowly and unobtrusively a positive force in the neighborhood, and subtly influence the behavior of those around him.

About 6:45 Harry S. brought over a pastry which his mother had just made and sent over for me. It is perhaps a return gift, acknowlegement of the fact that I give Chris (then aged 3½) a bun when I get my tea. Chris, when I first knew him, was an ill-clad neglected-looking child who was always out in the streets. Impossible to approach, instantly on the defensive, and very aggressive. After a long period I established a friendship. He now waits for me to come—even on Sundays—he has become quite friendly and allows other adults to approach him. Lately he has been much better clad and receives more attention at home. Have been told by other children that he used to receive regular beatings at home.[34]

There is no easy definition of the "right" person for the job of playleader; he—or she—has to combine the loving attention of a parent, the technical abilities of an apprentice carpenter, the patience of a good teacher, and much more. As one authority has described the ideal leader, he must be a combination of ". . . mother and father, a policeman, and Robin Hood. He must be fond of children in a deep but unsentimental way. His greatest asset must be a capacity for just being there."[35] A British expert on adventure playgrounds has written of the ideal leader:

The successful leader of an adventure playground is one who has confidence in the children's positive attitudes to make and create things in their own individual way, and in their ability to make good relationships with each other. He is less concerned with their physical development, or with organizing them into "teams" for games or joint activities, or showing them "how to play." He does, however, act as a referee when a situation is in danger of getting out of hand, or when the children are unable to resolve their transient difficulties by themselves . . . Above all, he will be eager to praise any endeavor that has patently brought pleasure to a group of children, or indeed, to an individual child, and not show his despair when the whole thing is abandoned and never completed.[36]

Or as another British writer on play leadership has written:

The children are sovereign and the initiative must come from them. The leader can make suggestions, but he must never demand. He must obtain the tools and materials needed or requested by the children, but he must at any moment be prepared to give way to new activities. To organize and arrange programmes is to stifle imagination and initiative and preclude children whose lively curiosity and interests constantly demand new outlets.[37]

On an adventure playground—unlike a regular playground with organized sports events—the leader has other community-wide responsibilities. It will be his job to canvass the community to locate contractors, lumber merchants, and others, and not only convince them of the worth of this innovative play scheme, but also persuade them to make regular deliveries of materials to the site. His will be the ticklish position of possibly being paid by a local city department, having his work activities overseen by a voluntary committee of parents, and yet not permitting either to dictate to him what *they* feel should happen on the playground.[38] It will be his job to placate neighboring householders who may object to occasional excesses of noise, or smoke from bonfires, and to liaise with police to ensure that there is no after-hours vandalism on the playground. On a number of British playgrounds, in addition to all the above duties, the leader has regular contacts with the schools, welfare, children's, and probation departments to mutually refer to each other cases of neighborhood children who are in need.

In view of the above remarks, it is perhaps superfluous to say that no existing recreation leadership training in the United States, or elsewhere, supplies all the facets of training that a good adventure playground leader would require. And it is not surprising that, in documented British examples, the most successful leaders have emerged from varied nonrecreation backgrounds—ex-seamen, ex-teachers, ex-janitors, ex-actors. There is evidence to suggest that only especially gifted individuals have in equal measure the ability to relate to children and to the community, and that where possible, two leaders (preferably a man and a woman) who have complementary talents, should be appointed.

It is ironic that in the United States, where the training and supply of play leaders is very much better than in any West European country, the actual record of introduction of innovative play ideas is relatively poor. Undoubtedly the potential for the selection and training of excellent adventure-playground leaders exists; what is necessary is more understanding and acceptance of the concept of this kind of recreation.

THE FUTURE OF THE ADVENTURE-PLAYGROUND CONCEPT IN THE UNITED STATES

It is very clear that, as adults in the business of designing the environments in which our children live and play, we have made a set of distinct and rigid value judgments about what play "should" be about. We have only to look around us in any city at the stereotyped and unimaginative settings specifically set aside for play to read the message—"play is to be structured, limited to a range of physical activities predetermined by adults, and its chief purpose is to keep you healthy."

The core of public recreation—and therefore of the settings provided for public play—is physical coordination and team sports. If you raise the question with park and recreation planners of the needs of children to explore, build, destroy, engage in make-believe and fantasy, you are regarded as—at best—some kind of "kook," and —at worst—quasi-subversive.

Despite America's tradition for local involvement and grass-roots democracy, it seems that citizen groups pressing the bureaucrats to try out innovations in recreation are far more prevalent and successful in Europe than here. The reason for this may well be the strong Protestant ethic in the United States which relegates play, leisure, and recreation—even for children—to a considerably lower position in both personal and municipal hierarchies of values than is true in the Old World. It is small wonder that few citizens are concerned with play—and the professional recreation "suppliers" coast along on well-worn solutions.

But there seems to be another reason why the adventure playground, per se, is initially looked upon by recreation professionals with amazement bordering upon horror. It is that somehow it is perceived as appealing to a "lower level" of emotions than traditional forms of public recreation. Although the "child within" in almost every recreation planner responds to the view of the children digging, building, tunneling, lighting fires, and smashing up their own constructions—with joy and excitement, the "adult without" warns that such activities appeal to "primitive" instincts which somehow cannot be as "good" as those character-building instincts for team cooperation and public acclaim fostered by organized competitive sport. It is largely this "cognitive dissonance" between instinctual acceptance of an idea and professional rejection which accounts for the almost anguished reactions of professional recreation directors to the notion of the adventure playground. Some of these reactions are discussed below.

To bring about the general acceptance of an innovation, its first adopters must do a good selling job in convincing their colleagues of its worth and merits. To do something for promoting and selling the idea in the San Francisco Bay area, the author made a short movie of a successful London Adventure Playground in the summer of 1967, and has shown it since to many neighborhood and professional groups, students, parent–teacher associations, etc. What follows is a brief account of how two groups—who were afterwards asked to answer a number of questions—responded to the ideas in the movie. These were a group of fifty-eight Park and Recreation Directors from California cities and counties, who met for their annual Institute at Asilomar in November 1969, and a group of seventeen landscape architecture students who were just completing a course taught by the author at the University of California, Berkeley, in December 1969.

When asked, "What is your 'gut level' response to the idea of an adventure playground? How does it appeal to you as a human being—forgetting for a moment your role as a professional in the recreation/landscape field?," more than half (57 percent) of the parks and recreation responded enthusiastically. Just over a quarter approved of the idea with some limitations, and 15 percent strongly disapproved. As might be expected, the students responded even more enthusiastically, with 94 percent strongly approving of the concept and only 1 percent of the group disapproving.

When the recreation and parks directors were then asked how they responded as *professionals,* the proportion who thought it unworkable rose from 15 percent to 47 percent. The chief objections were that the community wouldn't support the idea, and that insurance companies would not insure it. A few responded that they personally would strongly resist such a playground in their community.

My community would reject it totally. They would see an adventure playground as a breeding ground for vandalism, criminality, narcotics use, etc.

As a professional, I would strongly resist this kind of project on public property in my city.

It would be political suicide. People are geared to nice clean manicured play areas with shiny brightly painted equipment, even though they are not used.[39]

Nevertheless, just over half the recreational directors thought such a playground, or an adaptation of it, would be worth trying, though some admitted the "selling job" might be difficult.

Another question asked of the parks directors was, "Supposing a person were to present the idea of an adventure playground to your city council, what do you think their chief objections would be?" The objections most frequently mentioned (in order of numbers of mentions) were public liability and insurance (58 percent); unsightly appearance (49 percent); public would not accept, would fear loss of property values near playground (19 percent); too radical a notion, not what is usually provided (12 percent); cost (7 percent). Other, less frequently mentioned, objections were —fire hazards, problems of sex crimes and drug

trafficking, vandalism, the disorganized nature of the leadership on playground, and children's structures which wouldn't conform to building codes!

The next question was "Can you think of any ways in which these objections might be overcome?" Some 18 percent of the respondents thought there would be no way to convince them, but others suggested a variety of ways. One-third thought the best way would be by a good presentation, showing the films to the council or parks commission, taking them to see successful examples, producing statistics on accident rates, etc. Another one-third felt the best way was to modify the idea, to propose it as a temporary pilot program, and to find a site well out of sight. A few thought the support of other city departments and/or the academic community would be useful. About one-fifth felt the best way was not to try and convince the *council*, but to educate and convince the community and then have them pressure the council to provide such a playground, or to get a private group to sponsor and run such a playground and show the council that it worked. A few thought the best way was not to ask the council at all, but just to go ahead and do it, or as a last resort—"get rid of the council."

In a final question, respondents were asked if in fact there was a possibility they *would* propose or support a proposal for a playground incorporating some of the ideas of the adventure playground in their community. At the start of the questions, when asked their reaction as a professional, only 52 percent thought the idea was "worth trying," but in answer to this latter question, as many as 79 percent said they might propose such a playground in their community. The explanation of this increase in supporters may be that, when asked the question, few would want to rule out the possibility that they might try it some time in the future; but another explanation may be that the very exercise of responding to questions concerning the advantages and disadvantages of such a playground as well, as means of overcoming the objections, had the effect of people convincing themselves that the notion was worth a try.

This is an important pointer to the whole problem of selling innovations—get people talking, arguing with each other about the problems and merits, and in the process, they may begin to convince each other—and themselves—of its worth. One participant wrote after the movie and discussion, "My first reaction to the concept was very definitely negative . . . but eventually a feeling of acceptance and excitement overcame the negative attitude and the concept became a challenge."

Writing from the heart about the problems of innovation acceptance, one participant observed:

The key to the speaker's presentation was the acceptance of change, not only in the areas of playgrounds but in our interaction with people and communities.

Audience reaction to the presentation was of interest to me. I sensed group acceptance of what the speaker (and film) were saying, and yet there was a comic atmosphere. This combination is significant to me in that we tend to joke about significant things. It becomes easier to be light-hearted about many critical problems, with the idea in mind that with time they will disappear. I think that the group, myself included, experienced great frustration in listening to the speaker—not because of what she was saying, but because we are often unable to implement innovative ideas. . . . Issues that create controversy or draw criticism are often tucked away for further study. We may wish to practice what we hear but we do not. What do we gain by procrastination? The administration who is insensitive to change as a matter of self-preservation may ultimately be toppled by prevailing outside forces. . . . Without listening, learning to change, we risk far greater future losses than are presently imaginable.

Another participant echoed the feelings of many when he noted:

We seem to worry about "backlash" and not of the children who are the users of our product.

And the following theme was one expressed by many:

Our playgrounds must serve and meet the needs of our children—and not preconceived adult concepts. . . . Now is the time to make our voices heard . . . by upholding children's rights. . . .

Some wrote of a more hopeful, changing climate in local government that is more open to innovation than in the past.

Up until three years ago, the policies of our city's administration towards recreation was one of . . . "circle the wagons and we will make a stand here." Little thought was given to planning a park that would meet the needs of the people. We had set guidelines and standards that would have been outdated in the 1930s. . . . We had X number of swings, X number of trash cans, and X number of rest rooms—and all of these were placed in the same general area in each park. . . . Needless to say we had parks that are seldom if ever used to capacity. No one ever thought of asking the people in the neighborhood what they wanted. . . . I'm not sure we built the parks for use by the public.

Our city's administration has now changed . . . we have been given a challenge and we are striving to meet it. . . . We are trying to plan for the children and their needs and not just put in a bunch of pretty new equipment. . . . We have gone into the neighborhood and talked to the kids. We have observed them at play . . . in the streets, supermarket parking lots, vacant lots, and front yards. . . . We will be doing a lot of experimenting. . . . We have been given the tools, the ideas, and the money; now it is up to us to produce.

It should be stressed that the whole purpose of presenting innovative ideas to a professional group is not necessarily to persuade them to adopt them—lock, stock, and barrel—but rather to stimulate them into thinking in new ways. The final quotation is from one participant who did just this, and who had come up with what may be an excellent adaptation of the adventure-playground concept for the American scene:

The experience with creative play in Copenhagen proved to me that its great success was partly due to the inherited instinct of the children. Their ancestors were masters in design and woodworking, and they bring this ability to the playground with them. I can see great success with creative play in this country if we will also take a look at what our children have inherited. Practically every American child from the day he's able to sit up is involved in playing with mechanical things. We may do well to use this knowledge in attempting to get the creative play idea started here. I can see a play area designed to allow young people to build mechanical things such as go-carts or other motorized conveyances. An area designed as a building area with storage garages and material bins could be next to another area or track for the kids to run them on. How many kids do we see in this country working on some mechanical gadget in his yard without a place to test it?

The emphasis here on the merits of the adventure versus the regular playground does not mean there is no place for swings and slides and jungle gym with which we are all familiar. Adventure playgrounds should not be thought of as *substitutes* for conventional play areas, but rather as very important *supplements* which hopefully round out the recreational experience of the contemporary urban child.

The extent to which "problems with children's play" turn up again and again as a major complaint in moderate and high-density urban housing developments suggests that our current provisions for play in these areas are *not* fulfilling the needs of children or of their parents.

We try to deter children from manipulating elements of the nature environment—earth, water, fire, wood, plants—but trees climbed, holes dug, houses built in the landscaped areas of housing projects, parks, and suburban subdivision bear witness to the fact that children desperately need a place they *are* permitted to do these things. An important creative experience is being denied them.

In addition, the fascination for children of streets, parking areas, vacant lots, empty buildings, and other potentially dangerous locales suggests to us that another crucial element is missing from the play areas we presently provide—the element of challenge. The adventure playground provides these ingredients of creativity and challenge, as well as much more that is missing in the conventional playground.

The verbatim responses of some Berkeley landscape architecture students after seeing the adventure playground movie express succinctly why this is something we ought to try out:

I think the idea is fantastic. It allows the children to be creative in their own way and allows them an escape.

I think it's a wonderful idea. When I was watching the movie I was wishing I could be there, too.

Fascinating and yet so human. A great way for kids of all races to get together. Reminds me of my childhood.

Wow! Frightening-creative-dangerous-warm-human. Strange and wonderful. It has a kind of eerie fascination.

I wanted to be there. I remembered my childhood and how I liked to do those things.

Wow! Far out! We need it here! Now! Change some heads! All power to the imagination!

It was perfect!! Kids building, climbing, breaking, digging. These people will have a chance to live.

There is no time like now for experimentation. Are we going to deny our children the experiences which we most enjoyed when we were young? If we do, each of us must have it on our conscience that in this most affluent of countries we have deprived our children of something they want and sorely need.

It is not a question of dollars or space or regulation, but of our own limitations. We tend in both our personal roles and our professional life to define ourselves by our limitations . . . "Well, that's not appropriate behavior because I'm a man" . . . or . . . "We can't do that because the parks departments have never done that before." But we grow personally and professionally when we challenge those self-imposed limitations, when we recognize that anything and everything is possible. Like children at play, we too are unconsciously looking for challenges which will help us expand. We should not let the challenge of adventure playgrounds go unanswered. It could make a vital difference to a whole generation of children growing up in the city.

BIBLIOGRAPHY

Note: It is perhaps not without significance that 70 percent of the items in this bibliography are European—mostly British—in origin. This does not, I think, reflect a chauvinistic bias on the part of the (British) author, but rather is an indication of where much of the practical work and writing on outdoor play and play design is going on. My hunch as to why this is so is that—in general—Western European countries move more quickly and pragmatically to fulfill the needs of minorities than does the United States. One has only to look at the record of legislation on, for instance, free health care, subsidized housing, the repeal of capital punishment, legalization of abortion and homosexuality to see that the United States often lags one or two decades behind. Children too are a minority—in the sense of having no power over the decisions which affect their lives. The United States, despite its professed self-image of a somewhat child-oriented society, has still to recognize this.

1. Abernethy, W. D. "Playgrounds." National Playing Fields Association, London (no date).*

2. Abernethy, W. D. "Playleadership." National Playing Fields Association, London (no date).*

3. "Adventure Playgrounds: A progress report." National Playing Fields Association, London, 1961.*

4. Lady Allen of Hurtwood, *Planning for Play*. London: Thames and Hudson, 1968.

5. Lady Allen of Hurtwood. "Adventure Playgrounds." National Playing Fields Association, London, 1961.*

6. Benjamin, Joe. "In Search of Adventure: A Study of the Junk Playground." National Council of Social Service, London, 1966.*

7. "Children and Planning." Special issue of *Town and Country Planning,* Oct.–Nov. 1968.†

8. Dattner, Richard. *Design for Play*. New York: Van Nostrand Reinhold Co., 1969.

9. Gans, Herbert. "Recreation Planning." Ph.D. dissertation, University of Pennsylvania.

10. Goldman, Nathan. "A Socio-Psychological Study of School Vandalism." *Crime and Delinquency,* July 1961.

11. Hole, Vere. *Children's Play on Housing Estates*. National Building Studies Research Paper 39. London: Her Majesty's Stationery Office, 1966.

12. Huizinga, Johan. *Homo Ludens: A Study of the Play Element in Culture*. Boston: The Beacon Press, Inc. 1950.

13. London Adventure Playground Association. Information sheets on the setting up of adventure playgrounds—including (British) costs, salary scales, insurance, draft constitution of playground association, relevant publications, etc. ‡

14. Loizos, Caroline. "Play in Mammals." In P. A. Jewell and C. Loizos, *Play, Exploration and Territoriality in Mammals*. New York: Academic Press Inc., 1966.

15. Lynch, Kevin, and Alvin Lukashok. "Some Childhood Memories of the City." *Journal of the American Institute of Planners,* Summer, 1956.

16. Mays, John Barron. *Growing Up in the City: A Study of Juvenile Delinquency in an Urban Neighborhood*. Liverpool: Liverpool University Press, 1954.

17. Mays, John Barron. "Adventure in Play." Liverpool Council of Social Service, Liverpool, 1957.*

18. Millar, Susanna. *The Psychology of Play*. Baltimore, Md.: Penguin Books, Inc., 1968.

19. Moore, Robin. "An Experiment in Playground Design." M.C.P. thesis, MIT, 1966.

20. Parr, A. E. "Lessons of an Urban Childhood. In *The American Montessori Society Bulletin,* Vol. 7, No. 4, 1969.

21. Opie, Iona and Peter. *Children's Games in Street and Playground*. London: Oxford University Press, 1969.

22. Owen, Rowland. "Insurance: A Survey of Insurance Aspects of Playground Management." National Playing Fields Association, London (no date).*

23. Spencer, John. In collaboration with Joy Tuxford and Norman Dennis, *Stress and Release on an Urban Estate: A Study in Action Research*. Part IV, "The Upfield Adventure Playground." London: Tavistock Publications (1959) Ltd., 1964.

24. Spivak, Mayer. "The Landscape of Fantasy and The Real Live Playground." Paper presented at the

*Obtainable from: Housing Centre Bookshop, 13 Suffolk Street, London S.E.1., England—priced as follows (number refers to those in Bibliography). 1: 75 cents; 2: 60 cents; 3: 25 cents; 5: 25 cents; 6: $1.25; 17: 40 cents; 22: 25 cents. (All prices *not* including postage).

†Obtainable from: Town and Country Planning Association, 28 King Street, London W.C.2., England, price 75 cents; not including postage.

‡Obtainable from: London Adventure Playground Association, 4 Lansdowne Road, London W.11, England, at nominal cost.

44th Annual Meeting of the American Orthopsychiatric Association, Washington, D.C., Mar. 1967.

25. Stevenage Development Corporation. "Study of Playgrounds in Stevenage." Mimeo, 1969.

26. "The Ignoble Experiment." *Progressive Architecture,* Aug. 1967, p. 47.

27. Zimbardo, Philip G. "The Human Choice: Individuation, Reason and Order vs. Deindividuation, Impulse and Chaos." Nebraska Symposium in Motivation, March, 1969. Report from the Experimental Social Psychology Laboratory, Department of Psychology, Stanford University.

NOTES AND REFERENCES

1. Kevin Lynch and Alvin Lukashok, "Some Childhood Memories of the City," *Journal of the American Institute of Planners,* Summer, 1956.
2. Lady Allen of Hurtwood, "Adventure Playgrounds," National Playing Fields Association, London, 1961, p. 3.
3. For further details on this playground established by Robin Moore, see the chapter on "Adventure Playgrounds" in Lady Allen of Hurtwood, *Planning for Play,* London: Thames and Hudson, 1968, pp. 72–77; and Robin Moore, "An Experiment in Playground Design," M.C.P. thesis, Massachusetts Institute of Technology, 1966.
4. For more information on this playground, write Mrs. Lovie McIntosh, Director, People Pledged for Community Progress, 705 Bissell Avenue, Richmond, Calif.
5. John Barron Mays, "Adventure in Play," Liverpool Council of Social Service, Liverpool, 1957, pp. 6–7.
6. W. D. Abernethy, "The Importance of Play," in *Children and Planning,* special issue of *Town and Country Planning,* Oct.–Nov. 1968, p. 471.
7. There are various theories as to why children from all cultures engage in play that imitates the behavior of adults. Groos suggests that it is a form of instinctual play in which the animal or human is training itself for roles it will have to play in maturity. Others maintain that play recapitulates the development of the entire race. Freud suggests, in *Beyond the Pleasure Principle,* that children repeat in their play everything that has made an impression on them in life, and that they become masters of these situations they have observed by constant repetition in play. However, it is not the purpose of this paper to answer the question "Why?" concerning children's play. We are taking the fact of imitative and adventurous play as a "given" and suggesting ways to better provide for it.
8. These observations were made by the author standing at one vantage point in the playground and noting down everything that was happening for a half-hour period; the number of children on the playground at the end of the period was 45. The ages are estimated.
9. Vere Hole. *Children's Play on Housing Estates,* National Building Studies Research Paper 39, London: Her Majesty's Stationery Office, 1966.
10. Lady Allen of Hurtwood, "Adventure," p. 13.
11. John Spencer, with the collaboration of Joy Tuxford and Norman Dennis, "The Upfield Adventure Playground," Pt. IV of *Stress and Release in an Urban Estate: A Study in Action Research,* London: Tavistock Publications (1959) Ltd., 1964, p. 261.
12. "Adventure Playgrounds: A Progress Report," National Playing Fields Association, London, 1961, p. 18.
13. *Ibid.,* p. 8.
14. Stevenage Development Corporation, "Study of Playgrounds in Stevenage," mimeo, 1969, p. 30.
15. "The Vandal, Society's Outsider," *Time,* Jan. 19, 1970.
16. Philip G. Zimbardo, "The Human Choice: Individuation, Reason and Order vs. Deindividuation, Impulse and Chaos," Nebraska Symposium on Motivation, Mar. 1969. Reprinted as a report from Experimental Social Psychology Laboratory, Department of Pyschology, Stanford University, p. 50.
17. Nathan Goldman, "A Socio-psychological Study of School Vandalism," *Crime and Delinquency,* July 1961.
18. "Adventure Playgrounds: A Progress Report," p. 18.
19. Stevenage Development Corporation, *op. cit.*
20. Lady Allen of Hurtwood, *Planning,* p. 16.
21. Information from conversation with Donne J. Buck, leader of Bandley Hill Adventure Playground, Sept. 1969.
22. Playleaders on the Richmond, California adventure playground were paid through the National Youth Corps.
23. Spencer, *op. cit.,* p. 243.
24. The reactions that follow were those relayed to the author after showings of a short movie on a British adventure playground to low- and lower-middle income neighborhood groups in the San Francisco Bay Area, 1968–1969.
25. Joe Benjamin, "In Search of Adventure: A Study of the Junk Playground," National Council of Social Service, London, 1966, p. 14.
26. Lady Allen of Hurtwood, *Planning,* p. 62.
27. Lady Allen of Hurtwood, "Adventure."
28. Mays, *op. cit.*
29. Verbal report from teachers at a PTA meeting, Le Conte School, Feb. 1970.
30. Iona and Peter Opie, *Children's Games in Street and Playground,* London: Oxford University Press, 1969, pp. 13–14.
31. This section is summarized from three sources: Lady Allen of Hurtwood, "Adventure Playgrounds," Chap. IV of *Planning;* London Adventure Playground Association fact sheets; Stevenage Development Corporation, *op. cit.*
32. For greater detail on the site planning and build design at at Notting Hill Gate playground, see Lady Allen of Hurtwood, *Planning,* pp. 64–69.
33. Spencer, *op. cit.,* p. 221.

34. *Ibid.*, p. 257.
35. W. D. Abernethy, *Play Leadership,* National Playing Fields Association, London (no date), p. 24.
36. Lady Allen of Hurtwood, *Planning,* p. 56.
37. Benjamin, *op. cit.,* p. 12.
38. A revealing account of this problem situation can be found in Spencer, *op. cit.*
39. This quote and those that follow are from the final exam papers of participants in the Institute, where they were asked: "Select any single general topic (i.e., planning, design, decision process, etc.), or any single presentation or paper given by a speaker at the Institute, and answer in no more than 1,000 words: As a park administrator (planner, designer or —————), (1) what does the essence of this topic or presentation mean to you, and (2) why is it important?"

The Political Collapse of a Playground*

Mayer Spivack

LISTEN, HIDE, BUILD, SING, AND DIG

It is perhaps the fault of the Protestant ethic that we so habitually, as adults, separate the activities of children into play and work. For the child, however, things are not quite so clear; given proper conditions, children, in the name of play, will become thoroughly invested in enterprises that would make many a strong man a work-shirker. However, on a visit to nearly any public playground in midsummer we are likely to encounter a meager population sitting discouragedly on swings or near the edges of the playground, leaning against a fence, or perhaps aimlessly riding a bicycle around in circles. The often expensive and "esthetically pleasing" equipment purchased by adults for children with the best intentions stands either unused or unusable because of vandalism.

*Reprinted from *Landscape Architecture,* July, 1968.

Lately there has been much attention given to the subject of public playgrounds in urban areas. In Boston the Metropolitan District Commission has for several years been constructing its version of improved playgrounds for children. Manufacturers have sprung up nationally to add their notions of proper and beautiful play equipment for children. Annually architects, sculptors, and designers are invited to enter one of several competitions for the design of better playground "sculpture."

Well-intentioned as such efforts certainly are, the greater part of them miss the point. Playgrounds, if they are useful at all, must serve many purposes, only one of which is the satisfaction of a child's needs to play in the conventional sense.

Children are rarely conscious of the fact of their playing, which may consist of intense learning and the satisfaction of curiosity about the natural world and the human one. It may involve testing of social roles, development of physical coordination and strength, and competition with age mates in contests of skill of various sorts. Fantasy-based play may or may not be accompanied by the physical manipulation of objects in the environment—the "working out" or "playing out" of conflicts, fears, and other troublesome emotion-related material. In children's play we may see a wide range of behaviors.

Against this rather sketchy background of what children may do while playing, consider the range of settings available to an urban child in a "modern" playground. Most often playgrounds are designed to be miniature athletic fields or do-it-yourself amusement parks, in which the child is challenged only in the physical modes of his play behavior. There are bars to climb and hang on, slides to slide on, and swings on which to swing. But for a child who wants to build or dig, hide, sing or tell stories and listen to them, there is no proper setting. It is true that children are capable of modifying almost any setting to their needs, but on a playground where other children are flying and kicking there is often little quiet space in which to sit tranquilly and play with a tiny toy or immerse oneself in dreams or fantasies.

Most playgrounds being built today resemble huge squirrel cages. They challenge and exhaust the child with a variety of intriguing and enjoyable muscle-testing experiences. This is satisfactory if it does not have to fill the play-space needs of the same child or children day after day throughout the year. Unfortunately this is the kind of playground so widely photographed and discussed in Sunday supplements, and most often used as a model by cities and towns. A playground at a school or in a community mental health center, or in an urban or suburban neighborhood, must be capable of serving many requirements, especially if the group of children using it remains fairly constant. For the child in a dense urban area, ability of the space to provide a variety of play settings

may be of superlative importance to his well-being.

When a child *makes* something, or attempts to change his environment, he becomes invested in the object and in his work on it. The act often symbolizes his power to change himself. To deprive a child of this opportunity may work unnecessary hardships on his efforts at self-realization and self-definition.

The esthetics of the adult, and the basis for these esthetics, appear to rest on criteria very different from the esthetics of the child. And so adult-designed playgrounds tend to be neat, clean, flat surfaces with sculpture-like objects firmly attached to concrete or tar paving. But children like to play in the rather loosely organized vacant lots that adults seem to dislike.

Neighborhood play areas probably require the greatest setting adaptability of any designed environment anywhere. And manipulability of the environment appears to be their essential property for play behavior that is fluid, changing, and unpredictable.

A few years ago, while working as a city planner, I became involved in the design and construction of a neighborhood playground located in a very dense old urban area near Boston. I had for some time been interested in the problem of designing physical settings for children which could provide a spectrum of play satisfactions.

My new play facility was to be constructed on the site of an older one whose originally uninteresting and meager equipment had been further incapacitated by vandalism. The city under whose auspices I was working agreed to supply tools and earth-moving equipment and specialized labor where it was required, as in the installation of water supplies and drainage pipes, and drivers for the heavy equipment.

The city also made available a small amount of money (under $2,000) from a special fund. It was our intention to build an inexpensive, appropriately designed play world with the aid of children as designers and constructors. My services were available as a kind of technical consultant to both the city and the children.

For two or three weeks prior to the beginning of construction, and while involved in measuring the site and drawing up tentative proposals for its use, I was able to observe the play and intensity of use on the old playground and to become friendly with the children.

School had let out for the summer and yet in none of my visits to the site were there ever more than three or four children on the playground. Characteristically, they would sit disconsolately in a corner against the chain-link fence in the shade—for it was already quite hot on that black desert—or they would ride bicycles in lazy figure 8's, obviously bored. The space was huge in relation to the scale of a child, and totally flat. Broken pavement showed where old, damaged swings and slides had been torn out and the holes had been left unpatched. One could have turned it into a parking lot without altering a thing.

There were children of all ages, from tots through advanced teens everywhere on the streets, sitting in doorways, and leaning on lamp posts. When I talked about the idea of rebuilding the tot lot for the small children, the teenagers left no doubt in my mind that they had felt unfairly treated when, in the presence of an official from the Recreation Commission, they had been ejected from the old space. They soon told me that, reacting to this kind of treatment, they had found it satisfying to tear out the jungle gym, to break the slides, and to steal the swings used by the younger ones. In response to this the Recreation Commission had given up trying to maintain the area.

The neighborhood was populated in the main by working-class Italians. Many of the children had no access to the interiors of their own houses during the day while their mothers were away working. Children were put in the charge of other

families, left to themselves or in the care of some other, older child. The only play space, possessable space, or homeplace that they could hope for was that which the city would give them. They looked for space in someone else's backyard or alley, or in the street. These children had no place to keep anything of their own, in which to hide their toys, or to use them.

As often happens in such close old neighborhoods, children were noisily and actively discouraged from using vacant lots next to houses, side alleys, and backyards by the abutting property owners who feared the litter of broken glass, vandalism, and the noise.

Between us, the children and I devised a plan for the playground whose layout was based upon safety requirements and on the necessity to separate more violent active play areas from those needing some peace and security. The equipment was designed to be built by and for children with materials they could, with a little help, manipulate and control. Our goals were very limited and simple. Given the budget, we were restricted to using industrial surplus materials and to scavenging what we could. The city would provide us with fencing material, with paving, water pipes and conduit, and with fill.

Within a few weeks we had accumulated on the playground stocks of railroad ties, telephone poles, cable drumheads, and many truckloads full of wood chips. These were to be our raw materials; they would also to some extent dictate esthetic.

In addition, the playground was a kind of compromise or halfway point between the athletic field amusement park and the intimate play space required at various times.

The plan represented that compromise by providing the older children with such facilities as a basketball court in return for their guarantee of protection and maintenance of the playground for the younger children. It was hinted by the older children that if this were not the case they would not protect the facilities that they were not interested in. I learned quickly and gave them their due. In return, they more than kept to their bargain, throwing themselves into the work of building the whole playground with an intensity reserved only for play. There were no further problems with vandalism, and the playground began to have a life of its own.

Arrival of the first construction equipment carrying the hulk of a strong tree-trunk galvanized the whole community. The tree-trunk was placed on its side in temporary storage and within seconds after it was maneuvered into position it became the property of the playground population, which had risen to about twenty-five or thirty children. The new high level of use and involvement was maintained throughout the summer. Many of the children had court records, some of them by the age of nine. I had been warned by city officials that it was impossible to do anything with or for these children for they were hardened delinquents and would destroy anything that we gave them.

Perhaps we were all fortunate that our plan made it necessary for the children to match, by giving their effort and involvement, whatever the city and I gave on our side. In the course of the summer there never occurred an incident of theft or of willful damage to materials on the playground. The children were on the job every morning long before I arrived. Nearly every day I would find the children had torn down and completely rebuilt their little city. The first of these structures, ambitious quasi-shelters constructed of railroad ties, appeared in a shaded corner of the lot and, as I approached, one of the littler kids came running out, pleading, "Mr. Spivack, Mr. Spivack, you're not going to tear it down, are you?" That was their image of "adult authority" and of "city hall," each of which I represented to them.

As the summer progressed this same structure, modified time after time into new forms, would reappear. I was amazed at the ease with which these kids could move the railroad ties, some of which were 17 feet long and weighed over 300 pounds. I suspected adult collusion for I never saw them building this way in the daytime: apparently construction was a nocturnal act.

Building the playground became play. The only fights I observed were over the privilege of using a shovel or a pick, or some other tool, for there were not enough of these to go around. As the children built the space it became clear that they were building themselves as well. Pride in accomplishment, in competence, and just plain pleasure were almost always visible on the faces and in the movements of the children while they worked. Having invested themselves so obviously and so thoroughly in a community-sponsored, valued project, they also developed a sense of identification with and responsibility for the publicly owned property. The work and the playground were theirs.

They became visible members of a child community which had a certain amount of effect on, and esteem from, the adult community. They learned to get along with older people because they worked and played with them. They had the chance in a short span of time to participate with adults in the conception, planning, and implementation of a complex piece of work which had obvious and tangible consequences in their world. They widened their repertoire of social roles and contexts within which they could experiment and search for new notions of self-identity. They became, in a very real sense, political actors whose opinions were valued, whose responsibilities were clear; citizens of a small, organized, functioning community—leaders and followers at once. They experienced a sense of community.

Since much of the work and its planning was the responsibility of the children, problems encountered during construction and planning were often unanticipated, and the children, when challenged, time and time again had problems of organization and process which required considerable resourcefulness individually and as cooperating groups in their solution. Perhaps more important, they generated the problems which they encountered in the course of their work on their own initiative. They were not told what to do unless they asked for advice.

Average children discovered in themselves abilities to lead and found that they had attitudes and aspirations toward leadership that might otherwise have been undeveloped. They were glorious in the eyes of younger children and therefore became natural nominees for leadership roles, although such roles were never formalized. Hero worship patterns, however, could easily be observed.

The work–play fusion was complete. Work was played and play was worked. Builders must plan on a job like this or it will not be done well. This is an easy, natural way to a good working habit or at least a good attitude toward work, where work comes to be viewed as an experiment with oneself and an exploration of one's stocks of resourcefulness and one's limitations. Children who, for one reason or another, participated less in the building process came to the playground every day anyway, and in the course of the summer saw their playmates scheme and plan and convert an ugly pile of raw materials into wonderful structures. They watched and they learned vicariously and they enjoyed it immensely.

By late August the land had been molded and distinct activity areas or zones had taken shape. We were within a few weeks of completion. Raw material stockpiled for so long was now being used in construction. It became apparent that we intended to use these materials in their final form without refinishing them. The children were perfectly happy with the materials and may even have thought them beautiful. Their parents and neighbors, however, considered telephone poles and railroad ties as industrial surplus, or as one of them put it, "a bunch of junk."

This esthetic conflict became the issue which

was destined to destroy the project. I remained naively unaware that the neighbors were beginning to resent the fact that other areas of the city received shiny new playground equipment while their area was given used, ugly, wooden cast-offs. My original attempts to arouse substantial adult community involvement and support for the project had never been very successful. The neighborhood obviously preferred to have things done for them as was the case elsewhere. (Community action programs were at that time relatively new.) Their preconception also appeared to involve some notion of gaining, or at least not losing, status by having the services of the city performed for them by "servants" as was the case in middle-class and upper-income areas.

Thus without the support and involvement of the neighborhood, and without feedback, we were completely taken by surprise when one Monday morning in early September the children and I appeared at the site to find the project demolished and replaced by a perfectly flat, black, hot, top paving. We now had the equivalent of a parking lot. Later, in a conversation with a city councilor, I learned that an irritated property owner had persuaded him to "eliminate the mess" and that he had done so, even though previously he had been enthusiastic about the work and had gone so far as to propose to me other sites in his area which might be similarly transformed by neighborhood children.

Now, in the wisdom of retrospection, I understand how differences in esthetics are closely tied to concerns about community status and to the relatively different value structures held by the adults of the community, their children, and myself, the "expert consultant" or technician. Had I identified these differences as conflicts early enough and effectively dealt with them the project might not have failed so drastically.

Perhaps the lessons of failure are the more profoundly learned. If so, then the children have learned as well. For them, a positive image of City

Hall and government formed through the optimistic period of their work and participation was inexplicably and insidiously shattered. A truly democratic experience was negated by the powerful gestures of one or two people who remained unidentified.

Most of the children were acutely disappointed and were either unwilling or unable to understand the underlying reasons for the collapse of their efforts. They became uncommunicative and resentful.

Soon the city installed some shiny new fencing and playground equipment. Within days unmistakable signs of vandalism were visible. Fence posts were bent to the ground and the new paving covered with broken bottles. A new kind of junkpile had been created.

Even though the project failed, many ideas we explored concerning the spatial requirements of play behavior and the nature of play behavior itself have been an impetus to my continued thinking and research.

The Theory of Loose Parts[1]

Simon Nicholson

Creativity is for the gifted few: the rest of us are compelled to live in environments constructed by the gifted few, listen to the gifted few's music, use gifted few's inventions and art, and read the poems, fantasies, and plays by the gifted few.

This is what our education and culture conditions us to believe, and this is a culturally induced and perpetuated lie.

Building upon this lie, the dominant cultural elite tell us that the planning, design, and building of any part of the environment is so difficult and so special that only the gifted few—those with degrees and certificates in planning, engineering, architecture, art, education, behavioral psychology, and so on—can properly solve environmental problems.

The result is that the vast majority of people are not allowed (and worse—feel that they are incompetent) to experiment with the components of building and construction, whether in environmental studies, the abstract arts, literature, or science: the creativity—the playing around with the components and variables of the world in order to make experiments and discover new things and form new concepts—has been explicitly stated as the domain of the creative few, and the rest of the community has been deprived of a crucial part of their lives and life style. This is particularly true of young children, who find the world incredibly restricted—a world where they cannot play with building and making things, or play with fluids, water, fire, or living objects, and all the things that satisfy one's curiosity and give us the pleasure that results from discovery and invention; experiments with alternatives, such as People's Park, Berkeley, have been crushed or quashed by public authorities.

The simple facts are these:

1. There is no evidence, except in special cases of mental disability, that some young babies are born creative and inventive and others not.

2. There is evidence that all children love to interact with variables, such as materials and shapes; smells and other physical phenomena, such as electricity, magnetism, and gravity; media such as gases and fluids; sounds, music, motion; chemical interactions, cooking, and fire; and other humans, and animals, plants, words, concepts, and ideas. With all these things children love to play, experiment, discover and invent, and have fun.

All these things have one thing in common, which is variables or "loose parts." The theory of loose parts says, quite simply, the following:

In any environment, both the degree of inventiveness and creativity, and the possibility of discovery, are directly proportional to the number and kind of variables in it.[2]

It does not require much imagination to realize that most environments that do not work (i.e., do not work in terms of human interaction and involvement in the sense described), such as schools, playgrounds, hospitals, day-care centers, international airports, art galleries, and museums, do not do so because they do not meet the "loose parts" requirement; instead, they are clean, static, and impossible to play around with. What has happened is that adults—in the form of professional artists, architects, landscape architects, and planners—have had all the fun playing with their own materials, concepts, and planning alternatives, and then builders have had all the fun building the environments out of real materials; and thus has all the fun and creativity been stolen: children and adults and the community have been grossly cheated and the educational–cultural system makes sure that they hold the belief that this is "right." How many schools have there been with a chain-link and black-top playground where there has been a spontaneous revolution by students to dig it up and produce a human environment instead of a prison?

If we look for a moment at this theory of loose parts, we find that some interesting work supports it and in particular that there has been a considerable amount of outstanding recent research by people not in the traditional fields of art, architecture, and planning. Much of this research fits into five categories.

DESIGN BY COMMUNITY INTERACTION AND INVOLVEMENT

Ten years ago, a special issue of the magazine *Anarchy*[3] was published in which nearly all the fundamental educational, recreational, and community advantages of adventure-playground environments were described, including the relationship between experiment and play, community involvement, the catalytic value of play leaders, the relationship between accidents and the environment, and indeed the whole concept of a "free society in miniature." Later, in 1967, the facts on adventure playgrounds and play parks were taken and discussed in the context of the architecture and planning professions in an article in *Interbuild/Arena*.[4] Although the implications of the concepts and facts outlined in these researches are only now being widely disseminated, the process of community involvement has evolved very fast in both Europe and the United States. Outstanding among these have been some of the educational facilities "charettes" such as those in East New York,[5] and the Shelter Neighbourhood Action Project (SNAP) in Granby, Liverpool, recently described in an unusual article in the *RIBA Journal*.[6]

The interesting aspect of the evolution of community involvement—in the area of recreation in particular—is that the really meaningful programs soon appear to leave play, parks, and recreation by the wayside and become social organizations for community action in all aspects of the environment. Pat Smythe, for example, a pioneer in this field, worked for nine years on adventure playgrounds and then became fully involved in the revolutionary Neighbourhood Council project in

Golborne.[7] In terms of loose parts we can discern a natural evolution from creative play and participation with wood, hammers, ropes, nails, and fire, to creative play and participation with the total process of design and planning of regions in cities.

BEHAVIORAL PLANNING AND DESIGN

Parallel with the development of community involvement there has been a growth in behavioral planning, i.e., the study of human requirements and needs as the basis for the design of the manmade part of the environment. A recent example outlining this approach to design is Constance Perin's in her book called *Man in Mind*. Another example where the use of behavioral data is being used as a design determinant is the pattern language at present being developed at the Center for Environmental Structure, Berkeley.

The relationship of behavioral planning to the theory of loose parts is a direct one since the theory itself derives from it: however, one of the problems of loose parts is that the range of possible human interaction is an exceptionally wide one and many behavioral studies have only gone so far as to state very broad and general requirements (such as the statement, for example, that "children like caves") and have not explicitly described the more subtle forms of behavior that may occur—to use an analogy—"inside the caves." The behavioral generalizations of the 1970s often resemble the generalities or "laws" of the pioneers of social anthropology and merely state what we already know to be true.

The process of community involvement is actually inseparable from the study of human interaction and behavior: for example, to carry the previous analogy further, the study of children and cave-type environments only becomes meaningful when we consider children not only being in a given cave but also when children have the opportunity to play with space-forming materials in order that they may invent, construct, evaluate,

and modify their own caves. When this happens we have a perfect example of variables and loose parts in action and—more important—we find that a behavioral methodology of design, related to this example, has existed for some years: the methodology—involving what is called the "discovery method," has been developed by a unique group of researchers working in curriculum innovation for elementary schools. The obvious pattern of behavior that can be identified here is a self-instructional pattern—namely, that children learn most readily and easily in a laboratory-type environment where they can experiment, enjoy, and find out things for themselves.[8]

THE IMPACT OF CURRICULUM DEVELOPMENT

The principle of variables and loose parts has been acknowledged by most educators since the 1960s: when *Mathematics in Primary Schools* was first published in England in 1966 by H.M.S.O., to quote the Advisory Centre for Education, "It was a bombshell." The discovery method that it described has since then been wonderfully exemplified by the Nuffield Foundation, the elementary Science Study, and several other organizations.[9]

The E.S.S., for example, has now produced thirty of the most imaginative curriculum units ever devised: their format (as is that of the Nuffield Mathematics Program) is almost totally interdisciplinary, and concerns visual art and music as much as mathematics and the natural sciences. But this is not all, for another characteristic of these programs is that they break down the distinction between indoors and outdoors, a feature that had hitherto been experimented with mostly in the progressive schools of the 1930's. By allowing learning to take place outdoors, and fun and games to occur indoors, the distinction between education and recreation began to disappear.

The introduction of the discovery method has

been accompanied by intense research into the documentation of human interaction and involvement; what did children do with the loose parts? What did they discover or rediscover? What concepts were involved? Did they carry their ideas back into the community and their family? Out of all possible materials that could be provided, which ones were the most fun to play with and the most capable of stimulating the cognitive, social, and physical learning processes?

It was educational evaluation that provided the missing element in the design process and completed a system that is a perfect methodology for designers and which pre-dated the recent application of behavioral studies to urban planning—while the emphasis on real-life problems, frequently outdoor and off the school premises, was the beginning of a natural trend toward deschooling and environmental education.

ENVIRONMENTAL EDUCATION

It is hard to talk about environmental education without mentioning that the whole educational system, from preschool through university, is on the verge of changing: for who needs these institutions in their present form? The prototype for education systems of the future are almost certainly those facilities that take children and adults out into the community and, conversely, allow all members of the community access to the facility.

There are several groups in the United States which have been experimenting with this process with children—by far the most comprehensive being the Environmental Science Center in Minnesota[10]: a detailed bibliography of publications and environmental curriculum materials has recently been compiled for a new course at the University of California, Davis.[11] Environmental education (as opposed to conservation education, or the understanding of preservation of the non-man-made environment) means the total study of the ecosystem, i.e., man, his institutions, and his structural, chemical, etc., additions included. The subject of human ecology, our values and concepts, the environmental alternatives and choices open to us—in the fullest sense—has recently become a dominant factor in some educational programs. To express this in the simplest possible terms, there is a growing awareness that the most interesting and vital loose parts are those that we have around us every day in the wilderness, the countryside, the city, and the ghetto.

ART AND SCIENCE EXPLORATORIA

Finally there are groups of people experimenting with the theory of loose parts in art galleries and the science museums: (A simple example leading to this interest was the discovery that the most worn tiles on the floor of museums were usually adjacent those exhibits involving the maximum amount of variables and human interaction.) In 1970 the first comprehensive exhibition of interaction works, titled "Play Orbit," was held at the Institute of Contemporary Art in London. This was recently followed by an exhibition of work (parts) by Robert Morris at the Tate Gallery: to quote a critic's review of the exhibition, "the public got into the party spirit—a somewhat overzealous participation. They were jumping and screaming, swinging the weights around wildly—the middle aged in particular. The children were the most sensible of all the visitors" (!) We are beginning to realize that there are more ways to interact with art than to be solely contemplative (i.e., there exists the possibility of more loose parts and "variables" than via visual perception alone) and that although it is fine to allow scientists and artists to invent things, how about allowing everybody else to be creative and inventive also?

THE IMMEDIATE FUTURE

The whole idea of loose parts raises some fundamental questions about the way we design things: if you are an inventor or designer yourself, what parts or proportion of an environment—or components for an environment—can you legitimately invent yourself, and how much, for example, can children or adults in the community invent and build? How are variables and loose parts introduced into the world of newly born children, and what functions do the variables have on cognition and perception? If contemplation is merely one of the many possible forms of human interaction, what exactly are the other ways we can interact with our environment? Is society content to let only very few of its members realize their creative potential? It is the purpose of this article to propose that it is not, and that if we know that creativity is not just a characteristic of the gifted few, a crash program of educational, recreational, and environmental improvement must be started. I would like to propose the following four-part program, using the loose parts principle, whereby this could be achieved.

1. *Give top priority to where the children are*. All children—and particularly many of the most needy, such as those living in an urban ghetto or who are disadvantaged—spend a lot of the most important time of their lives in elementary schools, day-care, preschools, and children's hospitals: these are the environments that need immediate transformation.[12,13] This holds true even in innovative school districts that have extended or abolished the classroom walls—simply give top priority to the environment of the new "classroom" or "playground," whether it be a mobile unit, exploratory museum, ecological reserve or study center, or wherever the children may be. Ten years of vest-pocket parks, concrete plazas, and adventure playgrounds have failed to do this: we must solve this problem. Even if a local community is sold on the idea of a pocket park or adventure playground, it is still better to use the asphalt area of an elementary school for it, for this is where the children are.

2. *Let children play a part in the process*. Children greatly enjoy playing a part in the design process: this includes the study of the nature of the problem; thinking about their requirements and needs; considering planning alternatives; measuring, drawing, model making, and mathematics; construction and building; experiment, evaluation, modification, and destruction. The process of community involvement, once started, never stops: the environment and its parts is always changing and there is no telling what it will look like. Contrary to traditional parks and adventure playgrounds, the appearance of which is a foregone conclusion, the possible kinds of environment determined by the discovery method and principle of loose parts is limitless. The children in the neighborhood will automatically involve all their brothers, sisters, and families: this is design through community involvement, but in the total community the children are the most important. It is not enough to talk about a design methodology—the methodology must be converted into three-dimensional action, or it is worthless.

3. *Use an interdisciplinary approach*. In early childhood there is no important difference between play and work, art and science, recreation and eduction—the classifications normally applied by adults to a child's environment: education is recreation, and vice versa.[14] For professional architects and landscape architects, this means a first-hand experience and knowledge of children's behavior and an understanding of their physical and social needs and cognitive learning processes. The revolution in curriculum innovation, mentioned briefly above, was undertaken by researchers acquainted with real human needs, not by researchers employing behavioral consultants on the side: such an interdisciplinary approach is a prerequisite to the solution of the problem.

4. *Establish a clearing-house for information*. We

desperately need an international clearing-house for information on children's environments, from maternity onward, dealing with all aspects of their growth, education, curricula, and play, and—in particular—information on human interaction and involvement with loose parts in the environment. The time lapse for dissemination of research and evaluation is at present about 5–10 years and should be reduced to the near-instantaneous. The information should be available in the form of newsletter, demand-printing, microfilm, audio- and video-cassette, and video-cassette systems linked to CATV and satellite and communicated to school districts all over the country, from which it could be distributed, either free or by subscription, to members of the community, elementary schools, day-care centers, and any other person or institution needing it.[15] Much of this evaluation, filming, and videotaping can be experimented with, recorded, photographed, and played back by the children themselves.

Where does all this lead us? There are a lot of suggestions and recommendations in this article. Maybe more than can be acted upon at any one time. But we need to act on all of them if we are to build a society in which individuals and communities have greater control over the loose parts with which their environment may be constructed—loose parts that are at present controlled and fixed by an inflexible education system and cultural elite. The problem is a critical one when we consider young children. Most of the existing design methodologies do not take into account the theory of loose parts and thereby fail. The four-part program could act at least as a start toward solving the problem of cultural availability of bits and pieces of the environment—in both the software and hardware sense—and the extent to which a new generation will be able to invent new systems with the parts.

NOTES AND REFERENCES

1. The "Theory of Loose Parts" was originally published in *Landscape Architecture Quarterly,* Oct. 1971, and in 1972 was awarded the Bradford Williams Medal by the American Society of Landscape Architects. It has since been reprinted in many countries, in the *Bulletin for Environmental Education,* the Town and Country Planning Association, London; in *Human Previews, International Bulletin of Information Exchange 2,* Instituto Ricerche Applicate Documentazione e Studi, Rome; in *The Sentinel,* Provincial Association of Teachers in Quebec, Canada; in *The Center for Curriculum Design,* Evanston, Illinois; in *Studies in Design Education and Craft,* University of Keele, Staffordshire; and in *Man/Science/Technology, Journal of Industrial Arts Association* in Washington, D.C.; and the journal of the Society for Emotionally Disturbed Children in Montreal, Canada.

   An expanded version of this paper has been published in a new book entitled *Community Participation in City Decision Making,* by Simon Nicholson and Barbara Katharina Schreiner (Unit 22 DT201 "Urban Development"), New York: Harper & Row, Publishers, June 1973.
2. Simon Nicholson, "What Do Playgrounds Teach?," *The Planning and Design of the Recreation Environment.* University of California Extension, Davis, Calif., 1970, pp. 5-1 to 5-11.
3. Colin Ward, "Adventure Playground—A Parable of Anarchy," *Anarchy,* Sept. 1961, pp. 193–201 (entire issue on this subject).
4. "United Kingdom—Whose Playgrounds?" in *Interbuild/Arena,* Dec. 1967, pp. 12–19.
5. John Darnton, "Residents and Architects Plan Local Center in Brooklyn," *The New York Times,* Jan. 6, 1971.
6. Roger Barnard, "Community Action in a Twilight Zone," *R.I.B.A. Journal,* Oct. 1970, pp. 445–453.
7. Des Wilson, "Democracy Begins at Golborne," *The Observer* (London), Apr. 11, 1971.
8. Simon Nicholson, "Structures for Self-instruction," *Studio International Journal of Modern Art,* June 1968, pp. 290–292.
9. *I Do and I Understand,* and curriculum materials. The Nuffield Foundation, New York: John Wiley & Sons, Inc., and "Introduction to the Elementary Science Study" and curriculum materials, Education Development Center, Newton, Mass.
10. "Environmental Studies for the Elementary School," and curriculum materials, Grades 3-6, Environmental Science Center Distributing Co., Golden Valley, Minn.
11. Simon Nicholson, "Environmental Education in Early Childhood," University of California Extension, Davis, Calif.
12. "The School Playground as an Outdoor Learning Environment—a Community Project to Extend the Elementary School Curriculum to the Outdoor Playground," Office of Project Planning and Development, Berkeley Unified School District, Berkeley, Calif., June 23, 1970.

13. The first example of the low-cost conversion of an existing K-6 elementary school in northern California took place at Valley Oak School in 1970: see "Domain for Creative Play at Valley Oak Playground," *The Davis Enterprise,* Davis, Calif., July 17, 1970.
14. "Everett Interim Preliminary Report, Education/Recreation, General Analysis and Recommendations" (Appendix 2), Lawrence Halprin and Associates, City of Everett, Wash.
15. The quickest way to get some preliminary information is at present "Big Rock Candy Mountain: Resources for our Education," Winter, 1970, Portola Institute Inc., Menlo Park, Calif. For information on communications, see "Radical Software," Raindance Corporation, New York: Edition 1, pp. 11–12; Edition 2, p. 16, and Edition 3, p. 6, Edition 4, "Education Alternative Programming," pp. 14–16, and Michael Shamberg, *Guerrilla Television,* New York: Holt, Rinehart and Winston, Inc., 1971, pp. 46–48.

SELECTED BIBLIOGRAPHY

Apart from ERIC (Education Resources Information Center), which is academically oriented, there have been few attempts to create a nation-wide system of environment-information, especially in the area of early childhood, elementary and secondary education. Most of the work at assembling data has been restricted to compiling book titles—a method which has proven practically useless. Most people do not have the time to check off bibliographies. Some examples are as follows.

"A Bibliography of Open Education," Education Development Center and the 'Advisory for Open Education', 55 Chapel Street, Newton, Mass., 1971 (primarily a list of EDC and EDC spin-off publications).

"Big Rock Candy Mountain," Portola Institute, Menlo Park, Calif. This is the best interdisciplinary compendium so far—especially the issue of September 1971.

The Last Whole Earth Catalog: Access to Tools. New York: Portola Institute, Inc./ Random House, 1971. This book, and others like it may have more meaning for the average citizen and community, as they are not merely literary.

Martin, Fred W. "Bibliography of Leisure: 1965–1970," Program in Leisure Education, Recreation and Related Community Service, Teachers College, Columbia University, Jan. 1971.

Nicholson, Simon. "Environment Education—A Bibliography." Environmental Education in Early Childhood, UNEX, University of California, Davis, Calif., 1971.

Sleet, David A. "Interdisciplinary Research Index on Play; a Guide to the Literature." Department of Physical Education, The University of Toledo, Ohio, May 1971.

Open Space Learning Place: School Yards and Other Places as Communal Resources for Environmental Education, Creative Play, and Recreation*

Robin Moore

Beginnings

In 1966, I conducted a real-live experiment in playground design in Boston which resulted in the development of several operational concepts applicable to the design and management of play environments.[1] Through this experience, I realized that play and learning are completely intertwined in the reality of a child's behavior; that the learning dimension can be greatly extended through interaction with *people resources* and that both can be enormously affected by the quality and diversity of the *physical setting*.

In Berkeley, I have found the opportunity to apply and extend these realizations in two

*Much of the stimulus for this paper is the result of my association with Herb Wong, Principal of Washington School and Assistant Coordinator of the University Laboratory Schools, University of California, Berkeley. An endless stream of his ideas have become inextricably interwoven with my own. Reprinted from *New School of Education Journal,* Vol. 2, No. 4, and Vol. 3, No. 1, 1973.

elementary school settings; first, at Thousand Oaks in North Berkeley and for the past year and half at Washington (a University Laboratory School) near the center of town. In both cases the aim has been to make the school yard a communal place for learning, recreation, and creative play for the school population and everyone in the wider school community. Both projects were initiated through the growth of an environmental education orientation among teachers and parents, who viewed their yard as a potential outdoor extension of the school environment.

Environmental education is a process approach to learning, springing from an interdisciplinary – intercommunal consciousness and utilizing the real-live indoor – outdoor environment (people and objects in space and time) as the primary stimulus and motivation. In the school-focussed process, the kids, their parents and teachers, and the spaces they occupy are key components, plus all other people and places of the community.

PROCESS EVOLUTION

The physical changes at Thousand Oaks were made by a dedicated group of parents and students in environmental design during 1970 – 1971. I learned a tremendous amount simply through being there as a *participant designer*; plus several evaluations of user response were made of the new environment which then became specific inputs to the work at Washington.

The overt purpose of project WEY (Washington Environmental Yard)[2] is to function as a vehicle for the development of an environmental education process within the total school community. A highly complex, multifaceted cyclical process is entailed in changing the attitudes and behavior of all participants. Progress can only occur at the rate at which a shared consciousness of what is happening evolves. In this respect physical change on the yard has been instrumental in changing the behavior of kids (instantly) and teachers (slowly, but surely), a process which eventually results in curriculum change.

I do not intend to dwell in any more detail on the process-vehicle aspects of the yards, although this is a very fascinating part of the story. For example, both Thousand Oaks and Washington function as research field stations and interdisciplinary training grounds for university students in environmental design, conservation and natural resources, education, and many other fields.[3]

TRANSFER

My purpose in this paper is to share with you the excitements and feelings of a specific strand of my experience and what I think I have learned from it, stemming from my role as *action-research designer –manager*. By "design" I mean the expression of social purposes in physical change, including its ongoing long-term management as purposes change; by "action" I mean joining with others — school and university students, parents, teachers, and all other potential users—and "doing it"; by "research" I mean learning from the doing.

In the following discussion, I would like to point out and reflect on some of the potentials which have struck me and which help increase our consciousness of the possibilities of environmental learning with and without the help of adults. I in no way want to sell the idea that "it should all happen in school years on school yards." Learning and play should happen all the time, everywhere where children and people are — in the streets, shopping centers, factories, parks of our cities, etc. Let us hope that ultimately kids can move away from school into a richly diverse, accessible city where they can regain some of the freedom that overinstitutionalization and the automobile have taken away. School yards are a good place to start because of their accessibility and simply because they are such an obviously unused resource.

In an attempt to help you develop an understanding of the role the real-live physical environment can play as a vehicle for learning, I offer as a basis for discussion a set of *qualitative design concepts* that I believe to be critical to the evolution of a viable play and learning place. As you will see the qualities are by no means mutually exclusive, as is the nature of environmental education itself; they interconnect and overlap, all in one! But hopefully each quality gives a different focus and orientation . . . like moving around some intricate multidimensioned object, where each new view gives a fresh understanding . . . .

ENVIRONMENTAL QUALITIES FOR A PLAY AND LEARNING PLACE

To succeed, any child environment has to be a "place," has to have an elusive quality of *placeness* — a set of feelings and good vibes evoked by the character of the general domain. In part these feelings will result from particular qualities in particular places . . . each kid has a favorite spot out there: secret places, private places away from big kids, soft places to roll around in, hard places to play ball, high places for overviews, holes in the ground for hiding in with a group of friends. Positive vibrations can also arise from overall qualities, common to the whole territory: Like, is it inviting, open . . . free? Does it feel warm and comfortable, are there lots of things to do and can everyone do what they want?

For a lasting "sense of place,"[4] two characteristics must be present. The place must be relevant to kids, i.e., they must enjoy doing something there; and it must have a strong sensory identity— be able to make a lasting impact through the child's senses. The retention of a strong mental image will help reinforce the memory of happy events. A climbing structure, for example, located to give a strong, clear silhouette against the sky or a large uniquely shaped rock placed in the center of a grassy setting area could result in the "object," in both cases, becoming a "place."

Clearly not every place should have a strong identity. Perhaps a few pieces of "nowhere land" should be left over; otherwise, how will children learn to discriminate between place and non-place?

A rich diversity of school-yard places opens up many possibilities for sensory exploration and assessment. Children can test and compare their senses together . . . . How do you feel here? Is it too dark? Too light? Too warm? Too cold? Do you like the smell? What's your favorite place on the yard? What do you do there? What's your favorite place at home? In the neighborhood? How do they compare? How would an Eskimo feel here? An Indian? Your mother? Your grandmother? What's the noisiest place on the yard? The most peaceful? What is peace?

Sensory dimensions can be exploited in all kinds of ways in the design of objects and places, utilizing color, texture, light and shadows, smells, sounds . . . a whole outdoor acoustic environment could include giant instruments — bells, gongs, chimes, and whistles—things for kids to play and for the wind to play as it pleases.

On a typical school yard, there's seldom even a comfortable place to sit down. Yet learning is communication and it can be greatly helped by providing places where it can happen. A great deal of environmental experience is a communal affair. Kids are naturally social animals and need to share experiences with others (adults included) as they happen. They often need to sit down right on the spot to talk about what happened a moment before. Conversation places need to be quiet, shady, and sheltered (in California) and of an intimate size, consistent with the laws of social distance for small groups. For some groups a geometric formal setting may be required to initiate and sustain interaction, e.g., in the case of outdoor "performances."

Many such places can also serve the school's surrounding community. Thus some of the places should be large enough for community meetings, concerts, flea markets, and similar events. In this way yards can become an open meeting ground for school and community to interact; where knowledge and understanding of each other's spheres can intermingle . . . . Who lives in your community? What do they do? Where? Why?

Some of the most intensive learning-through-direct-experience-of-the-environment occurs through the peaceful focus of the individual child alone. Above all, kids need places where they can be privately at peace, alone, or with a friend. Imagine how hard it is for a young urban child to do this nowadays. It certainly can't happen in a typical school. Out of school there are parents and siblings to contend with, at home or in endless environmentally alienating auto ride-arounds. In our larger cities kids desperately need places where they can exert their autonomy as free individuals.

Placeness qualities represent the sum of comfort and well-being that may or may not grow in the user over a period of time. The sense of place we are talking of is that which deepens and mellows with use. Like Gertrude Stein's "there," it is the love of the place for its own sake that grows slowly from knowing . . . from repeated and tested experience. But also, like adults, children can flash their basic feelings about a place in the first few moments of experience, sensing as it were, a longer term image. There appear, however, even at an early age, marked differences in environmental response based on differences in cultural style and value systems. At Washington, which is centered in a particularly diverse community, there are very obvious differences in style, attitude, and behavior between say the "hippie kids" who wear odd assortments of old clothes to school, and the kids of newly middle-class families who come to school dressed in carefully considered suits and boots. With these guys, there's a very obvious conflict between their intrinsic desires as kids and their cultural values. For example, they *talk* about how "junky" the playground is, but nonetheless play in the junky areas; and when their clothes are messed up become really upset! In some cases the cultural values are too strong, preventing the child's natural behavior, and result in self-deprivation. With the exception of these isolated examples of severe cultural indoctrination, kids still seem generally to operate at a more basic level. Their needs are more universal, no matter where they come from . . . First, Second, or Third World; City or Suburbs.

In summary, *placeness* seems to depend on the number of things you can do "in" and "with" the environment; generally, the degree of psychological stimulation and physiological comfort and on the remaining intrinsic qualities we have yet to discuss. Actually, in a positive sense, cultural differences add tremendously to the richness of the human scene.

TIME AND CHANGE: IN ALL THINGS

Space, time, and objects are the key components of any learning environment. Space places we have just discussed. Time and change of objects (including people) form a twofold dimension that relates to everything, even though it is often played down.

Interpretation and utilization of the environmental time dimension require a certain level of consciousness. I am not sure how this is acquired, although it seems there are a growing number of people in this *aquarian* age who are in touch with the temporal dimension, from the "cosmic" on down (or is it "up"?).

This is an aspect of every other quality I shall discuss later. Clearly it can be "designed into" the learning environment, in many ways on many scales. A first basic point is that a school yard, rich in resources, will greatly conserve time by reducing the need for field trips!

At a less obvious level, people need lots of time to come to know each other. Kids need time to experience the amazing richness of the environment. We all need time to wander and wonder. In some places users should be forced to move s-l-o-w-l-y, to — look — with — loving care — at — every—small—detail—as—if—it—was—their — last — moment — on — earth.

With time, questions come without asking . . . the attributes of animate versus inanimate objects. . . . Do rocks change? How about mountains? How about piles of dirt? How about sunflowers . . . oak trees . . . pine trees . . . pole beans . . . butterflies? Did the Berkeley Hills always look like that? . . . .

Seasonal change is a natural dimension that can enter the design of the learning environment in all kinds of ways: The selection and location of plants and trees—for example, a red exclamation mark of fall maple; the positive utilization of rain

... a designed "flood," rather than letting the water escape down the nearest drain; a variety of shady, protected, open places will make users aware of microclimate through their own responses at different seasons; chimes and noisy plants such as bamboo for the windy season; mud patches, squelchy or hard-baked and cracked, depending on the season — the possibilities are endless! Utilization of the seasonal and daily path of the sun is another dimension . . . light, shadow, reflections, filters, photography, hot, cold, chlorophyl, and so on.

The diverse social implications of change can also be built into the childs' surroundings. Thus some places *can be fixed,* permanent and unchanging, providing familiarity, a sense of security, and a stable identity (an important psychic function in today's ever-changing environment); other places *can change* day to day, or even moment by moment according to the whims of the users. If some resources are loose, this will happen inevitably and with extraordinary rapidity. At Washington, where we have tried to keep options open in the initial phases, an enormous amount of creative activity has been generated from loose and ephemeral resources — a whole hunk of experience that is completely invisible to a casual visitor to the yard.

MOVEMENT

Movement is a mix of space and time. Most obvious physical movement invites social interaction — it is a beautifully predictable situation . . . and social interaction engenders mutual knowing, understanding, feeling, exploration, and compassion among kids. Movement depends on specific characteristics of the physical environment; they must be present for the social consequences to follow. Movement is also pure, sensory, kinesthetic pleasure for the individual child, as his or her body moves through space.

The kinesthetic sense can be stimulated in many different ways, e.g., the rhythmic up and down, growing amplitude of traditional swings (still a universally popular item, even in new-style playgrounds); the back-and-forth, round-and-round motion of swing ropes; the simple, small-scale, bouncy motion of a spring board; the quick, one-way downward flash of a slide; the circular, speeding-up-slowing-down gyrations of a merry-go-round. In this case users must designate themselves as "pushers" or "riders" for operation . . . a situation of human cooperation which is expressed perhaps in its purest form in the beautiful, socially interdependent see-saw . . . we need each other to do this thing! We must learn to work together for this teeter-tottering world to keep going . . . play and learning; what's the difference?

The diversity criterion can be extended in each particular component. Swing ropes for example can be long, suspended far above the ground, giving a long incredible *woosh* — moving through a big space with each swing. They can be short — a fast-moving, back-and-forth, round-and-round

Figure 1
Movement and interaction: inner-tube "spider's web" (Project WEY).

kind of ride. Double-hung, pendulum on pendulum, gives movement in two vertical planes at the same time — wild! Hey, what's a pendulum anyway? . . . gravity . . . the earth . . . rhythm . . . here we go again . . . .

Slides, can be high, low, fast, slow, narrow, wide, bumpy, smooth, straight, or curvy. You can slide on, over, under, through, between, beside, above, alongside, around . . . . The experience and contrast of each of these variations can produce a new awareness of movement, to be discussed, written about, compared, evaluated — a takeoff to who knows where . . . Why do your pants get warm? What is friction? Energy? How many calories is your slide?

Movement can be a self-learning process of body awareness and an acquisition of psychomotor skills. The physical environment should provide for a variety of possible movements, recognizing that individual users have different skill levels. Furthermore if different elements are physically connected in a variety of ways, the user will be able to engage in tarzanlike sequential motion . . . where mind and body are one. Climb . . . swing . . . jump . . . climb . . . slide . . . run . . . swing . . .; up, down . . . round and round . . . to and fro . . . . In this body-flowing pleasure, all kinds of possibilities open up for kids to explore their senses, especially in the company of finely tuned adults.

What muscles do you use for what? What are muscles? Do you have any sore ones? Do all creatures have muscles? Do plants have muscles? Fish? What does a muscle do? How does it work? Why is it important to keep our muscles exercised? What *is* good health? Can you balance on that plank? What does balance mean? How do you write it? What other things can you find that balance?

Movement raises questions of perception of time and space—fast and slow, near and far—all is relative! How far do you live from school? How long does it take you to get here? Who prefers to walk, who to ride . . . why? Do you know how far

some birds can fly? How fast some animals can run . . . what's the slowest animal you've ever seen? What's the furthest you've ever been? Hey, that rhymes! Let's make some poems . . . about speed . . . cheetas . . . humming-birds . . . rocks . . . pebbles on the beach . . . the sea that moves . . . calm and rough . . . waves and cycles . . . rising falling . . . the moon — round and round.

Rhythm is the beat of life . . . in the "age of rock" need this point be labored? Cycles: the heaving ocean . . . the universe . . . 24 hours to a day, 60 seconds to a minute, 3.7 people to a family, 6 beats to a bar, 2,000 cars per hour, 22 inches of rain a year, round the sun each year, probability and improbability, the cyclical view of history . . . this could go on forever . . . is eternity repeatable?

MANIPULATION: ADVENTURE PLAY– ADVENTURE LEARNING

If the "stuff" of the environment can really be moved around at will, pulled apart and recombined, then things really begin to happen. Kids really get to know the environment if they can dig it, beat it, swat it, lift it, push it, join it, combine different parts of it, make things with it. This is what adults call "creative activity," it's what artists do . . . a process of imagination and environment working together. By this token all children become artists once given access to physical resources they can freely mess around with. Simon Nicholson has aptly called this the "theory of loose parts"[5] *(included in this volume).*

The loose parts can encompass an endless diversity . . . milk crates, railroad ties, sand, dirt, water, oil drums, sheets, strips, blocks, wedges, packing crates, circles, cubes, planks; baulks of lumber, big and small. Logs, stumps, branches of trees, palm fronds, bamboo, eucalyptus sprouts. Sheets of cardboard, cloth, carpet sponge plastic, sheet plastic; soft and hard; big and small; flexible and inflexible; . . . ad infinitum . . . . European adventure playgrounds are a type of play – learning place that is completely based on a freely manipulable environment—an idea that sadly hasn't caught on in America yet. Clare Cooper[6] *(included in this volume)* has written an excellent account of the theory and practice of the adventure playground idea: sand, water, naked dirt, scrap lumber, shovels, hammers, saws and nails; and sensitive supervising play leaders are the basic resource requirements. Then let it happen . . . .

How did you make your house? Did your parents make your "real" house? How did Indians make houses? Or Africans? How do you use a saw? Who here can hammer nails in straight? Where does wood come from? Why is this wood rotten? What does rotten mean? Is your house big enough for you? Do some people live in houses that are too small, or bigger than they need? Do animals do the same thing? Where do animals live? Let's make a bird house.

Adventure play is a child-controlled process of community development. The provision of a free, open, changeable environment enables children to develop their own society and its physical habitat in a completely integrated two way process. As the society changes so does the physical environment in an endless cycle of growth and decay. The kids learn how to use their hands, bodies, heads, and each other as physical resources; they learn cooperation, law, fun, responsibility, initiative, respect, love; and they make lasting contact with the basic elements of earth, air, fire, and water. It is a situation of learning-by-living, beyond school—even the most interdisciplinary. By setting up their own experiments in "adventure learning" kids get an intuitive grasp of how the world works that can be translated into adult concepts later. To me this is an "alternative education" rather than the marginally different possibilities usually discussed. In adventure play, kids learn how to control their own lives and environment, so that in later life they won't get pushed around by the establishment and professional experts like architects, planners, and engineers![7]

OPENENDEDNESS

If fully fledged adventure play is beyond the means of parents or insurance engineer, many parts of the adventure process can still be provided for in fixed, permanent components. Openendedness, for example, is a quality in the environment that urges exploration . . . setting free the mind to wander wherever the environment leads it, into new areas of imagination and experience. Open ends can be specific places which kids can physically add to in their own way. "Edges" and "corners" are good examples; this is where kids will start building if they have materials. Big holes in the ground are good too . . . or simply a post . . . or the bowl of a tree . . . or between or against anything. Open ends need to be mentally open and undesignated. A certain degree of abstraction is required . . . an indefinite yet evocative meaning, a richness of feeling and identity . . . places where kids can make their own meaning— which is precisely what present-day "rocket-ship" and "pirates galleon" playground structures fail to do!

The most powerful part of an openended, communal process is the way kids hit off each other's imagination . . . a kind of corporate, shared creative process — a truly communal act of sharing

Figure 2
Open-endedness: dirt area (Project WEY).

each other as resources as they learn, play, and interact with the environment . . . and interplay with each other's feelings, emotions, and ideas. The more manipulable, diverse and openended the environment is, the more intensive, extended, and varied this process is likely to become . . . . "What's that?" "A dinosaur's bone." Let's go hunting dinosaurs . . . got the spears . . . where do they live . . . I once saw a saber-toothed tiger . . . in caves . . . over there, we could make a tiger trap in the corner. Let's dig a pit . . . . Who's got a spade . . . ? Did stone-age people have spades? We could make our camp behind those rocks . . . They got some wood and string . . . . We could use that for the trap door. Get to work you slaves. We'll use the pipe for a spy hole. No! It's a boat . . . Let's go looking for whales . . . . Do they still hunt whales? We saw a film about whales with Mrs. Jones yesterday, there's lots of different kinds, they make perfume from one . . . . My sister uses perfume . . . . Do you have a girl friend?

Openendedness can extend into an environmental education curriculum orientation where kids and adults work together in an unending sociocognitive process using the environment as a "constant vehicle"; teachers and resource people can greatly extend this open process by becoming part of it, sharing their ideas and knowledge, sometimes leading the exploration, sometimes sitting back and letting it go; sometimes acting with the group, sometimes staying out until called upon. Different roles are open at different times — leader, facilitator, friend and confidant, provider of tools, organizer of materials, safety supervisor, wildlife expert, lifter of heavy weights, and so on.

The nearest analogy to this kind of adult – teacher – resource is, in fact, the adventure-playground play leader. The need for human resources in an open environment is absolutely critical to its productive management, maintenance, and full utilization as a domain for human development. The need for outdoor people as well as indoor people has in general not been understood by the educational establishment. Thus most "open school yards" are having a rough time, scraping along as best they can with "bits" of people here and there. Unless something changes, enormous potentialities are going to remain untapped for a long time to come.

SCALE

If the mixture of scale (the comparative size of objects and the spaces between them) is varied, then the range and number of possibilities open to the users appears to increase. Thus, some areas can be small and intimate, others big and challenging, many areas should mix big and small together. For example, big towers can be built out of cable spools; and by knocking out a couple of boards from each central drum "escape spaces" result, which only very small people can fit into.

A close mix of scales in the whole psychomotor environment is very necessary because the degree to which children are prepared to take risk is not correlated with age, rather it depends on psychological and bodily characteristics, e.g., it is common to find a little seven year old doing things that would scare the heavier built ten year old.

Figure 3
Scale interaction: Tower of a Thousand Rooms (Thousand Oaks yard).

Kids continually want to test their capabilities and skills in relation to their peers — a form of self-evaluation which is a necessary aspect of growing up. It is very different from a formalized competitive situation with "I am better than thou" overtones. Rather it is an informal "sparring" kind of scene, where kids are saying to themselves, "can I or can't I?" "She can, I wonder if I can too?" "Hey, can you do this?" If the challenge is "stepped" at different heights at jumping and swinging places, then kids of different abiity (and age) can participate in the same situation, can

progress by stages and not feel hopelessly intimidated by a challenge which they cannot cope with.

But let's not forget that small people, (especially girls) five and six years old, like small intimate spaces where they can pursue their fantasies undisturbed. They can find a whole world in a few grains of sand or in the cracks between some rocks. What's the smallest place in the yard . . . the biggest . . . who lives there . . . are some places changing in size . . .? What's the difference between scale and size? How many people can fit in that space?

Figure 4
Scale interaction: Permanent structures (Project WEY).
Photo: Marty Bovill.

INTERFACES

Interface and interaction is another concept where a diversity principle applies and as with scale it is a relative measure. For environmental education the people–nature interface is the most relevant. Our aim is to have school sites with a broad spectrum of situations where nature is protected to varying degrees from human access and impact. At Washington a haven is planned for the roof where a fragile environment can flourish unmolested. Ground-level, mini-animal sanctuaries are also planned.

Along with a large number of subtly differentiated interfaces which also take into action the effect of nonhuman factors: sun, shade, water, soil, drainage, etc. The aim is to create a balanced spectrum of protection where people and other living things can coexist. In itself the situation is an ongoing experiment and lesson. Everyone has to face "us or them" choices all the time and will continually need to probe real-live physical situations to see why in some cases "they" win and other cases "we" win, and what, if anything, should be done to change the balance.

At Thousand Oaks, minigardens are flourishing

Figure 5
Interaction: The Delta (Thousand Oaks yard).

in small planters outside each classroom. Because the plants are two feet above the level of the surrounding asphalt, kids can't run across them. Other small planting places are at ground level and have not survived; but bigger places have, all of which provides us, and the children, with a useful spectrum of environmental impacts.

AN ANIMATE, LIVING DOMAIN

For a renaissance in environmental understanding and respect to occur in the future, kids (*who are future adults!*) must grow up in constant contact with the real-live processes of life. Environmental values will only grow in children if based on direct experience of living nature. It is imperative that primary school sites, because of their day-to-day, moment-to-moment accessibility, be provided with a diverse animate environment, one which kids can taste, touch, see, and feel at any moment of their school day. This is "level one" of environmental education. Once it is present then some of the latest books, kits, games, curricula, and other paraphernalia produced by the education industry may be relevant or even essential to a higher understanding of the environment. But affective – sensory interaction must always precede and intertwine with the cognitive understanding of concepts, relationships, implications, and so on.

Plant a flower and watch it grow. How long does it take to surface . . . what shape are the leaves . . . texture . . . how *many* . . . what *size*? What's the *rate* of growth? What's the difference between the plants in the sun and those in the shade? Graph it . . . measure it. Who saw the first one . . .? *Draw* it . . . describe it, *write* about it . . . *read* about it . . . What other flowers do you know? Do you have some at home? Where do you live? Do your parents like flowers? Why do you wear flowers on your dress? Let's wear flowers in our hair . . . Let's make daisy chains . . . Do flowers have feelings? Is this one dead? What does "dead" mean? How do you feel when you look at the flowers? How do they smell? What lives in the flowers? Wow, all kinds of things . . . Do you like honey? Who's tasted honey?

Are flowers useful? What are they for? (Japanese girl talks about flower arrangements.) Let's go to a flower store . . . a flower farm . . . a flower market . . . a perfume factory. Let's eat some sunflower seeds. What's a seed? Let's save some to plant next year . . . Cycle . . . Recycle . . . .

Is the sunflower a flower or a vegetable? What are vegetables anyway? Have they always been here? When did they arrive? What did the Indians eat? Where from? The ancient Chinese . . . Who were they? Measure, count, weight, describe,

Figure 6
(a) A living domain: planting the garden for the new season (Project WEY). (b) Interface: flower planting (Project WEY).

touch, taste, eat, cook, nutrition, health . . . You are what you eat . . . What's good for you? Where do they come from . . . a supermarket? Let's take a trip to a vegetable farm . . . Canning factory . . . Orchard . . . fruit! Are the plums on the yard ripe yet? You found a 6½-inch bean! . . . Jane wrote a story about a giant bean; let's listen to her read it.

If plants and vegetables can grow right outside the classroom, there's a whole new scene going! In fact consider the possibilities for developing a complete educational alternative around the concept and reality of a garden. "The Garden School: Where you grow your own and grow yourself . . . a kind of urban-learning-farm."

Ponds are an essential resource because they go through a whole complex cycle each year; the learning and curriculum potentialities are unending. Again they are an element where a diversity criterion needs applying: big ponds, small ponds, year-round and vernal (dry up in summer), still water and running, water falls and fountains, gorges and islands; some for boats and some for birds, some for fish, some for people, (and some for dogs!). Ponds need to be as "natural" as possible — a complete entity with dirt, mud, rocks, cattails, weeds, birds, butterflies, trees, lily pads, fish, pollywogs, dead leaves; the cold-damp winter stillness; nothing moving; the warm vibrant summer. A REAL PLACE with all the "level one" feelings to stick in a child's mind to promote lasting understanding.

RICHNESS, DIVERSITY, CHOICE

It is a basic concept of ecology that diverse environments are resilient and productive. Kids too, seem to grow well in rich, choiceful, supportive surroundings. The more diversity, the more possibilities . . . The more likely that each person or group will find their own particular "turn on" and the less chance that anyone will start disrupting someone else's scene as a result of boredom.

Diversity is a concept that can be applied to everything in the child environment, including the

qualities already discussed: place, space, time, change, movement, manipulation, openness, scale, interface, nature, sensory dimensions. All these can be subject to infinite variations, *some* of which have been noted . . . . A crude maxim might be: if in doubt, add it. Everything in the world has potential and will be used by someone for something, sometime.

If learning is the flow of ideas and excitement that comes from such diversity, education's role should be to facilitate the flow rather than hinder it. Kids may then grow up to demand a more supportive and balanced environment. In the final analysis, learning is not a question of the score on some attainment scale, but has to do with the development of a whole human person, of feelings and emotions, about and toward other people and all other things; of being able to understand and know oneself and to solve problems with ingenuity and humor. Environmental education, perhaps, is the generation of happiness that comes from such balance and process.

NOTES AND REFERENCES

1. Robin C. Moore, "An Experiment in Playground Design," thesis in City and Regional Planning, Massachusetts Institute of Technology, 1966.
2. Background and conceptual basis can be found in the *Project WEY Brochure,* obtainable from Washington school, 2300 Grove Street, Berkeley, Calif. ($1.50 post free) or the Department of Landscape Architecture, 202 Wurster Hall, University of California, Berkeley, Calif.
3. For further information see Robin C. Moore, "Teacher-Learner-Environment-Play," mimeo, Department of Landscape Architecture, 1972, and the *IDS 120 File of Environmental Activities,* Robin Moore and Carole Rollins (eds.), Department of Landscape Architecture, $7.50 ($5.00/students), post free.
4. A term first articulated in relation to larger places in the city by Kevin Lynch in *The Image of the City,* Cambridge, Mass.: The MIT Press, 1960.
5. Simon Nicholson, "The Theory of Loose Parts," *Landscape Architecture,* Vol. 62, Oct. 1971 (*and this volume*).
6. Clare Cooper, "Adventure Playgrounds," *Landscape Architecture*, Vol. 61, Oct. 1970 (*and in this volume*).
7. For anyone interested in seeing a real-live adventure playground, there is a fine one in Milpitas, California; call the city's Parks and Recreation Department for details and directions.

**THE CITY AS AN OPEN LEARNING
ENVIRONMENT**

Any attempt to formulate real alternatives in education must differentiate between education and schooling. The articles in the previous section illustrate some of the possibilities for nonschool learning to occur within the immediate boundaries of a child's neighborhood. This limited geographic range is both the strength and weakness of these options. The articles in this section are concerned with how the extent and diversity of learning resources can be expanded in both space and time.

In the first article Everett Reimer defines education as "increasing awareness for individuals and groups of their laws, ideologies and institutions, and increasing ability to shape these laws, ideologies and institutions, to their needs and interests." By this standard it is clear that existing schools are "dominating institutions" in which children are miseducated to the extent that they come to accept schools as the definers of their educational needs. If education as Reimer defines it is to ever take place, it is necessary to create "democratic institutions" which foster the ability of every in-

dividual to regain control over his own lifelong education.

What would a democratic institution look like? Are there any existing institutional arrangements that could serve as a model? According to Reimer,

Democratic institutions offer a service, satisfy a need, without conferring advantage over others or conveying the sense of dependence that institutions such as welfare agencies do. They take the form of networks rather than production systems—networks that provide an opportunity to do something rather than make and sell a finished product.[1]

By this standard, public utilities, such as public transportation systems, the mail and telephone, and electricity, water, and gas distribution systems provide examples of democratic institutions. In all of these, the user of the service initiates access to the system and participates in the system as long as he decides it is necessary for him to do so. Rather than inducing unsatisfiable needs, these utility networks provide access to universally necessary resources and they tend to remain responsive to their clients' changing needs.

The Illich–Reimer alternative to schools can be described as four interrelated networks of learning resources that would be operated much like existing public utilities: (1) networks of educational objects: books, records of all kinds, tapes, communications media, offset presses, and so on; (2) networks of skill models: people who have both the willingness and ability to demonstrate a skill; (3) networks of peers: individuals who share the same learning goals and previous level of experience; and (4) networks of educators: which would include experts and general pedagogues. To finance these learning webs, it is proposed that the money which now supports schools be distributed, in the form of lifelong educational accounts, to every U.S. citizen. This is similar to the voucher plan except that these credits could be applied to other learning options in addition to the existing schools.

While advocating his own radical alternative to schools, Reimer asserts that the educational methods of Paulo Freire are to be given first priority because they are more direct, efficient, and disruptive of unconscionable political relationships. For this reason, the Illich–Reimer opportunity networks, which are less overtly political, may be a more practical alternative.

Finally, using his definition of education as a criterion for evaluating learning alternatives, Reimer assesses the problems and potential of free schools and modern media. Once again these are viewed as viable alternatives only to the extent to which they become democratic rather than dominating institutions. For free schools this means gaining political and economic freedom from the public education system, and for the communications media this means gaining learner control over both the production and reception of messages.

Despite the persuasiveness of the Illich–Reimer deschooling thesis it is clear that a school system that accommodates approximately 45 million students taught by more than 2.1 million instructors is not going to be easily "disestablished." It is more likely that the schools will change and other options will be added.

Perhaps the true value of the Illich–Reimer proposal is that this utopian vision of learning in a just society can provide some guidelines by which to judge whether or not reform is moving in the right direction. Will a particular innovation enable people to shape rather than be shaped by their "laws, ideologies and institutions"? Is there greater access to learning resources? Are students increasingly responsible for defining their own educational goals and the means to achieve them? Are learning options more diverse, numerous, and relevant to individual needs?

Measured against these standards, Philadelphia's Parkway Program, a school without walls for high school students, operationalizes many of the basic ideas of a deschooled learning network. As authors Finklestein and Strick point out, ". . . students learn in the physical resources of the city itself—museums, businesses, libraries, hospitals, churches, stores—wherever they can find out what they want and need to know." By using the city as a vast network of educational resources, this highly successful program makes formal learning virtually indistinguishable from living. And, as a result of involving the community in the process of instruction and educational policy making, Parkway achieves a highly individualized program that is responsive to the needs of all the participants.

While schools without walls can make select resources of the city accessible to select groups of learners, they do not, as Jim Zien observes, "alter the general inaccessibility of urban environments to public scrutiny, urban activities to public participation, and urban objects to public use." A complementary strategy for making the city more generally accessible is to design the city itself as an educative environment. It is in this task that close collaboration between educators and designers becomes most essential and most fruitful.

The articles by Jim Zien and Michael and Susan Southworth are descriptions of case-study projects that demonstrate how designers can enhance the "educative potential of urban spaces." Zien describes an action–research project that attempted to discover ways in which the public transportation system can be designed to facilitate the child's free learning through his own independent exploration of the city. Research such as that undertaken in the Open City Project adds to our knowledge of how children conceive of and use the urban environment, providing new insights into the ways in which design and policy decisions can help to create new opportunities for public learning. The article by the Southworths, who are planners and designers, reviews two projects which illustrate how designers can "... [increase] physical access, [make] vivid the history of the city, [uncover] the activities of the city, [express] its social character, and [communicate] the city's form and structure." Efforts such as these, which facilitate user-initiated access to real world people, places, and processes constitute a basic nonschool alternative in education.

The last article in this section of Part Two focuses on ways in which opportunities for learning can be greatly expanded by appropriate redesign of the "relationships between people and the information in their environments." Dr. Chase presents two case studies in which basic principles of learning systems design are applied: the first is an infant learning environment that allows for new channels of communication among infants, their caretakers, and professional child-care specialists; the second is an exercise conducted with college students which generated a nonhierarchical learning situation "by selecting, organizing, formatting, and making accessible information that has relevance to the interests of a group."

Based on these examples, Chase attempts to outline the nature of the interdisciplinary mix that will constitute the environmental designer–educator–manager of the future, and to suggest how the "principles of learning systems design can also be applied to the evolving redesign of our culture." This article clearly demonstrates that educational policies and communications policies are merely different aspects of a strategy for making free learning a real possibility.

In one way or another all the articles in both Part One and Two seem to be moving us in the direction of a "deschooled" society. Perhaps Ronald Gross, poet, planner, and noted educational writer, best sums up the meaning of these trends when he states that

we are involved in a various, halting, impulsive, sometimes violent groping toward better ways of learning, growing, developing our potentials. My hope is that through the gradual weakening of the constraints of schooling we will so loosen its fabric, and so strengthen the opportunity to learn from other sources, that it will become impossible to separate learning from life, and students and teachers from friends learning together. For this we need a real flowering of other options, other avenues of growing up, other milieus in which to become more human.[3]

NOTES AND REFERENCES

1. Everett Reimer, *School Is Dead: Alternatives in Education* Garden City, N.Y.: Doubleday and Co., Inc., 1971, p. 108.
2. See Judith Areen and Christopher Jencks, "Educational Vouchers: A Proposal for Diversity and Choice," in *Restructuring American Education: Innovations and Alternatives,* Ray C. Rist (ed.), New Brunswick, N.J.: Transaction Books, 1972.
3. Ronald Gross, "After Deschooling, Free Learning," in *After Deschooling, What?,* Alan Gartner, Colin Greer, and Frank Riessman (eds.), New York: Harper & Row, Publishers 1973, p. 150. This collection of reactions to the deschooling thesis provides a good critical review by major writers in education today.

Freeing Educational Resources*

Everett Reimer

Since this article is committed to controversy, if not by its title then by the outlook of its author, it is important to define early what is at issue. I do not regard schools as truly educational but, more nearly, as an institutional perversion of education. Schools not only prevent true education from occurring, they actually miseducate, in my opinion.

They teach not what is relevant and true but what is irrelevant and untrue to the interests of their students. They do this, however, in the service of a society of which they are a central institution and a major bulwark. They effectively adjust their students to the requirements of this society, which has as its basic principle the maintenance of power and privilege differentials among nations, classes, and individuals, but which attempts

*This article was written for a study prepared for the International Commission on the Development of Education, at UNESCO, and published in *Prospects: Quarterly Review of Education,* Vol. 2, Spring 1972; © Unesco 1972.

to disguise this principle by promising all things to all men. One of the main purposes of schools is to make this false promise appear plausible.

Schools do this partly by appearing to be open to all comers while in fact they reserve their higher levels for the winners of the competition of the early grades. Since only those who succeed in school get access to the higher levels of consumption, influence, information, and respect, schools serve to ration the goods and services which technological societies pretend to be able to supply to everyone.

By convicting their dropouts of failure, schools justify the limitations under which they are subsequently forced to live. Since everyone with less than a Ph.D. is by definition a dropout—and actually limited in what he can earn—the schooled society could keep its promise only by keeping everyone in school for twenty years. Since this would expose the myth of schooling, we propagate instead the myth of genetic deficiency. To make the goods that man has learned to produce abundantly available to all would violate the law of God—this has to be the basic rationale for the present organization of affairs.

The actual rationale, that production is limited by manpower skills, is patently false as myriads of production restrictions, if nothing else, make amply clear. There are some real limits—ecological and other limits—on how much can be produced, but they do not provide a convenient rationalization for the distribution of the social product.

I define education as the conscious use of resources to increase people's awareness of the relevant facts of their lives, and to increase people's abilities to act in their own true interests. Of major importance to most people are the laws that govern them, the ideologies which influence them, and the institutions, and institutional products, which determine the impact of their laws and ideologies upon them. Practical education, then, is increasing awareness for individuals and groups of their laws, ideologies and institutions, and increasing ability to shape these laws, ideologies, and institutions to their needs and interests.

This definition of education need not exclude the teaching of respect for existing laws, ideologies, institutions, and other facts of life. So long as what *is* can meet the challenge of what *should be*, respect and critical awareness are compatible. It is not permissible, however, to give respect priority over truth since this is to induce respect for falsehood.

To argue that the youth of students makes this unavoidable is to beg the question. Until the present century youth was given no prior claim on educational resources nor can the current priority be justified except in terms of the present functions of schools, which are to shape the young to the requirements of a social system which cannot, itself, bear critical appraisal.

These statements assume the possibility of an objective test of truth, and I am not unaware of nor unimpressed by the "sociology of knowledge." I believe that objective truth can exist only in a just society, but I believe, also, that the prevision of such a society can induce the shadow of a criterion of objective truth. I define justice as the lifetime opportunity of every individual to enjoy at least his share of the universal values of his society and only as much more as will not inhibit the opportunity of others. Only in such a society would people have a relatively undistorted view of social reality.

In this article I shall present and recommend two radical educational alternatives to schools and evaluate two more. Paulo Freire's method of "conscientization" and an "alternative," which Ivan Illich and I have developed, are the two programs I shall recommend. *Free schools* and *modern media* are the two alternatives I shall evaluate.

Description and documentation will be concentrated almost entirely upon the first of these alternatives. They are much more specific, less well known in general and much better known to me. Free schools and modern media are subjects too broad and diffuse to be definitively discussed, or usefully documented, in an article of this size. Broad evaluation of their educational meaning and potential may, however, serve to increase slightly the scope and balance of a paper which might otherwise be judged too narrowly parochial.

As topics, free schools and modern media include many of the more commonly suggested alternatives to schools. An evaluation of them, in the light of the two recommended alternatives, may have implications, therefore, which go beyond the direct statements of the article.

PAULO FREIRE'S "CONSCIENTIZATION"

Paulo Freire's philosophy and method is, in my opinion, the most completely worked out and generally most satisfactory approach to education in the modern world. While I try to incorporate it into my own proposals, I feel that this incorporation does Freire less than full justice. My reason for going beyond his ideas at all is that in today's world these ideas may have only limited political possibilities.

While Freire's practice has been confined largely to illiterate agricultural workers, this is not only the most numerous clientele in the world but also the one most in need of education. Many members of the elite world would also agree that it is the most critical, since it contains the key to the growth of world population.

Conscientization is a general approach, however, applicable to any client population. Freire is too well known to require summary exposition and his system is too complex to be safely summarized. I shall concentrate, therefore, on the promise and feasibility of his approach, which is best illustrated by his own experience. Freire taught Brazilian peasants to read in from twenty to thirty hours of instruction by discovering a vocabulary highly relevant to their critical interests. As soon as they learned to read, Freire's peasants organized leagues and tried to bargain with their employers for improved conditions of life and work.

Freire's method is, clearly, highly effective and economical educationally, and, equally clearly, it is disruptive of existing political relationships where these are unjust and oppressive. Since most political relationships today are of this kind, the Freire method may appear to have limited application except in the hands of revolutionaries. Many governments, however, ideologically at least, regard revolutionary activities as legitimate and even necessary so long as they remain within certain bounds and do not constitute an immediate threat to the existing order. In principle, the Freire method, which achieves educational efficiency by selecting subject matter in terms of the students' true interests—as manifested in the students' own response—should be acceptable everywhere. In fact it would be and is widely acceptable when not applied to major populations suffering extreme injustice, or in otherwise highly sensitive situations.

In most countries dissemination of the Freire philosophy and principles and the training of a "teaching" cadre would probably not encounter political opposition. While such dissemination clearly has a revolutionary potential, it is the kind of potential which many governing elites would tolerate and some would even welcome. Few members of the elite today deny the inevitability of revolutionary changes in social organization and many ask only that it be achieved rationally. While this is in most cases a disguised plea that the cup pass them by, personally, it is also an attitude which permits preparatory action for revolutionary change to occur peacefully within the context of existing power structures.

First priority on any list of radical educational proposals should go to worldwide dissemination of the education philosophy, principles, and practices of Paulo Freire. It goes without saying that the widespread application of these practices should be carried as far as local situations will allow.

THE ILLICH–REIMER ALTERNATIVE

Second priority should go to the proposed treatment of educational resources outlined by Ivan Illich and myself, in materials which have been published by the Centro Intercultural de Documentación, and are in the course of more extensive publication.

Educational Accounts

We call first of all for a distribution of the public financial resources which now support schools to the entire citizenry of the political entities providing this support. We propose lifetime educational accounts, with credit accrued to each citizen in equal annual instalments. Unused educational credit would accumulate, possibly at interest, to be used whenever the individual desired. The account could be used for any kind of educational expenditure—which would have to be defined by each jurisdiction but which should be defined as broadly as possible. It would initially be defined, in all probability, to include schooling, although most school costs are incurred for custodial care and other noneducational functions of schools.

In order to assure an adequate supply of real educational resources, which would give the holders of educational credit educationally efficient options, Illich and I recommend the establishment of four educational resource networks, to be operated as public utilities. These are described below.

Network of Educational Objects This network might be described as a vastly expanded system of libraries, cataloguing and, in some cases, storing educational objects. These objects should include not only books but all types of records, equipment for the production, dissemination, and decoding of all kinds of records, examples of all types of energy converters (insofar as costs allow), examples of all kinds of natural and artificial objects, stressing those with the highest educational value for the entire population (considering the probable use as well as the potential value of the object if used).

An initial inventory of educational objects would, of course, have to be decided upon by educators, but subsequent use of this inventory, by students, should be the major determinant of the distribution of the ultimate investment among educational objects. It cannot be too much stressed that while libraries offer a good model of the directory and access services to be provided, current libraries and museums are hopelessly elitist in their selection and treatment of inventory and clientele.

A department store would, in many respects, provide a better model except that profit potentials outweigh human interests and needs in the selection and display of department-store goods. In the case of expensive objects, it would not be necessary that the public utility administering

the network acquire ownership but merely that it provide directory information and ensure success. Rivers, mountains, farms, and factories are examples of objects which it might not be feasible to acquire but which are educationally important. Laboratories, which now are often closed to public access, might be particularly important.

Network of Skill Models Next to educational objects, skill models are the most indispensable resource of the potential learner. Skill models need not be teachers but may be merely people able and willing to demonstrate a skill. In addition to necessary objects, this is all that most people interested in learning a skill really require. A directory of skill models should include all kinds of skills which may legally be practiced and no requirement in addition to the ability to demonstrate the skill in question should inhibit the listing of a willing model. Other characteristics could be listed in addition for the guidance of potential learners. The administration of a skill-model network would consist, centrally, in the maintenance of convenient directory service. Supplementary services could be offered, but they should avoid constraining or limiting the widest possible choice of the learner in selecting models and, equally, of models in deciding whom they will serve.

Network of Peers After skill models the most necessary human resources for learners are fellow-learners. Education, in the original sense of the word, implies more the use of skill to explore unfamiliar terrain than the mere acquisition of skills. For such exploration peers are frequently indispensable, persons with the same learning interests, similar preparation for the learning in question, and compatible secondary characteristics. Since interest and preparation for learning are usually both specific and ephemeral, the central problem of a peer network is to continually match and rematch individuals in groups which may vary in size from 2 to 1 million (see the medieval crusades and the recent popular music festivals in the United States).

Methods of peer matching may vary from the local bulletin board to the computer, with various kinds of publications in between. The user of a peer-matching system would identify himself by name and address, describe the activity he wanted to share and his preparation for this activity. A computer, or other medium, would send him back the names and addresses of all who had inserted similar descriptions. With the computer it would be possible to ensure that people using the system would become known only to their potential peers.

Network of Educators   Educators are the least essential of the major learning resources, less essential than objects, skill models, and peers. They may, nevertheless, be valuable at times, especially if they can be dissociated from schools. There are two kinds of educators, those who provide general guidance to a learner regardless of what he wants to learn and those who are experts in a content area.

The first we call pedagogues. Given educational credit and ample supply of educational resources, many people, especially parents who have been abdicating their educational responsibilities to schools, might want advice and assistance in the development of educational programs for their children. An independent profession practicing as medical doctors used to do, would constitute one network of educators. The other, made up of experts in all fields of activity, would parallel and overlap the network of skill models.

Administratively the network of experts might be treated as a subset of the network of skill models although, in some areas, there might be divergences. Educationally the difference is that skill models are needed by those who are beginning to learn a skill. Experts or leaders are needed by learners either perfecting a skill or using it in exploratory endeavor. In practice skill models, peers, and experts would all overlap, but it is important to distinguish them so as to avoid the practices by which schools have rendered plentiful resources scarce.

The Economics of Educational Resources

In relation to the number of potential learners there is an ample supply of educational objects, skill models, peers, and experts at every level of skill. Only the improper combining of these resources and other artificial barriers, including monopolization by a privileged class of students, make educational resources scarce. Removal of irrelevant restrictions, adequate comprehensive directories, and universal personal educational credit are all that is needed to make as much education available to everyone as he wants— wants enough, that is, to make the reasonable effort which learning sometimes requires.

Part of the money now going to the support of schools would have to go to the organization and basic maintenance of the networks described above. The rest, as much of the total as possible without jeopardizing the comprehensive character and efficient maintenance of the networks, should go to citizens in the form of educational credit, as above described. The use made of this credit in acquiring access to the resources administered by the networks should provide major, but not total, guidance to their operation. The public interest, as reflected in political rather than market behavior, should also have a voice.

The money now spent on public schools would, probably, be more than enough to provide as much education as people would want. There are three major sources of savings in comparison with the support of schools. First, school budgets are spent largely in the provision of custodial care for persons old enough not only to look after themselves but able to perform a large variety of socially useful services, the performance of which would also be highly educational. There is, thus, not only a large saving to be made on custodial care, but the realization of positively useful social services from those who are now cared for. Under the proposed plan there would be a further enormous saving in that learning would occur at the initiative of the learner—he would learn what and when he wanted.

Learning under these circumstances would be many times more efficient than now. Finally, the real price of educational resources would be greatly reduced by the removal of artificial restrictions on the supply and by the economics of scale implied in increasing the effective demand.

Criteria for Judging Educational Innovations

The two alternatives to schooling which I have discussed provide a basis for evaluating other innovations. The essence of the above proposals is that they counteract the tendencies of today's institutions, including the school, to shape men to the requirements of institutions rather than preparing them to shape institutions to meet human needs. I give priority to the Freire approach because it provides a positively countervailing force, exposing and otherwise offsetting existing institutional forces for the domination of man.

The proposal developed by Illich and myself is, if more general, relatively neutral. It merely frees and redistributes educational resources so that men can use them as they wish. Since it is neutral rather than directly opposed to the purposes of existing institutions it may have a better chance of adoption even while these institutions still prevail. In time, implementation of our proposal would also free men from their present bondage, although not as quickly or effectively as the Freire method if that were given free rein. The criterion on which other innovations should be judged is their potential for freeing men from the bondage of their present institutions, i.e., from the bondage of the institutional habits and attitudes which they exhibit as clients, employees, or citizens.

FREE SCHOOLS

One weakness of the free-school movement is that it is largely ancillary to schools. Most free schools exist as freeloaders, economic parasites, on schools. Their faculty services, particularly, are usually donated by individuals who draw pay from a nearby school. Their students, also, are assembled by existing school systems.

Free schools have not yet found, nor proposed, a method of financing which would make them independent of existing schools and, thus, a full-fledged alternative to them. They remain an ameliorative institution and, from the record so far, a fairly weak and transient one. The more fundamental weakness of the free school lies in its being still a school, in most important respects. It remains a means by which a privileged elite, highly selected by the very school system to which free schools are a supposed alternative, attempts to achieve alternative certification to elite occupations.

There are a few free schools dedicated to education, as such, or to education aimed at the reconstruction of society. Only schools whose students, in the main, renounce their use as status ladders can make this claim. Such free schools offer true alternatives. Some might even fit into what I have designated as the Freire approach. They would, then, of course, be subject to the political problems faced by that approach.

In principle, free schools have the potential of reviving the community of scholars which was the original university and perhaps its only valid form. In fact, this eventuality appears highly unlikely so long as free schools develop in the context of a school system which monopolizes educational resources. If these resources were distributed to individuals in the form of universal educational credit, free schools might very likely develop into and survive as true communities of scholars.

MODERN MEDIA

Modern media are, in fact if not in principle, a more important educational innovation than free schools. McLuhan goes too far but there is much in what he says. Both the main asset and the principal liability of modern media, as an educational alternative, are that they are so unpredictable. This is an asset in that they promise to free education, regardless of anyone's intentions, of many of its present strictures. People who do not learn to read will not, therefore, be condemned to ignorance nor, necessarily, to ineffectiveness. Elvis Presley and the Beatles would probably be just as effective if they could not read. People can also learn computer programming without being literate, sometimes perhaps even better than if they were.

The main problem in evaluating the educational impact of modern media is the difficulty of predicting, and therefore of controlling, their development as media. Most modern media are, on the other hand, highly susceptible to centralized control of program content—or, more generally, message selection. The medium is by no means the total message.

Monopoly of message control in modern media is in fact one of the major threats to man's freedom. There appears to be only one general way of avoiding the total control of men's minds which a monopoly of modern media threatens. This is true education of those who receive the messages. Some of this education may be achieved, inadvertently, by the media themselves. It is entirely possible that intensive exposure to television, early in life, may produce adults with high ability to disregard television. It would be extremely dangerous, however, to depend upon the media inoculating against themselves.

The critical educational question, with respect to modern media, is whether they will become resources for individual learners or instruments for institutions. Telephones and videophones which permit individuals to communicate are one thing, a captive television audience is another. Proliferation of movie cameras and offset presses, permitting anyone to make movies and print leaflets, is one thing. Passive clients hooked on commercially or governmentally produced movies and magazines are another.

The problem is not so much who controls the message—there is relatively little to choose between governments and corporations if the degree of monopoly is the same. The important point is that messages not be institutionally controlled. Establishments of school, of press, of sight and sound should be prohibited, just as establishments of religion are now prohibited in almost every democratic constitution. All such establishments are equally prisons for the mind of man.

If the objects required to produce and transmit as well as to receive messages of all kinds are widely available; if access to models of the skills involved in producing, transmitting, and receiving these messages is widely available; then modern media can significantly contribute to educational efficiency. If critical objects and/or skills are monopolized, on the other hand, the educational process will be that much more efficiently perverted by the development of modern media—shaping man to conformity with the requirements of existing institutions rather than preparing him for the shaping of these institutions to his needs.

CONCLUSION

It may appear that this paper poses a dilemma for an existing institution dependent for support upon other institutions, among which many of the most powerful are dedicated to the maintenance of privilege rather than to the equalization of educational opportunity. In major part this charge must be admitted. Nevertheless, there are in every institution degrees of freedom. Many individuals, occupying key roles in all of the most powerful institutions in the world, are deeply ambivalent. They recognize that the present struggle for power and privilege cannot long continue its present course and even that any such continuance is fraught with grave dangers for mankind.

Furthermore, the ideologies which most institutions propound already express the values which these institutions subvert in operation, and the proclamation of these ideologies is not wholly hypocritical. There is room for maneuver, therefore, and while not everything is possible, much can be done to free educational resources from their present shackles, and even to use them in weakening these shackles further.

Learning in the City*

**Leonard B. Finkelstein
and Lisa W. Strick**

A study of life in a large American city is a study of paradoxes and of opposites. From the time that the rapid growth of industry and technology first created the need for a concentrated labor force, people have been drawn to cities as centers of profitable activity. As populations grew, cities emerged as primary centers of culture, education, and sophisticated society as well as of trade, business, and industry. The lure of the city was opportunity on several levels, and the call was answered by many who wished a better future for themselves and their children.

The cities were where the jobs were, and where the money was. A whole new class of people grew out of the commercial economy of the cities—a "middle class," which made its money

*Reprinted by permission of UNESCO from *Prospects: Quarterly Review of Education,* Vol. 2, Spring 1972; © UNESCO 1972.

in manufacturing and trade. These people both lived and worked in the cities, and their industry ensured for many years the cities' prosperity.

Yet almost from the beginning, cities drew more people than they could support. And as the cities spawned a new middle class, they also created a new population of disadvantaged citizens— people who, though surrounded by a concentration of wealth and resources unique to city life, had meaningful access to few of these things. Of those drawn to the cities by a continued hope for a better life, more and more of the less-educated, less-skilled newcomers found themselves unable to find work. Clustered together in what we now call urban ghettos, these people became part of a trend toward social polarization which is today such a prominent feature of city life.

Perhaps it it ironic that it is this last group which now stands to inherit America's cities, as the middle class in increasing numbers leaves to make homes in the ever-growing suburbs, returning to the urban community in many cases only to work, make money, and take it away again. Social polarization in many large cities is now all but complete, as the advantaged who work in the city, and the disadvantaged who live there, eye each other with suspicion and hostility across the widening gap between them—a gap which is quickly extended by virtue of the new highways and heavily subsidized mass-transportation facilities.

Caught in the midst of this conflict is the urban educator, whose task it is to provide meaningful education for growing numbers of students (despite the suburban exodus) with decreasing amounts of tax revenue to do it with. The quality of urban education, reflecting the quality of urban life, has declined steadily in recent years. It is estimated that today nearly 40 percent of urban students do not complete secondary school, and it is doubtful if many who do, get much in the way of adequate training. The cities' educational systems are collapsing—yet the resources which once made the cities great are for the most part still there. Colleges and universities, museums and cultural institutions, business and industries and professional organizations continue to make cities their base. Somehow an urban environment still favors the growth of some of these institutions. No one is more acutely aware than the urban educator, however, how little these institutions contribute to the quality of life in the city—how separate urban professional, residential, and educational activities have become. Yet it is not only the urban resident who needs freer access to the city's resources. More than ever, the city needs the resources of its citizens, needs trained, skilled, educated, and informed citizens and employees. It is the function of the school to help provide these citizens. Yet urban schools have traditionally received only minimal support from the community institutions whose needs they are attempting to serve.

In Philadelphia, we have operated for three years a public secondary school and attempted to make the responsibility for educating children a shared responsibility, involving the community's cultural, business, and professional organizations in the educative process. There is in Philadelphia a growing awareness of the fact that everyone in the city has a stake in training the city's young people. The Parkway Program provides an avenue for turning that awareness into action.

PHILADELPHIA'S PARKWAY PROGRAM

In the Parkway Program, the city is both our campus and curriculum. Instead of studying in a school building, Parkway students learn in the physical resources of the city itself—museums, businesses, libraries, hospitals, churches, stores—wherever they can find out what they want and need to know. Conventional classes are taught in some of these facilities by our staff. However, about half the courses in our curriculum are taught by professionals in community organizations: we have architects teaching architecture, hospital employees teaching medical careers, businesses offering students training in clerical and management jobs. Our art classes meet at the Philadelphia Art Museum. We have sixteen-year-olds studying government at City Hall, law with attorneys, and cooking in restaurants. A student interested in learning car mechanics may go to a local garage for an apprenticeship; a student interested in anthropology may attend classes at one of five major universities in the area. A student capable of advanced work in chemistry might work in research at a local pharmaceutical house. So vast are the resources of the city that we now offer roughly 300 such opportunities for the 540 students enrolled in our program, enabling each student to completely individualize his curriculum.

CITY AS VAST EDUCATIONAL CENTER

The quality of instruction students are receiving in these institutions is encouragingly high. Because of the numbers of organizations and individuals participating in our Program, class size is seldom above fifteen and is often as low as two or three, allowing a degree of individualization in instruction which would be impossible in the overcrowded traditional schools. The materials and facilities which the community has opened to our students are unique, and could not possibly be duplicated on any school budget: a city library containing over 1 million volumes; art and science museums with world-renowned resources; laboratories containing the best modern equipment. Also, at the Parkway Program, we are taking advantage of the fact that most of the city's resources are concentrated within a limited geographical area, making it possible for a student to work within several different institutions in the course of an eight-hour day. Traveling by foot and by public transport, our students now treat their city as one vast educational center in which learning can take place any time, anywhere, and in many different forms.

The diversity of the city is reflected in our student body as well as in our curriculum. We draw our students from no special group, but select them at random from volunteers representing virtually every segment of the city's population —interestingly, we have attracted many applications from the suburbs as well. Not only have many of these students never been exposed to the city's resources, but in many cases they have had no exposure to each other. The very heterogeneity of our student body is one of the most unique things about the Parkway Program, where it has become almost axiomatic that the ability to learn to work with different kinds of people is

as basic a survival skill for urban life as the ability to read or write or work with figures.

Outside of the area of instruction, a significant contribution made by community institutions to our program has been to provide new sources of motivation for students who had formerly been poor learners in traditional school settings. At a time when the traditional school curriculum is being regularly condemned by students and educators alike as "irrelevant," and criticized for failing to keep up with the pace of modern civilization, community professionals are often in a better position than teachers to provide education which is timely, comprehensive, and responsive to students' needs and concerns. Students who failed to respond to education in traditional settings often find themselves doing far better when permitted to go "where the action is." Many students who were potential dropouts have, through our curriculum, become exposed to new fields, and acquired a new interest in even traditional subjects. Some of these students are now thinking in terms of college and professional careers which they learned about at Parkway. There is an element of "discovery" for students here, as they go from building to building, subject to subject, and there is little chance for them to become bored by monotonous routine.

INVOLVING STUDENTS AND COMMUNITY IN POLICY DECISIONS

When the Parkway Program first opened, doubts were frequently expressed about the ability of secondary school students to handle the freedom and responsibility which our program allows. It is true that few of these students, in the past, had to take as much responsibility as they must here. We ask them to design their own curriculum, select their courses, find their way to their studies regularly, and fulfill necessary obligations faithfully, all with a minimum of supervision and enforcement from the organization. After nearly three years, it is clear that not all are capable of doing this—but the majority of students learn to handle the situation very well. While some students seem to find the Parkway conditions frightening, or even threatening, and opt to return to traditional settings, most respond to the challenge favorably. The students who remain in the program tell us that what they learn here far transcends mere subject matter: they are, they tell us, expanding their general awareness of themselves and of others, increasing their understanding of their community, and undergoing a growth in confidence and maturity which would normally be delayed until they had gone on to jobs or college.

The ability of even our average students to act responsibly in situations where a minimum of adult supervision is provided raises serious questions about the wisdom of maintaining school systems in which students are allowed virtually no say in decisions which affect their education, and given almost no opportunity to take an active role in determining the direction of their own learning. Educators in schools in which students seem passive, apathetic, even disruptive, might well look into what opportunities their school organization allows for students to learn any other kind of behavior. Our experience is that students are both anxious and able to participate fully in decisions pertaining to their studies, and that allowing students to help make these decisions encourages a level of student involvement and responsibility which is conducive to learning.

Even with the many resources we have tapped —we feel that there is a great deal of room to grow—we have barely scratched the surface of the resources, both physical and human, available

in our city, which has a total school population of nearly 300,000. The city can still be a center of opportunity for those who have the skills and education to cope with the city's uniquely challenging way of life. More and more, Philadelphia's professional individuals and organizations are recognizing that they can and should play an important role in providing training in those skills. The realization that their future and the city's future are permanently linked is leading them to open their doors, to give time, facilities, money, materials, and instruction to students in the Parkway Program. They are rewarded, not in money, but in the knowledge that their commitment to education will help alleviate those forces which make the city weak, and contribute to those which make it strong. As it now seems fairly clear that the social and economic patterns of our cities— be they ascending or declining—offer an accurate prediction of the future of the countries in which they operate, the investment of these institutions in education may be considered of national importance. We expect that the community-based Parkway model will have implications for a broad range of communities and educational systems as it grows larger, including those in nonurban areas. The basic principles on which we operate—placing students in the community, involving both students and community in educational policy making, spreading the educator's burdens over a wider area—would probably be effective anywhere where students, educators, and community members are willing to work together toward what are, after all, essentially common goals.

Children in Transit: The Open City Project

Jim Zien

I. THE CITY AS A PLACE FOR LEARNING

In and around Boston, the subways, elevated trains, streetcars, and busses of the Massachusetts Bay Transportation Authority traverse urban and suburban environments of every character and kind. The Open City Project administered by the Children's Museum of Boston and funded by the federal Office of Environmental Education, undertook an intensive investigation of the metropolitan transit system with the help of 45 eleven-to fourteen-year-old residents of diverse Boston-area communities.

The project was inspired by recent efforts in the fields of education and design to develop the educative potential of city environments. Project activities were built upon the assumption that for children to benefit from the resources of the city for learning and enjoyment they must be able to move through its public paths with skill, confidence, and a degree of independence.

The Environment as Teacher: Historical Notes

"Learning has always been the most powerful lure of the city," maintains city planner John Dyckman:

The city as a work place was expected to inculcate skills, and the city as a play place was expected to provide vices that were at least slightly instructive. The city as a show place was a place to wander about in and gape at. . . . The educative uses of the city have always been too numerous to be comprised in the curricula of the schools.[2]

"When I grew up in Fayetteville, New York [circa 1900]," remembers Caroline Pratt, founder of the progressive City and Country School in Greenwich Village,

no one had to tell us where milk came from or how butter was made. We saw wheat ground into flour in the mill in our stream. We could learn the secrets of half a dozen other industries merely by walking through the open door of a neighbor's shop. School was not very important to children who could roam the real world freely for their learning.[4]

In the burgeoning New York City of the early twentieth century, Caroline Pratt later aided her elementary City and Country School pupils to observe the elemental activities of a more complex urban life—the making, buying, and selling of things; the performing of services; the rapid alteration of the environment itself—through regular walks in the streets of lower Manhattan. The students asked questions of the people they met and occasionally even participated in the activities they observed.

By midcentury, specialization, technology, and sheer physical growth had reduced city visibility to nearly zero. Doors ajar afforded views of plant-filled lobbies rather than tool-filled workshops. All the lawyers had abandoned their storefronts for the twenty-fifth floor. The hole in the construction site fence was consistently out of reach across four lanes of snarled downtown traffic. Children live today amid urban environments described by city planning professor Kevin Lynch, of the Massachusetts Institute of Technology, as displaying "many ambiguities, confusions and discontinuities; significant activities are hidden from sight; history and natural setting are obscured. The language of the cityscape is as baffling as a news release."[3]

In 1956, a group of architects and educators proposed a novel education program to the readership of *School Executive* magazine: include the human, environmental, and material resources of the living community in the curriculum of high school students. The proposal described an imaginary town in which many citizens assumed educational roles, students learned in diverse settings, and a new type of school facility functioned as a home base, meeting ground, and special resource center.[5] More than ten years passed before the first "school-without-walls" actually opened its doors on the world. Since the 1968 inception of Philadelphia's pioneer Parkway Program, however, similar experiments have proliferated from coast to coast.

But can organized student forays into the world of work alter the general inaccessibility of urban environments to public scrutiny, urban activities to public participation, and urban objects to public use?

In his 1961 essay on "The Changing Uses of the City," John Dyckman suggests reinforcing the naturally instructive aspects of the city through "conscious design of the metropolis as an educational experience."[6] City planners Stephen Carr and Kevin Lynch have speculated as to what this might mean in practice:

In an industrial area, factories would be encouraged to let their machines be seen in action, to label raw materials, to distinguish different kinds of operatives and explain what they do, to exhibit finished products, to make their transportation containers transparent. Thus the city, like a good museum, would be designed to increase the physical and perceptual accessibility of its contents. . . .

Particular areas in the city would be devoted to self-testing. Adolescents or adults might try themselves against a graded series of challenges and difficulties—cognitive, physical, artistic. . . . Many of these activities can emphasize mutual dependence and trust on the model of Outward Bound. . . .

We would provide an ubiquitous network of open space . . . uncommitted to prescribed users. Dumps and vacant lots would be in this inventory, as well as woods, fields, waterways and marshes. In these open areas, actions and explorations are permissible that would be intolerable on developed sites. Anything might be constructed from the material available —temporary sculptures (as on the mud flats of San Francisco Bay) or tree houses . . . Raw materials and technical advice might be available on call, much as in the junk playgrounds of Scandinavia.[7]

In recent years, designers and planners have cooperated with educators to generate concrete designs for projects that demonstrate the educative potential of urban spaces. Michael Southworth's "Lowell Discovery Network" in Lowell, Massachusetts, described elsewhere in this volume, is one such venture.

The Welfare Island new town in New York City's East River features meeting spaces for learners of all ages dispersed throughout its residential and commercial environments. An educational park at the island's end is proposed as a jumping-off place for explorations of the total island environment, natural as well as man-made, by students from schools throughout New York City. For the Minnesota Experimental City the goal is a lifelong learning system for the entire community: "When a family comes into [the Experimental City] . . . we ask if they would consider being resource people. We ask what skills do you have, what are your interests, your hobbies, what can you share with others? This goes into a computer which can be accessed later by learners."[8]

A "Streets for People" renewal plan for downtown Washington, D.C., would create continuous covered mall space punctuated by artistic and cultural exhibits, education and entertainment programs, and devices for retrieving information concerning other Washington environments and activities. In Montreal, a "Metro/education" program camps on underused public spaces near stations of the city's new subway system. Thus movie theaters usually idle in the daytime become auditoriums for film and lecture presentations to Metro students.

School-without-walls opportunities for students, and programs of planning and design based on educational criteria, represent first steps toward the radical notion of a "deschooled" society put forth by educational–social philosopher Ivan Illich.[9] In a fundamentally inaccessible urban culture where "rich and poor alike are artificially kept away from most of the things that surround them," Illich would foster public encounter with material resources for learning by liberating educational objects from the constraints of private ownership and the clutches of professional educators. In Illich's deschooled society, everyone would be entitled to "special access to ordinary things" (e.g., machines in a local factory), as well as "easy and dependable access to special things made for educational purposes" (e.g., a computer programmed to teach reading):

In a city opened to people, teaching materials which are now locked up in storerooms could be dispersed to independently operated storefront depots. . . . The corner biology store could refer (its) clients to the shell collection in the Museum or indicate the next showing of biology videotapes on a certain viewing booth.[10]

Illich also suggests a variety of techniques, from computer listings to billboards, for the bringing together of people who wish to learn with the people who have knowledge and skills to share.

Whether or not the deschooling of American society is, as Illich believes, inevitable, it seems clear that the imaginative thought and experimentation of the past decade-plus has established a trend toward greater involvement of students with city life, and greater openness of urban environments to public learning. As evidence of the trend, the 1972 International Design Conference in Aspen, Colorado, assembled educators, architects, designers, planners, government officials, and students to discuss approaches to making "The Invisible City" observable and understandable.

City Travel as a Learning Resource

Kevin Lynch has pointed out the value of travel through the city as an aid to perceiving urban form and pattern: "[The] system of paths along which people move . . . is their observation platform for seeing the city, their principal means of comprehending it. It is from the path network that the city dweller . . . becomes familiar with the city's landmarks and develops a sense of being at home instead of lost in the city's immensity."[11]

City travel is clearly a requisite to learning from the urban environment. Caroline Pratt and her childhood friends could "roam the world freely for their learning"; traversing the modern city is more complicated and costly. For the young and the poor these factors are major barriers to educative use of the city. A recent *New York Times* news article illustrates the situation with appropriately embattled wording:

ALL NEW YORK BECOMES SCHOOL

Armed *with subway and bus tokens, high school students will begin their "learning experience" at cultural, artistic and scientific institutions throughout the city.* [Roman added.]

Although most high school students may stand a fighting chance of winning the public transportation battle, their less seasoned younger brothers and sisters are at a decided disadvantage. Except for reduced student fares, effective in Boston only during school hours, transportation agencies offer no assistance to children in coping with their services. The schematic form and verbal content of maps and signs are not meaningful to children who relate more easily to pictures. Places that children like, or might like if they knew about them, are seldom identified in transit information.

Nor are there special transit services for children comparable to wrong-way expressway buses for rush-hour commuters, the ballpark express for fans from the suburbs, or ride-and-shop circuits for supermarket customers. In fact, youth as a class barely made the bottom of a list of "Transportation Disadvantaged Groups" published by the federal Urban Mass Transportation Administration in 1971: "59.8 million or 29.6 percent of the total population between 5 and 19 . . . is included because they are simply too young to drive."[12]

The mobility needs of this large segment of the population deserve greater attention, not only because children are entitled to encounter the opportunities of the total environment but also because the total environment cannot support many more generations of 60 million car freaks who have outgrown their "transportation disadvantage."

II. CHILDREN'S EXPERIENCE WITH TRAVEL IN THE CITY

In a doctoral dissertation on the city experience of ten- to twelve-year-old boys from Cambridge, Massachusetts, Michael Southworth relates his subjects' desire to travel more widely in the city than their previous neighborhood-centered experience had allowed:

You should know what the city looks like . . . some kids don't even know where they live in it . . . it's good to know in case someone asks you, in case you want to tell someone about it.

[*You should travel*] *so when you grow up and want to go places you know where to go and how to get there, instead of just searchin', searchin'. . . .*[13]

"Going places" was also a valued, though infrequent activity for most of the eleven- to fourteen-year-old participants in the Open City Project. Family outings and school field trips were their principal sources of encounter with environments outside their own neighborhoods. Of the available means of beyond-neighborhood travel, automobile rides from compliant adults were the least strenuous, most direct, and apparently safest way to reach a desired destination, but could not always or even often be counted on. The bicycle allowed the greatest freedom of movement and was popular for traveling with no particular destination in mind, but traffic hazards and parent worries restricted most cyclists' range. Many city residents used public transportation in a limited way for trips to school, to the downtown shopping district, and to houses of friends and relatives in other neighborhoods. Some suburban residents had never been inside a subway station; others who had in-town friends used public transportation on occasional weekend visits to the city.

Collectively, Open City participants had traveled much of the far-flung transit system. Individually, however, none had had significant transit experience beyond a few accustomed routes. Participants' limited exposure to nonneighborhood settings was reflected in freehand city drawings "showing places you know, with your house in the middle." Characteristically, names or sketches of familiar places appear in the drawings at random, with little suggestion of geographic relationships, intervening sections of the city, or paths of travel. By contrast, participants' neighborhood drawings are map-like, reasonably accurate, and often detailed with respect to buildings, streets, significant activities, and patterns of circulation. The variety of city travel experiences which Open City participants brought to the project is reflected in the following excerpts from group leaders' notes.

Group of Cambridge Girls: *All the girls have been close friends for numbers of years. They play together every day and do most of their traveling together. The girls know their neighborhood very well and travel a great deal within it, mostly by bicycle or on foot . . . With their parents they travel by car now and then to all the museums and other cultural points of interest . . . They know how to get to the Aquarium and Science Museum by train, have all ridden the nearby Red line* [a subway] *in its entirety (this was done one day as an adventure, to ride to the end of the line, see what was there and test the new train), and take it frequently to go to downtown Boston . . . This is the first year Chris and Jane have been allowed to travel on their own while the rest have been doing limited travel for several years. None are free to travel wherever and whenever they wish due to parental concern and supervision. They all seem to accept these restrictions and feel they are too young and lacking in sufficient knowledge to be totally free in their travel . . . I would characterize them as being novice travelers who are just beginning to know how to get around when off the paths previously established by a parent or older brother or sister.*

Group of Roxbury Girls: *Within their neighborhoods all the girls walk and ride bicycles . . . They ride to downtown Boston often by train, without adults. They all know the Orange line* [an elevated train] *since this is the route between home, school and downtown; and they know the buses in their neighborhoods which connect with the Orange line . . . It does not appear that the kids travel much outside of trips downtown.*

Group of Roxbury Boys: *Their travel experiences in the city, outside of adult-supervised excursions, are quite limited. There are places to go on bikes in local parks and in the neighborhood, but the range of travel possible on a bike is strongly delimited by major traffic arteries, and their sense of the hazards inherent in riding through someone else's neighborhood—turf problems. Their parents keep close tabs on them. There are strong reasons not to travel, especially if travelling means going through Dudley station after dark. They are unlikely to travel for the sheer fun of travelling. It will take something forceful, like the pull of a job or school or the need to make a major purchase downtown, to get them in motion. A Red Sox or Celtics game might also be*

strong enough to do that. There are not a lot of places they know of that they can get very excited about going to. They have been saturated with trips to the Science Museum and the Aquarium. They don't do much shopping by themselves yet.

Group of Lincoln Boys: *The boys reside in rural-suburban Lincoln about ten miles from downtown Boston. The last station on the longest line of the transit system is fifteen superhighway minutes away. A commuter train runs from Lincoln center to a central Boston railroad and transit station. With the exception of one boy who had previously lived in Boston and visits relatives and friends often, the boys' city excursions are infrequent. However, all have experienced the rapid transit system in the course of city visits with parents and school groups. They know a few transit routes from the center of the city to popular and functional places like the Science Museum, the Aquarium and the airport. The question, If it were easier to get to Boston from Lincoln, would you go more often?, is not particularly meaningful because the boys' familiarity with the city is largely limited to institutional attractions, which all have visited before.*

The Open City participants' drawings and their group leaders' observations reveal that most of these early adolescent children had previously experienced a number of city environments beyond their neighborhoods, including a constellation of institutional and commercial sites commonly familiar to nearly all participants regardless of their places of residence, and had traveled to some via public means; with only one exception, however, the participants neither demonstrated nor claimed a general ability to find their way around the city, even to some places they had visited more than once with parents or school groups.

That these pre-high school children have a fragmentary knowledge of the city, which they are unequipped to expand, hardly comes as a surprise. In interviews with his subjects' parents, Southworth determined the average age at which they permitted their children to travel outside the neighborhood to be eleven years. During an International Design Conference discussion of high-school-without-walls experiments, a school-without-walls student commented on the tendency of many of her peers to "freak out" over their newly acquired freedom and responsibility to choose among the urban opportunities available in the program. Such choices she felt "should start with grammar-school-aged kids. There is no reason why not, kids are a lot more intelligent than people think."

III. THE OPEN CITY PROJECT

Rationale and Objectives

Children often complain of boredom, nothing to do, and no place to go. The problem is particularly acute for early adolescents, eleven, twelve, and thirteen years old, who have exhausted their interest in child play, investigated every nook and cranny of their neighborhoods, and possess neither the patience nor the status to qualify for the teenage establishment activity of just being cool and hanging out. The potential benefit of opportunities to explore the city and discover environments of personal interest is perhaps greater at this stage of increasing independence in young people's lives than at any other.

The Open City Project experimented with a variety of methods for helping early adolescent children to visualize the physical extent of their familiar environment; to perceive the pattern of their activities within it; to recognize their neighborhood as an element in the city fabric linked with other, less familiar elements by threads of transit; and to use the transit system to discover the city.

Participants

In selecting forty-five participants, the project sought to assemble a population that included extremes in access to public transportation. Additionally, it was hoped that each of the working groups of four to six participants could be made up of friends who lived in the same neighborhood, spent their free time together, and were likely to be travel companions. Finally, we wished to work with both school-affiliated and nonschool groups.

Thirty junior high school students from inner-city Boston neighborhoods and suburban Lincoln, Massachusetts, participated in the Open City Project in conjunction with a public junior-high-school-without-walls experiment known as "Sidetrack." For these students Open City was one of several "community electives" in which they were involved weekly. The cross-section of urban and suburban Sidetrack students who elected to participate in Open City met our first criterion of extremes in access to public transportation. However, the innovative, voluntary nature of the Sidetrack program had attracted a fair number of "loners" who resided in widely separated neighborhoods. Because the Sidetrack population was not comprised of neighborhood friends, the students who elected to participate in the Open City project were grouped on the basis of geographic proximity and "ability to work together," as indicated by the Sidetrack staff. The contingent comprised three groups of boys and two groups of girls from inner-city Boston neighborhoods, and two groups of boys from suburban Lincoln. Only one suburban girl expressed interest in our program of city travel.

The remaining fifteen project participants, eleven-, twelve-, and thirteen-year-old residents of low-to-middle-income neighborhoods around the Open City storefront headquarters in Cambridge, worked with the project after school, on their own time. Each of the four Cambridge groups, two comprised of girls and two comprised of boys, met the criteria of shared neighborhood and friendship. The Cambridge groups were recruited in the streets near the headquarters. Potential individual participants were asked to invite three or four friends to spend one afternoon a week with Open City. After they had signed on, the Cambridge participants were told they would be paid for their participation in each session, as they would be doing research which might eventually be published for others' benefit. The Sidetrack students, although not paid in cash, were receiving academic credit for their participation.

Each of the ten Open City groups met weekly with a member of the part-time project staff, which included one community-center youth worker, two graduate architects, one theology school dropout, a city planner, and a museum director of community services. An official of the Massachusetts Bay Transportation Authority facilitated the making of special transit arrangements, including the underwriting of all project travel.

Project Design

Funded in mid-1971 by the federal Office of Environmental Education, the Open City Project was a hybrid of two earlier proposals that failed to win the support of the agencies to which they were submitted.

The first proposal had outlined an elementary and junior-high-school-without-walls program to be initiated in a Boston public school district with funds under the innovation provisions of the Elementary and Secondary Education Act, Title III. The second proposal had been written in conjunction with the Massachusetts Bay Transportation Authority and submitted to the federal Urban Mass Transportation Administration. It requested support for a "demonstration project . . . to make transportation systems more understandable and usable for children."

The Open City Project embodied the city-discovery theme of the former proposal and the concern of the latter for facilitating children's travel through components concerned with: (1) documentation and discussion of familiar environments and activities that comprised participants' life spaces, (2) projection of fears and problems related to travel in the city, (3) travel to favorite city destinations, and (4) travel for creative purposes. Travel within each of these categories occurred in alternation with storefront sessions in which participants documented and evaluated their city experiences.

Life Space   The project commenced with a focus on participants' prior urban experience, particularly in their neighborhoods, which enveloped 99 percent of their activity and were clearly the most significant urban environments in their lives. Prior to engaging in wide-ranging encounters with new environments, participants drew, photographed, and discussed the places, activities, and boundaries of familiar territory. They also attempted in a drawing to depict more distant familiar environments in the city in relation to their neighborhoods, and to show paths or means for moving beyond their neighborhoods. In theory, these exercises were to have provided participants with a visual image of their effective *life space*—the constellation of places, activities, and pathways in the Boston region that comprised their experience with the city to date.

In practice, the notion of using a knowledge of present life space as a foundation for building future experience with the city was too abstract to engage participant interest. Consequently, participants benefited little from life-space exercises, although the project staff gained knowledge of their group members' impressions of the city which later proved useful in devising travel activities.

Travel Fears and Problems   In spite of the fact that the participants had had relatively little experience with the city and travel, or because of it, they had numerous concerns about its pitfalls. The project attempted to provide outlets for participants to project fears and problems, to perceive that many were held in common, and to test them against the reality of actual travel. Participants were encouraged to express opinions, likes, and dislikes about city places, the transit system, and the kinds of people they encountered.

The principal opportunity for participants to express travel fears and problems was the making of a Monopoly-style illustrated game about city travel. On the game board, certain squares represented desirable or undesirable city places, while the other squares represented situations a traveler might encounter during a city outing. The content of all squares was provided by the participants themselves. Highly spirited games evolved, the object of which was to "capture" a prescribed number of desirable city places by landing on the appropriate squares. Fun to play, the games also revealed graphically the three principal problems participants had with travel in the city: fear of getting lost, fear of transit mishaps and consequent injury, and fear of harassment by strangers. To deal with the fear of getting lost, the project challenged participants to a "get-lost trip" (described later) the object of which was to get found. The ease with which all groups accomplished the task provided a significant reality test of their fear.

The potential for small- and large-scale accidents involving transit equipment preoccupied many participants. Most had heard the story of Boston's Great Molasses Disaster of 1923, in which a tidal wave of molasses from a factory explosion pulled down a nearby elevated train structure. Occasional news reports of more recent mishaps and breakdowns spurred their already vivid imaginations to new plateaus as they looked out of fast-moving trains in dark subway tunnels or high atop the "el." Participants' game-board drawings show arms caught in closing train doors, electrified humans frying on the third rail ("Danger: Third Rail Alive" read ominous anthropomorphic signs in the subway), head-on subway crashes, and other spectacular events.

In actual travel these fears occasionally manifested themselves in a kind of kamikaze bravado, which included standing close to the station platform edge when a train was coming, playing at pushing one's friend onto the tracks, watching for thrown objects to fizzle on the electric rail, and pretending to pry open train doors when riding.

Obviously, real dangers exist in the transit environment, as they do in perhaps greater degree on the road in an automobile, a form of travel not feared. In the course of the Open City project, repeated safe experiences with transit helped to allay participants' fears of its technology, at least to the extent that they were less verbal or demonstrative about them in actual travel.

Fear of encounters with hostile people is a general problem for city users of all ages. It is particularly critical for children, who have not sufficiently experienced the city to know which of its environments are truly dangerous and which are not. Here again, positive experience helps, as illustrated by a group leader's observation that: "swimming, one of Mark's major interests, provides a strong impetus for travel. This interest moves him into situations where other kids perceive dangers. The Boys' Club is generally seen by the group as a place where older kids can take advantage of you, but Mark is there frequently and does not seem worried about getting hurt or robbed."

A secondary but more specific people problem for some Open City participants was their relationships with transit personnel, who they felt were unresponsive to inquiries or downright hostile. Often, of course, the kids created their own problems, trying to sneak into subway stations, playing on escalators and being generally boisterous. As observed by Open City group leaders, transit personnel seemed to maintain an attitude toward kids consistent with the attitude of the transit environment as a whole: although their presence is cautiously tolerated, kids are not bona fide clients of public tranportation.

Travel to Favorite City Destinations One project objective was to assist participants to learn transit routes to places they knew and liked but had previously reached only by car. Not surprisingly, participants could think of few favored destinations other than familiar institutional places usually visited on school field trips and family outings. From time to time throughout the project, groups took advantage of unprogrammed sessions to learn their way to some of these well-known attractions by a process of travel trial and error, which grew more sophisticated as the project progressed:

Trip to the Aquarium: *We asked a kid on the train where to get off going to the Aquarium. He said Charles Street, but the girls didn't think so–they boasted they had gone to Revere Beach once on their own and remembered passing Aquarium Station on the way. When he was on the spot it became clear he wasn't sure, so he in turn asked people across the aisle. They said Park Street.*

We got off at Park and asked a man on the stairs where to go. He said upstairs. When we got up there Dorothy thought we should take the Cleveland Circle train. We went to that side of the station, then the man we had asked on the stairs came up, said we were in the wrong place, and authoritatively gestured where we should go: downstairs and up on the other side. When we got on the second train after pounding on the half-closed door, a kid wearing a leather peace symbol who had the manner of a forty-year-old lawyer asked what was going on. Then he explained that to get to the Aquarium we should follow him out the train at Government Center (Dorothy had known we had to get to Government Center somehow). When we got out the lawyer told us to follow him downstairs —he was quite well informed about where we should go—so down we went. At that point the clear Eastbound/Westbound signs and the new maps with stops clearly marked made the decision easy as to which side of the tracks to stand on (the kids knew the Aquarium had to be east, since it is on the ocean —would kids coming from the other direction be confused by having to take a Westbound train?) After getting off at Aquarium Station we wandered about the parking lot until someone saw the Aquarium building, which we headed for across a fairly dangerous intersection.

Trip Back: *Got on the train, asked someone where to get off and were told Government Center. Everyone remembered that was right. At Government Center a lady first told us not to take the Westbound train, then changed her mind and said to take it one stop, which we did and got off at Park Street. A cop came up and asked the girls where they were going, then clearly told them to go to the sign for Cambridge and go down the stairs.*

Dorothy led us down stairs under a sign with no mention of Cambridge —she didn't bother to read it because the stairway was the same one we had come up on our trip from Cambridge. We got on a waiting train quickly. The loudspeaker announced "Washington, next stop," but no one was listening. Washington came and went. Dorothy had an idea we had "made a boo-boo" but wasn't upset by it. When we got to South Station they were convinced we were going the wrong way, so we got off the train.

Dorothy wanted to go out one of the revolving exits; Gertrude thought we should ask somebody. Dorothy won out. We went outside and were confused by a Hayes-Bickfords cafeteria across the street, just like the one across from the stop in Cambridge we were trying to get to. Bewildered, we asked a transit man for assistance and finally got on the right train in the right direction.

Creative Travel   Because thinking of good destinations was not all that easy for participants, once the familiar list of school and family visit places had been exhausted, engaging non-destination-oriented travel activities were needed that would uncover new places of interest and provide a more generalized experience with the transit system.

The notion that using transit in the city could have any other purpose than reaching a given single destination was foreign to Open City participants. What point could there be in a trip that did not end up in some worthwhile place? Three Open City activities had "points" that were not concerned with visiting singular destinations, but rather with encountering many environments in the course of wide-ranging travel.

Moderately successful to this end was a city-scale version of the Monopoly-style game previously described. The new game, a kind of urban environment scavenger hunt, required participants to bring back photographic evidence of having visited five city places, drawn at random from a hat.

More engaging, and perhaps the best Open City activity from the participants' point of view, was the production of a slide tape that tells an adventure story against real backdrops in the city. This activity best represented Open City's fundamental objective, facilitating city discovery through travel.

Themes for the slide tapes covered a wide range of participant interests and concerns, including television-inspired science fiction, home and family situations, drugs, and even a tale of intrigue and greed leading to the near-shutdown of the transit system. Photographing the scenes for these diverse stories involved searching for environments with special characteristics not necessarily associated with institutional settings that comprised participants' principal experience with the city: harbor frontage, an airplane interior, a derelict building, a cemetery. Moreover, familiar places and spaces were used in new, interpretative, and more personal ways: fish in the Aquarium became characters in a flood scene, sculptures on City Hall plaza became attacking monsters, half-demolished buildings became ruins in a space war, the oldest subway cars became time capsules to the past.

Participants traveled widely to photograph their stories. They stopped not only at places for which they already had scenes in mind, but also in parts of the city where they had never been before, simply to see if anything near the transit station might inspire a new element in their stories. Group leaders noted that the making of the slide shows, about midway through the project, helped participants for the first time to perceive transit and encounters with unfamiliar settings as personally useful resources rather than as occasionally necessary, but not particularly attractive, aspect of getting someplace: *"The girls, after frequently using the Blue line, obtaining directions from the beautiful new wall maps, and several times using the station as scenes in their story, became very upset when one week someone began to destroy the maps and murals. Since the girls had had pleasant and useful experiences in these places, they had a hard time understanding why someone would want to destroy them."* Because participants had the opportunity to interpret city environments imaginatively, to see their interpretations in living color, and to share them with others, those environments became invested with meaning that they had not held before.

Documentary Travel A principal project goal was the creation of a guide to the Boston-area rapid transit system that would help children comprehend its structure and learn about accessible environments worthy of exploration. Open City

participants, engaged as researchers for the guide throughout the second half of the project, collectively investigated areas of metropolitan Boston within a five- to ten-minute walking radius of nearly every subway, elevated train, and streetcar stop.

Travel to research the guidebook was both the most and least structured Open City activity. On the one hand, the transit system had to be "covered," a well-defined goal toward which progress could easily be measured by simply marking off completed stops on the storefront transit map. On the other hand, the basic research task for a group session, to uncover the interesting elements of an unfamiliar and as often as not uninspiring environment, had a needle-in-the-haystack quality.

Yet needles were found. A bookstore on a tawdry arcade street in the shadow of a highway on-ramp yielded the best collection of *Mad* magazine paperbacks in town. The old Custom House clock tower was discovered to have a free outdoor balcony with a magnificent harbor view. A museum at Harvard that nobody knew about had stuffed animals nobody ever heard of. Other opportunities were encountered to see ocean liners close up, sit in on court proceedings, sample noise pollution from low-flying jets, read 200-year-old newspapers on microfilm, and chew on the bark of a cinnamon tree. The standard attractions everyone was familiar with—the Freedom Trail, the Swanboats, the Bruin's ice, Filene's basement, Harvard Square, the museums—were reviewed in terms of their transit locations.

The results of participants' travel research, drawings, photographs, and commentary on the places and activities they discovered were incorporated into a forthcoming guide to the exploration of Boston via rapid transit.

Project Evaluations by Participants and Group Leaders

After six months of weekly sessions, an analysis of life space, travel to familiar and attractive destinations, games in transit, and field research into transit-accessible environments, what outcomes did the group leaders feel to be most significant? What did the participants themselves think they had gotten out of the Open City Project?

Leader: *Mobility (or the lack of it) seems to be a function of something other than race, place of residence, or economic status. It does, however, reflect a kid's maturity. Without exception the black, white, urban, and suburban kids who traveled freely and widely were the most mature.*

Participant: *I didn't learn very much because i all ready know how to get to different places, by train and bus. But it is fun going places and doing things.*

Leader: *One could say that suburban kids are less mobile, but the statement has to be qualified. In general, suburban kids use public transportation less simply because it doesn't exist. In several instances in Open City a child took a trip by himself for the first time and was proud to announce it to me.*

Participant: *I did not know anything about the "T"* [*the transit system*]. *I go to Boston a lot more than I used to.*

Leader: *The kids reaction to parts of the program was that they were having fun, but they did not really think they were learning anything. It may be that they could not associate having fun with what adults usually call "learning."*

Participant: *I'm not sure whether I learned anything or not, because I won't know until I use the information. Besides I had a good time so nothing else really matters.*

Leader: *For all the kids, travel was the* raison d'etre *of Open City. For the kids, travel was* not *school. It was freedom, rapid and short periods of stimulation, noninstitutional, unrestrained. I think it was during travel times that I learned most from the kids.*

Participant: *I have learned pretty much all of the "T" lines and a lot of interesting places around the city. I can now get around without being scared of getting lost.*

Leader: *The kids' skill in using transit has improved and some of their travel fears have decreased. They have learned how to acquire accurate travel information more effectively, e.g., who to ask for directions, how to read a transit map. They are generally more familiar with the large stations where lines intersect; consequently, they are more able to take routes that necessitate a change of trains.*
Likewise, the kids have greater knowledge of city places available to them through transit. We traveled to favorite places which the girls had previously been able to get

to only by automobile. They were often surprised and pleased to find they could get to so many of these places without having to wait for a ride.*

Participant: *I never knew there were so many ways to get to so many different places.*

Leader: *Kids would like to be able to travel easily, quickly, safely, and without hassles, to attractive destinations. The major need they have is for a self-explanatory, comfortable transit system. They need to be able to think of the transit system as something they can use to their own ends, not a hostile force which moves them around mysteriously.*

Leader: *Kids like to feel they are in complete control of the situation. This means never showing you don't know where you are. This was especially true for the more mobile kids. They felt their credibility with me and the other members of the group would decrease if they admitted to being lost even for a minute. Kids need information if they are to be able to navigate by themselves.*

IV. ACTIVITIES FOR HELPING CHILDREN TRAVEL IN THE CITY

With the aid of sympathetic adults, early adolescent children can gain skill and confidence in city travel. To this purpose the following activities can be done by any adult with any small group of youngsters. Some of the activities are also suitable for high-school-aged youth, many of whom have little more experience with transit and city travel than their younger brothers and sisters.

The methods are suggestive rather than exhaustive under the assumption that they will have to be adapted to the particular environments and transit systems of their users. With small groups these methods cost small amounts of money, mostly in transit fares, and do not require any special equipment. They are not sequential and can be done independently. The common characteristic of the activities, in addition to being engaging for children, is that they focus participants' attention on the process of travel—a focus generally missing from typical adult-led children's trips —while each possesses at the same time a concrete "point," a destination, achievement, or visible product, through which the travel process takes on meaning. Individually, the activities respond to a variety of wishes, needs, and problems expressed by children concerning the limitations of their daily experience and the possibilities for new, more expansive adventures.

The Go-Someplace Trip

Get together a list of places your kids would like to go to. The list can be compiled over a period of time, gleaned from overheard remarks, from conversations with individual kids, or, more formally, from a group discussion. Add in places you can think of that the kids did not, but might like to go to anyway. Post the list in a visible place where kids can add to it as ideas arise. Do not place any arbitrary restrictions on the kinds of places that can appear on the list, either in distance or in kind (i.e., Grand Canyon is O.K. and so is the local amusement park). However, acquire street and transit maps of your city and devise a simple method for distinguishing on the list places that can be reached via transit, and thus traveled to at will, from those which cannot, and therefore require special arrangements and more than a little money. The list will become a vehicle for kids' projections of travel desires; it will help you to learn about their interests and add accessible places accordingly. The list is also, of course, a tool for decision making on trip days.

On or before the day of a trip, let the kids choose their destination from the transit-accessible places on the list. Explain before they choose that the trip will be led by them; getting to the destination will be their responsibility and you will just be along for the ride. (The first leg of travel from an outlying suburb might have to be by car to the nearest transit access point.) Plans should allow enough time to compensate for possible travel difficulties and still permit a reasonable visit once the destination is achieved. The group should discuss the intended route as much as the members feel is necessary, and should be supplied with aids—maps, a phone book, etc.—only if they ask for them.

You and/or the kids should have sufficient money to pay fares—extra money, in fact, in case of mistaken detours. Your familiarity with transit system transfer privileges will help to assure that your group does not pay more than necessary for its travel. (In Boston, for example, children may obtain transfers from trains to busses during school hours, whereas adults may not.) Some form of classroom, community center, or family travel fund might be established specifically for paying transit fares. ($25 could support up to 125 round trips for kids, or 25 trips for a group of five, under the Boston transit fare structure.)

Go-someplace trips help their takers build a repertoire of known routes to places they like. The trips can recur often, interspersed with other trips that place less emphasis on singular destinations.

The Get-Lost Trip

The get-lost trip has been described previously as an activity that helps children test the reality of becoming irretrievably lost in the disordered maze of streets and buildings which comprises their physical image of the city. The get-lost trip demonstrates the notion that transit routes eventually will carry you to a familiar place no matter where you enter the system.

For this trip, you have to select a place to get lost in. If your city has a major transit locus that most kids are likely to have experienced before, as, for example, Boston's downtown Hub, where all rapid transit lines intersect, you should choose a removed get-lost site; in any case, the site preferably should not be near a transit line that provides direct or well-known access to the intended point of return. An appropriate location for the beginning of the get-lost trip can be selected through comparative use of street and transit maps. Starting points in parks or residential streets that do not provide immediate clues as to the identity of the community create a maximum need for information gathering by the travelers.

Obviously, public transportation cannot be taken to the get-lost site or the challenge would be inconsequential. Therefore, the first leg of the trip requires an automobile, which is either left at the site for later retrieval or driven by an assistant. The automobile ride sets the tone of this adventure. Travelers are blindfolded and asked to use their remaining senses to try and determine the path of the journey to the get-lost site. The educated-guessing game that ensues is not only fun, but also helps participants to push their visual image of familiar territory to its limits as the car turns beyond recognized corners, sounds, and smells.

Upon arrival at the chosen starting point, the children remove their blindfolds, hold a strategy session, and commence to determine their whereabouts and find their way back, while you assume the position of a nonparticipating observer.

Upon the group's successful return, it is interesting to trace on a street map the automobile route to the get-lost site so that the travelers can determine the accuracy of their blindfolded observations. (These turned out to be quite accurate for most Open City groups.) Also useful is a tracing of the return route on a transit map—a way of confirming that there are methods, permanent enough to appear in print, for making one's way through the city's madness. Most Open City participants denied that their powers of return had been significantly challenged.

There is some game potential in the get-lost activity. Two or more travelers could pick get-lost sites for two or more others in challenges of escalating difficulty and distance from familiar turf. Subsequent to Southworth's study of Cambridge boys' conception and use of the city, one subject enjoyed riding his bicycle until he felt lost, finding his way home, and tracing his route on a street map hung in his room. In this way he substantially expanded his cycling range.

The Treasure-Hunt Trip

The language of most public tranportation systems, difficult enough for adults to understand, can be undecipherable for children, who often ignore maps and signs, and rely instead in imprecise advice like "go to the next corner and take the first bus that stops there." A further problem is that well-meaning informants sometimes provide inaccurate information. For this reason, blind people learn to ask directions in specifics: "What number bus goes to Symphony Hall?" rather than "How do I get to the concert tonight?"

The treasure-hunt trip involves kids in following accurate directions to a mystery destination.

Select a destination from the kids' list of desirable places that requires at least one transit change to get to. From the point at which the trip will begin, establish precise written instructions for reaching the destination, including how many blocks to walk to which street corner, which number and name of bus or train to catch, which direction, etc., and concluding with reference to the location of the destination, but *not* the destination itself. ("Then walk two blocks in the opposite direction that the bus you were on was going, and the place will be on the side of the street you're on, exactly across from a First National Bank building.")

At the beginning of the trip, each traveler should receive a copy of the instructions, review them, and ask any questions that occur with respect to the clarity of the wording. Once the trip begins, travelers may seek additional information from passersby, but you will allow no further inquiries. After the destination has been visited, the travelers will be responsible for navigating the return journey, whether by following the written directions backward or by some less formal means.

If the first treasure-hunt trip proves enjoyable (it should not be too complicated or trivial), participants might themselves devise directions to unnamed favorite places for their fellow travelers to follow. Doing so would necessitate a research trip to collect appropriate instructional details.

The Production Trip

The production trip involves visual storytelling using city environments as narrative backdrops. The activity is less focussed on transit use than most of the others; transit becomes simply a means of reaching settings for on-location photography. Yet the activity both requires and enlarges participants' knowledge of environments accessible via transit.

In Open City the activity involved slide photography with the least expensive "instamatic" camera available. These cameras are common, and one can likely be easily borrowed. If so, the cost of the activity in film and processing plus one magnetic recording tape for the story narration, would be $10 to $20, depending upon how many slides are taken. Open City productions were an average of sixty slides long after editing.

The production trip is an almost totally open-ended activity, which begins with the making up of a story or at least a theme for a story. One Open City group wrote an entire script, designated parts, and methodically went about locating appropriate sites and photographing just the scenes they needed. Another selected an Alice-in-Wonderland theme, which was simply to begin with an unexpected plunge into a subway tunnel. No other scene was planned; instead, a random selection of locations was scouted for eye-fooling or bizarre photographic possibilities. The final story was made up in the editing process, with the taped narration providing continuity.

The Open City slide shows are five to ten minutes long, with frequent slide changes to sustain visual interest. Our method of synchronizing the taped narration with the slide sequence was first to arrange the slides in the proper order in a slide carousel, and then to record the narration as the slides were shown. Slide changes are indicated

on the tapes by audible (sometimes piercing) vocal "beeps" made by the kids themselves. Because the Open City shows are not cued electronically, they require a projectionist to advance the slides at the sound of the beep.

The Open City slide shows have been presented to numerous audiences with great acclaim, and represent an excellent synthesis of travel, city discovery, and personal involvement with previously unfamiliar environments. The extra cost and relative technical complexity of the activity as compared with the others are well worth it.

Research Trips and Design of Travel Aids

The verbal-schematic spaghetti of existing maps and signs in most transit systems is not particularly useful to children who cannot associate the words and lines with real places of interest. However, children can create their own, more visual travel aids by drawing upon their experiences from previous trips and by further exploration of transit-accessible environments.

Needed is a mural-sized, simplified rendering of the city transit map with routes which serve kids' home, school, and/or community-center neighborhoods clearly identified. This mural will become a repository for images and impressions of environments encountered in travel: drawings, photographs, mementos and written comments will be affixed to the mural at appropriate locations.

"Holes" in the mural, areas of the city that have received little exploratory attention, can be systematically investigated, or they can be visited informally at times when kids feel like just traveling to "nowhere in particular" for a look around. In either case, the mural should be displayed in a conspicuous location, where images can be added at any time and where kids uninvolved in the travel program can view their peers' image of the city and the transit system.

As a variation on this theme, kids can research

the city for all the environments that relate to a subject of particular interest to them—animals, for example, which can be seen not only at the zoo everyone has visited, but also at duck ponds, the humane society, pet stores, the fish pier, and the university museum of comparative zoology. After determining the transit routes to these places, the researchers can design a set of animal-trip posters (or park, sports, music, or joke-shop posters), which show how to get to all the places in the particular category and which illustrate the places' attractions.

Pocket versions of the mural map and trip posters could be done in mimeograph form—"A Guide to the Harvard Square–Dudley Station Bus Line (#1)" or "A Guide to Visiting Animal Places by Public Tranportation"—but these would have to be primarily verbal, since large drawings, photographs, and mementos would be difficult to include. (On the other hand, if the group contains a particularly skillful artist, he or she might be able to "reduce" the mural or posters while maintaining the visual spirit.)

V. PUBLIC TRANSPORTATION FOR CHILDREN AND OTHER LEARNERS: POLICY PERSPECTIVES

For large numbers of early adolescent youngsters to gain mobility and realize greater benefits from the resources of urban environments, transportation agencies must adopt policies responsive to young people's needs. The principal policy areas in need of youth-oriented attention are fares, information resources, and route planning.

Fares

In his 1961 essay "The Changing Uses of the City," John Dyckman presents strong arguments for treating and designing urban environments as educational resources; "an essential minimum requirement for the creation of an educative city," according to Dyckman, is free public transit. Par-

ticularly where children are concerned, the lowering or elimination of prohibitive and increasing fares can open the way to wider experience with attractive environments for learning and recreation. As discussed earlier, transit fares for elementary and secondary students in Boston are reduced during school hours; the one-way fare for children up to age twelve is ten cents at all times. This policy needs to be extended to recognize the educative value of travel after 3:00 P.M., on weekends, and during the summer, at least for all young people under driving age. Transit agencies might also authorize nonschool educational places—artistic, cultural and scientific institutions, community centers, historic sites, factories with tours, and other organizations offering specific learning opportunities—to issue a certain number of badges carrying their names for free transit use by young people involved in their programs. Schools should be able to issue free passes for student travel associated with course work.

Clearly, fares at any level are a problem for children of poor families, who nevertheless must rely on and do use transit more than middle-class youngsters, often by sneaking into stations or vehicles rather than paying. Poverty-level children should receive passes for free travel.

Information Resources

Children's difficulties with the conventional artifacts of transit orientation have been discussed. Specific information concerning places children like does not exist in the transit environment, but should. Signing and transit maps are needed that incorporate pictures and symbols easily associated by children with destinations of interest. Effective color coding of maps, signs, and vehicles would simplify map and sign reading, as well as the following of spoken instructions.

Major transportation junctures should contain an information booth that dispenses travel aids and advice to all travelers, but especially to children. Available materials could include pocket-sized cards that illustrate routes from the juncture to places of special interest; illustrated maps of the transit system and guides to individual lines particularly rich in destinations for children; dittoed treasure-hunt trip instruction sheets, which change from week to week; and accurate, understandable information about the technology of the transit system and safety precautions. Large cities could maintain transit-travel resource centers that would offer AAA-like trip-planning services to children. Such centers could employ well-traveled youngsters as guides for others not confident about making their way alone. These "organizations for going places" are potentially self-supporting through $1 or $2 per year membership fees from users of their services; all new members might receive a book of coupons good for free or discounted entry to diverse city attractions.

In neighborhood settings, information about transit is virtually nonexistent, and should be disseminated through schls, community centers, libraries, corner stores, and other children's gathering places. "Take-one" travel ideas, proposing trips and providing instructions, would be easy to distribute widely. Principal neighborhood bus stops could be sites for kiosks plastered with instructional trip posters showing interesting places accessible on the bus routes that traverse the neighborhood, and giving illustrated directions for animal, beach, or science trips on a changing basis. Kiosk space should be also available for kids to post their own bills relating trips they have taken and liked. At some central point in every neighborhood, an illustrated city map should be on view. The map should highlight the location of the neighborhood within the city and should show key transit routes from the neighborhood to the city's major transit junctures and transit-travel resource centers.

Route Planning

It is possible to reach numerous, if not most, city sites of interest to children via transit—even-

tually. But transit routes are customarily planned to facilitate travel for workers and shoppers rather than for discoverers and learners. Consequently, there is a whole lot of time, not to mention distance between where children are and where they would like to be. Needed are routes specially planned for learning and enjoyment. Such routes could connect groups of nearby community centers or schools with constellations of parks and museums; or they could tie many educational, cultural, and recreational sites together. A precedent for this kind of service in Boston is a hospital bus, which originates in a community of high healthcare need and stops at a variety of medical facilities. In Seattle, a ten-cent "Fun Run" connects museums, the waterfront, and other visitor attractions.

The most attractive transit improvement envisioned by Open City participants concerned provisions for safe bicycle travel to transit facilities and for transport of bicycles on busses and trains (this was possible on some 1890s street railway cars, which featured bike racks along one side and seats along the other).

Developing Youth-oriented Transportation Policy

The development of policies, services, and education programs that foster wider use of public transportation—and broader city experience—by young people should attract diverse advocates. Planners for public transit agencies plagued by costly youth vandalism should consider services that give young people a greater stake in their systems. Environmentalists will be interested in seeing city-dwellers form energy- and air-conserving transit habits at an early age. Social engineers will want to maximize children's opportunities for exposure to cultural and economic diversity. Educators who would extend their curricula into the living city must clearly add a fourth "R" — riding transit — to the traditional three.

Parents, concerned that their children benefit

educationally and socially from positive encounters with people and places beyond the confines of their neighborhoods, would favor safe, well-organized children's travel services. Nearly all parents interviewed by Southworth in his study of Cambridge boys' city experience felt travel to be an important part of growing up:

It's important for kids to travel so that they will become interesting people.

Children have to learn how to handle themselves.

Boys will be boys—they have to explore.[14]

Most important of all interest groups, of course, are kids themselves, who are eager to move out, have new adventures, and feel more in control of themselves and their environment.

Practically speaking, implementation of youth-oriented transportation policies and resources would be largely in the hands of transportation agencies, which ideally would incorporate youth-service departments into their organizational structures. These departments should have staffs comprised of educators and environmental designers and planners concerned with children, as well as tranportation personnel; they should involve youngsters in their work as consultants and researchers. Youth-service departments might contract with other specialized city organizations to devise travel programs specifically related to learning, recreation and social service needs.

Initial efforts would likely take the form of demonstration projects, which might be funded by the Service Development division of the Urban Mass Transportation Administration (this division is responsible for the aforementioned list of "transportation disadvantaged groups"); by the federal Office of Environmental Education; by the Architecture and Environmental Arts program of the National Endowment for the Arts; or even under the Law Enforcement Assistance Act ("Safe Streets"), which has been widely supportive of youth education and recreation programs.

Conclusion

A truly "open city" is a city totally accessible for learning and enjoyment. Access to city environments can and does occur on many levels. Visual access to the street environment is free and unrestricted. Physical access to most stores and offices is also uninhibited, although access to people and things inside may be limited or forbidden. School-without-walls programs help students gain access to "inside" people and things under the umbrella of formal education. Designers and planners have envisioned or are actually building environments that show themselves off, incorporate access to pertinent information about their elements, and invite passersby to participate in their activities.

For children, none of these levels of access to the city is reliably available because the fundamental act of getting around is characteristically limited to neighborhood settings. It was the experience of the Open City Project that children eleven, twelve, thirteen, and fourteen years old can overcome some of the barriers to experiencing the city by learning to use the public transportation system to reach and discover environments of interest.

As work in the fields of education and design progresses toward making city environments more publicly accessible, more observable, more participative, and more understandable, children should be in a position to benefit from the results. Their ability to do so will depend critically on their ability to use public transportation, which in turn will depend upon modification of the transit environment itself for greater accessibility to young people and other learners.

NOTES AND REFERENCES

1. The staff of the Open City Project included Stephen Carr—architect, planner, and principal in the firm of Arrowstreet, Inc., Cambridge, Mass. (architects)—project codirector; Lee Jacobson—graduate, MIT School

of Architecture—group leader; Jane Kamps—Children's Museum Community Services staff—group leader; Stephen Tilly—graduate, MIT School of Architecture, staff member, Washington, D.C., "Streets for People," project of Arrowstreet, Inc., Cambridge, Mass.—group leader; and Doug Tueting—Children's Museum Community Services staff—group leader.

2. John Dyckman, "The Changing Uses of the City," *Daedalus,* 1961, pp. 111–130.
3. Kevin Lynch, "The City as Environment," *Scientific American,* Sept. 1965, pp. 209–219.
4. Caroline Pratt, *I Learn from Children,* New York: Cornerstone Library Publications, 1970.
5. "Random Falls," *The School Executive,* Mar. 1956.
6. *Op. cit.*
7. Stephen Carr and Kevin Lynch, "Where Learning Happens," *Daedalus,* 1968, pp. 1277–1291.
8. "Making the City Observable," *Design Quarterly,* Vol. 86/87: issue devoted to the 1972 International Design Conference in Aspen.
9. "Education Without School: How It Can Be Done," *The New York Review of Books,* Jan. 7, 1971, pp. 25–31.
10. *Ibid.*
11. Lynch, *op. cit.*
12. "Service Development Program, Fiscal Years 1966–70" Urban Mass Transportation Administration, Washington, D.C., 1971.
13. Michael Southworth, "An Urban Service for Children Based on Analysis of Cambridge Boys' Conception and Use of the City," Ph.D. dissertation, Massachusetts Institute of Technology, 1970.
14. Southworth, *op. cit.*

The Educative City

Michael Southworth
Susan Southworth

Environmental education has now become a public concern, but the educative role of the environment itself is seldom considered. That the urban environment—now the nursery of 40 million children under thirteen years of age—is an important force in child development goes without question. Yet urban environmental policy ignores this role and the special environmental needs of this major social group.

Before the days of universal public education and before the automobile age, the city environment served a crucial educational function. Along streets and in parks children were exposed to all aspects of social and economic life, obtaining a good understanding of society and their role in it. But today children are cut off from such direct participation. Much of their experience is vicarious, filtered through media. Architecture has become impenetrable to observation and experience; mirror facades and concrete walls deter curiosity,

and urban dispersal removes activity from the public street. The wealth of activities, places, people, and processes in the city, although now often hidden or incomprehensible, could become an intriguing firsthand source of knowledge, which would help present the diversity of experience that seems critical to early mental growth.

In making possible urban scatteration, the automobile has eliminated diversity, the opportunity for a child to walk to the store, the factory, the theater, or the park from his home. The child's world has been reduced to his yard, street, playground, and school. Of course, the dangers imposed by the automobile also make it nearly impossible for children to travel anywhere by themselves. It is not surprising that children frequently complain about lack of things to do and places to go. The neighborhood offers little choice, and children's knowledge of people and settings outside the neighborhood is limited, although there are many places that would be potentially attractive to them. Research indicates that one serious consequence of their limited city exposure is their strong bias against most unfamiliar places and people.[1] At the very least, a city should be designed to help children learn how to make their way about in it and to discover its life. Travel without adult supervision is particularly needed—it is the best way for a child to learn about himself and to come to know the city. Institutions, industry, businesses, and police now do little to help children use the city and often discourage their curiosity. Transportation agencies in particular could do much to aid children in city discovery. Children are often afraid of getting lost, busses and trains often do not go to the places they like, and travel is expensive. Moreover, the city is now represented in complex maps and words—remote nonsensual languages difficult for children to interpret. The skills of using the city and learning from it could be communicated to children, however, and could help them discover new realms of experience. Information systems that provide for children's needs will be of value and use for others, as well, since the elderly and handicapped have many of the same accessibility needs as children. Even the general public has a need for orientation information that is currently unfilled.

Several kinds of elements, short of building a total environment, could be manipulated to increase the educative effectiveness of the city: (1) play areas and other open spaces, (2) schools or recreation centers, (3) transportation systems, (4) selected activities, for example, industrial, commercial, residential, or entertainment, and (5) information systems. The costs of manipulating elements 1 through 4 would clearly be expensive for even a single city district. Manipulation of public signing seems most economical and allows one to encompass a larger district of the city than would any of the other possibilities. Signing can also be used to increase the informativeness of elements 1 through 4 with minimal change of those elements themselves. But to design an environment that will become far more informative through an information system alone requires innovation in what a sign can be: what its form can be, where it can be placed, and what it can say.

Two projects—the Park Square Information Center and the Lowell Discovery Network—illustrate approaches to creating an educative city. Several techniques are used for making the city more understandable and more accessible to direct experience—techniques for increasing physical access, for making vivid the history of the city, for uncovering the activities of the city, for ex-

Figure 1

pressing its social character, and for communicating the city's form and structure.

The first educative city project, the Park Square Information Center, was built in a gray area of Boston in the center of the hotel and transportation terminal district. We wanted to acquaint visitors and other users of the area with the wide range of activities and sites located nearby. The center was built as a design experiment that lasted for thirty days.[2] The construction of the center was a learning event in itself, attracting considerable attention. It provided life on a street that had previously been devoted to traffic.

The center was a series of kiosks, each of which communicated a different aspect of the city: travel, shopping, entertainment and cultural events and institutions (Figure 1). In addition to providing information to visitors, the center's fanciful form made a lively urban place to meet, to chat, to pass the time of day. Several visitors remarked that for the first time they had felt at home in a strange city. At night the glowing plastic spheres and illuminated tubes with maps and directories provided a lively focus for an otherwise chaotic street. Large pictorial maps of the district and revolving directories listing establishments in the area aided orientation. Slides and films presented contrasting images of local events and places. These were reinforced by a background of sounds recorded in the district, creating a sense of vitality in and around the center. A teletype printer gave instant news, a recorded message reported daily events, and a telephone allowed visitors to comment on the center and to hear others' comments. Visitors were particularly interested in a computer-like machine that printed answers to their questions on travel and history in Boston.

Extensive evaluations of the center's impact were conducted by means of interviews and observation. The success of the center is indicated by the number of visitors it received—about 3,000 per day. Previously this space had been largely unused by pedestrians.

The form of the center was designed to attract attention from a distance so that visitors could easily find it and would be drawn to it. The kiosk unit is adaptable to a variety of situations. The large plastic sphere may be removed and replaced with a flat or slanted top. Tubes may have a solid surface for applied graphics, or may be punctured to accommodate a variety of equipment. They may be used singly or in groups of varying number. Arrangements of kiosks may be centrally focused or linear. Boston is planning to implement a network of these centers throughout the city for the U.S. Bicentennial Celebration.

Lowell, Massachusetts, is the site of our second educative city project. Lowell was the first planned textile producing city in the United States, and it achieved international renown for its progressive ideas in the early nineteenth century. In reaction against industrial conditions in England, Lowell was planned to be an ideal industrial community with fine housing, cultural programs, and high moral standards. Although Lowell was at one time called the "Venice of America," the economy has been steadily disintegrating since the American Civil War and the flight of the textile industry to the South. Today Lowell is classified as one of the most economically depressed areas in the country, having an unemployment rate of nearly 15 percent.

The streets are grim reminders of the decline of the textile industry in New England. Relics of the early American industrial revolution remain decaying in the city. A vast man-made network of canals built in the nineteenth century to power the looms still stands as tribute to the engineering achievements of the period. These canals, however, have become overgrown and forgotten and are now used as open sewers.

Our work began in Lowell in the late 1960s when we were asked to solve an educational

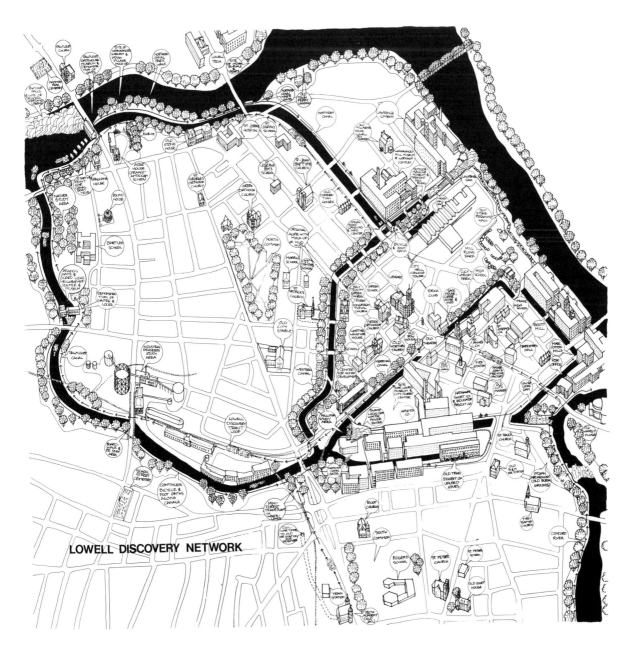

Figure 2

problem.[3] We felt the solution must go far beyond the schools and, in fact, lay in building upon and giving meaning to the environmental heritage, which was quickly being destroyed. By that time more than half the significant sites had been demolished and other sites sat neglected. The result was a city with almost a ghost-town feeling, depressing and unstimulating. The primary desire of most citizens was to escape Lowell. Somehow new meaning and value had to be created in this environment to renew its spirit, to change its course.

We decided to capitalize on the canal network and develop it as a linear cultural park to serve as an educational environment for residents. We also designed it to serve as a tourist attraction to help regenerate the Lowell economy. The canal network is very extensive—almost 5 miles long. Being a continuous network, it provided a new mode of movement throughout the city. Continuous bicycle and pedestrian paths are proposed along the canals, as well as a "Discovery Transit Loop" (Figure 2). This automated transit system would contain eight- to ten-passenger tracked vehicles and would provide views of historic Lowell to visitors as well as to Lowell children. The movement and open-space network would extend along the canals and the banks of the Merrimack River, north to the town forest less than a mile away, and south to Boston along the route of the old Middlesex Canal. Most of the remaining historic buildings lie along the canal network: some corporation houses, the textile mill buildings, an historic city market, an old fire station, and about eighty other sites. Use of this canal system as the structure for the park provides a continuous open-space and movement network, which will be accessible to many more people than would a centralized development. Because it is linear, it can be achieved with minimal interference with existing development. Major paths and transportation interchanges would fit into a network of child-oriented maps, pictures, and spoken and written directories describing the city's places, things to do, and how to get there. To help children understand the relation of the local place to the larger city, views or films of the place from the air would be displayed. Images and use of the same setting by different groups would be presented to encourage children to see the city from other viewpoints. Surfaces of major paths will be marked so that children can simply follow a color or symbol. Selected paths will be designed to explain local history, industry, and architecture, and others will be adventure and exploration trails.

"Discovery centers" located along the network would provide opportunities for open learning in the city. Among these is a series of power dams located along the canals that display picturesque control houses and tremendous flows of water. Francis Gate, one of the many dam and gate-house structures, has retained its original wooden gates. These have not been operable for many years but could be made to function again. The plan is to open the site to the public so that the workings of each of the parts are made apparent. Canal tour boats will take visitors through the locks to other sites in the park. On a small central island an outdoor museum of machinery would be displayed.

Another dam site would dramatize the fall of water, demonstrating hydrodynamic principles by means of water sprays and mechanisms that could be manipulated by visitors. Children could experiment with an Egyptian water clock or with a scale model of the dam in which the flow of the water could be changed. All of these would encourage learning in the city.

Among the most fascinating city activities are the large-scale systems of transportation, power, or communications. One effective way for teaching about these would be through outdoor models large enough to walk through. For example, a model of the transportation or power systems could demonstrate principles of flow with illuminated channels that change in color or sound with changing conditions. Observers could control the system and test the consequences of varying rates of movement or channel capacity. Other models could be made to explain social migration in the city or the ecology and geography of the entire region. A model of the entire canal system of Lowell would allow children to become familiar with its configuration and distribution of power from the natural waterfalls through the canals and power dams. Similarly, on an acre of land there would be an outdoor walk-through model of the central city having miniature constructions of facades and landmarks of the various districts of the city. A pedestrian could walk through the model and very quickly grasp the organization and character of the entire city (Figure 3).

Throughout its history Lowell has attracted immigrants from many locations: Greece, Ireland, French Canada, Puerto Rico, Armenia, Poland. The cultural roots of Lowell should be made more apparent. A migration map is proposed for the wall of an ethnic club or restaurant showing the origins, family names, and dates of immigration. Before the arrival of the early American settlers, Lowell was the home of the Pawtucket and Pennacook Indians who had lived there seasonally for centuries. Although several of these Indian sites have been identified, most residents are not aware of Lowell's Indian past. These sites might be made visible and accessible, with attractions such as an Indian village or Indian archeology digging areas. The sites occur along the banks of the Merrimack River, especially near the falls where fish were more plentiful. Environmental demonstrations are proposed here to teach Indian agriculture, fishing, food preservation, dwelling construction, and medicine.

Less than 1 mile from the city center is a forest that is very little known and rarely used by Lowell residents. Here we propose a Discovery Center in the form of a treetop walk, which begins underground with displays behind glass of root structures, soil composition, and underground life. The

path continues across the forest floor and then above ground level and into the treetops to a viewing platform above the trees, where the city, the countryside, and the stars may be viewed. Along the path there would be enlarged views of leaves, branches, trunks, and animal life, with highlights pointed out. A similar but horizontal walk is proposed for the swamp.

Of the many handsome mill buildings that once existed in Lowell, only a few remain, but these are often mistreated. Only one is still an operating textile industry; others are used for warehousing or manufacturing. They will be renovated with respect for their architectural and historical tradition. The fine old mill courtyards will be converted to public exhibition and events spaces. New uses that are economically viable are being sought for the large amounts of empty interior space. Some of these empty spaces are to be used as city learning places: a loom room where one could observe and try operating mill machinery, a com-

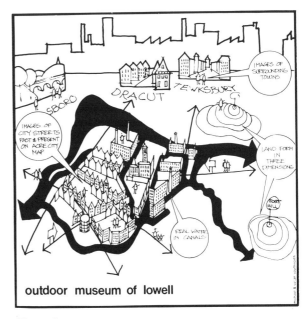

Figure 3
Miniature Walk-through City.

munity workshop of crafts, a costume room where one could don garments of the mill era, a time line of textile development to teach about the evolution of the trade that was so important in Lowell's history. A section of a mill would be established as a school–workshop, where one could immerse himself in nineteenth-century mill society, and learn how to produce fabric from the raw cotton down to the finished printed fabric, using methods and machinery of the era. These skills are still known by a few Lowell people who are eager to share them.

Some of the mill buildings have interesting manufacturing operations today. An example is the Hathaway Shirt Company, where we envision public access so that visitors can observe the complex process of making shirts. Nearby, another factory still produces "Father John's Medicine" just as it did 100 years ago. The factory desires to communicate its processes to the public. They are intriguing and from them one can learn to identify the scents of exotic oils and spices used in this elixir, as well as some principles of chemistry and marketing.

Industrial forms such as gas tanks also have great potential, and they conceal fascinating functions. Pipe and tank structures might be painted to communicate what is happening inside the tanks. Similarly, the windows of factory buildings can be made to communicate interior processes by means of simple platforms or periscopes, which bring the inside outside.

Although much of the mill architecture has been destroyed, the ruins are often very evident. Several sites of mill ruins are designated as exploration fields for architectural and industrial archeology.

How can the impact of an educative environment be assessed? Many of the consequences (e.g., the effects on skills such as reading or on general traits such as self-reliance or creativity) can only be evaluated over a long period of time, and even then with great difficulty. But there are

several important effects that can be evaluated in a short time with relative ease. (1) What educative city facilities or activities are most used? When? By whom? In what way? With what difficulties? (2) What are children's evaluations of educative city facilities and activities? (3) What are the effects of the system on children's city knowledge, places, activities, city structure and form, history, and people? (4) How do children's city activity patterns and travel territory change? (5) How are children's environmental values affected?

Although programs such as described here have many values, there are certain risks. There is the problem of control. Who is to decide what the content of the programs should be? The techniques of the educative environment could become a powerful propaganda weapon if they were misused. However, it is expected that this possibility would be minimized by means of a decentralized control system whereby many groups, especially children, contribute to program control and management. A reliable body would have to monitor contributions to prevent child exploitation.

Conflicts might develop with the public school system. If the educative city became too successful, many children, especially those who dislike school, would be more attracted to the city than to school. If that time were to come, public schools might have to change, perhaps relocating many of their programs in the educative city facilities. Until then it is best to view an educative city as a supplement to formal education, not as a substitute.

Still other limitations could be named; the costs are uncertain; management of such a decentralized program may be difficult; businessmen and police may object to the increasing numbers of unchaperoned children on the streets. The greatest danger is that the environment might become overexplained, and much of the mystery and pleasure of discovery would be lost. Some might worry that the city would become a vast dull school. We hope this outcome is unlikely. Explanation of the city would in most cases not be the aim; rather, the primary purpose would be to lead children to places and to let them develop their own interpretations.

NOTES AND REFERENCES

1. Michael Southworth, "An Urban Service for Children Based on Analysis of Cambridgeport Boys' Conception and Use of the City," Ph.D dissertation, Massachusetts Institute of Technology, 1970.
2. The Park Square Information Center experiment was supported by the U.S. Department of Housing and Urban Development and was administered by Signs/Lights/Boston and the Boston Redevelopment Authority.
3. The Lowell Discovery Network was supported by the Department of Housing and Urban Development through its Model Cities Program.

Information Ecology and the Design of Learning Environments*

Richard Allen Chase

INTRODUCTION

This paper is about learning and ways in which we can improve opportunities for learning to occur. Major attention will be given to the design of relationships between people and the information in their environments. Two case studies of designed learning environments will be presented first, followed by general discussions about information, learning, and environmental design.

*This paper has been adapted from an address delivered at the 1973 meeting of the American Association for the Advancement of Science as part of the Chairman's Symposium: Human Learning Capacities in Neurobiological Perspective. All the papers presented at that Symposium are to be published in book form [Philip C. Ritterbush and Karl H. Pribram (eds.), *Human Learning Capacity in Neurobiological Perspective,* New York: Plenum (in press)].

A LEARNING SYSTEM FOR INFANTS AND THEIR CARETAKERS

Five years ago, a group composed largely of members of the faculty at The Johns Hopkins University School of Medicine began to design an education program on infant development that could be used by parents to increase their competence as caretakers.[1] By reviewing both the available technical literature on infants and the research and clinical experiences of our own group, we identified several hundred facts about infant development that we felt could be of use to parents. This information was then translated into everyday language. In addition, we decided to convey each point of information by using clusters of photographs selected to communicate all major aspects of behavior development in infancy. The photographs are arranged on paper maps. There is a separate map for each three-month period from birth to twelve months. Basic aspects of caretaking, such as feeding, clothing, bathing, and schedules for well-baby clinic visits and immunizations, are shown on the top horizontal portions of the map. Below this is a major horizontal section devoted to each of the following categories of behavior: seeing, hearing, making sounds and language, touching and holding, moving, play, and a general category called "things children do." Scanning the map from left to right along any one of these horizontal sections will show the way in which behavior in that category changes as the infant matures. Most of this information is conveyed directly by the photographs. Text is limited to brief captions that call attention to the most important points being conveyed by the photographs. The maps can be personalized in a variety of ways. There are places for parents to put their own photographs, and simple tables that help parents make their own observations, such as on the kinds of responses an individual infant makes to the sounds of the doorbell, telephone, television, and radio.

Some photographs provide basic information about behavior development, such as the changes that occur in the way an infant holds objects during the first year of life. Some provide information about ways in which parents and older children can assist the intellectual and social development of infants through play.

Our efforts to design play materials for infants begin with information about infant behavior. This information initiates a preliminary effort to design three-dimensional objects that will have learning value. Four criteria are used in the design of infant play materials. Each piece of material is to be (1) as safe as possible; (2) low in cost; (3) effective in eliciting, reinforcing, and enlarging specific patterns of observable behavior; and (4) useful in a variety of ways and over long periods of time in the life of an individual infant. Information about ways in which the materials might best be used with infants of different ages, and the behaviors that can be observed when infants make use of the materials, is included in each package designed to hold play materials.

The parent education maps and the infant toys have been designed as a system. The parts may be used alone or in combinations. For example, the map covering the period from birth to three months could be used alone in the classes held for new mothers before they leave the hospital. Kits of maps combined with play materials could be used by parents in their own homes. The same kits could be used in parenthood education courses in high schools, or courses in child growth and development for medical students, nursing students, health-care assistants, and college students taking courses in developmental psychology. Practicing pediatricians could make use of the information parents record on the maps to help in their assessment of growth and development, and the basic-care portions of the map could simplify some of the pediatrician's communication with patients about health care. The staffs of day-care programs could use the maps and materials for training purposes, program development, and home-visit activities. We have designed the infant-care system so that it can be used by all professional groups in the field of maternal and child health. The same system can be used by parents in their own homes. If health-care and day-care program workers make use of the same information system about infant growth and development that parents are making use of, communication between parents and professional workers could become more accurate and more efficient. At the present time, most parents with new infants are often uncertain about how behavior develops and how the environment can be designed to facilitate learning in infancy.

Although many child-care manuals are presently available commercially, it is difficult for most parents to separate the high-quality items from the others, and there are many parents who are not used to reading lengthy books in order to gain practical information. We have relied heavily on the use of photographs in our system so that the same body of information can be shared with large numbers of parents as well as with the professional workers who help to care for their children.

It is meaningless to think about optimal learning environments for infants without giving prominent attention to the role of the mother and other caretakers. The presence of a positive, interested, concerned, supportive set of attitudes on the part of the mother significantly increases an infant's opportunities for learning. In addition to disposing the mother to use play materials to support behavior development, these attitudes make the mother responsive to the infant's individual expression of interests and skills. This responsiveness, communicated by smiling, touching, holding, and vocalizing, provides powerful reinforcement for the infant's behavior. The parent education and play materials that we have designed are intended to increase the competence of the caretakers and, thereby, the satisfaction and enjoyment of those reciprocal relationships with infants that constitute the essence of a competent early learning environment.

EXPERIMENTAL LEARNING ENVIRONMENTS FOR UNIVERSITY STUDENTS

In the Spring of 1971, D. Michael Williams and I were invited to work with members of the faculty at Cornell University who were teaching a course in environmental analysis.[2] We were to organize a series of exercises on the design of learning environments for a class of 190 students drawn from all undergraduate levels, as well as the graduate divisions of architecture, engineering, and biology. Three of these exercises will be discussed below. In all the exercises our principal objective was to show how the information available to members of a group can be vastly increased by appropriate redesign of the communication systems used by the group. As in the case of the learning system for infants and their caretakers, we were trying to show how opportunities for learning can be significantly increased by selecting, organizing, formatting, and making accessible information that has relevance to the interests of a group.

Instead of the fixed-seating amphitheater normally used by this class, we met our students in a large lounge area of the student union building. The center of the room had been cleared of furniture. Each student was asked to make and wear a name tag. We did this because students taught in large groups in conventional lecture halls usually do not know each other's names. Each student was asked to come to this special class session prepared to teach something. An explicit methodology was to be used, involving a clear statement of the behavioral objectives each student hoped to achieve through implementation of a carefully designed learning experience. Students were asked to be modest in their planning, and to provide all the materials that they would need to execute their plans. Each student was to teach several other students during the fifty-minute special class session, as well as to be taught by several students. Students raised their hands when they were available for teaching and lowered them when they began working with a new student. Although the rules for the exercise suggested working in pairs, small groups kept forming around student–teacher pairs. There was constant movement and animated conversation throughout the period. This class could be easily observed by students passing through the main lobby to the student union building. Many students came into the room to see what was happening, and some of them remained as participants in the exercise. In this way the boundaries of the class community kept changing in just the same way as the boundaries of the groups within the room kept changing. These changes were not dictated by a complex, predetermined schedule. They represented self-organizing properties of the experience.

Most of the student teaching plans involved efforts to shape specific motor performances. Since students were free to select their own behavioral objectives, the exercise was biased in favor of students selecting things that they could do well and had high interest in.

This exercise represents a radical alteration in the economics of information exchange within large class groups. We had, through this exercise, created a faculty of 190 people—each teaching something that he or she knew a good deal about and had interest in. The sharply hierarchical pattern of communication that operates when a large class takes notes on a lecture being delivered by a single individual gave way to a constantly changing array of group interactions, each characterized by a great deal of information exchange. When the amount of information being exchanged fell below critical levels, individuals simply withdrew and attached to other individuals or groups. In this way, each group interaction lasted as long as it was useful, and was reorganized when it stopped being useful. Decisions about interest and usefulness of available information were made by the participants through reciprocal interaction with their peers. The resulting patterns of change are not resisted simply because they involve changing a partner or group affiliation or mode of communication. They are accepted as necessary for the creation of new learning opportunities. In this sense, the group is more inclined to support productive patterns of communication, rather than to maintain particular structures of group organization. Group process becomes more important than group structure.

The exercise in which students taught other students was limited in time by the conventions of class schedules. However, the opportunities that were made possible through that exercise could be extended in time by creating a catalog describing the things that students were willing to teach each other.

Students were provided with one ditto master sheet and asked to describe the things they were willing to teach. Information concerning the amount of time, money, or special equipment necessary for the proposed learning experiences was also to be provided. Each statement was signed and contained information about how to get in touch with each student offering to teach.

The personal resources catalog consisted of 158 pages with 260 separate entries that could be classified into 131 categories. A few examples include automobile repairs, batik, calculus, drafting, embroidery, fencing, flying, guitar, knitting, map reading, piano, roulette, scrimshaw, trampoline, weaving, hair cutting, and yoga.

We provided each of our students with a second ditto master sheet and requested information concerning resources in the Cornell–Ithaca environment that might be of interest to other students. Each member of the class had explored the surrounding environment independently, and no matter how idiosyncratic individual explorations might have been, they are likely to have yielded information that would be of interest to at least some of the other students.

The environmental resources catalog consisted of 143 pages, with 569 separate entries that could be classified into 182 categories—for example: Greek restaurants, coffee houses, antique shops, candle wax, leather scraps, free maps, indoor and outdoor study areas, lounges, meeting areas, gardens, parks, bowling, films, ice skating, squash, tray sliding, bird sanctuary, foundry, graveyards, libraries, museums, wineries, zoo, birth-control information, cabs, computer laboratory, mystic, printers, check cashing, kittens, seminars, music practice facilities, and parking areas. The environmental resources catalog represents a mapping of resources within the Cornell–Ithaca environment that are of particular interest to university students. The catalog provides each student with a larger amount of information about environmental resources than could possibly be assembled through individual effort. In addition, the catalog describes the interests of the group and individual members within the group.

PRINCIPLES OF LEARNING SYSTEMS DESIGN

A competent learning environment must contain information that is relevant to the interests and needs of its users. The designer of learning environments must know a great deal about the people who will use an environment. He must have particularly accurate information about their interests, the kinds of problems that engage them and the kinds of solutions they seek, the conventions and styles of communication that are already being used to exchange information, and the kinds of effects on their environment that they are now seeking to realize. This information provides a framework within which the designer can make decisions about the kinds of information that should be available, the forms in which it will be most useful, and the delivery or access systems that will work best.

A great deal of information is available concerning behavior development in infancy, but this information is dispersed through the technical literatures in medicine, psychology, and education. For this reason, it is impossible for most mothers to understand it, even if they are highly

educated. The Cornell students had a great deal of information about the resources in their own immediate environment, but before our classes with them it was not readily available. It was diffused throughout the group, and no convention existed for the accumulation and organization of this information. We designed that convention and, in so doing, made a great deal of relevant, comprehensible information readily available to a large number of people.

INCREASING THE ACCESSIBILITY OF INFORMATION IN THE ENVIRONMENT

Information can be made more accessible by labeling. Traditionally, one comes to know about the location of informational resources through years of individual exploration. Individuals living in large cities rarely know where all the libraries, museums, and schools are located. Even when the locations of informational resources become known, it is hard to be sure who is welcome to make use of them. Clarification of these matters requires further investigation. The whole process is inefficient and favors those who are most skilled in information seeking and information utilization, leaving those most in need of developing these skills least likely to come in contact with the informational resource systems that could help them to learn. Of course, constant efforts are made to label informational resources. Most great libraries, museums, and schools have their own catalogs, designed to inventory their informational resources and to make clear the rules that govern their use. We now have quite a number of catalogs that inventory classes of information resources, and, by so doing, refer to many independent information resource centers. I have listed a few such catalogs in the "Selected Bibliography" at the end of the article.

Maps can show the location of informational resources with great clarity and economy. Many of the maps used principally for road location purposes also show the locations of schools, museums, and libraries. Figure 1 shows a particularly clear informational resource map—in this case, the location of libraries in New York City.[3] The

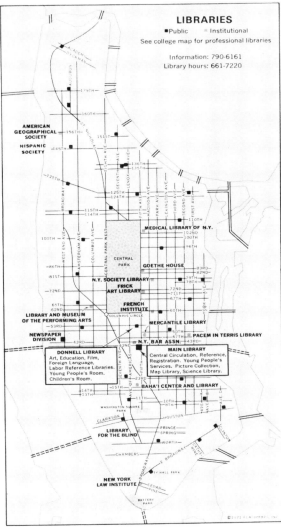

Figure 1
A map showing the geographical locations of major libraries in New York City. [**From Toy Lasker and Jean George.** *New York in Maps* **(rev. ed.), New York: Ballantine Books, Inc., and Flashmaps, Inc., 1972. Reproduced through the courtesy of the publisher.**]

improvement of mapping conventions for informational resources could significantly improve the extent to which informational resources are accessible to larger numbers of people. The map of libraries in New York City could be complemented by other informational resource maps and located on kiosks distributed throughout the city in convenient indoor and outdoor locations. If the conventions for representing and displaying informational resources were standardized on an international basis (in much the same way as information about transportation is now being treated), each person would learn, in the most immediate and familiar environments, the same conventions for the labeling of informational resources that would be in use in all other places. As conventions for the labeling of information evolve, it should be possible to go well beyond identifying the locations of schools, libraries, museums, theaters, etc.; it should become possible to identify the kind of information, amount of information, quality of information, and the relationship between particular kinds of information and the needs of particular user groups.

Information can be made more accessible by moving more of it through existing distribution channels. In Great Britain, the Open University is making major use of national television for information delivery on academic subjects to individual students. The University Extension Division of the University of California at San Diego is now initiating a program called "Courses by Newspaper."[4] Distinguished scholars have been invited to write 1,400-word lectures examining various aspects of the American experience and its implications for the future of man. There will be twenty such lectures in the first course ("America and the Future of Man"), and they will be published by newspapers throughout the world. The course will be available to the casual newspaper reader at no charge other than the cost of the newspaper itself. Those who wish to explore the subject more intensively can send for a $10 kit of supplementary resource materials. Those who wish to take the course for credit will be able to do so by registering with cooperating local colleges and universities.

Channels that are used for transportation have great potential for information delivery. Figure 2 shows a nineteenth-century British railroad map designed for the use of passengers traveling be-

RAILWAY CHRONICLE
TRAVELLING CHARTS;
FOR PERUSAL ON THE JOURNEY:

IN WHICH ARE NOTED

THE TOWNS, VILLAGES, CHURCHES, MANSIONS, PARKS, STATIONS, BRIDGES, VIADUCTS, TUNNELS, CUTTINGS, GRADIENTS, &c., THE SCENERY AND ITS NATURAL HISTORY, THE ANTIQUITIES AND THEIR HISTORICAL ASSOCIATIONS, &c. PASSED BY THE LINE OF RAILWAY.

Constituting a Novel and Complete Companion for the Railway Carriage.

LONDON TO TUNBRIDGE WELLS
(ON THE SOUTH-EASTERN).

MAP OF THE SOUTH-EASTERN RAILWAY, WITH ITS BRANCHES.

The South-Eastern line, instead of pursuing the old coach-road through Rochester and Canterbury, as was proposed, was compelled by the benighted, and now repentant, opposition of the inhabitants of North Kent to make a circuitous route through the Weald of Kent.

Starting from the London Bridge terminus, the first mile and a half of the journey is on the Greenwich Railway proper, which is now leased in perpetuity to the South-Eastern. The Greenwich line was begun in 1833, and opened to Greenwich in 1838. That line consists throughout of a viaduct of about 1,000 arches. The next eight miles were constructed by the Croydon Company, and opened in 1839; and the Brighton Company continued the line to Brighton. The portion of the line from the 15th mile to Reigate has been sold to the South-Eastern for about 300,000l., and it is at Reigate, 20¼ miles from town, that the South-Eastern begins its eastern course. This portion, as far as Tunbridge, was opened for traffic in May 1842. A further opening of the main line to Folkestone took place in June 1843; and in February 1844, the whole line was opened to Dover. The branch to Maidstone was opened in September 1844; that to Tunbridge Wells in September 1845; and that between Ashford and Ramsgate in April 1846.

Travellers on these branches should have their wits about them, to see that they get into the carriages marked for their destination, or that, if they do not, they alight at the proper station. For the Maidstone or Tunbridge Wells branch, they must alight at Tunbridge; for Canterbury or Ramsgate, at Ashford.

The TRAFFIC is increasing largely, and yields on the average about 10,000l. weekly.

The ELECTRIC TELEGRAPH is established along the whole of the South-Eastern and its branches, whereby the safety of travelling, even without it more safe than any previous mode, is further enhanced.

Every viaduct, bridge, river, pathway, cutting and tunnel is marked by the proper diagrams.

⌐⊐ represents a bridge passing *above* the railway in a cutting;

◻ | | ◻ a bridge passing *beneath* the railway on an embankment;

⊥⊥⊥ a level road or pathway;

▦ a tunnel;

▦ | | ▦ a stream passing beneath the railway.

The scale is an inch to a mile.

The names of the stations are inserted across the line; the principal stations in capital letters, as CROYDON; the intermediate in smaller type as Merstham. The distance of the chief places

near to each station is given: thus Nunhead Cemetery is 1 mile from the New Cross station.

This railway has excellent regulations respecting luggage. The traveller should see a ticket affixed to his luggage before entering the carriage. He may also leave his luggage at the station with perfect safety, by paying a penny each package and obtaining a check ticket.

The GEOLOGY of the line will be found noted where changes occur. The railway begins on *London Clay*, which passes into *Plastic Clay*, near Anerly 7¼ miles. *Chalk* begins at the 12th mile and extends nearly to Reigate, where the *Greensand* commences. After Bletchingley Tunnel we enter on the *Oaktree Clay*, which continues to Pluckley. Hence to beyond Hythe station, the line is on the *Sand*, which yields the Kentish rag stone. Crossing the *Greensand* again, for about 3 miles, the line is tunnelled through *chalk* into Dover.

This line offers peculiar attractions for PLEASURE EXCURSIONS. The tourist in search of picturesque and varied scenery, or national antiquities, may alight at Reigate, Godstone, Edenbridge, Penshurst, Tunbridge, Tunbridge Wells, Maidstone, Canterbury, Westenhanger, Folkestone, and will find at each an abundance. For details we refer to our separate 'Pleasure Excursions.'

Figure 2
Nineteenth-century British railroad map designed for the use of passengers traveling between London and Tunbridge Wells (Victoria and Albert Museum, London, England).

tween London and Tunbridge Wells. The map has pictures of places and buildings along the train route, and provides a brief historical description to accompany each picture. This simple traveler's map provides information relevant to the common experience of all travelers on the train. It not only makes more meaningful the comprehension of the places observed along the route,

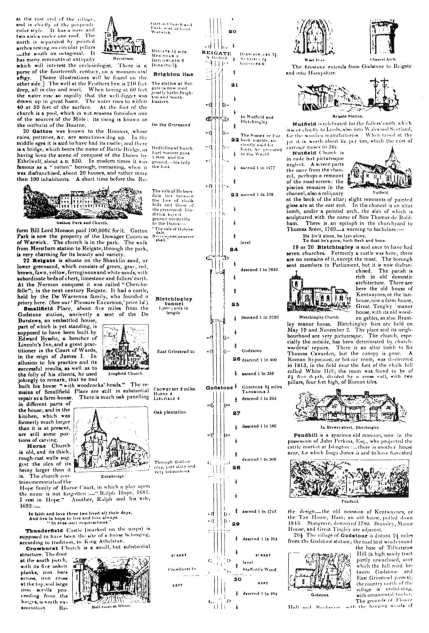

but it also facilitates the direct sharing of information among the passengers.

There are dining cars on trains. Should there be learning cars as well, places where those who wish could share information about their common travel experience more fully through the use of additional visual material and the availability of facilitators and resource people who could stimulate discussion? The learning car need not, of course, restrict its attention to information about the trip itself, it could attend to any area or topic that attracted the attention and interest of the group.

Underground transportation systems have a good deal of fixed space in which people must wait for considerable periods of time. Many underground systems now have clear maps of routes and station locations. The London Transport Underground System is particularly advanced in this respect. The photographic murals that are now being placed in subway stations in the city of Boston are designed to orient the traveler to some of the major aspects of the environment around the station.

These efforts merely scratch the surface of the possibilities for using the vast time–space dimensions of transport terminals to deliver information to the traveler in a way that will enhance opportunities for learning. The murals in the subway systems could be far more detailed. The public gardens in Boston have a rich social history and many amenities for public use. Detailed representation of such information could be added to the basic orientation graphics system. Motion pictures and slides could be used to complement the fixed photographic murals. Recorded commentaries could be delivered into parts of the station for use by those who want additional information about that region of the city. Rail and air transport terminals afford sufficient space for sophisticated information delivery systems in permanent learning environments. The frag-

mented efforts of the travel companies, local industry, and local chambers of commerce to convey messages to the traveler through a scattering of booths, posters, and printed literature could be coordinated to create learning environments in transport terminals that could provide travelers with a broad orientation to the region.

Information can be made more accessible by designing and managing new types of information resource facilities. One new type of information facility is the store that provides rapid printing services, usually through the use of electrostatic copying and photo-offset printing. Stores of this type have spread rapidly in recent years, primarily in university and business areas. Some "instant printing" establishments offer design and composition services also.

A new store in Greenwich, Connecticut (Leisure Learning Centers, 50 Greenwich Ave., Greenwich, Conn. 06830) states in its brochure:

We started with the idea that learning should be fun, convenient, and successful for everyone. When you enter our ultramodern learning center, you'll discover an abundant variety of educational products for all ages and interests: Toys that teach children; memorizing aids; adult mental stimulators and games; science, computer, and ecology kits; thought-provoking books-records-tapes; home-study kits; plus an assortment of craft items. The most unique aspect of our learning center is our "school" without classes. Subjects are taught to all age groups on the latest electronic audio-visual teaching machines . . . Everything is individualized. You never get lost or left behind. You come to our center at your own convenience when you are most motivated to learn.

Whether this form of self-access learning center will be most useful or whether some other format would work better will be decided by user acceptance. The entrepreneurial model seems to be well adapted to providing critical tests of the extent to which new learning resource facilities meet widely felt needs for access to information.

Information can be made more accessible by allowing a variety of information-rich environments to be used by students in the same way that they use conventional schools. Many urban high schools now allow students to work in existing community facilities, such as museums, factories and shops, law offices, architectural offices, and government agencies.[5] Many of these community facilities maintain training programs for their own personnel and accept graduate students for internships. These networks of dispersed and specialized learning resources could be amplified considerably in number, kind, and comprehensiveness of the learning opportunities offered. One example of continued development of learning resources of this type is provided by the recent decision of the Massachusetts Board of Higher Education to approve the authority of the Arthur D. Little Company (a diversified consulting firm) to award the academic degree of Master of Science in Administration.

The design of multifunction centers facilitates information dissemination by allowing each person who comes to the center because of one of its functions to observe at least some of the other functions contained in the total complex.[6] The Human Resources Center in Pontiac, Michigan, provides a good example of such a center.[7] It contains space for four schools, the operations of community agencies, and a broad spectrum of amenities to be shared by school and community alike: theater, exhibition area, public restaurant, community lounge, library, seminar rooms, gymnasium, arts and crafts workshops, etc. Many student unions located on university campuses provide good examples of single facilities that have a multiplicity of spaces designed to accommodate the major needs and interests of the communities they serve.[8] Generalization of multifunction community service centers could provide a major new network of resources for learning. The network could provide a mixture of the latest technology for information generation and transmission, along with the conditions for social inter-

action that have always been essential to the broadest possible encouragement of learning.

THE MANAGEMENT OF LEARNING ENVIRONMENTS

A learning system can, at one time, provide readily accessible information of high quality which is relevant to the interests of the users being served, in a social environment that allows the use of the information to have constructive consequences. But the same system may, at a later time, fail to meet one or more of these criteria. Such dysfunctions in a learning system can persist, become aggravated, and result in considerable stress. These considerations point to the need for environmental management. The environmental manager constantly monitors the performance of the system. This requires close observation of the behaviors of the people using the system. Are they finding the kinds of information that they need? Is it comprehensible? Does its use have significant and constructive consequences? If the system is not performing properly, it is in need of change. It should be possible to identify the changes that are needed well before the system is stressed to the point of producing discomfort, disaffiliation, and inefficiency in the learning process. This is one of the responsibilities of the environmental manager.

The environmental manager must understand the interrelationships between physical facilities and social process; the conditions under which learning is facilitated; and the ways in which information can be generated, stored, used, maintained, and renewed. We do not at present provide the training that would allow this competence to be achieved by a single individual. Most individuals who approximate the role we are defining for the environmental manager are presently concerned about political aspects of decision making in social systems, or else they are specialists in "orderliness," and give their major attention to the condition of facilities and the plans for operating facilities, rather than the condition of the people who use them. We have not yet achieved general recognition of the importance of environmental management as an essentially apolitical and nonobsessive role that requires competent technical understanding of the major ways in which people and resources can be most constructively interrelated. The role requires a synthesis of physical and social systems analysis, design, and management skills. The environmental manager must, in addition, be mindful of the history of individual communities in order to understand their aspirations for growth and change—aspirations that are projected, in part, in the form of learning environments. The environmental manager functions in the service of the public—equally sensitive to new opportunities for and impediments to constructive growth and change. The environmental manager provides constant monitoring of the man–environment system to assess the extent to which it is taking full advantage of the opportunities available to it. His interventions are consistent with, and facilitating of, the constructive patterns of human behavior that evolve through the self-organizing properties of functioning man–environment systems. The principal objectives of the environmental manager are consonant with those of the environmental designer. These objectives have been well stated by Forrester as follows:

Good planning based on a deep insight into the behavior of complex systems will attempt to release the internal power, initiative, driving force, enthusiasm, and human potential of the people in the system. It will do this instead of heaping more work, more discipline, more repression, and more co-ordination on them in an effort to push back a social system that is still trying to go in the wrong direction.[9]

Unlike the environmental designer, the environmental manager remains a part of the operating, evolving man–environment system. Just as the environmental manager must be well trained in the skills of environmental design, it is hard to conceive how the training of an environmental designer could be considered complete without his serving as an apprentice environmental manager.

INFORMATION, LEARNING, AND THE DESIGN OF CULTURE

The amounts and kinds of information available to individuals have continued to increase in a significant way through the twentieth century. We have, in earlier parts of this paper, discussed ways in which the environmental designer might make information even more accessible to larger numbers of people. However, we have given little attention to the conditions under which individuals maintain their interest in communication and learning. It is the patterns of social interaction within communities that define values and goals for the group, and the values and goals that are shared by groups give meaning and purpose to the behavior of individuals. In this way communities shape and are shaped by communication. This dialectic provides the framework within which meaningful commitments to learning are sustained.

These relationships were a matter of great concern to John Dewey, and the following series of brief quotations from his book, *The Public and Its Problems,* serves to clarify the need for the designer of learning environments to understand social process and cultural change.

To learn to be human is to develop through the give-and-take of communication an effective sense of being an individually distinctive member of a community; one who understands and appreciates its beliefs, desires, and methods, and who contributes to a further conversion of organic powers into human resources and values.

The essential need, in other words, is the improvement of the methods and conditions of debate, discussion and persuasion. That is the problem of the public. We have asserted that this improvement depends essentially upon freeing and perfecting the processes of inquiry and dissemination of their conclusions.

There is no limit to the liberal expansion and confirmation of limited personal intellectual endowment which may proceed from the flow of social intelligence when that circulates by word of mouth from one to another in the communications of the local community. That and that only gives reality to public opinion. We lie, as Emerson said, in the lap of an immense intelligence. But that intelligence is dormant and its communications are broken, inarticulate and faint until it possesses the local community as its medium.[10]

The most recent centuries in the evolution of Western man have shown steady growth in emphasis on professional work roles, and diminution in shared public life in favor of the private life of the family. Within the family, major attention has been given to the education of children in a manner that would put them at the greatest advantage in the development of individual careers and the continued growth of resources within their own families. Information has been largely viewed as a commodity that is important in the advancement of an individual life career. Institutions of education have proliferated to serve the growing ambitions of individuals to compete more successfully for increasingly complex jobs. Individual families have gained material advantages at the expense of broader patterns of social interaction within the community.[11] Status is expressed, in part, by obtaining increasing isolation from the community through the purchase of more private space, more widely distanced from the private spaces held by others. This process has strengthened suburban development at the expense of continued maintenance and growth of cities. The individual family home is well stocked with information products: television, telephone, radio, typewriter, tape recorder, phonograph, cameras, books, tapes, films, slides. The amounts of information that find their way into individual homes are impressive and unprecedented in quality and variety. But there is a paradox in this history—the

growth of information available to individuals is increasingly delivered to individuals in isolation—cut off from patterns of social interaction that give definition to how information should be utilized selectively to enhance the meaningfulness, satisfaction, and productivity of the human experience. Without the rich fabric of social experience needed to define values and purposes, needs and priorities, information becomes stockpiled like any other commodity that can denote status. Under these conditions, information not only fails to enrich the public life—it further intimidates patterns of individual growth for lack of a broadly meaningful orientation to its use.

Childhood was barely recognized in the Middle Ages. It was psychologically hazardous to become too attached to the young because their chances of survival were always questionable. If they lived, economic necessities required early sharing of the responsibilities of adult work. Protection from infectious disease and the growth of technology have resulted in progressive recognition of the state of childhood and of the disposition of children to investigation, exploration, and play. We now recognize that the child is something of an information-seeking machine whose behavior is influenced by patterns of early experience.[12] This understanding has resulted in important investigations into the ways in which early experience influences behavior.[13] However, the increasingly elaborate formal systems for the education of children have resulted in extended separation of the life of children from the life of the adult community. It is not until graduation from high school or college that "children" begin to share in a meaningful way in the activities of the adult culture. Their learning is then facilitated by sharing responsibilities.

Increased development of community life could allow children to have these advantages earlier—by allowing them to learn within existing community enterprises other than schools, not only as students but as peers. It would also seem to be possible, and desirable, to encourage adults to continue to develop the capacity for curiosity, exploration, and play that characaterizes so much of the behavior of very young children.[14] Surely the abrupt attenuation of these characteristics at the time adult work roles are accepted is as amenable to cultural change as the medieval denial of childhood.

The rules that govern the relationships between people and information reflect, in part, the needs of a society. Education in colonial America stressed moral and religious training.[15] During the eighteenth century, American universities moved toward secular education. The need for competence in government, law, medicine, business and trades, agriculture, science, and engineering continued to grow and increasingly influenced the character of the American university.[16] Changing needs within a society produce changes in education. Systems of education that prove most adaptive are discovered by judicious experimentation. We are engaged in such a process at the present time. What can we say about the changing needs of our society that have set this experimentation in motion? And what can we say about the new learning systems that are most likely to serve us best?

We are becoming increasingly aware of a problem that is unique in its proportions in the evolution of human populations. This is the problem of complexity.[17] Human populations have continued to grow, and the number and size of the social organizations needed to support them have also grown. The idea of growth had become equated with progress itself. However, a number of experiences have sharply challenged this view in recent years. We have become aware of the life-threatening consequences of uncontrolled exploitation of natural resources. We have also been humbled by the realization that growth in social institutions cannot be equated with increased capability—for the facts are often quite opposite.

How do we gain an understanding of the behavior of vast, complex systems?[18] How do we reintroduce feedback pathways that have stopped functioning as increasing scale has placed unbridgeable distances between parts of systems that need to be closely influenced by each other? How do we reestablish the regulation of systems by the consequences of their own behavior? The vast scale and complexity of contemporary social institutions now require planning and deliberate design to achieve these objectives,[19] and the most important aspects of these planning and design efforts may well be the ways in which people and information are related. This issue has concerned us throughout this paper. We have seen that learning system design can make schools more interesting, allow parents to help their infants to learn, and provide ways for students to make better use of the informational resources in their surrounding communities. We can now see that principles of learning system design can also be applied to the evolving redesign of our culture.

The planning and design of complex social systems requires large amounts of high-quality information. Good planning makes use of the information being generated as a system performs, to assess the needs for change and the character of the changes that might be most useful.[20] The better individuals are informed, the better they can contribute to this process of regulating the performance of social systems by the consequences of their behavior. The better individuals are informed, the better they can manage the planning requirements of their individual lives as well.

We can begin to see the prospect of a society devoted to learning in a way that has never occurred before. Education has been largely shaped by economic and political constraints. It now appears that the chances for survival and growth of human social organization will hinge on our ability to establish balanced and harmonious relationships between human populations, other life systems, and the physical environment. Under these circumstances it becomes important for everyone to have greater access to high-quality information and to become more skillful in its use.

It seems, at this point in the history of human populations, that the search for new planning systems and the search for new learning systems are simply different aspects of the same process of cultural evolution.[21] The obilgation is clear: that environmental designers and environmental managers become serious students of human ecology and human culture; that every individual come to understand more fully the ways of intelligent planning and design; and that the breadth of learning required to achieve these objectives be supported by the fullest possible development of opportunities to share information in every way that hard effort and fertile imagination can achieve.

NOTES AND REFERENCES

1. The group consisted of Shirley P. Borkowf, Department of Pediatrics; Doris W. Welcher, Department of Pediatrics; Richard Allen Chase, Department of Psychiatry and Behavioral Sciences; and D. Michael Williams, Art Department, C. W. Post College, Long Island University.
2. R. A. Chase, D. M. Williams, and J. J. Fisher, "Exercises in the Design of Learning Environments," in *Control of Human Behavior, Vol. III; Psychology and Education,* Roger Ulrich, Thomas Stachnik, and John Mabry (eds.), Glenview, Ill.: Scott, Foresman and Company, 1974.
3. Toy Lasker and Jean George, *New York in Maps* (rev. ed.), New York: Ballantine Books, Inc. and Flashmaps, Inc., 1972.
4. "Courses by Newspaper," University of California Extension, San Diego, Calif., 1973.
5. J. Bremer and M. von Moschzisker, *The School Without Walls,* New York: Holt, Rinehart and Winston, Inc., 1971; Ruth Weinstock, *The Greening of the High School,* New York: Educational Facilities Laboratories, Inc., 1973; R. Wurman, *Making the City Observable,* Cambridge, Mass.: The MIT Press, 1971, pp. 66–67. (Philadelphia's school without walls.)
6. C. Alexander, Sara Ishikawa, and M. Silverstein, *A Pattern Language Which Generates Multi-service Centers,* Berkeley, Calif.: Center for Environmental Structure, 1968.
7. Weinstock, *op. cit.*
8. P. Butts, *State of the College Union Around the World,* Ithaca, N.Y.: Association of College Unions-International,

1967; E. Sternberg and Barbara Sternberg, *Community Centers and Student Unions,* New York: Van Nostrand Reinhold Co., 1971.
9. J. W. Forrester, "Planning Under the Dynamic Influences of Complex Social Systems," in *Arts of the Environment,* Gyorgy Kepes (ed.), New York: George Braziller, Inc., 1972.
10. J. Dewey, *The Public and Its Problems,* Chicago: Gateway Books, 1946.
11. P. Ariès, *Centuries of Childhood: A Social History of Family Life,* Robert Baldick, (tr.), New York: Random House, Inc.—Vintage Books, 1962.
12. R. L. Fantz and S. Nervis, "The Predictive Value of Changes in Visual Preferences in Early Infancy," in *Exceptional Infant, Vol. 1: The Normal Infant,* Jerome Hellmuth (ed.), New York: Brunner/Mazel, Inc., 1967; J. Kagan, "On Class Differences and Early Development," in *Education of the Infant and Young Child.* Victor H. Denenberg (ed.), New York: Academic Press, Inc., 1970; M. Lowenfeld, *Play in Childhood,* New York: John Wiley & Sons, Inc., 1967; W. A. Mason, "Early Deprivation in Biological Perspective," in *Education of the Infant and Young Child,* Victor H. Denenberg (ed.), New York: Academic Press, Inc., 1970; S. Millar, *The Psychology of Play,* Baltimore; Penguin Books, Inc., 1971; Ina C. Uzgiris, "Ordinality in the Development of Schemas for Relating to Objects," in *Exceptional Infant, Vol. 1; The Normal Infant,* Jerome Hellmuth (ed.), New York: Brunner/Mazel, Inc., 1967; Susan Zegans and L. S. Zegans, "Fear of Strangers in Children and the Orienting Reaction," *Behavioral Science,* Vol. 17, No. 5, 1972, pp. 407–419.
13. Mary D. S. Ainsworth and Silvia M. Bell, "Attachment, Exploration, and Separation," *Child Development,* Vol. 41, 1970, pp. 49–67; J. Bowlby, *Attachment and Loss, Vol. 1; Attachment,* Baltimore, Md.: Penguin Books, Inc., 1971; Bettye M. Caldwell, "The Effects of Psychological Deprivation on Human Development in Infancy," in *Annual Progress in Child Psychiatry and Child Development,* Stella Chess and Alexander Thomas (eds.), New York: Brunner/Mazel, Inc., 1971; Harriet L. Rheingold and Carol O. Eckerman, "The Infant Separates Himself from His Mother," *Science,* Vol. 168, 1970, pp. 78–83; M. Rutter, *Maternal Deprivation,* Baltimore, Md.: Penguin Books, Inc., 1972; E. S. Schaefer, "Need for Early and Continuing Education," in *Education of the Infant and Young Child,* Victor H. Denenberg (ed.), New York: Academic Press, Inc., 1970; E. S. Schaefer and M. Aaronson, "Infant Education Research Project: Implementation and Implications of a Home Tutoring Program," in *The Preschool in Action: Exploring Early Childhood Programs,* Ronald K. Parker (ed.), Boston: Allyn and Bacon, Inc., 1972; D. P. Weikert and D. Z. Lambie, "Early Enrichment in Infants," in *Education of the Infant and Young Child,* Victor H. Denenberg (ed.), New York: Academic Press, Inc., 1970.
14. Millar, *op. cit.*; C. Price, "The Fun Palace," *The Drama Review,* Vol. 12, No. 3, 1968, pp. 127–129.

15. R. B. Nye, *The Cultural Life of the New Nation: 1776–1830,* New York: Harper & Row, Publishers—Torchbooks, 1960.
16. *Ibid.*
17. J. G. Miller, "Living Systems: The Organization," *Behavioral Science,* Vol. 17, No. 1, 1972, pp. 1–182.
18. Walter Buckley (ed.), *Modern Systems Research for the Behavioral Scientist,* Chicago: Aldine Publishing Co., 1968; F. E. Emery, (ed.), *Systems Thinking,* Baltimore, Md.: Penguin Books, Inc., 1970; Forrester, *op. cit.*; R. L. Meier, *A Communications Theory of Urban Growth,* Cambridge, Mass.: The MIT Press, 1970; Miller, *op. cit.*; L. von Bertalanffy, *General System Theory,* New York: George Braziller, Inc., 1968.
19. R. L. Burgess and E. Bushell, Jr., "A Behavioral View of Some Sociological Concepts," in *Behavioral Sociology,* Robert L. Burgess and Don Bushell, Jr. (eds.), New York: Columbia University Press, 1969; W. W. Harman, "Context for Education in the Seventies," mimeo, Educational Policy Research Center, Stanford Research Institute, Menlo Park, Calif., 1969; W. W. Harman, "Alternative Futures and Educational Policy," mimeo, Educational Policy Research Center, Stanford Research Institute, Menlo Park, Calif., 1970; W. W. Harman, "Planning Amid Forces for Institutional Change," *Man-Environment Systems,* Vol. 2, No. 4, 1972, pp. 207–220.; B. F. Skinner, *Beyond Freedom and Dignity,* New York: Alfred A. Knopf, Inc., 1971; R. G. Studer, "Human Systems Design and the Management of Change," *General Systems,* Vol. 16, 1971, pp. 131–143; "Toward a Social Report," U.S. Department of Health, Education and Welfare, Washington, D.C., 1969.
20. Forrester, *op. cit.*
21. *Ibid.*; Harman, "Planning"; R. M. Hutchins, *The Learning Society,* New York: The New American Library, Inc.—Mentor Books, 1969; I. Illich, *Deschooling Society,* New York: Harper & Row, Publishers, 1971.

SELECTED BIBLIOGRAPHY: INFORMATION RESOURCE CATALOGS

Alternatives in Print: An Index and Listing of Some Movement Publications Reflecting Today's Social Change Activities. Columbus, Ohio: Ohio State University Libraries, 1971.

Center for Curriculum Design, (ed.), *Somewhere Else: A Living–Learning Catalog.* Chicago: The Swallow Press, Inc., 1973.

Educational Opportunities of Greater Boston for Adults: 1972–73. Catalogue No. 50, Cambridge, Mass. : The Educational Exchange of Greater Boston, 1972.

Floodlight: Guide to Evening Classes 1972–73. London: Inner London Education Authority, 1972.

Hobman, D. *A Guide to Voluntary Service.* London: Her Majesty's Stationery Office, 1969.

Lasker, Toy, and George, Jean. *New York in Maps* (rev. ed.). New York: Ballantine Books, Inc., and Flashmaps, Inc., 1972.

Library and Reference Facilities in the Area of the District of Columbia. (7th ed.). Washington, D.C.: Library of Congress, 1966.

Shaw, R. *New York for Children: An Unusual Guide for Parents, Teachers and Tourists.* New York: Outerbridge & Lazard, Inc., 1972.

Tarshis, B. *The Creative New Yorker: A Participant's Guide to Arts, Crafts, Music and Theater in New York.* New York: Simon and Schuster, 1972.

Wurman, Richard (ed.), *Yellow Pages of Learning Resources.* Cambridge, Mass.: The MIT Press, 1972.

PART THREE
ENVIRONMENTAL
EVALUATION

Since the end of World War II there has been a growing awareness that the traditional methods of planning and designing are no longer adequate to the increased scale and complexity of environmental problems. Rather than ignoring these problems or leaving them for others to solve, many environmental design professionals have begun to reassess their roles and functions and to look for and develop better methods of problem solving.

As might be expected, this search has brought the realization that systematic approaches (e.g., systems analysis, production engineering, and operations research) have been effectively applied to certain large-scale military and business problems and might be successfully adapted to the needs of designers and planners. Throughout the 1950s and 1960s the education of architects, industrial designers, engineers, and city planners

has been increasingly focused on the discovery, testing, and evaluation of "new" design methods, most of which were already developed and in use by other disciplines concerned with technological development.

In many ways the search for new design methods today is analogous to the historic shift from "craftsmanship to draughtsmanship" which became institutionalized as a result of the profound social, economic, and technological changes caused by the Industrial Revolution. Before that time products such as farm wagons, saws and axes, rowing boats, cooking utensils, and musical instruments were the result of a process of trial and error in which the object was slowly brought into a close fit with the needs of its user. Because design information could not be codified into symbolic form (e.g., books), the education of craftsmen was by long apprenticeships during which exact information about the traditional product shape and the process of its making was learned by direct experience.[1]

Although this process of "craft evolution" was ideally suited to the slowly changing needs of an agricultural society, it was most inadequate to the rapidly changing needs of an urban–industrial nation. Craft evolution, which is based on precedent and trial-and-error modification of the actual product, did not provide for either complete reorganization of the form as a whole or for the development of completely new forms for completely new needs.

It was in response to the need to overcome the limitations of a craft evolution technology that the method of designing by use of scale drawings and models emerged and along with it a new class of form-givers—professional designers. This radical innovation allowed (1) production work to be split up into separate pieces made by many relatively unskilled people; (2) planning of objects too large for fabrication by a single craftsman, such as large buildings; and (3) accelerated rates of production arising from the ability to coordinate the flow of energy, materials, and labor. The method of design by drawing, because it externalized design information and decision-making processes and allowed more people to participate in the whole production–consumption cycle, was well suited to the demands of industrialization. In fact, today designing and planning is no longer solely what architects, city planners, landscape architects, and other design professionals do: it is also what educators, economists, systems managers, legislators, consumer advocates, real estate developers, and many others do. We are living in a planning culture in which all our institutions, whether or not they are public or private and whether they are concerned with the production of goods or services, find it necessary to engage in a systematic planning and design process: (1) to explicitly define their problems, (2) establish goals and priorities, (3) explore alter-

native ways of achieving desired outcomes, (4) evaluate and select an action to be taken and a strategy for doing so, and (5) to continually *assess* and *evaluate* the implemented plan or action in terms of new definitions of the problem and new goals and objectives. Obviously, such a comprehensive approach to planning is a complex multidisciplinary activity which is increasingly less concerned with the design and production of products and more concerned with the design and management of systems of relationships among people, places, and things.[2]

Clearly, design by drawing is only appropriate to a small portion of this expanded design and planning process. All the articles in Part Three are reactions against sole reliance on this ubiquitous design method. Most importantly, a scale drawing does not convey "anything about the needs of users or about the problems of manufacturers."[3] Drawings do not allow the designer to judge how the product will function in actual use, and, as is increasingly the case, if the product is not a single object but a system, drawings may be of no help. Also, scale drawings can only be used by one person at a time, usually the chief designer, making it impossible for other people, such as expected users or other professional experts, to participate in making the most important design decisions. As in the case of methods of craft evolution, traditional design methods are only appropriate to relatively stable design problems. When the nature of the problems change, as they are now doing, so does the nature of their solution.

Any attempt at systematic planning and design is based on an ability to anticipate the effects of proposals for change and to devise alternative courses of action that are compatible with desired outcomes and achievable within cost limitations. A planning process based on a strategy of "research and development" represents just such a marriage of science, technology, and economics. Central to this approach is the notion of system evaluation, which is aimed at assessing whether or not the implemented plan is achieving desired outcomes. This, of course, implies the need for a publicly stated definition of the problem and description of the nature of the solution, and the establishment of a set of specific objectives that can be used to judge the actual success of the operating system. Through time, such a process of systematic learning allows the planner or designer to devise more effective strategies for solving problems.

When compared to this somewhat simplified sketch of a research-and-development approach to planning for change, it becomes clear that the missing link in traditional design methods is *evaluation*. At best, an architect or landscape architect makes only a casual, nonsystematic evaluation of previous projects, and this is usually based solely on ambiguously stated visual criteria. Even the fee structure for professional services fails to provide compensation for evaluation of the fit between the design "solution" and the needs of the users. This situation is further exasperated by the fact that, as in the case of most institutional settings, such as schools, hospitals, and office buildings, the client is not even the expected user of that setting. It is amazing that, in a science-based postindustrial society, billions of dollars are spent designing and constructing for people whose needs are barely recognized and whose satisfactions are never determined. In short, using only traditional design-by-drawing methods of designing, we have no clear understanding of design intentions in terms of desired behavioral outcomes, and no way of evaluating whether we have succeeded or failed.

The five articles in this section are representative of some of the first primitive attempts to develop techniques aimed at making environmental design and planning more systematic and, therefore, more accountable to public scrutiny.[4] They all seem to share at least two major concerns: (1) concern for the introduction of design criteria based on the behavioral needs of the expected user client (in this case, children), especially where this group is different from the paying client; and (2) a concern for the development of more powerful, research-based theories of person–environment relations that will allow for more accurate predictions of the effects of alternative courses of action, and therefore provide a firmer basis for evaluation and selection of plans to be implemented. Implicit in all these proposals is the need for collaboration between designers and behavioral scientists, and the need to make evaluation research a standard part of a comprehensive professional service.

The first article, by Michael Ellis, addresses an issue that is crucial to any research-based planning and design process: What is the role and function of the scientist and how can the findings of research be useful in the day-to-day activities of practitioners? His answer is that science, which is concerned with the development of generalizable knowledge codified in the form of theories, and practice, which is concerned with the application of general knowledge to the idiosyncracies of a specific situation, are inherently complementary activities. Echoing a recurrent theme in this section, Ellis asserts that fruitful collaboration between researchers and practitioners is dependent on the ability of designers and planners to externalize their goals, objectives, and decision-making procedures in order to provide a basis for systematic postimplementation evaluation and communication to others of both research findings and design process. Applying these ideas to the activity of child play, he proceeds to review existing theory and empirical findings that relate to the problems of designing and managing play environments. The result is a set of heuristic (rule-of-thumb) principles for design decision making and a set of issues for further research.

Based on a three-year research study, the article by Kritchevsky, Prescott, and Walling is primarily concerned with the ongoing redesign and management of physical space for group child-care programs. Having discovered a strong relationship between program goals, the attributes and organization of physical milieu, and the quality of the total child-care program, the authors present their scheme for analyzing the content of the physical environment as it relates to program goals. Since the users—teachers and children—as well as the original designers of these settings were largely unaware of the influence of physical space on behavior, the findings of this study serve an important environmental awareness function. If such an approach was used by all the participants in the total design–research–evaluation–management process we could begin, perhaps, to develop a body of cumulative knowledge about the complex functioning of learning environments for children. This article clearly illustrates the importance of a field experimental approach to design and the need to conceive of the environment as a dynamic system of relationships among human behavior, purposes, and physical settings.

At present the design process is not organized to facilitate user input by children, since they are seldom the paying client. As a result, design decisions are apt to reflect adult conceptions of what children find, or *should* find, attractive, satisfying, and necessary in play–learning environments. Peterson, Bishop, and Michaels are concerned with developing research methodologies that allow children to represent their own views concerning what is desirable in environments designed for their use. This article clearly demonstrates that such techniques, drawn largely from the area of market research, are available and that findings from such studies can provide a firmer basis for design decisions. To support the need for such inputs, and to test the assumption that adult designers *know* what children prefer, results of research undertaken by the authors are presented which show that (1) children's environmental preferences can be measured, providing

consistently reliable and valid information useful to designers; and (2) adult designers are consistently poor predictors of what children find attractive. The article concludes with a plea for more research in order to better understand differences among children and to develop more powerful design principles.

Our culture is moving steadily in the direction of behavioral management and control in order to achieve "socially" defined goals, and, whether intentional or not, designers and planners are making daily decisions which have the effect of shaping behavior. Rather than denying this fact or ignoring it, Asher Derman asserts that the design process should make public the basis for decisions that affect behavior. This is especially important when designing environments for children since adults (as pointed out in the article by Peterson et al.), who base their judgments on their "intuitions" about what children want, are quite likely to introduce adult biases which can have the effect of controlling children rather than supporting their developmental needs. From this perspective it is argued that "intentionally considering design as an experiment (in the scientific sense)" is to be preferred to the " 'unintentional' human experimentation" which is the outcome of intuitive problem-solving methods.

As a first step, Derman undertakes a critical review of the state of the art of existing play theories and design paradigms (the set of beliefs and issues perceived to be relevant, and methods of problem solving shared by a given community) for play-facility planning. His conclusion is that neither our current theoretical understanding of play behavior and its social or cognitive function nor our present largely intuitive design methods allow us to engage in meaningful evaluation research. In an attempt to improve on this state of affairs, Derman cites examples from his own research suggesting that design intentions be stated in terms of observable activities rather than abstract concepts such as play. Such a minimal statement of design objectives will at least allow evaluation research to assess whether or not desired outcomes have been achieved. In this way designing begins to move in the direction of field experimentation based on an explicit, publicly accessible, and replicable paradigm.

Although there is an enormous body of information on the needs and behavior of the developing child, its value to designers and planners is limited. As knowledge in our society becomes more and more specialized and stored in the form of private languages that are intelligible to fewer and fewer experts, the problem of interdisciplinary communication becomes central. Drawing on her own research and design experience, Anne-Marie Pollowy describes how the performance approach to design programming (problem definition, and statements of goals, objectives, and evaluation criteria) and the use of "activities" as a unit of analysis can provide a basis for integrating behavioral research into the design process. Such a general codification scheme and design strategy, according to Pollowy, can be applied not only to the systematic design and evaluation of environments for children, but also can be adapted to the design and management of environments for all age groups.

The heart of all these articles is the recognition of the need for the environmental design professions to systematically evaluate the effects of their actions. To do so, of course, implies the related need to clearly articulate design intentions in terms of desired effects on human behavior, attitudes, and values, and human purposes as embodied in institutions. The effect of this trend is to move the design activity in the direction of experimental science, which is itself a form of social learning. Such changes can be viewed positively to the extent to which they make the process of social and technological development more accessible to control by those who are significantly affected by the outcomes of design decision making and to the extent to which the outcomes themselves become more supportive of "the greatest good for the greatest number." However, since many of these specific techniques as well as the values and assumptions that underlie them have been adapted from existing planning models in the military and manufacturing sectors, optimism must be tempered by sober reflection. Perhaps the most dangerous assumption would be that the application of science and "rational" decision making based on more and better information will make our schools better places, our cities more habitable, our air and water fit for human use. Clearly, this has not been the result of previous, expert, informed decisions. Although research can help to inform us about possible outcomes of alternative courses of action, our design and planning decisions have always been and will continue to be made on the basis of values, and such judgments are inherently political. Issues of environmental quality, just as issues concerning the quality of life, must ultimately be determined by our collective image of and desire for a better future.

NOTES AND REFERENCES

1. The conceptualization and analysis of the progression from craft evolution through design by drawing to systematic methods is owed entirely to J. Christopher Jones. The best single book on the history, theory, and applications of new design methods is J. Christopher Jones, *Design Methods: Seeds of Human Futures,* New York: John Wiley & Sons, Inc. (Interscience Division), All designers and planners should have a copy.
2. *Ibid.,* pp. 16–20.
3. *Ibid.,* p. 23.
4. For an excellent collection of readings on the behavioral and social basis for design decisions see Harold Proshansky, William Ittelson, and Leanne Rivlin (eds.), *Environmental Psychology: Man and His Physical Setting,* New York: Holt, Rinehart and Winston, Inc., 1970. Two books by Robert Sommer are also basic reading. *Personal Space: The Behavioral Basis of Design,* Englewood Cliffs, N.J.: Prentice-Hall, Inc., 1969 and *Design Awareness,*

San Francisco: Rinehart Press, 1972. The second of the two includes a particularly useful section on evaluation which attempts to help users (user self-surveys) and designers conduct their own research. Sommer is a psychologist who has worked with designers for over a decade and he is most sympathetic to the time and budget limitations of professional practice.

Play: Theory and Research[1]

Michael J. Ellis

Science is concerned with knowing; practice with doing. The communication gap between practitioner and theoretician in the management of play seems to be wide. This is because many of the people concerned with either the management of play or theorizing about it are confused about their roles. It is the responsibility of the scientist to produce principles, laws, and theories that can be used generally to relate cause and effect. The scientist is concerned with removing the specificities from a problem so that his findings may achieve general application.

On the other hand, practitioners are responsible for adding the specificities to the mix in order to maximize a goal. Practitioners are concerned with value judgments and peculiarities. The output of the researcher–theoreticians is their input. Practitioners need this input so that they may evaluate the products of their practice. If practitioners cannot conceptualize and communicate

their procedures, they cannot evaluate whether they reached their goal and they cannot communicate the process to others. Without communicable principles of design and evaluation we will stay stuck in a morass of opinions and feelings.

So the roles of the scientist and practitioner are complementary, one dealing with generalizations and the other specificities. Both are intimately concerned with the search for principles of play behavior that will enable an upward spiral in the quality of play management to begin. So endeth my sermon on our roles which I hope explains the purpose of this paper, which is to try to communicate why animals and people play, and some things we have found that might be useful.

Now to some theory that will, I hope, simplify the bewildering task of designing and managing play environments for people. Older theories of behavior still work well when there is some need to be satisfied. Each need is signaled by some sensor that sends signals of increasing urgency as the need increases. When the animal responds and satisfies the need, it is rewarded by the elimination of the signals for a time. These need-reduction theories of hunger, thirst, etc., are built on an assumption that the animal's goal is quiescence. Need reduction is work, and it is assumed that when all the work is done the animal sits quietly till the next need rears its head. It is clear that many animals do not seek quiescence when satiated. They continue to behave. The behavior is not work; therefore it is—let's call it "play."

To return to the quiescence notion; some animals do seem to follow the need-reduction model, but others do not. The differences between these groups suggest some important concepts concerning play. I am going to borrow some material that has been published elsewhere that says what I want to say here.[2]

These two classes of animals can best be labeled the "generalists" and the "specialists."[3] Specialists are animals that are very well adapted to a particular environment doing the few things necessary for their survival extremely well. When not performing their limited number of responses they relax, uniquely adapted to the status quo. They are exemplified by snakes, frogs, etc. Generalists are quite different. They are not adapted exclusively to any particular niche but are capable of adapting to a variety of environments. They are opportunists living by their wits. They maintain a large variety of responses and are forever testing and probing the environment, playing with it, even when not hungry. By this process they keep abreast of change and the more up to date ones tend to survive. The generalists' curiosity, their tendency to explore, manipulate and control the environment is characteristic of rats, bears and primates, etc. Man is the prime example.

Generalists have an abhorrence of sameness; in our terms they become bored. They need constant opportunities to deal with the environment. If they are deprived of opportunities to do this, then they create them. Men cannot tolerate the absence of stimulation, and may be considered to play when they maintain their interactions with the environment after insuring their immediate survival. Play can be seen, then, as a type of arousal-seeking behavior. It prevents boredom and generates a base of information about the environment from which to operate.

Animals are changed by their experience and become more complex as they get to know things. Things that become completely known cease to be interesting. Only things that are somewhat new, or to some extent uncertain, are interesting. Thus, with increasing experience an organism's interactions with its natural environment gradually increase in complexity. A dumb generalist in a rich environment is limited by its own capacity to get to know the environment, whereas a sharp generalist in a limited environment soon knows it well and begins to suffer from stimulus deprivation.

Play seems to be arousal-seeking behavior that leads to an increasing complexity of the players and their play. Further, the evidence suggests that appropriate opportunities to deal with unknown elements in the environment are crucial to the development of our children. If you accept the above, then shed a tear with me for the opportunities we have lost to enrich our children's lives.

Luckily for our planners and manufacturers children will play with a cardboard box, a scrap of wood, and playgrounds. Their propensity to play ensures this. Yet a hard-nosed look at usage patterns of our conventional playgrounds show that they do not sustain the attention of their clients. For example a recent study in a variety of different locations in Philadelphia[4] showed that children visited only once per day and then for only fifteen minutes. Children in the most depressed environment with presumably least opportunities for play and perhaps greatest need showed the same pattern. Further, the study showed that on the average the play apparatus was vacant at least 88 percent of the peak time. The conclusion that playground activity features low on the behavioral popularity poll and are used only when nothing else is happening was confirmed by Dee and Liebman[5] in their study of attendance at urban playgrounds. It is possible to compare the behavior in many traditional playgrounds to those aimless stereotyped mechanical responses of our furry relatives pacing their cages in chronic boredom.

The golden rules for design need to be based on a theory and, frankly, the one outlined in brief above is the theory of play that recommends itself by seeming to explain much of what is happening during play. To use it then leads to the following:

1. *Children play for the stimulation they receive not just to burn up energy.*
2. *Children need to indulge in activities that become increasingly complex with time.*
3. *As a by-product children learn about their physical surroundings, and about their own roles in a social group.*

The essential characteristic for a playground is that it should elicit new responses from the child as he plays, and that these responses increase in complexity as play proceeds.

For new responses to be elicited, the objects in the play environment must be manipulable by the child. Currently much apparatus merely allows the child to manipulate himself by swinging, or whirling, etc. This is important, but goes only half way. The items that sustain attention and generate the greatest number of responses are those that are manipulable. The items manipulated should by their interactions demonstrate relationships that exist in the physical world, and some should lead to social organization among the players. Finally, in Utopia, the playground would change regularly, say once a month, so that the children it serves are regularly challenged to explore a new environment.

Most of the concepts contained above are exhibited by adventure playgrounds, those delightful areas filled with bricks, lumber, dirt, scrap metal. Here the children can dig, build, change their environment and undertake cooperative projects that can last a whole summer. If we can add to those kinds of playgrounds the new devices as they are developed that seek for specific goals by leading the child to learn by his own actions, then we have achieved the pinnacle of our current state-of-the-art.

With the above in mind the following questions might be asked about items being considered for inclusion in a play area.

Which manipulates the child in the greater variety of ways?

Which allows the child to manipulate it in the greater variety?

Which preempts the behavior of the child least?

Which allows for cooperation between children?

Which seems to be capable of teaching most, or which seems likely to teach what you want the children to learn?

Moving to a higher order of question:

Which combination of items maximizes the variability of behavior exhibited?

Which set or combination will allow rearrangement of the setting to extend the possibilities for play either by the introduction of change, or by increasing its complexity through a season?

These central ideas stated in general terms can be taken by a planner and applied to the particular set of conditions that exist for his clients. A set of questions stemming from a definition of play as arousal-seeking behavior is derived whereby play-things or -grounds can be rationally considered from the viewpoint of the child. No particular items are condemned but much of the apparatus produced by the industry does not stand up well to the questions established as guides to plan-

ning. Finally, at this time there is no single answer to any planning decision. Within limits there are many solutions to a local need and a healthy diversity of solutions coupled with evaluation of each product is the ony way we shall evolve a technology sophisticated enough to reflect the complexity of play behavior.

Based on the theoretical system described above have been a series of studies that have investigated the novelty and complexity of the play environment. These studies showed that with increased exposure the reduction in novelty that ensues alters behavior. Wuellner et al.[6] first showed that the activity in a group of boys and girls playing on the same material in our play research laboratory usually diminished steadily over time. Then both Jeanrenaud[7] and Lovelace[8] showed that the time taken to resolve the conflict between the desire to approach a novel play apparatus and play and the desire to cautiously avoid interaction with a strange object diminished as the object became more familiar. Both of these findings are consistent with the concept that the information inherent in the setting is consumed by children as they interact with it.

Literally, in another direction, Karlsson[9] attempted to quantify the height preferences of children at play to study the theory and to produce information relevant to the design of play environments. She hypothesized that Wuellner's findings were caused by the children changing their behavior from interaction in a horizontal plane to vertical activity or climbing over time. To test this the height preferences of nursery school children were studied over a series of five free-play sessions using the height to which the children climbed as the measures. The apparatus in the playroom utilized the full 9-foot height of the room and was of three basic types: flat (boxes), barred (trestles), and unstable (rope net). The children's height preference was measured in two ways; height to the point of support and the height to their eye level. Play on these apparatus presented differing task complexities which created different height preferences measured both ways. As expected, the more complex the item the lower the children played. The expected trend toward an increased preferred height over time did not occur, supporting Wuellner's original assertions that the quantity of behavior diminishes as the setting becomes familiar. However, it may be merely that five sessions were not enough to show a trend as the children became more daring.

These kinds of studies have become possible because satisfactory methods have been developed for studying the behavior of children in a play environment. One useful method for collecting data concerning the position of playing children in time–space has been developed in our laboratory. The data are collected automatically, photographing the play space at intervals through a fisheye lens mounted above the area. The resulting 35mm film strip is then projected onto a grid that accounts for the distortions introduced by the lens. The grid enables the positions of the various children in the horizontal dimension to be scored by hand.[10] The coordinates recording position in space for each time sample are then punched on cards. The computer is then used to derive from the same basic raw data such measures as total distance covered, frequency of use of various items in the room, distances between children, time on apparatus, etc.[11]

The camera system is reliable, objective, unobtrusive, simple, and is not costly to run (relative to the employment of several observers). Its only disadvantage is that it is time-consuming for one scorer.[12]

The methods described above have led to much experimentation that has given equivocal results indicating that play behavior of children is extremely complex, which is something we already know well. The results also point out that it is difficult to proceed with the sophisticated ex-

perimentation that will precede the control of that behavior. The methods, however, lead to three types of derived dependent variables, best categorized as activity measures, equipment-use measures, and measures of the social structure in the play situation. So this method holds promise for application in a variety of situations, including the evaluation of playgrounds.

A different and coordinated set of studies, derived from the fact that the play of children is always shaped to some extent by the physical environment in which it occurs, has been carried out in our laboratory. Stimulus properties of play objects comprise a crucial portion of the child's environment. The effects of specific stimulus factors on play should hold great interest for the basic researcher concerned with fundamental questions relating to play and for the designer working to optimize children's play environments. Necessary research should divine as well as measure the effects of variation within and between stimulus features of play objects. Such investigations of stimulus properties of play objects has been pursued at our laboratory and two sets of findings have been replicated. The first is that children exhibit a preference for using a play item placed in the center of a play area. This "centricity" effect indicates position as a powerful stimulus parameter.[13]

Furthermore, a second group of studies involving standard school size play blocks showed no basic color preference among the nursery school children tested, but some indication of preference for blocks was determined by their being placed in the outer piles in a semicircular array of four piles.[14]

This approach was also applied to the common observation that children like to play in encapsulated spaces. The reasons for children's propensity to play in cardboard boxes, old refrigerators, under tables was examined by Gramza.[15] By manipulating the number of open sides in a series of hollow 2-foot cubes (the degree of enclosure) in an experiment, the children's preferences for complete enclosure was clearly demonstrated and has been replicated on other sizes of capsules.

This study of encapsulation was extended to ask the question, what were the attributes of a capsule with only one open side that was attracting usage? With size (32-inch cubes) and material (Plexiglas) being held constant, visual aspects (stimuli) of the boxes were varied. When sides were made transparent, translucent, and opaque, it became possible to answer whether the capsule was attractive because of darkness, visual separation, or because it merely provided a tactile (touchable) bounding of space. In this study both opaque and translucent boxes were preferred over the transparent boxes, indicating that in addition to a preference for occupancy of a touchably finite space there was additional attractance created by visual separation.

Another series of studies conducted in the same setting described the relative attractance of complex versus simple apparatus. The theoretical basis for this work stemmed from research showing that stimulus complexity is an important parameter for preferences and from characterizations of play as stimulus or arousal-seeking behaviors.

This research has considerable relevance for play environment design and suggested an empirical test using objects that were similar to the climbing playthings appearing regularly in playgrounds. The study progressively complexified one of two 8-foot-tall climbing trestles. Repeated exposures were given to allow for separation of novelty from complexity in children's preferences. The outcomes, as usual, were not straightforward. For example, the effect of position appeared again to complicate the issue, and boys tended to maintain exclusive use of a favored trestle over girls.

However, initially the first stage of the two-stage complexification created greater usage, but after a while the simpler trestle was used more. The second stage of the complexification process resulted in lasting preferences for the complex trestle. To explain this experiment, Gramza et al.[16] suggests that the first stage of complexification was actually a simplification. In the first stage large sheets of plywood with foot holes were bolted to the sides of the trestles. While this was novel, the children preferred it, but as the novelty wore off it was revealed that the series of bars to which the sheets were bolted were not available to sustain a variety of climbing and swinging behavior. The second-stage complexification involved smaller sheets, platforms, ramps, and ropes that added to the behavioral possibilities rather than subtracting. Accordingly, the second stage was sustainedly more attractive.

These effects exemplify the need for knowledge of apparatus stimulus parameters before a technology for manipulating play behavior can be developed.

The data and theoretical formulations exist, and we face a twofold challenge to continue our work and to interpret the findings in a way that makes them useful. Our best bet seems to be to build a theory and to support that theory with hard data on the effect of various design decisions of children's play behavior.

NOTES AND REFERENCES

1. This article is based on a presentation made under the same title to the National Symposium on Park, Recreation and Environmental Design on February 16, 1971, in Chicago. The paper has been prepared from research conducted by M. J. Ellis, A. F. Gramza, R. E. Herron, K. A. Karlsson, R. J. Korb, P. A. Witt, and L. H. Wuellner while they were on the staff of the Motor Performance and Play Research Laboratory. The research was supported in part by a research grant to that laboratory via the Adler Zone Center, by the Department of Mental Health of Illinois, and by USPHS Research Grant MH-07346 from NIMH.

2. M. J. Ellis, "The Rational Design of Playgrounds," *Educational Products Information Exchange Institute Product Report,* 1970, 3, Vol. 8–9, pp. 3–8.

3. Morris[17] originated this differentiation with the use of the words "neophilia" and "neophobia," literally, novelty-liking and novelty-avoiding animals. However, the words generalist and specialist express the idea more directly.

4. G. R. Wade, "A Study of Free-play Patterns of Elementary School-age Children in Playground Equipment Areas," master's thesis, Pennsylvania State University, 1968.

5. N. Dee and J. C. Liebman, "A Statistical Study of Attendance at Urban Playgrounds," *Journal of Leisure Research,* Vol. 2, 1970, pp. 145–159.

6. L. H. Wuellner, P. A. Witt, and R. E. Herron, "A Method to Investigate the Movement Patterns of Children," in *Contemporary Psychology of Sport,* G. Kenyon (ed.), Chicago: The Athletic Institute, 1970.

7. C. Jeanrenaud, "Approach Behavior in a Novel Situation," master's thesis, University of Illinois, 1969.

8. G. E. Lovelace, "Responses of Educable Mentally Handicapped Children to a Unique Plaything," master's thesis, University of Illinois, 1971.

9. K. A. Karlsson, "Height Preferences of Children at Play," master's thesis, University of Illinois, 1969.

10. Wuellner, *op. cit.*

11. R. E. Herron and M. J. Frobish, "Computer Analysis and Display of Movement Patterns," *Journal of Experimental Child Psychology,* Vol. 8, 1969, pp. 40–44.

12. M. J. Ellis, "Quantification of Gross Activity of Children at Play," paper read at the NRPA Congress, Chicago, Sept. 1969.

13. P. A. Witt and A. F. Gramza, "Position Effects in Play Preferences of Nursery School Children," *Perceptual and Motor Skills,* Vol. 31, 1970, pp. 421–434.

14. A. F. Gramza and P. A. Witt, "Choices of Colored Blocks in the Play of Preschool Children," *Perceptual and Motor Skills,* Vol. 29, 1969, pp. 783–787.

15. A. F. Gramza, "Preferences of Preschool Children for Enterable Play Boxes," *Perceptual and Motor Skills,* Vol. 31, 1970, pp. 177–178.

16. A. F. Gramza, J. Corush, and M. J. Ellis, "Children's Play on Trestles Differing in Complexity: A Study of Play Equipment Design," unpublished paper, 1971.

17. D. Morris, "Occupational Therapy for Captive Animals," *Collected Papers of the Laboratory Animal Center,* Vol. 11, pp. 37–42; D. Morris, "The Response of Animals to a Restricted Environment," *Symposium of the Zoological Society of London,* Vol. 13, 1964, pp. 99–118.

Planning Environments for Young Children: Physical Space*

Sybil Kritchevsky
Elizabeth Prescott
Lee Walling

INTRODUCTION

What is in a space, a room, or a yard, and how it is arranged can affect the behavior of people; it can make it easier to act in certain kinds of ways, harder to act in others. We do not ordinarily think to take out a deck of cards at a dinner table set for six, even though the number and arrangement of people suggest a poker game. The whole setting gives us cues about expected behavior, and generally we do what we have been invited to do—eat and chat in usual ways. The extent to which we can be involved and interested in the setting—dinner party for six—will depend in large part on our hunger, the amount and kind of food, and the attitudes and interests of ourselves and our companions.

*Reprinted from *Planning Environments for Young People: Physical Space,* Washington, D.C.: National Association for the Education of Young Children, 1969.

In a similar way, particular settings invite children to involve themselves in particular activities, and the extent of children's constructive participation in the activity will depend in large part on how well certain concrete, measurable aspects of the surrounding physical space meet their "hunger, attitudes, and interests." It is with these spatial cues that this article is concerned—what they are, and how they can be used to support goals for young children.

Our awareness of the relationship between space and the resultant behavior of those who live and play therein was the outcome of a research project conducted by members of the Pacific Oaks faculty, funded by the U.S. Children's Bureau. The goal of this three-year study was to increase knowledge about programs for children in day-care centers, and especially to examine factors which might be predictive of differences in program quality which could serve as guides in the improvement of programs for groups of young children.

In the course of our study, we began to see that space was, in many instances, severely limiting the amount of choice which could be given to children and teachers. Moreover, teachers and directors obviously were unaware of this influence. We then began to see a relationship between a clear understanding of the influence of physical space and clarity of goals. If program goals are so clear to staff that they can be stated in behavioral terms, it is much easier to see how the space can be developed to support these goals.

Of course, physical space cannot be considered apart from other dimensions of program such as scheduling, grouping procedures, and the teacher's choice of activities. We have found, however, that an examination of program along the dimension of space provides an objective tool for analyzing program and enables the staff to engage in group problem solving with a minimum of personal criticism.

There is now a wide variety of group programs for young children. They differ in purpose and in clientele served. Their basic differences generate a wide variation in other factors which determine the nature of a program, such as number of days and hours during the day in which the program is offered, the number and kinds of adults who participate, the type of grouping practices, etc. For example, day care is different from a parent cooperative, and both differ from Head Start. Even within a program category, important differences may exist; for example, a Head Start program for non-English speaking children cannot be identical to one designed for children who do speak English.

Although all of these programs share a common goal of fostering the growth of young children, it seems crucial to us that the goals for each program be stated in specific and concrete terms which emphasize its unique purpose, rather than in vague global terms which emphasize its similarity to all other programs. For instance, one goal for a particular Head Start program may be to help young children learn to pay attention to teachers, not only as adults whose directions should be followed, but as warm, trustworthy sources of needed and useful play ideas, information, and help. Under these circumstances, space should not encourage children to go off and manage on their own. The necessity and usefulness of teachers-as-resource might be maximized by limiting the number of easily available play ideas in the space and by increasing the ratio of teachers to children. Narrow age-range grouping might also support this goal, since it would tend to negate the learner – teacher (follower – leader) relationship which often develops between younger and older children. Scheduling special trips may also help make the usefulness of teachers obvious to children.

Goals in day-care programs will often be conconcerned with providing the sort of warm, affectionate, individualized attention offered by home and mother. With a ratio of one teacher to up to fifteen children, space which encourages children to go off and manage on their own will free the teacher to meet the needs of individual children as they occur. Wide age-range grouping may well provide a homelike feeling and allow some of the older – younger, teacher – learner relationships which can characterize a home atmosphere. The number of staff may be increased at times such as lunch, so as to allow for small groups in which the level of adult attention to children can be high.

A cooperative nursery school program probably has primary concern with such things as helping children develop social skills, creativity, and self-sufficiency. Cooperatives also typically need to provide opportunities for parents to learn more about children and child development. Space in a cooperative, with the usual one to five ratio of adults to children, needs to be roomy enough to accommodate all these adults in a nonintrusive way, so that development of self-sufficiency is not impeded. Space should also keep children involved and interested, not only with equipment, but with each other, so that social development can be supported. In this kind of program, which often meets only two or three mornings a week, a smaller group with a narrow age range may also help support social development.

To make space work for a program then, it is very important to have a clear and realistic idea about the goals to be achieved. Consequently, we have referred throughout much of this article to particular goals as they relate to the particular aspect of space under discussion.

In much of our discussion we are assuming that play space should allow for self-direction of children.[1] In a program emphasizing teacher direction of children's activities and closely restricting choices by children, the principal criterion for supportive space is that it not distract attention from the teacher. Teachers who arrange inviting activity centers and then require that children ignore them in order to pay attention to the teacher for extended periods are setting the stage for discipline problems. As we will discuss below, however, some programs which rely heavily on teacher direction reflect spatial constraints rather than educational goals. In many instances these constraints can be modified in the direction of greater flexibility for both children and teacher.

HOW TO ANALYZE PLAY SPACE

Space communicates with people—in a very real sense it tells us how to act and how not to act. What it tells us to do is related to what is in the space and how these things are arranged or organized. Just as adults behave in one way at a table set for a formal dinner, and in a very different way at the same table set for a poker game, children tend to behave in ways suggested by spatial contents and arrangement. If play space is interesting to children, they are likely to play in an interested

way, provided the rest of the setting is not excessively distracting. Even the talented storyteller presenting a favorite tale is likely to find the activity disrupted by the unexpected presence of a lively and friendly dog; and children in a play room well equipped with interesting materials are likely to shift their attention frequently if the area is congested.

In other words, it is necessary to understand both the parts of a play space (the contents and the empty space around the contents) and how these parts function as a whole, since it is apparently the total setting which children perceive and to which they respond.[2]

THE CONTENTS OF PLAY SPACE

The contents of play space which appear to matter most to children are *play units* and *potential units*.

Potential Units

A potential unit is simply some empty space which is surrounded in large part by visible and/or tangible boundaries. For instance, an empty table, the empty corner of a room or yard, a shady area under a tree or umbrella are all potential units to which it is easy to add play material of one kind or another. Potential units can be used for greater spatial variety from day to day and thus provide flexibility for the staff. However, a staff-unrecognized potential unit can be a source of trouble. Access to space under stairs, if off limits, may need to be boarded up. If children are attracted to cozy play in an off-limits closet, a high hook may need to be placed on the door.

Play Units

Play units, in contrast to potential units, contain something to play with, and may or may not have visible and/or tangible boundaries. The sides of a play house or shelves surrounding a block play area do provide tangible boundaries, but much equipment needs some surrounding empty space to function effectively. For example, the jump-off-walk-around space surrounding the slide, the space outside a jungle gym where children swing their legs and stretch their arms, the space surrounding a table where children shift their chairs or stand just watching all belong to the respective play units. This surrounding empty space is not really free for other uses. If other children need to use this play unit space to move through a room or yard, there will quite naturally be conflicts and interruptions of play.

Types of Play Units: Complexity Play units can be classified in two major ways. In the first place, they can be classified according to differences in the kind of activity in which they invite children to participate: climbing, digging, building, etc. These differences are discussed below under the heading of *variety*. In the second place, they can be classified according to differences in what we have called relative *complexity:* the extent to which they contain potential for active manipulation and alteration by children. Elaborating on this distinction, it is possible to discern three types of play units—simple, complex and super, which vary both in their relative capacity to keep children interested, and in the relative number of children they can accommodate at one time. Our basis for classifying play equipment considers its possible use based on its internal complexity.

1. *Simple:* A play unit that has one obvious use and does not have subparts or a juxtaposition of materials which enable a child to manipulate or improvise. (Examples: swings, jungle gym, rocking horse, tricycle.)
2. *Complex:* A play unit with subparts or juxtaposition of two essentially different play materials which enable the child to manipulate or improvise. (Examples: sand table with dig-

ging equipment; play house with supplies.) Also included in this category are single play materials and objects which encourage substantial improvisation and/or have a considerable element of unpredictability. (Examples: all art activities such as dough or paints; a table with books to look at; an area with animals, such as a dog, guinea pigs or ducks.)
3. *Super:* A complex unit which has one or more additional play materials, i.e., three or more play materials juxtaposed. (Examples: sandbox with play materials and water; dough table with tools; tunnel, movable climbing boards and boxes, and large crates.)

A super unit can be likened to a large sponge which soaks up a lot of water; it accommodates the most children at one time and holds their interest longest. A complex unit is like a smaller sponge and ranks second in degree of interest and number of children it is likely to accommodate at one time. A simple unit is like a paper towel, indispensable but short-lived, and ranks third.

The relative complexity of a space or setting (the number of complex and super units) is a measure of the capacity of the space to keep children continuously interested. Except for an occasional spring-horse, tumbling mat, or pull toy, simple equipment is not often found indoors in California. Outdoors, however, many play units tend to be simple. If children are expected to play in an area for any length of time, high complexity seems virtually essential.

Complex and super units can be formed most easily by rearranging simple units and/or adding props of some kind. A crawl barrel, a large crate, and a couple of old benches might be used to surround a dirt area and create a complex unit. Children could climb up, over, through, around, and in—and maybe do some rearranging of their own. If shovels or trucks or dramatic play props such as parasols or costumes were added, a super unit would be formed. Boxes and boards added to the jungle gym make a complex unit. A box with a steering wheel becomes complex if engineer hats are added. To be complex, trikes need some place to go, or there must be an interesting way of going. If crates and boxes can be arranged so riders can thread their way through, or stop and go signs added, trikes become complex.

Children often create their own complex or super units. A table with kitchen equipment placed a foot or two from a sandbox is a super unit to a child, and if sand must stay in the box it is wise to move the table, either away from or into the sandbox. Some conflict in preschool settings is related to the presence of complex and super units unrecognized by staff.

It is probably obvious that if children are expected to stay in any area for only a short time, high complexity may well lead to unhappy children unwilling to leave their play. But if children are expected to stay in a play area for a long time without complexity, teachers probably will need to compensate, through their own active participation, for the failure of the setting to provide enough play ideas.

Types of Play Units: Variety   The other important way in which play units can be classified is according to the particular activity they invite from children. The number of different kinds of units (only in terms of differences in activity, and regardless of whether they are simple, complex, or super) can be called the degree of variety and is a measure of the relative capacity of the space to elicit immediate interest from children. Some of the categories we have used are rockers, digging areas, vehicles, climbing units, and house play units. For example, a play yard with twelve vehicles, a rocking boat, a tumble tub (all single); a jungle gym with boxes and boards and a dirt area with scooper trucks (both complex); and a well-equipped sand table with water (a super unit) have only four different kinds of things to do. Even though there are seventeen separate play units, and two complex and one super unit, the space offers choice only of riding, rocking, digging, or climbing.

Occasionally, though a space does contain a healthy variety of things to do, a disproportionately large amount of one kind of thing overwhelms the eye, so that the choice may seem to be between climbing and digging, and climbing and riding, and climbing and swinging, and so on. Or, for example, so much shelf space may contain blocks that other things to do may fade into the invisible category of "toys."

Possibilities for increasing variety often exist within the framework provided by what is already present. For instance, some play units which have potential for more than one kind of activity. If there are two units which invite children to crawl inside and be cozy, such as a crate and a crawl barrel, it might be expedient to exploit the climbing potential of one and the containing potential of the other; or routinely, to introduce different kinds of play ideas by adding props like trucks, hats, etc. If there is an excessive number of certain toys such as trikes or blocks, some might be stored away, or traded for other needed equipment, or dismantled and their parts used in novel ways. Like complexity, variety appears of greatest importance when children are expected to play freely for some length of time and make their own choices about what to play with.

Complexity and variety then, are measures of interest. Complex and super units invite children to make an ongoing series of meaningful choices in altering the contents of a particular play unit, and thus tend to keep them continuously involved. Wide variety invites children to make choices among many different kinds of activities, and thus tends to elicit immediate interest from children who are ready to find something to do.

Amount To Do per Child

A particular space may contain a wide variety of units, including many complex and super units, and thus appear to provide a good deal of choice to children. Still the question remains: Given the number of children expected to use the space, what is the likelihood that these play units will actually be available for children's choices? Based on the relative value of simple, complex and super units, we devised a method for approximating what might be called the number of play places that a room or yard actually has. To do this we assign a value of 4 to complex units, on the basis that complex units will generally accommodate about four children at once. Considering the unique potential of super units, we felt that they were worth two complex units, and so we valued them at 8. Though many simple units can be used by more than one child at a time, the fact that they are continuously less interesting than complex units led us to assign a value of 1 to simple units. When the total number of play places of a yard or room is determined, this sum can be divided by the number of children expected to use the space. This ratio gives the approximate number of play spaces available to each child at any given time. The table shown describes a play yard with a total of 30 play spaces.

If the yard had 15 children, there would be 2.0 play places per child; if the yard had 25 children, there would be 1.2 play places per child.

The implications of this dimension are most easily expressed through an analogy in which play is likened to a game of musical chairs. However, for the puroses of the analogy we shall assume that the objective of the game is not to eliminate participants, but to provide each child with a chair each time the music stops. In a game with twenty chairs and ten children (two chairs per child), when the music stops children can easily find an empty chair without help. If there are ten children and fifteen chairs (one and a half chairs per child), some children probably will have difficulty finding an empty chair. The closer the number of chairs are to the number of children, the more likely it will be that a teacher will need to help children find the empty chairs. If there are fewer chairs than children, either some one (or more) must stand every time the music stops, or children must double up on chairs. If the teacher is in charge of the music, shifting from chair to chair will take place for all children at once and be much as described above. However, if the teacher wants the children to listen to their own "inner music," further difficulties are introduced. When the number of chairs is close to one per child, and a child wants to change chairs, choice will be severely limited,

Number of Play Units	Type of Unit	Number of Play Places
12 vehicles	Simple	12
1 rocking boat	Simple	1
1 tumble tub	Simple	1
1 jungle gym with boxes and boards	Complex	4
1 dirt area plus scoop trucks	Complex	4
1 equipped sand table with water	Super	8
	Total play pieces	30

and the teacher probably will need to help. If several children want to change chairs in close succession, the demands on the teacher and the limitations on the children will be extreme. Through this analogy, the importance of having enough to do per child can perhaps be felt.

The amount to do per child in a space can be increased most readily either by scheduling smaller groups of children in the space, or by adding complex and super units.

The Importance of Contents

Complexity, variety, and amount to do per child as aspects of play ideas available to children have been discussed. Unless staff have a clear conception of the relationship between goals and the play environment which they have created by their choice of contents, they may force behavior which acts against the achievement of desired goals. For instance, teachers may want to support the development of autonomy by giving children many opportunities to make their own choices, and yet the amount to do per child may be so low that choice is constantly thwarted. Or teachers may want to support the lengthening of attention span by actively helping children remain interested in their self-chosen activity, and yet the complex or super type of play unit which invites doing lots of different things within one play unit (i.e., invites children to stay with an activity for a long time) may virtually be absent. It becomes important then, in examining space, to be sure the content necessary to support the goals is present.

THE ORGANIZATION OF PLAY SPACE

The ways in which potential units and play units function in a given space will depend very much on how they are organized. The criteria for good organization are a clear path and adequate empty spaces.

Paths

A path is the empty space on the floor or ground through which people move in getting from one place to another; it need be no different in composition from the rest of the surface. A clear path is broad, elongated, and easily visible. Paths are very difficult to describe in words, but when they are well-defined they are easily seen. If an observer looking at a play area cannot answer readily the question, "How do children get from one place to another?," probably the children can't either, and there is no clear path.

Paths can be unclear for a variety of reasons, but the result is always the same: there is interference with children's seeing, moving to, and/or staying with a play unit. Sometimes a path is clear except for an overlapping boundary between adjoining play units so that children can reach across to one another. For instance, a climbing ladder next to a swing can be an invitation to a youngster to yank the chain on the swing and watch the ensuing activity—a screaming child and a rescuing teacher.

Sometimes units are just far enough away to avoid interference, but it is still not possible to walk through the room or yard without entering space which rightfully belongs to a play unit. A child may set out across the yard to the sandbox, but may wind up climbing because he arrived inside the surrounding use space of the jungle gym first.

Occasionally, a path is clear but does not easily lead to certain units. To come unexpectedly upon something intriguing around a corner or to see a familiar play unit from a new angle can stimulate play, but units are sometimes permanently hidden. One center had a well-equipped but rarely used play house area. At child's eye level it was apparent that, though children could see most of the play units in the room, they simply could not see over or around the rather large dividers intended to provide coziness.

The adult who kneels down himself and places his eyes at the child's level can better see just where and how clear the path really is. In one large yard, children often ran through a centrally placed sandbox. From adult height the sandbox certainly was visible. But from the height of the child, looking at the inviting high-climbing equipment beyond, the sandbox was very difficult to see and it made perfectly good four-year-old sense to run straight across the yard, through the suddenly present sandbox, and on to the jungle gym. The same sort of principle seemed to be operating where children regularly walked under a U-shaped climbing and hanging ladder. Here children were sighting tricycles beyond the ladder unit, and with eyes focused at trike level they were walking under the apparently unseen ladder in a direct route to their goal.

Sometimes, in order to provide adequate visibility for the path, the teacher must plan to make play units and their boundaries more clearly visible. Jungle gyms, ladders, and the like occasionally camouflage themselves, and it may be necessary to surround them with more empty space, or place them near the backdrop of a solid fence or tall green bushes in order to make them clearly visible. The sandbox described above would benefit greatly from a high open-lattice roof; sun could still shine through, and the several roof supports and the roof itself would make the sandbox clearly visible. (Sandbox roofs need to be high enough to give the children the sense of freedom they need to stand and stretch and move with ease.)

A total absence of path, because of too much equipment placed too close together, is very disruptive. The adult cannot see a path and neither can the children. There is always some empty space in which children move around, but in this kind of room or yard children will bump into one another and will interfere, accidentally and often, in one another's play.

Some yards and rooms lack a path for another reason. They have what we have called dead space, a large amount of empty space, roughly square or circular in shape. Dead space is usually at least partly in the center of the room or yard, and in contrast to a potential unit, dead space does not have any visible or tangible boundaries. Play units may be far enough from one another to create partial paths here and there, but entering this dead space becomes a special kind of trap for children. Partial paths will lead children into, but not out of, dead space; instead, disorganized running and wrestling activity often develops, and adults have to restrict and/or redirect the children involved. This is a hard concept to put into words, but we feel teachers with experience in this kind of space will readily recognize it.

Dead space can be eliminated in a variety of ways. The addition of a play unit may help, or the moving of a fence. It is sometimes possible to extend other units into the space; boxes and boards can be added to a jungle gym or a rug placed in front of a play house. Much equipment can be shifted, extended, or added so as to develop an adequate path. But it seems to us that somewhere worth going (interesting, varied equipment) is needed to make a clear path function at its best.

The Amount of Empty Space per Child

Just as it is necessary to consider the amount to do per child in determining the adequacy of content, it is necessary to assess the amount of empty space per child in determining the adequacy of organization. The question here is: Given the number of children expected to use the space, how well can a particular clear path function? Good organization provides ease of movement throughout a room or yard. Larger numbers of children need not only a larger total square footage, but they also appear to need a larger proportion of empty space. The findings of our day-care study suggest that the range of no less than one third to no more than one half uncovered surface is appropriate to good organization. Larger numbers of children appear to need the extra space provided by having more empty surface.

From the teacher's point of view, organization also relates to ease of supervision and efficient placement of storage units. It is important that the shape of the space and the distribution of objects in that space allow teachers to see and be seen with ease. It is also very important that materials be stored close to their point of use.

Another aspect of space which is important is its potential for long-term variety—its capacity for reorganization and/or use of contents in novel ways to allow the teacher to enrich children's experiences. Tables, porches, partly bounded corners (potential units), all can be used for different activities at different times. Some equipment is easily moved for rearrangements—boxes and boards make a fine "store," or can turn the jungle gym into a "fire station," or can be lined up to provide a challenging trike path. Novel dramatic play props can be added to certain multiple-use units, such as crates, crawl barrels, and jungle gyms.

When play space is being developed, therefore, careful thought should be given to the placement of permanent equipment such as swings, climbing equipment, storage cabinets, and other nonmovable equipment. Often decisions about such placement appear to be made by persons with little knowledge of program, and the teaching staff must live with the consequences. Movable equipment gives the staff much more control over the physical setting and probably should be judged superior to permanent placement.

As an additional source of enrichment, many centers use the natural assets in the surrounding community. Groups of children and their teachers periodically visit parks, playgrounds, stores, etc. In one center, children go to a nearby gas station where the air hose is used to inflate their collapsed wading pool—a most exciting trip indeed. In other centers, groups of children accompany staff members on shopping trips—perhaps for needed juice, perhaps for just the right brushes for a painting project. Still other centers visit parks, beaches, etc.

SUMMARY: EVALUATING PLAY SPACE

When space is good, the content and organization (and absence of special problems) help achieve goals in two ways. On the one hand, the space makes it easy for goal-related behavior to occur; and on the other, the space itself neither forces behavior which is contrary to goals, nor does it force the selection of otherwise unimportant or inappropriate goals as a means of coping with space-induced negative behavior.

One result of good space, then, is that goals can be freely developed in terms of an informed view of the real children and staff who will participate in the program. A second result is that the staff has greater freedom of choice in its own teaching activities. When children are involved in self-directed activities in good space, much of their behavior tends to be such that teachers can respond or not as they see fit. This is not to say that conflict or the inability to become interested in play will not occur. Such problems are simply far less likely to occur with unmanageable frequency in good space. A teacher may see a free activity period as a time for children to learn to get along with one another, and she may assume the role of observer or mediator; or she may see this time as her prime opportunity to relate to individual children and get to know them better and thus spend much of her time involved with children. In both cases, because the space is actively directing and guiding constructively, and providing play ideas, the teacher has a large amount of what we have called "discretionary time." She can act out of her own choices made in terms of her knowledge, experience, and sensitivities, just as the children are acting out of their own choices. In addition, when the teacher wants all children to participate at the same time in a directed activity, the availability of good play space nearby means that the directed activity need last no longer than the group's genuine interest. It is not necessary for staff to provide directed activities as a compensation to spatial inadequacy. Good play space thus maximizes freedom of choice for the staff as well as for children.

NOTES AND REFERENCES

1. We also use the term "play" consistently. Educators who prefer the term "work," but use it in a format that encourages choice by children, may substitute it for "play" throughout.
2. There is another side to a child's response to particular space which relates to the child's background. For instance, what is spacious and roomy and provides ease of movement in a familiar way to one child may be apprehended as cold and distant and even unpleasantly threatening to another. This is still a very speculative area.

Designing Play Environments for Children*

George L. Peterson
Robert L. Bishop
Richard M. Michaels

INTRODUCTION

The Design Problem

From the point of view of the energy involved, it might be argued that all human activity is profitless, serving only to accelerate the overall trend toward disorder in the universe. As seen by the physicist, man is just another phenomenon that consumes order and spews forth disorder, helping to bring about the decay of energy and—more recently—the decay of matter into energy.

*The principal financial support for this research was provided by the Environmental Control Administration of the U.S. Public Health Service. The time-lapse photography was financed through the Design and Development Center of Northwestern University by a grant from the Sloan Foundation. The cooperation of elementary schools in the Chicago metropolitan area also contributed to the success of the project. Much of the research reported here was done as part of a doctoral dissertation under the direction of Peterson and Michaels.

From the human point of view, however—and surely this is the one we are interested in—man is a conscious creature capable of enjoyment. His freedom to enjoy is sensitive to a number of things, including the degree of cooperation between his needs, aspirations, and sensations, on the one hand, and his environmental objects, conditions, and tools, on the other.

In our quest for the freedom to enjoy, then, we may well be causing the decay of energy as the physicist claims, but hopefully we are thereby creating a more humanly comfortable order among other things. We have found that some arrangements in the environment are more to our liking than others, because they increase the probability of survival, improve the efficiency of our efforts, or simply stimulate feelings of satisfaction. Perhaps this feeling of satisfaction is an ultimate criterion, built into the creature to prod it to surround itself with benevolent conditions. This may be a mandate that nature delivers as an ultimate human function, the function of design, to bring to pass an order that is more to our liking.

In rising to this mandate, the environmental designer is concerned with the creation of devices, objects, and conditions that perform desirable functions efficiently. He should be guided by an understanding of the functions to be performed as well as by an understanding of the natural principles governing efficiency. But usually the thing he is designing must be used by someone before it can perform its function. Suppose that the sense of need for the function is not compellingly urgent, that it is difficult for the potential beneficiary to recognize his need, or that the opportunity is in competition with other more accessible or subjectively appealing, but actually less effective, alternatives. Furthermore, suppose that use is voluntary. In such a case the designer should also understand the principles of attractiveness, so that his design may draw users to it, thereby obtaining the opportunity to perform its function.

In summary, the designer of environments is trying to create things that satisfy needs as measured by functional criteria. He should also try to make them attractive, so that they will be put to use and provide satisfaction. It follows that he needs to understand how to make his designs attractive and enjoyable, as well as the more technical question of how to make them perform their mechanistic tasks.

Designing the Child's Play Environment

Formulating design requirements involves an interaction between the potential user and the designer. Often this interaction is complicated by additional interested points of view, such as those of politicians, administrators, builders, and nonuser publics. With public works, and often with private ventures as well, this interaction occurs by political transaction in which information is exchanged and values established. The political process can be and often is enhanced by technical assessments of attitudes and preferences, but final decisions tend to be made by political means.

When the potential users are children, however, criteria of attractiveness and satisfaction tend to be based on what someone believes would attract and please the child. One reason for this is that it is difficult to gather meaningful information from children. Another is that the interaction processes are not organized to allow direct participation of children in representing their own interests. If they are represented at all, it is usually through adult "advocates," who are understandably preoccupied with considerations of the children's health, safety, and morals, and who also believe that they understand the child's point of view.

The situation is aptly described by Dattner in his discussion of children and the design of urban facilities that affect them:

Although they (the children) are the most deeply affected groups of users, they are presently the least able to influence the design of their environment. Not only are children seldom consulted about these matters, but their needs are almost completely forgotten when the facilities are being designed. The important decisions are made by another group at the other end of our spectrum of users.[1]

Children are not the only group of environmental users likely to suffer from a gap between the users' actual requirements and the values that guide design. Craik[2] argues that decision makers in general are likely to have values and dispositions different from their clients. Recently this problem has emerged in the outdoor recreation literature.[3] If designers in general are guided by their own values, their designs are likely to fall short of their potential degree of usefulness. But nowhere is this more critical than with children, perhaps the ultimate politically inarticulate minority group. Clearly, if environments for children are to be attractive and satisfying to their users, as well as functionally constructive, means must be invented for sensing and representing the child's point of view.

Toward More Powerful Design Principles

Another reason to look for improved ways to communicate with children about their environment is the need to develop more powerful design principles. The decision maker who knows what children want, in terms of specific objects or conditions, is in a better position to be responsive to criteria of attractiveness and satisfaction than one who does not. But he still is not acting as a designer. He is acting as a selector who chooses from among available alternatives. A true designer is a creator of new alternatives, an artist who causes something new to become available. At present, and as far as children are concerned, this is accomplished by reproducing forms that have succeeded in the past, perhaps with minor modifications due to the designer's personal style. If a major innovation proves to be successful, we are at a loss to explain why. Likewise, failure is difficult to explain. All too often, the designer prances merrily along, dropping the products of his fancy along the way without ever looking back to see what has happened.

We desperately need principles that explain why the child finds one thing attractive and shuns another, why he is satisfied in one setting and left wanting in another. The "what" of it is important, but the "why" of it is the source of more power. With play equipment, we have very little to guide us in the synthesis of new forms of play. The equipment must be attractive, or it will not be used, unless it enjoys a monopoly. But why is one slide more attractive to the child than another? Why is a slide more attractive than a seesaw, if it is, and how can this be translated efficiently into more effective and perhaps totally different innovations? If we do conceive of something new, how

can the child's response be predicted without an understanding of the processes by which the reaction occurs? Even the child himself cannot provide the answer, if he is asked, because it is something he has not experienced.

The answer lies in environmental design research. First, there is a need to search out the knowledge about children that lies scattered throughout a variety of scientific disciplines. The theories, facts, and principles that have been gleaned thus far need to be consolidated so that answers can be applied and unanswered questions identified. These unanswered questions, together with the available theories, become the framework for a program of meaningful research.[4]

One avenue of needed research is concerned with identifying what is attractive in specific settings and analyzing the reasons. Designers then can deal with the attributes of their designs to which the child is sensitive.[5] This may not be the complete answer, because of gestalt problems, but it certainly promises to be fruitful. A necessary part of such research is methodology for articulating the preferences, perceptions, and satisfactions of children.

VALIDATION OF MEASUREMENT METHODOLOGY

For purposes of environmental design research, probably the best way to articulate children's preferences, perceptions, and satisfactions is to measure them. This is easily said and sounds perfectly logical, but we must first have a yardstick with which to measure. The problem is further complicated by the fact that these are psychological variables that cannot be observed directly. Therefore, one must resort to methods that measure indirectly through observation of behavioral effects of the psychological variables we are interested in.

Measurement is a process of assigning numbers to a variable (e.g., preference), in such a way that changes in the magnitude of the variable are described by relationships among the numbers. Thus, in measuring preference, we would like to assign large numbers to objects that are highly desirable and small numbers to objects that are less desirable. If several play devices can be arranged in order from least to most desirable, a sequence of increasing numbers can be assigned to them, resulting in what is called "ordinal" measurement. Ratios and intervals among the numbers are not meaningful, however, which means that additions, subtractions, multiplications, and divisions are not strictly valid.

In order for additions and subtractions to be valid, the amount of difference or "preference distance" between play devices must be measured, resulting in an "interval" scale that also retains ordinal properties. An example is the Farenheit scale of temperature, which has an arbitrary zero point. If such an interval scale is shifted so that its zero point coincides with absolute absence of the variable being measured (e.g., the Rankine temperature scale), we have a ratio scale. Multiplications and divisions among the numbers are then meaningful.

Methods for measuring preferences, perceptions, and satisfactions are well developed in the psychometric literature.[6] Unfortunately, many of these methods, and especially many esoteric methods now in vogue, share a common disadvantage when the subject is a child. They require rather complex decisions and sophisticated skills, and there is good reason to doubt that they can be used with children. The problem is to find methods that are simple enough for a child to use, yet reliable and valid. If the method is reliable, it will consistently yield the same results when repeated measurements are made. If it is valid, it will measure what we want to know: what a child is actually attracted to do. In combination with experimental control, we can then use such a method to observe the sensitivity of preference to variations in design variables, thereby gaining the opportunity to develop explanations of preference and, consequently, powerful design principles.

The research reported in the following pages was aimed at validating and applying a measurement technique. The first step in selecting a method for testing was to apply the criterion of simplicity. The simplest method we could find is the method of pair comparisons based on the "law of comparative judgment" originally developed by Thurstone.[7] Thurstone scaling seems recently to have fallen into disrepute in some circles, owing mainly to work by Stevens.[8] However, we believe that the benefits of simplicity of the task required of the subjects far outweigh the negative arguments in this case. Furthermore, because we are interested in developing measures of relative attractiveness rather than specific functional forms, the arguments against Thurstone probably are unimportant.[9]

In any case, pair comparison seems feasible with children, and this is of primary importance. The method asks the child to choose between only two alterantives at a time. Given a set of alternatives, they are combined pairwise and presented to the child with the instruction that he should decide which one he likes best. When this method is used with a group of children having similar preferences, or repeatedly with the same child, it can be determined statistically whether there is a consistent ordering of preferences among the alternatives. If there is, an interval scale can be constructed that can subsequently be used to explore reliability and validity, Stevens notwithstanding. A disadvantage with the method is that it is not convenient to use with large numbers of alternatives, because of the number of pairs that must be created.

In the hope of overcoming this problem, we decided to explore the method of rank order also. In this method, the child is presented all the alternatives at once and asked to decide which one he likes best. This one is then removed, and he is asked to pick the best of those that remain, and so forth. If the two methods agree and yield valid preferences, the more convenient method of rank order can be used to research preferences in a variety of experimental situations.

For maximum validity, the methods should be used with real environments. This approach did not fit our budget, however, and we found it necessary to use color photographs of the alternatives being tested. This raises a question of the validity of photographs as simulations of real environments: how well do preferences for color

Figure 1
Photographs Used for Validation of Measurement Methodology

photographs agree with actual preferences for the object photographed?

In order to test reliability and validity, we studied a playground containing six pieces of play equipment of simple conventional design. We used six color photographs, corresponding to the black-and-white renditions in Figure 1, to measure preferences by means of rank order and pair comparison. For this phase of study, the sample consisted of forty-five eight-year-old children. Preferences were measured by the two methods at two different times, separated by a three-month interval.

To test validity, a time-lapse movie camera was set up unobtrusively to record the population in the same playground at one-minute intervals. Several thousand observations were obtained under a variety of use conditions. No attempt was made to control the children entering the playground, so the camera was recording play decisions of a group different from the one in the photo-preference study, and more varied in age. Thus, agreement between scales constructed from the photo preferences and those constructed from playground observation has forced itself not only through reliability and validity questions, but also through population differences. Conclusions based upon observed agreement are therefore conservative.

This experimental design allows reliability to be measured by comparing pair comparison and rank order over time. Validity is tested conservatively by comparing photo preferences with observed choices. Details of the design and analysis have been reported previously.[10]

Results of the Test for Consistency and Reliability

Both methods, rank order and pair comparison, produced statistically meaningful interval scales with ordered preferences among the six alternatives. This indicates that something was measured. When the scales were compared across method and over time, the orders were identical, and the intervals agreed within the statistical limits allowed by sample size. This remarkable finding demonstrates that children's preferences, at least for color photographs, can be measured by these methods with excellent reliability. The method of rank order has been shown to give the same results as pair comparison. If the measurements also have validity for predicting actual play behavior, rank order is to be preferred because of its ability to handle larger numbers of alternatives.

Figure 2 shows the correlation between the two methods. The horizontal axis is the scale of attractiveness derived by the method of pair comparison. The vertical axis is the scale of attractiveness derived by the method of rank order. If the photographs occupy the same relative numerical positions on both scales, they will lie on a straight line inclined upward to the right through the origin (the point of intersection between the two scales). Departure from such a straight line is measured by the correlation coefficient. The open circles represent the scale values resulting from measurements taken in October 1970; the solid black dots indicate January 1971 observations. The correlation between methods is 0.97, which means that the scales produced by the two methods have $(0.97)^2 \times 100$ percent, or 94 percent of their variation in common. If we distribute the "error" equally between both methods and use the correlation between methods as an estimate of reliability, we can expect the correlation of each scale with the set of true scores to be $\sqrt{0.97}$, or 0.98![11] Figure 2 shows the correlation between the two methods, and also shows the variation over time.

According to these results, the order of attractiveness for the photographs is (1) swings, (2) slides, (3) horizontal ladder, (4) monkey bars, (5) seesaws and (6) horizontal bars, from most to least attractive, respectively. This will be discussed later.

The reader should remember at this point that we are not trying to predict the behavior of individual children. If that could be done at all, it would require a completely different (and more complex) approach to measurement. Rather, we are interested in predicting the relative attractiveness of a piece of play equipment, its ability to compete for users.

Results of the Test for Behavioral Validity

Although we have demonstrated a powerful way to measure children's preferences for color photographs of play equipment, the question remains whether these preferences bear any resemblance to what children would choose in a real play situation. Can actual attractiveness of play equipment be predicted from preferences for photographs? After careful sampling design, the time-

lapse films of playground behavior were sampled in several different ways and frequencies of use recorded for each of the six devices. Several different samples were taken, because conceptual analysis turned up questions about what to count and what not to count. It was often difficult to determine whether a child was using the apparatus "legitimately" for the function it was designed to perform, or for some other purpose. For many frames, it was also difficult to determine whether a child was using one of the devices or merely observing the use of it. These and other questions suggested that the films could be sampled according to several different sets of criteria, and there was no way to determine which was most "correct." When the children viewed the six photographs in the interviews, were they thinking of "legitimate" use only, or were they viewing

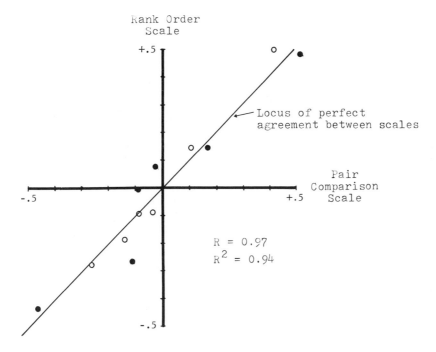

Figure 2
Reliability of Measurement Methods: ○, October 1970; ●, January 1971.
(See text for explanation.)

the pictured equipment as play objects that were attractive in a variety of ways, no matter what their design function?

After examining the results of several different sampling strategies, stratified according to the suspected source of variation, it was found that two samples adequately represented the range of differences. The first consisted of 452 frames with no illegitimate or questionable use. The second consisted of 550 frames, including frames with illegitimate or questionable use, but only clearly legitimate use was counted. Frames containing fewer than two or more than twelve children were excluded from both samples, and all frames were separated by at least three-minute intervals.

The two samples chosen were used to generate estimates of the probability that a given device would be occupied when there are children in the playground. The two scales differed only in terms of the relative attractiveness of swings and slides. In the 452-frame sample swings and slides were equally attractive, while in the 550-frame sample swings outranked slides. Still, we do not know whether the criteria used for either sample are the same as those used by the children when choosing among the play devices. Thus, it must be concluded that the time-lapse films produce only an estimate of behavior, perhaps close to the truth but not necessarily perfect.

In order to compare photo preferences with the time-lapse estimate of attractiveness, the four preference samples of forty-five observations each were pooled to produce a 180-observation estimate of the probability that a child would select a given photograph when asked to choose among all six. Figure 3 compares the interview estimates with the playground estimates of attractiveness. The playground estimates predict the following: (1) swings are most attractive, followed in order by (2) slides, (3) seesaws, (4) monkey bars, (5) horizontal ladder, and (6) horizontal bar.

This order of attractiveness differs from that predicted by the photo preferences only with respect to seesaws and horizontal ladders, which have switched places. The correlation between estimated probabilities is 0.77 over the six devices. If the two estimates of attractiveness are both 95 percent reliable, the observed correlation could not be expected to be above 0.90, even with perfect behavioral validity. This suggests that there is considerable behavioral validity in the photo preferences, albeit less than perfect. In fact, the validity is probably better than these results indicate, for the reasons already discussed.

Considering only the agreement between the two approaches, the following conclusions are justified:

1. Swings and slides are the most attractive alternatives, with swings probably having an advantage over slides.
2. The horizontal ladder, monkey bars and seesaws occupy a mid-range of attractiveness, but we cannot differentiate among them from the photo interviews.
3. The horizontal bar is least attractive. In fact, according to the playground observations, it is used only about one-tenth as frequently as the swings.

It is interesting that the two most attractive alternatives involve the child in solo motion, while the least attractive seems more concerned with strength and skill. Might there be suggestions of principles here that would aid the designer in predicting and improving the attractiveness of his creations? Given the excellent reliability and reasonable behavioral validity of the photo-preference method for measuring attractiveness, the next step is to use the method in experiments aimed at identifying the sensitivity of attractiveness to selected design variables.

TOWARD THE SYNTHESIS OF DESIGN PRINCIPLES

Already it has been shown that some devices are more attractive than others, given equal treatment with respect to color and originality. To explain exactly why this is so would require understanding of the psychology of play, which is beyond the scope of this study. Need-less to say, it offers a challenge for future research. Instead, we turn now to studies aimed at testing hypotheses about the sensitivity of attractiveness to specific design variations. Given that a decision has been made to design a climbing apparatus, for example, what variations of form, theme, color, etc., will produce the greatest attractiveness? A recent study by Gramza, Corush, and Ellis[12] demonstrates that preschool children are attracted by functional complexity.

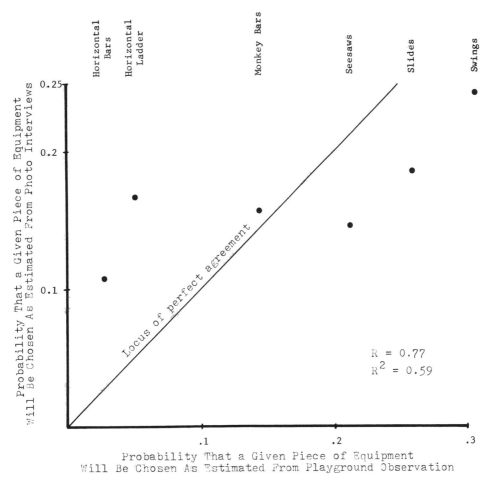

Figure 3
Agreement Between Photo Interview Results and Observation of Actual Playground Behavior

We designed studies to test hypotheses about slide design variations and climbing design variations. The approach was to select a set of fifteen color photographs of each of the two functional types. Only available designs were used, and selections were made for covering the range of variation from (1) natural and spontaneous (uncontrived) opportuinities through (2) traditional and unadorned designs to (3) highly complex, colorful, and thematic devices. Black-and-white renditions of the photos selected for slide design variations are shown in Figure 4. The climbing design photos are shown in Figure 5. Several other sets were also included in the study, but they will not be discussed in detail for the sake of brevity.

Figure 4
Photographs Used To Test Slide Design Variation

Sample Design

A sample of 200 eight-year-old children was used to study responses to the two sets of photos. Because of the possibility that sex, ethnicity and social rank might influence the child's response, the sample was stratified by male–female, black–white, and suburb (Evanston)–central city (Chicago), with twenty-five subjects in each of the eight classes. For comparative analysis, each of the three variables of classification (sex, ethnicity, place) was examined under the four conditions defined by the other two variables. For example, sex differences were examined for Chicago, Evanston, blacks and whites. This is less powerful than permitted by the three-way experimental design, but it allows scales to be based on sample sizes of fifty observations.

Figure 5
Photographs Used to Test Climbing
Design Variation

Differences Among Children

For slide design variation, sex, ethnicity and place of residence did not cause significant differences in the preference scales. The correlations are shown in Table 1. If there are differences among children with regard to the attractiveness of the slides, they must be caused by other variables not measured.

For climbing design variation, however, there were important differences. The correlations are shown in Table 2. The greatest differences are between males and females. This is strongest for blacks; and in the central city. Weaker sex differences exist in the suburb, and for whites. That sex differences in play preference should be greater for blacks than for whites agrees with our findings for high school students.[13] Apparently the sex differences are deeply rooted. Although the correlations for slide design in Table 1 are all very high, it must be noted that their magnitudes have the same order, from lowest to highest, as for the climber photos (i.e., black, Chicago, Evanston, white). This was noted with anther photo set as well.

The correlations for ethnic difference in Table 2 show that there is considerable disagreement between blacks and whites in the suburb and for females. For males, and in the central city, there is much less, if any, disagreement. In general, differences in preference between blacks and whites are not as great as between males and females. Differences related to place of residence are weakest of all, but sufficient to be important for whites and for females.

These results show that different groups of children may respond differently to alternative play devices. It also seems that the difference process may vary for different classes of equipment (i.e., there were important differences for climbers, but not for slides). Where differences in preference do exist across sex, ethnicity, social rank, or some other variable, they should be understood by the designer. If the differences are not understood, the result may be discrimination on the one hand, or poor satisfaction for everyone when averages guide design. This is a fertile field for further research.

Some Tentative Design Principles

For slide design variation the most preferred was slide 1, a giant, colorful, and cage-like robot with the slides being tubes that form the robot's arms (see Figure 4). Second choice was a giant, undulating slide with capacity for six riders in parallel (slide 7). Third choice was an innovative and colorful spiral slide (slide 8), and fourth was a colorful, planet-like combination slide and climber with holes in it through which children could crawl (slide 3). Three traditional slides were included (14, 11, and 13), which were preferred twelfth, thirteenth, and fourteenth, respectively. Of these three traditional designs, the most

Table 1

Similarity Among Different Types of Children with Regard to Attractiveness of Slide Design Variations

Type of Difference	Classification	Correlation Between Preference Scales
Sex	Black	0.91*
(male vs. female)	Central city	0.94
	Suburban	0.96
	White	0.97
Ethnic	Suburban	0.91
(black vs. white)	Female	0.93
	Central city	0.96
	Male	0.97
Place	White	0.93
(central city	Female	0.94
vs. suburban)	Black	0.97
	Male	0.99

*For example, 0.91 is the correlation between the average preferences of black male children and black female children. It is the correlation across sex for black children; likewise, the second number, 0.94, is the correlation across sex for central city children; and so forth.

preferred has the ladder parallel to the slide, and the child passes through a canopy at the top. The next one (11) is a conventional design with two slides, and the third (13) is a similar design with only one slide. They appear to be ordered in decreasing complexity. A natural mud slide on a grassy hill (15) was rated in last place by the children. In general, attractiveness appears to be enhanced by complexity, novelty, color, thematic design, and excitement of ride (height, complexity, etc.). Garishness seems to be more important than a tasteful aesthetic design, as though "stimulus-seeking"[14] were an important motive.

For climbing design variation, the observed differences among types of children make the job of describing preferences difficult. Averages are questionable, if not meaningless. All groups did agree that photos 2, 3, and 5 are among the most attractive. Photos 2 and 3 are colorful solids with holes and cavities for climbing in and through. Number 5 is a geodesic lattice. Photos 6, 7, 8, 9, and 10, rather traditional lattice or bar-type climbers, were much more attractive to black females

than to black males (see Figure 6). They were also more preferred by Chicago females than by Chicago males.

On the other hand, photos 11, 12, 13, 14, and 15 were more attractive to males than to females among blacks and in Chicago. Apparently the rustic and tree-like theme has male appeal for these groups, whereas the more traditional climbers have female appeal. The tree-like climbers also appeal more strongly to whites than to blacks (see Figure 7), and more to suburban children than to central-city children. In Chicago, the children seem more attracted to the conventional lattice and bar designs.

Translation of these findings into useful design principles will require more research. Perhaps the results are more interesting for social or psychological reasons than for design purposes. Let the designer beware, however, lest he try to feed meat to his horses and hay to his cats. Another problem worth considering is whether the cultural differences observed among these eight-year-old children should be accommodated and reinforced

Table 2
Differences Among Children with Regard to Attractiveness of Climbing Design Variations

Type of Difference	Classification	Correlation Between Preference Scales	Percent in Common
Sex (male vs. female)	Black	0.43	18
	Central city	0.50	25
	Suburban	0.75	56
	White	0.79	62
Ethnic (black vs. white)	Suburban	0.63	40
	Female	0.73	53
	Male	0.88	77
	Central city	0.91	83
Place (central city vs. suburb)	White	0.67	45
	Female	0.78	61
	Male	0.88	77
	Black	0.92	85

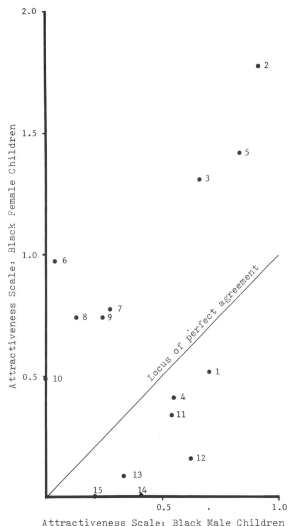

Figure 6
Sex Differences Among Black Children for Attractiveness of Climbing Design Variations; *R* = 0.43

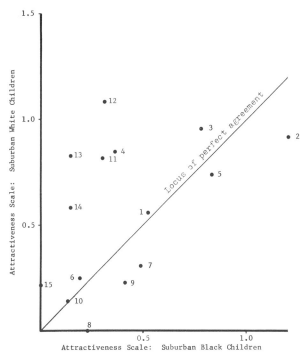

Figure 7
Ethnic Differences Among Suburban Children for Attractiveness of Climbing Design Variations; *R* = 0.63

or deliberately diffused. The designer cannot provide the answer, but he must face the choice!

In general, and allowing for the major differences described above, the preferences again tend to be ordered in favor of color, complexity,

novelty, and thematic design. Swiss-cheese-type objects seem to have special appeal, although this could be coincidental. Girls prefer the bars, whereas boys are attracted to tree themes. Surprisingly, the tree itself was relatively unattractive to everyone, even the boys, perhaps due to its well-groomed and somewhat institutional setting.

Other studies concerned with activity variation and variations of the playground were not as well controlled as those for slides and climbers, but several additional hypotheses were suggested: (1) Children choose recognizable and thematic designs over aesthetic architectural creations. (2) Vacant lots, junkyards, and construction sites are not substitutable in the children's minds for contrived playgrounds. They seem to be regarded

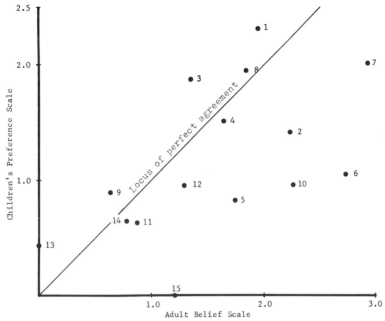

Figure 8
Comparison of Children's Preferences and Adult Designers' Beliefs About Children's Preferences for Slide Design Variation; $R = 0.56$

as a different kind of activity, and generally seem less attractive. (3) Complexity, color, and recognizable thematic innovation again seem to be important attractors.

ARE ADULT DESIGNERS RESPONSIVE TO CHILDREN?

A criticism commonly leveled at this kind of research by professional designers is that there is no point trying to discover by elaborate scientific and statistical means what a good designer already knows by training or inherent creative talent. The truly successful designer may well be partly a product of natural selection, whereby designers with incorrect beliefs are weeded out. But, as mentioned earlier, there are plenty of reasons to believe that designers' tastes differ

from those of their clients, especially when the clients are children. A more interesting question is whether the designer's beliefs about his clients' tastes are correct. Rather than speculate about this, we attempted to answer the question directly.

Using the same photographs to which the children responded, and a sample of fifty adult designers and decision makers, we measured beliefs about what is attractive to children. The results are extremely enlightening.

Slide Design Variation

Because there was good agreement among the children for this set of photos, it makes sense to make a single comparison between the children and the adults. Figure 8 shows emphatically that

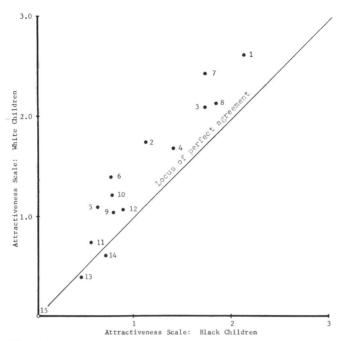

Figure 9
Comparison Between Black Children and White Children: Attractiveness of Slide Design Variations; $R = 0.96$

the adults are poor predictors of what a child finds attractive. In fact, as shown by Figure 9, we are better off using the preferences of white children to guide design for blacks than to consult the adults, at least for slide design.

The greatest discrepancy was for the mud slide. Adults rated it ninth, but it was last for children. Slide 3, the globular satellite, was vastly underrated by adults. Slide six, an architecturally imaginative slide with the theme of a house ruin, was greatly overrated by the adults, perhaps because the children had difficulty understanding it. The adults also failed to recognize the appeal of the garish robot slide (1), the rocket slide (4), and the spiral slide (8). They overrated slides 2, 5, and 10, in addition to the mud slide and the house theme. The only thing they agreed upon is that the plain traditional designs, which are also the

most common, are relatively unattractive. The conclusion seems to be that if you want to know what appeals to the child, ask the child, not the designer.

Climbing Design Variation

The differences in preference among types of children are large enough for climbing design variation that it makes no sense to compare adult beliefs with the average preferences for all children. Rather, Table 3 is presented, which shows the correlation between adult beliefs and child preferences for all children, as well as for the six categories of classification: male–female, white–black, and suburban–central city. Correlations in these categories are shown for five sets of photos, including slides and climbers.

Table 3
Correlation of Adult Beliefs About Children's Preferences with Preferences Expressed by the Children

Photo Group	No. Photos	Child Type						
		All Children	Male	Female	White	Black	Suburban	Central City
Slide design	15	0.56	0.63	0.49*	0.65	0.46*	0.63	0.49*
Climbing design	15	0.28*	0.60	−0.05*	0.43*	0.08*	0.41*	0.10*
Activity variation	15	0.56	0.75	0.22*	0.61	0.48*	0.57	0.47*
Contrived environment	11	0.82	0.88	0.74	0.87	0.73	0.84	0.79
Uncontrived environment	4	−0.72*	−0.64*	−0.75*	−0.64*	−0.78*	−0.69*	−0.75*

*Correlation not significantly different from zero at the 0.05 level. (These correlations have probability greater than $1/20$ of occurring by chance in a random sample taken from a population in which the correlation is zero.)

For climbers, the correlation varies from a high of 0.60 for male children to a low of −0.05 for female children. For the overall average, the correlation is 0.28, which is not statistically different from zero. Following through the pattern of correlations, we see that the adults are closer to male children than to females. They are also closer to white children than to blacks, and to suburban children than to those from the central city. Apparently the adults are most responsive to white, male, suburban children, and least responsive to black, female, central-city children.

There are several plausible explanations for this lack of correlation. Forty-four of the adults were white males, five were white females, two were black females, and only one was a black male. All were middle-class types. Clearly, this suggests that we are observing not only adult–child disparity, but also sex and ethnicity biases. Although it might be argued that this is poor experimental design, it seems stronger to argue that the sample closely represents the true distribution of adult types involved in making decisions about the child's play environment. Would the results be

better if parents in the respective categories, rather than designers, were consulted? This is a question for future research.

Regarding how the adults and children differed for climbing design, it is too complex a matter to discuss completely here, given the differences among children. Clearly, the adults were using different criteria than were the children, and this is most evident for photos 11, 12, 13, 14, and 15. These all could be interpreted as tree-like, and were greatly overrated by the adults. Can it be that the time-honored love affair between the child and tree is a myth?

The Overall Pattern of Responsiveness

The overall pattern of correlation between children and adults shown in Table 3 indicates that the conclusions observed for climbing designs persist, albeit more weakly, with all the other photo sets. The differences among correlations are often too small to be significant, but the consistent direction of the results is most unlikely to have occurred by chance. We would conclude that for all sets of photos, the adults are more responsive to males than to females, to whites than to blacks, and to suburban children than to those from the central city. The results also suggest that for all but the uncontrived play environments (vacant lots, junkyards, and construction sites) there is a positive, though usually weak, relationship between adults and children. This positive correlation is quite strong for contrived playgrounds, but the correlation is strongly negative for the uncontrived environments. We can say in this case that we are better off to provide the opposite of what the adults believe will be most attractive to the children.

The problem with uncontrived playgrounds is interesting in that it further emphasizes the fact that adults and children apparently use quite different criteria to evaluate attractiveness. During the interviews and after the preference choices had been recorded, the researchers informally asked the subjects why they made the choices they made. Adults seemed to respond in terms of the variety of things that could be done in each place. Comments about the most preferred uncontrived play environments indicated that the adults believed they were "exciting and interesting places to play." On the other hand, children seemed more concerned about personal safety than about whether it would be a fun place to play. A junkyard stimulated comments about dirt, junk, rats, and the possibility of getting hurt. A construction site was also described as dirty, messy, and dangerous. Apparently, the children are more mature in their evaluations than the adults would like to believe. At least, this is one possible interpretation.

CONCLUSION

In summary, the study reported here was designed for three purposes: (1) to test reliability and validity for a proposed method for measuring children's preferences for play equipment and environment; (2) to measure the relative attractiveness of controlled variations in selected design variables toward the synthesis of design principles; and (3) to test the hypothesis that adult designers and decision makers have correct beliefs about what is attractive to children. The study was motivated by two basic problems that confront the designer of environments for children: (1) Children do not express their preferences effectively in the decision-making arena, either economically or politically, and their preferences are difficult to measure. (2) Environments and devices intended for children should be attractive and satisfying from the child's point of view. One of the principal purposes of the play environment is to provide the child with enjoyment. But even if the functions are more technically concerned with physical or mental education, the designs should be competitively attractive if they are to be used.

The results of the study reinforce the proposition that design principles are needed. We have shown that, in many of their beliefs, the adult designers are in error about what is attractive to children. If designs and decisions are based on these beliefs, the products will not be as attractive and satisfying for the children as they might be if appropriate design principles were available. It has also been shown that there are many complicated differences among children with regard to their preferences. Sex, ethnicity, and place of residence have been shown to modify what the child finds attractive. It is not clear whether these differences should be reinforced by selectively aiming designs toward the appropriate groups, or whether there should be a conscious social effort to reduce these differences, which apparently have cultural origins. From the designer's point of view, we have at least shown the need for variety of choice that spans the spectrum of differences, so that every child has the opportunity to play in the constructive ways he has learned to enjoy.

These strong needs for design principles, on the one hand, and for a better understanding of differences among children, on the other, combine to create a demand for research. One important requirement for this research is an ability to measure what is attractive to children. This study has demonstrated that the relative ability of play devices to compete for users can be measured with reasonable validity using color photographs and the methods of rank order and pair comparison. Attractiveness of the photographs can be measured with excellent reliability, and reasonably good predictions about actual play behavior can be made from the measurements. The user of such methods should be cautious, however, to be sure that the things photographed can be recognized and interpreted by the children. Predictions about totally new devices or environments should be based on principles, not direct measures of attractiveness. Completely new devices may be ambiguous and, therefore, unattractive to the child until he has had a chance to experience them. A more interesting application of the demonstrated measurement methods is in controlled experiments aimed at the synthesis of design principles.

In a preliminary application of this idea, our study has pointed toward such principles. In general, attractiveness is enhanced by complexity, novelty, color, and theme. Sensations of motion seem to be preferred over opportunities requiring strength and skill. Conventional unadorned designs are unanimously regarded as the least attractive of the alternatives tested, both by adults and by children. Several interesting questions have also been raised. Why were the children so attracted to climbing devices that are solids with holes and cavities, rather than to lattices? Is this a hint of an important principle, or is it merely coincidence? Why were trees and climbers with tree themes downgraded by many of the children, and why were sex and other differences among children so strong in this regard? Why were the children not able to place uncontrived playgrounds in the same category as contrived playgrounds, and what are the implications of this for some of the modern trends toward "adventure playgrounds"?

At a much more fundamental level, some extremely important questions need to be answered. How stable are the preferences (and differences) that have been measured? Are the differences largely the result of exposure? If so, how quickly will the children learn to prefer new things? Which attributes of play equipment can become attractive through a quick process of learning or adaptation? Which, if any, are the objects of more deeply rooted motives that are resistant to change?

Perhaps the study has raised more questions than it has answered with respect to the reasons why children respond the way they do. We believe that it has taken some important steps, however, in the direction of improved methods for answering such questions. If the reader is in the business of designing environments for children, it is hoped that we have given him reason to question his own beliefs and begin to search for better answers. It is also hoped that our results have provided some useful insights and some helpful, albeit general and tentative, design principles. In the meantime, much detailed research is needed.

NOTES AND REFERENCES

1. R. Dattner, *Design for Play,* New York: Van Nostrand, Reinhold Co., 1969, p. 33.
2. Kenneth H. Craik, "The Environmental Dispositions of Environmental Decision-Makers," *Annals of the American Academy of Political and Social Science,* Vol. 389, 1970, pp. 87–94.
3. R. N. Clark, et al. "Values, Behavior, and Conflict in Modern Camping Culture," *Journal of Leisure Research,* Vol. 3, No. 3, Summer, 1971, pp. 143–159; George L. Peterson, "A Comparison of the Sentiments and Perceptions of Wilderness Managers and Canoeists in Boundary Waters Canoe Area," *Journal of Leisure Research,* Vol. 6, No. 2, Spring, 1974.
4. B. L. Driver, "Potential Contributions of Psychology to Recreation Resources Management," in *Environment and the Social Sciences: Perspectives and Applications,* J. F. Wohlwill and D. N. Carson (eds.), Washington, D.C.:

American Psychological Association, 1972, pp. 233–248; George L. Peterson, "Psychology and Environmental Management for Outdoor Recreation," *Environmental Design Research,* Vol. 1, Wolfgang F. F. Preiser (ed.), Stroudsburg, Pa.: Dowden, Hutchinson & Ross, Inc., 1973.

5. Kelvin J. Lancaster, "A New Approach to Consumer Theory," *Journal of Political Economy,* Vol. 74, Apr. 1966, pp. 132–157; George L. Peterson and Edward S. Neumann, "Modeling and Predicting Human Response to the Visual Recreation Environment," *Journal of Leisure Research,* Vol. 1, No. 3, Summer 1969, pp. 219–237; George L. Peterson, Jan U. Hanssen, and Robert L. Bishop, "Toward an Explanatory Model of Outdoor Recreation Preference," prepared for the Symposium on Consumer Behavior and Environmental Design, American Psychological Association meetings, Washington, D.C., 1971.

6. J. C. Nunnally, "Psychometric Theory," New York: McGraw-Hill Book Company, 1967; Warren S. Torgerson, *Theory and Method of Scaling,* New York: John Wiley & Sons, Inc., 1958.

7. L. L. Thurstone, "A Law of Comparative Judgment," *Psychological Review,* Vol. 34, 1927, pp. 273–286; *The Measurement of Values,* Chicago: University of Chicago Press, 1959.

8. S. S. Stevens, "A Metric for Social Consensus," *Science,* Vol. 151, Feb. 4, 1966, pp. 530–541; "On the Operation Known as Judgment," *American Scientist,* Vol. 54, No. 4, 1966, pp. 385–401.

9. Nunnally, *op. cit.,* chap. 1.

10. Robert L. Bishop, and George L. Peterson, "A Synthesis of Environmental Design Recommendations from the Visual Preferences of Children," Technical Report #2, Outdoor Recreation Opportunity: Needs and Desires, Grant No. 5 RO1 EC 00301 from the U.S. Public Health Service, Department of Civil Engineering, Northwestern University, Evanston, Ill., 1971; Robert L. Bishop, G. L. Peterson, and R. M. Michaels, "Measurement of Children's Preferences for the Play Environment," in *Environmental Design: Research and Practice,* William J. Mitchell (ed.), Los Angeles: University of California, 1972; George L. Peterson, R. L. Bishop, R. M. Michaels, and G. J. Rath, "Children's Choice of Playground Equipment: Development of Methodology for Integrating User Preferences into Environmental Engineering," *Journal of Applied Psychology,* Vol. 58, No. 2, 1973, pp. 233–238.

11. Nunnally, *op. cit.,* chap. 6.

12. A. F. Gramza, J. Corush, and M. J. Ellis, "Children's Play on Trestles Differing in Complexity: A Study of Play Equipment Design," *Journal of Leisure Research,* Vol. 4, No. 4, Fall 1972, p. 303–311.

13. Peterson, Hanssen, and Bishop, *op. cit.*

14. George E. McKechnie, "Measuring Environmental Dispositions with the Environmental Response Inventory," *EDRA TWO,* proceedings of the 2nd Annual Environmental Design Research Association Conference, Charles Eastman and John Archea (eds.), 1970.

Children's Play: Design Approaches and Theoretical Issues*

Asher Derman

Poetry for some may be like child's play, but perhaps it is time to stop the poetry of maximizations and/or optimizations of child's play through poetic-methodological approaches if children's development and behavior are to be of legitimate and generalizable concern. If that is the case, it then becomes necessary to consider whether in fact enough is known about child's play to study means by which it can be facilitated through "design," or whether enough is known about play itself that we might be able to describe its occurrence—or to say something about its potential value for the development of the child—or for that matter about its value to our social systems.

A number of problems must then be considered at equal levels of concern. First, because of the need to design environments for children's

play, designers and designer–behaviorists (of varying degrees) have begun to publish papers in the form of experimental reportage, proposals for methods of approach, and in some cases a number of larger works attempting to contribute to the design of play facilities through descriptions of what has already been accomplished.[1] These works must be scrutinized carefully for their merits, for they may otherwise represent casual but nevertheless gross misapplications of theoretical positions and experimental findings.

Second, in some of these works[2] there are theoretical oversimplifications which endanger the role that behavioral science might play in contributing to the study, evaluation, and specification of children's play environments.

Third, a number of recent works[3] suggest that difficulties concerning the definition of play behavior are far from being resolved. The implication is that it may be pointless to design *play* en-

*This study was supported, in part, by a grant from the Gulf Oil Company.

vironments unless there is a consistent willingness to deal with definitional matters in terms of procedures guaranteeing a minimum of generalizable methods and data for comparison or relationship to other similar efforts.

Fourth, the role of adult attitudes in the design of play facilities is in need of study, as Bishop[4] suggests (the preceding article in this volume, by Peterson, Bishop, and Michaels, is based on this publication). Attitudinal dimensions are of general concern to any designer or planner—given his implicit task of establishing methods by which user requirements may be described and implemented in physical form. But in the design of children's play environments this issue is more critical because of two factors—intuitive design procedures and special interest groups. Children are not capable of externalizing their behavioral requirements through most extractive (verbal) methods now available. These factors are perhaps most instrumental in permitting design (given the present state-of-the-art in designing children's play environments) to continue to be a highly intuitive nontestable process. And, because of this intuitive problem-solving mode, attitudes of the designer and other adults who may participate in the design process require analysis in order that the goals of play environment design can be directed as much as possible away from adult bias and toward children's behavioral requirements, as those requirements may be defined through objective methods and studies of children's behavioral development. Special interest groups in the form of agencies, organizations, or institutions, as aggregates of "adult designers," also become deeply committed to the achievement of play-oriented goals, which may be in the interest of the developing child; but they may also confound the goal of facilitating play behavior by incorporating excessive child-control measures or programs that simultaneously attempt to accommodate other behavioral requirements.

Fifth, we appear as a culture to be hesitantly moving in the direction of management and control of behavior to achieve socially defined goals. This hesitancy is strangely covert, for overt design decisions are continually being made that *do* manage behavior. The hesitancy then becomes not only incongruous, but confusing as well, to those participating in the goal of providing environments for children's play. Consider that those who are most insistent upon the value of play behavior to "freely" developing children are not necessarily disposed to minimize other concurrent goals in their design attack, for example, control of children, learning skills, cooperative behavior, and other social skills.[5] Studer[6] has been one of the few theorists to explicitly state that there must be an overt move in the direction of establishing a planning oriented culture so that both the goals of individuals and those of society might be brought into (at least an iterative) alignment. He is also one of the few to alert designers to the need to structure and evaluate decisions of behavioral and environmental significance according to a testable paradigm. Therefore—and most importantly—once behavioral management is the expressed goal of design (whether through physical or behavioral means), it must be stated in the form of experimental paradigms that will yield useful data regarding both success and failure encountered in the process of goal achievement. Design, according to Calhoun,[7] is the creation of meaning. But there is no meaning without a response (to the meaningful event), which can be categorized as a change in the recipient system. What this change may be, or whether it can be observed or verified, is an experimental function. Therefore, when we design environments for children, we are forming composites of assumed-to-be-meaningful elements and anticipating behavioral changes in the children processing such input. Without intentionally considering design as an experiment (in the scientific sense), we shall merely perpetuate the confusion and waste that has resulted from a tradition of "unintentional" human experimentation.

THESIS: DESIGNED ENVIRONMENTS FOR CHILDREN'S PLAY

Both Friedberg[8] and Dattner[9] are deservedly prominent figures in the design of children's play facilities and have displayed great innovativeness in generating environmental configurations for children's activities in many diverse contexts. These designers are to be complimented on the design results they achieve within an intuitive problem-solving framework. However, it is when intuitively based designers begin to explain the rationale behind their intuitively derived decisions that questions of appropriateness to broad-scale application (in the hands of others) begin to arise. The question is then most obvious: Are such intuitive problem-solving methods generalizable? Is a contribution being made to the public forum where workable knowledge is exchanged, particularly with regard to the facilitation of children's play behavior and general development?

It would be informative if the underlying structure of design decision-making processes was revealed in some direct fashion. To do so would involve a minimal statement of the objectives of designing for children's play in such a way that the specification of goals, methods, and means of verifying or evaluating the results would be clearly outlined in the form of a paradigm. A paradigm, more broadly defined, "stands for the entire constellation of beliefs, values and techniques . . . shared by members of a given (scientific) community."[10] A paradigm also represents the *sharing* of a disciplinary matrix composed of (1) symbolic generalizations (e.g., formulas), (2) values concerning prediction, and (3) exemplars (e.g., classic experiments or propositions). The design products of both Dattner and Friedberg could be held as exemplars of children's playgrounds, but their

values concerning prediction (e.g., do children play in those environments according to specifications formulated in the preliminary design conception?), and the "formula" or procedure for arriving at their behavior–environment solution are not generalizable. Studer[11] proposes one set of operations that answers this need. Briefly, his paradigm requires, (1) definiltion of those behaviors that are to be supported, facilitated, or managed, (2) specification of the physical form or configurations that might facilitate the defined behaviors, (3) execution of plans for the physical facility, and (4) verification that the behavior–environment relationship hypothesized in items 1 and 2 is occurring as planned. (Following such a format, a reconstructed outline of the design paradigms *possibly* employed by the authors referred to in this paper is provided in Table 1.)

1. Linked Play Environments

The paradigm for playground design that can be extracted from Friedberg's work[12] may be characterized first by a definition of play as a form of "research" that a child engages in to evolve relationships between himself and the world. To facilitate such play behavior, a series of "linked play" forms with an emphasis upon complexity (to increase potential choice) is recommended. Since there are many diverse settings of varying scales that will require play facilities, a priority may then be given to the development of modular designs permitting diverse combinations of basic elements. Another advantage of a modular system is that it could be utilized by Friedberg (or other designers) to design many different facilities, or the system could be utilized by communities (as designers) to "create any desired, overall form." With regard to the testing of a facility, it is considered that research and evaluation methods suitable for use are "rare," and therefore the validation of any design through testing cannot be included in the original design

Table 1

Reconstructed Design Paradigms Utilized by Authors Referred To in the Text

Author	Behavior To Be Facilitated or Supported	Specified or Realized Physical Properties or Environment	Method of Verifying or Evaluating the Behavior–Environment Relationship
Friedberg and Berkeley	1. Children's play. 2. "Play is the child's work ... play is the research by which he explores himself and his relationships to the world." 3. Learning.	1. Linked play environments. 2. Use of modular design. 3. "... the more complex the playground the greater the choice and the more enriched learning experience."	1. Inspection or casual observation by designer. 2. "Unfortunately research is rare ... evaluation of existing play designs is also rare ...."
Dattner	1. Children's play. 2. "Play is the way in which children develop intelligence." 3. Play behavior consistent with developmental level, e.g., practice play, symbolic play, games (with reference to Piaget, 1962).	1. Adventure Playground. 2. Design criteria based upon the premise that intelligence and learning consist of creative interaction between the individual and his environment. 3. "A playground should be like a small scale replica of the world, with as many possible of the sensory experiences to be found in the world included in it."	1. Inspection or casual observation by designer.

Burnette	1. Acquisition of increased amounts of confident, competent, explorative behavior.
	2. Acquisition of a coherent cognitive world model.
	3. Assist the formation of strong social relationships between infant–peers and infant–adults.
		1. Infant learning landscape for day-care settings.
		2. Environment composed of elements representing five symbolic form classes:
		  a. Countryside–recreation.
		  b. Council–chamber–sacred place.
		  c. Work.
		  d. Highways.
		  e. Social settings; eating areas, meeting place.
		  f. Various other sensory inputs.
			1. None specified.

Cooper	1. Children's activities determined by age, background, and individual competencies (i.e., motor coordination, social behavior, etc.).	1. Adventure playground. 2. A bounded space, for privacy. 3. Space alloted to individual child. 4. Diverse materials and equipment. 5. Supervisor's office, hygienic facilities, storage, permanent shelter.	1. None specified.

Table 1

Author	Behavior To Be Facilitated or Supported.	Specified or Realized Physical Properties or Environment	Method of Verifying or Evaluating the Behavior–Environment Relationship
Ellis	1. Children's play defined as arousal-seeking behavior. 2. Facilitate acquisition of new responses, responses that increase in complexity through play. 3. Facilitate social groups. 4. "... as a byproduct (of play) children learn about their physical surroundings and about their own roles in a social group."	1. Experimental use of novel or complex play apparatus. 2. "... opportunities to deal with unknown elements in the environment." 3. "... stimulus complexity is an important parameter for preferences." 4. "The essential characteristic for a playground is that it should elicit new responses from the child as he plays ..." 5. "The items manipulated should by their interactions demonstrate relationships that exist in the real world."	1. Scientific methods: i.e., hypotheses tested through experimentation following rules of operational definition, generality, control observation, repeated observation, confirmation, consistency, and with reference to existing theory and findings.
Berlyne	1. *Extrinsically motivated exploratory behavior:* search for stimuli necessary to guide subsequent acts with biologically valuable consequences. 2. *Intrinsically motivated exploratory behavior:* search for stimuli that do not influence what an organism does next—stimuli sought for their own sake. 3. Other behaviors associated with exploratory activities: a. *Receptor adjusting responses* —changes in posture directing sense organs to stimulus source. b. *Locomotor exploration* — movement toward source of stimulation. c. *Investigatory responses* — seek to effect some change in environment through actions directed at objects, e.g., manipulation.	1. Stimulus novelty. a. How often similar (relevant) patterns have been experienced before. b. How recently similar patterns have been experienced. c. Other "collative" properties: *Change* or movement that occurs while stimulus acts on receptors: *surprisingness* and *incongruity*.	1. Scientific methods (see above).

Table 1

Author	Behavior To Be Facilitated or Supported	Specified or Realized Physical Properties or Environment	Method of Verifying or Evaluating the Behavior–Environment Relationship
Hutt	1. Exploratory and play behaviors of children. 2. *Specific exploration* a. Rewarding through arousal reduction. b. Extrinsically motivated, is stimulus-oriented. c. Essential for survival; a means of obtaining information about variation in the environment. d. Stereotyped responses with minimum variability. 3. *Investigatory responses* a. Synchrony of visual and tactile receptors. b. Intent facial expression. c. Stereotyped sequence of behavioral elements. d. Behaviors of long duration elicited by novel stimuli. 4. *Diversive exploration* a. Moderate arousal increments are rewarding. b. Serves no specific organismic function—is expenable. c. Is response-oriented; composed of activities that increase stimulation regardless of source—dependent upon capricious factors. d. Characterized by response variability. 5. *Play* a. Characterized by asynchrony of receptors (hands, eyes). b. Relaxed facial expression. c. Behavior elements are brief and variable or idiosyncratic in their sequence. d. Does not occur in the presence of novel stimuli. e. Requires a secure environment.	1. Experimental environments permitting control over number of children, time of exposure to stimuli, type of stimulus objects (commercial toys and specially designed novel objects), and controlled observation.	1. Scientific methods (see above).

requirements. In effect, the designers evaluate the success of the final product through inspection or casual observation.

2. "Adventure Playground"

To reconstruct a paradigm for Dattner's[13] design decision-making and evaluation process, one has to proceed through a theoretical formulation regarding the development of play (based on Piaget[14]), a set of design criteria derived from or assumed to be consistent with that theoretical formulation, and an evaluation of the facility through casual observations over time. Play behavior is then typified as ". . . the way in which children develop intelligence . . . [it is] . . . a child's way of learning." Therefore, design criteria for play environments must be rooted in the premise that the individual and the environment must be placed in interactive conditions which facilitate intelligence and learning. To accomplish this end, the playground should assume a form that replicates the "real world" at a small scale. However, once the condition of abundant experiential potential is actualized through physical forms, ". . . we must encourage the interaction of the child with them." Also, since it is not a desirable goal to generate environments that permit children complete freedom, physical design must exercise a certain degree of control over the range of behavioral possibilities. This is consistent with Dattner's assumption that "control of children's play is one way in which a society prepares the child to participate eventually in the world of adults."

Utilizing the adventure playground in New York City's Central Park as an example of a play facility derived from criteria such as those described above, Dattner proceeds to evaluate it through a comparison with an immediately adjacent "standard" playground and through other casual observations. It was noted that children did exhibit a preference (determined by some approximate count of children) for the adventure playground by a use rate of 12 to 1. The popularity of certain playground elements was also noted. It was re-marked that the children's use of various elements did not seem to follow any pattern, but where activities indicated preferred elements which were located too near each other (to the point that they might be defined as crowded), it was suggested that future planning might deal with such problems through better spatial arrangements.

Obviously, this design model has provided many novel children's play environments. Just as obviously a problem exists between that type of paradigm which may be used for intuitive problem solving and one which may be required for testable problem-solving solutions with generalizable findings.

In neither Friedberg's or Dattner's paradigm is there provision for making their methods accessible, even though they have published their rationale. Both authors invite others to learn from their process and products when in fact there is nothing to be learned per se, since the process is completely intuitive and the product evaluated by subjective (nongeneralizable) casual observation. However, neither designer should be judged too harshly, for behaviorally oriented designers often employ similarly untenable paradigms when confronted with designs for, evaluations of, or utilizations of theory concerning children's play.

3. Play in Experimental Settings

Ellis,[15] included in this volume, has reviewed some recent investigations by his associates regarding the relationship of novelty and complexity to play environments. Play is defined as (1) an arousal-seeking behavior that operates to reduce boredom in the child while (2) also assisting to reveal certain informational characteristics of both the physical and social environment. (However, the latter, learning effect is considered a by-product of play behavior.) Attached to the concern for facilitating play behavior is a parallel concern for increasing the complexity of possible activities in which children will participate. Within this conceptual framework, play is seen to have the capability of facilitating increases in the behavioral complexity of children. Put into rudimentary design criteria, these sequences of behavior should be capable of being supported by an environment that functions to elicit "new responses from the child as he plays." Also, there should be evidence of increases in the complexity of a child's behavioral repertoire in response to the play environment.

Considering conditions of environmental novelty (but with regard to some unspecified types of novelty), Ellis reports that there is diminution of children's play activity in response to unchanging material. In another condition, where (an undescribed) novel piece of apparatus first elicits (undescribed) cautious or avoidance types of behavior, it is eventually interacted with after a period of familiarization. This finding is generally consistent with the literature dealing with novelty and exploration.[16]

D. E. Berlyne,[17] a major formulator of theories regarding exploratory behavior, considers complexity to be the most "impalpable" concept that he attempts to define (when compared to the concepts of novelty, uncertainty, and conflict). Nevertheless, three definitions are advanced: complexity "increases with the number of distinguishable elements," "increases with dissimilarity between elements," and "varies inversely with the degree to which several elements are responded to as a unit." Complexity, like novelty, uncertainty, and/or conflict, must be considered capable of eliciting arousal increments under some conditions that have the potential to elicit distress or fear responses in children exposed to such stimuli. However, without any apparent theoretical trepidation some (undescribed) studies have been carried out by Ellis's associates exploring the "relative attractance of complex versus simple apparatus." Their justification for such a study is that it relates to (unreferenced) "research showing that stimulus complexity is an important parameter for preference

and . . . characterization of play as stimulus or arousal-seeking behavior." In a study related to the perception of complex patterns. Berlyne[18] has shown that "there was a significant tendency for more complex patterns to be rated *less pleasing* but more interesting," that "these are also the patterns that . . . are more arousing or disturbing," and that "patterns judged more pleasing tend to be the . . . [less complex] . . . ones to which subjects prefer to expose themselves when given a choice after adequate acquaintance with the alternatives . . . ." A further point to be made is that play may be a form of arousal-seeking behavior, but if in fact play does occur after exposure to a complex apparatus, it will occur *only* after a preliminary state of heightened arousal, which is diminished through extrinsically motivated specific exploratory behaviors. Whether "attractance" is in any way related to preference or exploratory behavior is debatable. If, however, by attractance it is meant that a child fixates, or observes, a complex object, attractance may be a function of the other collative properties (novelty and the like) of the object. If, on the other hand, preference by a child for a *previously habituated to* complex object is indicated by increasing behavior directed at the object, it may be more a function of what the child wants to do with the object than a function of what the object does to the child.

The Ellis paradigm, because of its experimental orientation, should be amenable to translation in terms typical of the scientific method. However, the primary problem encountered in Ellis's review is that it derives from theory and empirical findings (assumed to support theory), but fails to reference sources related to theory or to describe with clarity the nature of the experimental treatments employed. For example, what type of novelty typifies a particular apparatus, what type of complexity typifies another piece of equipment, assuming that these facilities were designed with those variables in mind. Also, and most importantly, if play behavior is defined as arousal seeking in children, how was arousal-seeking behavior instigated so that similarities between exploratory and play behavior could be distinguished or explained?

4. The Infant Learning Landscape

Although not concerned directly with children's play behavior, Burnette[19] provides an informative example of an attempt to derive physical environmental configurations that are assumed to be consistent with children's developmental capabilities as defined by Piaget's[20] cognitive development theories, Bruner's[21] concept of competency, and Lynch's[22] postulations regarding how internal representations of environment are developed. Two infant environments are detailed by Burnette. One is a crib-type environment for the very young infant. The other is an environment accessible to infants capable of rudimentary locomotion. It is the second environment which will be of concern in the discussion that follows.

The infant learning landscape is presented as a physical hypothesis that is meant to facilitate the achievement of several types of behavior goals in a public or privately supported child day-care setting. These goals are facilitation of increased amounts of confident or competent explorative behavior, facilitation of development of a coherent cognitive world model, and facilitation of "strong" social relationships between peers and between infant and adults. The physical hypotheses intended to implement these goals are organized into five "elemental" form classes; each class is symbolic of some aspect of the world in which the child will progressively develop and function. Thus, there are elements in the infant learning landscape representing "countryside and recreation," "council chamber or sacred place," "work or factory," "highway," and other

social environments such as an eating area and a place of meeting. Other functions are accommodated by changing stations, cribs in sleeping areas, and spaces designed to permit the interaction of a caregiver with three infants. Also, these areas are designed to permit study (the form of which is unspecified) of the hypothesized effects that the setting will have upon infants' developmental behavior.

Burnette's design paradigm is well stated in its initial stages of defining what classes of behavior are to be supported through physical form. It states that there are developmentally determined levels of infant–environment relationships that can be assumed to be capable of enhancement through the design or manipulation of physical environmental features (as well as through infant–infant and infant–adult interactions). The paradigm does not specify how information is to be gathered regarding the testing of hypotheses; consider, for example, the problem of pretesting infants to determine their developmental level and cognitive abilities, and their history, short as it may be, in terms of exploratory behaviors before any experimental exposures are permitted. Nor is there any indication of what measures will be made to determine how a child's responses may be attributed to contacts with specific elements of the designed environment. Also, how is the infant's increased development or cognitive ability to be measured after exposure to the learning environment? The problem with Burnette's paradigm, as with others discussed previously, is that there is ample theory to describe infant development, and ample hypotheses regarding how design or management might go about facilitating the development of children—as evidenced in scores of built playgrounds and day-care facilities—but there is little said regarding how child's play or learning behavior is to be defined (and/or measured) as having increased by some amount as a result of the hypothesized environment. A partial explanation, in this case, of why there is difficulty in realizing the level of evaluation required to produce worthwhile (generalizable) information may rest upon Burnette's assumption that the environment can be manipulated so as to *reinforce* the occurrence of particular behaviors.

In Burnette's design of the infant learning landscape it is assumed that specific physical or other experiential features of the environment may be configured and utilized for their deliberate reinforcing effects upon the mental development of the infant. This assumption requires an explication of why it is necessary to design special environments to serve reinforcing purposes, since it is quite conceivable that (say) a park, or new apartment, or motion picture might serve the same function for an infant. One reason presented by Burnette rests upon the evaluation of traditional child-rearing environments as being inadequate to the task of fulfilling the developmental requirements of the infant, since they may represent the expedient needs of the adult before those of the infant. However, this is still an inadequate explanation of why one environment reinforces cognitive development more, and another environment less—they are both adult determined. Also, the environment—the "real" world—as it stands in one particular moment is the real world of potential experience for both infant and adult, even though it may vary with regard to available information and possible action. To encompass that world of possibility into a fixed and highly minimized replica based upon what is man-made and what is natural is, first, a *reduction* of experiential possibilities and, second, a series of artificial and arbitrary decisions as to what exists. How one can follow this reduction of form types with guesses to the effect that one form will have reinforcing effects upon an infant's cognitive development to a greater extent than all other possibilities is difficult to comprehend.

What developmental theories have described, regardless of variations in points of view, is that the growth of the human organism can be partitioned into stages of physical and mental changes of structure and function that are highly dependent upon genetic endowment and experiential factors. But no theory has stated that the attainment of developmental stages is achieved at the same time for children of the same age or even accomplished in intraorganism systems in fixed time relationships. For the individual child at any given time there is great variability between it and other children and variability in its receptivity and reactivity to experience.[23] If the function of identifying the developmental stage of an infant is to attempt to bring it closer to some developmental norm (for whatever reason), then various types of reinforcement may be one such tool—remembering that reinforcement can only be utilized with any effect if the child has been well described and studied beforehand so that reactivities to reinforcement may be predicted.

Systematic reinforcement is dependent upon the identification of behaviors that are to be reinforced through particular schedules designed to increase the probability of their occurrence.[24] There is within this format a *fixed-ratio* reinforcement schedule (as with the reinforcement of, say, the tenth response) and a *variable-ratio* reinforcement schedule (where reinforcement is applied at a fifth response in one treatment, a seventh response in the next treatment, etc.). There are also reinforcement schedules based upon time: *fixed-interval* schedules, where reinforcement occurs at constant intervals (say, every two minutes) and *variable-interval* schedules. Combinations of both interval and ratio schedules are also used. Obviously, it is implicit in the reinforcement concept that certain reinforcers are rewarding and serve to facilitate the acquisition of behavior, whereas in other situations reward may be withheld to extinguish already learned behavior. It should be emphasized that in this type of treatment the reinforcing agent is extrinsic (i.e., coming from outside the organism).

Burnette has not evidenced a concern for specific types of reinforcement schedules to facilitate the acquisition of competent exploratory behavior, the achievement of cognitive schema, or social behavior. However, he has provided for activities that can be considered suitable for types of exploratory behavior—variations in color, sound, shape, objects, surfaces—to which an infant may respond with explorative forms of behavior. But what happens when an infant's range of exploratory behavior has been executed in response to the new environment? True, to the extent that a number of exploratory behavior repertoires come with the infant, they will be reinforced through their suitability within that environment. And, perhaps, additions to that repertoire may also occur. Thus, if exploratory behaviors have been adequately reinforced through physical or interactional devices, in part by organism necessity, what remains to be reinforced as determined by adult necessity—more of the same? In increasing complexity? Obviously the answer lies in the direction of intrinsic rewards for the infant achieved through intrinsically determined modes of behavior classed as either exploration or learning.

Bruner[25] has stated that the goal of directing a child so that it may best develop its cognitive abilities is not to be achieved through increases in exposures to extrinsic reward systems (as is the case with reinforcement schedules), for those systems tend to develop patterns of conformity and make the child highly dependent upon environmental contingencies. Instead, the problem is to free the child "from the immediate control of environmental rewards and punishments." Arriving at such a step, the child can then be "in a position to experience success and failure not as

reward and punishment, but as information." It is then such information that determines the degree to which a child can achieve competence or control over its own behavior. Bruner has argued that the infant learns because of intrinsic "intentions" or strategies—and does so with greater rapidity than behavior-shaping techniques permit. The role of reinforcement in this process is not that of eliciting new responses, but rather to increase the skill by which existing routines are performed. One direction that Bruner's studies may suggest for behavioral management (whether through behavioral or physical strategies) is to devise means by which behavior may be first monitored (for its emergence and the identification of component parts), and then to attempt its exercise within contexts that will reduce the need for extrinsic reinforcement. The design problem is then to find those elements that will facilitate the practice of existing skills in response to problem situations whose "solution" will produce gratification derived from coping with such problems. (Extrinsic reinforcement techniques are not disregarded, for they may play a more important role in dealing with behavioral disorders that may interfere with the attainment of individual development.[26])

Bruner[27] has also stated that "the unique terminus of human growth is that to survive, humans, like other animals, must take their places as members of the species. In the case of humans, this is quite a special order: to become members of linguistic and mythologically instructed communities, to join a common data base, to use a pool of technology, etc." It is possible that a statement of this sort *could* be interpreted as pointing to the need for establishing special learning systems that may accomplish those goals. Also, the earlier an individual can be exposed to systematic experiences designed to facilitate the acquisition of behavior appropriate to those goals, the higher the level of social functioning such an individual is assumed to exhibit at various developmental stages. It is suggested that Burnette's design paradigm derives somewhat from this type of direction in its attempt to provide symbolic equivalents for countryside and recreation, council chambers, sacred places, work places, factory, etc., as well as an assumed range of appropriate behaviors to be reinforced (i.e., cognitive schema based upon these categorizations). If this is so, then it is further suggested that Burnette has created an approach to infant learning that is counter to Bruner's complementary concern for the infant's achievement of individual competence by providing a gross segmentation of the world within a small symbolic frame of reference, which may very well offer too much of a simplified representation of cognitive mapping possibilities. To then seek to reinforce such a categorization may not necessarily have later social value. For example, a requirement for a hard-surfaced road in the infant learning landscape (symbolic of highways) may very well foster concepts of world organization that have already proved deleterious to society— efficient as such systems are for maintaining various types of social interaction. If it must be assumed that there will always be some form of "road" efficiently connecting environmental components, it is *not* required that the appropriate behavior be always, with equal efficiency, to follow it. Perhaps the function of design for children's environments, which could be derived from Bruner's studies, is to demonstrate that the longer route, or some other way to the same goal that is arrived at through competence-increasing behavior, has the greater potential for facilitating the development of individual potentialities.

5. The Adventure Playground Concept

The previous arguments have tended to emphasize the conceptual inadequacy prevalent in designing for children's play behavior, whether deriving from the efforts of architects or designer–behaviorists. Essentially, it would seem that it is impossible to design and evaluate environments for children's play because there is no adequate definition of that behavior that in scientific or design terms permits the reliable observation of play. These are definition and/or operational problems regarding exploratory and play behavior, which are reviewed in detail by Welker[28] and will be discussed shortly. However, one further example of an attempt to design settings for use by children is required to establish the polarity of design intervention possibilities— in fact to establish what may be defined as the role of minimal design intervention or manipulation. This is the adventure-playground concept as reviewed by Cooper[29] (included in this volume) and should not be confused with Dattner's use of the same term.

In contrast to efforts to design fixed environments for children's activities, the adventure-playground concept permits children access to a defined area where various materials are made available for their use in construction, manipulation, or any self-directed activity. The constraints imposed are a staff member who is present to provide some supervision regarding the use of materials, primarily to offset any potential hazards. The children who participate in this environment do so at their own pace, at their own level and/or need for social or cooperative interaction, and most importantly, enter and manipulate the environment at their own level of general behavioral competence. Competence-increasing behavior may be achieved, again at a pace determined by the child, through self-selection of different materials, tools, projects, and amounts of social participation. Although no immediate demands are built into such a program regarding the facilitation of learning or various social behaviors, such behavioral increments are of concern and most likely do occur. (Cooper does argue that such environments can offset children's experiences of stimulus-poor environments, particularly in urban settings.) It is interesting to note that Dattner, Friedberg and Berkeley, Ellis, and Burnette all express a concern that their designed environments represent the "real" world, whether in symbolic or actual form. The adventure-playground concept would seem to solve that problem through lack of design: the "real" world is not fabricated as a *fait accompli* (". . . a place overflowing with things to see, touch, smell, hear, and taste . . ."[30]) and then populated by children (as response systems); instead, it is constructed in miniature by the children themselves—which would seem to be experientially loaded with greater sources of internal and external reality.

The paradigm for an adventure playground requires that (1) children's activities be determined by their age, background, and individual behavioral competencies with various materials, equipment, and social relations, and (2) the facility be (preferably) a neighborhood space, bounded for the sake of privacy and control, with equipment storage space, a supervisor's office, adequate hygienic facilities, and (at a maximum) a sheltered area for poor-weather activities. The behavior–environment interaction is controlled by the allocation of a space to a child, the availability of material and equipment, and some ratio of number of children to space and available materials. At this time no studies or proposed methods of study seem available to verify the efficacy of such an environment for, say, increasing a child's motor or social competencies, or to determine if such an environment facilitates particular children's activities better than does a more conventional playground. Although the adventure playground concept may be antithetical to conventional design of playgrounds by permitting children the freedom of environmental manipulation, it is more particularly the antithesis of adult concepts of environmental order and control (as expressed in insurance restrictions, fear of sur-

rounding property devaluation, and comments regarding the apparent disarray of such sites[31]).

The Play–Learning Dichotomy

Berlyne[32] defines two major forms of exploratory behavior that appear to be part of the behavioral repertoire of most animal species including man. These are extrinsically motivated specific exploration, which allows an organism to deal with changes in its environment that are potentially critical to its survival, and intrinsically motivated diversive exploration, which is a search for stimuli without apparent necessity for organism survival. Behaviors associated with both these systems of exploration fall into three major classes: (1) receptor-adjusting responses, which permit the organism to achieve the most efficient orientation to the source of stimulation, (2) locomotor exploration, which permits the organism to select the best vantage points for further contact with the stimulus source, and (3) investigatory responses, which are concerned with attempts by the organism to extract further information from a stimulus through manipulative behavior.

Stimuli that elicit exploratory behavior are defined by Berlyne as novelty and complexity. However, before definitions are presented it must be kept in mind that no organism is without some degree of sensory experience, which by its nature orders sensory input so that some internal representation (or "schema") is retained. Thus an organism responds to new input with respect to whether or not that input fits its internal representation of past experience (see Kagan[33] regarding the emergence of this phenomenon in infants). How similar or dissimilar the input, or how recently similar input was experienced, define the degree of novelty inherent in the stimulus situation. Novelty *is not* a stimulus characteristic per se; it is ". . . a transactional concept that relates a current stimulus to previous experience with either that stimulus or with one similar to it."[34]

Another critical variable in eliciting specific exploratory behavior is the condition under which stimulus material is being perceived; for example, is the condition unfavorable, or is there confusing symbolic material that must be dealt with? Also, conditions of novelty may not be capable of fitting well within an organism's existing schema. All these conditions will elicit a state termed "uncertainty" or "conflict," which will then determine whether or not an organism will explore the stimulus material or withdraw from the source of stimulation. If the organism withdraws from the condition of uncertainty or conflict, it may be concluded that the condition is aversive (distressing, anxiety or fear producing), and defensive response systems have become effective to reduce discomfort. If the organism deals with the uncertainty or conflict, it is because a state of *curiosity* has been elicited, which then determines a sequence of specific exploratory behaviors whose function is to provide adequate information for the construction of schema.

The function of both the defense and exploratory response systems is to reduce the level of organism arousal caused by external stimulus conditions. Also, in both cases the reduction of arousal (which is rewarding,[35]) is dependent upon the exposure time required by the organism to form a representation of the stimulus event. The use of such a representation in future encounters with the same or similar stimulus material permits the organism to modify or direct its behavior appropriately—in effect to learn—to respond in a particular way to aversive stimuli (through withdrawal behavior), to already known stimuli (with disregard or appropriate behavior), or to novel stimulus conditions (with exploratory behaviors of possibly increasing efficiency).

Stimulus complexity is defined by Berlyne[36] as (1) the amount of variety or diversity in a stimulus pattern, (2) increasing with the number of elements in that pattern and with the degree of dissimilarity among elements, and (3) varying by the extent to which elements may be responded to as a group or class. An organism responds to complex stimuli with the same repertoire of behavior types that it uses for novel stimulus conditions: receptor-adjusting behavior, possible locomotor exploration, investigatory responses, and if the complexity of the stimuli is too great, with defense responses. Again the function of these behavior systems is the reduction of organism arousal through sufficient exposure to facilitate habituation and/or learning.

Experiments concerned with establishing the role of specific and diversive exploration in the behavior of children have been carried out by Hutt over the past decade.[37] These studies have controlled the environment which children explore (specially designed rooms), the objects children manipulate (standard commercial toys and specially designed objects), the exposure time permitted, and the number of children participating. Observations were carried out through use of behavior checklists, by motion picture for later checklist reduction, and in one experiment by electroencephalographic equipment.[38]

Hutt's studies tend to support Berlyne's general statements regarding exploratory behavior. For example, specific exploration is considered directional and concerned with the acquisition of information regarding environmental change. If the goal of exploration is to reveal the properties of an event, the process of habituation and/or learning should result in decay of explorative behavior over time, and this has been demonstrated for single children in a novel environment. However, another important feature of children's specific exploration is that they will not readily explore a new environment on their own. The presence of an adult or other children is required to facilitate the onset of exploration. This has been demonstrated by high amounts of child–observer interaction concurrent with low amounts of child exploratory behavior during early experimental sessions involving children's exploration of a novel room. Specific exploratory behavior is also typified by Hutt[39] as composed of stereotyped responses by children with minimum variability.

The response to novel stimulus conditions and complex stimuli is highly dependent upon the intensity of the stimuli. For the most part, novel stimulus conditions that are of intermediate intensity are those which will elicit the conditions of uncertainty, conflict, and curiosity, and then exploratory behaviors. (Stimuli of high intensity will elicit defensive responses; stimuli of low intensity will elicit brief exploratory behavior, or possibly disregard.) The investigative response component of specific exploratory behavior serves as a means of increasing the amount of information about a stimulus object or event through manipulative behavior directed at the stimulus source. Hutt indicates that behavioral events associated with investigation in children are composed of (1) stereotyped sequences of behavioral elements, (2) synchrony of visual and tactile systems, (3) intent facial expressions, and (4) generally long behavioral involvement with novel stimuli (objects). Both the synchrony of hands and eyes and the intent facial expressions can be considered as strong indicators of information acquisition and learning.

In sharp contrast to statements that describe children's play as research or exploration,[40] or as "the way in which children develop intelligence,"[41] Hutt[42] observes that "while investigative exploration demonstrably results in the acquisition of information, in play such learning is largely incidental," and, furthermore, that "by being repetitive play is by definition a highly redundant activity, and can actually prevent learning." Further reasons why learning and play may be considered dichotomous within the con-

fines of explanation based upon explorative behavior are to be found in the explanation of diversive exploratory behaviors.

Diversive exploration has been described as arousal-seeking behavior, which may take the form of entertainment, actions that will relieve boredom, or a search for new experiences—providing that the stimuli contain some *correct* proportion of properties (incongruity, surprise, novelty, etc.) determined by an organism's tolerance or preference for levels of stimulation.[43] According to Hutt,[44] actions that may be taken to relieve boredom, or that are executed for their own sake, or that tend to increase stimulation without regard to their source (e.g., gesturing or locomotor behavior)—actions dependent upon capricious factors—generally occur during those times when an organism is not concerned with activities higher on the motivational hierarchy (e.g., alleviation of hunger, reduction of intermediate arousal through exploration, or reduction of high states of arousal, such as fear).

Whereas behaviors such as synchrony of eyes and hands and intent facial expressions are characteristic of investigative exploration in children, in play there is an observable lack of synchrony between visual and tactile systems, relaxed facial expressions, and variable and idiosyncratic sequences of behavior of short duration.[45] Furthermore, when specific and investigative exploration was observed to occur upon contact with a novel stimulus condition (environment or object), diversive exploration and play *did not* occur in the presence of novel stimuli or in an environment that was not known.[46] A picture of the relationship between investigation and play in response to a novel object is provided by Hutt.[47] During the first sessions of children's exposure to the novel object, the ratio of time spent in investigative activities to time spent in play behavior was approximately 7 to 1 and was maintained for the successive two sessions. However, during the fourth session the ratio became 7 to 3, during session five 7 to 8, and finally during the sixth and last session 6 to 9. The critical point to be made from these observations is that exploration for the sake of gaining information—or learning—precedes the possible occurrence of play and is a behavior set distinct from play as typified by its ordered (stereotyped) and synchronized behavioral elements. On the other hand, the behavior set typical of play may be composed of similar behavioral elements, but in a fragmented, incomplete, abortive, or disjunctive sequence.[48]

The adaptive value of play, its ability to contribute to survival of the organism, is a question that cannot be readily answered and will probably remain so until more definitive experimentation is undertaken. As Hutt[49] has demonstrated, there are questions regarding whether play can be considered instrumental to learning. Bruner[50] has also commented upon the incompatibility of play behaviors with the direct utilization of tools or skills. Piaget[51] similarly has stated that within practice play there is no new learning; after the acquisition of some new behavior pattern, all new objects a child may encounter are bent to fit that pattern regardless of suitability. However, it is at the point at which Piaget's observation and theory regarding cognitive development make their greatest contribution, to the comprehension of symbolic behavior, that these processes become least observable—at least at a scale where designers of children's environments could use observations of behavior to validate or test physical hypotheses. Hutt's work on exploratory and play behavior has selectively attempted to avoid an involvement with symbolic play, possibly for similar reasons. (This issue will be discussed later in the context of observing children's activities.)

The adaptive value of specific exploratory behavior is that it permits an organism to deal with environmental events that are different from its own representations through learning more about what is occurring or what responses (from its repertoire) are most appropriate to deal with that event. It is important, however, that the concept of environmental novelty not be oversimplified, since generalizable information exchange is threatened if labels are applied to behavior sets that are inconsistent with the theory and empirical findings from which such terminologies have arisen. For example, specification of environmental novelty (of importance to designers and behaviorists alike) must account for at least two facets of novelty: the past experience of the organism and the context wherein the novel event is occurring. A review of experimental works concerned with experiential variables, such as "absolute novelty" (properties of a stimulus never experienced by an organism previously), "relative novelty" (familiar stimulus elements in a combination or pattern new to the organism), "long-term novelty" (stimulus not encountered for some time), "short-term novelty" (stimulus not encountered for a period of minutes or hours), has been presented by Cantor,[52] and many of the operational problems encountered by experimenters at that time are still germane. Extending Hutt's[53] contextural recommendation that novelty be used more specifically with regard to whether or not an object is referred to or an aggregate of events in relation to an organism, a number of criteria of possibly novel interactions are offered: (1) *organism–self* interactions or events, (2) *organism–organism* interactions or events, for example, between younger child, peer, older child, or adult, (3) *organism–group* interactions or events, (4) *organism–object* interactions or events, (5) *organism–environment* (as an aggregate of natural or man-made objects or events) interactions, (6) *organism–other organism* (of a different species) interactions or events, (7) *organism–symbol* interactions or events (as with language or pictorial symbols), and (8) other combinations of these contexts as are required to define more complex interactions and phenomena.

The ability to describe phenomena and to present theory to explain such phenomena in terms that have relevance for psychophysiological systems is what makes Berlyne's and Hutt's contributions to exploratory behavior theory of great value. This is not to say, however, that the theory and description of exploratory behavior is by any means complete or resolved, especially where infants and children are concerned. For a more thorough view of these issues, the reader is referred to Cantor's review[54] of experimental work dealing with children's responses to complex and novel stimuli; Hutt's review of specific and diversive exploration in children; the work of Cox and Campbell[55] dealing with infant explorative behavior; Collard's work[56] dealing with variables such as birth order, exposure to adults, and their relationship to children's exploration; and the work of Thomas and Chess,[57] dealing with variables such as infant individuality or "reactivity" and resultant behavior–environment interactions.

OBSERVING WHAT IS MOST OBSERVABLE

Comments by Friedberg and Berkeley[58] that research applicable to evaluating the design of children's play environments is "rare" is grossly misleading. For example, in a recent compilation[59] of works on children's play twenty-three articles were presented, incorporating in total over 1,000 references to other works of significance. Even granting redundancy in citations, one must accept that the number of works potentially applicable to either specification or evaluation of environments for children's play is far from rare. What may be more realistically argued, as the foregoing has attempted, is that specifications for physical play facilities which derive from complex behavioral theory are not necessarily criteria that are amenable to operation and verification in design paradigms. In effect, it is pointless to build for behaviors that cannot be observed with confidence, but not pointless to build for what is observable and potentially relatable to behavioral theory. This position more specifically proposes that *unless* there is a willingness to construct workable design paradigms (1) hypotheses regarding the facilitation of learning (which cannot be specified) by specific playground designs should be considered spurious, (2) hypotheses regarding play as a facilitator of learning must be used with extreme caution, and (3) hypotheses regarding the facilitation of exploratory behavior by novel physical apparatus or configurations should be subject to qualifications regarding the type of exploratory behavior, the length of time these facilities are expected to function, and the anticipated rate of use by different children. In other words, to arrive at any assumption regarding the behavior–environment interaction of children, it may be more appropriate for designers (with a generalizable paradigm) to ask simpler, more useful questions regarding *activities,* which can be observed within the context of their designed facility. This statement should in no way be construed as limiting the freedom to develop any environmental configuration; the only limitation sought is that for each configuration "estimates" should be made regarding the kind of *activity* children are expected to engage in, and that these *activities* be operationally defined so as to be observable and generalizable. For example, to ask if a particular form was designed to facilitate (some amount of) group behavior, and if it does so by (some amount of) observed group behavior, is the simpler question to ask and the simpler piece of data to collect (e.g., by time-lapse photography) than, say, equivalent questions and data for validation of the occurrence of "fantasy play" or "make-believe play." If, in this example, the children were a constant population for some fixed period of time, further questions could be asked about the relationship of group activity to exploratory behavior by re-ordering the data on a day-to-day basis with a view to determining whether a decrease in activity occurs over time (as the theory of exploratory behavior predicts).

The proposal to specify and evaluate environments for children's activities in terms of *activity* measures is indirectly suggested in the work of McGrew,[60] which is concerned with developing a taxonomy of motor behavior patterns to describe the activity of four-year-old preschool children. For that taxonomy, 111 distinct items were developed concerning five classes of movement (visual fixation, posture, locomotion, manipulation, and gestures). From the data presented by McGrew, one may rank order these as to frequency of occurrence as follows: ranking first in total number of observations were actions defined as manipulative. Ranking second was walking, third were actions concerned with picking up the arms, fourth were actions concerned with placing objects, and fifth were actions concerned with turning (i.e., rotation of the trunk beginning with the face). These observations, it should be noted, represent 46 percent of all activity observed. Continuing in descending order were actions defined as standing up, running, bending, pouring, and scooping, which represented an additional 12 percent of all observations. Thus ten activity types represent 58 percent of all motor behavior observed. With the addition of fifteen more activity categories (e.g., stepping up or down, reaching, sitting down, pulling, climbing, and specialized manipulation), twenty-five types of motor behavior were observed to account for 77 percent of all children's motor activity.

If more data were available regarding the context wherein these motor behaviors occurred (this was not the intent of McGrew's study), it would be possible to observe similarities or differences in motor patterns for groups (i.e., all boys, all girls, or mixed) or for isolated children. It could be anticipated that the motor activity would exhibit sex-specific differences as to rate of occurrence, type of activity, or perhaps as to "style" of exploration. If these behaviors were observed to occur within the context of some novel environment (or pieces of equipment), they would serve as an important index of behavior–environment interaction, which might serve as a validation of design or as a generalizable description of events for future study (can the data fit, or be explained by some theory of learning or exploration).

A small example of how operationalization of children's activities may be used to describe (and eventually evaluate) their interaction with a "designed" play environment can be taken from a study by the author (in progress).[61] During the summer of 1972, twenty-three children in a preschool program (with a mean age of five years) had access during "free play" to an outdoor space 60 by 65 feet with grass, concrete surface, and a large sand area where four specially designed pieces of equipment ("forms") were installed. The "free play" periods lasted for one hour per day and continued for ten consecutive days, at which point the forms were replaced by another set. This process was repeated three times and permitted observation of children's interactions with twelve different forms. Data were collected from an observation point overlooking the outdoor space by fixed-interval 35mm color-slide photographs (taken every two minutes) and fixed-interval videotape recordings (two minutes of tape on a form, thirty-second interval, two minutes on another form, in rotation).[62] The slide data from this study are of interest to this discussion, since they are equivalent to the use of time-lapse photography as an unmanned observation device for, say, a public playground, and also confronts the issue of operationalizing children's behavior as "play" or "activity" for designer evaluational paradigms.

Consistent with previous statements regarding the definition of play behavior (i.e., the relatively nonsymbolic forms), it would seem to be extremely difficult to describe, from still photographs, behavior that is fragmented, incomplete, abortive,and/or disjunctive in sequential character,[63] or behavior involving asynchrony of eyes and hands, relaxed facial expression, or elements that are brief, variable, or idiosyncratic in their sequence.[64] However, what is observable from the slides are indicants of where children are (location), how many children are isolated or in some group (social behavior), type of motor activity (designated "high" or "low" motor activity), and what objects the children have freely brought to the environment (a potential indicant of investigatory activity). More specifically, "location" was designated by "form" (including a 16 by 16 foot area around each form defined by a painted line), or "grass" (an L-shaped area approximately 39 percent of the total site), or "other" (a concrete surface outside the painted boundaries around the forms (approximately 34 percent of the total site). The group behavior of the children was defined as either "isolate" (boy or girl), "groups of two to four children," or "groups of five or more children." A "group" was taken to be a cluster of children at least three feet from each other (regardless of postural orientation), and was further classified as boys, girls, or mixed. "Motor activity" was defined as "high motor" (consisting of walking, climbing, jumping, or active use of some object) or "low motor" (sitting, kneeling, laying, standing). "Object use" included any piece of equipment the children freely chose to bring into the outdoor area from within the preschool. These were categorized as "large toys" (push toys, wagons,

furniture), "containers–tools" (pails, plastic bottles, shovel, utensils), "costume–dolls," and "other" (small toys, books, or unidentifiable objects).

There are a number of interesting trends in the data under analysis at this time. These must be considered as very preliminary findings, but they do demonstrate some important issues regarding the definition of children's activity in response to novel environments.

The children's behavior in response to the four experimental forms indicated high amounts of group activity (that could be directly tied to the children's mean age of five years). A major portion of this group activity (495 observations) consisted of children in mixed groups (68 percent); boy groups accounted for 17 percent of all observations and girl groups accounted for the remaining 14 percent. In addition it was found that in 55 percent of all observations of self-selected object use, at least one object was associated with a group. These objects, it may be recalled, consisted of push toys, containers, costume, etc. Whether or not the co-occurrence of object use and group formation could be specifically described as "house-play" or "make-believe" may not be as significant as the implications of those events to investigatory activities in general. That is, children through contact with the objects engage in the manipulation of diverse stimulus material (the object itself, the object and aspects of the designed environment, the object and other children) to increase information. The importance of investigatory activities occurring as a possible function of peer-group activity is a factor generally unmentioned in studies more concerned with the behavior of a single child.

A further look at the separate observation of self-selected object use tends to bear out the importance of these interactions. Out of a total 563 observations of object use of all types (where one or more objects may have been

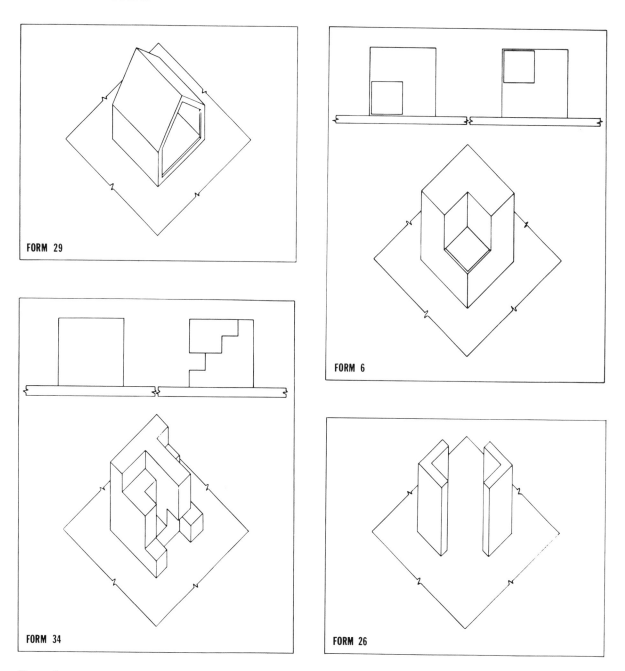

FORM 29

FORM 6

FORM 34

FORM 26

Figure 1

counted per observation), 60 percent were in the context of a group and 40 percent with an isolate child. The trend for greatest object use was found in mixed groups (45 percent); isolate girls were found to be associated with an object in 22 percent of these observations, and isolate boys accounted for 18 percent.

It is premature to generalize at this time, but still worth speculating that the self-selected use of objects by "children" can provide some indication of the plasticity of an environmental design for children's activities. If an environment were "complete," there would be no reason for anything else to be added to it other than children (and the range of behavior–environment interactions could be predicted). However, since such a condition is unrealistic (although well-planned environments may seek to achieve such a completeness of material and equipment), some degree of unpredictable environmental change must be anticipated as the result of children's manipulative behavior through object use. To foster such possibilities (if one is concerned with the facilitation of learning) may require that the fixed physical facility be somewhat "impoverished" so as to permit more varied manipulations through object use. This would be in alignment with Bruner's[65] concept of competency-increasing behavior, since the children's skills, in relation to object use, would become the source of environmental change.

Of the four pieces of equipment (see Figure 1) used in the third and last experimental set, form 29 is likely the *least* novel to children's experience since it is shaped as a simple house with sloping roof (4 by 4 feet at the base and 4 feet to the apex of the roof, with the front surface completely open). Compared to forms 6, 34, and 26, it received the greatest record of observed motor activity, object use, and group formation. Of interest is the fact that whereas all activities on the other forms tended to be highest during the

first three days of exposure and then decreased over the remaining seven days [see Figure 2(b)–(d)], the house form activity rate was similarly high during the first three days, increased during the next four days, and then decreased[66] [see Figure 2(a)]. Explanation of these changes in activity rate can be sought in the context of exploratory behavior theory, which states that in response to novel stimulus conditions an organism will seek to diminish the arousal caused by such an encounter through behaviors which will increase information input and so facilitate habituation.[67] However, as habituation increases, the amounts of organism activity in response to the novel stimulus condition are expected to decay over time.[68] This may adequately explain the decrement in children's activity for the three other forms, but not the increase of activity associated with the house form.[69]

Earlier in this discussion novelty was considered a variable dependent upon an organism's previous experience with classes of stimuli similar to the stimulus event being experienced.[70] Children's encounters with forms 6, 34, and 26 may represent a condition of absolute novelty (properties of stimuli never experienced previously by the children), or a condition of relative novelty (familiar stimulus elements in a pattern new to the children). If the condition were one of absolute novelty, one might expect that children's initial behaviors would be tentative, then increasing in frequency, and then diminishing. However, the data suggest that forms 6, 34, and 26 might have presented a condition of relative novelty to the children (with respect to shape or appearance), since they were responded to with behaviors of decreasing frequency. Looked at another way, on a day-to-day basis the decrease of initial activity could be attributed to a process whereby relatively novel forms (6, 34, 26) become phenomena considered by the children—*through increasing exposure*—as conditions of decreasing short-term novelty (stimuli somewhat habituated to, but not encountered for a short period of time).

The house form (29), on the other hand, described as somewhat minimal in terms of the relative novelty of its appearance, had associated activity increase over time which suggests that the condition of relative novelty may have shifted contexts from physical characteristics to child–child contexts or child–group contexts,[71] until whatever repertoire of behavior the children brought to these contexts began to wane (particularly during the last three days; see Figure 3 for a schematic representation of activity trends in response to novel stimuli).

Although the ten-day exposure to the experimental forms may not represent an adequate study length to determine the capability of specific forms to support children's activities over more extended periods of time, it does seem to

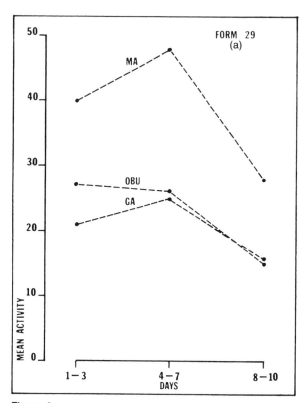
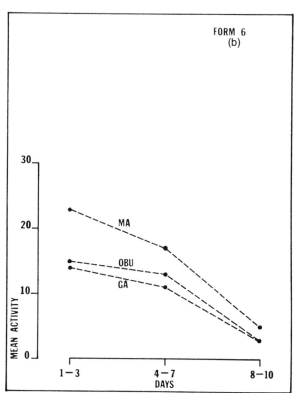

Figure 2

(a) Mean activity associated with Form 29 during ten-day experimental period (MA = motor activity, OBU = object use, GA = group activity). (b) Mean activity associated with Form 6 during ten-day experimental period (MA = motor activity, OBU = object use, GA = group activity).

suggest what may be a designer's dilemma: novel forms will elicit decreasing amounts of children's behavior as habituation increases. Whatever behavior occurs after habituation need not be considered a result of physical design as a motivator, but of children's ability to initiate their own activities. In other words, the designed environment must become boring so that stimulus-seeking behaviors (intrinsically motivated exploratory behaviors) begin to appear with greater frequency. However, with a constant group of children it would not be expected that the activity rate increase greatly, but rather that it level off. The possible success of some public playgrounds, in terms of this argument, may often be the results of (1) constantly changing children who respond to the facility as a novel condition (see Dattner's statements describing how non-neighborhood children are bused by schools or taken by parents to his adventure playground[72])

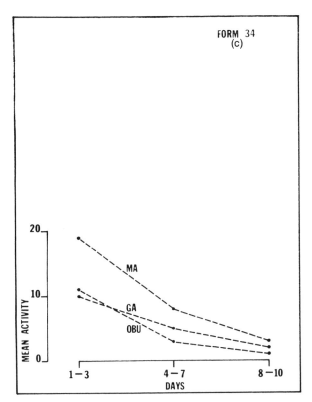

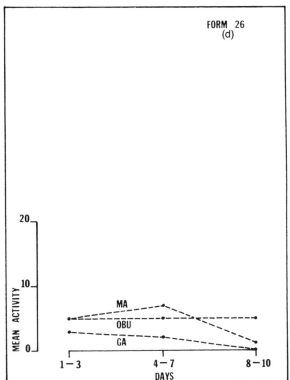

(c) Mean activity associated with Form 34 during ten-day experimental period (MA = motor activity, OBU = object use, GA = group activity). (d) Mean activity associated with Form 26 during ten-day experimental period (MA = motor activity, OBU = object use, GA = group activity).

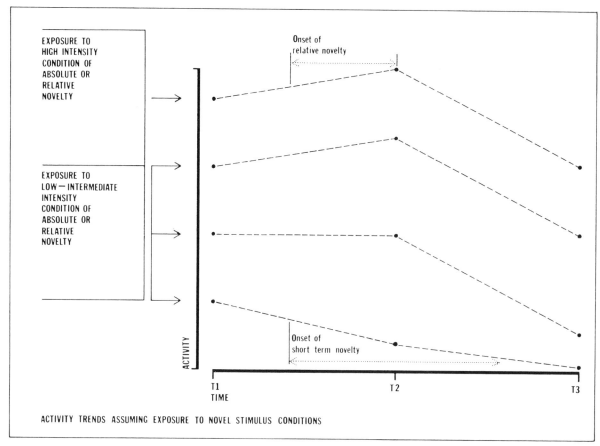

EXPOSURE TO HIGH INTENSITY CONDITION OF ABSOLUTE OR RELATIVE NOVELTY

EXPOSURE TO LOW — INTERMEDIATE INTENSITY CONDITION OF ABSOLUTE OR RELATIVE NOVELTY

Onset of relative novelty

Onset of short term novelty

ACTIVITY

T1
TIME

T2

T3

ACTIVITY TRENDS ASSUMING EXPOSURE TO NOVEL STIMULUS CONDITIONS

Figure 3

or (2) other children already habituated to a physical facility responding to the novel condition of other new children.

The fine points of children's response to novel environmental form may seem to be an esoteric concern for those interested in more practical and immediate problems of design or evaluation. To a great extent even the "design" of children's play environments executed by architects is similarly esoteric, for according to a recent study by Pyatok et al.[73] of 120 day-care facilities sampled in a survey throughout Pennsylvania, 90 percent had adapted to, or were located within, structures that were not designed for such use. Another point made by the Pyatok survey was that many of the decisions regarding the relationship of programs to physical space were generally made by day-care staff without the help of designer-experts. The evaluation of behavior–environment interactions within the context of those day-care facilities would most likely be the last capability expected of staff. However, it is suggested that the use of activity measures of children's behavior in response to physical form (e.g., specially ordered equipment and arrangements of equipment within a room or outdoor site) does

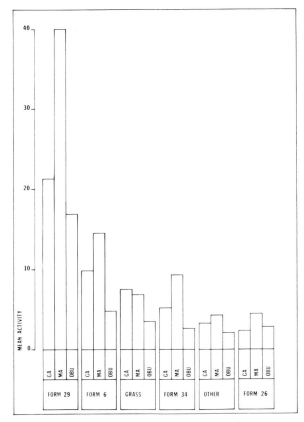

Figure 4
Children's activities throughout experimental environment during ten days (MA = motor activity, OBU = object use, GA = group activity).

make simple observation and evaluation accessible to those interested in knowing more about what behaviors typify responses to their best intended environmental decisions. For example, even a use profile, based upon frequency of observed occurrences of social, motor, or object-use activities, has the value of making known what is occurring and at what rate (see Figure 4). The value of further detailing and partitioning observations into time segments is that it permits the description of behavioral changes as a result of habituation. For a fixed population of children responding to a fixed number of environmental features, strategies for the inclusion of new objects or events could then be planned to counter excessive habituation in the form of boredom, or to sustain some activity rate consistent with the goals of the designers of the environment program through interventions that enhance or reestablish novel conditions (see Figure 5). Planning *without* evaluation based on observation can have "interesting" effects, but planning because of evaluation can be a powerful instrument to foster children's development.

CONCLUSION

The work of Friedberg, Dattner, and Ellis in their concern for designing environments for children's play, and Burnette's concern for designing infant learning environments, are representative approaches that demonstrate the difficulties encountered in attempting to link physical design with behavioral theory. A major issue which emerges from these efforts is that our competencies for physical manipulation of the environment far outstrip our competencies for either evaluating the built environment or integrating behavioral theory into design paradigms. This is not a weakness unique to designers, but rather a problem that derives from utilization of theory and operational definitions of children's behavior that vary with the disposition of designers and researchers alike. For example, both Piaget[74] and Berlyne[75] have made major theoretical contributions applicable to the study of play. However, Piaget-based studies have focused on developmental and cognitive issues that are exceptionally difficult to translate into measures of children's play occurring within a public playground (e.g., observed through time-lapse photography, an observational tool that could make design evaluation feasible); and Berlyne-based studies have dealt with varieties of human explorative behavior that are primarily visual (two-dimensional stimulus patterns) and occur in highly controlled settings.

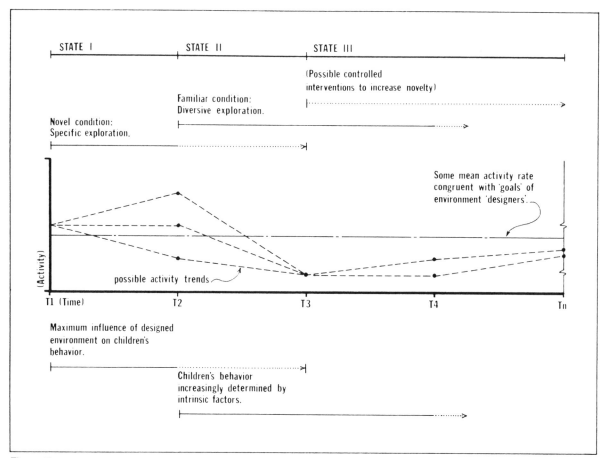

Figure 5
Children's activity trends elicited by an idealized "play" environment that is programmed to be responsive to the effects of novelty on children's behavior.

Hutt has been one of the few researchers to demonstrate the various behaviors that are associated with children's play behavior, but it would be difficult to extrapolate her methods to evaluation of large-scale play environments. Play behavior has also been associated with creative behavior, and studies of child's play that elicit unusual uses of objects or the production of statistically infrequent responses are typical of this approach.[76] But again, such investigations are not easily applicable to the evaluation of behavior–environment interactions at a large scale. Further complications arise when children's play is seen as a set of phenomena accessible to control and manipulation for the purpose of advancing the child toward more adult modes of behavior. Operating under such a mandate, designers (as adults, educators, architects) configure environments and programs consistent with the achievement of "appropriate" behavioral prototypes. The behavior-set "play" thus becomes subservient to the goals of social games, standard manipulation of objects or tools, constructive use of equipment, etc.

Reduction of the confounding issues that seem to follow the search for defining and supporting *play* behavior is no simple matter. However, it does seem possible to achieve some *clarity of purpose* if steps are taken to separate the goal of defining and explaining play from that of creating environments for children's *activities*. It is therefore suggested that, when children's behavior is to be described with reference to their free-choice access to the built or natural environment, such behavior be generically labeled "free activities," "free-choice activities," or just "activities," and then partitioned into subsets such as motor, social, exploratory, and/or investigative activities, according to the needs of evaluation. Further subdivision of those activity types would, of course, be dependent upon the methods of observation (i.e., on-site observers, film, or videotape) and scope of the evaluation (evaluation of total facility or specific segments). If activity definitions were selected (as opposed to the less observable and generalizable "creative play" or "fantasy play") in the specification of a facility, there would be few children's free-activity settings that could not be evaluated with inexpensive and easily used observation tools and some mathematics at the level of addition and division. The term *play* should be used only to describe behavior with reference to new or existing *theory* and that it be used to represent attempts at operationalizing aspects of those theories. This rather simple format permits designers of children's environments to design for behaviors they can measure and evaluate, regardless of the degree of environmental novelty or complexity that they wish to hypothesize as appropriate to the support of children's activities. However, if *play* behavior has the value that all our collective concern and efforts would seem to indicate, it must first reach adequate definition so that it may achieve levels of generalizability, and then relatedness to other behaviors. Only at such a point can programming, planning, and design be carried out to foster children's play. Until that time, however, activity measures may provide a useful evaluative format for design paradigms concerned with facilitating children's motor, social, and explorative behaviors.

NOTES AND REFERENCES

1. R. Dattner, *Design for Play,* New York: Van Nostrand Reinhold Co., 1969; P. Friedberg and E. P. Berkeley, *Play and Interplay,* New York: Macmillan Publishing Co., Inc., 1970; A. Lederman and A. Trachsel, *Creative Playgrounds and Recreation Centers,* New York: Praeger Publishers, Inc., 1968.
2. C. H. Burnette, "Designing to Reinforce the Mental Image, an Infant Learning Environment," in *Proceedings of the Environmental Design Research Association,* J. Archea and C. Eastman (eds.), 1972; M. Ellis, "Play: Theory and Research," in *Proceedings of the Environmental Design Research Association,* J. Archea and C. Eastman (eds.), 1972.
3. For example, C. Hutt, "Specific and Diversive Exploration," in *Advances in Child Development and Behavior, Vol. 5,* H. W. Reese and L. P. Lipsitt (eds.), New York: Academic Press, Inc., 1970; S. J. Hutt and C. Hutt, *Direct Observation and Measurement of Behavior,* Springfield, Ill.: Charles C Thomas, 1970.
4. R. L. Bishop, "Measurement of Children's Preference for the Play Environment," in *Proceedings of the Environmental Design Research Association,* J. Archea and C. Eastman (eds.), 1972.
5. See Dattner, *op. cit.,* and Ellis, *op. cit.*
6. R. G. Studer, "Human Systems Design and the Management of Change," paper prepared for the Second International Conference on the Problems of Modernization in Asia and the Pacific, University of Hawaii, 1970.
7. J. B. Calhoun, "Promotion of man," paper presented to the symposium on Global Systems Dynamics, University of Virginia, Charlottesville, Va., 1969.
8. *Op. cit.*
9. *Op. cit.*
10. T. S. Kuhn, *The Structure of Scientific Revolutions,* Chicago: University of Chicago Press, 1970.
11. *Op. cit.*
12. *Op. cit.*
13. *Op. cit.*
14. J. Piaget, *Play, Dreams and Imitation in Childhood,* New York: W. W. Norton & Company, Inc., 1962.
15. *Op. cit.*

16. D. E. Berlyne, *Conflict, Arousal and Curiosity,* New York: McGraw-Hill Book Co., 1960; Hutt, *op. cit.;* Hutt and Hutt, *op cit.*

17. *Ibid.*

18. D. E. Berlyne, "Measures of Aesthetic Preference," in *Psychology and the Visual Arts,* J. Hogg (ed.), Baltimore, Md.: Penguin Books, Inc., 1969.

19. *Op. cit.* This work is also included in Jon Lang, Charles Burnette, Walter Moleski, and David Vachon, *Designing for Human Behavior,* Stroudsburg, Pa.: Dowden, Hutchinson & Ross, Inc., 1974.

20. J. Piaget, *The Construction of Reality in the Child,* New York: Basic Books, Inc., Publishers, 1954.

21. J. Bruner, *Studies in Cognitive Growth,* New York: John Wiley & Sons, Inc., 1966.

22. K. Lynch, *The Image of the City,* Cambridge, Mass.: The MIT Press, 1960.

23. See R. R. Collard, "Social and Play Responses of First Born and Later Born Infants in an Unfamiliar Environment," *Child Development,* Vol. 39, 1968, pp. 325–334; A. Thomas and S. Chess, "Behavioral Individuality in Childhood," in *Development and Evolution of Behavior,* L. R. Aronson et al. (eds.), San Francisco: W. H. Freeman and Company, Publishers, 1970.

24. See A. Bandura, *Principles of Behavior Modification,* New York: Holt, Rinehart and Winston, Inc., 1969.

25. J. Bruner, *Processes of Cognitive Growth: Infancy* Worcester, Mass.: Clark University Press, 1968.

26. See Bandura, *op. cit.*

27. *Processes.*

28. W. I. Welker, "Ontogeny of Play and Exploratory Behavior," in *The Ontogeny of Vertebrate Behavior,* H. Moltz (ed.), New York: Academic Press, Inc., 1971.

29. C. Cooper, "The Adventure Playground: Creative Play in an Urban Setting and a Potential Focus for Community Involvement," Working Paper 118, Center for Planning and Development Research, University of California, Berkeley, Calif., 1970.

30. Dattner, *op. cit.*

31. See Cooper, *op. cit.*

32. *Conflict.*

33. J. Kagan, "On the Meaning of Behavior: Illustrations from the Infant," *Child Development,* Vol. 40, 1969, pp. 1121–1131; "Attention and Psychological Change in the Young Child," *Science,* Vol. 170, 1970, pp. 826–832.

34. Welker, *op. cit.*

35. Berlyne, *Conflict.*

36. *Ibid.*

37. C. Hutt, "Exploration and Play in Children," in *Play, Exploration and Territory in Mammals,* P. A. Jewell and C. Loizos (eds.), New York: Academic Press, Inc., 1966; Hutt, "Specific and Diversive Exploration"; Hutt and Hutt, *op. cit.*

38. See Hutt and Hutt, *ibid.*

39. "Specific and Diversive Exploration."

40. Friedberg and Berkeley, *op. cit.*

41. Dattner, *op. cit.*

42. "Exploration and Play."

43. Berlyne, *Conflict.*

44. "Exploration and Play"; "Specific and Diversive Exploration."

45. Hutt, "Specific and Diversive Exploration."

46. Hutt, "Exploration and Play."

47. *Ibid.*

48. Welker, *op. cit.*

49. "Specific and Diversive Exploration."

50. *Processes.*

51. *Play.*

52. G. H. Cantor, "Responses of Infants and Children to Complex and Novel Stimulation," in *Advances in Child Development,* L. P. Lipsitt and C. C. Spiker (eds.), New York: Academic Press, Inc., 1963.

53. "Specific and Diversive Exploration."

54. *Op. cit.*

55. F. N. Cox and E. D. Campbell, "Young Children in a New Situation with and Without Their Mothers," *Child Development,* Vol. 39, 1968, pp. 123–131.

56. *Op. cit.*

57. *Op. cit.*

58. *Op. cit.*

59. R. E. Herron and B. Sutton-Smith, *Child's Play,* New York: John Wiley & Sons, Inc., 1971.

60. In Hutt and Hutt, *op. cit.*

61. "Designer–user congruence in the selection of play environments for preschool children": The major thrust of this study was investigation of adult ability to judge scale models (¾ inch = 1 foot) of some thirty-five examples of "proposed equipment" for preschool children's outdoor play. The process was a simulation of the simpler steps in an intuitive design procedure where the designer presents proposed physical solutions to the problem of children's play equipment to a group of concerned adults —the client—for their evaluation. One formality imposed on this process was that the adults (eighty-five in number) rate each model on a numerical scale, indicating their judgment as to the amount of behavior they thought each piece of equipment would elicit from preschool children in an outdoor setting (i.e., high-to-low amounts of "social play," high-to-low amounts of "motor play," high-to-low amounts of "investigatory activities"). Based upon these (cumulated) adult ratings, twelve "designs" were selected as representing the highest and lowest facilitators of social, motor, and investigatory activity, and were constructed at full scale for outdoor use by children in sets of four (an experimenter decision based upon space available, number of children, etc.). The operational definitions outlined reflect the need to permit comparison between judged amounts of behavior and actual occurrences of behavior.

62. Analysis of videotapes will provide comparative data to test the accuracy of observations from slides.

63. Welker, *op. cit.*

64. Hutt and Hutt, *op. cit.*

65. *Processes.*

66. With the exception of object use, which tended to be relatively constant during the first seven days and then decreased.
67. Berlyne, *Conflict.*
68. Hutt, "Exploration and Play."
69. If the house form were not identified as a house per se, the associated activity rate would fit the model of organism response to novel stimulus conditions that are somewhat aversive: initial cautious approach behavior, subsequent increases of explorative behavior, and then a general decrement in activity (see Figure 3).
70. Berlyne, *Conflict;* Cantor, *op. cit.*
71. This is indicated by the relatively constant rate of object use during the first seven days, while the rate for motor and group activity increased during the same time [see Figure 1 (b)].

72. *Op. cit.*
73. M. Pyatok et al. "Pennsylvania Day Care Physical Facilities: Preliminary Report 1," Center for Human Services Development, Pennsylvania State University, University Park, Pa., 1973.
74. *Play.*
75. *Conflict.*
76. E. P. Torrance, *Guiding Creative Talent,* Englewood Cliffs, N.J.: Prentice-Hall, Inc., 1962; M. A. Wallach and N. Kogan, *Modes of Thinking in Young Children,* Holt, Rinehart and Winston, Inc., 1965; J. N. Leiberman, "Playfulness and Divergent Thinking," *J. Genet. Psychol.,* Vol. 107, 1965, pp. 219–224.

The Child in the Physical Environment: A Design Problem[1]

Anne-Marie Pollowy

INTRODUCTION

Two major problems exist when it comes to designing for the child in the physical environment. The first one relates to the design profession; it seems that trailing behind educators, psychologists, and other social scientists, the designers of our environment have not yet accepted children's activities and their play as the most necessary function of early life: developmental functions through which they learn to become adults, and for which adequate and supportive facilities have to be provided. It is remarkable how very little conscious programming effort has been concentrated on understanding, identifying, and satisfying the requirements of the young child, and how considerations for their activities are dismissed from planning and design concepts with the provision of some safety factors and of child facilities, such as playgrounds, daycare centers, schools, etc.

The second problem is that the design profession cannot be totally blamed. There is a grave lack of communication between the scientists that know about the child and the designers, this communication gap being not only one of language and of concepts, but also of general method and approach; the designers search for generalizable information, the scientists search for specific data. This is only too obvious if we note that man–environment research in general has concentrated either on the child within a given, specific setting or on some preidentified class of activities, such as social patterns. Few researchers have attempted to comprehend and derive functional requirements from existing situations, to qualify critical fit and misfit areas in the child–environment domain and thereby obtain design information usable in the elaboration of more supportive physical environments. (The exception is data dealing with human comfort.)

In this paper an attempt is made to identify an information-transfer framework to establish communication between the design and the social sciences. In it, it is presumed that (1) existing relevant data stemming from either developmental research or from environmental research can be utilized to provide information about the child's spatial requirements and about his use of space, and (2) these data can be formulated so as to be usable in the design process.

CONCEPTUAL DISTINCTIONS

Let us start with a basic assumption: the young child has a right to develop and to grow according to his inner dictates; he needs to play, to socialize with other children and adults, and to explore the world around him. Let us then take a parallel between contemporary educational philosophies and this life-style, and consider the child as an active learner, the physical environment as a living–learning environment, and the child's life as a development cycle through which he and his family evolve, and which requires certain congruent opportunities and facilities. If we are aiming at physical congruence between the child and the built environment, information has to be obtained about his spatial requirements, and this information has to be usable in the design process. This objective requires a holistic problem-solving approach in which the process of child development and the process of design (for the physical environment) are dealt with in the same terms, and the information derived from a variety of involved disciplines can be integrated. Furthermore, since such an approach must be operational to be effective, the information has to be available in a format usable in the design process

at the initial programming stage, at the conception stage, and eventually at the evaluation stage. To deal with the process of design and the process of development in the same terms, we must first open a channel of communication between the design and the social sciences. This requires an initial differentiation between the terms "activity" and "behavior."

To proceed systematically, we first have to clarify what we mean by development: Hart and Moore[2] (1973) suggest that the term "development" should be reserved for the ". . . qualitative changes in the structural organization of behavior. . . ." Following the behavioral line of thought, Studer[3] suggests the use of "behavior" for operationally defining "need," so that, consequently, developmental needs could be expressed in terms of developmental behavior patterns. Yet "behavior" is a psychological identificator that does not clarify or directly relate to environmental conditions. That behavior is affected by the built environment is readily accepted in all research; yet we have to be conscious of the fact that our knowledge of behavior is arrived at by the identification and categorization of observed *activities* and interpersonal exchanges. Behavior is an important information source, but a knowledge of behavior alone is not sufficient for evolving design concepts, and it has to be ultimately related to the physical environment in which it occurs. Therefore, instead of attempting to re-relate behavior to the built environment, the unit of analysis should be activities: they represent the most directly quantifiable and qualifiable relationships between the child and the built environment. Also, in most environmental investigations the use of the term "behavior" is interchangeable with that of "activity." For example, Canter[4] states that ". . . in the great majority of cases behavior and the places in which it is carried out seem appropriate to one another. It is generally accepted that people sleep in bedrooms, sit in sitting rooms, do clerical work in offices, and so on . . .": "sleep," "sit," and "do clerical work," although classified as behavior, can be considered as activities, and the appropriateness of the environment can be related to the activities performed therein. To further clarify, activity concerns itself with *what* is being done, *how* is it being done, *where* is it being done, *when* is it being done, *with what* is it being done, and *with whom* is it being done, whereas behavior extends the sphere of inquiry to question *why* is it being done. The question of why, although extremely important, is not directly relevant to the design process unless the causes are identifiable environmental conditions. The design process, also concerned with what, how, where, and when, can therefore obtain the required information about child–environment situations from statements derived from the study of activities.

ACTIVITY PATTERNS AND CHILD DEVELOPMENT

Developmental theories indicate that some elements in the child's development are always clearly represented by activities. Furthermore, these theories suggest that we could represent some aspects of child development by activity development, and therefore design-oriented developmental requirements could be identified in terms of predictable developmental activity patterns. For example, Piaget's experiments indicate that ". . . our adult understanding and representation of space results from extensive manipulations of objects and movements in the physical environment . . ."[5]; ". . . learning is dependent on the *activity* of the learner . . ."[6] (added italics). Gesell's[7] experiments perceive development as a series of events governed by laws and forces. These are described in terms of normative *activity patterns* in the description of the "behavior day"[8]; *play activities*, acknowledged as being direct reflections of developmental stages, are classified according to developmental levels. Since there is a direct relationship between play activities and learning, similar relationships exist between play and deprivation.[9]

Within the scope of "normal" child development, we identify three categories of activities:

1. Self-initiated activities result from the maturation of the organism. We refer to activities that are alike in all human infants, such as the typical reflexes, crawling, creeping, and walking.
2. Self-initiated directed activities are motivated by physical and social environmental conditions. We refer to habits that the normal infant may or may not acquire where "exercise has a considerable influence upon the development of such activities. . . ."[10] We presume a stimulus–response condition in which we classify these activities as the desired response or output, and the physical environment as part of the stimulus or input. For example, in nursery schools, self-initiated directed activities are a function of the available materials, of environmental conditions, and of social interactions.[11] Also, if we observe playground activities, the available equipment, as well as peer-group involvement, motivates certain types of activities that we classify as self-initiated directed activities. Therefore, to satisfy and stimulate design-based developmental requirements, the relationship aimed for is the optimization of physical environmental stimulus to encourage predictable developmental activity patterns.
3. Directed activities are performed in response to explicit directions. For example, when a child is told to paint, listen to stories, play with blocks, etc., at a given specific time, the choice of the activity and of the timing of the activity is extraneous to him.

An environmental focus toward "self-initiated directed activities" (in play theories these are referred to as *unstructured play*) has to be emphasized in an environmental design goal since "... young children learn through their own exploration and activity, realize themselves through the impact they make on the world, and extend their understanding through rehearsing and reliving experience through play. This philosophy is very much in tune with the basic concepts of Piaget, who seems to suggest that structured play is not adequate, especially when we are working with the pre-school child."[12]

ACTIVITY PATTERNS AND THE BUILT ENVIRONMENT

Research in psychology, physiology, education, and mental hygiene has concentrated until recently on the effects of built environment on *behavior*. Direct effects have been demonstrated on early learning processes, aggressive behavior, territorial behavior, etc.[13] (Jersild and Markey, 1935; Johnson, 1935; Markey, 1935; Murphy, 1937; Muste and Sharpe, 1947; Body, 1955; Munn, 1965; Hutt and McGrew, 1967). The experiments of Hutt and McGrew[14] relate various aspects of child behavior to well-described environmental conditions: density conditions and room sizes and shapes are identified and can be correlated with activity patterns within the physical environment, resulting in clear environmental cause–effect relationships. More recently, in a study of a children's psychiatric hospital, Wolfe and Rivlin[15] qualify some relationships between the development of use patterns and specific conditions in the life history of the building. However, it is apparent that research into this type of relationship is still in the embryonic stage.

In an exploratory investigation attempting to identify direct linkages between activities and environmental conditions, Pollowy[16] observed and recorded quantifiable child–environment interactions in three different physical environments.[17] These interactions are identified as dis-cernible physical contacts between the child and his surroundings, that is, tactile relationships between activities and components of the built environment. In this context, the built environment is considered as those parts of the child's surroundings acting on him or submitting to his actions.[18] These parts are limited to those to which activity could be physically related (i.e., floors, walls, toys, tables, chairs, etc.) and which are or can be engaged in an activity. These are generically labeled *equipment,* and activity is then defined as the *use of equipment*. The relationships investigated are specified as patterns composed of tactile interactions between *activity* and *equipment*.

Three direct components of any activity–equipment interaction are identifiable:

1. *Equipment*
   (a) A primary group E_1, consisting of physical components such as floors, walls, partitions, stairs, and furnishings (built-in or free standing). E_1 is that part of the built environment to which all activities must relate; that is, any activity consists first, and possibly only, of an interaction between the child and equipment group E_1.
   (b) A secondary group E_2, being equipment usually referred to as "play equipment" or "play material." Activities engaging E_2 are optional, equipment usage being related to a specific activity. This equipment group is in turn subdivided into three categories according to the type of physical activity involved and the area or space assumed to be required for equipment usage.
   $E_{2\cdot1}$—swings, parallel bars, jungle gyms, etc.
   $E_{2\cdot2}$—large building blocks, large trucks, trains, tractors, etc.
   $E_{2\cdot3}$—scissors, crayons, paste, paint, clay, dough, puzzles, books, dolls, etc.

2. *Activity or equipment use:* Equipment use is the interaction between a child and a component of an equipment group. As defined in the classification of equipment groups, there cannot be any interaction between the child and an equipment E_2 without a direct involvement of an equipment E_1.

Furthermore, all interactions between child and equipment are identified as either "expected" or "nonexpected." In other words, in an expected interaction, the equipment is used in a manner consistent with its design purpose; in the nonexpected interaction, equipment usage is different from the expected design purpose. For example, in a child–chair interaction, the child is expected to sit on the chair; it is nonexpected that the child will stand on or crawl under the chair.

Figure 1 illustrates all the possible courses of action each child has for the use of all available equipment, when governed by either one of the two established usages, expected or nonexpected.

3. *Child location:* The position of the child within the environment, in reference to the equipment, and his relation to the equipment.

In the investigation the greatest variety of interactions (activities) occur during "free play" periods (periods of self-initiated directed activities motivated by environmental conditions). Generalizing, the following activity–environment relationships are identified:

1. The number of activity–equipment interactions increases with the available floor area *and* with the visual identification of specific activity areas. This implies that visual identification (by the child) of specific activity areas is necessary to encourage activities, and that physical accessibility *only* is not sufficient.

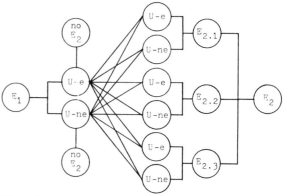

Figure 1

Interactions between expected and nonexpected uses of equipment group E_1 and E_2. This figure indicates that all interactions are of equal importance and weight. Such factors as motivation, accessibility of equipment, etc., are not taken into consideration. U-e: "expected" use of equipment; U-ne: "nonexpected" use of equipment; E_1: equipment group 1; E_2: equipment group 2; $E_{2.1}$, $E_{2.2}$, $E_{2.3}$: subcategories of equipment group E_2

2. In areas where children's activities are restricted by equipment layout and distribution, a high degree of teacher (or supervisory) involvement is necessary. This implies that the types of activities as well as supervisory involvement are a function of environmental conditions (floor area, activity area location, furnishing distribution and density, etc.).

3. As the floor area increases, its spontaneous use for various nonexpected activities also increases, but the expected usage of tables and table-related equipment (puzzles, crayons, etc.) decreases. In addition, personal observations suggest that child initiative in the choice of activities might be related to this increased usage of floor or floor-related equipment, and that the function of some equipment (such as tables) should be reevaluated in view of the limitations it might impose on nonexpected usage in the built environment.

For programming purposes, the major implication of the study is the apparent feasibility of deriving qualified and quantified design determinants from the analysis of activity–environment relationships. Also, it appears possible to qualify specific relationships between activities and characteristics of the built environment, so that activities may be encouraged or discouraged according to the physical characteristics of the built environment. This study empirically supports the stimulus–response, environment–activity hypothesis, and although the observations were carried out in the limited environment of a nursery school, it would seem possible to enlarge the experiment to geographical levels.

IDENTIFYING ACTIVITY PATTERNS

The previous arguments presented the hypothesis that activity patterns could be used for identifying some characteristics of the developmental cycle and for relating to environmental research. Accordingly, the child's activity requirements can be derived from two parallel approaches. First, using existing normative child development data, some developmental spatial requirements of the child can be identified. The objective here is to clarify the overall development pattern, whereby the physical parameters of motor, spatial, social, and personality growth are related as a function of gross chronological age and of development stages. From this, a normative *activity pattern* model can be established, identifying and relating developmental stages to physical conditions. For example, if we look at the average four year old, a series of patterns is apparent: we know that he is fully mobile, can walk and run, enjoys play groups and new experiences, but is not yet quite capable of the attention required for crossing streets or visiting friends on his own. From this we can derive for design programming that he may require easy and protected access to a play group in order that he may develop his sense of independence or autonomy. Physically, this implies certain general relationships between the play space, the home, and in the paths between the two. However, each statement has to be further clarified in terms of conditions relating to a specific activity pattern and to the interaction of different patterns.

The second approach is the use of existing environmental studies. Although there is a lack of field observations that could identify specific child–environment conditions, it is possible at this time to identify some critical fit and misfit areas in the child–activity–environment domain. A number of studies contain activity–environment information in reference to the child's and the family's behavior under various urban conditions,[19] and these have to be clarified and synthesized. For example, it is well known that "a mother cannot look out for her kids if they are fifteen floors down in the playground."[20] In this one statement of a misfit situation, a number of activity-restricting physical problem areas can be identified: (1) the vertical distance between habitat and play area, (2) the lack of direct communication between habitat and play area, and (3) the discongruence between the mother location and the child location. All are recognizable problems in high-rise multifamily housing with playgrounds located on ground level when a family with small children lives beyond a given height or communication range. These conditions result in restricted exploration and socialization opportunities for the child and in problematic surveillance situations for the adult, and are identifiable by nonsatisfied or *dysfunctioning* activity patterns. Based on an activity pattern analysis within this situation, we may derive some general physical relationships such that (1) a distance X should be considered as maximal for a vertical relationship between habitat and playground, and (2) within that distance, some form of interpersonal contact (visual, auditory, or mechanical) should be available to mother and child. Here again, only general notions are presented, and a finer activity pattern recognition is still lacking.

To this point, what is being discussed is the use of a vast scope of existing research information. To proceed, an operation of synthesis must be undertaken relating, through the use of activities as a common denominator, the empiric research information about the child's developmental activity requirements to the environmental survey information about child and family activities and activity problems in actual settings. This synthesis is to result in a comprehensive model of both positive and negative activity patterns, where positive activity patterns are those considered desirable from a developmental or cultural point of view, and negative activity patterns are those which inflict undesirable stress conditions on either the child or in the family's relationship with the child.

To date, very few connections have been made between the two outlined sets of materials or approaches, and very little information from either has been channeled into the design process. However, it is obvious that the scope of the undertaking, from looking at the various conditions about the child to identifying and relating the type of information applicable to each condition is vast. It is obvious, for instance, that the two previous examples are related, so that a playground problem for a mother and child differs vastly with the age (or general development) of the child. This implies that every situation has to be looked at from several vantage points: from the given physical situation and its variations to the age and related characteristics of the child involved. In other words, an activity pattern has to be stated and described in terms of the physical conditions involved and the relevant child developmental data.

AN OPERATIONAL FRAMEWORK FOR INFORMATION TRANSFER

It is assumed then in this approach that certain developmental, psychological, social, and environmental data can be identified in terms of spatially related activity patterns, either as factors of specific physical conditions, of geographic distance, of activity boundaries, or the like. It is important to recognize, however, that the information available is for the most part very soft, for in many cases both the internal validity of research data and their generalizability could be questioned. Yet we should not dismiss these data with the ever-available scientific criticism and scepticism, and an attempt must be made to accumulate, compare, and synthesize information. If this is not done, we shall forever be in our present situation in which research is comparable to narrow, deep holes of knowledge bored into the general sphere of inquiry, where this sphere lacks an overall surface crust made up of the connections between researches. Until these connections are made, and no matter how thin the resulting crust, man–environment research and most other man-related research will be of very little use to the designers of our environment, and shall continue as scientific exercise.

What is proposed then by channeling research into a well-defined operational framework is, at a first level, the identification of (1) what is known, (2) the connections between knowledge units, and (3) the gaps in knowledge or continuity. [Boulding[21] stated quite accurately that there is a gap of communication between the various disciplines which consequently creates gaps in the overall knowledge of a problem.] At a second level, the operational framework should provide the means for establishing coherence and continuity between information about the child's spatial requirements, the statement of user requirements, the design process, and the designed product (the built environment).

Particularly when developmental and environmental research information is to be related to the design process, physical as well as nonphysical parameters and also measurable and nonmeasurable properties will have to be considered. To ensure that all relevant parameters are taken into account, it is suggested that we approach the child in the physical environment through systems thinking, trying to attain a workable model of the "whole." If the child in the physical environment is to be viewed as a holistic system, the major components of the system are the child, the family, the peer group, and the physical environment. The interactions among these parts create the following four subsystems in whose framework data from existing literature can be organized.

1. Child–environment, in which normative developmental data about the child, his play preferences at various ages, danger conditions, etc., could be identified.
2. Child–family/environment, in which anthropological data such as child-rearing practices, attachment behavior, etc., could be related to environmental situations.
3. Child–peer/environment, in which peer social development, environmental "city use" research, sociological research, etc., could be stated.
4. Child–family–peer/environment, in which again different aspects of anthropological research, of social research, etc., could be identified.

It is obvious, however, that only data having implications for the physical environment should be included. But since to date only very few studies (e.g., play-equipment preferences) deal directly with this type of data, the material source encompasses nearly the whole realm of existing research, and limitations should be established according to specific interests.

As previously suggested, activity patterns or environmental dysfunctions can be identified from this literature and integrated through a process of synthesis. Once these activity patterns have been identified alone, or in terms of environmental dysfunctions, they can be related to the design process. This process ". . . can be considered from the present point of view as the fitting of a physical form to a complex pattern of human objectives, activities and requirements. This necessarily involves identifying the requirements, devising the form and finally appraising the fit . . . Before the fit can be objectively appraised, it is necessary to decompose the ultimate objective into the sub-objectives and to define appropriate activities conducive to the achievement of each (objective) and the requirements that these activities generate."[22] This statement presumes that within the process the initial design program, in which user requirements are identified in environmental terms, provides a means of prescribing these requirements and of evaluating both design solutions (the form) and the built environment (the "fit").

The use of the performance approach throughout the process appears to be the only means to satisfy this range of requirements. Its basic premise is to demand a statement of environmental or physical performance in terms of function, where in this case the function is identified in terms of activity patterns. Also, ". . . the performance concept is an organized procedure or framework within which it is possible to state the desired attributes of a material, component or system (the environment) in order to fulfill the requirements of the intended use (the activities) without regard to the specific means to be employed in achieving the result (the actual design)."[23]

Generally, the performance organization is hierarchical to ensure the required continuity, and it follows through six levels:

Level 1: *An overall goal statement is made. This goal is basically a general statement of ultimate intent which relates to the specific social, economic, and environmental conditions that prevail in the context of the problem. For example, we could state that our goal is the improvement of urban housing conditions in view of the requirements of child development.*

Level 2: From the goal, distinct objectives are identified. Objectives, by definition, have to be reachable, and one must be able to predict that means to achieve these objectives are available or could be developed.

Level 3: As a matter of convenience, each objective can be divided into as many subobjectives as are necessary to make the problem manageable.

It should be clarified what the objectives or subobjectives should express and in which terms they should be expressed. In the previous section the argument for using "activity patterns" as the means for describing the interface between child–environment interactions was presented. Therefore, objectives (and subobjectives) have to be described in terms of the explicitly stated sets of activities that are expected to take place in the intended environment. For each objective or subobjective there will be one set of activities; however, similar activities could be present in various sets (as we know from set theory). Within each set, the basic activities for that set have to be identified with their paradigms. These are the inflections of the basic activity, indicating its various aspects: how the activity is taking place, where the activity is taking place, how many participate in the activity, etc. (In the paradigms, the procedure should be statement by exception, only the relevant inflections being identified.)

The overall continuity could be illustrated by the following example:

Objective: motor development

One of the subobjectives: large motor activities for three year olds

One of the identified sets of activities aimed at: experimenting with "play" equipment

Basic activities in the set: 1. using a tricycle, 2. climbing on structures, 3. using a ball, etc.

Paradigms of basic activity 1 — using a tricycle
how: 1. pushing the tricycle, 2. climbing on the tricycle, 3. riding the tricycle, etc.

where: 1. interior, 2. exterior, 3. open space, 4. enclosed space, etc.

when: should indicate the frequency of occurrence of the activity

how many: 1. alone, 2. with one other child, 3. with one adult, etc.

Once all the activities have been established for the various objectives, exhausting the range of possibilities, the next phase (levels 4 and 5) can take place. This consists of relating activities to environmental conditions by developing *performance requirements* and *performance criteria* to arrive at comprehensive *user requirements performance specifications*. Through this process, characteristics the built environment should offer are identified so that the performance of the environment satisfies the conditions in which the activities are to take place.

Level 4: The performance requirements are the quantified and/or qualified characteristics of the built environment that result from the analysis of the user's activities. They are comprehensive narrations stating which conditions are required to satisfy the various activities. The performance requirements shall only be concerned with what is the problem and what shall be achieved, and in no way should they include a statement that implies or indicates a means to achieve the ends.

Level 5: Once the performance requirements have been stated, reference principles (performance criteria) for the evaluation of proposed solutions have to be established. The key to the development of performance specifications is the identification of significant criteria that characterize the environmental performance expected. The purpose at this level is to isolate, identify, and select measurable properties or characteristics for each performance requirement, and to single out relevant performance evaluation techniques or, if these are not available, to develop new evaluation methods. When the nature of the problem does not allow for quantifiable principles of judgment, performance criteria are replaced by performance requirement guidelines, *relying on expertise evaluative techniques for final judgment.*

The procedure used for channeling the information of levels 4 and 5 to the party or parties the solution is sought from consists of the documentation of the performance requirements and performance specifications. The product of this process would be the user requirements performance specifications. (Some basic user requirements, such as health and safety, will not be directly related to specific activities, and should be expressed as general requirements.) In its final form this contains all information and data relevant to three types of statements: (1) the statement of the problem (performance requirements), (2) the acceptable levels of performance (performance criteria) the solution is to meet, and (3) the evaluative techniques to be implemented.

The user requirements performance specifications will identify all the environmental parameters relevant to all described activities. These parameters are to be specifically categorized into families of environmental conditions, such as spatial requirements, perception of the environment, acoustical condition, physiological condition (illumination, atmospheric control), etc. However, for the various requirements identified, the relative hierarchical value or weight (according to evaluated importance) should be indicated in order to allow the designer a range of options in the choice of criteria during the design process.

Level 6: *It is at this point that the designer takes over. Analyzing the relationship between the proposed function of the built environment and the built attributes that perform these functions, he identifies the design factors he will respect in order to meet the user requirements performance specifications. He determines these design factors by relating the user requirements performance specifications, the contextual constraints (economic, climatic, code regulations, etc.), the state of the art (technology) and the available resources, and the design variables.*

FEEDBACK

In addition to the fact that feedback is necessary to any operational framework, it is absolutely essential when the user and the built environment are approached as a whole. The available holistic methods of evaluation are based on empiric techniques (simulation) that lead in most cases to posterior evaluations whose results are available only during the operational stages of the built environment. This, of course, is not sufficient. Within the described framework, feedback is possible at four stages: (1) in developing a solution the designer at all times refers to the user requirements performance specifications as a means of evaluating his choices of attributes; (2) in evaluating the complete solution the whole of the user requirements performance specifications and the program can be referred to, verifying if the designer has fulfilled his mandate (it must be recognized, however, that a mandate may change during the design process); (3) from the closed cycle, where posterior evaluations are made from the built environment designed and implemented through the complete performance approach, which provides feedback on the environment as well as on the process itself; (4) from the evaluation of *any* built environment, new empiric data on activity–environment relationships can be incorporated into existing user requirements performance specifications, hence becoming immediately applicable to new environmental problems.

With the use of the performance approach, evaluation and feedback can be an ongoing process, since it provides a conceptual checklist through design and a performance-evaluating guide for operation evaluation, at which time, in a major feedback process, relevant changes may be made in the main body of the performance guidelines.

CONCLUSIONS

This paper has attempted to outline an approach for relating the design and the social sciences. Arguments were presented for using *activity patterns* as a common denominator for stating developmental and environmental research data relevant to identifying the spatial requirements of the child in the physical environment. (Where activity patterns are not readily identifiable, specific dysfunction statements can be made about child–activity–environment conditions.) Furthermore, it was suggested that with the use of the *performance approach* as a vehicle, activity patterns (and dysfunction statements) can be interpreted for use in the design process: for programming, for design, and for evaluation. The scope of the work is such, however, that this framework presumes that a large-scale activity and performance program is developed for a specific user group from which specific bits of information can be drawn for particular design problems.

Although the example provided herein deals exclusively with the problem of the child in the physical environment (since, as a specific user group, a great deal is known about him), the general approach appears applicable to all user groups where a sufficient body of data has been gathered. The main points, viewing the user in the environment as a system, using activity patterns or environmental function or dysfunction statements for identifying specific user–environment relationships, and then stating these relationships in terms of environmental performance requirements, can be considered a general notion.

One last point has to be made: it will appear to many readers that on one hand the value of the "designed object" has been raised in the Pollowy study (1969), while on the other hand here the framework is to attempt to formulate a means for arriving at design solutions from a better knowledge of children's spatial requirements. The two ideas are not as incompatible as it may appear at first glance: since the "designed object" or even the majority of the built environment is conceived with only minimal notions of children's requirements, and although nonexpected activities may be a desirable goal, we should first know how and what to provide for expected activities. Then we

may at least partially satisfy the range of activities of the developing child by creating a more supportive physical environment.

NOTES AND REFERENCES

1. This paper explores further some concepts presented by A. M. Pollowy and M. Bezman, "Design-Oriented Approach to Developmental Needs: An Operational Framework relating Activity Patterns to Environmental Requirements through the Performance Approach," in *Environmental Design: Research and Practice,* William J. Mitchell (ed.), 1972, proceedings of the EDRA 3/AR8, UCLA.
2. R. A. Hart and G. T. Moore, "The Development of Spatial Cognition: A Review," Place Perception Research Report Number 7, The Environmental Research Group, Chicago, in *Cognitive Mapping: Images of Spatial Environment,* R. M. Downs (eds.) Chicago: Aldine Publishing Co., 1973.
3. R. Studer, (1969); *The Dynamics of Behavior-Contingent Physical Systems in* Broadbent, G. and Ward, A. (eds.), *Design Methods in Architecture,* London: Lund Humphries, and New York: Wittenborn, Inc., 1969.
4. D. Canter, (1970); *The Place of Architectural Psychology: A Consideration of Some Findings,* Proceedings of the Second Annual Environmental Design Research Association Conference, October 1970, Pittsburgh, Pa.
5. Hart and Moore, *op. cit.*
6. M. Brearley and E. Hitchfield, *A Teacher's Guide to Reading Piaget,* London: Routledge & Kegan Paul Ltd., 1970.
7. A. Gesell et al. *First Five Years of Life: A Guide to the Study of the Pre-school Child,* New York: Harper & Row, Publishers, 1943.
8. A. Gesell et al. *Infant and Child in the Culture of Today: The Guidance of Development in Home Nursery School,* New York: Harper & Row, Publishers, 1943.
9. O. Weininger, "Unstructured Play as a Vehicle for Learning," in *International Journal of Early Childhood,* OMEP, Vol. 4, No. 2, 1972, pp. 63–69.
10. N. L. Munn, *The Evolution and Growth of Human Behaviors,* Boston: Houghton Mifflin Company, 1965.
11. A. M. Pollowy, "Investigation of Use Patterns in Pre-school Facilities," unpublished study, 1969.
12. Weininger, *op. cit.*
13. M. K. Body, "Patterns of Aggression in the Nursery School," *Child Development,* Vol. 26, 1955, pp. 3–11; C. Hutt and W. C. McGrew, "Effect of Group Density upon Social Behavior in Humans," unpublished study, 1967; A. T. Jersild and F. V. Markey, "Conflicts Between Pre-School Children," *Child Development Monograms,* No. 21, 1935; M. W. Johnson (1935); "The Effect on Behavior of Variation in the Amount of Play Equipment," *Child Development,* Vol. 6, 1935, pp. 56–58; F. V. Markey, "Imaginative Behavior of Pre-school Children,"

Child Development Monograms, No. 18, 1935; Munn, *op. cit.;* L. B. Murphy, *Social Behavior and Child Personality: An Exploratory Study of Some Roots of Sympathy,* New York: Columbia University Press, 1937; H. M. Muste and D. F. Sharpe, "Some Influential Factors in the Determination of Aggressive Behavior in Pre-school Children," *Child Development,* Vol. 18, 1947, pp. 11–28.

14. Hutt and McGrew, *op. cit.*
15. M. Wolfe and L. Rivlin, (1972); "Evolution of Space Utilization Patterns in Children's Psychiatric Hospital," in *Environmental Design: Research and Practice,* William J. Mitchell (ed.), proceedings of the EDRA 3/AR8 conference, UCLA.
16. Pollowy, *op. cit.*
17. To obtain comparative data in the form of activity–equipment interactions for different physical environments, three nursery school settings were selected so that (1) diversity in physical characteristics such as size and layout was obtained, while (2) similarity in the socioeconomic and ethnic characteristics of the children, in the apparent educational attitude, and in child–staff ratios were maintained.
18. L. Couffignal, *La Cybernétique,* Paris: Presses Universitaires de France, 1953.
19. A. Bengtsson, *Environmental Planning for Children's Play,* London: Crosby Lockwood & Son Ltd., 1972; G. Coates and H. Sanoff, (1972); "Behavioral Mapping: The Ecology of Child Behavior in Planned Residential Settings," in *Environmental Design: Research and Practice,* William J. Mitchell (ed.), proceedings of the EDRA 3/AR8 conference, UCLA; A. Sharp, "Children's Play Observations in Paddington," Sociological Research Section, Ministry of Housing and Local Government, England, 1970.
20. E. T. Hall, *The Hidden Dimension,* Garden City, N.Y.: Doubleday & Company, Inc., 1966.
21. K. E. Boulding, "General Systems Theory—The Skeleton of Science," *Management Science,* Vol. 2, No. 3, Apr. 1956.
22. R. J. Mainstone, L. G. Bianco, and H. W. Harrison "Performance Parameters and Performance Specification in Architectural Design," Building Research Station, Ministry of Public Building and Works, England, 1969.
23. CIB Working Commissions, W60.

ADDITIONAL READINGS

CIB Working Commissions W31 and W58.

Hunt, T. M. *Intelligence and Experience,* New York: The Ronald Press Company, 1961.

Isaacs, S. *The Children We Teach,* London: University of London Press Ltd., 1950.

SER 1 Environmental Abstracts, University of Michigan, Ann Arbor, Mich., 1965.

Index